National Traditions of Opera

Italian Opera

National Traditions of Opera
General editor: John Warrack

National Traditions of Opera is a series which aims to study the development of the genre in individual European countries. Volumes planned and in preparation cover France, Russia and Germany. Since each country has made a very different contribution to operatic history, no systematic pattern of treatment has been imposed on authors; rather they have been asked to find the methods that will best provide an account of the manner in which each country's opera has reflected its character, history and culture. Considerations that have been borne in mind are therefore not only musicological but literary, historical, political, social and economic, in an attempt to determine what it is that has shaped each particular tradition. Other matters discussed have been language, in some cases folk music and folk traditions, national epic and legend, the growth of national musical institutions, and much else that has had a bearing on the expression of national character in opera. Naturally it has also been necessary to view these matters in the context of the international development of opera. It is intended that the books should be of value to the opera goer no less than to students and scholars.

Already published:

Czech Opera
John Tyrrell

Italian Opera

DAVID KIMBELL

Professor of Music
University of Edinburgh

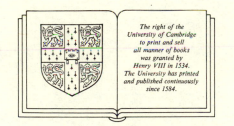

The right of the
University of Cambridge
to print and sell
all manner of books
was granted by
Henry VIII in 1534.
The University has printed
and published continuously
since 1584.

CAMBRIDGE UNIVERSITY PRESS

Cambridge
New York   Port Chester
Melbourne   Sydney

Published by the Press Syndicate of the University of Cambridge
The Pitt Building, Trumpington Street, Cambridge CB2 1RP
40 West 20th Street, New York, NY 10011, USA
10 Stamford Road, Oakleigh, Melbourne 3166, Australia

First published 1991

Printed in Great Britain at the University Press, Cambridge

British Library cataloguing in publication data
Kimbell, David R. B.
Italian opera – (National traditions of opera)
1. Opera in Italian
I. Title
782.1'0945

Library of Congress cataloguing in publication data
Kimbell, David R. B.
Italian opera / David Kimbell.
p.   cm. – (National traditions of opera)
Includes bibliographical references.
ISBN 0–521–23533–2
1. Opera – Italy.   I. Title.   II. Series.
ML'733.K55   1990
782.110945 – dc   89–17414   CIP

ISBN 0 521 23533 2 hardback

CE

To Ottó Károlyi and our friends and colleagues in the
Music Departments of the Scottish Universities

Contents

Contents

Illustrations

Preface

'I no longer believe that there is such a thing as "the Italian operatic tradition".' Reinhard Strohm's avowal, in his distinguished collection of *Essays on Handel and Italian Opera* (Cambridge 1985), was just the tonic I felt I did not need as I approached the completion of this book; for my purpose has been – it can hardly be denied or disguised – precisely that of describing some of the manifestations of the Italian operatic tradition as it evolved over a period of rather more than 300 years, from the late Renaissance to Puccini. It would be sad if I had indeed pursued a chimera. But even then there might be, I venture to hope, some interest in telling the story of Italian opera, or to be more strictly accurate the story of opera in Italy, with a particular view to exploring the social, philosophical, literary and musical forces that shaped it.

A moment's reflection will explain one of the peculiar problems of the enterprise and the point of the insistence on 'opera in Italy'. For the greater and more productive part of its history, Italian opera was an international art-form; at various times London, Paris and St Petersburg; cities all over the German-speaking heartland of Europe; Madrid, Lisbon and a number of centres in the New World, were the scenes of much Italian operatic activity. To survey it all in the space of a single volume would scarcely have been possible, even had I known more about it than in fact I do.

It is certainly the case that in many, if not all, of these non-Italian centres, the character of the operas produced was to some extent conditioned by the local 'national traditions', musical, social and historical. Nevertheless, the frontiers between Opera in Italy and Italian Opera are shadowy and ill defined, to say the least. At certain periods, perhaps for political or financial reasons, ultramontane cities – notably Vienna and Paris – have been so central to the operatic experience even of those composers resident in Italy that it was impossible not to make them an integral part of my narrative. At other times some of the very greatest composers of Italian opera have worked in centres that made little or no impact on the practice and evolution of opera in Italy – Handel in London, even Mozart in Vienna; to such composers I have been able to make no more than passing reference. The dilemma is intractable, and I certainly do not claim to have found a definitive solution to it; brief reflection on the not

entirely dissimilar question, What constitutes a History of English Literature?, may enlarge the reader's indulgence.

My book is in principle a work of history. But I take it that one of the
primary objects of studying the history of music is to help us attune
ourselves culturally and ideologically to remote, or vanished, or mysterious
worlds, so that we can approach a performance of Monteverdi or Pergolesi
or Rossini as an 'ideal spectator' of the composer's own day might have
done. And for that reason the historical narrative is punctuated with a series
of critical essays in which I have tried to put that presumption to the test. I
have chosen for this purpose operas that are – as far as possible – accessible
in score and/or recording, and which have shown a lasting vitality in theatre
performances. For the final section of the book, 'Cosmopolitanism and
decadence', that procedure no longer seemed feasible. In writing the
history of this period, I have discussed fewer operas but written about them
in fuller detail; the operas themselves are more clearly distinct in ethos and
physiognomy, and it was scarcely possible to select any one of them as a
summa of the tendencies of the age without a degree of arbitrariness that
would have been self-defeating.

Few readers are likely to wish this book any longer; there may be some,
however, who feel that the decision to end it with Puccini needs explanation. Briefly, it ends there because, however beautiful, interesting or
remarkable the operatic and quasi-operatic works of younger Italian
composers may have been, it is difficult to feel that anything that could
properly be described as an Italian operatic tradition survived much
beyond the First World War. As will become apparent, this tradition had
depended upon such things as composers willing and able to work fluently
and imaginatively within a broadly accepted musical *lingua franca*; an
uninhibited delight, at once naive and mystical, in the expressive power of
the singing voice; a central role for the opera-house in the social and
cultural life of the peninsula. I cannot see that any of these things survived
the combination of self-conscious modernism and radical antiquarianism
typical of much of the music composed by the next remarkable constell-
ation of Italians, sometimes known as the 'generazione dell'ottanta':
Ildebrando Pizzetti (1880–1968), Gian Francesco Malipiero (1882–1973),
Alfredo Casella (1883–1947).

Though I should like to think that the conception of the book is to some
extent my own, its size and scope inevitably mean that, for the materials
that sustain it, I am even more beholden to the work of fellow scholars than
academic authors usually are. The Bibliography might appropriately be
described as my List of Sources, and I am indebted to all whose names
appear in it. They will, I hope, forgive me if, to leave the narrative as
uncluttered as possible, I have referred to them in the body of the text only

when I have quoted them or, on occasion, when I owe them new information or new ideas available in no other source.

It is a pleasure to acknowledge my indebtedness to the Gladys Krieble Delmas Foundation of New York for the award of a research fellowship that enabled me to spend several weeks working on opera manuscripts in Venice; and to the University of St Andrews for the award of two periods of study leave and travel grants for several expeditions to Italy. I thank too the librarians and custodians of the following institutions for their hospitality, courtesy and assistance: *Casa Ricordi* and the *Museo teatrale della Scala* in Milan; the *Museo Donizettiano* in Bergamo; the *Biblioteca nazionale marciana*, the *Archivio di stato* and the *Fondazione Giorgio Cini (Istituto per le lettere, la musica e il teatro veneto)* in Venice; the *Istituto di studi verdiani* in Parma; the *Biblioteca communale Carlo Magnini* in Pescia; the library of the *Conservatorio di musica San Pietro a Majella* and the *Biblioteca nazionale Vittorio Emanuele III* in Naples; the Bodleian Library, Oxford; the National Library of Scotland and the Reid Music Library, Edinburgh; the University Library, St Andrews.

I am grateful to a number of friends and colleagues who have read and commented on sections of the book in typescript, particularly to Raymond Monelle, Matteo Sansone, Roger Savage and Frederick Sternfeld. And a special word of thanks is due to the general editor of the series, John Warrack, for his unfailingly tactful support and encouragement throughout the book's unconscionably protracted gestation. My wife Ingrid has again performed heroic deeds of deciphering, typing and indexing; my mother in Kent and my mother-in-law in Hamburg have vied with one another to provide me with ideal conditions for extended periods of writing-up.

These acknowledgements must end on a less customary note. I have written this book over a period of seven or eight years during which I have been the first and, for the foreseeable future, only holder of an established Chair of Music in the University of St Andrews. It might have been a better book, it would certainly have been finished sooner, had these years not coincided with 'The Cuts', the economies in British Higher Education during which it was for long suggested and finally insisted upon that the St Andrews Department of Music was surplus to requirements. On the other hand it would not have been finished at all had I not been blessed with three departmental colleagues, Christopher and Elizabeth Ann Field, and John Kitchen, abundantly endowed with resilience and idealism. In the Arts Faculties of the Scottish Universities, with their long tradition of a broad-based inter-disciplinary study of the humanities, the academic study of Music ought to be as securely founded as anywhere in the civilized world. But as I write it seems in fact more precarious here than anywhere. I judge it therefore appropriate to dedicate this book to all my colleagues in the Music Departments of the Scottish Universities who still believe in that tradition and struggle to maintain it, and in particular to my friend Ottó Károlyi, Senior Lecturer in Music in the University of Stirling.

A note on Italian prosody

The standard textbook on Italian versification, on which the following remarks are based, is W. Th. Elwert, *Italienische Metrik*, Munich 1968.

The technical terms used in the description of Italian verse depend upon the number of syllables in the line. Thus *quinari, senari, settenari, ottonari, novenari, decasillabi, endecasillabi, dodecasillabi* are, respectively, lines of 5, 6, 7, 8, 9, 10, 11 and 12 syllables. This simple principle is, however, complicated by the fact that lines of Italian verse normally have feminine endings. If a line in fact ends with a strong syllable, or is extended by means of an additional weak syllable, these abnormal circumstances are ignored in counting the syllables but acknowledged in an additional descriptive term, either *tronco* – 'truncated' – or *sdrucciolo* – 'sliding'. The following lyric from Metastasio's *Olimpiade* thus combines normal *quinari* (lines 2, 4), *quinari sdruccioli* (1, 3, 5), and *quinari tronchi* (6):

> Più non si trovano
> fra mille amanti
> sol due bell' anime
> che sian costanti,
> e tutti parlano
> di fedeltà.

The 'classic' line of Italian verse is the *endecasillabo*; it forms the basis for the *terza rima* (three-line stanzas) of Dante's *Divina Commedia*, for the sonnets and *canzoni* of Petrarch, and for the *ottava rima* (eight-line stanza) of Ariosto and the epic poets. Verses written entirely in non-rhyming *endecasillabi* are known as *versi sciolti*, the Italian equivalent of blank verse. More loosely, the term *versi sciolti* is often used in an operatic context to mean the kind of verse written for recitative. But that is normally a mixture of *endecasillabi* and *settenari* with the occasional rather casual use of rhyme, and should perhaps more strictly be described as *versi a selva*.

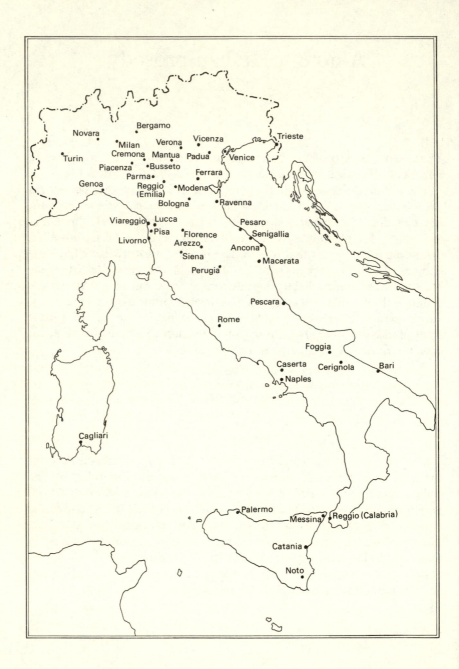

Introduction
The Italianness of Italian Opera

Italy was the birthplace of opera, and has always seemed its most natural habitat. It was there that the speculations and experiments took place that led, in the years around 1600, to the first attempts at composing opera; and for at least 300 years after that, Italian musicians were continuously involved in its development, and made uniquely significant contributions to the art.

Italy's concern with opera has been both longer-lasting and more whole-hearted than that of other nations. Italian composers and dramatists have created a huge proportion of the world's store of opera; Italian singers taught the world the arts of musical representation; Italian audiences found in opera a perfect gratification for their tastes and a complete fulfilment of their ideals and aspirations. It is, of course, perfectly possible for a rational being to prefer Rameau to Scarlatti, or Wagner to Verdi, or Janáček to Puccini; but it is the Italians who represent the mainstream. The Italian tradition is the central tradition, from which Frenchmen and Germans and Slavs have drawn inspiration and sustenance; which they have imitated, refashioned or rebelled against. Italian opera is opera in its quintessence – opera in its purest, most unadulterated and characteristic form.

Humanism

If we go back to the last decades of the sixteenth century, to the period of incubation that preceded the first attempts at opera, one characteristic of Italian art that it seems proper to regard as a national characteristic, is unmistakable. At that time – indeed from the beginning of the Italian Renaissance – educated Italians were obsessively preoccupied with the world of Classical Antiquity. They were, moreover, firmly persuaded that they were themselves the heirs of that world, and that this was an entitlement to be proud of. For while it may have been the Jews that had been the chosen people in the sense of having an unusually developed religious awareness, an acute sense of the presence of God, the ancient Greeks and Romans had been no less a chosen people in the sense of possessing unique human gifts – such gifts as those of wisdom, imagination, creativeness, character. To be a disciple of that ancient Graeco-

1

Roman humanist wisdom was a vocation scarcely less noble than to be a disciple of the Judaeo-Christian religious revelation.

Few Renaissance Italians doubted that they owed the flourishing of civilized living and the wonderful artistic developments witnessed in their land since the late fourteenth century to the rediscovery of that Ancient World, to the study of its authors and the pondering of its philosophy. And that the Renaissance – the phenomenon that the Florentine Matteo Palmieri described as 'this new age, so full of hope and promise, which already rejoices in a greater array of nobly-gifted souls than the world has seen in the thousand years that have preceded it' (*Della vita civile*, 1531–38, in Woodward 1906: 67) – should have come about in Italy was due, they felt, to Italy's uniquely intimate relationship with the Ancient World. Until comparatively recent times, Latin had been the common language of the Italians, who were otherwise linguistically separated from one another by a multitude of mutually unintelligible dialects; the Italian landscape was full of visible and tangible relics of the glories of the Classical past; and from the time of the Council of Florence (1439), and especially after the fall of Constantinople to the Turks (1453), Italy had also become the principal seat of Greek learning. In the eyes of Renaissance Italians, Ancient History was their history, Classical mythology their mythology. Florence, the city at the heart of the Italian Renaissance, liked to think of itself as the 'New Athens on the Arno'.

Of all the ideals inherited by Renaissance Italians from the Ancient World, none was more important than the belief in – to quote the title of a famous fifteenth-century treatise by Gianozzo Manetti – 'the dignity and excellence of man'. Manetti's panegyric is typical of the many essays of the age that established the conviction that man was the supreme glory of the created universe. He speaks of his 'upright carriage, of the beauty and harmony of his body, of the skill and genius by which he has created all the arts of civilization, of his capacity for virtuous living, and of his unique place in the creation as spectator and interpreter of the other works of God' (Robb 1935: 40–1).

What such Renaissance Italians as Manetti felt about the potentiality of human personality could be traced back almost in its entirety to the poetry and philosophy of Classical Antiquity. Greek drama had placed man's capacity for acting on his moral decisions at the centre of its concerns ever since Pelasgos, in Aeschylus' *Hiketides*, had wrestled with the ethical dilemma posed by the refugee suppliants who had come to his city; from the Stoics had come ideals of virtue and glory that sprang from reason, self-knowledge and will-power; from Plotinus and the neo-Platonists a metaphysical justification for man's love and admiration for beautiful things. In the Italian Renaissance the world became man-centred once more. Man – virtuous, heroic, beautiful and passionate – was the central overwhelming fact of God's creation; 'Man', as the sophist Protagoras had said, '[was] the measure of all things'. This is the fundamental meaning of the word 'Humanism', and in the fifteenth and sixteenth centuries it was very largely Classically inspired.

Italian opera originated in a world whose attitudes were conditioned by humanism; and as far as serious opera is concerned, it remained faithful to that ideal throughout its history. Even in the earliest years, when opera was ostensibly mythological, the 'dignity and excellence of man' was the true theme. Orpheus, in Monteverdi's opera, may be a 'Semideo', as the shepherd claims in the first scene of the opera. But when his hour of glory is come, when Charon has been vanquished and the journey into Hades accomplished, what the chorus sings is 'Man undertakes no enterprise in vain.' 'Orpheus . . . moved the audience . . . because he was a man', declared the composer (Arnold 1963: 116). As long as the tradition survives, this humanist inheritance remains a vital ingredient. In Italian opera politics are rare, magical or metaphysical dramas virtually non-existent, mere escapist entertainments commendably few. Man is the theme; the individual personality is the hero; and his deeds, his passions, his pleasures and his sufferings are all treated with an absolute conviction of their reality and seriousness. Of Italian opera specifically we may say what Luigi Barzini said about Italian life in general: 'The pleasure of Italy comes from living in a world made by man, for man, on man's measurements' (1964: 57).

The fact could be illustrated from any of the great repertoires within the Italian tradition – from Venetian opera, or *opera seria*, or *verismo*. My examples are the closing scenes of two Verdi operas, *Rigoletto* and *La traviata*. Each ends with what might be described as a kind of *Liebestod*. To be sure, it is not a Novalis-cum-Schopenhauer-inspired *Liebestod*; rather one in which the afterlife is seen in sentimentalized Christian terms. Both Gilda and Violetta envisage themselves in Heaven, at their prayers among angels and the dear departed. They die in a mood of serene rapture, to that extent resembling Isolde; but that is the limit of the resemblance. In *Tristan und Isolde*, that 'opus metaphysicum of all Art', the Liebestod resolves the unendurable tensions of the drama in what Wagner apprehended as a metaphysical truth. For the Italian artist, the fact of death, whatever mood it may be approached in, is starkly tragic. More precisely, the annihilation of personality appals and terrifies. *Rigoletto* and *La traviata* conclude not in the supreme tranquillity of *Tristan und Isolde*, but with howls of anguish and dismay: 'Ah, la maledizione!'; 'O mio dolor!' This world is the world that matters; the characters whose lives have been devastated by fate are our final concern. Human personality in its human environment, whether flourishing or destroyed, remains the central and ultimate reality of Italian opera.

Sistemazione

A favourite Italian imprecation or threat is 'te sistemo io', which may be rendered approximately as 'I'll sort you out'. The verb 'sistemare' and its derivative noun 'sistemazione' are important words in Italian, with rather more complex and interesting associations than such English phrases as 'sorting out' or 'putting in order'. 'Order' carries with it connotations of pattern, proportion and symmetry. Italians enjoy giving form to things and then embellishing those forms with elegant and decorative surfaces. What foreign visitor to Italy has not been impressed, perhaps initially even repelled, by the geometrical formality of the Italian garden? And can the inspiration of perspective and mathematics be easily forgotten in the paintings of Renaissance Florence? What an incomparable stroke of musical *sistemazione* it was, when Vivaldi divined the ritornello form in the confusion of variegated colours, antiphonies in space, and contrasting levels of technical prowess that had been typical of the early concerto. Dante, the greatest of Italian poets, creates patterns out of Hell itself. In Italy 'to *sistemare* all things is considered to be the foremost, perhaps the unique, mission of man on earth' (Barzini 1964: 112).

This enthusiasm for formal lucidity, this tendency to reduce the multitudinous activities of mind and hand to forms and patterns, is inseparable from the Italian genius for decoration. For the obsession with creating patterns presupposes a love of the patterns themselves; and what Italians love they have adorned with all the abundance of their exuberant fancies. Thanks to this decorative flair the mere pattern becomes a work of art; even the trivial formalities of everyday life can become at least elegant rituals. 'Everything must be made to sparkle, a simple meal, an ordinary transaction, a dreary speech, a cowardly capitulation must be embellished and ennobled with euphemisms, adornments and pathos' (*ibidem*: 75). Against the French pride in the *mot juste*, we may set the Italian delight in pattern, ritual and adornment. This delight I would claim as a second *Leitmotiv* in Italian opera.

It has always been recognized as such by perceptive critics. Has there ever been a better evocation of the character of Rossinian *opera buffa* than Stendhal's, who called it 'chaos organized and made perfect'? Einstein writes of Verdi's *Macbeth* that 'where with Shakespeare mist arises, with Verdi something takes on form' (1947: 277). And what is Boito's celebrated article on form and formula in Italian opera but the same insight expressed from a hostile point of view? 'Since opera has existed in Italy down to our own times, we have never had true operatic form, but always only the diminutive, the formula' (quoted Walker 1962: 451). All great Italian artists have abhorred disorder. No matter how violent or complex the action, no matter how frenzied and manic the passions, Italian opera has resolved them into patterns in sound, ritualized and decorative structures – 'formulas' if one will – which tame their wildness and civilize them.

Since the whole Italian tradition of opera is pervaded by such *sistemazione*, it does not much matter where we look for examples. The very earliest operas, in theory, took their form from the text; it was a case of *prima le parole, dopo la musica*. But one need not spend many minutes with the score of *Orfeo* to see that this is simply not true. The whole opera is a glorious monument to the Italian genius for *sistemazione*, a rich pattern of ritornellos and refrains and variations. Of course the pattern is congruous with the drama, but in no way can it be described as a necessary consequence of the drama. *Opera seria* is another case in point. There are several perfectly sound aesthetic arguments in favour of its schematic structure and of the ubiquitousness of the so-called *da capo* aria, and they will be discussed at the appropriate point in this book. Meanwhile let it be observed that, for all that, the *opera seria* is another manifestation of the national love of ritualized order.

What is true of Italian opera in its broadest outlines is no less true of the details of its musical forms. There cannot be many operatic scenes more emotionally turbulent than that of the quartet in Act III of *Rigoletto*. Set at night, at a derelict riverside tavern on the outskirts of Mantua, a thunderstorm brewing in the distance, the scene depicts a complex turmoil of conflicting passions. Within, the libertine Duke flirts with the harlot Maddalena; their conversation is overheard by the seduced and betrayed Gilda, lurking outside in the street with her father, the hunch-backed jester Rigoletto, who meditates revenge. Yet in the great ensemble that distills the emotions of this harrowing scene, Verdi creates a beautifully poised form, an exquisite pattern of lights and shades, of symmetries and contrasts in perfectly balanced equilibrium.

The primacy of song

It was, of necessity, in Italy that the opportunities and problems inherent in the blending of drama and song were first recognized. And it is a critical commonplace to recognize that, very rapidly, Italian composers found a more conspicuous role in opera for song than composers working in any other tradition. What is perhaps less generally recognized is that a certain sleight of hand was necessary to bring about this state of affairs. In so far as early opera was an attempt to revive the tragic drama of the ancient Greeks, song in the sense of formal aria had no real part in it: in principle, the essentials were recitative and chorus. But in fact, consciously or unconsciously, musicians and poets compromised the spirit of tragedy with the spirit of pastoral drama. They did this in order to make more natural, or at least more plausible, that fusion of poetry and song that haunted their imaginations, and which, they were convinced, represented the most perfect achievement of Classical art.

The pastoral world was the appropriate world for the realization of such dreams. It is one of the principal functions of the pastoral convention to undo the corruption and decadence of 'real' life, to circumvent even the Fall itself, and to create an Utopian dream of man's life as it might have been, a vision of a Golden Age in some far distant time or place – often identified as Arcadia – where ideals of love and beauty are untarnished and all the most poignant yearnings of the human spirit may be stilled. In such a world, poetry and song were as natural to the nymphs and shepherds and demigods who peopled it, as conversational prose is to the decadent here-and-now. And for centuries artists played upon this deeply ingrained belief, filling their 'pastoral' novels with exquisite lyrics, as Boccaccio was already doing in *Ameto* in the fourteenth century; and filling their 'pastoral' poems and dramas with song and dance, as, to cite simply the most momentous example, Poliziano did in his *Orfeo*, first performed in Mantua in 1480. It was largely in order to justify a profusion of song and dance that the composers of the first operas employed pastoral themes, concerning themselves almost exclusively with that pre-lapsarian Golden Age when 'language was flowery and sweet, so that it had melody in every part . . . when music was natural and speech was like poetry' (G. B. Doni, quoted in Solerti 1903: 203). It is no mere chance that finds the earliest operas full of nymphs and shepherds, and with such heroes as Apollo and, above all, Orpheus, the semi-divine shepherd, who, according to legend, was the most magically gifted musician of all Antiquity.

While the operas of Rinuccini, Peri and Caccini are ostensibly attempts at reviving the Greek tragic drama, they in fact relied heavily on the pastoral convention to motivate the conspicuous role they assigned to music. Greek tragedy may have been sufficient justification for the chorus and for the recitative style. But the precise philosophy behind the use of virtuosic and enrapturing song was a little ambiguous; it depended upon a mixing of the genres, and on peopling the drama with characters of the right kind, like Orpheus. Such problems and ambiguities were, however, rapidly resolved. The primacy of song and a magnificently sure intuition of its function in the new art are already unmistakable in Monteverdi's *Orfeo*.

It will be remembered that, while the prologue of Rinuccini and Peri's *Euridice* is assigned to an allegorical figure representing the spirit of Tragedy, Striggio and Monteverdi's prologue is sung by *La musica*. The significance of this shift of emphasis from tragedy to music has often been commented on. Equally important is what Music tells us about herself:

> I am Music, who with my sweet accents
> Can soothe every troubled heart,
> I can inspire – now with noble rage, now with love –
> Even the coldest hearts.

Singing to my golden lyre
I sometimes soothe the ears of mortals;
And in this manner incline their souls
To desire the harmonies of the celestial lyre.

Song may have symbolized a vanished pastoral paradise, but Music assures us that it has more direct and urgent functions in drama. It soothes, it enchants, it elevates and inspires. But especially song stirs the passions, it enflames 'even the coldest heart now with noble rage and now with love'. Ever since Monteverdi, Italian and Italianate composers of opera have fulfilled the promises of that prologue almost as if it were a manifesto. Of course all have recognized, in a variety of ways, that opera is a form of dramatic *Gesamtkunstwerk*; but within that *Gesamtkunstwerk* the Italian composer has always regarded his principal task as being that of stirring the passions by song. Italians in their singing, remarked Mersenne, 'represent for all they are worth the passions and affections of the mind and soul, for example, anger, fury, rage, spite, swooning and several other passions, and they do this with incredible violence' (Fortune 1954: 211). Scarlatti in the eighteenth century would have endorsed Music's claim, and so would Puccini have done in the twentieth. But no one proclaimed the creed more trenchantly than Bellini, who, exasperated by the intellectual pretensions of Carlo Pepoli, the librettist of *I Puritani*, cried, 'Carve in your head in letters of adamant: *the music drama must draw tears, inspire terror, make people die*, through singing' (1943: 400).

The primary role played in the Italian tradition of opera by impassioned song has very much conditioned composers' attitudes to the types of drama that might be employed. If the characters are continually to indulge in what W. H. Auden called 'a form of public outcry' (1968: 88) about their emotional life, clearly a very particular style of drama is postulated. Italian opera demands a wide range of moods – without that, chronic monotony would set in at an early stage; and it demands character-types that are energetic, articulate and passionate. Introspective, secretive or frigid types would be a contradiction in terms. The matter is epitomized in Verdi's attempts to turn Shakespeare's greatest tragic heroes into operatic figures. (*King Lear* we will leave out of consideration as too complex an enterprise to be described in summary terms.) *Othello* yields a towering masterpiece, *Macbeth* a fascinating and high-minded but in the end not quite convincing problem-opera, *Hamlet* an utterly abortive project, abandoned the moment it was seriously thought about.

A language for singing

There can be few music libraries which do not have their copies of Mozart's *Il flauto magico* or Meyerbeer's *Gli Ugonotti*. Apt to provoke little more today than a condescending smile, these Italian translations of the standard

German and French operas are certainly relics of an age with different priorities from our own. I merely observe that in the days when the quality of the singing was the fundamental issue in the operatic experience, virtually all connoisseurs were of the opinion that Italian lent itself uniquely well to the purpose. 'There can be no doubt' – asserted Vaccai in his classic textbook of vocal method, the *Metodo pratico* of 1832 – 'but what the Italian language . . . by virtue of its euphony, is best suited to the art of singing' (Vaccai 1978: 3).

Italian is a Romance language, one of the family of languages derived from the Latin spoken throughout most of south and west Europe during the centuries of the Roman Empire. Indeed, for obvious geographical and historical reasons, it has remained the most central Romance language; not only retaining many Latin elements, but periodically delayed or diverted in its natural vernacular development by the readoption of Latinisms. This process might be seen as beginning as early as 825 when Lotario (the Frankish Emperor Lothair I) attempted to re-establish a cultivated Latin by instituting eight royal schools in northern Italy; but it was most marked during the fifteenth and sixteenth centuries, when humanist scholarship continually encouraged emulation of the classics.

One other historical peculiarity of Italian must be mentioned: the quite exceptional degree to which it became a language cultivated for literary and artistic purposes, rather than for everyday use. It was only in the wake of the *langue d'oil* and the *langue d'oc* of the trouvères and troubadours that the vernacular dialects of the Italian peninsula began to gain literary respectability. The first was Sicilian, which was widely read, copied and imitated during the thirteenth century; while Tuscan attained the status of a great literary language with Dante (1265–1321). Tuscan too were Petrarch (1304–74) and Boccaccio (1313–75), so that, by the end of the fourteenth century, their vernacular had acquired a prestige unique among the Italian dialects. Dante, Petrarch and Boccaccio came to be treated like the Latin authors of the classical past, monumentalized as exemplars of grammar, diction, imagery and style. By the fifteenth century 'the terms "vernacular", "Florentine", "Tuscan", "Italian", were used promiscuously and apparently indifferently' (Migliorini and Baldelli 1964: 123). Thereafter, the introduction of printing, the scholarly care devoted to editorial work on the Italian classics of the fourteenth century, humanist debate in the academies, more centralized and bureaucratic governments in place of the communes of the Middle Ages, all encouraged the development of a more standardized, educated Italian. These tendencies came to a climax with the appearance in 1612 of the *Vocabulario* issued by the Accademia della Crusca, the first great, comprehensive dictionary to be produced for any modern language. But the *Vocabulario* was not concerned with 'Italian as she is spoken', rather with 'strict adherence to the criterion of an archaizing Florentinism' (Migliorini and Baldelli 1964: 195).

The corollary to this attitude to the Italian language as an achievement of art remote from the needs of mundane, everyday communication was the intense and highly individual development of a multitude of regional dialects. Given the low level of literacy in Italy there was nothing to check this development until the Unification of 1861. At the Unification less than a quarter of Italians were literate; and the number who spoke 'Italian' was probably less than 10 per cent.

Meanwhile, largely insulated from the needs of real life, Italian writers were free to cultivate a language which they felt to be uniquely pure, sweet and euphonious. Certainly it is a language that lent itself superbly to song. It has an unusually high proportion of vowels to consonants, especially of those clear bell-like vowels, the 'a' and 'e' sounds that resonate in the roof of the mouth; and that is, in Rossini's words, 'the transmitter par excellence of beautiful sounds' (Michotte 1968: 115). What the seventeenth-century composer Ottavio Durante called the 'odious vowels', 'i' and 'u', which constrict the emission of sound, or push the singer towards a falsetto style, are never so frequent that the composer cannot avoid placing long notes or coloratura passages on them – in 1624 Crivellati compared roulades on 'i' and 'u' with quacking and howling (Fortune 1954: 216). At the same time, Italian is strongly accented and decisively articulated. While the clusters of consonants that fracture the flow of tone are largely avoided 'yet the articulations of its consonants, are more firm, vigorous and poignant, than in any other language'; and 'a neat, clear and articulate pronunciation of consonants is as necessary to the intelligence of what is singing, as open vowels are to its being well sung' (Burney 1789: 502). The cantabile qualities of the language are much enhanced by virtue of another factor: 'the passage from one word to another can be made with the greatest fluency, since all its words, whether nouns or verbs, end in a vowel, a few monosyllables excepted' (Arteaga 1785: 84). This was an asset that came to be fully realized in the eighteenth century when, under French influence, Italian poets learned to eschew Latinate inversions, and to cultivate a simple sentence construction in which 'the linear phrase tended to replace the architectonic' (Migliorini and Baldelli 1964: 230): this unaffected syntax was surely one of the sources of the fabled singing quality of Metastasio's verse.

Not the least musical feature of the language arose from the temperament with which it and its related dialects were used by native speakers. Comparing, perhaps somewhat gratuitously, the vivacious and imaginative Italians with the 'impassive' Muscovites and the 'bellowing' Swiss, Arteaga noted that their language 'seems full of interjections, of exclamations, of distinct and perceptible tones' (*suoni spiccati e sensibili*) (1785: 103). Burney commented that 'every dialect has peculiar inflexions of voice, which form a kind of *tune* in its utterance' and that Italian had 'a greater compass and variety of intervals in this colloquial *tune* or *cantilena*, than any other [language] with which I am acquainted' (1776–89: 500). Modern phoneticians confirm that 'Italian seems to be sung, with sinuous pitch movement over two octaves' (*Encyclopaedia Britannica* 15th edn, s.v. 'Romance Lan guages'). When Burney conversed with Metastasio 'on the euphony of languages', and commended Italian as 'more favourable . . . for Music, than any other European tongue', the poet cried out 'È la musica stessa'[1] (Burney 1776–89: 500).

One must also record some reservations. In any age when the enchantment of opera was primarily due to the magic of great singing, it was a source of nothing but gratification that Italian avoided the non-cantabile elements of other European languages. It suffered neither from the mutes and nasals of French, nor from the guttural consonant conglomerations of German, nor from the hissings and chewed diphthongs and backward consonants of English. Its brilliance and sonorousness as a singing language were indeed beyond compare; but as Gounod said, 'is brilliance and sonority everything in music?' What about the nuance, the half-shadow, the understatement? These, it may be conceded, have not been the strengths of Italian opera. The language has contributed its part to a tradition that has been more notable for an extrovert, flamboyant, rhetorical kind of theatricality. Gounod continued, 'Do you know what I compare the Italian language with? A magnificent bouquet of roses, peonies, crocuses, rhododendrons . . . but wanting heliotropes, mignonettes, violets . . .' (Reichenburg 1937: 98–9).

By the second half of the nineteenth century there were also those who noticed that the facility with which the Italian language could be turned into full-throated song was having a detrimental effect on composers' rhythmic resource. The strong accentuation and the pure, resonating vowels led to a convention of word-setting that Boito was to denounce as a 'cantilena of symmetry . . . that mighty dowry and mighty sin of Italian prosody which generates a meanness and poverty of rhythm within the musical phrase' (Budden 1978: 16–17). This was in the context of an essay in which he commended Verdi for seizing the opportunity offered by the French language in *Les Vêpres siciliennes* for escaping into more fluid and varied rhythmic patterns.

Conviviality

The last of these national characteristics that have dictated the tone of Italian opera is a quality I would describe as conviviality. It was less a feature of the operas themselves than of the atmosphere and environment in which they were performed. But since opera is supremely a social form of art, the conviviality of the setting did affect the work of art in a number of ways.

Conviviality developed a little more slowly than the other qualities I have been describing. The Italian language, obviously, was there from the start; the humanist sensibility too; *sistemazione* and the primacy of song are accomplished facts within the first decade of opera's history. Conviviality was perhaps not an established condition before the second half of the seventeenth century. Thereafter it is constantly present, surviving until the early decades of the present century, when it was destroyed, largely by the work of Toscanini.

Three crucial steps taken during the Italian phase of Toscanini's conducting career epitomize this rooting-out of conviviality. First, at Genoa and Turin, in the early 1890s, we find him refusing to countenance any longer the *ad hoc* orchestral ensembles that were assembled to accompany the opera in many Italian cities at this time. At his insistence, orchestras and later choruses became as thoroughly professional as the soloists; no one was admitted to them any longer without a rigorous audition. Secondly, during the 1906–07 season at La Scala, Toscanini banned the encore; and thirdly, at the beginning of the great decade 1920–29 during which he restored La Scala's reputation as the first opera-house in the world, he brought about a complete reorganization of the principles of theatre life, one of the results of which was the abolition of the old box-system. No longer were the boxes in the theatre private property, passed down in the wealthy families of the city from generation to generation; they became available to any member of the public who cared to pay the appropriate admission fee. No bungling amateurism, then, no encores, no private boxes: Toscanini's ideals were those of uncompromising professionalism, of the integrity of the work of art, of the theatre as a temple sacred to the muses, not merely a social amenity.

The box-system that Toscanini dismantled in 1920 had been the backbone of Italian theatre life for the best part of 300 years. From Venice, where it had first evolved as a form of insurance, it had spread rapidly to the other cities of Italy. Where it was not commercially necessary, as at some of the court operas, it was nevertheless retained because to have one's box at the opera was recognized as a charming social asset. Considering the fact that the system survived for three centuries in many cities very different in social and political character, it underwent remarkably few modifications; and it affected the whole Italian attitude to theatre-going. Above all a box of one's own, a supernumerary drawing-room as it were, which just happened to be at the theatre, did encourage people to go to the opera regularly, night after night, as a matter of course. The box was their public salon: there they could meet their friends, there they could mingle with the best society of the town.

The effect of the box-system on theatrical manners is not immediately apparent from such seventeenth-century reports as survive. The diarist John Evelyn, for example, visited the opera in Venice frequently during his stay in the city in 1645. He was amazed by the spectacle, and enthralled by the singing of the *castrati*; but he has nothing to say about the social life of the theatre. Perhaps the art form was still too new, too fascinating and too surprising, at least for a visitor, for him to notice anything but the essentials. But by the time we come to the eighteenth-century accounts, France, Germany and England all have their own operatic traditions. Visitors can compare theatre life in Venice or Naples with theatre life in Paris or London, and they begin to evince surprise at some of the practical consequences of the system. 'The pleasure these people take in music and the theatre is more evidenced by their presence than by the attention they bestow on the performance', writes Charles de Brosses in 1739. '. . . Chess is marvellously well adapted to filling in the monotony of the recitatives, and the arias are equally good for interrupting a too assiduous concentration on chess' (Grout 1947: 197–8). In Venice, in the 1790s, reports a German traveller, Johann Christoph Maier, 'there is a constant noise of people laughing, drinking, and joking, while sellers of baked goods and fruit cry their wares aloud from box to box' (*ibidem*). But perhaps the most interesting of the eighteenth-century accounts is that of Giuseppe Baretti, who in 1769 published a book on Italian manners, specifically designed to correct the misleading impressions given by the reports of casual visitors, particularly those of the surgeon Samuel Sharp, author of a volume of *Letters from Italy*. When it came to opera, Baretti did not deny the talk and laughter and inattention. On the contrary, his defence of his fellow countrymen was to assert that this kind of behaviour showed their good sense.

Singing is only a diversion, and attended to with no more seriousness than a diversion deserves. I have told you already, that we have so great a plenty of music in Italy as to have very good reason to hold it cheap; and every sensible Englishman must wonder at [Mr Sharp's] solemnity of scolding, as if we were committing murder when we are talkative in the pit, or form ourselves into card-parties in our boxes . . . When we are at the opera we consider [the singers] in the lump as one of the many things that induced us to be there; and we pay the same attention to their singing which we pay to other parts of that diversion . . .   (Baretti 1769: 302–3)

When we reach the nineteenth century the picture does not change, it only becomes more vivid and in some respects more surprising, because the men and women who used the boxes were no longer rationalists like Baretti, sceptical of the real worth of opera as an art-form, but often real enthusiasts. A good example is Stendhal. From his *Life of Rossini* and his journal *Rome, Naples and Florence in 1817* we know that Stendhal adored music, was deeply moved by it and wrote about it with unique perception. Yet this is what he has to say about the opera-going habit:

Introduction

Every day I go to Signor di Brema's box at La Scala . . . It is an entirely literary society
. . . I bring these gentlemen news of France, anecdotes about the retreat from Moscow,
Napoleon, the Bourbons; they pay me back with news of Italy . . . I don't know
anything in Paris to compare with this box where, every evening, one sees fifteen or
twenty distinguished men sit themselves down one after another; and if the conversation
ceases to be interesting one listens to the music.

(Stendhal 1817, entry for 12 November 1816)

The impression given so far of the working of the box-system must be
qualified. In republican Venice in the eighteenth century, in such liberal
cities of the nineteenth century as Milan and Florence, it was certainly the
case that the possession of a private box encouraged an extraordinarily
casual attitude to the opera. The music was there if one required it: if one
did not, one could draw the curtains and withdraw into an entirely different
world, visiting and being visited, entertaining oneself in whatever way most
suited the mood of the moment, calling for refreshments. But until the
unification of Italy several of the leading opera-houses in the peninsula,
notably those of Turin and Naples, were court theatres. There etiquette
was distinctly more starchy: in the presence of the court, laughter and
conversation, even applause, were strictly proscribed; there could be no
question of drawing the curtains of the boxes; the company sat formally
dressed and brilliantly illuminated and submissively mannered for the
whole evening.

If the box-system was the most important single factor in giving the
Italian opera-house its remarkable social character, a second was probably
the fact that much of the music was in the hands of amateurs. A few
opera-houses had fully professional orchestras – La Scala and the San Carlo
in Naples in the nineteenth century, perhaps La Fenice in Venice. But in
the majority of cases, the professors, as they were called, formed only a part
of the whole. In cities that had schools of music the better students were
conscripted for the local opera; elsewhere numbers were swelled by such
local dilettantes as were available, men prepared to play for a pittance, a bit
of pocket money or nothing at all. At Lucca towards the end of the
eighteenth century Mrs Piozzi was shocked to find an abbé playing in the
opera orchestra 'for eighteenpence pay' (Rosselli 1984: 114). The situation
with chorus singers was even more redolent of present-day amateur
operatics: not only were many of the singers non-professionals; in smaller
theatres there was no money for dressing them, and they had to supply their
own costumes. And probably only a minority of such theatres were as lucky
as the Teatro Regio in Parma in the middle decades of the nineteenth
century, which had, in Signor Toscanini senior, a professional tailor among
their amateur *coristi*.

Such conditions naturally imposed limitations on what could be done
with choruses and orchestras. In most places complex choral writing of the

kind associated with the Paris Opéra was completely out of the question. Orchestras, too, outside Milan, Venice and Naples, often left much to be desired. Particularly notorious in the early nineteenth century were the Roman orchestras, which Berlioz described in memorable terms:

formidable and imposing in the manner of the Monégasque army, possessing every single quality that is normally considered a defect. At the Valle Theatre the 'cellos number precisely one, a goldsmith by trade, in which respect he is more fortunate than one of his colleagues, who earns his living by repairing cane-bottomed chairs.

(1969: 186)

What concerns us in the present context, however, is not the effect such amateurism may have had on the quality of the performance, but the extent to which it contributed to the growth of conviviality. For the opera was, clearly, a convivial social occasion. The music was the pretext that drew people to the theatre, but once there they enjoyed it in their own way. Some, like the amateur singers and players, joined in the performance; others listened, intent and enthralled; others again were largely engrossed in the social life of the opera-house and cared little for the music. But, for whatever motive, the entire community was drawn together in a single celebration; art, sometimes great art, was a central, everyday concern.

The convivial environment was not without its influence on the critical and appreciative faculties of Italian audiences. When the modern music-lover goes to the opera-house his conduct there, thanks largely to the triumph of what may be described as the Wagnerian attitude to opera, more resembles that of the worshipper at a religious service than that of the family man relaxing at home. For an Italian of the pre-Toscanini era the reverse was generally the case. The theatre was as familiar to him as his own sitting-room, and there he passed judgement on the compositions and performances that were offered him, with absolute confidence and total absence of reserve. The Irish tenor Michael Kelly describes Roman audiences in the 1760s like this:

The Romans assume they are the most sapient critics in the world; they are certainly the most severe ones: – they have no medium – all is delight or disgust . . . The severest critics are the Abbés, who sit in the first row of the pit, each armed with a lighted wax taper in one hand, and a book of the opera in the other, and should any poor devil of a singer miss a word, they call out, 'bravo bestia' – 'bravo, you beast!' Should any passage strike the audience as similar to one of another composer, they cry, 'Bravo, il ladro' – 'bravo, you thief'.

(1975: 32–3)

And here is Stendhal describing a typical Italian audience of forty years later:

These are men possessed of seven devils, determined at all costs, by dint of shrieking, stamping and battering with their canes against the backs of the seats in front, to enforce the triumph of *their* opinion, and above all, to prove, that, come what may, *none but their opinion is correct.*

(1956: 112)

14

Delight was expressed with equal abandon. Spohr tells us that at the precise moment a Rossini crescendo reached its climactic *tutti*, audiences invariably 'exploded with cries of "bravo" and frenzied applause' (1860: 330). A neatly executed cadenza or trill apparently had the same effect. At successful performances of the finest operas there seem to have been extraordinary scenes of communal rapture.[2]

Clearly the relationship between the composer and his audience was very much more direct and real than anything with which we are familiar today. It was not refracted by an Arts Council policy, nor manipulated by expert critics. The connoisseurs who decided whether an opera was a good opera or not were the audiences who sat in the theatre, enjoying it or not enjoying it. If a composer wrote operas that thrilled or delighted people all over Italy he was a great composer; if he didn't he wasn't, and it cut no ice to read in the newspaper next day that his modulations were sublime, or his instrumentation deeply scientific.

The characteristics I have outlined in this introduction combined to give opera in Italy its national distinctiveness. Almost always it has been notably unproblematic; almost always it has been effective theatrically and widely popular. At the same time it has had a basic human seriousness, and its sense of style has often been the envy of composers working in less well founded traditions. The way in which these qualities have manifested themselves through the centuries may now be investigated.

Part I
The origins of opera

1 · The Renaissance *intermedi*

The role of the *intermedi* in Renaissance festivities

Of the virtues commended to the faithful by St Thomas Aquinas none was more gladly embraced by the princes of Renaissance Italy than Magnificence: they were never happier than when giving ostentatious form to their most generous impulses. Royal weddings, birthdays, state visits, diplomatic coups – all were celebrated 'with pomp, with triumph, and with revelling'. The form of these revels varied widely; there were masques and ballets, processional pageants, jousts and banquets. And increasingly during the sixteenth century there were theatricals, of which historically the most momentous were those revivals of the Latin comedies of Terence and Plautus that took place at Ferrara, beginning in the last years of the fifteenth century under the enthusiastic protection of Duke Ercole I. 'Carmina te dicent scenam instaurasse poetis',[1] prophesied the court-poet Battista Guarini (Flechsig 1894: 12).

The inclusion of dramatic performances at court feasts grew out of the long-established custom of the 'entremets', the purpose of which – as, for example, at the Burgundian court on the occasion of the Feast of the Pheasant in 1454 – was to provide respite from the gormandizing with entertainments of song, dance, mime and recitation. Towards the end of the fifteenth century, when a liking for more regular types of drama was developing, the songs and dances that were so well received as *entremets* were not abandoned. Instead, by analogy with the chorus of the Classical Greek theatre, they were used to frame and articulate the play, appearing at the ends of the acts – 'intermedii a li acti', to use a form of words that appears for the first time in Niccolò da Correggio's *Cefalo* of 1487 (Pirrotta 1969a: 66). For those who did not share Duke Ercole's passion for Classical drama these *intermedi* became the most enjoyable part of the performance: Isabella d'Este, in a letter to her husband, was the first of many to confess how welcome was the relief they provided from the austere and recondite pleasures of the drama (Flechsig 1894: 12).

Ferrara was not alone in its cultivation of spoken drama with *intermedi* of dance and song. Indeed for the later history of the *intermedio*, and hence for the history of opera, a more important tradition evolved in Florence, where, from the Restoration of the Medici in 1513, the most ostentatious forms of art were being laid under contribution to help the consolidation of the dynasty. For, as has been observed, 'before the invention of the mechanical mass media of today, the creation of "monarchs" as an "image" to draw people's allegiance was the task of humanists, poets, writers and artists' (Strong 1973: 19). The greater dynastic occasions called for entertainments on a truly sumptuous scale, as is shown by the calendar of events to celebrate the wedding of Francesco de'Medici and Joanna of Austria in 1565.

December 16: formal entrance of the bride into Florence. The cortège proceeded from the Porta al Prato, through a city decked out with triumphal arches, to the Palazzo Vecchio.
December 18: solemn nuptial ceremonies in the cathedral.
December 25: performance of the comedy *La Cofanaria* by Francesco d'Ambra in the Salone dei Cinquecento . . . G. B. Cini composed the interludes (*intermedii*) on the theme of Cupid and Psyche.
February 2: allegorical cavalcade, the *Trionfo de'Sogni*.
February 17: siege of a fortress erected in the Piazza Santa Maria Novella.
February 21: the procession of the *Genealogia degli Dei*, with 21 floats and 392 mythological or allegorical figures.
February 26: the *Mascherate delle Bufole*.
March 10: a musical and theatrical representation of the Annunciation in the church of Santo Spirito. (Nagler 1964: 14–15)

At the peak of their development in the 1580s, the plays and *intermedi* alone were formidable logistic exercises. During the preparations for Bardi's *L'amico fido* in 1586, the scenographer Buontalenti had 400 artists and craftsmen working for him – though of course not all dramatic performances were on that scale.

The *intermedio* began as an element in some feast or celebration. Drama in the proper sense of the term was therefore subordinate to panegyric; a central motif in the entertainment was always the formal homage to the guest of honour. A good example is provided by the *Trionfo* performed on 6 July 1539 as part of the festivities for the nuptials of Cosimo I. This included a kind of allegorical revue, in which the principal cities of Tuscany paid loyal tribute to their grand duke:

appearing to pay homage to Cosimo and Eleanora, Flora, the patron goddess (of Florence), stepped before the Duke and sang a *canzone* composed by . . . Festa. She then drew herself up sideways to permit the appearance of Pisa, who, escorted by three nymphs and a grotesque Triton, now drew attention to herself. The nymphs brought the bridal couple products of their respective regions modelled in coloured sugar. After Pisa's canzonet . . . followed the appearance of Volterra with five nymphs, whose costumes and kettle-shaped head-pieces pointed to the Tuscan mining-industry . . . Then followed Arezzo, Cortona, Pistoia, the Tiber and even Lady Rome.
(Nagler 1964: 9)

The artists who devised the *intermedi* never entirely abandoned this kind of laborious and superficial symbolism. But at its best – in the 1589 set for example – the *intermedio* worked at a deeper level, in which the formal tribute was indistinguishable from a Platonic vision of cosmic harmony: both the artistically ordered proportions of musical harmony (*musica instrumentalis*, to give it its mediaeval name) and the well ordered government of social and political life (*musica humana*) were parallel microcosms of that *musica mundana* which God had implanted in His universe; the one – *musica instrumentalis* – therefore became an entirely natural symbol of the other – *musica humana*. Jacopo Sansovino made the point quite specifically in explaining why he had depicted Apollo on the *loggetta* of the campanile of St Mark's, Venice: 'because from the union of its Magistrates there issues extraordinary harmony, which perpetuates this admirable government, Apollo was depicted' (Fenlon 1979: 26).

Drama and allegory

In the early history of the *intermedio* its essence was to be found in its pantomimic dancing. As with the *entremets* of an earlier age, impresarios did not flinch from mixing together the most incongruous ingredients – 'buffoons and tumblers . . . morescas comic and exotic . . . mythological evocations and moral and political allegory' (Pirrotta 1969a: 72). The coarser and more farcical elements never quite vanished from the *intermedi* and in due course this strain becomes one of the sources of Italian comic opera. But in the sixteenth century dance and mime gradually yielded pride of place to music and spectacle; spectacle which was often of formidable allegorical density and inspired by the loftiest philosophical intentions.

A relationship was sometimes claimed between these allegorical *intermedi* and the naturalistic world of the plays they framed. The *intermedi* were understood to give a metaphysical explanation of the action, as the scenes of divinities were to do in seventeenth-century opera. Of the *intermedi* which accompanied Francesco d'Ambra's *La Cofanaria* (1565) Grazzini wrote, 'all the *intermedi* were taken from the story of Psyche and Cupid' and had been treated with such skill 'as to make it appear that those things which the Gods performed in the plot of the *intermedi*, were also done, as if under constraint of some higher power, by the mortals in the comedy' (Pirrotta 1969a: 229). But the fact that in 1589 the same *intermedi* could be performed with three quite different plays – Bargagli's *La pellegrina*, an anonymous *La zingara*, and Isabella Andreini's *La pazzia* – makes it clear that such interrelationships can rarely have been significant. By then the virtuosity of scenographers and machinists was the dominant factor, not relevance to the play. In describing Giovanni Bardi's work on the 1585 *intermedi*, Bastiano de'Rossi, best known as the first secretary of the Accademia della Crusca, explains that their composition posed a dilemma for Bardi, precisely because of the conflict between his own preference for thematic coherence and the obligatory 'varietà' of music and spectacle demanded by the *intermedi* (Walker 1963: xxix).

The favourite source for the themes of the *intermedi* (and of early opera) was that great compendium of Classical mythology, the *Metamorphoses* of Ovid. Particularly popular were those myths with musical connotations, and none haunted the imagination of the age more fruitfully than the myth of the Golden Age (*Metamorphoses* Book I). Its aptness for a quasi-dramatic form, one of whose principal functions was panegyric, is clear – a Golden Age is always anticipated when the future of the dynasty is secured – and it became a kind of *Leitmotiv* running through virtually the whole century, from the Florentine theatricals of 1513 to the *intermedi* master-minded by Bardi in 1586 and 1589. The madrigal 'Or che le due grand'alme' (text: Strozzi, music: Malvezzi), from the fourth *intermedio* of 1589 provides a succinct summary of those Golden Age manifestations that were to be hoped for: it looks forward to the flourishing of virtuous enterprise – 'ogni alma al ben oprar s'accende e punge'; to the banishing of care – 'volane lunge la cagion del pianto'; and, not least, to the return of music as a spontaneous and natural art – 'e felice ritorna eterno canto'. (Why music needed to return, will be explained in Chapter 2.)

The Florentine tradition of *intermedi* came to a climax in the entertainments devised by Bardi in 1586 and 1589. No one was better fitted than he to exploit the allegorical complexities of the medium; in his hands its poetic, musical and figurative resources became a mirror in which was reflected a transcendent Platonic vision. In 1586, the theme of his *intermedi* for *L'amico fido* were the four elements of earth, air, water and fire, of which the universe was believed to be formed. These four elements or, to be more precise, their four 'kingdoms' – earth and heaven, sea and hell – recurred in 1589, and here Bardi's philosophical intentions were even more apparent, the emphasis on Platonic imagery and on musical allegory even more unmistakable. Bardi was attempting 'to make visible the profoundest mysteries of the universe as shadowed forth in Plato and Horace' (Warburg 1932: 281). *Intermedi* I, IV and VI were allegories of the *musica mundana*, while *Intermedi* II, III and V were illustrations of the force of *musica instrumentalis* in the age of mythology. No detail of text, scenery or costume was too trifling for Bardi's attention; and his colleague Rossi was put to work as a mythological exegete, providing a 'prologo scientifico' to explain the author's intentions to the audience.

In the first *intermedio* of 1589 Bardi draws on the myth of Er, son of Armenius, of the race of Pamphylia, a story recounted in the tenth book of Plato's *Republic*. It takes the form of an allegory of that *musica mundana* by which the order, the rhythm and movement of the cosmos is maintained. We are shown 'the spindle of Necessity, by means of which all the circles revolve'; the 'planets' on their eight circles – fixed stars, Sun, Moon,

Saturn, Mercury, Jupiter, Mars, Venus is Plato's order – whose Sirens emit the musical notes that create the Music of the Spheres; and the three Fates, the daughters of Necessity, who sing 'Lachesis of what has been, Clotho of what is, and Atropos of what shall be'. The opening music of the *intermedio* is sung by the figure of *Armonia Doria*, the Dorian being that mode most revered in the Ancient World. In the beginning was Harmony, one might almost say; and Harmony speaks the Word which brings forth cosmic order.

Against this vision of the *musica mundana* one may set the image of *musica humana* and *musica instrumentalis* in the sixth and last *intermedio*. In Plato's *Laws*, Jupiter authorizes Apollo, Bacchus and the Muses to bring mankind music and dance as a comfort and a refreshment from labour: men were to be given 'the power to perceive and enjoy rhythm and melody'. And this Platonic myth combines with the Ovidian vision of the Golden Age. With the wedding of Christina and Ferdinando, the Golden Age returns; and oak-trees distil honey and the streams flow with milk; the Gods descend to earth bringing 'il bello e'il buon Ch'in ciel si serra Per far al Paradiso ugual la terra',[2] and the dance and song gifted to mortals help them to make the *musica humana* a perfect image of the *musica mundana*.

Dance and song

Dance had played a central role in the *intermedio* from the first. But in this context it will be sufficient to emphasize just one aspect of the balletic art of the Renaissance, which is that by the second half of the sixteenth century it was as richly conditioned by Classical lore as any of the arts. The third *intermedio* of 1589 included a representation of the Pythian games honouring Apollo. It is lost; sadly, for Rossi's account makes it sound one of the most interesting pieces in the score:

In this *intermedio* the poet wished to represent the Pythian battle in the form taught us by Julius Pollux, who says that when this fight was represented in ancient music it was divided into five parts: in the first Apollo looked to see that the place was convenient for the battle, in the second he challenged the serpent, and in the third, in iambic verse, he did battle: in the fourth, which was in spondaic verse, was represented the death of this serpent and the victory of the god. And in the fifth, he danced a joyful leaping dance, signifying victory. (Warburg 1932: 286)

In contrast the ballet in the sixth *intermedio* has been described as a 'striking reversal of humanist values', on the grounds that, while its inspiration may have been Platonic, the way in which it was worked out flatly contradicted the principles one normally associates with Bardi and his circle or indeed with any of the other humanist groups of the age (Walker 1963: xxvii). Apparently the choreography was devised first; then the music was composed; and only finally was the text written. But even if this

Plate 1 The first *intermedio* to Bargagli's *La pellegrina*, performed in Florence, in the Uffizi theatre, 1589. Engraving by A. Carracci

was so, was it necessarily a procedure unworthy of humanists? Must the word, the concept, necessarily have priority over the image – is it indeed any more completely adequate a metaphor for the reality? If the theme of this *intermedio* is the bridging over of the chasms that separate the different orders of music – *mundana*, *humana* and *instrumentalis* – then a medium that is able to make the divine mathematics visible and audible can surely quite properly take precedence over the verses in which these mysteries are conceptualized.

Next to the ballet the most important musical element was the madrigal, or in earlier years the *frottola*. Pirrotta is confident that many *frottolas*, particularly those published in Petrucci's Book VI (1506) and later, originated in the *intermedi*: he comments on the frequency with which the singers introduce themselves, explaining who they are, how they are dressed, why they have come, etc. (Pirrotta 1969a: 79). Such representational devices as mime and onomatopoeia are frequently suggested. By the middle of the sixteenth century Italian madrigalists had already acquired an expressive range appreciably wider than English madrigalists would ever achieve, or see any reason to attempt to achieve, and in the theatrical context of the *intermedio* they did not quail before the most grisly expressive tasks. In the fourth *intermedio* of *La Cofanaria*,

two anthropophagi made their appearance playing trombones. Each of them was escorted by two Furies carrying whips and other instruments of torture . . . [which were camouflaged] musical instruments. The Furies' bodies were covered with wounds, from which hot flames seemed to spit; they were girdled with snakes and their arms and legs were in chains. The figures on stage [Discord, Cruelty, Rapine and Revenge as well as the anthropophagi and Furies] danced a galliard and sang a madrigal composed by Corteccia, with a brazen, warlike melody.   (Nagler 1964: 20)

At about the same time, in *intermedi* performed in 1567 and 1569, the elder Striggio was beginning to dramatize the madrigal in another way, exploring its resources of timbre, distributing and subdividing the voices to create vivid effects of musical dialogue.

Even in the 1589 *intermedi*, where a leading role was played by men associated with Bardi's Camerata,[3] the madrigal remained the central form. Surprisingly, in view of the historical reputation of these men, the style is a predominantly festive one, little affected by progressive ideals either in language or technique. The music provides a careful declamation of the text in a sonorous chordal style, but it is harmonically plain and unsophisticated in texture. Even Marenzio is expressively restrained in this festive style. Such pieces as 'O valoroso Dio' and 'O mille volte' from the third *intermedio* are in his simplest and most hedonistic Roman manner.

Indeed, the only madrigal in the entire score that seems seriously touched by the ideals of what was later to become known as the *seconda prattica*[4] is Bardi's own 'Miseri habitator' in the fourth *intermedio*. It is rather like one of the more extreme late madrigals of Rore. The verse structure is reflected in the clear-cut phraseology of the music; the rhythms reflect with fair fidelity those of the words; the upper voice moves within a tiny range – which one may see either as a reflection of the doctrine that melody should arise from the diastematic imitation of the text, or alternatively as the result of Girolamo Mei's teachings on the subject of Greek melody – and the harmonies in some measure lend their colour to intensify the sense of the words (Ex.I.1). But elsewhere musical values clearly outweigh poetic or dramatic values; the singers of the madrigals rarely even impersonate the characters they represent. In the second *intermedio*, for example, the nine Pierides are represented by a choir of six singers, the nine Muses by two choirs of six voices apiece, and the three Graces by another six-voice choir. Perhaps the moral is that, as with the closing ballet, one runs the risk of exaggerating the narrow-mindedness of humanist musicians. Given its preponderance in the 1589 *intermedi* we must assume that the festive madrigal style was enjoyed and approved of by Bardi. In any case, what he can have hardly failed to notice, listening to such a piece as 'A voi reali amanti', is that – all theoretical considerations notwithstanding – only an old-fashioned madrigal style, with its throbbing sonorities and its spacious antiphonies, could evoke in the imagination the vision of a universe resonating with harmony.

Compared with the madrigals, the monodies are few in number, a fact

. . .the horror and the torment will be eternal. . .

Ex.I.1 Bardi, 'Miseri habitator'. *Intermedio* IV (1589)

that has sometimes surprised historians. And indeed some of these few, 'Io
che l'onde raffreno' from the fifth *intermedio*, for example, are really
madrigals performed as accompanied solos. Those that are unmistakably
monodic in conception have ostensibly little to do with the austere ideals
which Galilei and Bardi proclaimed in their theoretical writings, for all of
them are of a truly virtuosic floridity. The interesting point emerges when
we consider what function these florid solos performed; for then we see that
each of them is in some sense an epiphany, a meeting point between the
divine and the human: 'Dalle più alte sfere' (*Intermedio* I) is an allegorical
representation of the divine attribute of harmony descending to earth in
order to be comprehensible to men; 'Io che dal ciel' (*Intermedio* IV – see
Ex.I.2) represents a 'medium' – a sorceress – in communion with the
divine; and 'Dunque fra torbid'onde' (*Intermedio* V) is the song of a divinely
inspired artist. Clearly florid solo song was the medium for vatic rapture.
Its virtuosity is of an inward kind; it is not addressed to an audience to
create a brilliant and astonishing effect; rather it gives the effect of an
improvisation, a self-communing by one in thrall to the divine afflatus. And
because the supporting accompaniment avoids a steady rhythmic pulse the
music is freed from its most earth-bound element; hovering above simple
and almost imperceptibly moving harmonies, this effortless torrent of song
acquires an 'ethereal and crystalline serenity' (Pirrotta 1969a: 267). These
monodies look back to the Orphic singing of the fifteenth century (see pp.
65–6) and forward to 'Possente spirto' in Act III of Monteverdi's *Orfeo*.

I who might make the moon fall from heaven give command to you who
are aloft and see the whole heaven. . .

Ex.I.2 Caccini, 'Io che dal ciel'. *Intermedio* IV (1589)

The Renaissance *instrumentarium*

No aspect of the music of the *intermedi* was more important for early opera, particularly for Monteverdi's *Orfeo*, than what we may, somewhat anachronistically, describe as their orchestration. *A cappella* madrigal singing was rare in the *intermedi*; generally the voices were supported by groups of instruments and these groups became larger and more multicoloured as the century progressed. The Florentine *intermedi* of 1539 required approximately eight singers and eight instrumentalists; fifty years later the numbers had risen to approximately sixty and thirty, respectively (Brown 1973: 77). Of the instrumentalists some performed backstage in a kind of 'orchestra'; others were costumed and played their instruments – often camouflaged – on stage as part of the *tableau vivant* of the *intermedio*.

Instrumentation was an art based on the consort. The favourite instruments – viols, recorders, flutes, trombones etc. – were built in families, and in principle, in the earlier part of the century at least, a piece of instrumental music was played by one such family or consort. But pure consort scoring of this kind came to be modified in two ways (quite apart from the question of the combination of instruments with voices). In the first place, the weaker or more awkward members of the consort were replaced or strengthened by instruments from other families – cornetts often replaced high trombones, for example, and solo viols were often used to highlight the treble and bass lines. Secondly, it became common practice to add to the consort one or more foundation or continuo instruments. These would have been particularly valuable in helping maintain good ensemble despite the increasingly elaborate antics in which the on-stage instrumentalists found themselves involved. Brown estimates that by 1565 'foundation-scoring' was as important a principle as consort-scoring, and certainly by 1589 a vast array of continuo instruments was in use: lutes, *chitarroni*, harps, keyboard instruments, and lyres. Both these developments – the highlighting of the outer voices and dependence on the continuo – point toward seventeenth-century instrumental practice.

Certain types of tableau recurred again and again in the *intermedio*: celestial scenes, set among the divinities of Olympus, infernal scenes among the tormented souls of Hades, pastoral scenes and so on. A style of instrumentation which was dominated by distinct family groups encouraged composers to associate these families with particular categories of scene. Where the modern art of orchestration depends upon the expressive blending of instrumental colours, composers of the sixteenth century chose their instrumentation on associational grounds. Olympian scenes called for a resplendent *copia sonorum* in which only reed instruments and percussion were lacking; it was, one may say, a universal harmony from which, however, all trace of vulgarity was banished. The sixteenth-century

Olympian orchestra is described most explicitly in Bottrigari's *Il desiderio*, where the author conceives

an *armonia celeste* performed by a group founded on the solid continuo of a harpsichord and a great spinet and divided into three sections: plucked strings (three lutes and a double harp), bowed strings ('a great quantity of viols' to which must be added two small rebecs and a lyra) and wind instruments ('another great quantity of trombones' whose harmony is completed by appropriate numbers of great recorders and transverse flutes, and one straight and one curved cornett). (Weaver 1961: 369)

Pastoral scenes were accompanied by reeds, whose associations with the pastoral milieu were traced back to Classical mythology – to the story of Pan and Syrinx. Pipes, crumhorns, dulcians and bagpipes were the characteristic instruments, supplemented and eventually (but only in the seventeenth century) superseded by recorders. The distinctive sonority of infernal scenes came from the combination of viols and trombones. They were distinguished from Olympian scenes by the lack of plucked strings, harpsichords and high wind instruments, and from pastoral scenes by the lack of reeds and high strings. The appearance of Phlegyas – from Dante's *Inferno* – in the second of the 1586 *intermedi* prompts a typical piece of associational instrumentation. He was 'a horrible old man with a scraggly beard, naked and covered with flames, [and] sang a song once he had brought his boat to a standstill. Trombones and bass viols lent a suitable accompaniment. Then he readied his bark to receive the Evil Ones. While he rattled his chains, they sang a madrigal of lamentation' (Nagler 1964: 68).

It is not always easy to see that the finer details of sixteenth-century instrumentation had a clear symbolic purpose. Presumably, given the temper of the age, they had; but what is one to make of, for example, the appearance of the nine Muses in the Florentine *trionfo* of 1539? Thalia (comedy) carries a trumpet; Euterpe (music and lyric song) a dulcian; Erato (love-poetry) a violone; Melpomene (tragedy) a *piffero* (shawm); Clio (history) a flute; Terpsichore (dance) a lute; Polyhymnia (sacred poetry) a *storta* (crumhorn); Urania (astronomy) a cornett; Calliope (epic poetry) a small rebec (Nagler 1974: 7). Nevertheless the grisly myth of the contest between Apollo and Marsyas provided a Classical precedent for at least one kind of more individual instrumental characterization. The story of a competition between the lyre and reed-pipes clearly symbolizes a much more profound conflict, between 'noble mathematical music' and 'guttural lascivious music', between reason and passion, the realms of Apollo and Dionysus (Winternitz 1979: 97). We see in this story the prototype of those instrumental antagonisms that Monteverdi was to exploit so masterfully in *Orfeo*. Thanks to Apollo, it was the lyre that carried its symbolic and characterizing associations most unmistakably; but the real point is that composers might already be aware of the dramatic and psychological

29

potential of instrumental colour. Brown's comment on the use of the crumhorns in the *intermedi* repertory seems to bear this out: they are, he writes, 'normally played for those kinds of scene where their buzzing nasal timbre appears to be appropriate even to modern musicians', and he cites their use to accompany Calumny, Ignorance and Fear in the 1568 *intermedi* (Brown 1973: 68).

Stagecraft and scenography

Virtually all the visual delights that charmed the seventeenth-century opera-goer had their origins at the court festivals of the Renaissance: vistas that drew him into dreamlike realms of enchantment, miraculous trans-formation scenes and prodigious machines, superb costuming. Develop-ments in these fields were rapid during the sixteenth century, and the *intermedio* was the forcing ground. In 1500 stagecraft was still almost entirely mediaeval; by the late 1630s when opera was taking hold in Venice as a public entertainment, practices had been developed that survived into the nineteenth century. The motive power behind these developments was provided by, first, the desire to emulate the stage practices of the Ancient World – the rediscovery of Vitruvius' *De architectura* in the mid-fifteenth century and the publication of Alberti's *De re aedificatoria* in 1485 were the chief stimulants here; and, second, a dawning recognition of the fact that the discoveries of perspective drawing might with advantage be applied to stage design.

The basic necessities of mediaeval staging had been 'mansions' – small practicable structures representing the various scenes of the drama – and an open acting area. In number and character the mansions varied, but almost always they included one representing Heaven and another representing Hell. All were simultaneously visible, and the action of the play migrated from one to another according to need; the sets, like the dramas them-selves, were innocent of any aspiration towards an Aristotelian unity. Other valued resources included movable floats on which might be exhibited *tableaux vivants*, and the so-called *ingegni* – precursors of the machines of early opera – which were complicated mechanical contrivances for hoisting the performers into the air or to different parts of the stage.

Before the end of the fifteenth century the first moves were being made in the direction of a more unified type of stage. By 1483 Pomponius Laertus' Academy at Rome, seeking to revive a style of staging strictly modelled on the Ancients, had framed the mansions with a series of decorative columns – the *frons scenae*. This had the effect of building them into a single practicable, though hardly realistic, street. Not so dissimilar was the kind of set that Povoledo suggests we call the *città ferrarese*, which made its appearance at a performance of Plautus' *Menaechmi* in 1486. Essentially it was still a series of mansions but, thanks to the unity of the dramatic theme, these mansions could all be straightforward houses organized into a single comparatively realistic location.

It was surprisingly late before perspective was applied to the art of scenography. The reason, presumably, was that perspective is a form of realism, and realism was an aesthetic value irrelevant to the panegyric forms of theatre – *trionfo*, *mascherata*, *intermedio* etc. – and perhaps to Renaissance views of Classical comedy too. The realistic perspective set arrived with realistic modern comedy, at the première of Ariosto's *Cassaria* at Ferrara in 1508. According to the report of the chronicler Prosperi, the scenery comprised 'a street and the perspective of a landscape with houses, churches, bell-towers and gardens, which one can never tire of looking at because of the variety of things in it, all of them cunningly wrought . . .' (Flechsig 1894: 22). A few years later, in 1513, at the ducal palace of Urbino, this kind of perspective backcloth was combined with practicable sets on the front part of the stage. The new conventions spread rapidly; so did new conventions for the accommodation of the audience. By 1489, on the occasion of the wedding of Isabella d'Este and Francesco Gonzaga, the performance had moved from the open air into a hall in the palace, and the layout of the hall had already assumed the form that was to remain standard for more than a century. The specially constructed stage occupied one end of it, and round the other three walls were placed the tiers of seats for the spectators. A wide aisle between the stage and this seating accommodation, together with the central floorspace of the hall, were left free for the dancing before or after the performance; also perhaps for the manoeuvring of the *ingegni*, and the entry of groups of performers for the *intermedi*.

People were soon taking delight in stage sets for their own sake, coming to think of them as works of art addressed to the sense of beauty and the erudition of the spectator. A letter of Alfonso Paolucci describes a performance of Ariosti's *I suppositi* in Rome in 1519 for Pope Leo X. The stage design – a perspective of Ferrara – was by Raphael, and when the curtain fell to reveal it, the Pope examined it long and admiringly through his eyeglass; not until he had gazed his fill was the performance allowed to begin (Flechsig p. 66).

By the fourth decade of the century, scenography was an important enough art to figure extensively in Serlio's treatise on architecture (1537–47), one of the most influential works in the whole history of Italian stage-design. 'Among the other things made by the hand of man' – writes Serio – 'which can be viewed with enjoyment of eye and contentment of mind is (in my opinion) the uncovering of a stage apparatus, where within a small space one may see, created by the art of perspective, proud palaces, vast temples, divers houses and near and far spacious squares adorned with various buildings . . .' (Povoledo 1982: 311). Serlio inherited from Vitruvius and Alberti the idea of three standard types of set: the tragic, which represented a palace built in stone; the comic, which represented a house built in wood; and the satyric (pastoral) which represented a forest and was created in embroidery, since most performances were in winter when real leaves and flowers were in short supply. Where Serlio departed from Vitruvius and Alberti was in depicting these scenes, not by means of the Classical *periaktoi*, but on a succession of flats laid out in depth to the back of the stage. Although the number gradually increased, the idea of a handful of standard stylized genre sets was to remain basic to Italian opera into the nineteenth century.

But even as Serlio was writing, the stylized and unified Classical sets for tragedy, comedy and pastoral were being undermined, not least by the taste for *intermedi* and the variety of stage pictures which they commonly demanded. Already by 1539 in the *intermedi* for *Il commodo* we read of the action of the *intermedi* moving about the perspective set; prologue and epilogue began in the sky and descended to the proscenium, and the *intermedi* took place either on the set, or in the 'piazza of the theatre', that area between the stage and the tiers of seating. Such proceedings quite destroyed the rationale of the single perspective set and in due course the movable set became indispensable. It made its appearance in 1568; the changes of scene took place in full view of the audience, and *periaktoi* were revived to achieve them. These were rotating triangular constructions – two or more on each side of the stage – on each face of which part of a different scene would be painted: with one rotation of all *periaktoi* the palace could thus be transformed into a street of single houses for comedy or into a wood for pastoral (Figure 1). It was not until about 1600 that the *periaktoi* dropped out of favour again, superseded by sliding wings.

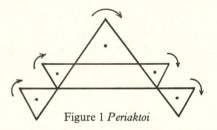

Figure 1 *Periaktoi*

By the time of the great *intermedi* of the 1580s the art of the scenographer had begun to outstrip the needs of the dramatist. When the cunning of the artist's hand, and the imaginative use of machines, and transformations that took place in the twinkling of an eye made it possible to evoke worlds of fantastic enchantment, realism and unity came to seem drab ideals. The invention of the curtained proscenium arch, which shut off the stage world from the real world, underlined the flight from reality; as did the

Skriabynesque drugging of the audience's senses by the diffusion of sweet perfumes in the 1565 and 1586 *intermedi*. But if the rational poise and harmonious coherence of the finest Renaissance art were being lost, the *intermedi* were certainly according due recognition to the claims of the imagination and the senses.

2 · The elements of early opera

Aristotle as mentor

As well as providing the Renaissance world with philosophical, moral and educational ideals, the rediscovery of the Classical past had specifically artistic consequences. Musicians, poets and men of the theatre were indebted to humanist learning for any number of insights into the aesthetics and techniques of their art, and many of these insights have a direct bearing on the origins of opera.

To begin with, the very idea of a 'work of art' designed for 'the recreation or relaxation of the mind, its noble diversion through the appreciation of beauty . . . purgation and moral instruction' (Hanning 1980: 25–6) is a Classical one. Classical Greece was historically the first civilization to record works of art intended primarily for aesthetic pleasure, and the first to discuss the philosophical and technical questions they prompted. As far as Christian civilization is concerned, it was not until the sixteenth century, in Italy, that these issues again became a matter of urgent concern. Aristotle's *Poetics*, a work practically unknown in the Middle Ages, acquired virtually the status of a sacred text, and occasioned a flood of critical discourse, in which the concept of the work of art, and such technical problems as subject-matter, form, imitation and catharsis were debated with unwearying relish.[1]

What Aristotle called the 'first principle' of poetics was that art was mimesis, an imitation or representation of life. In the Ancient World critics were apparently unanimous in their assent to this proposition, and in Renaissance Italy it could not be otherwise. The consequences for all the arts were everywhere apparent. Dance began to be imitative; lyric poetry was justified as being an imitation of the passions; composers of motets and madrigals devised musical metaphors that enabled them to imitate the ideas in the texts they set. But in view of the almost universal acceptance of Aristotle's principle of mimesis, it is hardly surprising that many critics felt that the loftiest form of art must be that which was most fully and indisputably representational: the drama.

It is beyond the scope of this book to discuss the Renaissance debates on the nature of Classical drama. But a few pointers can be given to show how much opera owed to those debates. To begin with, it was in the *Poetics* that

34

the humanists found drama defined as a form of *Gesamtkunstwerk* that employed poetry and music, mime, dance and spectacle in a single work of art. This, as the prefaces to the first operas almost invariably show, was one of the chief justifications for the attempt at composing opera. From Aristotle too came the idea that tragedy worked its effects on an audience not by appealing to their reason, but by stirring their passions; in particular by moving them to fear and pity. Once composers had satisfied themselves that music could wonderfully intensify such effects of pathos, the progress towards opera was irresistible. The type of idealizing characterization we find in early opera, indeed in by far the greater part of the Italian repertory, is another of its debts to the Classical heritage. 'The first and most important point', said Aristotle, 'is that the character should be good' (*Poetics* XV.1); tragedy differs from comedy in showing men as being 'better than they really are' (II.7). In an age so enthralled with the potentialities of personality it is not surprising that the Aristotelian precept awakened sympathetic responses. Tasso's *Gerusalemme liberata* is, among much else, a demonstration of the widely held belief that 'the central character of a heroic poem should exhibit exemplary behaviour in respect to one of the moral virtues, and that the ideal hero should be a composite of all the virtues needed in a prince or leader' (Hathaway 1962: 144). When Malatesta Porta produced a mildly eccentric variant of this doctrine, according to which the hero of an epic or drama should rather be characterized by excess of emotional experiences, he brings us even closer to a recipe for the principles of characterization that were to be observed in Italian opera. Finally there was the chorus; this too became an integral part of the idea of opera only because of Aristotle's description of the essential role it played in Greek tragedy. So the establishing of opera as a type of music-drama which employed both soloists and chorus, which is heroic and idealistic in tone, and which achieves its effect by stirring and soothing the passions of the spectators, was very largely a work of neo-classical emulation.

By 1600 Italian dramatists and critics had been eager students of the extant repertory of Greek tragedy for the best part of a century. Between 1502 and 1518 the entire corpus had been published by Aldo Manuzio, and translations began to be issued at much the same time, at first into Latin, later into Italian; at first sporadically, later, towards the middle of the century, with increasing regularity.[2] The first attempt to compose an original Italian tragedy in the Classical style was Trissino's *Sofonisba* of 1515. Very rarely were such translations and imitations staged: the interest they excited was primarily literary and critical. As far as theatrical practice was concerned the Latin repertory was better known than the Greek, and within that repertory the comedies of Plautus and Terence were staged more frequently than the tragedies of Seneca. Nevertheless, among those who pondered the aesthetic problems associated with drama, among those who wrestled with the meaning of the *Poetics*, and dreamed of reviving the glories of the Aristotelian *Gesamtkunstwerk*, there is no doubt that Greek drama, particularly Sophocles, enjoyed the higher esteem. In bringing opera to birth a largely bookish knowledge of the Greek repertory was far more significant than a wide practical experience of the Latin.

The role of the chorus

The impact of Greek dramatic practice on the theatre of the late Italian Renaissance in general and on early opera in particular is most clearly seen in the matter of the chorus. As usual the authoritative statement on the subject was to be found in Aristotle:

The chorus too must be regarded as one of the actors. It must be part of the whole and share in the action, not as in Euripides but as in Sophocles. In the others the choral odes have no more to do with the plot than with any other tragedy. And so they sing interludes, a practice begun by Agathon. And yet to sing interludes is quite as bad as transferring a whole speech or scene from one play to another.

(*Poetics* XVIII. 19–20)

Italian authors in search of models for their own choric practice were left in no doubt, then, that they should look to Sophocles. More problematic was the question of how these choruses should be set to music. All Classical scholars were agreed that the choruses of Greek tragedy would have been sung, but since no Greek music from the Classical period had survived they knew next to nothing about it. So while the dramatic principles underlying a Sophoclean chorus could be grasped from real examples, its musical qualities remained – within the limits laid down by theorists and philosophers – matters of speculation. Nevertheless, the mere theory was powerfully suggestive: in particular, its revelation that text, melody and rhythm had formed an indivisible unity. Spoken Greek had already employed pitch accent and quantitative syllabification – had in fact possessed an inherent melody and rhythm. In the declamation of verse in tragic drama these qualities were simply heightened and drawn out. Music was a more explicit realization of qualities already latent in the language; poet and musician were one and the same person.

Of the various sixteenth-century attempts to recreate the lost dramatic art of Classical Greece, the revival of Sophocles' *Oedipus tyrannus* at Vicenza in 1585 is, for a number of reasons, quite the most interesting: as an admired translation, by Orsatto Giustiniani, of the most perfect surviving specimen of Sophoclean tragedy; because it was staged in the Teatro Olimpico, newly built to designs which the greatest Italian architect of the day, Andrea Palladio, had based upon a reconstruction of the Roman theatre at Orange. The historian of opera remembers it above all for the

Plate 2 The Teatro Olimpico in Vicenza, 1580–85

music composed for its choruses by Andrea Gabrieli, which survives virtually in its entirety. (Schrade 1960 includes a modern edition.)

Edipo tiranno, to give it its Italian name, was staged under the direction of Angelo Ingegneri, a respected man of the theatre; and, to judge from a treatise he was later to publish on the production of drama, his views on the role of music in tragedy had some influence on Gabrieli's setting. Ingegneri insisted that there must be a sharp distinction between the kind of music written for theatrical *intermedi*, where a delectable variety of styles and a colourful array of instruments might very properly be employed, and the kind written for the choruses of a tragedy, which should be 'in the simplest style, such as seems hardly different from ordinary speech' (Schrade 1960: 58). No secular music from the sixteenth century comes so close to this ideal. In Ingegneri's view, to which Gabrieli conforms, only those formal lyrical movements sung and danced when the chorus is alone on stage should be set to music – the *parodos* (accompanying the entrance of the chorus), the *stasima* (between each episode of the drama) and the *exodos* (accompanying the exit of the chorus). But in fact, and apparently rather arbitrarily, Ingegneri decreed that the last of these should not be sung. The grounds given were that, by the final scene, the emotion has reached such a pitch of desperation that music can add nothing – a tell-tale remark which shows how even the most ardent humanists still found it impossible to conceive that indivisible oneness of word and tone which in theory they so admired. Gabrieli's music for *Edipo tiranno* eventually amounted to four extended choruses, a *parodos* and three *stasima*; and it was sung, an eye-witness reported, 'by fifteen people, seven on each side and the leader in the middle; the said chorus executed its task with pleasing declamation and harmony, in such a way that virtually all the words could be clearly understood; and that is something very difficult to effect in tragedies' (Schrade 1960: 50).

Gabrieli's choruses are indeed like nothing else in sixteenth-century music. Under Ingegneri's guidance the composer strove to create a contemporary idiom commensurate to the humanist idea of what Ancient Greek music might have been. That is not to suggest that *Edipo tiranno* in fact bears the remotest resemblance to the music that would actually have been heard in fifth-century Athens. For one thing, Ingegneri had persuaded Gabrieli that no instruments should be used. Though he admitted that instruments had a role to play in Classical times, he thought that was simply 'to cover up errors in the singing – and in particular to create a more impressive and emotional effect' (Schrade 1960: 61); in modern conditions they would simply obscure the words. For another, when Giustiniani made his translation, the pattern of strophes and antistrophes in the original choruses had not been recognized. Gabrieli's settings of the very free *canzoni* into which Giustiniani rendered Sophocles' verses could therefore have no structural similarity to the real Classical chorus. Most important, obviously, are the sonorous and harmonic possibilities available to Gabrieli. He breaks the *canzoni* into short sections which he sets for anything from unaccompanied solo voice to six-part choral ensemble. But while this latter resource is something of which Sophocles himself could never have dreamed, Gabrieli uses it not at all in the way one might expect. The sonority may be contemporary, but the manner of treatment makes it clear that he is still striving for a Classical ideal of word-setting. Anything in the way of characteristic and beautiful melody is avoided; of counterpoint there is absolutely no trace – not even so much as is required to create a cadential suspension. The music consists of a chordal declamation of the text in which all voices, all the time, move in identical rhythms, those rhythms being modelled on the way in which the text might ideally be declaimed (see Ex.I.3).

There is nothing to suggest that Gabrieli's music was widely known, and in any case the idiom he evolved for *Edipo tiranno* could scarcely have served as the basis for an operatic art. But the piece is of extraordinary historical interest as a demonstration of the authority which the Classical

Sacred oracle of Jove, who breathe so sweetly, with what tidings do you now come from the lofty, golden temples of Delphi to noble Thebes?

Ex.I.3 Gabrieli, *Edipo Tiranno* (1581), choro primo

world exercised in humanist circles. Gabrieli was one of the most accomplished and eminent musicians in Italy, a past master of every modern effect of colour and expression. Yet his most substantial work is a piece of musical archaeology, a piece in which he shows himself willing to abandon all his acquired resources of skill in an attempt to create a new idiom inspired by what antiquarian scholarship could tell him about the music of the Ancient World.

The supernatural powers of music

Speculations on the role of music in Greek tragedy were a key factor in the evolution towards opera. No less vital in preparing the way for the new art was another humanist obsession: the accounts in the Classical poets and philosophers of the supernatural powers of Ancient Greek music. A good illustration is provided by the 'Discourse on ancient music and good singing' which Bardi addressed to Giulio Caccini probably in 1578.

> Now that we have given the definition of music according to Plato (a definition in which Aristotle and the other scholars concur) and have said what music is . . . let us turn to the marvels of music, in discussing which Damon, the teacher of Socrates, says that, being chaste, it has the power of disposing our minds to virtue and, being the contrary, to vice. And Plato says that there are two disciplines – one for the body, which is gymnastics, and one for the good of the mind, which is music; he also tells us that Thales the Milesian sang so sweetly that he not only influenced the minds of certain persons, but also cured illness and the plague. And we read that Pythagoras cured drunkards with music, and Empedocles insane persons, and Socrates a man possessed. And Plutarch tells us that Asclepiades cured delirious persons with the symphony, which is simply a mixture of song and sound. And it is said that Ismenias cured sciatic persons and the fever with music. And Aulus Gellius writes that those who suffered from sciatic gout were healed with the sound of the tibia, likewise those who had been bitten by serpents.
>
> (Strunk 1950: 292–3)

The most beautiful of these myths and legends were those told of Orpheus. Orpheus, the semi-divine musician of Thrace, was said to have tamed wild beasts and charmed even the rocks and trees with his music; so intensely moving was his singing that when Eurydice his wife died and descended to the underworld, he was able to follow her, and by softening the heart of Hades itself to bring about her restitution; in other legends Orpheus is revered as a founder of cities.

The layers of meaning in these stories are many and deep and some of them will have to be considered when we come to an examination of Monteverdi's *Orfeo*. At present it is sufficient to note that they presented musicians with formidable problems, problems compared with which those attached to the revival of the forms of Sophoclean tragedy were trifling. Few humanists cared to dismiss as incredible the effects attributed to ancient music, but none could deny that such effects were no longer achieved by sixteenth-century composers. Could there be any doubt where their duty lay? Surely in bringing about a reform of music so that it might once again have the power to 'arouse and control passions, inculcate and preserve virtue, even cure disease and ensure the stability of the state' (Walker 1941: 8). Such at least were the ambitions of some. It was well that – true men of the Renaissance – they lacked nothing in self-confidence, even to the extent of being ready to dismiss as folly and self-deception the entire development of the art since the beginning of the Christian era.

The Florentine Camerata

The 'Camerata' was a group of artists and scholars that used to gather at the Florence home of Giovanni Bardi, Count of Vernio. Bardi, his son tells us,

took great delight in music and was in his day a composer of some reputation; [he] always had about him the most celebrated men of the city, learned in this profession, and inviting them to his house, he formed a sort of delightful and continual academy from which vice and in particular every kind of gaming were absent. To this the noble youth of Florence were attracted with great profit to themselves, passing their time not only in pursuit of music, but also in discussing and receiving instruction in poetry, astrology and other sciences which by turns lent value to this pleasant converse. (Strunk 1950: 363)

Who exactly the members of this Camerata were is still debated. At one time or another the poets Guarini, Chiabrera and Rinuccini are all likely to have been associated with it; and 'the most celebrated men of the city, learned in this profession' of music may be supposed to have included those who were to work with Bardi in the 1585 and 1589 *intermedi*, such as the elder Striggio and Malvezzi (Palisca 1972: 208). But the only certain information we have identifies as leading members – apart from Bardi himself – the aristocratic dilettante composer Piero Strozzi, the singer and composer Giulio Caccini, and Vincenzo Galilei, like Caccini a singer and composer, but better known as a musical theorist and indeed as the father of Galileo Galilei. The Camerata assumes a place of honour in every history of opera, though in point of fact its members were not in the least bit interested in the idea of music drama. Like all the musical humanists they deliberated upon the music of the Ancient World, and enjoyed speculating about its possible nature. But at no point in his theoretical writings did Galilei discuss the musical problems associated with the revival of Greek tragedy, and when opera did materialize, Bardi himself took no pleasure in it (Palisca 1963: 352). He remained loyal to the established sixteenth-century format for dramatic music, that of the spoken play with *intermedi*.

But if the musical reforms preached and practised by the Camerata were certainly not directed towards the idea of restoring Greek tragedy they did ultimately and indirectly make a contribution to opera of the profoundest significance. The *stile rappresentativo*, the dramatic recitative style without which no operatic art could have taken wing, was an offshoot of the typical genre of the Camerata, the 'monody', the accompanied solo song. And for this reason alone the operatic historian must pay homage to Bardi and his friends, and pause to reflect on their work both theoretical and practical.

Bardi was a man of many parts: a social historian, who had published a history of Florentine football; an ardent Platonist whose correspondence with Francesco Patrizi influenced one of the major aesthetic treatises of the period, Patrizi's *Della poetica deca istoriale*; a scholar of linguistics and prominent member of the Accademia della Crusca who took an active part in the controversies surrounding the work of Tasso; we have already met him as the mastermind behind the magnificent *intermedi* of 1585 and 1589. But nothing Bardi did was of greater historical importance than his presidency of the Camerata during the 1570s and early 1580s and in particular the inspiration he gave its two most radical musicians, Galilei and Caccini. Galilei made Bardi the main interlocutor in his *Dialogo della musica antica e della moderna*, the fullest theoretical statement of the principles underlying the monodic style; and in the preface to the *Nuove musiche*, the first published collection of Camerata-inspired monodies, Caccini avowed that he had learned more from the discussions of Bardi and his friends than he had from thirty years' study of counterpoint.

There was of course nothing unprecedented in the Camerata's interest in accompanied solo song; even in the days of the *prima prattica* – the classic polyphonic art of the Renaissance – polyphonic masses, motets and madrigals by no means monopolized composers' attention. At an Italian Renaissance court or academy, even in the first half of the sixteenth century, one might have heard virtuoso singers performing madrigals in arrangements for solo voice and lute, or improvising musical declamations of lyric or epic poems to such traditional *arie* as the *romanesca* or the *ruggiero*. Nor were such performances one whit less esteemed than those of vocal polyphony. Indeed the pattern-book for the Italian courtier, Baldassare Castiglione's *Il cortegiano* (1528), singles out such solo song for special commendation,

because all the sweetness consisteth in one alone, and a man is much more heedful and understandeth better the feat manner and the air or vein of it when the ears are not busied in hearing any more than one voice . . . singing to the lute with the ditty (methink) is more pleasant than the rest, for it addeth to the words such a grace and strength that it is a great wonder.   (Strunk 1950: 284; the translation is by Sir Thomas Hoby, 1561)

But nothing of this takes away from the importance of the Camerata. It was their talents, their proselytizing zeal and their timeliness that made the monodic style in all its ramifications a central and indispensable part of the language of music.

To a modern musician the fame enjoyed by the Camerata will in all likelihood seem disproportionate to their gifts. The reason for their prestige, however, is entirely typical of the time and place: they were articulate and combative, and possessed of a deep learning in Ancient musical lore. Both Bardi and Galilei were musical humanists of considerable scholarly attainment, familiar with the best musical philosophy and musical theory of Ancient Greece; and behind all their deliberations in this field, a kind of corresponding member of the Camerata, mentor and counsellor and the source of many of Galilei's ideas on music, lurked Girolamo Mei, a scholar of formidable erudition and the greatest living authority on the music of the Ancient World.[3]

A new ideal of song

The members of the Camerata surpassed other Italian musicians of the period not merely in learning, but in a very special kind of idealism. They never let fade from their minds the memory of the wonderful powers attributed to music by Classical authors, and they were determined to bring about a restoration of these powers. The pitch of their ambition may be gauged from the passage I have already quoted from Bardi's 'Discourse' (cf. above p. 40). It was his and Galilei's dream that such magical arts might be revived, that musicians might once again aspire to move the passions, to compose the soul, to spellbind the very forces of nature. Their programme of reform set out from the observed fact that, as yet, modern music had succeeded in doing none of these things. They did not deny that in music, as in all other forms of human activity, there had been admirable developments over the previous 150 years, that the barbarism of the dark ages had been extirpated in music as in so many other realms of the spirit. However, what they did contend was that, for all their virtues, Glareanus and Zarlino and the other sages of modern music had not, as Galilei put it, 'restored [music] to its ancient state, or . . . attained to the true and perfect knowledge of it' (Strunk 1950: 303). This the Camerata sought to do.

The musical Renaissance had failed because it had been based on false premisses. Virtually none of the musicians of modern times had been able to escape from a fatal inheritance which Mei traced back to the collapse of the Greek Classical tradition in Plato's day. That was the origin of the sensuality and virtuosity that had de-natured music and rendered it unfit for the noble ethical and spiritual tasks that were its by right. The professional instrumentalists of Plato's time had, Mei taught, corrupted music by indulging themselves in 'diminutions and passages and other such variations, all things imagined and thought up by the artificers themselves to satisfy their ambitions, while vying with one another to find a way of giving maximum pleasure to the ear without any longer caring for the intellect' (Palisca 1960a: 15). And the art of counterpoint that had developed in recent centuries, no matter how skilful or delightful to the senses, was nothing more than a contemporary manifestation of this age-old folly. Galilei himself had nothing against the polyphonic style for instrumental music, but accepted Mei's teaching that, as far as vocal music was concerned, a quite new 'Poetics' was required.

Some members of the Camerata saw hints of such a new Poetics in certain types of music cultivated by their predecessors and contemporaries: in the later declamatory madrigals of Cipriano de' Rore, for example, or in the declamations to the *lira da braccio* of such virtuoso *improvvisatori* as Serafino dall'Aquila. But in principle and as a matter of course, deep-rooted reform in Renaissance Italy had to seek its guidelines in Classical Antiquity. The

Camerata believed that the secret of the miraculous musical art of Ancient Greece was to be found in the identity of poet and musician. Like almost all musical humanists they believed, with Zarlino, that 'il Musico non era separato dal Poeta, ne il Poeta dal Musico'[4] (Walker 1941: 6). Make the composer not a contrapuntalist but a poet, and then one might again experience the oneness of poetic metre and musical rhythm, the various modes might recover the intrinsic emotional and ethical qualities that Plato had described, and hidden melodies might emerge unbidden from a line of verse. If the Camerata could realize a manner of song in which, for the first time since Plato, the words and the music were truly inseparable, mutually dependent and mutually illuminating, then the age of miracles might return.

In one respect, however, they accepted the fallen condition of modern music as an accomplished fact which no reform could remedy. The poet *was* now separate from the composer, and the composer from the poet, and nothing in the writings of the Camerata suggests that they ever expected this divorce to be undone. Galilei and Caccini did not aspire to become poets, nor Chiabrera and Rinuccini to become composers. The crux of the matter therefore became the attitude of the composer to an already existing poem.

This was a topic that during the course of the sixteenth century had become increasingly important to many musicians; the Camerata differed from other Italian humanists only in the radicalness of their solution. Even composers and theorists of the *prima prattica* accepted 'the rule that, in Plato, Socrates lays down for melodies: that the musician ought to make the melody follow the words, and not the words the melody' (Johann Ott (1539) in Strunk 1950: 256). 'Prima le parole, dopo la musica' was a watchword for Zarlino as well as for the Camerata. But under Mei's tutelage Galilei interpreted the maxim more austerely, declaring that music existed not in its own right, for mere sensuous pleasure, but that its function was to serve the word, to lend its eloquence to the task of intensifying the meaning and the mood of the verse. Bardi, Galilei and Caccini all proclaimed their belief that the poet's words were the nobler and more fundamental element of a song. 'In composing, then', said Bardi, 'you will make it your chief aim to arrange the verse well and to declaim the words as intelligibly as you can . . . for you will consider it self-evident that, just as the soul is nobler than the body, so the words are nobler than the counterpoint' (Strunk, p. 295). And it was Caccini's boast, in the *Nuove musiche*, that he had

conformed with the manner so much praised by Plato and other philosophers, who asserted that music was nothing more than speech and rhythm and lastly tone, in that order . . . the idea occurred to me to introduce a kind of music in which one might, as it were, speak in harmony, employing a kind of noble negligence of song.

(Solerti 1903: 56–7)

The art of monody

In describing in more specifically musical terms the characteristics of the monody[5] developed by the Camerata, we must emphasize three features. The first and most obvious is the exclusion of polyphony. The only way in which the poetry can be presented clearly and faithfully is by a solo voice. Such simple harmonic support as the melody may require will be provided not by a polyphonic ensemble of voices but by an instrument, ideally a member of the lute family, and ideally played by the singer himself. Secondly, the character of the sung melody – its rise and fall in pitch, its patterns of short and long note values, its accelerations and ritardations – will arise not from any purely lyrical impulse on the part of the composer but from the words alone. Finally, in what Galilei called 'the most important and principal part of music', the Camerata proposed a shift of emphasis in the way the composer aimed to express the words. What have come to be known as 'madrigalisms' – details in the musical setting that act as analogues to details in the poem – are to be avoided. The important thing is for the composer to penetrate into the spirit of the verse, and then to intensify that spirit with the resources of his own art. If we turn to the passage in the *Dialogo* in which Galilei discusses this matter, we shall see why, as far as opera is concerned, this was far and away the most important aspect of the monodic style. Bardi is speaking:

Our practical contrapuntists . . . will say that they are imitating the words when among the conceptions of these there are any meaning 'to flee' or 'to fly'; these they will declaim with the greatest rapidity and the least grace imaginable. In connection with words meaning 'to disappear', 'to swoon', 'to die', or actually 'to be extinct' they have made the parts break off so abruptly, that instead of inducing the passion corresponding to any of these, they have aroused laughter and at other times contempt . . . At another time, finding the line:

He descended into Hell, into the lap of Pluto,

they have made one part of the composition descend in such a way that the singer has sounded more like someone groaning to frighten children and terrify them than like anyone singing sense. In the opposite way, finding this one:

This one aspires to the stars,

in declaiming it they have ascended to a height that no one shrieking from excessive pain, internal or external, has ever reached.   (Strunk 1950: 315–17)

For such imitation of the words, Galilei has no time. And in a passage that provoked the scornful ire of the veteran Zarlino he goes on to propose that such musical metaphors and haphazard similitudes be superseded by a style of imitation that can best be described as histrionic:

When [composers] go for their amusement to the tragedies and comedies that the mummers act, let them a few times leave off their immoderate laughing, and instead be so good as to observe, when one quiet gentleman speaks with another, in what manner he speaks, how high or low his voice is pitched, with what volume of sound, with what sort of accents and gestures, and with what rapidity or slowness his words are uttered. Let them mark a little what difference obtains in all these things when one of them speaks with one of his servants, or one of these with another; let them observe the prince when he chances to be conversing with one of his subjects and vassals; when with the petitioner who is entreating his favour; how the man infuriated or excited speaks; the married woman, the girl, the mere child, the clever harlot . . . From these variations of circumstances, if they observe them attentively and examine them with care, they will be able to select the norm of what is fitting for the expression of any other conception whatever that can call for their handling. (Strunk p. 318)

Such a conception of song is already very close to music-drama. The polyphonic madrigal had delighted its hearers – even more its performers – by the wit and inventiveness with which the composers created a musical metaphor for the poem. When a poem is set as a monody, it becomes a miniature *scena*, the singer impersonates an imagined character in an imagined situation, and the object of the performance is to exert an emotional and ethical force on the audience. While madrigal-singing is music-making, the singing of monody is an exercise in rhetoric. 'If the musician has not the power to direct the minds of his listeners to their benefit, his science and knowledge are to be reputed null and vain, since the art of music was instituted and numbered among the liberal arts for no other purpose' (Strunk p. 319). It is certainly no accident that both Mei and Bardi were also members of the Accademia degli Alterati, some of whose most interesting debates were on the aesthetic writings of Aristotle and his doctrine of catharsis. The Alterati's conclusion that the task of the creative artist was to 'awaken in himself the emotional estate he wants to express and . . . call forth the images and forms that will awaken it in others' (Palisca 1968: 36), corresponds precisely to the understanding of the Camerata and points up again the proximity of monody and drama. 'Si vis me flere, dolendum est primum ipsi tibi.'[6]

Caccini's musical publications at the very beginning of the new century emphasize still more the analogy between monody and drama. Indeed in the preface to *Euridice* he specifically claims that in such early monodies as 'Perfidissimo volto', 'Vedrò il mio sol' and 'Dovrò dunque', all published in *Nuove musiche* in 1602, he was employing a style which Bardi had recognized as being 'that used by the ancient Greeks in performing their tragedies' (Solerti 1903: 50). The concept of *sprezzatura*, the 'noble disdain of song', is surely intended to give an impression, not just of the casual ease of the well-bred courtier, but also of the freedom and impulse of the improviser, of the character therefore for whom song is a natural and spontaneous form of self-expression, not something learned and then performed. Even the *gorgia*, the ornamentation that Caccini describes so carefully in the *Nuove musiche*, may be seen at least in part as a quasi-dramatic resource, underlining and high-lighting the most significant elements in the text. Caccini himself compares *gorgia* with the figures of rhetoric (Solerti p. 75). But when all due emphasis has been laid on the dramatic characteristics of the monody, it must be repeated that the Camerata themselves did not set out to recreate a music-drama comparable with that of the Greek tragedians, and that opera would never have emerged from their unaided efforts.

The rise of pastoral drama

A further indispensable element of the early opera is pastoral, in particular pastoral drama. Pastoral is a genre which depicts an idealized world where shepherds and nymphs, untroubled by the material and moral problems of the 'real' world, disport amorously in a landscape of perfect beauty beneath a Mediterranean spring sky. Despite its apparent preciosity and narrowness, pastoral was a favourite dramatic form in sixteenth-century Italy, and its importance for music was incalculable. For two centuries the Arcadia it celebrated was to remain an inexhaustible source of inspiration for opera, cantata, serenata and song.

Like most things in Renaissance Italy, the pastoral was Classical in inspiration. It took its origins from the Greek idylls of Theocritus and the Latin eclogues of Virgil. A substantial part of the Renaissance repertory of pastoral in fact continued to be composed in Latin, though it was not the part to which we need address ourselves here. As far as opera is concerned the crucial pastoral form is the pastoral drama; and of the period that preceded the appearance of the first fully fledged drama of this kind, Agostino Beccari's *Il sacrificio* of 1554, it need only be noted that drama was latent in pastoral even in its purely lyrical form. Virgil's eclogues, to name but the most admired ancient examples of the genre, were already potentially dramatic, couched in the form of dramatic monologues and of dialogues between two or three shepherds. In the pastorals written during the first half of the sixteenth century this inherent theatricality was slowly made more tangible. At Urbino in 1506, for example, Baldassare Castiglione and Cesare Gonzaga, dressed in shepherd's weeds, recited an eclogue in character before the ducal court. The development from such a performance to the pastoral drama proper was seen by at least one contemporary chronicler as being analogous to the development of tragedy and comedy in Ancient Greece: 'Even as the Muses grafted tragedy upon the dithyrambic stock, and comedy upon the phallic, so in their ever-fertile garden they set the eclogue as a tiny cutting, whence sprang in later years the stately growth of the dramatic pastoral' (Greg 1905: 427).

During the forty years that followed the first appearance of Beccari's play the form was much developed, chiefly by the absorption of elements from Classical drama. In Tasso's *Aminta*, written in 1573, the Classical apparatus is already considerable: the play is divided into five acts, each of which ends with a choral commentary; the principal characters are provided with confidants, and most of the action is presented in the form of descriptive narrative. In Battista Guarini's *Il pastor fido* (1580–84), the most admired and influential dramatic pastoral in the whole Italian repertory, the devices borrowed from the regular drama are still more numerous and portentous: dreams and omens and oracles, processions and sacrifices. Although the pastoral drama flourished in Italy for another 200 years, these two plays mark the climax of the tradition. Both were written for the north Italian court of the Estensi at Ferrara; indeed Ferrara had been the scene of most of the important pastoral dramas from Beccari onwards.

The pastoral convention

It is a common predicament for the modern reader to find the pastoral convention insipid and tedious. But for cultivated Italian audiences of the late sixteenth century, for the circles that is to say in which the art of opera was to be born, pastoral drama was a form of apparently inexhaustible fascination. There was in fact very much more to it than meets the eye, and until we have thought a little about it, the style it adopted and the ideas it was made to convey, we shall be in no position to understand its importance for Peri, Cavalieri, Caccini and Monteverdi.

It has been well said that 'essentially the art of pastoral is the art of the backward glance' (Marinelli 1971: 9). It arose and in some degree it continues to flourish in societies where the artist is painfully aware of a spiritual malaise. It is a genre that feeds on present discontent, and it purges that discontent by a form of escape. The watchword is Cowper's dictum that 'God made the country and man made the town'. For normally it is the squalor and materialism of the big city, or the vice, corruption and cynicism of the court, from which the artist longs to escape; and his escape takes the form of a flight back to an idyllic rural world where souls are pure, feelings spontaneous and pleasures simple. From cosmopolitan Alexandria Theocritus looked back through a roseate haze of memory to pastoral Sicily; in Imperial Rome Virgil dreamed of distant Arcadia – which thereafter became the favourite *locus amoenus* of the poets. Equally favourable to the cult of pastoral was the sense that 'il mondo invecchia, / e invecchiando intristisce'[7] (Tasso, *Aminta* 891–2). Any society, any individual, for whom life had lost its savour, whose appetites and pleasures had grown stale, could dream dreams of imaginary worlds where youthful raptures and eternal springtime never faded. Pastoral celebrates youth no less than it celebrates innocence: the youth of the individual life, the springtime of the year, the first age in the story of mankind – the Garden of Eden in the Judaeo-Christian tradition, the Age of Gold in the Graeco-Roman. Indeed this vision of an Age of Gold is its central preoccupation.

For the Italian Renaissance the classical portrayal of the Age of Gold remained that in the first book of Ovid's *Metamorphoses*. And when Tasso, in the most exquisite poem in the Italian pastoral tradition, the closing chorus of Act I of *Aminta*, seeks to evoke that age, he begins by paraphrasing Ovid quite strictly. The land of content flows with milk and honey; toil is unnecessary, for the earth yields up its harvests unbroken by the plough; the wild beasts of the forest are harmless; spring is eternal; man, happy within his own small plot of land, does not roam the world in search of commercial or martial exploit; and law is unnecessary, for all pleasures and desires are innocent.

If Arcadia is the setting, the predominant theme is love. A complicated love-intrigue had been the basis of Beccari's *Sacrificio*, and remained the *sine qua non* of most later pastorals. Tasso's *Aminta*, framed by a prologue spoken by Cupid (Amore) and an epilogue spoken by Venus, was essentially a dramatic analysis of contrasted conceptions of love. Its great sequel, *Il pastor fido*, was that too, as well as being the earliest Italian drama to present love-scenes directly on the stage. 'Come live with me and be my love' was the exclusive and relentless exhortation not just of Marlowe's but of every passionate shepherd.

But if the monotonousness of the preoccupation might be described as proper to the Golden Age, the actuality, as presented in pastoral drama, decidedly was not. How Tasso imagined the love of the Golden Age we read in the Act I chorus of the *Aminta*: Cupid carried neither bow nor torch, and lovers consequently experienced neither the wounds of love nor the fires of passion; they sat naked amid flowers and brooklets, murmuring amorously, caressing and kissing. The lovers in pastoral drama have a more complicated and – as a post-lapsarian man one is bound to feel – more interesting time. For love has absorbed the idealism and something of the concept of service from the world of chivalry, and recognizes that it will mature only if it is won through suffering and against denial. Love ceases to be something that just happens, and in response to which lovers need do nothing but enjoy one another; it becomes a transfiguring force, ripening, civilizing and ennobling. Sometimes another note too – one of bitter-sweet nostalgia – sounds unmistakably in this poetry; what is enjoyed is often enjoyed with an acute sense of its transience:

> Amiam, che 'l Sol si muore e poi rinasce:
> a noi sua breve luce
> s' asconde, e 'l sonno eterna notte adduce.[8]   (*Aminta* 721–3)

A theology of the sensible world

This belief in love as an elevating force was a corollary of the belief that beauty was an epitome of the Divine goodness. Both beliefs owe their central place in the thought of Italian Renaissance artists ultimately to

Plato, more immediately to the most articulate and influential of the Florentines of the Platonist Academy, Marsilio Ficino. Ficino was quite explicit that Eros was a medium by which the soul might approach God:

The divine beauty in fact creates love in everything; that is desire for itself. Since God draws the world to himself, and the world is possessed, there is a single continuous attraction . . . which, as if in a kind of circle, to the place whence it flowed returns again . . . In so far as it begins in God and is proper to him, it is beauty; in so far as it captivates the world in transit, it is love; in so far as it returns to the Creator and joins its work with him, it is pleasure. (*In convivium Platonis de amore commentarius*, in Cody 1969: 35)

If in real life such a synthesis of the sensuous and spiritual was difficult to attain, it was a magnificent programme for an artist. And where might such a programme better be realized than in pastoral, where the artist becomes a shepherd, in intimate communion with the world as God made it, and where, as apprehended by the pagan mythographers, each flowery grove, each silver stream and each lofty mountain had its resident deity?

One detail of this theology of the sensible world had particular relevance to the musician: the phenomenon known as pathetic fallacy. It was implicit in much Greek mythology, particularly in such stories as Echo and Narcissus, or Pan and Syrinx; and Virgil already observed, 'non canimus surdis; respondent omnia silvae'[9] (*Ecloga* X, 8). In Renaissance Italy pathetic fallacy was exploited more fully, for two reasons. In the first place, since Petrarch, her poets had become deeply self-conscious about the psychology of love. They lavished all their art upon the minute analysis of their feelings, upon expressing them eloquently and movingly. When the quality of emotion was so important to them, it is not surprising that they availed themselves of a literary device that enabled them to underline it and dramatize it by showing the whole world of created nature to be affected by it. Tasso's Aminta, Guarini's Mirtillo, Rinuccini's and Striggio's Orpheus all intensified and universalized their sorrows in some such words as these:

> . . . ma grideran per me le piagge e i monti
> e questa selva, a cui
> sì spesso il tuo bel nome
> di risonare insegno.
> Per me piagnendo i fonti
> e mormorando i venti
> diranno i miei lamenti . . .[10]   (*Il pastor fido* Act I scene 2)

More important even than this sentimental application of pathetic fallacy are its theological implications; theological, that is, in terms of the Platonic cosmology outlined in Chapter 1 (cf. above pp. 22–3). A shepherd, who in the pastoral convention represents the good man or the sensitive artist, is better placed than anyone to live that kind of life which Pater described so beautifully as 'a kind of listening' (Cody 1969: 47), to apprehend the harmony in the nature of the things, the divine voice speaking through the created universe. In the *Aminta*, when Dafne says to Silva,

> Stimi dunque stagione
> di nimicizia e d'ira
> la dolce primavera,
> ch'or allegra e ridente
> riconsiglia ad amare
> il mondo e gli animali
> e gli uomini e le donne? e non t'accorgi
> come tutte le cose
> or sono innamorate
> d'un amor pien di gioia e di salute?[11]   (*Aminta* 218–27)

she is really urging her to listen, to open her ears and eyes to the message of the *musica mundana*.

Music in the pastoral

One last consideration remains in the complex of ideas embraced by Renaissance pastoral; in some ways it is the most important of all, for it concerns the role in the world of art and the artist.

Before the passing of the Age of Gold man was instinctively good and did instinctively what was right. In the post-lapsarian world virtue has to be battled for, it is achieved by such constraints as law, self-discipline and education. The love that, in Tasso's vision of the Golden Age, was simply plucked and innocently enjoyed, now had to be purified by chastity, marriage and fidelity. Nor was it any different with beauty. Compared with the prodigal loveliness of Golden Age Arcadia, fallen man can respond only with a garden; the sweet murmurings with which a Golden Age swain beguiled the ear of his nymph can only be imagined and formulated now by a Tasso or a Marlowe; only the most artificial madrigalist can hope to evoke the memory of those 'dolci carole' sung amid 'fiore e linfe' by 'amoretti senz'archi e senza faci'.[12] In short, the Golden Age can be recaptured, and therefore the theology of the Platonic universe can be comprehended, only in the world of art. And in no form of art can one better apply oneself to such momentous tasks than in the pastoral. It was in the Classical eclogue that the poet first revealed himself as an idealistic dreamer of dreams, and this was to remain one of the principal functions of pastoral throughout its history.

All these pastoral preoccupations – the Age of Gold, the analysis of love, the cosmic harmony of the created universe, the belief that it was in art that these concerns might best be pondered – already go a long way towards explaining why pastoral drama was so congenial a field for the early composers of opera. But they perhaps do not fully explain how it was that by the end of the sixteenth century, men interested in the possibility of an art of music-drama had reached the point of feeling that, as Molière's dancing-master was to put it: 'Lorsqu'on a des personnes à faire parler en musique, il faut bien que, pour la vraisemblance, on donne dans la bergerie.' The belief that Arcadia was a pre-eminently musical world was apparently due to one of the few men of note actually to come from that inaccessible region, the historian Polybius. Guarini cites Polybius as the authority for his statement that 'all Arcadians were poets; their principal occupation was music, which they learned in childhood, as the law ordained' (Pirrotta 1969a: 337). It was this claim of Polybius, together with the fact that Pan came from Arcadia, that prompted Virgil to set his eclogues there. By the sixteenth century some Italian humanists were even prepared to claim that song was 'invented' in Arcadia.

But really it was the pastoral world in general rather than Arcadia specifically where music flourished. Theocritus' Sicilian shepherds are just as prone as Virgil's Arcadians to sing hymns and elegies, and to compete with one another in contests of song. The pastoral world expressed itself thus simply because it was that much closer to an Age of Gold, that much more aware of the gods' cosmic music. In pastoral the boundaries between reality and dream, life and art were easily crossed, and the tendency for prose to become poetry and poetry to become song was correspondingly marked. The prose pastorals of Boccaccio and Sannazaro and Sidney easily accommodate a profusion of poems; the exquisitely lyrical verse of Tasso and Guarini always hovers on the verge of music. And lest this seems vague impressionism, let it be recalled that the monologues and dialogues of *Il pastor fido* provided at least 125 composers with the texts for at least 550 madrigals (Hartmann 1953: 424). Obviously contemporary artists felt no less keenly than modern critics that in the 'languid and voluptuous' pastoral 'the vision floats before us as if conjured up by the strains of music rather than by actual words . . . a thousand pictures rise before us as we follow the perfect melody of the irregular lyric measures' (Greg 1905: 192). When an arena was sought for the first trials of a dramatic art in which were fused poetry, song and dance, it is little wonder that imaginations turned to Arcadia and its pastorals rather than to Athens and its tragedies.

3 · The beginnings of opera

'A truly princely spectacle'

The ideological and technical ingredients of early opera had been fashioned by humanist scholars and musicians in the last three decades of the sixteenth century. For the first forty years of its history the new art-form remained intimately bound to the kind of world in which such men had flourished: to aristocratic academies and art-loving courts. By the middle of the seventeenth century it was to become, in some cities at least, a widely popular commercial entertainment, but to begin with its home was the court – the Medici court at Florence, the Gonzaga court at Mantua, the Barberini household in Rome – and its function was to adorn such great festivities as royal weddings, princely birthdays, or state visits.

Peri's *Euridice*, the first opera to have survived in its entirety, owes its origin to such an occasion, the wedding by proxy of Maria de'Medici and King Henry IV of France in October 1600. Several of the musicians whose contribution to the new art has been discussed in Chapters 1 and 2 participated in the festivities that marked this event. Guarini and Cavalieri composed *La contesa fra Giunone e Minerva* to act as an interlude in the great banquet at the Palazzo Vecchio that followed the wedding on 5 October. Next day, in the Pitti palace, *Euridice* had its première, and on 9 October, what was probably regarded as the *pièce de résistance*, Caccini's setting of Chiabrera's *Rapimento di Cefalo*, was performed before an audience of 3,800 guests at the Uffizi. Much of Monteverdi's early dramatic music was commissioned for similar occasions. *Arianna*, the *Ballo delle ingrate* and the *intermedi* for Guarini's *Idropica* were all composed for the festivities held to celebrate the wedding of Francesco Gonzaga with the Princess Margherita of Savoy.

To begin with, opera was very much a connoisseur's entertainment. In the prologue of *Euridice* the spirit of Tragedy, 'who loves deep sighs and weeping', appears 'with smiling face' – for no shadow of sorrow must fall over the royal nuptials – and the promise of 'joyful notes' that will 'furnish delight for the noble heart'. Some noble hearts were, we may be sure, delighted by the opera, as Jacopo Corsi had been 'delighted beyond measure' by Peri's *Dafne* a few years earlier (Marco da Gagliano in Solerti 1903: 80). But they were probably few in number compared with those who revelled in the spectacle of the *intermedi* or in the boisterous intrigue of a spoken comedy. In a letter to Duke Ferdinand's secretary, Marcello Accolti, Cavalieri reported a resounding flop: 'boredom and irritation' among a group of visiting Roman clergy; 'the music tedious . . . like the chanting of the Passion'; and Giovanni Bardi was apparently incredulous that he should not have been commissioned to stage another comedy with *intermedi* on the model of the great festivities of 1589 (Palisca 1963: 351–2). The fact that both the libretto and the score of *Euridice* were published does not reflect a popular triumph; rather the determination of a group of prosperous and loyal Florentine noblemen to do honour to the great occasion.

For some years after 1600 opera was one of several musico-dramatic genres that might grace a festival. *Intermedi, mascherate* and dramatic ballets continued to flourish for many years, and may well have been more popular with the larger part of the audience. As we have seen, Bardi certainly preferred the spoken play with *intermedi* to the opera that he had involuntarily helped to bring to birth. And those noble amateurs who prided themselves on their accomplishments as maskers and dancers would have had even less cause to be partial to a form that depended so much on professional skills.

The long struggle in which opera asserted itself against the older established forms of courtly entertainment is reflected in the terminology of the new form. It was some decades before such simple generic titles as 'dramma musicale' or 'melodramma' were thought a sufficiently clear indication of the nature of the piece. The term 'opera' – actually 'opera da rappresentarsi in musica' – appears only in 1647, in the subtitle to a collection of librettos published in Ancona by Prospero Bonarelli (Solerti 1903: 248–9). Before that, a profusion of such terms as 'favola in musica', 'dramma pastorale recitato . . . con le musiche di . . .', 'tragedia rappresentata in musica', 'canto rappresentativo', 'favoletto da rappresentarsi cantando', etc. etc. had testified to the flexibility and variety of emphases with which men had blended drama and music.

But in an age that was fascinated by the possibilities of combining the arts, and particularly of recharging the traditional arts with dramatic movement, it was inevitable that sooner or later opera should come to be seen as the 'baroque art-form par excellence' (Robinson 1966: 13). In his address 'to the readers', Marco da Gagliano, the composer of *Dafne* (Mantua 1608),[1] praises opera in terms that were to be repeated, echoed and paraphrased by Italian theorists for more than two centuries:

a truly princely spectacle, pleasing beyond all others, since it is the form in which is united every most noble delight; such as the invention and arrangement of the story, judgement (*sentenza*), style, sweetness of verse, the art of music, the ensemble of voices and instruments, perfection of song, elegance of dance and gesture; and it can also be said that the art of painting, as in the perspectives and the costumes, plays no small part; so that the mind is able to enjoy at one time all the most noble feelings inspired by the most pleasing arts that the human mind has discovered. (Solerti 1903: 82)

The operatic synthesis

Opera was invented, experimented with, and established as an art-form in the period of about 15 years from the early 1590s to the Mantuan festivities of 1608, at which Monteverdi's *Arianna* was first heard. Its essential quality was the way it co-ordinated and synthesized a profusion of established art-forms – as Gagliano's panegyric makes clear. More specifically it arose when the relationship between music and drama, which had always been close, was reassessed in the light of those preoccupations and ideals discussed in the previous chapter – the neo-classic inspiration provided by Greek drama, the rediscovery of the affective powers of declamatory song, the cultivation of the pastoral. It was thanks to these things that the traditional types of dramatic music – where music was incidental to, or decorated, or acted as a diversion within the drama – gradually came to be superseded by opera – where music permeates the whole drama, where music is in fact the medium through which the drama is expressed.

There was scarcely one of the first generation of opera composers who did not rationalize the new genre by explaining that it was an attempt to revive the tragic art of the Ancient Greeks. Cavalieri's publisher, Alessandro Guidotti, Rinuccini, Peri, and Gagliano all allude to the belief that Greek tragedy was 'sung in its entirety', and describe their own music-dramas as experiments to ascertain whether or not modern music could achieve similar effects. No doubt there was something of mere humanist habit in such allusions; but it is not until we get to Vitali's *Aretusa* (Rome 1620) that we find a composer who refrains from it, and always the allusion is quite specific. Cavalieri, Peri and Gagliano would not have written music-drama had they not believed that the Greeks had written it.

Of the musical elements of opera quite the most important was what came to be known as recitative, and what at this early date is best described as monody or *stile rappresentativo*. The first opera composers could teach the older madrigalists nothing about the arts of choral writing, or of instrumental and balletic writing. But monody was a field in which they did develop new expressive and dramatic resources. The new art of singing lent itself particularly well to 'moving the passions' by heightening the emotional language of the verse. Gagliano was generous in his tribute to Peri's skill in this style: 'Signor Jacopo Peri discovered that artful manner of declaiming in song which all Italy admires . . . I should say that no one can fully understand the nobility and power of his arias who has not heard them sung by him himself; for he gives them such a grace, and imprints the emotions of the words on the hearers in such a way as to compel them to weep and rejoice as he wills' (Solerti 1903: 81). This power of monodic singing to move the affections was not infrequently seen as analogous to the way in which Greek tragedy stirred pity and terror.

But if Greek tragedy provided the inspiration for opera, and monody the technique by which the ideal of continuous music-drama might be realized, there is no doubt that pastoral provided the ethos in which the new form could seem natural. Perhaps in Ancient Greece Agamemnon or Medea did wrestle with their moral dilemmas in song, and perhaps the monodic style could have lent unbearable poignancy to the plight of Oedipus. But as long as composers were experimenting with music-drama they felt the need to work in a genre where music seemed as plausible a medium as possible. The pastoral provided this. As Doni explained, it was more poetic than comedies or sacred plays and as 'it consists almost always of amorous subjects and has a flowery and sweet style . . . it could be said to have melody in all its parts, especially as there are represented deities, nymphs and shepherds from that far distant age when music was natural and speech like poetry' (Solerti 1903: 203).

Prescriptions for and descriptions of the performance of early opera make it clear that it was essentially a chamber-music genre. It made little use of the spectacular scenic effects or of the sumptuous orchestral resources favoured in the *intermedi*. Several commentators insisted that it worked best, not in great theatres, still less in the open air – where much Renaissance theatre music was played – but in halls of a comparatively modest size. 'In rooms that are too large it is not possible for everyone to hear the words, so it would be necessary for the singer to force his voice, which diminishes the effect; so much music becomes tedious when the words are inaudible' ('A' lettori', *Rappresentazione di anima e di corpo*, in Solerti 1903: 6). Clearly Cavalieri's reason for recommending intimacy of scale was his belief that solo song in the new *stile rappresentativo* was the most important single element in dramatic music. Only when singing was uncluttered by elaborate instrumental ensembles, only when there need be no concern about audibility, could the actor-singer work the full magic of affective song on the audience. Pietro della Valle's encomium of the modern style of singing introduced by the Florentines is manifestly an evocation of the skills required in early opera: 'the art of piano and forte, of gradual crescendo, of graceful diminuendo, of expressing the passions, of judiciously underlining the words and their meaning; of brightening the voice or of making it sorrowful; of making it pitiful or ardent as required' (Solerti 1903: 162). The art of performing early opera was the art of performing monody, and the proper home for both was the princely chamber.

Pioneers and rivals

In the essay of della Valle from which I have just quoted, the Roman musician speaks admiringly of what he calls the 'good school of Florence'. But in point of fact there was about the pioneers of opera little of the closely knit fraternity that this term might seem to suggest. No love was lost between the musicians of the erstwhile Camerata and Peri, or indeed Cavalieri. Emulation was jealous, rivalry sometimes petty. The most startling manifestation of this contentiousness was the fact that, when Peri's *Euridice* was first performed, Caccini refused to allow those members of the cast who were pupils of his to sing his rival's music; instead equivalent passages from his own setting of the same text were substituted. For the historian, this rivalry has one invaluable consequence. Cavalieri, Peri and Caccini were all anxious to be recognized as innovators in what they perceived to be an event of the first magnitude in the history of music. And so they prefaced the printed scores and librettos of their works with dedications and addresses which give much indispensable information about these first stages in the history of opera.

Despite the confusion and sometimes nearly contradictory testimony of these prefaces, none of our protagonists can quite be detected in flagrant falsehood. Even the archrivals Peri and Caccini make slightly different claims, claims nicely differentiated by Pirrotta in his elucidation of the contrast between 'recitar cantando' and 'cantar recitando' (Pirrotta 1969a: 314–15). What Peri hoped to be remembered as was the first composer to have devised for dramatic purposes a kind of music 'imitating in song someone who speaks . . . a harmony as far elevated above ordinary speech as it is descended below melodious singing' (Solerti 1903: 45–6). He was the originator of dramatic recitative in a theatrical context, of 'recitar cantando'. Caccini's claim is slightly different, though there is no doubt that it was designed to belittle Peri's. He says, in a preface addressed to Bardi, 'in [my opera] you will recognize that style used by me on other occasions, many years ago . . . when your Camerata flourished in Florence' (Solerti 1903: 50). He may have thought that his monodic style was indistinguishable from Peri's dramatic recitative, but the modern critic is inclined to regard it as a recognizably different thing, and to acknowledge Caccini as the early master of declamatory song, or 'cantar recitando'.

There is a third claimant for priority, the Roman Cavalieri, and his claim is disputed by no one. Indeed Peri himself acknowledged that 'Signor Emilio de Cavalieri, before anyone else that I know, with wonderful invention enabled us to hear [our kind] of music on the stage. (Solerti 1903: 45). Cavalieri had staged three 'music dramas' in Florence before anything of Peri's in this line had been completed. Two, *Il satiro* and *La disperazione di Fileno,* both with texts by Laura Guidiccioni, were performed in 1590; the third, *Il giuoco della cieca,* presumably a setting of the famous scene from Guarini's *Pastor fido,* in 1595. All three are lost.

In the preface to the *Rappresentazione di anima e di corpo,* Guidotti, surely acting as Cavalieri's own spokesman, draws the inevitable analogy between these three pastorals and the dramas of the Ancient World. But they cannot disqualify Peri's right to be regarded as the first composer of opera. No doubt Cavalieri's pieces were sung in character, but to judge from Doni's description, they were really strings of songs, not genuine musical dramas. In fact he makes them sound more akin to madrigal-comedy than to opera: 'one must understand however that these musical settings are very different from those of today in the style generally called recitative, being nothing more than ariettas with many such artifices as repetitions, echoes and the like, which have nothing to do with the real, good theatre music . . .' (Solerti 1903: 208). So while Cavalieri may be credited with having been the first to have staged dramas in music, a fully fledged operatic idiom – to which Caccini's monody contributed not a little – emerged only in the works of Peri.

The first operas

The first real opera therefore was *Dafne,* the text written by Rinuccini, the music by Peri. Its first performance, at the Palazzo Corsi in Florence, took place, according to Gagliano and the earliest surviving libretto, during the 1597–98 Carnival (Sternfeld 1978: 131–2), though in the preface to *Euridice* Peri claimed that the work went back as far as 1594. It was twice revived, in revised form, before Rinuccini and Peri essayed a second opera. Then, in 1607, Rinuccini re-worked his libretto again for Marco da Gagliano. His setting formed one of the main attractions at the Mantuan festivities early the following year, and was likewise several times revived. In passing we may note that in 1627 the same *Dafne* was to become the first monument in the history of German opera: Martin Opitz's adaptation of the text was composed by Heinrich Schütz and performed at Torgau in that year.

Rinuccini, Peri and Gagliano all left their own accounts of the origins of *Dafne,* pointing the analogy with Greek drama, emphasizing the success it enjoyed, claiming – or in Gagliano's case conceding – that it was something quite different in kind from Cavalieri's earlier pastorals, and the true *fons et origo* of the new art that was to spring up in the early seventeenth century. Gagliano's story is the fullest and, if it is not quite the eye-witness account that the others are, may be presumed to be the most impartial.

After having many, many times discussed the manner used by the Ancients in presenting their tragedies, how they introduced the choruses, whether they used singing and in what style, and similar matters, signor Ottavio Rinuccini devoted himself to writing the drama of *Dafne,* [and] signor Jacopo Corsi, of revered memory, a lover of all learning and especially of music, so that he was very properly called its father by all musicians, composed some settings of parts of it. Delighted with these, and determined to see what effect they would make on the stage, he and signor Ottavio confided their thoughts to signor Jacopo Peri, an experienced contrapuntist and a most exquisite singer. He, hearing their plans, and approving that part of the arias that were already composed, busied himself with composing the others. They delighted signor Corsi beyond measure, and on the occasion of an entertainment during the 1597 Carnival he had it performed . . .   (Solerti 1903: 80)

The six surviving fragments of the music for *Dafne*[2] comprise formal monodies and choruses, not radically different in style from other theatre music of the late sixteenth century. But there can be no doubt that this was the work in which Peri forged his *stile rappresentativo*. The long description of that style which he gives in the preface to *Euridice* does not refer to *Euridice* itself, but to the discussions and the experiments with Rinuccini and Corsi that led to the achievement of *Dafne*.

Rinuccini and Peri were again the collaborators in *Euridice*, an enterprise in which Corsi contented himself with an entrepreneurial role. In character their second opera closely resembled their first. The poet selected a similar mythological fable, with a hero of song as his protagonist, and placed it in a similar pastoral setting. Structurally too *Euridice* resembles *Dafne*, each of its short scenes culminating in a strophic chorus. But emboldened by the success of *Dafne*, Rinuccini and Peri now felt confident that music-drama could be sustained on an altogether more ambitious scale; the new opera is almost twice as long as its precursor.

Despite its greater size *Euridice* is a purer example of pastoral drama than *Dafne*. The principal characters are fully absorbed into the Arcadian milieu and express themselves with an easy spontaneity in the language of song, chorus and dance. The pastoral inheritance is clear too in the long, descriptive messenger scenes, and in such set pieces as Orpheus' apostrophe to Nature, 'Antri, ch'ai miei lamenti', and his lament in Hades. Scenes like these are the direct descendants of the soliloquies of Aminta or Mirtillo, and in turn furnish the model for the great operatic monologues of later-seventeenth-century practice.

Above all Rinuccini fills his libretto with those thematic features that made pastoral so congenial for opera: with Golden Age imagery and with the depiction of a blessed and beautiful world where music is a way of life:

> Ma deh, compagne amate,
> Là tra quell'ombre grate
> Moviam di quel fiorit' almo boschetto.
> E quivi al suon de limpidi cristalli
> trarrem liete carole e lieti balli.[3]

with allusions to the power of music and with pathetic fallacies that endow the natural world with sentience or fill it with cosmic harmony. As Orpheus leads Eurydice back from Hades Aminta reports that:

Ardea la terra
Ardean gli eterei giri
Ai gioiosi sospiri
Dell'uno e l'altro innamorato core.
E per l'aer sereno
S'udian musici cori
Dolci canti temprar d'alati amori.[4]

In a singularly wilful piece of self-assertiveness Caccini began to make a rival setting of *Euridice* at much the same time. There are many resemblances between the two settings. While the contrast between recitatives on the one hand and aria and chorus on the other is less extreme than it was later to become, it is clear in both, in the 'dramatist' Peri's score no less than in the 'lyricist' Caccini's. Recitative is employed for soliloquy and dialogue; aria for song and dance, for those passages in the drama that would have been music even before the invention of opera. Of many more specific resemblances which suggest that Caccini knew Peri's setting and did not disdain to imitate it, three passages may be mentioned in which both composers use the strophic variation form: the prologue, the solo verses in 'Al canto, al ballo', the chorus at the end of the second scene, and the solo verses in 'Sospirate aure celesti', the lament that closes the messenger scene. The refrain in the latter piece is a choral recitative in Caccini as in Peri.

The real interest of the *Euridice* operas, however, lies in Peri's demonstration of the power and variety possible in the new *stile rappresentativo*. Caccini may have preceded him in the composition of monody, but when it came to the test of opera, his recitatives were nothing like so radically new or so dramatic. While Caccini followed the harmonic laws of the mainstream of sixteenth-century music, Peri was quite prepared to ignore them in his quest for the ideal of heightened but naturalistic declamation. His recitative is more boldly dissonant, more erratic rhythmically, more detailed in its reflection of the test (see Ex.I.4). In an interesting passage in the preface to the opera, he described his practice in these terms:

I recognized the fact that, when we are speaking, we sometimes make use of intonations which could serve as the basis for harmony, and that in the course of speaking we pass through many others that furnish no such basis, until we return to another implying some change to a different consonance. And having had regard to those styles and those accents which are used in grieving, in rejoicing and in similar things, I made the bass move in time with them, now more now less, according to the passions; and I held it firm against dissonances and consonances until, running through various notes, the voice of the speaker should arrive at what, fashioning the intonation according to ordinary speech, opens the way to a new harmony.   (Solerti 1903: 46–7)

This bold, radical style of declamation was to furnish the basis for Monteverdi's dramatic art, too. *Orfeo* is unimaginable without the example of Peri.

DAFNE

Las - sa che di spa - ven - to e di pie - ta - te ge-la-miil cor nel se - no Mi - se - ra - bil bel - ta - te, Com'in un pun-to, ohi - me, ve - ni - sti me - no

Alack! with terror and pity the heart freezes in my breast. Wretched beauty, in a moment, alas, how you have faded.

Ex.I.4 Peri, *Euridice* (1600)

Euridice was the purest manifestation of the Florentine humanists' urge to recreate the music-drama of Ancient Greece. But its style was too sparse and uncompromising for it to have established a tradition of opera that could survive the rivalry with the other musico-dramatic forms of the age. First in Mantua, then in Rome, the spirit of early Florentine opera was compromised – compromised in order to accommodate a more ample supply of virtuosity, of colour and of spectacle. In short, opera came to terms with the *intermedio*.

Rinuccini's next libretto, the *Arianna* that he wrote for Monteverdi in 1608, was perhaps the best example of the greater complexity and colourfulness of the operas of this phase. The setting is still basically pastoral, but the protagonists Ariadne and Theseus stand apart from the nymphs and fishermen as representatives of a higher order and a different way of life. What is more, the action is framed by scenes set among the gods, and concluded – apparently at the urging of a team of noblemen – by a spectacular apotheosis. The fact that the action of the opera takes place on several planes of reality gave scope for a wider range of musical styles, for the deployment of the multicoloured Renaissance orchestra, and for the full scenic resources of scenographers and theatre architects. Alas, save for the lament, *Arianna* does not survive – as deplorable a loss as any in operatic history. For there were many among the audience who felt that here at last the magical powers of Ancient music had been restored. As Aquilino Coppini, a Milanese friend of Monteverdi, put it, 'those effects we read about with such amazement in ancient sources should no longer appear strange . . .' for Monteverdi's opera too had the power 'of making the famous audience weep thousands and thousands of tears' (Schrade 1951: 240).

But Monteverdi's first opera, *Orfeo* (Mantua 1607), did survive. Here too he accepted the Perian principle of the continuous music-drama; but he transformed its character by absorbing into it all the multifarious musical resources of the other dramatic forms of the Renaissance. The result was the first great masterpiece in the Italian tradition.

4 · Monteverdi's *Orfeo* (Mantua 1607)

The theme: Orpheus and the music of Renaissance Italy

During the first twenty years or so of the history of the new form, operas in which Orpheus was the hero were remarkably numerous: Peri's *Euridice*, Caccini's *Euridice*, Monteverdi's *Orfeo*, Belli's *Orfeo dolente* (strictly a set of *intermedi* performed in conjunction with Tasso's *Aminta*), Landi's *La morte d'Orfeo* were all performed in various Italian cities between 1600 and 1619. This is too great a profusion to be attributed convincingly to mere coincidence. Let it be admitted that the Orpheus myth was a singularly beautiful and evocative one, and that his divine gifts – which in the English-speaking world are most familiarly memorialized in Shakespeare's 'Orpheus with his lute' – were eminently fitting for a hero of opera, nonetheless it is certain that in Renaissance Italy he was a character with deeper and richer and in a sense more operatic associations. Before examining Monteverdi's *Orfeo* in detail, it will be worthwhile to enquire briefly into these associations. When we do, we shall find that Orpheus is a figure so entirely congenial to the operatic medium that it would be only mildly hyperbolical to describe him as its inventor.

At the close of Plato's *Apology*, Socrates explains to his judges why he has no fear of death. Death must, he declares, be one of two things: either it is a state of oblivion comparable with a dreamless sleep – and there is nothing fearsome in that prospect – or it leads us to an afterlife, where we shall meet with a whole world of departed spirits. Foremost among the illustrious dead whom Socrates looks forward to meeting in any such afterlife is Orpheus; for the pleasure of conversing with him, with Musaeus, Hesiod and Homer, he would be ready to die many times (*The apology*, 41.A).

No less remarkable is the tribute to Orpheus in Horace's *Ars poetica*.

When men were still savage, Orpheus being the priest and interpreter of the gods deterred them from slaughter and violence. For this reason he is said to have calmed savage tigers and lions; and Amphion too, the founder of the city of Thebes, is said to have moved the stones by the sound of his lyre and led them whither he pleased by the sweetness of his voice . . . It was in song that the oracles were delivered and the way of life shown. *(Ars poetica* 391–5, 405)

We see that Horace revered Orpheus and his fellow-musician Amphion as nothing less than the founders of civilization, the first to create an orderly social intercourse among men. Music was not, as the philistine supposes, the fruit of leisure and prosperity; it was the first prerequisite for civilized living. And consequently the great musicians at the mythological dawn of history were to be regarded as something very much more than mere entertainers or performers. Quintilian expressed the attitude most succinctly when he described Orpheus as *musicus, vates, sapiens* – musician, seer and sage (*Institutionis oratoriae* Lib. 1.X.9). It was because the Classical authorities ascribed to him such awe-inspiring powers that Orpheus became a central figure in Renaissance thought about art and civilization. From what Plato, Horace and Quintilian had to say, it was clear that he was something other than or more than the celebrated mythological musician, who attempted to rescue his lost wife Eurydice from Hades.

In Ancient Greece, Orpheus was venerated as the founder of the religion that bears his name. Orphism was the source of some of the most influential strands in Greek philosophy, and both Pythagoras and Plato, to name but the greatest, were deeply indebted to it. Two elements are of particular interest to us. It taught that the soul was immortal, though unharmoniously conjoined with a decaying body, and that after this life it transmigrated to a place either of bliss or of torment. It was therefore one of the ancient religions that most obviously anticipated and prepared the world for the developed doctrines of Christianity. Secondly, according to the Neoplatonist Iamblichus, who wrote an account of Pythagorean philosophy, it was from Orphism that the Pythagoreans derived the belief that the structure of the universe was based on numerical proportions. Orpheus was, then, in the first instance, remembered as the founder and high-priest of an influential mystery-cult, as one of the deepest sources of wisdom. This was why Socrates, to judge from the kinds of pleasure he looked forward to in the afterlife, so much hoped to meet him: beautiful music did not enter into the philosopher's calculations.

Orpheus' association with music went hand in hand with his reputation as the founder of metaphysical mathematics. For like the great universe itself, musical harmony is based on mathematical proportion. The creation of the cosmos is one manifestation of the power of God the mathematician; music is another. And the mathematical order of the universe and the mathematical order of musical harmony reflect and image one another. The universe, as Maximus Confessor put it, is 'music performed by God'. In its most developed form, in Boethius for example, this belief in cosmic harmony distinguishes three degrees of music. To expand on the definitions given earlier, *musica mundana* is that harmonious order which God established when he created the universe in time and space. *Music humana* is the orderly intercourse of the civilized world, the proper functioning of a sane mind and a healthy body. Music as we know it, music sung, played, and enjoyed, *music instrumentalis*, is a microcosm of these great patterns and derives its philosophical justification from them. Such beliefs about the cosmic harmony Boethius derived from the Pythagoreans; from him they passed down to the great astronomer Kepler, and even to Hindemith in our own day. Their ultimate source, however, is Orpheus, Orpheus who was at once *musicus, vates, sapiens*.

The picture of Orpheus that begins to emerge helps explain something else that fascinated both the Ancient World and the Italian Renaissance. Both as high-priest of a mystery-cult and as mathematician and sage, Orpheus was in touch with the Divine. And those musical gifts that were reported in legend – his ability to tame wild beasts, to move the rocks and trees, to redeem Eurydice from Hades – are likewise clear tokens of divine inspiration. If he could do these things there could be no doubt that his singing was the result of the visitation of a 'frenzy', a god-given intoxication that bestowed upon him supernatural powers.

The classic statement on the subject of such inspiration is to be found in Plato's *Phaedrus*, where Socrates describes the poet-musician as one of the four types of person visited by divine frenzy. Besides him there was the mystic, the prophet and the lover, all of them similarly possessed. It did not escape the notice of some philosophers that Orpheus fitted tolerably well into most if not all of these categories. Certainly Marsilio Ficino thought so when, in fifteenth-century Florence, he pondered and elaborated the Platonic doctrine of divine inspiration. For him, therefore, and for the large number of his followers, Orpheus became the very type of the inspired artist, possessed in equal measure of spiritual illumination, sublime eloquence and superhuman passion. And these came to be the qualities expected of genius in its highest manifestation, of a Michelangelo, a Josquin or a Tasso. No wonder that in the Italian Renaissance the artist became a hero; nor that people saw in the stories of Orpheus the original portrait of the artist as hero.

In Classical times a special type of song and a special style of singing were particularly associated with Orpheus. The Orphic hymns, a repertory of ancient sacred odes, were believed by many to be actual examples of Orpheus' composition; while the art of declamatory singing to one's own accompaniment on the lyre, though it was a form of music-making by no means limited to cultic occasions, was often described as Orphic singing. This art of Orphic singing survived in some form or another into the Christian era, indeed into the fifteenth century; and at the time of the Council of Florence (1438–45), called to discuss the reunification of the Eastern and Western churches, one of the leading Greek representatives, Gemistus Pletho, introduced it to the West.

Given the enthusiasm felt in Florence at that time for every manifestation of Classical civilization, it is not surprising that Pletho's demonstrations aroused considerable excitement. Indeed Ficino rated the revival of Orphic singing with the revival of Platonic philosophy as the two supreme achievements of the early decades of the Florentine Renaissance. Since nothing of this music has survived it is not possible to describe it very precisely. But from contemporary accounts we may deduce that it was rhapsodic and improvisatory, that its rhythmic and diastematic character, while often employing traditional melodies, was intimately related to the words, and that the singer accompanied himself on an instrument which in the fifteenth century was generally the *lira da braccio*. It is best imagined as a kind of spiritual incantation: Ficino himself practised it 'as part of the religious discipline of *contemplatio*' (Cody 1969: 31). The most illuminating account of the perfect fusion of text and music in this Orphic singing is in a letter in which Poliziano describes to Pico della Mirandola the precocious skills of the young Fabio Orsini:

He then performed an heroic song which he had composed himself in praises of our Piero di Medici . . . His voice was not quite like that of one who recites and not quite like that of one who sings, but you could have heard both the one and the other and yet without distinguishing the one from the other. Sometimes it was plain, sometimes modulated, changing as the context required; now varied now sustained, now exalted now moderated, now calm now vehement, now slowing down now accelerated, always precise, always clear and always pleasing; and his gestures were neither indifferent nor dull, but nor were they exaggerated or affected.   (Pirrotta 1969a: 46–7)

The extent of the vogue is perhaps best gauged by the profusion of Italian paintings of the period depicting Apollo or Orpheus or 'Music' performing this kind of song (Winternitz 1979: 89–97); Leonardo da Vinci himself practised the style in his youth. Vasari tells us: 'for a little while he attended to music, and then he very soon resolved to learn to play the lyre, for he was naturally of an elevated and refined disposition; and with this instrument he accompanied his own charming improvised singing' (Bell 1965: 179).

The kind of singing admired by Ficino and Leonardo and Poliziano cannot have been so very different from the monodic style of the Florentine Camerata a hundred years and more later. And, let it be reiterated, its source was believed to Orpheus himself.

All the aspects of the Orpheus theme discussed so far derive from the Orpheus traditions of the Ancient World. But all of them were a living force among the artists of Renaissance Italy too, and the influence of all of them is to be felt in the earliest operas, especially in *Orfeo*. In particular the opera's great centrepiece, the aria 'Possente spirto' in Act III, explores the whole gamut of what the Renaissance would have understood as Orphic music. It is an expression of overwhelming human passion – Orpheus' yearning for the lost Eurydice; it is, as the singer summons all the resources of contemporary ornamentation, a supreme demonstration of the artist's cunning; and it makes manifest the ethical and magical powers of music, since it succeeds in melting the heart of Hell itself. What is more,

Monteverdi composed the aria in such a way as to suggest that he intended it not simply as an imposing specimen of Orphic song, but also as a microcosm of the harmonious mathematical order of the universe. For he has built the aria over a regularly recurring pattern of harmonies on the strophic variation principle, and by punctuating the phrases with instrumental ritornellos for violins, cornetts, and harp – it is the only movement in the opera in which voices and *obbligato* instruments are so interwoven – he contrives to evoke in the spectator a sense of the immanent music of the universe, the *musica mundana*, the music of the spheres.

It will be conceded that Orpheus was, for Renaissance Italians, a mythological hero of singularly rich allure. And his attractiveness as an operatic character will already be easy to understand. But one might go further and suggest that Orpheus was not just a good hero for an opera, he was almost the only possible hero; that it was only through him that opera became a feasible art. A famous Shakespearean passage will help illuminate this claim.

> . . . look, how the floor of heaven
> Is thick inlaid with patines of bright gold:
> There's not the smallest orb which thou behold'st
> But in his motion like an angel sings,
> Still quiring to the young-eyed cherubins;
> Such harmony is in immortal souls;
> But, whilst this muddy vesture of decay
> Doth grossly close it in, we cannot hear it.
>
> (*Merchant of Venice*, Act V scene 1 58f.)

Shakespeare is, of course, describing the music of the spheres, the *musica mundana*. Alas, it can only be described, since to fallen man it is inaudible; by implication, man's life of earth is not the *musica humana* it ought to be.

But there was a time when it was. In Eden one presumes that the *musica mundana* might have been heard; before the snake and the apple the *musica humana* would have formed a perfect concord. Running through almost the entire history of Western art is a vein of nostalgia for the wholeness of pre-lapsarian man, for that Golden Age of innocence. In the convention of the pastoral, man is in harmony with nature, he does perceive the music of the universe, and he is himself a being whose language is music and poetry. Given that convention, it is not surprising that at an early date Orpheus was being described as the son of a muse, as a companion of the nymphs, as – in the pastoral sense – a shepherd. And when he re-appears in the dramatic literature of Renaissance Italy the pastoral tone is even more emphatic.

The work in question is the *Fabula di Orfeo* written by Poliziano, and first performed at a Carnival banquet at Mantua in 1480. The *Fabula* is a short piece, a mere 352 lines, a dramatic sketch of a kind that commonly marked the climax of the *entremets* used to punctuate the Lucullan feasts of the age. Yet, notwithstanding its brevity, Poliziano's choice of subject and his way of handling it means that room is found for more music than is common in such a *fabula*. In the pastoral scenes *frottolas* and *canzonas* are sung by the shepherds; in the heroic scenes Orpheus addresses odes (for which he would surely have employed the idiom of Orphic singing) to the noble audience or to the powers of Hades; in the scenes of Bacchic ritual the maenads sing and dance. During the drama music is, then, allowed to function in three ways: as the natural expression of the pastoral world, as a civilizing or impassioning influence, as the proper embodiment of sacred rituals. It is hardly surprising that historians have seen Poliziano's *Orfeo* as the first clear foreshadowing of the art of opera; for these are precisely the kinds of musical function that make opera a feasible proposition.

After the *Fabula di Orfeo* the pastoral became a popular form of courtly drama, not least because of the scope it afforded music. But for the greater part of the sixteenth century the resources that might have been turned to the service of opera were diverted into the *intermedio*, and nothing more operatic than Poliziano's entertainment appeared for over a century. It would be easy to suppose, indeed it has often been supposed, that when this point was reached in the 1590s and dramatists and musicians deliberately set out to create a type of music-drama analogous to that which the Ancients were believed to have cultivated, their aim was to recreate Greek tragedy. Sometimes the authors claimed as much themselves. But it was not until Monteverdi's *Arianna* of 1608 that anyone ventured to describe a music-drama as a *tragedia*. Previous to that the usual term had been *favola*. The earliest operas had been pastorals – the pastorals of Cavalieri in the early 1590s, Peri's and Caccini's and Agazzari's fables in the years around 1600, Monteverdi's own *Orfeo*. It was in the pastoral world that opera was born, because it was only in such a world that music would seem an entirely proper medium of expression; it was not until it had proved itself in this style that Monteverdi or anyone else ventured to attempt operatic tragedy.

The reasons why Orpheus became the irresistible, inevitable hero of so many early operas should now be clear. It was not simply that the legend of the attempted rescue of Eurydice from Hades is one of the world's great stories, though that helps. So does the fact that this heroic enterprise vividly epitomizes the questing spirit of a humanist age. But the crucial thing is surely this: that Orpheus was the glorious exemplar of an artist operating upon the world in which he lived; raising up his fellow men to a state of civilization, and shaping destiny itself by the eloquence and beauty of his art. To that must be added the fact of his traditional association with muses and nymphs, with wild beasts, trees and rocks; for that made him at home within the pastoral convention, a central figure of a world in which the *musica humana* comes close to being a faithful imitation of the *musica mundana*. Opera was born in an age that ardently longed to bring back the Age of Gold by means of art: no protagonist could be found to whom such dreams might so confidently entrusted.

Alessandro Striggio's *favola*

The text written for Monteverdi by Alessandro Striggio the younger treats the Orpheus story in considerably greater detail than either Poliziano or Rinuccini had done. It is laid out not in a series of short scenes, but in five extensive and elaborately organized acts; three Pastoral acts (I, II and V) frame two Infernal acts (III and IV), and this whole five-act structure is in turn framed by the toccata and prologue at the start and the *moresca* at the close, conventional ingredients of all court theatricals of the period. This spacious structure was a boon for the composer, since without the least trace of diffuseness it accommodated a far wider range of dramatic expression than the *Euridice* of Rinuccini had done; a brief synopsis will make the libretto's scope clear.

Act I is an act of preparation. The wedding of Orpheus and Eurydice is soon to take place; the central characters are introduced and pledge their love, Hymen and the Muses are invoked, and at the end of the act the company departs for the temple to offer incense and prayer to the gods. Act II brings the first dramatic crisis: the joyful songs and dances in celebration of the wedding are interrupted by the arrival of the messenger, Silvia, a friend of Eurydice. She tells how the young bride has been bitten by a snake and died. An act that began in rejoicing thus closes in grief; dance and song give way to elegy. But Orpheus has resolved to rescue Eurydice from Hades; and in Act III we witness his descent into the Underworld in the company of the allegorical figure of Hope (Speranza), his encounter with Charon, the ferryman, and his successful crossing of the Styx into the kingdom of Pluto. In Act IV, thanks to Proserpina's intervention, Orpheus secures the release of Eurydice. But Pluto imposes a condition: he must not look back on his bride until he has led her back to the sunlight. He fails to abide by this condition and loses her a second time, irrevocably. Act V is dominated by Orpheus' lament for Eurydice. At the close of the act, however, Apollo (Orpheus' father according to some Classical sources) descends to comfort him and to translate him to the heavens, where he will be reunited with Eurydice.

The musical and dramatic scope afforded Monteverdi by Striggio's libretto is considerable. Each of the three central acts pivots round a critical dramatic encounter: that of the revellers with the messenger in Act II, that of Orpheus and Charon in Act III, that of Orpheus with the temptations of fear and passion which are to unman him in Act IV. In the first two acts, and in the fifth, Music can give a comprehensive demonstration of its powers of expression, both joyful and tragic.

Invaluable too from Monteverdi's point of view is the text's architectural coherence, a quality which can be observed in the broadest outlines of the opera and in the smallest details of its individual scenes. Whereas Rinuccini sets only one scene of *Euridice* in the underworld, Striggio sets two whole acts there, two acts of Infernal musical colouring and Infernal décor to balance the two Pastoral acts with which the opera had begun. Throughout *Orfeo* he shows his understanding of the fact that, even in forward-moving dramatic action, music needs opportunity for repetition and reduplication if it is to be intelligible. The reprise of two of the choruses in Act I; the refrain 'Ahi caso acerbo' running through the later stages of Act 2; the touches of rhetorical parallelism found in many of the longer speeches – such features as these show that Striggio understood that musical coherence was as much a desideratum for Monteverdi as musical eloquence.

Provision for the chorus

Of supreme importance to the character of this opera is Striggio's provision for the chorus. Since Monteverdi's time the chorus has – with a few exceptions – played a comparatively minor role in the Italian operatic tradition. But in these early days the situation was very different. The chorus was more important than the aria, as essential an ingredient in the opera as recitative; and for similar reasons: because the chorus was a medium for which there was a precise analogy and model in the Classical world. So far as the current musical idiom allowed, the operatic choruses of Monteverdi and his contemporaries in the years around 1600 were deliberate imitations of the choruses in Classical Greek tragedy.

There is no reason to doubt that in Monteverdi's time Aristotle's views on the chorus would have been accepted without question (cf. Chapter 2 above). The ideal model was Sophocles, because he, better than any other ancient author, understood how to involve the chorus in the action of the drama. In Sophocles the odes which the chorus sings might well be in some measure philosophical, and might well be of intense lyrical beauty; but above all they express the feelings of people intimately concerned with the fate of the protagonists. The Sophoclean chorus does not stand apart from the action as the Aeschylean generally does, and philosophize with objective detachment. Nor do its odes ever become merely ornamental and diversionary, as Euripides' sometimes do. Sophocles achieves the ideal of profound reflection in majestic lyrical language from a chorus deeply concerned with the course of the action. As far as this dramatic function is concerned, it is the choruses of Acts I and II that come nearest to the Aristotelian prescription. They are sung by nymphs and shepherds, the friends of Orpheus and Eurydice, who rejoice with them on their wedding day and weep for them at Eurydice's death. And while by no means all of the choruses are therefore Sophoclean in function or character – some are simple *balletti* or canzonettas – the two most substantial at least, 'Alcun non sia' in Act I, and that at the close of Act II, may certainly be regarded as imitations of the classical *stasimon*. 'Alcun non sia' is sung during the procession to the temple, and takes the form of a meditation on the action so far: no one should allow himself to be overcome by despair; when the storm-clouds have done their worst the sky clears; after the harsh frosts of Winter Spring returns to deck the fields with flowers. So Orpheus once fed only on sighs and drank only tears, but now he is so happy that there is nothing more for him to desire.

Altogether more problematic is the involvement of the chorus in the final act of the opera, which exists in two different versions. In the printed libretto, Orpheus' lament, which takes up the first part of the act, is cut short by the approach of a chorus of Bacchantes; in the printed score, however, the descent of Apollo and Orpheus' translation to the heavens bring the act to a close. Neither version is entirely satisfactory; indeed in neither is the sequence of events even entirely clear.

Nevertheless, in the version set by Monteverdi there is no doubt that the function of the chorus is the same as it had been before: to draw the attention of the spectators to the significance of the action they have witnessed. We cannot but be struck by the fact that the tone of the moral is strikingly non-mythological. The chorus bids Orpheus farewell as he journeys to a world where joys never fade and griefs are never felt. They who are left behind will devote themselves to his rites with altars, incense and votive offerings. In the second verses we learn that Orpheus' happy fate is the proper reward of one who did not recoil when the eternal god summoned him. One who has experienced hell on earth shall obtain blessings in heaven: he who sows in tears shall reap the fruit of grace. The tone, it will be observed, becomes progressively more Christian as the scene moves to its close, even to the extent of paraphrasing the Sermon on the Mount. In effect the Apollo scene provides the opera with one of those 'allegories' by which the humanists loved to redeem Classical mythology for the contemporary Christian.

For all the problems and puzzles posed by the final scene of the opera, it is clear that in the first, second and fifth acts of *Orfeo*, the chorus does in principle fulfil the Aristotelian requirements of a chorus. It is treated as a participant in the action of the opera, and the choral odes, however philosophically they may be developed, arise naturally from that involvement. In Acts III and IV its role is somewhat different. Both libretto and score describe it here as a 'chorus of infernal spirits'. That in itself would guarantee some greater measure of objective detachment from the fate of

Orpheus and Eurydice. But Striggio's text and Monteverdi's manner of setting it emphasize this detachment. With some qualification, which will become apparent in a moment, we may say that the infernal chorus stands quite apart from the action and that its utterances are more purely lyrical, philosophical and moralizing than those of the other acts.

In Act III the chorus sings only once. The infernal spirits, having taken no part in the action, appear at the close – or possibly speak as disembodied voices – to point out the moral and philosophical significance of what has taken place. Despite the undertones of burlesque in the encounter with Charon, Act III shows Orpheus at his most heroic. Character and art have enabled him to achieve an unimaginable deed. The end of this act is therefore the opera's ideal opportunity for incorporating a choric ode to the humanist ideal of heroism. For Renaissance man no undertaking is too bold; the laws of Nature herself are no longer inviolate from him. He ploughs the tempestuous waves, sowing the seed of his undertakings and reaping a rich harvest. His rewards are Fame and Glory which bestow upon him immortality: 'Nulla impresa per uom si tenta in vano.'[1] Striggio continued his chorus through two more verses, recalling the superhuman achievements of Daedalus, who flew up to heaven. But he concludes that nothing achieved before could compare with Orpheus' descent into the underworld.

Monteverdi's setting includes only one of the three verses, a drastic example of a theatrical impatience which is as characteristic of him as it was to be of Verdi 250 years later. Virtually all the large-scale choral movements in *Orfeo* use abbreviated versions of Striggio's text. If the verses become prolix, or if the philosopher in Striggio becomes so engrossed in pointing his finger at the moral that he looks like forgetting his story, Monteverdi cuts him short.

The composer emends the poet's scheme more fundamentally in the earlier stages of Act IV. At the point where Pluto accedes to Proserpina's entreaty and agrees that Eurydice may be restored to Orpheus, on condition, however, that he does not turn to look at her until they have left the underworld, Striggio had placed another chorus, spelling out the precise nature of the god's decree. But a chorus at this juncture would slow down the action at its dramatic climax, and perhaps distract attention from Proserpina's eloquence; and Monteverdi chooses to set it as a recitative. Or perhaps for mundane practical reasons – the cost of extra costumes, for example – he simply did not want to get his chorus of spirits involved in the action at all, choosing rather to reserve them for the detached moralizing role they had already assumed in Act III. Twice more in this act – immediately before Orpheus' song of triumph 'Qual onor di te fia degno', and at his 'breaking of the law' – Striggio composed stanzas for the chorus. But on both occasions anything suggestive of involvement in the action was turned by Monteverdi into recitative. All that is left of the three intended choruses is the single moralizing couplet

Pietade oggi et Amore
Trionfan ne l'Inferno.[2]

The metrics of the *favola in musica*

The last of the qualities of Striggio's text with which we need concern ourselves is its range of verse forms. For this, better almost than anything else, helps identify the sources on which early opera drew and clarifies our understanding of the tone and function of the various parts of the score.

The classic Italian verse-form was the *endecasillabo*, the eleven-syllable iambic line. *Endescasillabi* formed the basis of the Petrarchan sonnet, of Dante's *terza rima*, of the *ottava rima* of the Renaissance epic poets, and of the most elevated of Italian verse-forms, the *canzone*: in this last form, however, the *endecasillabi* were intermixed with *settenari*. If the poet, while employing a combination of *endecasillabi* and *settenari*, abandoned the strophic form of the *canzone*, and employed rhyme only casually and occasionally, the type of verse that resulted came to be known as '*versi a selva*', because metre and rhyme were 'as unorderly as trees in a forest' (Elwert 1968: 144). *Versi a selva* was first popularized, fittingly enough, in pastoral drama, in Tasso's *Aminta*, and from this source it was transferred to the early opera librettos of Rinuccini and Striggio. It remained the standard type of recitative verse down to the time of Verdi. Striggio's libretto illustrates very clearly some of its strengths. Not only was it flexible and varied in itself; one could very easily modulate from it to more formal or elevated types of verse: to the rhyming 'madrigal' – a one-verse *canzone* – for more consciously lyrical speeches, such as the Nymph's 'Muse, onor di Parnaso' in Act I, or to blank verse – the exclusively hendecasyllabic but non-rhyming *versi sciolti*, which were introduced in the sixteenth century in deliberate imitation of Classical verse, and which Striggio used for the most magisterial speeches in the libretto: that of the allegorical figure of Hope in Act III, and the climatic passages of Orpheus' lament in Act V. More obviously set-piece verses employ the Dantean *terza rima* (Orpheus' 'Possente spirto') or – another Classical imitation – the Horatian ode form (Prologue, and Charon's 'O tu ch'innanzi morte'). Like all Italian authors of the period who addressed themselves to the task of creating a modern analogy to the choral drama of the Greeks, Striggio followed the precedent established by Giangiorgio Trissino in *Sofonisba* (1515) of writing his choruses in *canzone* form – or, of course, in the one-verse equivalent as madrigals.

A complete contrast with all these elevated forms of verse is provided by the large number of lyrics which we may describe generically as examples of the *canzonetta melica*. In the hands of Chiabrera, its most zestful exponent, this form, with its short stanzas, short lines, dancing rhythms and emphatic rhymes, drew on a wide range of sources, notably Ronsard, but also on the tradition of popular verse represented by the *canto carnascialesco*, the *canzone a ballo*, the *frottola*, the *villanella*, etc. Monteverdi knew Chiabrera's verses well, using them extensively for the *Scherzi musicali* that are closely contemporary with *Orfeo*. And Striggio employs the *canzonetta melica* for all the dance-song episodes in the opera: the final chorus, Orpheus' 'Qual onor di te fia degno' in Act IV, and the revelries that make up the first half of Act II.

Act II of the libretto

One will not find Striggio's poetry represented in modern anthologies of Italian verse, and it may be that from the purely literary point of view he was little more than a well educated poetaster. Nevertheless so rich had the intellectual store of Renaissance Italians become, so profoundly had the layers of meaning in Classical myth been pondered, so thrilling was the inspiration provided by the potentialities and responsibilities of the artist-hero, that his *Orfeo* libretto turned out to be an artefact of almost limitless fascination. Wherever one dips into it one finds, over and above the eloquent and well shaped dramatic framework, intuitions, implications, overtones of enthralling richness. It would fall outside the scope of this book even to attempt to explore all these, but a closer examination of the libretto of Act II will at least help explain why that act of Monteverdi's opera is of a beauty, a subtlety and a nobility that in three hundred years of Italian opera was never surpassed.

In the songs and dances that begin the act, we notice at once the weight of the pastoral convention. Orpheus, the semi-divine shepherd, has an intensely companionable feeling for the world of nature. His first words are an affectionate greeting, not to his friends, but to the 'cara selve' and the 'piagge amate'.[3] When in his great song 'Vi ricorda' he looks back on the early stages of his love for Eurydice, it is to recall the sympathy, the fellow-feeling of the forests and rocks. This pastoral tone, the sense of the presence of nature's indwelling divinities, is sustained in the canzonettas sung by the shepherds within the frame of Orpheus' two songs. Now that Phoebus' rays are burning down from the sky, the shade of the beech-trees invites them: there they should recline and let the music of their voices mingle with the murmurings of the waters. This is a landscape where all the gods of the woodland are at home. Sometimes one can hear Pan lamenting his lost love – the echoes, the sighing of reeds and fir-trees – and here too the Napaeae come to gather flowers. No wonder that when Orpheus sings, the woods and meadows laugh for sheer joy at the beauty of it.

As the messenger arrives, bringing news of Eurydice's death, Striggio switches from *canzonetta* verse to *selva* verse. A cry of pain, generalized and rather abstract, breaks in upon the happy scene. And that generalized quality is a masterly touch, for when Silvia's tale is told, it will express equally well the feelings of every single nymph and shepherd, and those pungent cries of 'Ahi, caso acerbo! ahi fato empio e crudele! Ahi stelle ingiuriose! ahi cielo avaro!',[4] an arresting example of 'that high poetic art of making sonority meaningful, and meaning sonorous' (Donington 1981: 163), will recur again and again, resounding lamentingly through the whole second half of the act. Perhaps too, the abstraction of Silvia's first words reflect the fact that the gods have turned away their faces, the world has suddenly become an empty place, has lost that sense of numinousness that was so pronounced in the first part of the act and the whole of Act I. At all events the lines contrast strikingly with the matching lines in Rinuccini: 'Sospirate aure celesti, lacrimate o selve, o fonti.'[5]

But there are levels of meaning in these pages other than the mythological and pastoral. One surely is moral and philosophical. Earlier in the opera Orpheus has several times seemed guilty of what one might describe as emotional hubris, a tendency to blaspheme, so rapturous in his happiness. In 'Vi ricorda', for example, he forgets that Phoebus Apollo is the bringer of light, and transfers that god's attributes punningly to Eurydice, 'quel Sol . . . per cui sol mie notti han giorni'.[6] Similarly Fortuna has ceased to be a goddess, has become merely an abstract manner of speaking; it is Eurydice alone who is to be blessed for bringing an end to his suffering. There are surely grounds for Apollo's reproach in Act V, 'Troppo, troppo gioisti Di tua lieta fortuna.'[7] The impropriety of excessive passion, the sense of its being hostile to one's full humanity is again suggested when the shepherds comment that Orpheus' grief is so overwhelming he has been turned to stone (and he was once the man who made stones feel!). This strain in the scene culminates in the choral version of 'Ahi caso acerbo', which, starting from the same cry of despair, is developed into a philosophical madrigal text, a truly Sophoclean utterance that reduces the emotions and aspirations of the protagonists to scale. Let no man put too much faith in things that fade and perish; and let him not aspire too high, for the precipice is always close.

The act does not end here, as one might perhaps anticipate. Instead Striggio, who in the first two acts never puts a foot wrong, leads us back from the cold desolation of the central part of the act – where the emphasis is on 'caso', 'fato', 'destino' – to close once again in the world of pastoral. And for once one must regret that Monteverdi cut his poet short, eliminating from his setting the final stanza of the choral *canzone* that ends the act. For in these stanzas gradually the whole animate world of 'Arcadia' which had, so to speak, held its breath during the messenger scene, is brought back to life to give Eurydice the 'funebre pompa' which is her due. The act closes with a pastoral elegy. The nymphs and shepherds, who earlier had danced and sung with joy, now weep over their dead companion: the Graces and Muses, who had inspired mankind with kindness and good feelings, with the power of poetry and music, don black and loosen their hair to administer the funeral rites and sing dirges; the skies are overcast, and the very sun, glorious divinity that he is, can only hide himself in woe, shedding a faint, funereal light on the tomb. Nowhere is the rhetoric of pathetic fallacy worked out more consistently or more beautifully than in the second act of *Orfeo*.

The instrumental movements of *Orfeo*: creating an operatic architecture

Nothing differentiates *Orfeo* more startlingly from the earlier operas than the profusion, variety and importance of the instrumental music. In one sense all this music serves a similar kind of purpose. It is a pervasive trait of the classical Italian tradition of opera that springs from *Orfeo* that the action should be set out in a systematically patterned, almost architectural form, readily comprehensible as such to the listening audience. And it is primarily, though by no means exclusively, on the instrumental movements that Monteverdi relies to achieve this end in his first opera. They articulate, frame and make patterns out of the flux of incident and feeling, though as the diversity of names suggests – ritornello, sinfonia, toccata, *moresca* – they do this in different ways and on different scales.[8]

Simplest and most modest in function are the ritornellos. The word means 'refrain', and Monteverdi and his contemporaries generally use it to describe an instrumental movement which is played to introduce a song, ensemble or chorus, and recurs between each of its verses. At this early date the ritornello is rarely played after the final verse, so the number of recurrences of the ritornello corresponds with the number of verses. Ritornellos, then, show the composer's architectural preoccupations in miniature. They are attached to individual songs and choruses; they provide a frame that sets these movements clearly apart from what preceded them, and they introduce a strong element of patterning within that frame. But with one exception they do not affect the larger architectural pattern of the opera.

The exception is provided by the ritornello associated with the prologue. Obviously it is called a ritornello because in the first instance it is attached to the prologue, just as the later ritornellos are attached to their songs and choruses: it is played to introduce it, and between each verse of the prologue it recurs in a slightly abbreviated form. But Monteverdi assigns a second role to this particular ritornello. Because it is first played as the curtain falls to reveal an idealized pastoral landscape of trees and streams, singing birds and wafting breezes, it becomes powerfully associated in the audience's mind with that landscape. And so, from being simply the ritornello to the prologue, it becomes a musical emblem of that Golden Age pastoral world in which the prologue is set. After the Spirit of Music has sung the prologue and left the stage, the ritornello is played again in full to accompany the appearance of the nymphs and shepherds for the start of Act I. Later in the opera it is heard twice more: at the end of Act II when pastoral Thrace is left behind for Orpheus' journey to Hades, and at the end of Act IV when the action returns to Thrace after the failure of his mission to redeem Eurydice. In each case the ritornello acts as a musical corroboration of the pastoral spectacle, as a kind of pastoral signature-tune. The cumulative effect of these recurrences is to impose upon the entire span of the dramatic action an unmistakable, musically articulated symmetry.

The term 'sinfonia' has a much less precise etymological significance: it means really nothing more than a movement to be played by instruments. So it is scarcely surprising that the sinfonias in *Orfeo* should be more varied in style and function than the ritornellos. Two of them, that first played at the start of Act III, and that framing the chorus at the close of Act IV, are infernal sinfonias in the same sense that the prologue ritornello is a pastoral sinfonia. The former in particular, by virtue of its scoring, its dense, dark texture, and the very fact of its being first played as the scene changes to the banks of the River Styx, becomes a musical emblem of the underworld. Like the pastoral sinfonia, it recurs at certain dramatic turning-points to frame the action: towards the end of the act where, having beguiled Charon, Orpheus crosses over into Hades; and again after the final chorus of the act, to serve as a transition to Act IV. On the analogy of Monteverdi's treatment of the pastoral sinfonia, one might expect it to recur again at the end of Act IV, before the scene returns to Thrace. But Monteverdi prefers, presumably for reasons of expressiveness, to use a different sinfonia there. Triumph has been succeeded by tragedy; the hero who dared to challenge the very powers of Hell has been undone by the passions of his own heart. However, although Monteverdi frames the closing chorus of Act IV with a sinfonia in a different mode, it is certainly no coincidence that there is little else to differentiate it from the Act III sinfonia. It employs the same dense seven-part texture, the same orchestral colouring, and the latter part of it, with its overlapping ♩. ♩ ♩ imitations, is virtually interchangeable with the latter part of the Act III piece. As far as providing a structural frame for the infernal acts is concerned, the two sinfonias function as one. But by recomposing the material in a different mode Monteverdi matches the music more nicely to the change in dramatic atmosphere.

Sooner or later all the instrumental sinfonias also function as music incidental to stage action: Act II begins with a sinfonia accompanying

Orpheus' return from the temple to join his dancing and singing companions; later in the act there is a sinfonia for the exit of the messenger and so on. A particularly intriguing example is the sinfonia first played immediately before 'Possente spirto' and heard twice more later in the opera. This threefold recurrence might seem to relate it to the prologue ritornello and the infernal sinfonias, but is in fact of symbolic rather than structural import. The sinfonia is heard first as Orpheus prepares to summon the resources of his art for 'Possente spirto'; the second time, later in the same scene, it is played 'pian, piano' as the ferryman is lulled to sleep; its final appearance accompanies the descent of Apollo, the epiphany of the god from whom Orpheus has learned his divine art. Given these associations it seems plausible to suggest that 'it symbolizes the supernatural power of music' (Harnoncourt 1969).

While ritornellos and sinfonias are used by Monteverdi to frame the dramatic action and to create architectural patterns out of the very stuff of his drama, the toccata and *moresca* provide a framing of a more extrinsic kind. Almost all Italian opera is intimately linked to the environment for which it was composed, and *Orfeo* is no exception. It is at home, not in the theatre, but amid the gorgeous paintings, the glittering mirrors and chandeliers, the cultivated assembly of guests who on great occasions of state thronged the halls of a Renaissance prince. These two movements are part of the ceremonial that belonged to such an occasion. They provide a frame which sets the opera apart from the rest of the evening's entertainment, but they do not themselves form an integral part of the opera at all. The toccata summons the noble guests to the hall; the *moresca*, like Bottom's Bergomask, dismisses them at the close.

Two years later – in the *Vespro della Beata Vergine* – Monteverdi, by the addition of a choir of voices and the interpolation of contrasting episodes, was to turn an almost identical toccata into a brilliantly personal creation. In *Orfeo* it is a purely conventional signal. The trumpets are muted, presumably because of the smallness of the room in which the opera was performed; but apart from that, it is exactly the kind of piece that might have been played at any court occasion. The Mantuan chronicler Follino describes a similar fanfare at the performances of Guarini's *L'Idropica* in the following year. That too was played twice before the curtain opened, a third time as it did (Whenham 1986: 48). And one can hardly imagine that the three playings would have been continuous. They must surely have been spaced out at two- or three-minute intervals before the time due for the performances to start, like the warning bells of the modern theatre, or the brass fanfares from the balcony at Bayreuth, or, to go back closer to Monteverdi's own time, the First and Second Music of the seventeenth-century English theatre.

The matching part of the external frame, the closing *moresca*, was less formalized, though hardly less conventional. By 1607 it had been the favourite theatrical dance in Italy for over a century, appearing again and again in the *intermedi*. It no longer had any specific thematic associations, with Moors or with anything else, but was simply a stage dance, in costume, of such vigour that, according to Sabatini, it was advisable for the stage to be reinforced for it (*MGG*, s.v. 'Moresca').

Expressive and symbolic role of the instrumental music

While the toccata and *moresca* are purely conventional in character, all the other instrumental music is composed with an exquisite sense of its unique dramatic function. Several of the ritornellos do not merely introduce and frame a song; they consist of instrumental variants or elaborations of it. This is particularly noticeable in the ritornellos of such dance-songs as 'Lasciate i monti' (Act I), 'Vi ricordo' (Act II), and 'Vanne Orfeo' (Act V), where the rhythms, which have necessarily to be treated with some restraint for the singing voices, can be developed and decorated with splendid uninhibited verve by the five-part instrumental ensemble. The sinfonias, being independent of the vocal music in a way the ritornellos are not, depend for their expressive aptness on the character of their own material. A case in point is the wonderful sinfonia that accompanies the exit of the messenger in Act II. Into the most functionally concise design, without for a moment disturbing the aura of solemn decorum that pervades all the instrumental music in this courtly festival-drama, Monteverdi packs a wealth of chromatic and dissonant harmony perfectly conforming with Silvia's grief (see Ex.I.5).

Other movements, notably the framing sinfonias of Acts III and IV, achieve their expressive end by more indirect means. Hades is not only a fearful and gloomy place; it is a place where the rule of law is harsh and inexorable. Monteverdi, rather like Bach in some of the Old Testament episodes in his church cantatas, expresses an idea in which Law and Death are intimately interwoven by employing an antique contrapuntal idiom. In place of the dancing rhythms and the well aired phrase structure of most of the other instrumental music, these sinfonias are densely polyphonic, and their phrase structure is disguised by a web of overlapping melodic lines somewhat neutral in rhythmic character. Not only that: the harmonic idiom is purely modal, with no use of chromaticism. Even the dissonance treatment is of Zarlino-like strictness. An antique idiom, severely modal and contrapuntal, is also used for rather different purposes in the ritornello attached to the 'chorus' 'Alcun non sia' in Act I. Here the association may perhaps be with the music of the church liturgy, for it is heard first as Orpheus and his friends process to the temple to offer up incense and prayers. In *Orfeo* Monteverdi is putting to dramatic ends the divorce that

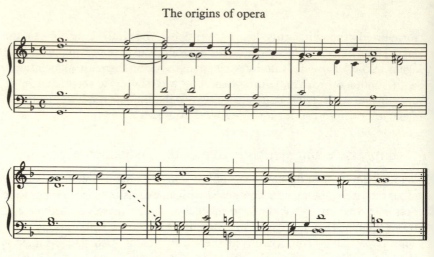

Ex.I.5 Monteverdi, *Orfeo* (1607), Act II

he has helped bring about between *prima* and *seconda prattica*, between the *stile antico* and the *stile moderno*.

The most obvious of the means whereby Monteverdi makes his ritornellos and sinfonias dramatically apt is instrumentation; it is also the most purely conventional. In *Orfeo* he employs just such a large, multi-coloured ensemble of instruments as would have graced any grand courtly festivity in late Renaissance Italy, and he employs it exactly as Malvezzi, or the elder Striggio, or any other of his courtly predecessors might have done. It is this very conventionality that makes *Orfeo* unique in the operatic repertory. Unlike the other very early operas, which make negligible use of organized instrumental ensembles, *Orfeo* calls for a resplendent array of instruments. But this 'orchestra' does not represent an imaginative leap into the distant future; rather a late, even posthumous, flowering of the Renaissance tradition of instrumentation.

The symbolic connotations of this style of instrumentation have been outlined in Chapter 1. In *Orfeo*, with few exceptions, we find that the instrumental music of Acts I and V employs an 'Olympian' style of scoring, that of Act II a 'Pastoral' and that of Acts III and IV an 'Infernal' style.

Monteverdi's Olympian orchestra is described most fully at the start of Act V: 'violins [that is the whole violin family], organs, harpsichords, double-bass, harps, large lutes ("chitarroni") and large citterns ("ceteroni")'. While it might be legitimate to add wind-instruments (cornetts and recorders are included in the *Orfeo instrumentarium*) for the toccata and *moresca*, it is clear that, in principle, that is the *tutti* that should be used for the prologue and the greater part of the instrumental music in Acts I and V. To add or subtract, still worse to substitute alternative scorings in the interests of further variety, is to mess about with the clear associative intentions of Monteverdi's instrumentation.

Throughout the sixteenth century the pastoral milieu had regularly been evoked by means of reed instruments; by crumhorns, dolcians, or bagpipes. But as musical taste became more self-consciously fastidious, less raucous timbres came to be preferred – rebecs, for example, or the higher members of the recorder family. In the first three ritornellos of Act II Monteverdi is obviously following this new fashion. To a basic continuo group of harpsichord and two large lutes he adds, for the first ritornello, two 'small French violins'; for the second, two violins and 'cello; and for the third, two recorders. He emphasizes the rustic flavour of these movements also by reducing the number of parts from five to three, the standard texture of such genres as the *villanella* and the *canzonetta alla napoletana*. It seems clear that when the five-part texture is restored later in the act, the Olympian orchestra should play again.

Most distinctive in timbre is the Infernal orchestra. At the end of Act II of the score, Monteverdi writes: 'Here the trombones, cornetts, regals enter, and the violins, the organs and harpsichords are silent.' The ensemble is not quite identical with those most often used in the sixteenth century. All the same, it was traditional that, in infernal scenes, the trombones should dominate the ensemble, as they do in *Orfeo*; and it was conventional that the harpsichords should fall silent. The appearance of the snarling regal as one of the Infernal continuo instruments is a brilliantly apposite stroke; I do not know that there was any tradition of such a usage in Renaissance Italy. In the third and fourth acts the basic representative colour is more often varied than in the others. The reason is obvious. Orpheus has come to Hades as an interloper; and when the instrumental music is closely associated with his songs or with his actions, the infernal orchestra yields to a more worldly ensemble. So, for example, at the end of the scene with Charon, the sinfonia is played 'very softly with violins, chamber organ and bass viol'.

With the exception of the toccata, the ritornello framing 'Alcun non sia' in Act I and the two Infernal sinfonias in Acts III and IV, all the instrumental movements appear to be composed in the style of, or at least to be strongly influenced by the rhythms of, Renaissance dance music. Only the *moresca* is avowedly a dance, but – to take just the two other instrumental movements in Act V – there is no mistaking the pavane character of the sinfonia accompanying the descent of Apollo, or the resemblance of 'Vanne Orfeo' and its preceding ritornello to the *balletti* of Gastoldi. Throughout the opera the association between the instrumental pieces and various kinds of dance and processional is in fact palpable.

The music of the choruses: dance-song and madrigal

The distinction between dance-song and madrigalian reflection, which Striggio mirrors in his employment of *canzonetta melica* and *canzone* or *canzone*-related verses, is clinched by Monteverdi's music. In all the dance-songs, the choral music is introduced or concluded by instrumental ritornellos, it is strophic in form and often resembles instrumental music in the details of its structural organization. The expressive correspondence between words and music is necessarily slight.

A simple example is 'Dunque fa degno', which employs the same music as the preceding duet, 'Qui le Napee vezzose'. Indeed it is a kind of 'realization' of the duet for five voices, and it is introduced by the same ritornello for recorders, *chitarroni* and harpsichord. Though consisting of a mere two phrases, it has the kind of minutely organized structure typical of the opera's instrumental music. For all its rhythmic and melodic charm and the fleeting suggestions of textural sophistication, the whole chorus is built over an unbroken reiteration of one-bar-long cadential figures in three slightly different forms. The ritornello is built over the same kind of bass pattern. Ex.I.6 quotes a passage from the duet section, 'Qui le Napee vezzose'.

The first chorus in Act I, 'Vieni, Imeneo', is distinct in both structure and style from the rest, the only movement in the entire opera which is faintly reminiscent of Gabrieli's choral writing in *Edipo tiranno*. Not only the melodic and rhythmic character, but also the structure of the music is dependent upon an ideal of scrupulously faithful word-setting. The chorus comprises three periods of $6\frac{1}{2}$, 4 and 4 bars (in the original barring), the second four-bar period being a reduplication of the first; and this overall scheme is obviously a reflection of the two unequal sentences which make up Striggio's text. But the smaller details of the design also prove to be reflections of the text: the $6\frac{1}{2}$-bar period is formed of 4 phrases of $1\frac{1}{2}$, $1\frac{1}{2}$, $1\frac{1}{2}$ and 2 bars respectively, which match the three short lines and one long line in the verse; similarly the $1\frac{1}{2}$- and $2\frac{1}{2}$-bar phrases of the four-bar period match one short and one long line of verse.

Despite the madrigal verse, this is music of which it might almost be supposed that Monteverdi had his imagination fixed on those venerated choruses of the Ancient World in which melody and rhythm are no more than a realization of the inherent music of the poetry. Particularly is this so with the first soprano part of the first period, which is essentially speech-song, the lower voices being used simply to harmonize. But throughout the chorus a discreet ♩. ♩ ♩ rhythm is used to help the music through the central long notes of the phrase; and in the final phrase of the final period a greater complexity arises when Monteverdi composes an enjambement into his first soprano, thus putting it out of step with the rest. He corrects the

Here the beauteous dryads, always a flowery band, were seen plucking roses with their white hands.

Ex.I.6 Monteverdi, *Orfeo* (1607), Act II

dislocation quite beautifully, by means of a cross-rhythm – 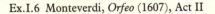 – which remains a natural derivation from the text, but at the same time, by its dance-like character, underlines the joyfulness of the words.

In 'Vieni, Imeneo' Monteverdi's harmonic style is generally as austere, and avoids dissonance as assiduously, as Gabrieli's in *Edipo*. But even this chorus provides one exception to the rule, in the biting sweetness of the cadence of the first period, where syncopations, a diminished interval in the bass and a sharp double suspension are matched to 'dì sereni', a characteristically Monteverdian piece of oxymoron. Also notable is the change of mode at mid-point from Dorian transposed to Mixolydian. This too is surely an expressive point, in musical analogy to the lifting of the shadows, the dispelling of sorrow, that follows upon the lighting of Hymen's torch.

There are passages of speech-song in several other choruses, some demurely observant of the metrical character of the text – as in the 'Qui miri il sol' section of 'Lasciate i monti' – others employing a more rhetorical style of delivery – as in 'Alcun non sia', where the words 'che disperato in preda'[9] prompt a violently jagged rhythm in the music. But whatever impression the opening chorus 'Vieni, Imeneo', may give, it is obvious that the Gabrielian ideal of 'Oratio harmoniae domina absolutissima' was not Monteverdi's, or at least that Gabrieli's way of realizing that ideal was not. Only one other chorus in the opera, 'Ahi caso acerbo' from Act II, is primarily notable as an example of musical declamation, and that only in its first part.

This section, the section subsequently recurring as a refrain, is a choral recitative. The idea is borrowed, like much in *Orfeo*, from Peri's *Euridice*, but executed far more boldly by Monteverdi. In Peri's opera, the lament that follows the death of Eurydice also culminates in a phrase of recitative, 'Sospirate aure celesti, lacrimate o selve, o campi',[10] sung by a solo voice. Immediately it is taken up by the chorus and sung again, fully harmonized; in this form it acts as a refrain running through the latter part of the scene. But while Peri makes it perfectly obvious what he is doing, Monteverdi works more subtly, putting the original monody in the bass and building the choral recitative above it. In the process the original rhythm has to be regularized slightly to eliminate the syncopations and breaks in the continuity, and to provide a firm harmonic foundation. The 'realization' is superbly done. Where the original rhythm is most distinctive – as in phrases 1 and 3 – it has been preserved, and is hammered out by all five voices in boldly chromatic and dissonant harmonies. Where it is less arresting the treatment is more complex; the second phrase incorporates touches of imitation in the upper voices, which give rise to some sombre dissonant passing notes; the final phrase is set in overlapping antiphony between low and high voices.

Between the extremes of speech-song on the one hand, and dance-song on the other, the majority of the choruses of *Orfeo* are set as madrigals, with all the variety which that term held for Monteverdi. Or perhaps not quite all; for while we have recitative madrigals like 'Ahi caso acerbo', and duet madrigals like 'Chi ne consola' ten years before such things appeared in the madrigal books proper, the style of the five-part madrigals is in many ways rather old-fashioned. The reason is clear. These madrigals are settings of philosophical and moralizing verses rather than of directly emotional ones, and in the case of the infernal choruses, in particular, the inexorability of the moral law is a central aspect of the theme. For such choruses it is entirely fitting that Monteverdi should employ a madrigalian style in which the colours are darker, the harmonies more severe, the textures more densely contrapuntal than was usual in the Italian madrigal repertory around 1600. In the second part of 'Ahi caso acerbo', and in the choruses of Acts III and IV, the idiom is not far removed from that of the great Netherlandish madrigalists of two generations earlier.

The best example is 'Nulla impresa per uom'. Like Lassus or the young Rore, Monteverdi achieves such expressive effects as are required by textural and rhythmic contrasts rather than by the harmonic or *parlando* techniques that are perhaps more typical of the *seconda prattica*. The harmonic style is of a grave, antique diatonicism – atmospheric rather than expressive – but textures and rhythms are sharply responsive to the text. The words 'l'instabil piano' prompt a rocking cross-rhythm; the scorn of the laws of nature implied by 'che sprezzò d'Austro e d'Aquilon lo sdegno' is underlined by a prolonged passage of syncopated stretto imitation; while a pause, followed by a massive five-voice declamation of 'che pose freno al mar con fragil legno',[11] puts, metaphorically speaking, quotation-marks round the imagined words of Fame.

It is in the duet and trio choruses of *Orfeo* that Monteverdi first masters the medium of the madrigal duet and madrigal trio in which he was to create so many of his late masterpieces. The beauty of the medium, particularly the duet medium, is that it is hardly less flexible than monody, but at the same time affords far richer resources to the declamation: a dissolance can be expressed wholly in vocal timbres; the recitative-like delivery of the text can be coloured by varying the intervals between the voices; there is even scope for imitative counterpoint.

The first verse of 'Chi ne consola' illustrates the style beautifully. Expressively erratic rhythms – as at 'turbo crudele' – are as vivid as in any monody, while the dissonances set up against the pedal-point bass – 'Chi ne consola . . . ne concede' – are the richer and more sounding by virtue of the fact that two voices are singing. Even the uneventful euphony at 'i due lumi maggiori' has a symbolic aptness. Virtually all the phrases of imitation are contrived with expressive intent; the drooping phrases of 'da poter lagrimar . . .'; the rhythmic contrasts to highlight the antithesis of joy and grief in the second period, 'in questo mesto giorno . . .';[12] the augmented chromatic interval, analogous to the bite of the snake, or the stab of grief, in the final lines.

Verse 2, 'Ma dove, ah, dove', contains similar characteristics in more complex form. Its first line is a marvellous example of a two-voice 'monody', the sweet-sour thirds of the voices tugging against the pedal notes of the continuo. At 'belle e fredde membra', Monteverdi holds up the flow of the music with a falsely accentuated '(bel)le e' in order to intensify the impact of the falling diminished fifth on to 'fredde'; and what a chilling effect is created when the voices cadence on a bare fourth! Even the simplest touches seem deeply expressive, as when one voice begins alone at 'andiam, pastori'[13] and the second voice joins in, not, it seems, to imitate, but rather to comply with the exhortation. Later phrases in the duet demonstrate the expressive power of comprehensive chromaticism. The movement ends with a marvellous series of anguished cadences – descending sixths, descending augmented fourths and diminished fifths overlapping between the two voices – an unforgettable musical simulacrum of the emotions aroused by the thoughts of Eurydice's lifeless body (Ex.I.7).

With such music as this in our ears it is not difficult to feel that, of all the vocal mediums of the period, the chamber duet was the most perfect and the most expressive. There is not one of the attributes of recitative that cannot be handled just as impressively – in some cases more impressively – in the duet form, while at the same time many, if not quite all, of the expressive resources of the madrigal are also in its grasp.

The duets at the close of Act II are among the few choruses in *Orfeo* for which the accompanying instruments are specified; here the continuo support is provided by chamber organ and *chitarrone*. In the other choruses instruments are specified only for 'Vieni, Imeneo' ('performed to the sound of all the instruments'); for 'Lasciate i monti' ('sung to the sound of five violins, three *chitarroni*, two harpsichords, a double harp, a double-bass viol and a sopranino recorder'); and for 'Nulla impresa per uom' ('to the sound of a regal, a chamber organ, five trombones, two bass viols and a doublebass viol'). But this evidence is sufficient to make it clear that the distinction between Olympian, Pastoral and Infernal scoring applies to the music for chorus too.

Recitative and aria: the composer as dramatist

Interesting as the instrumental and choral music of *Orfeo* may be, the crucial issue in these early years of opera was the dramatic potential of the monodic style – both recitative and aria. The mathematical and architectural powers of composers were not in doubt, nor was the charm of their lyricism or the persuasiveness of their rhetoric. The real question was, how successfully could the composer turn himself into a dramatist.

Prima le parole, dopo la musica; the old tag holds good for much of Monteverdi's score. He saw it as a first responsibility to reinforce and to heighten Striggio's text, and much of the beauty and much of the cunning of his music draws its inspiration very obviously and directly from the

Ex.I.7 Monteverdi, *Orfeo* (1607), Act II

no al cor - po e-san - gue.

gue al cor-po e-san - gue.

Let us go, shepherds; let us go, full of pity, to find (her), and with bitter
tears let due tribute at least be paid by us to her lifeless body.

Ex.I.7 *continued*

libretto. On the whole, even where it entails a mannered rather than a
natural delivery of the words, his recitatives punctiliously observe the verse
structure (including the caesuras) of Striggio's lines. Never does Monteverdi tire of the analogical devices formulated by the madrigalists of the
seconda prattica. Was diastematic rhetoric ever more felicitous than at
Orpheus' determination to redeem Eurydice from Hades, with its plunging
descent to the 'più profondi abissi' and the exultant return 'a riveder le
stelle'?[14] Were rhythmic 'madrigalisms' ever more beguiling than in the
fifth verse of the prologue, where Music charms the birds, streams and
breezes into stillness, and the progression of harmonies that has run
uninterrupted through the first four verses is continually held in suspense,
and broken by silences? So persuasively does Music speak that the verse
comes to a premature halt, spellbound on its dominant chord.

But the monodic style tempts Monteverdi into realms of musical rhetoric
scarcely imaginable in the madrigal. Particularly is this true of his
harmony. When a solo voice is singing and the accompaniment is provided
by continuo instruments, the harmony does not need to be under the same
kind of contrapuntal control as in a madrigal, and the intonation of the
ensemble is not a problem. Dissonance may therefore be bolder and
chromaticism more extreme – in the throes of emotional anguish, the solo
voice may tear itself away from the ostensibly supporting harmonies,
dragging behind them, plunging ahead of them, even straying altogether
from their orbit. The messenger scene in Act II is a *locus classicus* for this
kind of procedure, particularly the refrain, 'Ahi caso acerbo', and the
messenger's final recitative.

But the closer one investigates Monteverdi's musical rhetoric, the clearer
it becomes that we have broken out of a world circumscribed by the *prima le
parole* vision. It is music that enraptures and wounds the senses at 'Ah vista
troppo dolce', and it is music that thrills the imagination as Speranza
describes the 'campi di pianto e di dolore'.[15] Monteverdi is not simply
setting a dramatic text to music; he is in control of its emotional tone; his

is the medium through which we perceive the characters and their dilemmas. When we compare with Orpheus' 'Rosa del ciel' recitative (Act I), the following recitative of Eurydice, 'Io non dirò', so charmingly shy and modest in the measure of its harmonies, the regularity of its rhythms and its total absence of musical rhetoric; and when we perceive in the sequence of dance-songs at the start of Act II, how repetitions and reprises are used to differentiate Orpheus, the artist, from the rest of the nymphs and shepherds with their once-straight-through ditties; and when we hear Monteverdi's marvellous skill in getting inside the skin of his characters – for instance in the recitative 'Dove, ah, dove te'n vai' (Act III) where Orpheus, held in the vice-like grip of pedal-point harmonies, wrestles with despair – we see that the art of musical characterization is already with us.

Ultimately then the eloquence of the music moves on to a higher plane of expression than the eloquence of the poet-librettist. The same is true of the musical architecture; even in monody, even in recitative, Monteverdi felt the necessity or perhaps the charm of audible musical form. Needless to say the inspiration frequently comes from the text. Monteverdi never missed such opportunities for musical repetition and variation as are afforded by poetic parallelism, for instance in Proserpina's two recitatives

> . . . se da queste luci
> Amorosa dolcezza unqua traesti,
> Se ti piacque il seren di questa fronte . . .[16]

or

> sia benedetto il dì che pria ti piacqui,
> Benedetta la preda e 'l dolce inganno . . .[17]

In the absence of such form-giving qualities in the text, Monteverdi creates his own. Over and over again the recitative follows a threefold pattern which may be described as Declamation, Rhetoric, Arioso. The start of Act III provides a good example. It begins with a rather formal delivery of the text over static or slowly moving harmonies; at 'omai son giunto' the setting becomes more animated, and above all more attentive to the expressive detail of the text: finally at 'Ond' oggi' the rhythm steadies, and the music assumes a more lyrical and 'organized' character by virtue of melodic sequences and a more measured and linear bass (Ex.I.8).

The final claim for the new art of opera must be this: that just as it is the composer's expressive eloquence and the composer's sense of structure that really counts, so, in the final analysis, it is the composer who provides the organizing dramatic intelligence. Opera is not a form of drama accompanied or heightened by incidental music: the drama lives, or fails to live, in the music; it is through the forms, the textures and the colours of the music that the spectator experiences and understands the drama.

In its simplest form this music-drama is achieved by certain juxtapositions of instrumental timbre: one might, to clarify the dramatic

Ex.I.8 Monteverdi, *Orfeo* (1607), Act III

Accompanied by you, my good spirit, Hope, the only good of afflicted
mortals, now I am come to these shadowy, dismal regions where the rays
of the sun never reached. You, my companion and guide, by what strange
and unfamiliar ways you have directed my feeble, trembling step, so that
today I hope again to see those blessed eyes which alone bring daylight to
my eyes.

Ex.I.8 *continued*

analogy, describe them as 'confrontations' or 'encounters' of instrumental
timbre. And these are something quite distinct from the general principles
of instrumentation discussed earlier. In the messenger scene in Act II,
Monteverdi juxtaposes the colours of harpsichord and chamber-organ, the
one representative of the familiar pastoral world of the earlier part of the
opera, the other introducing a new note of ominous solemnity. In the
Charon scene of Act III the juxtaposition is of chamber-organ and regal, as
Orpheus' noble aspiration is confronted with the world of grisly horror. In
the scenes of the loss of Eurydice in Act IV the continuo accompaniment
fluctuates between chamber-organ and harpsichord. This is less a dramatic
confrontation than a psychological conflict – the clash of love and fear in
Orpheus' own mind. At each of the three crucial turning-points in the
action Monteverdi uses instrumental colour as a means of heightening
dramatic tension.

Orfeo demonstrates the primacy of the composer in numerous ways. It
was clearly Monteverdi who decided that Striggio was generally too abstract
and long-winded in his choruses and that sizeable chunks of many of them
had simply got to be omitted. And it was Monteverdi who decided that the
choruses in the early part of Act IV – 'O de gli abitator' and 'Pietate oggi' –
were disproportionate to their dramatic function, and needed lightening by
being set (except for the first two lines of the latter) as recitatives; or
conversely who saw that the Apollo–Orpheus dialogue in Act V must have a
musical setting to match its visual magnificence, and plucked the text for a

chamber duet out of a series of verses which Striggio had designed for recitative.

A rather different kind of example is provided by the organization of festivities at the start of Act II. This whole sequence is framed with G minor/G major ritornellos in five parts, each of them an orchestral elaboration of one of Orpheus' canzonettas. Within that frame further ritornellos and ariettas provide continual contrasts of key, colour and texture.

G minor	C	G minor	C/G	G
à 5	à 3	à 3	à 3/5	à 5
$\frac{3}{2}$	$\frac{2}{2}$	$\frac{3}{2}$	$\frac{2}{2}$	$\frac{2}{2}$
no scoring indicated	violini piccoli alla francese	violini ordinarii	flautini etc.	viole da braccio etc.

The structure of the libretto here is straightforward – eleven four-line stanzas, those sung by Orpheus in *ottonari*, those sung by the other shepherds and the chorus in *settenari*. Monteverdi has superimposed a rapid alternation of metre, timbre etc. which gives the scene vigour and exuberance, makes of it a kind of crescendo of joyfulness; all is movement, all colour. And it is by virtue of these qualities that we perceive the intense dramatic irony of it, placed as it is immediately before the arrival of the messenger, when dance and song, colour and movement are frozen in a bleak recitative.

The supreme demonstration of the commanding dramatic role of the composer is provided by the Charon scene in Act III. One feature of this – its instrumental colouring – has already been discussed; it remains to consider its structural organization, which takes the form of two interlocking sets of strophic variations.

In Charon's case, 'O tu, ch'innanzi mort'', these variations are surely a device of characterization. The form helps illuminate the comedy in his character – the suspicious, narrow-minded doorkeeper, an expert in demarcation disputes, who can never speak without consulting his book of rules and precedents. By setting his verses as strophic variations Monteverdi gives a vivid impression of a person incapable of independence of thought or freshness of response; who, however long he may hold forth, can never get away from the tried formulas of his prepared speech. The full extent of Monteverdi's dramatic initiative becomes apparent only later, after Orpheus' 'Possente spirto'. Charon's first verses had, after all, been formal stanzas in *quarta rima*, for which strophic variation form might be regarded as a perfectly normal equivalent (cf. the Prologue). After 'Possente spirto', however, his next lines are in recitative verse. Monteverdi ignores that. He wishes to sustain his character portrait, more specifically to make in music the dramatic point that Charon's 'valiant bosom' is impervious to Orpheus' song. So he takes these lines up into his strophic variation scheme: back come the same grave harmonies, the same melodic formulas as had formed the substance of his earlier verses.

If Charon's strophic variations are a device of characterization, Orpheus' in 'Possente spirto' are a device of art and rhetoric. Something of the aria's symbolic connotations has been explained in an earlier part of this chapter (see p. 66–7): its mathematical severity is a symbol of the belief that music functions as a microcosm of the *musica mundana* of God the musician-mathematician; the all-pervasive ritornellos – the only ones in the opera that do more than frame the stanzas – evoke the image of a cosmos reverberating with music; the florid song is not merely the result of Orpheus' superhuman efforts to win over Charon, it looks back beyond the 1589 *intermedi* to the whole tradition of Orphic singing conceived as a gift communicated by divine afflatus. But this explanation carries us only as far as the fourth of the six verses of *terza rima* which Orpheus has been given by the librettist. Just as Monteverdi had taken matters into his own hands with Charon, absorbing 'Ben mi lusinga alquanto' into the strophic variation scheme, so too he does here – but in reverse. As Orpheus reaches the climactic verse of his song, he forgets Charon and breaks into a rapturous apostrophe to the adored Eurydice; the whole symbolic and mystical apparatus of florid song, instrumental ritornellos and variation form is abandoned and he sings with heart-breaking directness. In the last verse Orpheus turns again to Charon and the strophic variation form is resumed. But now, with a psychological penetration that has often been commended, Monteverdi abandons all artifice, and the variations close in a style of unaffected simplicity. The whole scene is a marvellous illustration – the first in history – of the fact that in opera 'the dramatist is the composer' (Kerman 1956: 267).

Part II
The Venetian hegemony

5 · Opera in seventeenth-century Rome

Stile rappresentativo in Rome

Today we recognize Monteverdi's *Orfeo* as a 'real' opera, a magnificent demonstration of what the synthesis of music and drama achieved by Rinuccini and Peri was capable of in the hands of a great artist. But what of such pieces as the *Ballo delle ingrate* or the *Combattimento di Tancredi e Clorinda* or Cavalieri's *Rappresentazione di anima e di corpo*? These the modern musician is likely to regard as works somewhat different in kind, clearly related to opera but yet not quite genuinely operatic. The distinction would have been far less clear in the early decades of the seventeenth century. At that time there was no central, normative musico-dramatic tradition; opera in our sense was simply one of a whole range of solutions to the question of how best to co-ordinate the charms and the power of drama, music and spectacle. Ballets and masquerades, spoken plays with *intermedi*, pastorals in the *stile rappresentativo*, were all to be seen in any Italian city where wealthy patrons were moved occasionally to cut a figure by sponsoring costly and ostentatious entertainments.

Rome was no exception. By 1606 Pietro della Valle and Paolo Quagliati had introduced quasi-dramatic allegorical musical tableaux to be paraded round the city on floats during the Carnival (Ademollo 1888: 3–4). By 1620 Filippo Vitali had introduced pastoral opera, the *favola in musica*, *Aretusa*, composed in avowed imitation of Rinuccini, Peri and Caccini and performed in the private house of Monsignor Ottaviano Corsini, himself the poet. But in a city where humanist scholarship was the prerogative of priests and the religious, and where there was a well established tradition of sacred paraphrases of the classics, with 'princes and prelates of the Church [exercising] their tastes for fine literature with transformations of Pindar and Horace designed to inspire Christian devotion' (Murata 1984: 104), it was inevitable that the most typical forms of music-drama should be spiritual and produced under ecclesiastical protection. The Roman oratories, meeting-houses attached to some of the principal churches where fraternities of laity and clergy met for prayer and devotions, presented a wide range of quasi-dramatic musical spectacles out of which, in the middle decades of the century, the oratorio was to develop: Cavalieri's *Rappresentazione*, presented in the church of Santa Maria in Vallicella in 1600, was the most famous and most nearly operatic of these. The Jesuit conviction that drama could become a vehicle of spiritual enlightenment led – via the edifying *dramma pastorale Eumelio*, composed by Agazzari for the Seminario Romano in 1608, and Ottavio Catalani's *David musicus* of 1613, a Latin opera composed in honour of the visiting Bishop of Bamberg, Johann Gottfried von Aschhausen – to a whole repertory of sacred operas performed in palaces, colleges and monasteries during the first half of the century.

Sacred music-drama in one form or another was to remain characteristic of the Roman scene throughout the century. The reason is clear: in the early decades of the seventeenth century the Counter-reformation was still at full flood; Rome, as the seat of the papacy, was the capital city of a prince who claimed a more absolute authority than any prince in history had claimed before. For the Pope, in the name of God, demanded both the political and religious loyalty of his subjects. And this meant that he was bound to take a direct interest in all the ethical, philosophical, psychological and aesthetic questions that arise when the theatre aspires to something more than bland escapism. Opera could flourish in the Eternal City only if it had papal blessing.

The Barberini family as patrons of opera

It goes without saying that such blessing could not always be counted on. Art of any kind was most warmly welcome if it was active in the Counter-reformation cause; at very least it should aim to be edifying. Not all popes trusted opera to live up to these ideals; and because popes, in the very nature of the case, tended to reign for comparatively brief periods, the operatic history of seventeenth-century Rome was singularly erratic. However, between 1623 and 1669 all the arts experienced something of a Golden Age. Of the four popes who reigned during this period three were themselves poets, including Giulio Rospigliosi (Pope Clement IX, 1667–69), who before his elevation had distinguished himself as a dramatic poet and librettist. And the first of this quartet, Urban VIII, 1623–44, ranks among the very greatest patrons of art in the whole history of the papacy.

Urban VIII was a Barberini. A 'reckless nepotist', he decided, on his election to the papal throne, to appoint his brother Taddeo, and two nephews, Francesco and Antonio, to influential posts in the Vatican hierarchy, where 'he enriched them all so exorbitantly that in old age he felt conscience-stricken' (Kelly 1986, s.v. 'Urban VIII'). The family thus became the virtual rulers of the city, able to indulge their art-loving propensities without restraint. Pope Urban is best known today for his patronage of architects, sculptors and painters, among them Borromini, Bernini and Pietro da Cortona. But the family was no less generous to musicians, providing salaries or retaining pensions for many of the finest composers, singers and instrumentalists in the city. Given their close friendship with Rospigliosi it was inevitable that before long they would engage this multi-media team of talents in the production of opera.

The first Barberini opera, Rospigliosi and Landi's *Il Sant'Alessio*, was staged during an otherwise cheerless Carnival in 1631, when plague, war and famine had driven revelry from the streets (Murata 1981: 19). But it was with the opening of a newly built Palazzo Barberini in the Via Quattro Fontane in 1632, an occasion celebrated with a revival of *Il Sant'Alessio*, that the great age of Roman opera began. From 1632 to 1656 this palace and the Palazzo della Cancelleria, Cardinal Antonio Barberini's official residence as Secretary of State, were the sites of virtually all Roman opera productions, which were given either as part of the Carnival festivities or to celebrate some state occasion.[1] Their productions were occasions of imposing opulence, rehearsed with tireless thoroughness, superbly staged, accompanied by such manifestations of heedless luxury as gilt-bound printed arguments and the day and night playing of the palace fountains. Four performances of *Chi soffre, speri* in 1639, an opera far from spectacular by seventeenth-century standards, cost the family exchequer very nearly as much as 24 performances of Cavalli's *Antioco* cost the management of the Venetian Teatro San Cassiano twenty years later, even though the fees for the Barberini singers were nothing like so high (Bianconi and Walker 1984: 234). The Barberinis still abided by the Renaissance convention of creating temporary theatres in the great halls of their palaces. Contemporary reports tell us that more than 3,000 spectators could be accommodated in the theatre at Via Quattro Fontane, which was erected in what is now known as the *Sala delle statue* (Ademollo 1888: 10; Murata 1981: 21). It was symptomatic of the immaculate decorum to which Counter-reformation Rome aspired that from these productions ladies were normally excluded. There were however special performances which married women might attend, provided they were accompanied by their husbands (Ademollo p. 26).

It is not clear how long this custom survived; but by the time the operatic performances at the Palazzo Barberini came to a close in 1656 it had apparently been abandoned. This last great occasion in the history of the Barberini operas, in its combination of spiritual edification and baroque sumptuousness, may serve as an apt epitome of the Roman operatic tradition of the whole century. The opera in question, *La vita humana, ovvero il trionfo della pietà* with text by Rospigliosi and music by Marco Marazzoli, was presented to celebrate the arrival in Rome of Christina, former Queen of Sweden, who had abdicated the previous autumn, on her conversion and reception into the Roman Catholic Church. A contemporary chronicler, Gualdo Priorato, left a full account of the occasion:

In the evening of the last day of January an opera was performed, *Il Trionfo della pietà*, or *La vita humana*. The subject matter was entirely spiritual and very apt by virtue both of the scope it offered as spectacle, which was charming in the highest degree, and of the doctrines and beauties of the verse – and indeed of the sweetness of the music . . . This composition showed the arts and subterfuges by means of which Pleasure and Sin are always seeking to shake Innocence and Understanding.

Gualdo goes on to describe the allegory of the opera at some length, and concludes:

After she had enjoyed observing the nobility of the apartments and the richness of the furnishings in this royal palace, which is also adorned with excellent paintings, the Queen descended by a secret stair to the theatre, and in the middle of this, behind a grating and under a remarkable baldaquin, she savoured the morality of this drama with such attention and delight, that having deemed it very fitting for her rare understanding, she wished to attend it twice more.   (Ademollo 1888: 69–72)

Giulio Rospigliosi

Half-a-dozen or more different composers were involved in the Barberini operas – Landi, Michelangelo Rossi, Virgilio Mazzocchi, Marazzoli, Vittori, Luigi Rossi, Abbatini; and they essayed a range of dramatic styles extending from comedy to religious allegory. But all this activity centred around one pivotal figure, the poet Giulio Rospigliosi, who wrote all the texts except those for Vittori's *La Galatea* and Luigi Rossi's *Orfeo*. He did more than any composer to give Roman opera its distinctive tone. And his reputation was to survive remarkably long, into an age that had generally very little patience with the literary styles of the mid-seventeenth century. Crescimbeni, chronicler of the Arcadian movement (see p. 183–4), wrote of him that he 'understood so well how to adapt the prescriptions of poetry to the requirements of the theatre, that neither before nor since, has there been anyone more careful, more judicious than he, and more worthy of glory and fame' (Ademollo 1888: 81). Rospigliosi's work as a dramatic poet befitted an eminent churchman. It was inspired by a vision of the theatre as an institution both popular and wholesome. He shared nothing of the Renaissance humanists' ambition to resuscitate the dramatic styles of the pagan Ancient World, basing his libretti on the lives of saints, on stories of the heroes of the Crusades, or on simple moral tales. He aimed to wean drama-lovers away from the often lewd spectacles offered by the travelling *commedia dell'arte* companies, and to establish a form of theatre that was edifying without being tedious.

The primary model for accomplishing this mission was the old *sacra rappresentazione*, which had enjoyed its hey-day in the fifteenth century, but which, since the passion for imitating Classical drama had swept the more refined centres of Italian civilization, had now been driven into the cultural penumbra of monastery and convent. The hagiographical theme, the profusion of incident unconstrained by time or place, the lively delight in spectacle, the startling modulations of tone from the solemnly allegorical to the realistic, the humorous, the contemporary, were all to be hallmarks of Rospigliosi's dramatic manner. A second model he found in the *commedia dell'arte* itself. Here, however he may have deplored the bawdy, he clearly admired the sense of pulsating everyday life, the juxtaposition of a wide range of character types and the sheer theatrical pace. In *Chi soffre, speri* the *dramatis personae* actually include a whole troupe of *commedia* masks – Coviello, Zanni, Moschino, Colillo and Fritellino. A final influence came from Spain, where Rospigliosi resided from 1644 to 1653. There he became familiar with the type of romantic comedy of which Calderón and Lope de Vega were the masters, that *comedia de capa y espada* which blended elements of romance, tragedy and comedy in a fast-moving and realistic intrigue which had no more respect for the Aristotelian unities than the *sacra rappresentazione* or the *commedia dell'arte* themselves. Spanish models have been found for three of the four opera libretti he wrote after his return to Rome (Murata 1981: 50).

Rospigliosi fashioned from these models a type of operatic text that was neither tragic nor comic nor pastoral as these terms had hitherto been understood. From Solerti's bibliography of the first Italian operas, we can see that *Sant'Alessio* was described as a *dramma musicale* (Solerti 1903: 247); it was the first time this generic term 'dramma' had been used of an opera, and it was to continue to carry with it the associations that it seemingly had for Rospigliosi. The new type of opera mixed together aristocratic and plebeian characters, it juxtaposed high seriousness and uninhibited humour, it set off flights of idealism with descents to a very materialistic earth; and for all this Rospigliosi employed a comparably all-embracing poetic manner, ranging from a lofty rhetoric to a real adeptness in vernacular dialects. Furthermore in some of his operas the poet enlarged the scope of the genre by integrating into the dramatic action the kind of spectacle that had been characteristic of the *intermedi*. A huge proportion of the expense of the Barberini productions was devoted to the *mise-en-scène* (Bianconi and Walker 1984); Landi himself recorded the delight occasioned by this aspect of *Sant'Alessio*.

But what shall I say . . . of the scenic apparatus? The first appearance of the new Rome, the flight of the angel through the clouds, the appearance in the sky of Religion, were all works of ingenuity and machines, but they rivalled nature itself. The scene was most cunningly wrought; the visions of Heaven and of Hell marvellous; the changes of the wings and the perspective were ever more beautiful.   (Ademollo 1888: 18–19)

The range and variety of material packed into these operas sometimes overloaded the dramatic structure: a few of them – Rossi's *Il palazzo incantato* of 1642, for example – were recklessly episodic. But at their best the Roman operas introduce a new and important dramatic ideal: whether ostensibly sacred or comic or legendary or allegorical, they are essentially human. Rospigliosi's texts offer an edifying but down-to-earth vision of human potential, which does not disdain an indulgent smile for the humour and frailty of real life. Sometimes, as in *La vita humana* or *Sant'Alessio*, the spiritual message was obvious, oppressively so in the former; but even when his touch was lightest Rospigliosi had his sights set on serious matters, as his *Argomento* to *Chi soffre, speri* shows:

By Silvia is meant Voluptuousness, as the very name of Silvia can indicate, which derives from the woods, since men who are immersed in the deceptive pleasures of the senses are like wild beasts, hence it is that she is represented as having been Lucinda's Nurse; since through the allurement of pleasures, and through bad education, man quite often trespasses the proper bounds of self-respect.   (Reiner 1961: 278)

The musical resources of Roman opera

The survival, or reappearance, in Roman opera of elements borrowed from the *intermedi* and the *sacra rappresentazione* – chorus, dance, machines, supernature and allegory – has given the repertory a reputation in which the magnificence of the spectacle and the richly textured choral writing have been emphasized. In Domenico Mazzocchi's *La catena d'Adone*, Vittori's *La Galatea*, and Landi's *Sant'Alessio* the elaborate madrigalian choruses of Renaissance theatricals enjoy an Indian summer, as a brief example from Vittori's *La Galatea* may serve to illustrate (Ex.II.1).

Up to a point, the appreciation is just – it will be a long time before choruses half so fine reappear in Italian opera – but these movements do represent something of a sunset glow. In any case they are typical only of the earlier Roman operas. After 1636 (the last of the great choral operas was *I santi Didimo e Teodora*, an anonymous setting of a Rospigliosi text performed in both 1635 and 1636), as Rospigliosi became increasingly preoccupied with comedy and with the psychology of his individual characters, choruses came to be of minor importance, their place to some extent usurped by *intermedi* of dance or by solo arias. In fact, if one is looking for the most innovative aspects of this music, one might do better to look in a different direction altogether, at the recitative. For it is in Roman opera, particularly the comedies, *Chi soffre, speri* and *Dal male il bene*, that we find the beginning of that rather drably functional idiom commonly known as *secco* recitative, 'a quick-moving, narrow-ranged, sharply accented, irregularly punctuated, semi-musical speech, with many repeated notes sustained only by occasional chords' (Grout 1947: 80). Rospigliosi's

Ex.II.1 Vittori, *La Galatea* (1639), Act III

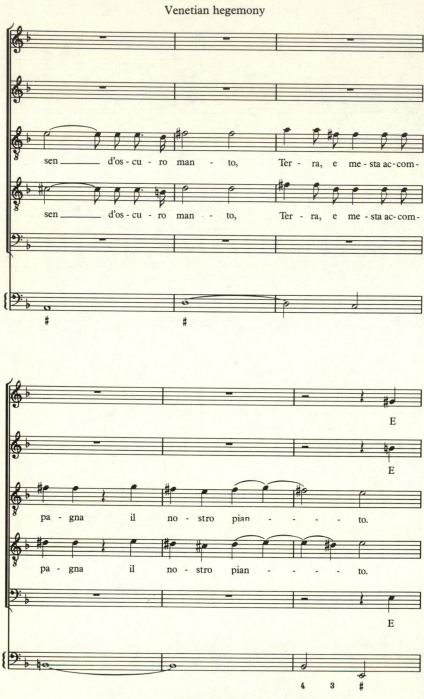

Ex.II.1 *continued*

Weep, grasses and flowers, weep for the eclipsed splendours. And thou,
oh earth, clothe thy bosom in a dark coat, and sadly accompany our
lament.

Ex.II.1 *continued*

style of drama, with its emphasis on action, naturalistic dialogue and pace, virtually forced his collaborators to create this prosaic medium.

The dramatic range of his texts prompted composers to explore a wide spectrum of styles. Particularly important for the well-being of a still comparatively new form which was competing to establish itself against, on one hand, the splendours of the traditional *intermedi*, and, on the other, the virtuoso performers of the *commedia dell'arte* troupes, was the solo aria. In Roman opera its expressive range grew much wider. The dance-songs and processionals that had been so central in *Orfeo* were still favoured, but they were joined by a number of aria types that can only be described as 'purely musical' forms. One type of song that became extremely popular was built on what one might describe as a quasi-ostinato principle; the bass, though in fact freely composed, moves with so regular a rhythm as to give the listener the impression of an ostinato, while the vocal melody above this apparently restrictive foundation unfolds with a delicious combination of cunning and fancifulness (see Ex.II.2). Laments, too, in which composers applied all the sophisticated, hot-house skills of the chamber-cantata in order to create for their operas that kind of emotional core that Monteverdi had given his *Arianna*, were much cultivated. The number and variety of these arias show how obsessed opera composers had become with the theatrical potential of the solo voice. The orchestra had already dwindled into relative insignificance. Landi in *Sant'Alessio* and Michelangelo Rossi in *Erminia sul Giordano* experimented with *canzona*-like sinfonias. But the multi-coloured instrumental ensemble of *Orfeo* belonged to a past age. The Roman opera orchestra was an exceedingly modest and virtually monochrome affair of strings and continuo (Bianconi and Walker 1984: 681). Expressiveness, colour, theatricality, and sheer sonorous thrill were provided in abundance by the great Roman *castrati*, tenors and basses, the finest singing voices of the age.

The clear-cut distinction between recitative and aria could have given the dramatic rhythm of the opera an ungainly, awkward quality. And for all the theatrical advantages of speeding up the delivery of the recitative, it could have resulted in a rather dull negligence in the relationship between words and music. Both these dangers were early recognized. In the index of arias added to the published score of *La catena d'Adone*, Domenico Mazzocchi wrote: 'there are many other "*mezz'Arie*" scattered through the work, which break the tedium of the recitative'. By 'mezz'Arie' or semi-arias, Mazzocchi appears to mean ariosi – short, expressive cantabiles, comparatively regular in rhythm but lacking the large-scale organization of the aria proper. By such means, something of the rhetorical eloquence of the great days of the *stile rappresentativo* was preserved into the age of the 'aria opera'. *Mezz'arie* could be used to heighten the dramatic impact of certain chosen episodes, to give force to the sententious maxims with which the

And so smiling hillsides, happy more for my happiness than for your own
flowers, may I breathe only through you, and abide only in you.

Ex.II.2 Mazzocchi, *La catena d'Adone* (1626), Act I scene 2

librettist Tronsarelli underlined the significance of his tale, or to act as a
bridge between the naturalistic pace of the recitative and the statuesque
stillness of the arias.

The decline of Roman opera

While Rospigliosi and the Barberinis had believed that it was possible for
opera to flourish in the service of morality and spirituality, many of the later
seventeenth-century popes saw the relationship between theatre and

morals as one of simple antagonism. The issue became that much more urgent with the attempt to establish regular seasons of opera on the Venetian model and the opening of a public opera house, the Teatro Tordinona, in 1670.

Rospigliosi's successor as Pope, Clement X, who came to the papal throne as the theatre was being built, at once showed his coolness towards this civic amenity by firmly refusing ex-Queen Christina's request to extend the theatrical season beyond the traditional weeks of Carnival (Ademollo 1888: 129). His fears were amply borne out. While it was open the Tordinona was so thronged with enthusiastic audiences that the impresario, Count d'Alibert, had promptly to enlarge and refurbish it for the 1671 season. But in a public theatre no trace was left of that strict decorum that had once distinguished the Barberini productions: there prevailed the most casual and promiscuous social intercourse, always noisy, sometimes riotous and indecent. Before giving permission for the theatre's reopening, Pope Clement issued a proclamation, requiring the strictest good behaviour from the singers; banning the taking of weapons into the theatres, 'even by clerics' (but excepting swords); prohibiting shouting, whistling, and interrupting the performances; and forbidding the admission of prostitutes. As all this failed to have any real effect, the next pope, Innocent XI, intervened more vigorously: he reinforced the ban on female singers, which seems temporarily to have passed into desuetude, he forbade men who sang in the opera to be professionally engaged in Roman churches, he had the partitions between boxes demolished in the hope of stamping out the unseemly intimacies they concealed, and he even imposed an *ad hoc* sumptuary law to trim down the ostentatious splendour of Christina's box. D'Alibert conceded defeat, and left Rome temporarily to purvey opera to the Turinese. The Tordinona remained closed from 1676 to 1690 and, as the *Avvisi di Roma* reported during the particularly dismal Carnival of 1679, 'in the gilded boxes of the Queen of Sweden, where cardinals once used to promenade, there are now only spiders crawling about in search of flies for Domitian' (d'Accone 1985: 8).

The election in 1689 of Pope Alexander VIII, a man charmingly described by Ademollo as 'eminentemente carnevalesco', led to a brief spurt of renewed operatic activity. But within two years he was dead, and his successor, having, as it were, given due notice by assuming the name Innocent XII, did indeed continue where Innocent XI had left off. The theatre was taxed in aid of church charities, then closed down, and finally, in 1697, demolished. It had become, reported Monsignor Battaglini, Bishop of Nocera, a place where 'extravagance, gluttony and every other most guilty form of intemperance triumphed, so that the resources of families were squandered, youth was corrupted, and pilgrims were scandalized' (Ademollo 1888: 196).

The troubled history of the public theatre encouraged private patronage. Much of the best Roman opera in the last part of the century was composed for the private pleasure of ex-queen Christina, or the Pamphilis or Ottobonis and their friends. It was in this kind of environment that Scarlatti learned to think of opera as a refined aristocratic art, subtly persuasive rather than clamantly theatrical. How passionately Roman music lovers yearned for what they were so often denied is perhaps made clearest by the extraordinary series of events attending Scarlatti's first opera *Gli equivoci nel sembiante* in 1679 – the brawls among those struggling for admission at the Collegio Clementino when Queen Christina arranged to have the production transferred there from the private house in which it had originally been staged, and above all the scandal that arose when the pope learned of performances continuing in private palaces for some weeks into Lent (d'Accone 1985: 13, 19–28).

The interaction of opera and sacred music continued throughout the century. If earlier forms of Roman music-drama had drawn much from the *sacra rappresentazione* and from the music of the oratorios, it soon began to repay the debt. Stricter members of the oratory brotherhoods were rather dismayed than gratified, and fought long and hard to keep their musical devotions free from the worldliness and sensuality of the opera.[2] But they fought an uphill battle, and the peculiar history of Roman opera in the second half of the century only served to increase its pressure on the style of the oratorios. When opera enjoyed papal favour, oratorio could be seen as a fitting Lenten substitute; when opera was suppressed, virtually the whole of its musical and much of its scenic apparatus could with impunity be applied to the oratorio.

6 · Opera comes to Venice

Roman singers

One aspect of seventeenth-century Roman music remains to be mentioned: the city was the home of great singing, the central source from which flowed an enormous number of performing artists who were instrumental in taking opera to most corners of the Italian peninsula. The excellence of Roman singers must have been due in large part to the Church. The city had innumerable churches which offered professional employment to musicians, many of its religious schools provided an excellent musical education, and not a few of the princes of the Church resident in Rome maintained an establishment of household musicians. The rigorous training of Roman singers is described in Angelini Bontempi's *Historia musica* published in Perugia in 1695: each morning they spent 'one hour in singing difficult and awkward things, to gain experience; one hour in the study of literature, and another in singing lessons and exercises done in the hearing of the maestro and in front of a mirror, to accustom themselves not to make awkward movements of the hips, or the face, or the eyebrows, or the mouth . . .' In the afternoon followed half an hour of theory, half an hour of counterpoint improvised against a cantus firmus, an hour of written counterpoint, another hour of literature; and the rest of the day was spent in practising the harpsichord or composing (Ademollo 1888: 33–4).

Roman singing gained its distinctive strength from the fusion of two traditions. Such at least is the impression given by Pietro della Valle in 1640. An older generation of Romans had cultivated a highly ornamented, florid style, in which the listener could not distinguish the sad from the gay because they 'sang so many notes and sang them so fast' (Fortune 1954: 213). Della Valle does not except even so great a singer as Vittoria Archilei from his censure. But, he continued, Cavalieri had introduced the Florentine style to the city, that is to say he had introduced all those subtle nuances of expression that arose from the philosophy of '*prima le parole, dopo la musica*', and since then Roman singing had been incomparable.

Though Rome provided attractive conditions for those able and willing to find professional satisfaction in the performance of Church or domestic music, it offered little security – for reasons that will have become apparent – for those who had succumbed to the fascination of opera, and it offered few prospects of any kind for female singers. Women were permitted to sing neither in Church nor in the theatre: a ban on the appearance of women on stage had been imposed by Pope Sixtus V in 1588 and was not withdrawn for the best part of 200 years, though occasionally, as in the early 1670s, it seems to have lapsed by default. And even the most successful male singers were not immune from those ups and downs of fortune and fashion that opera underwent as a result of the unique combination of artistic, political and religious circumstances that prevailed in the city. Altogether it is not to be wondered at that Roman singers formed the backbone of the touring troupes of musicians and theatre folk who, from the 1630s, began to circulate round Italy and beyond, and who were effectively responsible for the spread of opera to centres as far afield as Naples and Paris.

Touring opera troupes

Itinerant theatre companies were not a new phenomenon. For a hundred years *commedia dell'arte* troupes had led this kind of existence, and there can be no doubt that the opera-companies learned from them much about the problems and practicalities of touring. Rivalry was fierce between the two types of players and mutual influence was strong; on the whole it was *commedia* that suffered, never again quite regaining the esteem it enjoyed in the early decades of the century. Ivanovich reports that in Venice the vogue for opera completely undermined the popularity of the older spoken comedy (Ivanovich 1681: 383–4).

The best account of how such a touring opera-company functioned is provided by the Jesuit Giovan Domenico Ottonelli, writing in 1652: 'such professional companies', he explained, 'under the direction of one of their number, comprise virtuosos in the arts of singing, or playing, or dancing, or inventing new stage sets, or operating wonderful machines, or arranging and varying the scenes with graceful facility' and their womenfolk. They took with them a repertory of operas which they could normally cast from their own resources. But if their numbers were a bit short, they would descend on a city, 'and take steps to find out if there was a singer or player in the city, whether layman, or churchman, or monk, who could be invited with a reward, or besought with love, or indeed sometimes forced by the influence of powerful people, to take on one or more roles as a musical assistant . . .' (*Della christiana moderatione del Theatro*, in Bianconi and Walker 1975: 406–7). Clearly this mode of operation imposed some limitations on the type of opera performed: it is easier to take *Albert Herring* on tour than *Aida*. And if practicability was one factor in the mobility of an opera, another was the ease with which it could be adapted to the tastes of local audiences. So, for example, when Sacrati's *La finta pazza* (Venice

1641) became a standard item in the repertory of a touring company, the Venetian allusions in Strozzi's text had to be abandoned and its general literary style simplified, the scenic apparatus was necessarily reduced, and a larger role was given to the comic characters (Bianconi and Walker 1975: 424).

Like the *commedia* troupes, like the modern circus or fair, such a company was always on the move. It liked to base itself in a populous city at Carnival time, for then the whole citizenry was licensed to indulge itself in festive pastimes; it needed a keen sense of opportunism, to make the most of state occasions or dynastic events that might warrant an outburst of celebratory revels; otherwise it would be happy to perform wherever it could get a hearing. But the touring opera-company made its greatest cultural impact when it was invited into the heart of the intellectual and social establishment, to perform in a gentlemen's academy, or in the great hall of some prince's palace, or in a public theatre.

Benedetto Ferrari and Francesco Manelli were both musicians with Roman backgrounds. During the 1630s and 1640s, both of them, either singly or together, were involved in initiatives to introduce opera in a number of cities, including Parma, Modena and Bologna. But they and their company of musicians from Rome and the Papal States are best remembered for their visit to Venice in 1637 and their staging at the San Cassiano theatre of *Andromeda*, the earliest Venetian opera. It seems likely that they were invited there by the noble Tron family, proprietors of the San Cassiano. In April 1636 many of the Venetian aristocracy had been present at the production of the Marquis degli Obizzi's opera *Ermiona* in Padua, a few miles away. Obviously some of them at least had been impressed, for within a month, in May 1636, the Tron family had applied for and been given permission to convert their old theatre, a favourite venue of the *commedia dell'arte* troupes, into a 'Theatro de musica' (Mangini 1974: 37). A sequel to *Andromeda*, *La maga fulminata*, was performed at the same theatre the following year.

Before continuing the Venetian tale, we must briefly record the introduction of opera at Naples. The most famous and widely travelled of the itinerant opera groups was that known as the Febi armonici. They had taken opera to Piacenza and Lucca and other cities in north and central Italy, had even travelled as far afield as Paris. But their hour of greatest glory came when, in the early 1650s, they descended on Naples, at the time under Spanish rule. The Spanish viceroy in Naples, Count Oñate, had been a patron of the Febi armonici in Rome in the 1640s (*DBI*, s.v. 'Cirillo'), and was anxious to demonstrate to the Neapolitans the prestige value of opera; that is to say, he recognized its potential as a princely diversion that would do honour to his court and lend the eloquence of art to the most prosaic *ragioni di stato*. Oñate invited the Febi armonici into the royal palace, and there, in a hall previously used for ball games, staging and seating were erected for the performance of opera. Among the works given in these provisional, if luxurious, surroundings, may be mentioned Cavalli's *Giasone*, to celebrate the happy delivery of a son to the Spanish Queen in 1651, and the same composer's *Veremonda*, to celebrate the suppression of the Catalonian revolt in 1652. When Oñate demitted office, the Febi armonici moved from the royal palace to the Teatro San Bartolomeo, which, like the San Cassiano in Venice, was 'converted at great expense' from its earlier function as a conventional theatre to become the first of Naples' opera houses (Croce 1926: 82).

Opera in Venice: the first decade

Venice, unlike some Italian cities, did not treat the group that brought it its first taste of opera as a nine days' wonder. Surprisingly fast, opera really took root there, not as an occasional diversion but as an integral part of civilized life. Between 1637 and 1645, when they were closed down for three years in the stringent economy drive that marked the first phase of the Turkish War, four opera-houses were opened.

When Ferrari and Manelli brought their company to Venice the city could already look back on a long theatrical tradition. In the sixteenth century it had supported dozens of *compagnie della calza*, societies of wealthy nobles who organized mummings and theatricals to enliven banquets and festivals. *Commedia dell'arte* troupes frequently based themselves in the city. Hall and courtyards and cloisters had often been adapted for the players, and both Vasari and Palladio had been brought to the city to erect provisional theatres. All these activities were occasional and ephemeral, but in *c.* 1580 two Venetian families, the Michiel and the Tron, decided to build permanent theatres 'so that comedies could be performed there at Carnival time, according to the custom of the city' (Sansovino, *Venetia città nobilissima* (1581), in Mangini 1974: 20). The two theatres were at first more of a liability than their owners could have foreseen, for the vigorous opposition of the Jesuits resulted in the banning of the 'comedians' from Venice for the best part of thirty years. But by 1607 they were back in triumph, and several more theatres had been put up in the city before 1637 and the arrival of the new art-form that was to contribute so much to the *commedia*'s decline.

All these early theatres were built on the private initiative of wealthy Venetian noblemen: and all of them in due course were converted into opera-houses. This can best be shown in tabular form, as in Table 1. The idea of opening an opera-house as an economic investment will, these days, seem curious indeed. But that, in the seventeenth century, seems to have been at any rate a part of the story. It was a period of economic stagnation in

Table 1. *Chronology of the first Venetian theatres*

Theatre	Proprietary family	Original date of theatre	Conversion to opera-house
San Cassiano	Tron	*c.* 1580	1636–37
San Moisè	Giustinian/Zane	*c.* 1620	1638–39
San Salvatore (also known as San Luca)	Vendramin	1622	1660–61
SS. Giovanni e Paolo	Grimani	between 1635 and 1637	1638–39

Source: Mangini 1974.

Venice; and families who had traditionally had an interest in the leasing of property, investigated attentively the scope for new kinds of initiative opened up by the passion first for spoken drama, later for opera. Commercial opera was, of course, a risky enterprise, and different families pursued it with different financial means and different attitudes. The Giustinian/ Zane family lacked the means really to make a success of the San Moisè, which within a few years returned to its original function; the Vendramin family, notoriously prudent, hesitated for over thirty years before converting the San Salvatore for opera; on the other hand, the Grimanis pursued this new line of business with ruthless single-mindedness, opening new theatres and gaining control of existing ones virtually to the end of the century (Mangini 1973: 211). And this was not simply for economic motives: subtly tangled up with that factor was the idea of the theatre as a symbol of magnificence, an assertion of the family's economic and political clout within the city.

This period saw the establishment of opera as a commercial enterprise and as a public entertainment in the sense that anyone might buy a ticket for the performance. But it was not yet a popular entertainment. These public theatres accommodated far fewer people than the princely theatre in the Palazzo Barberini. Admission prices were not cheap – 4 lire, unchanged from 1637 to 1674 (Ivanovich 1681: 411), and 4 lire were twice the evening's wage for workmen employed in the theatre (Bianconi and Walker 1984: 227). It seems certain that, except for the servants who presumably attended on their masters and mistresses, the social standing of the theatre audiences was high. Even spoken plays – when they were performed in a permanent building – had excluded the real 'popolo minuto': in the late sixteenth century Alvise Cornaro had met with no success when he proposed the erection of a huge public theatre on a sandbank in the Canale della Giudecca in the hope of weaning the commonalty away from its brutish delight in bear-baiting (Mangini 1974: 27). But the opera had an altogether superior social tone; there was, Sir Philip Skippon was to observe, much less spitting into the pit than at the play (Glover 1978: 116).

This elegance was particularly marked at the last-erected of these early theatres, the Teatro Novissimo, established in 1641. Even the terms of the agreement in which the Dominican monks of SS. Giovanni e Paolo agreed to lease the land for it make clear the selective character of opera: it stipulated that 'on no account should clownish comedies or plays of any other kind be performed there, but only the aforementioned heroic operas' ('eroiche opere in canto', Bianconi and Walker 1975: 415). The Novissimo was unique among Venetian theatres, though parallels might be found at Bologna or Florence, where operatic initiative generally came from established 'academies'. In the first place it was a new building designed for opera from the outset; secondly it was not a commercial enterprise launched by a particular family, but rather a pastime for a group of like-minded friends, a pastime 'elevated to levels of princely magnificence' (Mangini 1974: 62). It was never designed to function profitably, but in its brief life it set new standards of opulence in the staging of opera, and was the scene of Giacomo Torelli's earliest and most influential experiments with theatrical machinery. Being an extravagant hobby rather than a business it was the first casualty of Turkish War economies and never reopened after 1647.

The blossoming of Venetian opera

The first years of opera in Venice had brought the city magnificent things: the last glorious flowering of Monteverdi's genius and the budding of Cavalli's; the astonishing spectacles devised by Torelli. Nevertheless the great age of Venetian opera really began only with the reopening of the theatres in 1648. Before the end of the century at least eleven more theatres had been opened, a few private, a few very short-lived, but almost all of them staging opera at some time or another. Opera, as Ivanovich made clear, became a major tourist attraction (1681: 392), and it gradually became available for a wider cross-section of the community. The productivity of librettists and composers was prodigious. In the last quarter of the century there were never fewer than seven new operas produced each year in the city, and in a vintage season, like 1682–83, there might be as many as twelve (Smith 1969–70: 62).

Several of the new theatres helped cater for the broadening audience by staging opera in humbler surroundings or on a less sumptuous scale. The Sant'Apollinare, scene of a notable collaboration between Cavalli and the Faustini brothers in the early 1650s, 'had been crudely converted from an old warehouse on the Grand Canal' (Glover 1982: 103). And there, spectacles of an apologetic modesty were provided for a largely middle-class audience. In 1674 the San Moisè, after decades of more or less continual crisis, was suddenly given a new lease of life by the impresario Francesco Santurini who, to the consternation of all rivals, introduced cheap productions and cut-price tickets at a quarter of a ducat each (Mangini 1974: 68).[1] The Sant'Angelo, another theatre offering cheap performances of economically staged operas, opened in 1677; the San Fantin, a tiny house often used by young singers at the start of their careers, in 1699.

But, it must be reiterated, we are in the world of enterprising businessmen, not of aristocratic aesthetes with a devotion to art that did not care to count the cost. Competition was fierce, and not all the families involved were able or willing to sustain it. Their problems were manifold. An unsuccessful opera was not, as it had been in the old days at the Medici court, simply a boring evening, it was a squandered investment. The policy of cheap tickets introduced at the San Moisè had to be emulated by the other theatres, and very much reduced profit margins. When owners put their theatres in the hands of impresarios, as happened increasingly, these far from signorial figures could find themselves at a disadvantage in dealing with noblemen who dragged their heels over the settling of their debts. There were compensating insurances and economies to which the owners sometimes resorted. They particularly liked to get a popular composer to act as a kind of house-composer: Cavalli was this at the Sant'Apollinare in the early 1650s, Pallavicino served the Grimani family in a similar capacity at SS. Giovanni e Paolo from the mid-1670s, while Legrenzi worked mainly in the Vendramins' San Salvatore. A favourite way of keeping the repertory fresh while avoiding the expense of a new production was to refurbish the score with new arias. The practice is illustrated by a 'second edition' of Pallavicino's *Galieno* staged at the SS. Giovanni e Paolo theatre in 1676 which omitted 33 of the original 71 arias and introduced in their stead 44 newly composed ones (Smith 1969–70: 65).

In this hard competitive world the Grimani family pursued their course with relentless single-mindedness. Indeed they came within sight of gaining a monopolistic control over the whole theatre business of the city. As we have seen, they owned one theatre, the SS. Giovanni e Paolo, before the Turkish War crisis in the late 1640s. Thereafter their theatrical interests expanded with unfaltering sureness of purpose. In the 1650s, as the Vendramins persevered with spoken plays in the San Salvatore (spoken plays were also performed occasionally at the San Cassiano), the Grimanis decided that they too should maintain a theatre for that form of drama, and opened the San Samuele in 1655. When the need to match the cut-prices at the San Moisè began to lower the income and perhaps the tone at the SS. Giovanni e Paolo, they decided in 1677 to open a second opera-house, the San Giovanni Grisostomo, which they could maintain as a kind of opera-house *de luxe*. Bonlini reports that 'it was built . . . with that magnificence appropriate to the house of Grimani . . . [a theatre] which, with the vastness of its superb structure, was able to rival the pomp of ancient Rome and which, with the magnificence of its more than regal dramatic display, has now gained the applause and esteem of the whole world' (Towneley Worsthorne 1954: 34). At the San Giovanni Grisostomo theatre cheap tickets were not available; but besides the spacious opulence of the surroundings, patrons could enjoy a large orchestra that contrasted markedly with the tiny chamber ensembles used in the other theatres (Bianconi and Walker 1984: 681), and the skills of a team of machinists who had mastered their craft in the Arsenal (Mangini 1974: 82). When in 1687 the performances at the San Salvatore had come to rival those in the Grimanis' prestige theatre, the family even managed briefly to gain control of that, by persuading the tenant impresario to sublet it to them; no sooner had this ruse been legally disqualified than they set their sights on taking control of the Sant'Angelo, which they did in 1688–89 through two placemen, the Bezzi brothers (Mangini 1974: 54 and 75).

The operatic businessman and his customers

In the early years of the Venetian opera-houses the families who had built them generally directed them personally. But after 1650, partly, one presumes, to save themselves bother, and partly to minimize financial risk, they followed increasingly the practice of placing their theatrical affairs in the hands of an impresario. The first man to distinguish himself in this capacity was the lawyer Marco Faustini, brother of the Giovanni Faustini who was Cavalli's favourite librettist in his early years. In 1650 the financially harassed Giovanni took a leading role in the partnership that launched the middle-class Teatro Sant'Apollinare. When he died suddenly, the following year, his brother took over, with such flair that for the next twenty years he became the leading figure in the 'industrialization of the theatre' (Mangini 1974: 40–1), advancing to the San Cassiano in 1657, and in 1660 being snatched up by the Grimanis to run the SS. Giovanni e Paolo theatre.

Traditionally theatre performances had been staged to mark a special occasion or a particular season of the year – we have seen that it was 'the custom of the city' to stage comedies during the Carnival. With the advent of commercial opera it became essential to give performances as frequently as possible, in order to redeem the initial investment made in the production. From this need arose the operatic season, focused on the Carnival, but extending that festive season backwards as far as the church calendar permitted, to 26th December – St Stephen's Day. Towards the end of the century autumn seasons were introduced; and that was a further blow to the *commedia dell'arte* troupes, who hitherto had had the theatres to

117

themselves in autumn. In the eighteenth century a third season was to grow up around the great Ascension Fair in May (Mangini 1974: 31–2).

Even in the seventeenth century the cost of running an opera-house was not inconsiderable. To begin with it had to be built (with no government subventions – but see below p. 119) and maintained. Except perhaps at the Novissimo and the San Giovanni Grisostomo, the cost of the actual staging was, for all the magnificence with which it was contrived, rather less than one might suppose (Bianconi and Walker 1984: 681). For it involved a single investment for a whole season during which only a tiny number of different works would be performed. The 1666 season planned for the SS. Giovanni e Paolo theatre, for example, involved only two operas, Cesti's *Tito* – a new work – and P. A. Ziani's *Doriclea* – a resetting of a libretto already composed by Cavalli twenty years earlier (Schmidt 1978: 443); and in any case the basic machinery on which the effects largely depended could be reused season after season. The real expense came from the musicians, even in those theatres that maintained only very small orchestras. The singers were highly skilled, salaried professionals, the finest voices in Italy, and they had to be engaged for months at a time. Competition between theatres to procure the best of them pushed salaries ever higher – with destructive consequences, incidentally, for the music in Venetian churches, even in San Marco. Good composers could also be expensive, especially those successful enough for impresarios to want to engage them as house-composers. When Cavalli was signed up for the San Cassiano in 1658 he was offered 400 ducats a year, twice the salary he received as organist of San Marco (Glover 1978: 23). And we may be sure there were various other expenses that are easily forgotten. For example, after the burning down of the San Salvatore theatre during the 1653 Carnival, all theatres were legally required to engage 'diligent watchmen obliged to sleep [there] every night during the season, to search the boxes and other places to protect them against fire' (Mangini 1974: 52).

On the other hand, there were ways of economizing on the overheads, even of reducing capital expenditure, that are not available in the modern organization of opera. Cavalli's salary at the San Cassiano may have been generous, but it covered more than the composition of operas. All scores, copies and parts were to be made at his expense; he had to supervise all rehearsals and make such alterations as might be necessary; he was precluded from composing for any rival theatre; and when the opera was ready he had to direct all the performances from the harpsichord – or in the event of illness provide a deputy at his own expense (Glover 1978: 23). The payment of librettists was also arranged in such a way as to eat as little as possible into the basic capital investment for the season. Ivanovich explained that, as payment for his labours the author of the drama is given everything that is earned from the sale of librettos – which are printed at his own expense – and from the dedication, which he may bestow as he will. These earnings will depend upon the success of the drama. In addition the author has free admission to the theatre every evening, authority to take with him a friend, and a box is put at his disposal. This is a courtesy practised by the Grimani theatres, and by various others that have followed their example.

(1681: 414)

Income came from the sale of admission tickets; from the hire of portable seats – there was no fixed seating either in the pit or the gallery and, as in a modern Italian café, if you wanted to sit down you paid extra – and from the sale of refreshments. In the 1690s the San Samuele introduced a highly profitable side-line in the form of a gambling room, an initiative much imitated in the eighteenth century (Mangini 1974: 72). But however popular an opera might be, these things in themselves would never have ensured the prosperity of the theatre managements. That was due primarily to the inspired devising of the 'box-system', a system for the financing of the theatre which, with modifications, survived into the twentieth century.

The Italian opera-house as it evolved in seventeenth-century Venice had a design strikingly different from theatres in other parts of Europe. There was a pit (where you could put your hired bench) and a gallery (often reserved, in part at least, for servants), but by far the greater part of the auditorium was occupied by tiers of enclosed boxes, three tiers in small theatres like the Sant'Apollinare, five tiers in the grander ones. And these boxes were not simply to accommodate spectators for single performances, they were for sale; indeed, they were for sale before the theatre was even built. When someone decided to open an opera-house he would approach various wealthy families in Venice inviting them to subscribe for a box. In this way a substantial proportion of the initial investment was provided by the people who subsequently became the customers. Once the theatre was built, the box-owners paid an additional annual rent for each season the theatre was open, and bought admission tickets each night they actually attended. So long as they continued to pay the rent, they could retain their boxes for themselves and their heirs, theoretically in perpetuity (Ivanovich 1681: 402). Even so it is unlikely that theatre-owners ever made much money in any direct or literal way out of opera (Bianconi and Walker 1984: 227). But they had certainly learned how to reduce their losses to a minimum; the balance was an investment eminently well worth making since it provided them with a princely entertainment, and enhanced immeasurably their prestige and influence in the city.

Another factor in the box-system may have been the wish to furnish each of the wealthy and powerful families in the 'Most Serene Republic' with the kind of privileged accommodation which, in a duchy or monarchy, the

119

ruler and his guest of honour would have enjoyed.[2] But by whatever calculations it was arrived at, the charms of the system were manifold. Boxes added immensely to the attraction of the theatre as a meeting-place; to have the noblest of diversions offered to you, at a modest price, in what felt like your own private apartment was to enjoy a matchless social amenity; and the curious condition of intimacy in a public place turned the theatre into an ideal centre for the exchange of commercial and political information. Boxes were in fact assigned to diplomatic residents in the city as one of the perquisites of the job – they had been from very early days when the San Cassiano was still a play theatre (Mangini 1974: 36–7). Under these circumstances the active interest taken by the Venetian state in what went on there is unsurprising. The Doge himself was responsible for the allocation of boxes to the diplomatic corps (Towneley Worsthorne 1954: 12), and political supervision of the theatres was organized by the State Inquisitors, who, so to speak, 'bugged' them by means of hired informers.

Already there were no doubt some music-lovers who appreciated the box-system on artistic grounds – as in later centuries Rousseau and Stendhal were to do. But that is not what the surviving documents record. They serve rather to show how the system fostered that extraordinarily casual attitude to the spectacle which was to condition the whole history of Italian opera down to Verdi. By 1678 the Tuscan ambassador was reporting that the spacious boxes of the new San Giovanni Grisostomo theatre had already been the scene of magnificently illuminated banquets on the one hand, and of brawls between masked men on the other (Mangini 1974: 80). And the 'many scandalous wickednesses' committed in boxes, of which the Jesuits complained at the San Cassiano as early as 1581, remained a matter of concern to the Council of Ten for the whole of the seventeenth century (*ibidem*: 21).

7 · The nature of Venetian opera

Public taste and the canons of art

When a city supports half-a-dozen or more public theatres, all run on a commercial basis, the effect on the character of the spectacle is bound to be considerable. In seventeenth-century Venice, opera came to be a commodity, offered for sale in a highly competitive market. Inevitably, therefore, its nature could no longer be dictated by a tiny cultured clientele sharing common presuppositions and aspirations. Once opera became a public entertainment its development was bound to reflect public taste, not the kind of philosophical and ethical ideals that had brought the art to birth. The note sounded by T. Fattorini in the preface to his libretto for Legrenzi's *Eteocle e Polinice* (Teatro San Salvatore 1675) recurred over and again in the librettos of the period: 'The author believed that he did not need to follow any other law than that of pleasure, neither has he aspired to any other object than that of universal gratification.'

The question that troubled many poets was whether this aim of 'universal gratification' was not being achieved at too great a cost. Could artistic and moral standards be maintained in a commercial theatre? Was 'putrid barratry' unavoidable? (The phrase is Ivanovich's, 1681: 429.) The theme of the debasement of music-drama in the pursuit of an easy popularity with the undiscriminating crowd became a critical commonplace, and was to remain one in discussions of seventeenth-century Venetian opera virtually down to modern times.

Late-twentieth-century taste finds it easier to sympathize with the reckless theatrical vitality of the operas of the mid-seventeenth century than with the reformed *dramma per musica* of Zeno and his successors (see Chapter 10); but there is no denying that havoc was wrought on the cultural ideals upheld by the first generation of opera composers. Almost as soon as opera arrived in Venice, those appeals to classical precedent with which Rinuccini and Peri, Gagliano and Monteverdi had graced their publications were abandoned. Giovanni Busenello, librettist of *L'incoronazione di Poppea* (Teatro SS. Giovanni e Paolo 1642), denied that the modern theatre poet had anything to learn about the writing of poetry for music from 'the strophes and antistrophes and epodes of the Greeks . . . [or] the Orphic hymns, or the Idylls of Theocritus and Anacreon' ('Lettera scritta . . .

intorno alla *Statira*', in Degrada 1969: p. 89–90). Vincenzo Nolfi was even more brashly contemptuous of the hitherto accepted canons of art:

You waste time, O reader, if, with the poetics of the Stagirite in hand, you go seeking out the errors of this work . . . the wits of our times not recognizing today Epicharme for father, nor Sicily as fatherland, nor Aristotle as law-giver anymore . . . Of the two ends for Poetry taught by Horace there only remains to delight.

(Preface to *Il Bellerofonte*, 1642, in Towneley Worsthorne 1954: 176)

The tone of Nolfi's remark would surely have shocked the Camerata. What might have troubled them more profoundly was the erosion of the status of the poet that the Venetian style of opera brought about.

However fond of opera they were, Venetians must sometimes have come to feel gorged to satiety by the profusion of works available for them. And it cannot always have been easy for poets and musicians to know how best to stimulate their jaded palates. In 1662 Aurelio Aureli, one of the most productive of Venetian librettists, remarked that 'these days the citizens of Venice have become so listless in their dramatic tastes that they no longer know what they want to see, and the intellect of the writer no longer knows what he can invent to gain the spectator's applause' (Preface to *Le fatiche d'Ercole per Deianira*). On the whole, authors were disposed to put their faith in various types of virtuosity: in dazzling spectacle, in increasingly obtrusive and flamboyant solo arias, in comic turns modelled on the *lazzi* of the *commedia dell'arte* (see Chapter 16).

Poets were quite frank about the radical upset in the hierarchy of the arts that such tendencies brought about. Poetry, once the soul of musical inspiration, was now but 'a cripple not to say a corpse . . . [unless] . . . sustained and animated by the architecture of Signor Carlo Pasetti and by the music of Signor Francesco Manelli' (Francesco Berni, *La palma d'onore*, Ferrara 1660, in Varese 1967: 543). And a dozen poets in scores of printed librettos deplored the way in which this tendency gathered a seemingly irresistible momentum as the years passed. 'To accord satisfaction to the many I have prejudiced my own', lamented Badovero; 'the current fashion for the multiplicity of the arias has caused materials to be dissipated in arias that would have made excellent recitative' ('ha fatto correr in aria le sostenze del più buono recitativo') (Preface to *Sesto Tarquinio*, 1679, in Smith 1969–70: 66).

The element of expediency in these developments is clearest when the poet addresses the reader not about public taste in general but about a specific opportunity that has arisen on a specific occasion. Giovanni Faustini contrived a mad-scene for Cavalli's *Egisto* (Teatro San Cassiano 1643) at 'the authoritative request of a powerful person' and 'to satisfy the genius of the performer of the role' (Belloni 1929: 423). A 'Signor Clemente' arrived in Venice too late to have a proper role written for him in Sartorio's *Gl'amori infruttuosi di Pirro* (Teatro SS. Giovanni e Paolo 1661), so, explained the librettist Aureli, he was fitted in here and there as best they could manage, 'so as not to deprive you of the pleasure of hearing the voice of so outstanding a virtuoso'. 'I pray you, gentle reader', urged G. C. Corradi, 'do not wonder to see Orpheus appearing on the Styx at the close of Act II. He is an accessory introduced simply to enable you to hear a famous violinist' (Preface to *Germanico sul Reno*, Teatro San Salvatore 1675). The general thrust of two centuries of criticism of Venetian opera is already quite clear in Ivanovich's contemporary diagnosis:

> In contrast with those princes who support the poetic decorum of their theatres with gifts and magnificence, here it has become a commercial transaction, which opens a thousand ways to the vexations introduced by a putrid barratry. One has to undertake a thousand missions just to get one's composition heard; and even if one attains to this good fortune one has to subject oneself to the judgement of many, and, well, the majority prevails, that is where defeat or success come from . . . It is regarded as a trifling error that heroic and ludicrous themes should be treated in the same style of language; that the pathetic, which is the soul of the drama, should be reduced; that the arias should occupy the place of the necessary recitative; that stage machinery should be added capriciously at will; that the crises of the drama should be resolved in the manner of those Ancients, criticized by Cicero: *Et cum explicare argumentum non potestis, ad Deos confugitis.* (1681: 429–31)

The loss of moral inventiveness

It was not simply public taste that undermined the standards of Venetian opera. Those citizens who went to hear the première of Pallavicino's *Carlo, Re d'Italia* at the Teatro San Giovanni Grisostomo in 1682 would have found that the librettist, Matteo Noris, had dedicated it, not to some wealthy prince of church or state, but to Fortune, 'sovereign Mover of earthly vicissitudes, lubric Fantasy of second causes, Accident deified by the plaudits of the unhappy man made happy . . . [etc.]'. Noris enjoyed cultivating a whimsical tone; but the world in which Venetian opera took root and flourished was often genuinely tormented by this same Fortune, and her minions, Chance, Mutability, Transience. Many of the more sensitive minds of the age were haunted by a recognition that the foundations of both mediaeval faith and Renaissance humanism had been undermined. In a world fashioned by the Reformation, by the New Science, and by Cartesian philosophical scepticism the old securities and values simply failed to hold fast. Some men felt that they could be sure of nothing beyond the struggles, the raptures and agonies of their own subjective existence. During the early decades of the seventeenth century, the stylistic coherence of the artistic world out of which opera had arisen was lost. The only criterion of art came to be the artist's or the audience's pleasure. Giambattista Marino, the most successful and influential Italian poet of the age, was charged by eighteenth-century critics such as Crescimbeni with responsibility for the 'licentious' incoherence of seventeenth-century Italian literature; because 'the ferment of his wit, not capable of remaining restrained within any limits, burst completely every dike; nor did he tolerate any other law than that of his own caprice' (Mirollo 1963: 104). Less dazzling talents than Marino, such as the poets of Venetian opera, frankly indulged themselves in the same way. In the prologue of Cavalli's *L'Erismena* (Teatro Sant'Apollinare 1656) Aureli presents a debate between Facondia (Eloquence), Bizzaria (Whimsy) and a 'choro di Capricci'. The *capricci* are at work composing an opera, and the prologue is in fact a brief ironic review of contemporary operatic aesthetics. How low in the scale of values those traditional virtues of eloquence, craftsmanship, sense of style (all surely contained in the concept of *Facondia*) had sunk is shown by her scornful dismissal by Bizzaria:

> Sò, che altrove i tuoi vanti
> Devi spiegar tù, che col dir soave
> L'alme incateni, e gli uditori incanti.
> La Facondia non ha tetto qui intorno,
> Capricci, e Bizzaria
> Sol qui fanno soggiorno.[1]

If Marino was the spokesman of his age in claiming the poet's caprice as the basis of all aesthetics, so was he in establishing those characteristics of style that followed from this self-indulgence. Of these none is more obvious than sensuality. Such flagrantly erotic specimens of his art as the 'Canti de' baci' and the 'Pastorella' promptly earned themselves a place on the Index of banned books. But such a fate only helped the poet to a more delicious notoriety among the younger Italian writers of his day; and he found a band of enthusiastic supporters among the Venetian Accademia degli Incogniti, founded by Giovanni Francesco Loredan in 1636. Among the roistering libertines of the Incogniti were several of the early Venetian opera librettists (Bianconi and Walker 1975: 418–19), including Busenello, whose *L'incoronazione di Poppea* introduced to opera an unbridled sensuality unimaginable in the Neoplatonic world of the earlier generation.

This note, heard at its most irresistible in the Poppea–Nerone duets, surely added much to the broad seductive appeal of Venetian opera. But in the hands of lesser artists than Busenello all sense of fitness was lost. Sometimes the result was a ludicrous hyperbole, as at the close of Cicognini's *Giasone* libretto, where,

> Fra nodi tenaci
> Rimbomban queste valli
> Al suon dei baci . . .[2]   (Varese 1967: 56)

sometimes, particularly by the 1670s, a calculated lubricity, which brought on stage things that were otherwise unheard of until the second half of the twentieth century. One example will suffice. In the third act of Pallavicino

124

and Corradi's *Il Nerone* (Teatro San Giovanni Grisostomo 1679) Nero, having fallen in love with Gilde, the wife of Tiridate, contrives a pretext for enjoying her. They are to take part in some private theatricals, a mythological play in which Nero is cast as Mars, Gilde as Venus, and her unfortunate husband as Vulcan. Act III scene 7 culminates in the following exchange (Mars and Venus are observed by Vulcan and Bronte):

Marte (Nero)	Già ch'ai baci m'inviti	
	Sovra letto di rose, il seno ignudo	
	Vieni a depor ò bella	
	A delitie maggior l'alma t'appella.	
Venere (Gilde)	Lieta ti seguo . . .	
Marte	Ma pria ch'a i dolci nodi	
	L'alma si stringa, e s'incatena il core	
	Qui deponiam le spoglie.	
Venere	Pronta ubbidisco	[Si dispoglie.]
Vulcano (Tiridate)	*Gilde havrà tant'ardire*	
Bronte	*Taci se vuoi son fintioni, o Sire.*	
Marte [Aria]	Quanto godo il mirar	
	La nudità del sen	
	Meno vezosa appar	
	L'Alba col suo seren.	
	Quanto . . .	
Venere	Basta così: vieni a soavi amplessi.	[S'inviano verso il letto, e ciascheduno di loro vi s'adagia sopra.][3]

At which point Seneca bursts in upon them with news of a rebellion.

Another trait in which Marino provides the model for the greater part of the century was his enthusiasm for exaggerated rhetorical device. Croce believed that the preoccupation with the unexpected and astounding, with virtuosity of rhetoric applied to no deeper purpose than itself, was the most characteristic vice of the 'baroque' style (Croce 1946a: 25). Certainly many seventeenth-century Italian artists, and not just poets, seemed bent above all on the bravura accomplishment of unprecedented tasks, on effects without causes. Marino himself declared his creed in the thirty-third 'whistle' of his *Martoleide*, a sonnet-war with Gaspare Murtola:

> È del poeta il fin la meraviglia
> (Parlo de l'eccellente e non del goffo):
> Chi non sa far stupor, vade alla striglia![4]   (Mirollo 1963: 25)

Of the effects of bravura essayed by Marino and his epigones, none was of greater moment for music than his cultivation of what he himself called his 'stile metaforuto', a style permeated by far-fetched and cunningly contrived metaphors. The metaphor of course had a venerable literary history, going back millennia before Marino. In his own aesthetics it held a place of honour because, in metaphor, the poet's wit and ingenuity afforded unexpected insights into the nature of things, and created an astonishment and delight which depended as much upon the means as upon the end. During the seventeenth century it came to be regarded as the indispensable adornment of poetry, 'the great mother of all wit' as Emanuele Tesauro described it in the most authoritative work of Italian 'poetics' of the age, the *Cannocchiale aristotelico* published in Venice in 1655; and he went on to acclaim metaphor as 'the most ingenious and shrewd, the most exotic and wonderful, the most joyful and serviceable, the most eloquent and fertile production of the human intellect' (Raimondi 1960: 32 and 73). Later in the century it occurred to the subtler mind of the philosopher Giambattista Vico that its particular value in poetry lay in what we might describe as its subconscious suggestiveness (cf. Towneley Worsthorne 1954: 14–15). It is hardly necessary to point out the advantage for opera of a device of rhetoric that is dependent upon analogy. In encouraging a delight in virtuosity and challenging composers to cultivate the art of tone-painting, the *stile metaforuto* was an important source of the full-scale operatic aria.

If the humanists' neoplatonic vision of the world had faded, old habits of thought survived for some decades. In the 1640s Count Bisaccioni was still extracting symbolic and allegorical significance from the stupendous stagesets which Torelli was producing at the Teatro Novissimo (cf. Towneley Worsthorne 1954: 46–7). And, particularly in more old-fashioned centres, printed librettos occasionally included an *Allegoria* – a philosophical and ethical explanation of the 'meaning' of the dramatic action. Sbarra's *Alessandro* (Lucca 1654) has five and a half pages of such an allegory, the conclusion of which is that

Alessandro, although passionately fond of Campaspe, finally, so as not to break faith with Apelles, yields her generously to him, which helps us understand how important it is for a great man to keep his word. And in depriving himself not only of Campaspe, but also of her portrait, he clearly teaches us that it is necessary to distance one's self from all occasions, however small, which threaten to deny the glory of the conquering of self.

But what Sbarra calls an allegory, is so banal that it can better be regarded as an example of 'precettistica', the art of coining philosophical and ethical precepts, which Croce diagnosed as the most characteristic form of philosophy of the age (Croce 1946a: 137–60). Croce attributed the flourishing of this preceptive style to the supreme position held by shrewdness (*l'accortezza*) in the hierarchy of moral values. Seventeenth-century Italy may have lost 'its moral inventiveness, the faculty of creating new and progressive forms of ethical life' (Croce p. 17); but in Church and state alike there was an unprecedented appreciation of the diplomatic and political skills. The precept, the lapidary, epigrammatic formulation of useful truth, was an apt symptom of a way of life dominated by dogmatic ecclesiastical conservatism and of political absolutism. P. Mattei took pride in having invented a new form of history in which 'the historical narratives are conjoined with political maxims' (Croce 1946a: 143, quoting Tomasi), and neither novels nor dramas escaped this tendency. When Virgilio Malvezzi describes the precepts with which he adorned his historical writings as 'necklaces of pearls' the relevance of all this to opera at once becomes clear. For as Tesauro himself pointed out, the precept, like the metaphor, was a literary grace (Raimondi 1960: 21), and it lent itself perfectly – its character after all was that of a detachable self-contained work of art – to emphasis, elaboration and adornment in an aria.

For decades Venetian opera was conditioned by a careless, unphilosophical hedonism. But a change of tone makes itself felt in the 1680s and by the 1690s is marked. It is epitomized in two consecutive early operas by C. F. Pollarolo, performed at the Teatro San Giovanni Grisostomo in 1692 and 1693. The first, *Onorio in Roma*, is described in the libretto, in the time-honoured self-depreciatory Venetian fashion, as a 'precipizio' – 'conceived in a matter of moments, plotted in a matter of hours, versified in less than a day, rendered harmonious by Sig. Carlo Pollarolo in little more than a week'. The second, Domenico David's *La forza del virtù*, is startlingly different; it reintroduces, with a seriousness reminiscent of the loftiest flights of Renaissance humanism, the idea of allegory; indeed the libretto is prefaced by an 'Allegoria del Drama', in which we read,

Since drama is a body manufactured by art it will acquire its fullest measure of beauty when it is composed, not merely of imitation, but of allegory as well. Imitation represents to the eyes and ears of the theatre audience a man's external actions: allegory displays to the spectators' intellect certain occult and prudent mysteries which, beneath the surface of the action, are wonderfully hidden in the innermost core.

And in a further address 'To the Reader', David goes on to reinstate the values so scornfully rejected by Nolfi fifty years earlier:

The former delights, the latter instructs, both together combining the useful with the pleasing, which are the two so important objects at which all the best teachings about poetry have directed their aim.

In the same theatre during the same decade Girolamo Frigimelica-Roberti reintroduced operatic tragedy, of which Venetian audiences had had no experience since the revivals of Monteverdi's *Arianna* in 1639. Each of these works, *Ottone* (1694), *Ercole in cielo* (1696), *Rosmonda* (1696) – all of them set by Pollarolo – has a solemn and erudite preface. The poet regards tragedy as a kind of 'mysterious panegyric of public liberty' because of the dismal fate that befalls its tyrant protagonists; he explains its high ethical purpose; discourses at length upon the varieties of Greek tragedy that he has taken as model; and prepares the audiences for the unprecedented toughness of the fare he offers them with complimentary allusions to their refinement of taste. With Frigimelica-Roberti we are on the threshold of a new age, an age in which the traditional type of Venetian

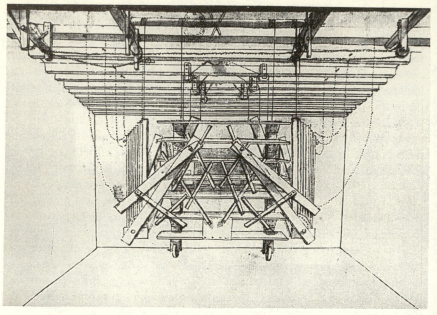

Plate 3 Descending cloud machinery without decoration, from *Germanico sul Reno*

Plate 4 Descending cloud machinery open, from *Germanico sul Reno*

opera was to be superseded by the reformed *dramma per musica* of Apostolo Zeno and the Arcadians (see p. 183–5).

The art of the machinist

The cult of bravura in seventeenth-century Italian art was vividly exemplified in the skills of the operatic scenographer and machinist. Of the sister arts involved in the production of an opera, spectacle began, from the 1640s, to establish for itself a position of primacy. In the already cited preface to *Bellerofonte* (p. 122), Nolfi professed 'not to have wished to observe other precepts than the sentiments of the inventor of the apparatus' (Towneley Worsthorne 1954: 176). But what Nolfi admitted with a cynical shrug of the shoulders, other artists were less willing to concede, and hints of their dismay at the pretensions of the machinist are scattered through the critical and exegetical writings of the period. An interesting example is found in the prologue to Cavalli's adaptation of Provenzale's *Ciro* (originally Naples ?1650) given in Venice in 1654. It is one of the earliest of several prologues in which the traditional mythological allegories are abandoned in favour of a *Capriccio*-like debate about the nature of opera. In the present case la Poesia, la Musica and la Pittura all express their dismay at the machines introduced into the opera by l'Architettura:

Pittura		Ahimè rovina il tutto
Musica	à 3	De' tuoi folli Compassi è questo il frutto.
Poesia		
Architettura		Ah! Ah! sciocche voi sete,
		Che gli artifici miei
		Precipiza credete.
Pittura		Novità peregrine
Musica	à 3	Saper farsi ubbidir dalle ruine . . .[5]
Poesia		

But the spectacle of opera became one of the most characteristic manifestations of the baroque imagination in Italy. For, as Dent long ago observed, the passion for building which had absorbed so many Renaissance Italians was now infused with a straining for bravura effects which aimed to give the impression, not of stability or of measured repose, but of inner animation: 'the ideal creation would have been an architecture not only of unlimited magnificence, but alive with perpetual movement in every part' (Dent 1960: 5). If in the Romantic age architecture was to be viewed as 'frozen music', in seventeenth-century Italy opera came almost to be regarded as a form of animated and sounding architecture, a sequence of transient but dazzling visions conjured up and as quickly dispersed again by the Prospero-like magic of the machinist's art.

Supreme among the machinist-magicians of the period was Giacomo

Plate 5 Detail of decorated Venetian machinery, from *Germanico sul Reno*

Torelli, the 'great sorcerer', as the French were later to call him. He had come to Venice originally to work in the Arsenal, and being a man 'impatient of ease' (*Il cannochiale per la Finta pazza* (1641), Bjurström 1961: 49), started to exercise his mechanical talents in the theatre as a hobby. There he devised means to enable gods and dragons and clouds to fly through the air in every conceivable direction, in 'chariots' whose workings were cunningly concealed with painted cloth or paper. But his most epoch-making innovation was a device to enable a single stage-hand to effect a transformation of a whole stage set. The grooves in which the wings were slotted were cut right through the floor of stage and the wings mounted on trolleys running on tracks in the area underneath. These carriages were attached by a system of ropes to a revolvable drum, so that they all moved smoothly, simultaneously and effortlessly at the switch of a lever. Torelli's theatrical colleagues had been accustomed to employing a team of up to sixteen stagehands, each responsible for pushing one of the wings into place for a change of scene, a laborious procedure which effectively limited transformations to those between acts. The invention of the simultaneous scene-change, achieved by a single operator in the twinkling of an eye, astonished, indeed mesmerized, the early audiences at the Teatro Novissimo, and was to become one of the most potent sources of theatrical 'magic' in the following decades.

Besides his mechanical innovations, Torelli played his part in the more general transformation of scenographical style. Further advances in perspective art were made by such devices as angled façades or views through arched frames, and in *Bellerofonte* Torelli became the first scenographer to manage a genuine interior set, closed in above with a ceiling. He was adept at integrating into his 'moving architecture' effects borrowed from artists working in different media: landscapes based on the pictorial traditions of tapestry (*Bellerofonte*, Act III); the decorative effect of shrubs in rows of urns, that had recently been introduced to Venetian gardens from the Orient (*Bellerofonte*, Act II scene 9); rocky caves, a favourite motif of contemporary landscape gardening (*Bellerofonte*, Act I scene 11) (Bjurström 1961: 58–72).

In most operas and in most theatres, spectacle continued to be concentrated in the framework of prologue and *intermedi*; and in some instances it remained quite extrinsic to the drama. But Torelli's invention of the simultaneous scene-change made it possible for the poet to make the boldest visual effects an integral part of his dramatic design. Gradually the dividing line between the spectacular interludes that opera had inherited from the *intermedio*, and the plot of the opera itself, began to blur and dissolve. Grandiose tableaux of song and dance, astonishing novelties in the manipulation of the stage machinery, continued to be spaced out at the turning points of the drama, but they became intrinsic to the action.

Faustini liked to bring his first acts to a close with a ballet in which the characters mingle with figures from mythology. Later in the century more recherché effects were sought. The first act of Sartorio's *Adelaide* (Teatro San Salvatore 1672) ends in an 'illuminated royal quarry' – where Adelaide has taken refuge. A miner sings an aria accompanied by 'the hammer blows of the labourers chiselling the marble'. Some of the miners begin to pay unwelcome attention to her, and finally,

Adelaide departs from the quarry . . . two miners want to follow and molest her, but are restrained by their other companions; becoming angry they quarrel among themselves forming a curious ballet in the form of a struggle which ends the first act. When this is finished the gunpowder which has already been laid in niches in the rock is fired, and with a noisy explosion (strepitosamente sbarrando) brings many chunks of marble crashing down in pieces, throwing down some of the labourers, and at the same time changing the scene.

In the prologue too the spectacular apparatus of myth and allegory was gradually dissolved to become part of the dramatic action. The process is clear in Sartorio's *Gl'amori infruttuosi di Pirro*, text by Aureli (Teatro SS. Giovanni e Paolo 1661), the 'Argument' of which ends as follows:

on the anniversary of the day in which Pyrrhus obtained his victory over Atreus, the action of the drama begins with a public festival celebrated by the people . . . in the majestic amphitheatre of Coleo in memory of so glorious a triumph. The machines devised for this popular festival serve as Prologue to the Drama.

The characters in this opening scene include Apollo on Pegasus, a chorus of Muses in the sky, Fame on the ground, and Pyrrhus and Hermione seated on a throne. Even when the mythological and allegorical elements disappeared altogether, composers and librettists liked to begin their operas with some kind of magnificent spectacle. In Cavalli and Minato's *Scipione affricano* (Teatro SS. Giovanni e Paolo 1664) the opening scene was designed as a gladiatorial contest, complete with processions of gladiators, a double-chorus of spectators, and the fight itself, which leaves 'some dead, some wounded, yielding up their arm to the victors'.

By the 1660s it was clear that this delight in spectacle was running quite out of control. In the preface to his libretto for Mattioli's *Perseo* (Teatro SS. Giovanni e Paolo 1665), Aureli complained that 'Venetian audiences have got to such a point that they no longer know how to enjoy what they see; nor do the authors know how to invent something to satisfy the bizarre tastes of this city' (Glover 1978: 59). Bizarre is indeed the word for the combination of whimsy, cunning and infantilism with which ever-new pretexts were contrived for ever-new scenic surprises. The prologue of Cavalli and Minato's *Antioco* (Teatro San Cassiano 1659) closed with a circus-like thrill, when an *amorino* is carried off over the audience's head by a flying swan. He falls off, but clings on to one foot of the swan, which thereafter 'continues on its course with a more laborious flight'. And could anything be more bizarre than Siface's escape from his tower of imprisonment in the same authors' *Scipione affricano*? His ally Asdrubale arrives at the foot of the tower dragging the mangled corpse of one of the gladiators killed in the contest at the start of Act I. From the top of the tower Siface waves a sheet, in which he proposes to 'collect the vehement breath of the courteous zephyrs'. He breaks into aria:

> Zefiretti qua correte:
> E rendetemi quei fiati
> Che più volte sospirati
> Voi da me raccolti avete . . .[6]

during which the sheet becomes inflated like a sail. Then exclaiming 'Mà già d'aura benigna Veggio gravido il lino. Mi consegno al voler del mio Destino!',[7] Siface parachutes over the parapet into the arms of the astonished Asdrubale (*Scipione affricano*, Act I scene 16).

Writing in the same decade Ivanovich remarked how the insatiable appetite for transformation scenes and machines was having a crippling effect on the finances of the opera-houses (1681: 408). Nevertheless when the Grimani family opened their *de luxe* opera-house at San Giovanni Grisostomo in 1677, they could think of no way out of the vicious circle and set out with the obvious intention of confounding the senses with bigger and better spectacle than opera-houses had ever witnessed before. The libretto of Pallavicino and Noris's *Amore innamorata* of 1680 proudly lists the 15 machines that are to be set in motion during the course of the drama (the composer does not get a mention). The sorts of spectacular incident that punctuated the San Giovanni Grisostomo operas were indeed of a fabulous magnificence. Act I of *Carlo Re d'Italia* 1680 – Pallavicino and Noris again – incorporated a sea battle accompanied by the discharge of fire-arms and the alarming attentions of a mouth-opening sea-monster. At the close of the scene the monster 'snaps its jaws shut, and there descends upon its head the great square of a Spanish city, with an army of Moors'.

By this stage Venetian opera did indeed do much to earn the scathing condemnation that was visited on it by the enlightened critics of the eighteenth century. The collapse of artistic standards, the surrender of genuine dramatic values, was unavoidable once those who produced the operas became so obsessed with 'the marvellous'. For, as Arteaga was to remark, since such effects were 'not founded on a credence publicly established by religion or history . . . they could have no law other than that of caprice' (Arteaga 1785: 248–9).

The themes of Venetian opera

Venetian opera began in that fabled world of Classical mythology that had served the first composers of opera so well. Such a piece as Cavalli's early

Nozze di Teti e di Peleo (Teatro San Cassiano 1639) exploits to the full the whole mythological apparatus: the semi-divine characters, the choruses of dryads, oreads and zephyrs, and that pastoral ethos where

> San pigliar sensi, & effetti
> Per godere a tuoi contenti
> Fino i sassi innanimati;
> Son festanti, son ridenti
> Per gioire a tuoi diletti
> Fino gl'Arbori insensati[8] (Act I scene 8; text Persiani)

Certain elements of this mythological tradition – the lament for example, which via the *Orlando furioso* derives ultimately from Ovid's *Heroides* – survived to enrich the whole subsequent development of opera (Bianconi and Walker 1984: 683). But generally speaking the taste for mythological themes barely survived into the second half of the century. The decline of interest in the traditional kind of prologue and *intermedio*, discussed above, is a symptom of this change of taste. What interested the Venetians was not the deities and heroes of Classical mythology, not even the spectacle of mankind as the plaything of the gods, but the purely human, or perhaps one should say the merely human. If further comment was called for on the antics in which the protagonists became involved it was likely to come, not in the form of philosophical reflection from the immortals, but of earthy moralizing from the comic or lower-class characters.

During the 1640s Cavalli's favourite librettist, Giovanni Faustini, began to abandon mythological plots for ones that were, in essentials, freely invented. Generally they depict the adventures through which one or more couples of princely lovers come to maturity and discover the treasure of perfect happiness. In these adventures the most formidable obstacles must be overcome; and this is achieved by cunning and courage, by the use of disguises, by the blindest fortuitousness. Symptomatic of the complex entanglements of Faustini's plots is his use of the *antefatto*, which makes it possible both to clarify and to exacerbate the complication of the story by tracing it back far into the past. The style of plot favoured by Faustini had several operatic advantages – it could encompass a wide range of moods and settings, and provide opportunities for the astonishing use of spectacle. Most important, as Donington noted, it gives opera the archetypal power, and the poetic suggestiveness, of a fairy-tale (Donington 1981: 255).

The movement of opera away from a philosophical world of myth into an enchanted world of fantasy helped prepare the way for a strong influence from Spanish drama. As early as 1641 in the preface of *Didone*, Busenello was citing the Spaniards as his model for the practice of representing time not in hours but in years. Perhaps his interest in their plays was stimulated by his membership of the Accademia degli Incogniti, for Loredan 'was renowned for his translations from the Spanish' (Towneley Worsthorne

1954: 125). But it was the Tuscan writer Giacinto Andrea Cicognini who released the full flood of Spanish influence into the Venetian opera-house with two operas, both performed in the year 1649: *Giasone*, set by Cavalli, (Teatro S. Cassiano), and *Orontea*, set by (?)Cesti (Teatro SS. Apostoli) (cf. below p. 163). Both proved more popular than any other Italian operas of the seventeenth century, and there can be no doubt that Cicognini's texts contributed largely to this success. Though he certainly had no high ethical purpose, he introduced to the Venetian theatre some of the same qualities as Rospigliosi had to the Roman: plots with little basis in history or legend, that combined romance, comedy, and intrigue; a wide range of character-types, high and low; fast-moving action expressed in natural dialogue. He did not entirely avoid the florid rhetoric of the age, but the general effect of his style is comic: among contemporaries he was known as the 'Terenzio toscano', and he earned a complimentary reference in Goldoni's memoirs: 'parmi les Auteurs comiques que je lisois et que je relisois très souvent, Cicognini étoit celui que je préférois' (*ES*, s.v. 'Cicognini').

During the 1640s and 1650s opera became more human and faster moving, its moods veering unpredictably between the gay and the poignant, the pathetic and the humorous. A type that was handled particularly well is exemplified by Cavalli and Faustini's *La Calisto* (Teatro Sant'Apollinare 1652). The opera hovers on the verges of mythology and comedy; it blends the poetry of the one and the naughtiness of the other in an extraordinary amalgam which, notwithstanding the trappings of Olympian deities, is in essence a hymn to the pathos and ecstasy of the human condition. Probably a taste for this kind of piece was connected with the fashion for mythological burlesque which originated in Francesco Bracciolini's *Lo scherno degli dei*, a much-admired poem published in 1618 (Pirrotta 1984: 327–8).

Monteverdi's *L'incoronazione di Poppea* introduced a further type of dramatic subject, the historical.[9] But it was not until the 1650s that such operas became common, largely through the work of the librettist Nicolo Minato. Minato, citing Aristotle as his authority (e.g. Preface to *Artemisia* (Teatro SS. Giovanni e Paolo 1656)), liked to differentiate between the historical basis of his plots, the Classical sources of which he often listed in his *Argomento*, and the fanciful fictional superstructure erected upon these foundations. The scrupulous allocating of the materials of the plot to 'quello che si hà dall'Istoria' on the one hand, and to 'quello che si finge' on the other was to remain standard practice in even the most fantastical operatic travesties of known historical fact, for a century and a half. Possibly this was a quirk of scholarly punctiliousness; more likely it reflected the widely held belief, expressed by Muratori among others, that imaginative poetry penetrated to deeper levels of truth than history could, and was therefore a 'more praiseworthy, more estimable, more philosophical' art (Muratori n.d.: 80 [1706]). Minato was not notably more accurate historically than Busenello had been in *L'incoronazione di Poppea*, but he did introduce into opera a more heroic note, and this became pronounced in the later decades of the century. Wolff (1975: 16) has postulated an influence from Corneille, whose *Le Cid* introduced into drama that conflict of love and duty and that preoccupation with magnanimity, of which *Poppea* was singularly innocent, but which was soon to become an obsession of Italian opera.

But almost certainly there was another factor to help account for the more elevated tone of the historical operas of the 1680s and 1690s. Bianconi and Walker have shown how the change coincides with a darkening of the political horizon, the flaring up once more of the Turkish problem and the founding of a 'Holy League' to combat the menace. Two principal suppliers of mercenary troops for this campaign, Johann Georg II of Saxony and Ernst August of Hanover, were both involved in the new style of heroic opera. A period of crisis and idealism seemed to Johann Georg just the occasion to re-introduce opera in the Venetian style in his own domain – Pallavicino's *La Gerusalemme liberata* (Dresden 1687) – while Ernst August on his visit to Venice in 1685 and 1686 was fêted in a series of grandiose and tendentious entertainments in the private Contarini theatre at Piazzola sul Brento (Bianconi and Walker 1984: 684).

If there was some prudential, ulterior motive in the cultivation of the heroic historical opera, no connoisseur of seventeenth-century Italy will be surprised. Outside the prologues, which often referred an opera to the specific occasion of its performance, there seem to be no examples in Venice of the detailed allegorical linking together of dramatic theme and political occasion that Minato was to practise in many of the operas written after his removal to Vienna in 1669. But the taste for historical opera was presumably not unconnected with the contemporary craze for historical books and pamphlets. The thrust of these was predominantly political, 'corresponding to the merely political interests of the period, and to the doctrine of the Interest of the State'; and some of the writing, taking its cue from John Barclay's *Argenis*, was in the form of the *roman à clef*, disguising modern events in the cloak of ancient ones (Croce 1946a: 136, 120).

The dramatic structure

During the 1640s the librettos of Venetian opera gradually assumed a new and distinctive physiognomy. The tableau-like formality of the earliest operas began to crumble, and gave way to a type of dramatic action that moved fluently and continuously, and which did this without interruption from the prologue to the end of the evening. For the introduction of the simultaneous scene-change meant that, even at act-ends, there was no need for breaks in dramatic continuity. (Cf. the end of Act I of Sartorio's *Adelaide* described above, p. 132.) Each of the tableaux of *Orfeo* and of *Il ritorno d'Ulisse in patria* had had not only its own distinct setting, but its own distinct group of characters and its own dramatic function. At its best, as in *L'incoronazione di Poppea*, the new type of libretto had a cohesiveness and a momentum that never slackened its grip on the spectator. And if Busenello had few peers, at least his contemporaries aimed at a dramatic construction in which all the characters and all the threads of the action were cunningly woven into a single pattern of exposition, complication, and resolution: *proposta, nodo, scioglimento*, as Strozzi labelled the three acts of his libretto for Cavalli's *Il Romolo e 'l Remo* (Teatro SS. Giovanni e Paolo 1645). The aim was not always achieved. Juggling with pretexts for spectacle, for song and for comedy, even the most skilful librettists were rarely able to avoid occasional lapses into the episodic, the irrelevant, or the flagrantly contrived. But about the complexity of their pieces they were unapologetic. 'Idiots may find confusing those stories which are only disentangled in the final scenes', exclaimed Faustini, 'but not connoisseurs, and the studious admire them since even the most curious intellects are held in suspense by such compositions' (*Eupatra* 1655, in Rosand 1975: 290).

In the early years, relics of Renaissance theatrical practice were still found. Cavalli's *Nozze di Teti e di Peleo* (Teatro San Cassiano 1639) began like the court theatricals of an earlier age with, to quote the printed *scenario*, 'an orderly harmony of concave orichalcs . . . [to] . . . dispose tongues to silence'. And at the end of Act I of Manelli and Ferrari's *Andromeda*, 'was sung, from behind the stage, a madrigal for several voices accompanied by various instruments, then the Intermezzo took place, which was performed by three youths dressed as cupids, who performed a most graceful dance' (Rossi 1637: 83–4). Even when the prologue and *intermedio* were abandoned as independent self-contained units, those effects of scenic and sonorous magnificence associated with them were still used to articulate and variegate the texture of the entertainment.

The crucial role in this task was played by transformation scenes and ballets. As a musical effect the chorus did not survive long in Venetian opera, but as a visual effect it lasted throughout the century. Legrenzi's *Germanico sul Reno* (Teatro San Salvatore 1676) includes no less than eleven 'choruses' in the list of 'personaggi muti'. It used to be said that the chorus declined for economical reasons. But Pirrotta has pointed out that the *intermedi* that replaced them can hardly have been any cheaper: they must simply have been preferred as a foil to the principal action. And he quotes Bonarelli's preface to *Solimano* (Venice 1620), where the author remarks that in so far as the chorus had served 'to interpose between the acts and to entertain the people, [its role] can be much more worthily supplied by other means, by *intermedi* . . .' (Pirrotta 1968: 54). It was the increasing popularity of characteristic and grotesque dances in these *intermedi*, and the use of comic characters to act as a bridge from the world of historical music drama to the world of bizarre spectacle, that prepared the ground for the comic *intermezzo* of the eighteenth century (cf. below, Chapter 17).

Nothing affected the structure of Venetian opera more fundamentally than the changing role of the music, particularly of the solo aria. Increasingly the dramatic structure came to be seen as a pretext for outpourings of impassioned song.

In the 1640s there is, as yet, little sign of this. Typical of Cavalli's earliest operas are long, long scenes of carefully composed recitatives. The arias that punctuate these operas are predominantly in varieties of strophic form with ritornellos and they are introduced only for the best of reasons; for Cavalli was a composer who 'having thoroughly absorbed the precepts of the *seconda prattica*, deemed it necessary to justify any surrender of text to music' (Rosand 1976a: 94–6). All the same it is a striking commentary on the extent to which music drama had established itself during Monteverdi's career, that the justification comes not from philosophical *a priori* suppositions associated with, for example, the pastoral convention, or Platonic metaphysics, but from the nature of the drama itself. The young Cavalli uses arias for such purposes as to depict the development of a character's thoughts and feelings at a moment of dramatic crisis, or to portray the vacillating relationship of two characters at a turning point of the action in a kind of aria dialectic, as in the little knot of arias at the start of Act II of *La Didone* (Teatro San Cassiano 1641) (Rosand 1976a: 94–6).

As soon as it was understood that the justification for the use of aria in opera was dramatic rather than philosophical, the scale of musical intervention in the action increased markedly. It also became more flexible. During what Jane Glover has taught us to regard as the 'peak period' of Cavalli's career, the 1650s, Venetian opera became a wonderfully integral musico-dramatic medium in which the fluid ebb and flow of the musical invention perfectly imaged the ebb and flow in the passions of the characters, and the tensing and relaxing of the dramatic action. But by later standards the operas of the 1650s were still 'grudging with ariettas, and for the greater part in recitative style' (Preface to *Il tiranno humiliato d'amore* (Teatro SS. Giovanni e Paolo 1667), in Smith 1969–70: 66), and a further shift of the balance from recitative to aria was generally welcomed. Cesti is commonly credited with bringing this about; with persuading his collaborators that from time to time the dramatic action should be suspended to make way for lyrical reflection and self-expression. So music was given scope to expand further, and, while it may sometimes have played a modest second fiddle to the spectacle, had certainly assumed the primacy in that more subtle relationship with poetry.

138

Cavalli lived not only to see but to practise this new type of aria-based opera: his last operas, like those of his younger contemporaries, employ arias more frequently and more formally, while the composition of recitative has clearly become a more perfunctory business. The Venetian fondness for arias approached the proportions of a craze. By the 1670s operas could contain more than seventy of them.

The dramatic pretext for them grew ever more slender, like the music-party Nero decides to hold in the middle of a civic riot in Pallavicino's *Nerone*, or more incongruous, like the bare-handed fight with a lion during which Narsete sings 'Pugnerò, vincerò' in the same composer's *Diocletiano* (Teatro SS. Giovanni e Paolo 1675). And whenever opera was imported into Venice from elsewhere, as Cesti's *La Dori* (Florence 1661) was in 1663, the paring down of recitative to make room for additional arias confirmed the city's operatic priorities (Schmidt 1975: 465–6). By the 1670s some operas, such as Sartorio's *Ercole su'l Termodonte*, text by Bussani (Teatro San Salvatore 1678), contain whole sequences of scenes in which the pattern of recitatives culminating in exit-arias is already as systematically organized as it was to be twenty years later in Zeno.

Arias in mid-scene were becoming rarer. Indeed the fusion of musical and dramatic values that such a mid-scene aria necessarily entailed was becoming unusual enough for a new terminology to arise. While arias at the beginning or at the close of scenes were commonly described as 'ariettas', Beregan in his libretto for Cesti's *Il Genserico* (Teatro SS. Giovanni e Paolo 1669) shows that the term 'cavata' was already in use for an aria that was preceded and followed by recitative. Out of this the term 'cavatina' was eventually to emerge; properly it signified a little song that was, so to speak, 'excavated' from the very stuff of the dramatic action.

8 · The development of the musical language

General considerations

I have observed that the personages of the drama are winds, *amoretti*, *zeffiretti* and sirens
. . . moreover that the winds – the west winds and the north winds – have to sing. How,
dear sir, shall I be able to imitate the speech of the winds since they do not speak? And
how shall I be able to move the passions by their means? Ariadne moved the audience
because she was a woman, and equally Orpheus because he was a man and not a
wind . . .   (Monteverdi, in Arnold 1963: 116)

Monteverdi's letter dates from December 1616; and he was explaining to
his old friend Alessandro Striggio his feelings about a libretto he had just
been sent, a *favola marittima* called *Le nozze di Tetide*. The Vision of the
Renaissance humanists was undimmed. The role of music in a drama was to
move the passions by a sublimated imitation of human speech, to give a
voice of song to all that was deepest in the experience of humankind.
Several more of Monteverdi's writings, notably the preface to the Eighth
Book of Madrigals of 1638, confirm that he was endlessly fascinated by
what came to be known as the doctrine of the affections – the attempt to
classify and find formulae for the expression of 'the principal passions and
affections of our mind'. He did not flinch from the toughest tasks of such
musical characterization, as is shown by the letters to Striggio, dated May
and June 1627, in which he discussed the musical imitation of madness that
he was attempting in *La finta pazza Licori* (Stevens 1980: 314f.).

The convincing and moving expression of the affections was to remain
the primary task for a composer of opera. Despite the rival attractions of
virtuosity and scenic pomp, the better composers among Monteverdi's
successors attached a deeper significance to impassioned singing than they
did to spectacle or to massed effects of choral song and dance: that is shown
by their partiality for bringing the opera to a close with a quiet climax of
passionate intimacy – a vogue Monteverdi himself had established with the
closing love-duets of *Il ritorno d'Ulisse in patria* and *L'incoronazione di
Poppea*. For Scarlatti at the end of the century no less than for Monteverdi
at the beginning the first requirement of a good libretto was that the
characters were placed in dramatic situations that wrung the heart. He
found Salvi's text for *Il gran Tamerlano* (Pratolino 1706) 'of the things for
drama which I have had through my hands, if not the best, at least among
the most choice and sure of good results, because it has a strong plot,

handled . . . in such a way that it is almost impossible, at the mere reading of it, not to feel the movements of the different passions which it contains' (Donington 1981: 263). Even in the decadent 1670s composers were judged for the skill they showed in bringing characters and their emotions to musical life: Pallavicino's *Nerone* was much admired by the correspondent of the *Mercure galant* for its 'elegance' and 'wit', and 'one cannot praise too highly the admirable skill he has of providing the characters in an opera with material that is suited to each' (Smith 1969–70: 63).

For some years the survival of the prologue and the periodic interventions of deities in the business of the drama enabled composers to preserve much of the musical richness of the Renaissance *intermedi*. Arnold remarks that just as 'Monteverdi crowded into [*Orfeo*] all the musical forms known in 1607, to express a totality of human emotion, [so] *Il ritorno d'Ulisse* does exactly the same thing in terms of 1640' (Arnold 1963: 120). There are chamber-duets, *madrigali guerrieri*, ballets, light ariettas in the latest fashion; nor is Orphic singing entirely dead. Indeed that kind of rhapsodic, florid arioso was to remain the favoured medium for the epiphany of divinities into the second half of the century.

By the middle of the century, however, this *intermedio*-like opulence was being pared down. There was obviously no alternative in the less well endowed opera-houses like the Teatro Sant'Apollinare where Cavalli did much of his best work in the 1650s. At the same time Venetian audiences were becoming besotted with the sensuous pleasures afforded by great singing, and admired the most eloquent of their virtuosos with a cultic fervour. Solo arias began to occupy more room, and to be composed in more brilliant and architecturally imposing forms. These tendencies encouraged the absorption of instrumental idioms into song. This was a feature of style latent in opera from the first, in the sequential quasi-instrumental dance-songs of *Orfeo*, and still more in the ostinato-based arias so numerous in *Poppea*. It became far more pronounced with the exploitation of virtuosity in the late 1650s; while the fondness of Sartorio and his contemporaries for introducing *obbligato* instruments, notably trumpets, in certain of the grander arias encouraged a concerto-like emulation between voice and instruments. By the last quarter of the century, the expressive range of opera depended not upon the variety of musical genres it accommodated, but on the variety of musical expression that composers had learnt to pack into the solo aria.

The elderly Monteverdi could still enjoy the challenge of creating a musical architecture out of the events of the drama. In the suitor's scene, Act II scene 5 in *Il ritorno d'Ulisse*, for example, he creates a rondo-like structure unified by periodic recurrences of the trio 'Ama dunque sì sì'. But music's role remained that of 'sensitively tracing the word in an emotive gesture' (Osthoff 1960: 113); and since with *L'incoronazione di Poppea* the

141

neoclassical drama was ousted by a fast-moving drama of intrigue there was to be little scope henceforth for that kind of architectural repose. Monteverdi's late masterpiece must have provided the inspiration for much of what was best in Cavalli's sense of operatic design. In the 1640s and 1650s he evolved an idiom of wonderfully flexible strength; recitative yielded to arioso and arioso to aria with little or no hiatus in the flow of music, so that the dramatic idea could be realized with seemingly effortless spontaneity and sensibility.

With the feverish cultivation of the solo aria in the second half of the century this structural fluidity was gradually destroyed: the music flowed with a less spontaneous and immediate response to the dramatic need. Recitative became increasingly a matter of functional declamation that had little time for the insinuating charm or the touches of rhetorical magic in which earlier generations had delighted. Arias, on the other hand, now often set apart from the dramatic action by formal ritornellos, tended to abandon themselves to flights of musical fancy during which the poetry and even the dramatic situation from which the aria took its rise were largely lost from sight. Despite this more emphatic distinction between recitative and aria, librettists and composers continued to the end of the century to enjoy some degree of flexibility in the way they laid out the scenes. But there was no overlooking the tendency to regard the aria as their climax and their primary purpose. As the French traveller Limojon de St Didier reported in 1680,

They that compose the Musick of the Opera, endeavor to conclude the Scenes of the Principal Actors with Airs that Charm and Elevate, that so they may acquire the Applause of the Audience, which succeeds so well to their intentions, that one hears nothing but a Thousand *Benissimo*'s together . . .   (Grout 1947: 103)

The resources of the recitative style

In the early years of Venetian opera much use was made of an expressive and rhetorical kind of recitative that came close to the ideals of the first opera composers. Few of the devices proved by Monteverdi were not taken up by the young Cavalli, albeit to be 'handled . . . in a less extreme manner' (*The New Grove*, s.v. 'Cavalli'). Narrative and conversational texts, questions and exclamations all had their matching musical manners; for the emotional heightening of the more pathetic scenes a whole array of devices could be drawn upon – word repetitions and obsessive refrains, carefully controlled harmonic intensifications, poignant chromaticisms and stark juxtapositions of unrelated chords, even Peri's celebrated pedal point style had lost little of its force in Cavalli's writing (see Ex.II.3); more flamboyant emphasis could be achieved by 'madrigalian' flourishes on individual words and phrases, or by eruptions of fanfare-like declamation in the style of the

Turn your pullulating leaves into ears, and listen, I beg you, listen to my
bitter and greater woes.

Ex.II.3 Cavalli, *L'Egisto* (1643), Act III scene 5

madrigale guerriero. An early Cavalli opera such as *Egisto* (Teatro San
Cassiano 1643) shows that recitative could still be rich and powerful enough
to hold an audience enthralled through a scene without any need for a
crowning aria. The first scene of Act III is an extended love scene for Lideo
and Clori the text of which is laid out to suggest a pattern of duet–
recitative–duet; but its closing section, its sensuous lyrical climax, is set in a
recitative-cum-arioso style. Later in the act the whole of Egisto's mad-
scene, including the lines in short metre, is likewise set in a style hovering
between recitative and arioso.

The importance of arioso in Cavalli's operas, particularly those he wrote
in collaboration with Faustini between 1642 and 1652, has already been
suggested. He used it to capture some spontaneous impulse of joy or
tenderness in the hearts of his characters, or to underline one of his poet's
aphorisms, or to act as a transition between the recitative and the aria.
Cavalli's younger contemporaries recognized arioso as a precious dramatic
resource and imitated it eagerly and resourcefully; sometimes they used it
in ensemble form. In Cavalli's own later music, particularly after his return
from France in 1662, his arioso style is affected by the 'instrumentalizing'
tendencies of the age, inclining to become more energetic, more systematically patterned and rhythmed, as may be seen in Ex.II.4. Much of
the treasury of expressive and rhetorical device stored up by Monteverdi
and Cavalli, particularly perhaps the option of gliding into and out of
arioso, remained current almost to the end of the century. Eloquent recitative and arioso is to be found throughout Sartorio, and in the early works
of Pallavicino and even of Pollarolo.

143

FARNACE

m'an-no - di 'l cor men - tre mi scio - - -

- gli il pie - de_____ etc.

. . .you bind my heart while you loosen my foot. . .

Ex.II.4 Cavalli, *Pompeo Magno* (1666), Act I scene 2

All the same, by the 1660s there is no doubt that it was becoming less common than it had been. Reasons are not far to seek. The fast-moving dramatic intrigue popularized by such librettists as Aureli and Cicognini in the late 1640s and 1650s demanded a more conversational delivery of the recitative. More life-like characterization was necessarily embodied in a less formal and elevated poetic tone, and that too inevitably pushed composers in the direction of what came to be the style of *recitativo secco*. The tendency was encouraged by the profusion and expressive variety of the arias. And with the development in the last two decades of the century towards a more systematic and rational libretto structure, in which pride of place was given to the recit→ aria type of scene, composers had even less occasion to indulge their fanciful, lyrical and expressive impulses in the recitative.

A word must be said about accompanied recitative. Cavalli had made occasional use of it (rarely more than once an opera) in the 1640s, and it retained its place as a very special dramatic resource throughout the century. Sometimes it was used for scenes of overwhelming pathos – a remarkable example is the scene of Euridice's death in Sartorio's *Orfeo* (Teatro San Salvatore, 1672) (Ex.II.5). But in general the accompanied recitative was valued not so much as a means of intensifying the passions of the singer as of bathing the entire scene in a peculiar, supernatural atmosphere: sleep scenes, magic scenes, scenes set in the underworld provided the best pretexts.

Alas, alas, ye Gods, I die; a cruel serpent kills me, a deadly poison closes these eyes in the womb of eternal cold.

Ex.II.5 Sartorio, *L'Orfeo* (1672), Act II scene 21

The language of song

Take up a score of Monteverdi's *Ritorno d'Ulisse* or *Poppea* and one cannot but be struck by a new phenomenon. Each of them contains a profusion of lilting, caressing arias in $\frac{3}{1}$ or $\frac{3}{2}$ metre. A classic description of this new style was given by Bukofzer, though we need not follow him in labelling it 'bel

145

canto' (Bukofzer 1947: 118–20). The exquisitely fashioned melodies, their elegant seriousness, the languorous ease with which they float up out of the recitative and dissolve back into it have often prompted comparison with the new cantata style cultivated in Rome at the time by Luigi Rossi and Carissimi. But the style was introduced to Venetian opera, as far as we can now judge, by the young Cavalli, one of the 'new swans' singled out by Bonlini in 1641 in his account of the origins of opera (Solerti 1903: 139).

In the early years a majority of these triple-time arias were short, simple and – where they were not framed by instrumental ritornellos – informal. No less than the recitative, they lent themselves readily to such effects as the expressive colouring of individual words by harmonic means; and 'madrigalian' touches of tone-painting were common too, touches that embellished or highlighted or imparted an extra poetic resonance to some detail in the text. But the feature that was perhaps most important for the future development of the aria was the tendency of these touches of musical imagery to break away from mere rhetorical functionalism and to become figures in their own right, extended and varied in flowing melismatic patterns that begin to give the aria an autonomous sense and shape. All the charm, all the telling expressive and symbolic detail, all the burgeoning lyrical impulses of the Cavalli style are found at the opening of *Statira* (Teatro SS. Giovanni e Paolo 1655) (Ex.II.6).

The origins of this type of aria are not yet clear. Perhaps they are essentially nothing more than amplifications of those brief episodes of arioso common in both the opera and the cantata of the period, and arise therefore from some dramatic or metrical point in the text. It will certainly do no harm to emphasize that for several decades yet composers were to depend on the forms as well as the content of the libretto for many of their musical ideas. At the same time the influence of fashionable dances and even popular song cannot be overlooked. The letters of a younger contemporary of Cavalli's, Pietro Andrea Ziani, who began composing for the Venetian theatres in the mid-1650s, show how aware he was of the public taste for 'canzonettas' (Wolff 1975: 39). If Cavalli's arias had often been redolent of minuets and sarabandes, Ziani and the later Venetians, notably Legrenzi, drew on a whole range of popular dance and song types.

The dancing rhythms and the more popular tone that became so pronounced a feature of the operas of Ziani and Cesti in the late 1650s and 1660s gradually drove out of fashion the fastidious lyricism of Cavalli. Nor could he keep pace with a more flamboyant kind of virtuosity. The madrigalian melismas through which his own arias had flowed so effortlessly, now paraded themselves altogether more ostentatiously (see Ex.II.7). It must have been a distressing and humiliating experience for the elderly master when his last two operas, *Eliogabalo* (1668) and *Massenzio* (1673), failed to reach the stage. What happened in the case of the former is

The musical language

Ex. II.6 Cavalli, *La Statira* (1655), Act I scene 1

re - no al   Sol

_____   al   Sol   al_____   Di - - e_____

Night, hide the treasures of thy twinkling, sparkling stars; let one star
only shine on me here on earth, and make my eyes renounce the
brightness of the sun and the daylight.

Ex.II.6 *continued*

unknown, but *Massenzio* was actually dropped during rehearsals, and a
commission to recompose the text given to Sartorio. Cavalli's setting had
failed to please, reported Dolfin, 'for lack of spirited ariettas' (*The New
Grove*, s.v. 'Sartorio').

The cult of the virtuoso singer, the rhythm of dance, the inflections of
popular song provided much of the inspiration for the brilliant and
ingratiating aria style of the last third of the century. It drew on two further
sources of energy. The first was still the poet's verses, particularly the
rhythm of the poet's verses. The *parlando* style of song favoured for comic
characters had long since introduced a kind of lean muscularity into certain
parts of the score. Increasingly this style was adopted by the serious
characters; their more exuberant numbers had a spanking vigour typified
by those driving up-beat rhythms on which the early concerto was to draw
so heavily. Pallavicino's *Messalina* (Act II scene 12) provides an example of
this (Ex.II.8). Still more crucial was the mutual interaction of vocal and
instrumental idioms. The somewhat impassive ostinato and quasi-ostinato
basses of Monteverdi and the young Cavalli began to absorb distinctive
figures, analogous to the 'madrigalisms' in the voice. So they became
livelier, more characteristic, and could be sustained in quasi-sequential
patterns that gave more energy to the aria, and set it more emphatically
apart from the recitative. And once the bass was so full of character, it
suggested to the composer all manner of possibilities for contrapuntal
interplay between itself and the voice, which in the hands of an imaginative
musical dramatist provided an invaluable resource for exploring complex
states of mind.[1]

Such an example as that shows that it is unnecessary to regard develop-

At the horrible glitter of your sword let the She-wolf of Romulus and the Ausonian Hills tremble and fall.

Ex.II.7 P. A. Ziani, *Attila* (1672), Act I scene 1

Happiness is close at hand, I feel my whole heart rejoice. . .

Ex.II.8 Pallavicino, *Messalina* (1679), Act II scene 12

ments in the aria style in the later seventeenth century as being necessarily anti-dramatic. The aria had become, potentially at least, more searching emotionally and psychologically, not merely more self-indulgent musically. And quite new types of aria had appeared. For certain particularly solemn scenes composers were likely to write in a fully contrapuntal style (see, for example, Pallavicino's *Messalina* (Act III scene 2) in Ex.II.9.) In *Il Titone* (Teatro SS. Giovanni e Paolo 1666), Cesti introduced a type of aria in which a widely arching cantilena slowly unfolds over throbbing repeated chords in the strings, a conception from which composers of Italian opera down to Handel were to draw some of their most sublime effects.

The forms of song

In origin the operatic aria was a strophic form. The first classic collection of 'arias', in Caccini's *Nuove musiche*, shows that the term was associated with a type of song in which, against a bass that remained constant from verse to verse, the voice discanted in continually varied melodies. Arias in this sense were introduced in the prologues of the first operas, including *Orfeo*, and were still being used for the same purpose in the first years of Venetian opera. But by now the musical structures tended to be more sophisticated. In *Il ritorno d'Ulisse*, for example, the variation strophes sung by L'Humana fragilità are set apart not only by orchestral ritornellos, but by contrasting episodes sung by other allegorical figures, Tempo, Fortuna and Amore. Strophic form was also common in more tunefully song-like arias. Often the number of verses is surprisingly large, though composers tended to leave some of them out, or set them as recitative. In Act II scene 1 of *Egisto*, Cavalli sets only four of the six verses Faustini provided for Egisto's 'Lasso io vivo'.

By the 1650s composers had become more conscious of the potentially undramatic effect of the strophic aria, and the form was altogether less ubiquitous. It continued to be used in the *intermedio*-like episodes of an opera, sung by the comic characters or the divinities who had no direct involvement in the central intrigue. But when the leading characters sang strophic songs it was in situations where they made good dramatic sense: lovers might express the union of their souls in a strophic song shared out between them; or the form might be used in dramatic monologues where time indeed stood still. In such scenes the old recitative-like aria was still in use. A fine example is found in Act II of *Calisto* where Juno (a principal character despite being a goddess) expresses her rage and jealousy in dignified *endecasillabi* which Cavalli has set in the strophic variation form of the prologues of old.

I die, yes, I die innocent. . .

Ex.II.9 Pallavicino, *Messalina* (1679), Act III scene 2

Among the strophic types of aria a very special place was held by the lament, the opera's 'principal object of curiosity' in the judgement of Ivanovich (Towneley Worsthorne 1954: 71). Like the immortal lament of Monteverdi's *Arianna*, the earliest examples in Venetian opera were in an impassioned recitative style. But Monteverdi left another model: the *Lamento della ninfa* published in his Eighth Book of madrigals, an

Note Four verses in all - each slightly varied

His weary soul faded away; alas, he breathed out his life; Coroebus, oh God, died and left me alone. He wanted me as his bride, and I weep here, left a widow before I was a bride.

Ex.II.10a Cavalli, *Didone* (1641), Act I scene 4

Trembling spirit, weak and drooping, leave me at once; let my soul go
there where gloomy Erebus greedily awaits it.

Ex.II.10b Cavalli, *Didone* (1641), Act I scene 7

unbroken flow of poignant soprano melody unfolding over a 34-times
repeated ostinato bass. The publication included some interesting remarks
on the performance of the piece, which must also surely apply to the
operatic lament of the period: it is to be sung at the speed suggested by the
passions of the soul ('a tempo del'affetto del animo') and not in strict time
('non a quello de la mano'). Such laments were introduced to the opera-
house by Cavalli early in his career, and at least one example is found in all
his scores from *Didone* (1641), his third opera, onwards. It is worth quoting
two of the remarkable laments from this opera to show the form at the point
of crystallization: Cassandra's 'L'alma fiacca' is not far removed from the
recitative origins; Hecuba's 'Tremulo spirito' on the other hand – in which
each phrase graphically illustrates her choking despair by breaking off
before the cadence – adopts the flowing $\frac{3}{2}$ lyrical style, the classic lament
manner until the end of the century (see Ex.II.10).
    Strophic variation forms and ostinato bass forms both with and without
orchestral ritornellos provided the mainstay of the operatic structure in the

1640s and 1650s. In passing it may be reiterated that many of the flowing triple-metre arias described earlier are subject to no strict formal organization; they are ariosi writ large in which the unfolding of the lyricism obeys the promptings of the text. Towards 1660, as arias came to assume a more dominant position in the opera, the structure of the individual arias became more expansive and more formalized. A wide range of formal types were employed, of which only one need be mentioned. In Faustini's librettos strophic verse had become less common; on the other hand he made much use of refrain texts, encouraging Cavalli to cultivate a ternary aria structure, an ABA pattern. Out of this, during the 1660s and 1670s the *da capo* aria was to evolve, a process conveniently illustrated in the work of Pallavicino. In his first opera, *Demetrio* (Teatro San Moisè 1666), a quarter of the arias are in effect *da capo* arias, though the repeat of the opening section is written out in full at the close. By the time of *Vespasiano*, composed 12 years later for the inauguration of the new Teatro San Giovanni Grisostomo, more than three-quarters of the arias are examples of the *da capo* form (Smith 1969–70: 66). At this period the decision to cast an aria in that form was often the composer's rather than the poet's. Two arias in Act I scene 5 of Pallavicino's *Messalina* have strophic verses which the composer has set in *da capo* form.

Venetian composers showed no very highly developed interest in ensemble singing. Such complex ensemble or chorus numbers as one does find in their scores – the opening chorus of mariners from Cesti's *L'Argia*, for instance – are commonly a sign that the opera originated elsewhere: in this case Innsbruck. In the local repertory they rather rarely attempted anything more grand than a duet, and these rare cases treat the voices generically rather than individually. In the Infernal scenes of Ziani's *Fatiche d'Ercole*, for example, there are several effective little trios for the damned souls of Sisiphus, Ixion and Tantalus.

If larger-scale ensembles were neglected, in most Venetian operas the love duet was likely to rival the lament as the *pièce de résistance*; and for the obvious reason that here too the composer could explore the power of lyrical song to express the passions of the heart. The clinging sensuousness of the duets that close Monteverdi's two last operas set a pattern that was to serve for most of Cavalli's career; but the duet, no less than the solo aria, was affected in the second half of the century by the growing taste for virtuosity, by the adoption of a more incisive, instrumental style of melisma, and by the reabsorption of contrapuntal principles. In the opening movement of *Orfeo* (1672) Sartorio composed a duet developed to the point where it could embrace simultaneously the brilliant and the gorgeous: this kind of piece is not far distant in style from Steffani's chamber duets (see Ex.II.11).

Ex.II.11 Sartorio, *L'Orfeo* (1672), Act I scene 1

155

- - - ge   al mio te - so - - -

m'u - ni - sce   al ben ch'a -

9 8   #   6

- - - - - - - - - - - (ro)

do - - - - - - ro

4 3

Dear and pleasing chain that binds me to my treasure. . . / that unites me
to the loved one I adore. . .

Ex.II.11 *continued*

The opera orchestra

The expansion of scale in arias and duets went hand in hand with a fuller
involvement of the orchestra; between 1640 and the end of the century,
there was a steady reduction in the proportion of arias accompanied simply
by the continuo instruments. At the beginning of Cavalli's career in the
theatre the orchestra's role in arias was confined strictly to the playing of
framing ritornellos. And several details in his autograph scores show that
well into the 1650s he hardly thought of these ritornellos as an integral part
of the aria at all: sometimes the decision to include them seems to have been
taken only after the aria had been composed, and regularly they are merely
cued in in some form of musical shorthand. During the 1650s, however, it
became increasingly his practice to involve the orchestra in the body of the
aria, punctuating, echoing, reduplicating the phrases of the singer; this
concertato-like antiphony of voice and orchestra was to remain standard
practice for decades. Only rather infrequently, even in Cavalli's latest
music, do the orchestral ritornellos and interjections and antiphonies flood
over into the sung sections of the aria. I quote one of these rare examples,
from *Pompeo Magno* (Teatro San Salvatore 1666), where in the space of a

156

dozen bars the orchestra functions as ritornello, *concertato* element, and sonorous background to the voice (Ex.II.12).

As composers began to recognize something of the structural possibilities of the emerging system of tonality the ritornello became an important factor in their modulatory strategy, used to clarify and reinforce the sequence of keys through which the music moved. 'Vaghi fiori' from Sartorio's *Orfeo* provides a succinct example (Ex.II.13). By this time too the ritornello was itself becoming a more organized limb of the structure, and in it much of the aria's potential for development was latent. A ritornello from Pallavicino's *Diocletiano* (Teatro SS. Giovanni e Paolo 1674) shows what was to become the standard ritornello design: an incipit that takes its shape from the decisive declamation of the opening line of text; a melismatic passage which is to be the source of much of the aria's momentum and virtuosity; and a cadence phrase (see Ex.II.14).

The appearance of the *concitato* style in Monteverdi's *Combattimento di Tancredi e Clorinda* has been claimed to mark 'the autonomy of the instrumental spirit, its calculated involvement in the dramatic action' (Osthoff 1960: 26). Those instrumental traditions that he had taken over into *Orfeo* from the Renaissance *intermedi* were abandoned. No longer was there any need for that profusion and variety of colour on which the old associational style of instrumentation was based, for now Monteverdi was in search of an instrumental musical language that could speak eloquently by virtue of its melodies, rhythms and harmonies. Here was 'the root of that thought which generated the doctrine of figures' – the *Figurenlehre* of the seventeenth- and eighteenth-century theorists (Weaver 1964: 88). In the Venetian opera-house, as in the Barberini theatre, the orchestra was reduced to a small ensemble of strings and continuo instruments.

If Weaver is right, the fruits of this quest for instrumental eloquence must, in most respects, be accounted disappointing. We certainly must not anticipate a generation of tone-poets in any Romantic sense. In the second act of *Didone* Cavalli essays a *sinfonia navale*, to accompany the 'shipwreck of a larger part of the Trojan fleet': in scale and conception it seems ludicrously inadequate (Ex.II.15). Nor were such opportunities seized more enterprisingly by a subsequent generation. Act III of Ziani's *Attila* requires a sinfonia for the 'play of the machines' during which Amore, Fama and Marte are whisked away into the heavens. Ziani's score provides three bars of figured bass. In so far as orchestral imagination did blossom it was in the context not of spectacle but of song: in those heroic trumpet arias in which Sartorio delighted, and particularly, in the 1680s and 90s, with Pollarolo, who of Italian opera composers was the first to establish the oboe as a regular constituent of the orchestra, and whose carefully calculated variety of timbre and textures shows a keen and new sense of the dramatic and psychological potential of orchestral colour.

157

POMPEO

So - no al - pestri

son spi - no - se di vir - tù le vie

sco - sce - se

Mountainous and thorny are the rugged paths of virtue. . .

Ex.II.12 Cavalli, *Pompeo Magno* (1666), Act I scene 11

EURIDICE

Va - ghi fiori, a - meni pra - ti,

Viola stave is blank

ver - di pompe d'odo - ro - sa Prima -

ve - ra fredda Borea coi suoi fiati mai non soffi, mai non

soffi in voi pro - cel - le

Ex.II.13 Sartorio, *L'Orfeo* (1672), Act I scene 16

ma se - re-ne in Ciel le (stelle)

etc. for a further 13 bars
accompanied by continuo
and closing:

dol - ce ru - gia - da

Pretty flowers, smiling meadows, green glories of the perfumed spring,
may cold Boreas with his winds never blow his tempests on you. . .but the
stars serene in the sky. . .sweet dew.

Ex.II.13 *continued*

Of the more formal independent orchestral movements – toccatas,
sinfonias, etc. – Monteverdi's late opera scores and Cavalli's often give only
the sketchiest details. Clearly they were worked out in full only after the
main work of composition was over, perhaps at rehearsal. Traditional or
improvised trumpet signals were still in use both as part of the dramatic
action and to summon spectators into the auditorium (Glover 1978: 111).

The two-movement sinfonia at the start of *L'incoronazione di Poppea* is a
comparatively familiar example of a form that was common at the period, in

Ex.II.14 Pallavicino, *Diocletiano* (1674), Act I scene 3

which a solemn chordal opening was transformed into a lively second movement by the kind of rhythmic variation procedure that was common in contemporary dance suites. By the 1660s the second movement was usually quite independent of the first and often more contrapuntal in style. This has sometimes been seen as possibly a result of French influence – the Lullian French Overture was well established by the late 1650s – but that is by no means a necessary conclusion. There was, after all, a flourishing tradition of instrumental music in Italy and, in one case at least, the habit of drawing on that repertory for the opera-house is clearly established: no less than eight of Legrenzi's operatic sinfonias are taken from his collections of instrumental sonatas (*The New Grove*, s.v. 'Legrenzi'). An interesting development in the sinfonia that was to survive to the time of Handel was that of fusing together the sinfonia and the opening scene of the opera. After the development of the three-movement sinfonia (a slow chordal opening, a quasi-polyphonic second movement, a dance-like finale), a form already popular by the 1660s, it became common practice to make the final 'dance' the ritornello of the opening vocal number; an early example is provided by Cesti's *L'Argia* (Innsbruck 1655, rev. Venice, Teatro San Salvatore 1669).

Sinfonia navale

Ex.II.15 Cavalli, *Didone* (1641), Act II scene 5

9 · Cesti's *L'Orontea* (?Venice 1649, Innsbruck 1656, Venice 1666)

An early repertory opera

In 1665 an opera-house was opened in Macerata, a small provincial city in the hills of the Marches. The inauguration was marked with a performance of *Orontea*, and in the libretto printed for the occasion the opera was described as 'the famous Orontea, which defying time and death still lives gloriously in the world' being performed 'in the noblest theatres of the chief cities of Italy' (Holmes 1968b: 115). That an opera just 16 years old should be described as 'defying time and death' tells us much about the ephemerality of the art in the mid-seventeenth century. But by the standards of the age the longevity of *Orontea* was remarkable; only Cavalli's *Giasone* could rival it as the most widely and frequently staged Italian opera of the century. By the time it reached Macerata it had enjoyed performances in – among other places – Genoa, Milan, Turin and Innsbruck; after the Macerata inauguration its fame spread further afield, from Brescia and Bergamo in the north of Italy to Naples and Palermo in the south; in 1678 it even reached distant Hanover (Bianconi 1982: 15).

Though it was first performed in Venice and/or Innsbruck, *Orontea* was an opera with Tuscan origins. It was the work of Giacinto Cicognini, a Florentine poet and playwright, and of Pietro Cesti, a Franciscan monk from Arezzo. Between 1643 and 1649 Cesti was attached to the cathedral at Volterra, first as organist, later as *maestro di cappella*, and it was during these years that he came into contact with some of the leading figures of a Florentine literary academy – the Accademia dei Percossi – one of whom, Giulio Maffei, owned property near Volterra (*The New Grove*, s.v. 'Cesti'). With two of the 'Percossi', the painter Salvator Rosa and the poet G. F. Apolloni – a fellow Aretino – Cesti enjoyed a close friendship. Cicognini, the most successful Italian dramatist of the age, the 'Tuscan Terence', was another member of the group. It was during these Volterra years too that Cesti became increasingly attracted to the operatic stage, a fascination that was soon to become scandalous and lead to a number of inconveniences with his ecclesiastical superiors. He appeared in a leading role in an opera staged at Siena in 1647 for the inauguration of the restored theatre there, and by 1650 had become such a celebrity in the world of opera that Salvator

Rosa could describe him as 'the glory and splendour of the secular stage' (*DBI*, s.v. 'Cesti').[1]

Towards the end of his life Cicognini wrote four opera librettos, of which *Orontea* (Venice, Teatro di SS. Apostoli 1649) was the third, and the last to be performed in his own lifetime. Scholars are unable to agree whether the music for this 1649 version was by the young Cesti, or by a still younger Venetian composer, Francesco Luccio (cf. *The New Grove*, s.v. 'Cesti'; and *DBI*, s.v. 'Cesti'). That is not an overwhelmingly important issue; what does matter is that something, whether in the text or the music, delighted and fascinated audiences irresistibly, and that Cicognini's *Orontea* was embarked on a long and extraordinarily complicated series of adventures and peregrinations.

We meet it next in Naples, where it was performed to open the first season of opera to be staged in a public theatre there, the Teatro San Bartolomeo, in 1654. The introduction of opera to Naples has already been described in Chapter 6. It was essentially the work of a group of musicians known as the Febi Armonici who had first come together in Rome in 1646 under the protection of the Conte d'Oñate, the Spanish ambassador. In due course they followed him to Naples, where since 1648 he had been viceroy, and for some years staged operas in the royal palace under the artistic direction of their 'virtuoso di canto e maestro compositore', Francesco Cirillo. Both at court and later for the Teatro San Bartolomeo, Cirillo composed operas of his own, but he also adapted for his company some of the finest Venetian operas, Monteverdi's *Poppea* and Cavalli's *Giasone* among them. *Orontea* was described as 'enriched with new music by F. Cirillo', which leaves unresolved the question of whether it was an original work or an adaptation of the 1649 score.

In the later history of the opera only two episodes need be mentioned. From 1652 to 1657 Cesti was employed at the Archducal court at Innsbruck. He was joined there in 1653 by his old friend Apolloni, who became court poet. During their years together in the Tyrolean capital they collaborated on a number of operas. *L'Argia* (1655) and *La Dori* (1657) were both original pieces; but between those dates Apolloni took up Cicognini's famous *Orontea* once more, revised the text slightly, and added a prologue of his own devising, an allegorical debate between Filosofia and Amore. Cesti reworked his 1649 score (or composed the opera for the first time), and it was staged during the Carnival celebrations in February 1656; it enjoyed another brilliant success. Ten years later *Orontea* returned to Venice where, at short notice, it replaced a planned revival of Cavalli's *Doriclea*. It was entirely typical of the period that the Innsbruck version of the score should be deemed insufficiently generous in its provision of arias, and four additional ones were borrowed for the occasion from *L'Argia*. This 1666 version of the opera is perhaps that preserved in the manuscript at Magdalene College, Cambridge and familiar from the recording directed by René Jacobs. It is the basis for the comments in the rest of this chapter.

Cicognini as librettist

Compared with most of the librettists of Venetian opera, Cicognini's output of texts for music was modest, a tiny proportion of his vast production of dramatic work. Yet of these four libretti two, *Giasone* and *Orontea*, were the most successful operas of the century. Their popularity and his more general notoriety as a man of the theatre meant that he had an impact on the development of opera out of all proportion to the extent of his involvement with it. And when the style of seventeenth-century opera fell into disrepute it was he who was made the scapegoat for its deficiencies. The scornful severity of Crescimbeni's denunciation was to re-echo throughout the eighteenth century:

In order the more to flatter with novelty the listless appetites of the spectators, which were nauseated alike by the baseness of the comic style and the gravity of the tragic style, [Cicognini] the inventor of dramas, united the one with the other . . . giving rise to a practice of unheard-of monstrosity, involving kings and heroes and other illustrious personages, and buffoons and servants and the basest of men. This muddle of characters was the reason for the total destruction of the rules of poetry, which so fell into disuse that no care was taken even over diction; the latter, constrained to be the servant of music, lost its purity, and was filled with idiocies.

(Quoted, in Italian, Holmes 1968b: 118)

Giacinto Andrea Cicognini lived from 1606 to 1651. He was a lawyer by training, but came from a stage-struck family. His father, also a lawyer, was himself an author of plays, an acquaintance and correspondent of Lope de Vega, and was traditionally reported to have had the whimsical notion of entrusting much of his son's education to Pier Maria Cecchini, a famous Fritellino of the day (*DBI*, s.v. 'Cicognini'). Giacinto Andrea, it transpired, needed little prompting to abandon a career in the law-courts for one in the theatre. He became a hugely productive author of comedies, tragedies and sacred dramas, many of them adaptations of Spanish classics by Calderón, Tirso de Molina and others, earning himself, among his Italian contemporaries, a reputation as the greatest dramatist of the century. The chaotic profusion of his writings and the brevity of his life made it easy for unscrupulous impresarios and authors to borrow his name to help ensure success for their own productions.

In seventeenth-century Italy Spanish drama enjoyed a popularity comparable with that of English drama in the Netherlands and northern Germany. From Naples, which for obvious political reasons was the major centre for Spanish culture, travelling theatre companies carried the repertory widely throughout the peninsula. With its complicated ravelling and unravelling of intrigue, its attempts at natural, lifelike characterization, its startling contrasts of mood and tone, the bombastic rhetoric of its purple patches, this Spanish drama found receptive audiences and eager imitators everywhere. It became a fundamental source of Cicognini's eclecticism as he came to terms with the philosophy and practicalities of what has been described as 'consumer-theatre'.

This was no bad background for someone coming to work in opera, and much of Cicognini's dramatic inheritance was in fact taken over into his librettos. They have many scenes of fast-moving, natural-sounding conversation and argument, with an animated and spontaneous give and take between the characters. The comic scenes are not partitioned off from the main action in *intermezzo*-like interludes, but are inextricably tangled up with it. Cast lists represent a real cross-section of life: in *Orontea* there are two pairs of lovers, one royal – Orontea, Queen of Egypt, and Floridan, Prince of Phoenicia (who spends almost all the opera as Alidoro, an irresistibly charming, blithely amoral painter, in whom, it has been suggested, there may be a trace of Salvator Rosa himself (*ES*, s.v. 'Cesti')) – the other from among the courtiers of the royal household – Silandra and Corindo; there are characters who interpret, encourage or oppose these romances, Tibrino the page-boy, the 'Cherubino of the piece' (Jacobs 1982: 13), and the severe philosopher Creonte; and there is a splendid trio of earthy comedy characters, the drunken servant Gelone; the lady-in-waiting Giacinta, who, for reasons into which we need not enter, spends the opera disguised as a man; and the aged and lecherous nurse Aristea. The deftness with which the experienced dramatist manipulates these elements is well suggested by Donington: 'almost every scene offers strong drama or strong humour, with plenty of excitement, and the liveliest blend of very funny comedy and very romantic entanglements – some cynical, some heartfelt, but all obviously destined to work out happily in the end' (1981: 255).

But Cicognini also saw that opera had its own peculiar problems and opportunities. He saw, for instance, that while entangled plots and disguises and mistaken identities might be a source of much of the thrill of the contemporary theatre, they needed to be more strictly disciplined in lyric drama. And so his librettos are 'not only more clearly constructed than his prose plays, but also simpler and more lucid than most other opera texts of that time' (*MGG*, s.v. 'Cicognini'). In his language too our author is far less self-indulgent than his eighteenth-century reputation might lead us to expect. When Alidoro thanks Orontea for his rescue and exclaims

> Comanda tu che sia
> Cinto il mio piede da servil catena;
> Ed in quei ferrati giri,
> Instupidito il mondo
> La tua clemenza, e le mie pompe ammiri[2]   (Act I scene 9)

he reaches a modest pitch of baroque rhetoric that is nowhere else in the libretto overtopped.

With a self-effacement remarkable in so distinguished an author, Cicognini recognized that in this particular type of theatre it was music that worked the magic, or – if one wishes to put it at its lowest – that gratified an audience's hedonism. The librettist's task was to fashion a drama of a kind that gave music ample opportunity to exert these powers. It must have been one of the attractions of the good-humoured comic tone of *Orontea* that it allowed more space to be made over to song. The principal characters – always excepting Creonte – are so spirited that ariettas flow easily from their lips, and genuine comic scenes – of which there are many – had always been the place for arias and ariosi. Act I scenes 6–8 and Act III scene 10 are examples of scenes in which the singing is interrupted by recitative only fleetingly. But the crucial desideratum for a seventeenth-century opera libretto, as Busenello and Monteverdi had perhaps already seen when they planned *L'incoronazione di Poppea*, was that the characters should be largely immune to the rational controls, the decorous or moral restraints of spoken drama. In Cicognini's libretti the action is 'raised up out of the everyday into a sphere of intensified feelings, supernatural forces, and sensuous self-indulgence' (Abert 1954: 156). Analogies have been suggested with the world of fairy-tales (Donington 1981: 255). Act III scene 14 provides a simple illustration of the way the characters tend to be swept along on the current of feeling, acting on the impulse of the moment, passionately asserting the first thing that comes into their heads. The courtier Corindo is protesting to Queen Orontea about the insult received from Alidoro the painter, whom – unbeknown to Corindo – the queen loves:

Orontea	In che t'offese?
Corindo	A duellar mi sfida.
Orontea	Ebben?
Corindo	Son cavaliero, egli è plebeo.
Orontea	Alidoro è plebeo?
	E chi tel' disse?
Corindo	È figlio d'un corsaro e tanto basti.
Orontea	Non più; io d'Alidoro
	Il nome renderò illustre e chiaro:
	Cavaliero lo pubblico e dichiaro.[3]

By whatever process of instinct or reason Cicognini arrived at his operatic style, *Orontea* was a land-mark in the evolution of that kind of song-saturated opera that was to inebriate Venetian opera-goers in the next decades.

The cult of song

Cicognini shared the taste of his contemporaries for aria texts with short lines – there are *quinari* and *senari* in abundance; likewise for an almost continuous fluctuation of metre during the course of the lyric:

> Com' è dolce il vezzegiar
> Amorosa beltà,
> Che cortese ti dà
> Quanto il cor sà bramar.
> E se dolce è quel piacer,
> Quant' è piu dolce nel suo sen goder.[4]   (Act I scene 7)

The most extended arias tend to be placed at the start of a scene, for nothing was more fundamental to Cicognini's sense of theatre than the care he took to make every entrance of every character a moment to be cherished, a moment bringing its particular *frisson* of surprise, delight, amusement, or excitement; and in opera an aria provided one of the best means of achieving this.

At the same time Cicognini could not have been unaware of the long-held, deeply rooted conviction that recitative was a more dignified and philosophical form of self-expression than aria: Creonte has no aria to sing anywhere in the opera. The proportion of aria to recitative is much lower in scenes for Orontea than in scenes for Gelone or Aristea. And when serious matters are being discussed, the librettist felt no compunction about writing longish scenes of recitative with little or no relief in the form of arias. It is in such scenes that he begins to make occasional use of a type of aria which, by the end of the century, had come to oust the entrance-aria almost entirely. In Act I scenes 9–11, for example, Cicognini builds a sequence of scenes round the central figure of Alidoro, depicting his first experience of life at the Egyptian court, of the vehement irrationality of the queen and the forward ways of her ladies-in-waiting. And here both lyrical numbers, the aria 'Destin, placati un dì' and the duet 'Donzelletta vezzosetta', are used to round off a phase of the action, to provide a highly charged summing-up of the emotional experience undergone in the pre-ceding dialogue. In many recitative scenes, particularly the comic ones, he likes to break up the customary *selva* verse[5] with metrical irregularities. These, one must suppose, would have been designed to stimulate the use of arioso sections, a practice in which Cesti needed little enough prompting.

With Cesti we have reached the point where the clear lines of demar-cation between what is sung and what is played by the orchestra are beginning to break down, a state of affairs which offers immense possi-bilities to a composer with a vivid dramatic imagination. The orchestra is small – two violins (sometimes perhaps doubled by recorders) and con-tinuo – but is employed in remarkably various ways. There are a number of simple continuo-songs, a number of continuo-songs framed or rounded off by orchestral ritornellos; two arias in Act II scene 17 – lullabies and therefore associated with the magical realm of sleep and dreams – are accompanied by strings almost continuously. But most characteristic of Cesti's arias is an antiphony of voice and orchestra, a pattern of statement and counter-statement, or sometimes of statement and variation, which much enriches the expressive potential of the form. In a few cases the antiphony becomes more animated, the mood of the music more thrillingly volatile; in others, notably Giacinta's lament 'Mie pene, che fate?', the singer seems sunk in intimate conversation with the orchestra, as if the old echo convention had returned to life in a more fashionable metempsychosis. Elsewhere the orchestra strikes in simply to add a further touch of gorgeousness to those episodes of caressing sensuousness of which Cesti was so fond.

The frequent fluctuations in the metre of Cicognini's lyrics often stimulated matching fluctuations in the metre of the aria, one of the most readily apparent signs of Cesti's vaunted '*souplesse*' (Bianconi 1982: 15). And this *souplesse* is, besides, a mark of the fact that he was not just one of the great charmers of seventeenth-century opera, but a composer with an acute sense of theatre. Many of his arias and duets cry out to be acted as much as sung. A case in point, one of the delicious highlights of the score, is the duet 'Spuntò in ciel' (Act I scene 8) of which it will be helpful to quote the text:

Corindo	Spuntò in ciel l'alba novella
	Ed io torno ad inchinar
	Te, dell'alba del ciel, alba più bella.
Silandra	Sorge il sol nell'alta mole,
	Ed io vengo a riverir
	Nel sol del tuo bel volto, un più bel sole.
Corindo	Silandra, io non ho core.
	Amor me lo rubò,
	E nel tuo seno i furti tuoi celò.
Silandra	Corindo, io non ho vita,
	Amor morte me diè,
	E vuol che viva la mia morte in te.
Corindo	Mio ristoro.
Silandra	Mio desio.
Corindo	Mio tesoro.
Silandra	Tutto mio.
à 2	Quanto cara è tua beltà
	Per te questo core
	Al cielo d'amore
	Beato sen va.[6]

The graphic rhetoric of the first two matching verses prompts music of an almost Handelian verve. Over a running bass unfolds a florid melody which, like many of Cesti's $\frac{3}{4}$ melodies, gains much of its character and much of its brilliance from 'madrigalian' touches of word-painting – the suggestions of a bright dawning at 'spuntò in ciel' / 'sorge il sol', the fussy little bowing phrase at 'ed io torno ad inchinar' / 'ed io vengo a riverir' (see Ex.II.16a). The metre in these stanzas is a mixture of *ottonari* and *endecasillabi*; in the second pair of stanzas Cicognini mixes *settenari* and *endecasillabi*, the metre of recitative. That was an opportunity not lost on

The sun rises up in lofty majesty, and I come to pay homage. . .

Ex.II.16a Cesti, *L'Orontea* (1666), Act I scene 8

Silandra, I have no heart; Love robbed me of it. . .

Ex.II.16b Cesti, *L'Orontea* (1666), Act I scene 8

My refreshment. My desire. My treasure. My all. How dear is your
beauty. . .

Ex.II.16c Cesti, *L'Orontea* (1666), Act I scene 8

Cesti, who brings his duet back to dramatic life with phrases of recitative
before the brisk cantilena is resumed (Ex.II.16b). The sweet intimacies of
'Mio ristoro . . .' seem to have evoked memories of Nero and Poppea, and
prompted another change of style to Cesti's most voluptuous sarabande
manner, starting over the same descending tetrachord bass as had served
for the finale of Monteverdi's opera (Ex.II.16c).

But if Cesti's arias often bring to life the character and the dramatic situation, and if they are often ingenious in applying the devices of musical rhetoric to give extra point to the sense of the word, they also, almost invariably, betray the master craftsman's delight in well-fashioned lyrical gems. One senses this in a partiality for contrapuntal play between voice and bass that goes well beyond what is found in Cavalli. And one senses it still more unmistakably in the shapeliness of Cesti's arias. Every one of them shows a highly developed formal sense. Often, as in the final quartet, he will round off an aria with a deftly varied reprise of the opening – a device that sometimes, but by no means always, is suggested by the libretto; in 'Il mio ben' (Act III scene 12) he composes a full-scale rondo in which a refrain in his favourite $\frac{3}{2}$ metre alternates with $\frac{4}{4}$ episodes in a more declamatory manner. But nothing shows his sense of form better than his happy skill in giving witty or expressive emphasis to the closing line or couplet of an aria. Cesti is too resourceful a composer for one to be able to define the procedure more narrowly than that, but Aristea's 'S' amore insolente' (Act II scene 6), a strophic song in two verses, may serve as an example of a practice he handled with inexhaustible variousness.

In this case the prevailing metre, which is of *senari*, changes to *endecasillabi* for the refrain:

> All'età non perdona il cieco Dio.
> E se ben vecchia son di carne anch'io.[7]

Cesti's highlighting of this is masterly. For the first line he breaks into recitative. Then at 'E se ben vecchia' he resumes the $\frac{3}{4}$ of the rest of the aria, but no longer in quite the flippant sing-song manner of the opening. Here the phrase is sung once in the dominant, then repeated in the tonic, but expanded with sequential repetitions both at the level of the phrase (a) and of the figure within the phrase (b). Finally the same idea recurs a third time in a clinching orchestral ritornello (Ex.II.17).

Mid-seventeenth-century recitative

In the prologue too we catch some glimpses of a composer with a highly developed sense of structure. There is certainly nothing remarkable about the fact that Filosofia's opening 'ode' – 'Sciolta il crin' – has its verses framed with a ritornello, for that had been standard prologue practice from the first, nor even that this ritornello recurs to round off the prologue at the close. What is remarkable is that Filosofia's first verse (Ex.II.18b) should take its thematic material from the 'sinfonia avanti il prologo' (Ex.II.18a), transforming its solemn harmonies into a declamatory recitative.

With this exception the opera has become a far more loosely organized form than it was in the days of Monteverdi; one feels that Cesti might

ARISTEA

Ex.II.17 Cesti, *L'Orontea* (1666), Act II scene 6

(RITORNELLO)

eto

I don't know what to do, if that's how Love wants it. The blind god does
not excuse old age. Even if I am old, I too am of flesh and blood.

Ex.II.17 *continued*

almost have improvised his way through the composition, reacting sensitively, imaginatively, wittily to the impulse of the moment, but rarely
planning out grand strategies that would embrace an entire act or even an
entire sequence of scenes. Frequently the musical choices he makes seem
not to tally with what Cicognini had envisaged. The strophic lyric that
Cicognini had written for Corindo in Act II scene 10, 'O cielo, a che son
giunto', is set as a recitative; and it is difficult to imagine that the librettist
did not expect Gelone's exit in Act III scene 9 to give rise to a merry song –

> Come adirato giura!
> Come mi minacciò!
> A smaltir la paura
> All'osteria men vò.[8]

In view of Cesti's reputation as an incorrigible lyricist it is curious to
discover that so many of these departures from what Cicognini might have
anticipated entail composing recitative where the text allowed for an aria.[9]
Even in the 1666 revision of the opera, with its additional arias from
L'Argia, there are a number of extensive passages of recitative with no
provision for lyrical singing at all, notably the crucial scenes 4–5 in Act III
in which Creonte persuades Orontea that she must renounce her love for
Alidoro. Clearly neither composers nor their audiences were yet so
uninterested in recitative as we have sometimes been led to suppose.

This is not altogether surprising, because mid-century recitative still
commanded a very considerable expressive range. Certainly there are
passages, most obviously – and aptly – in those scenes in Act III where the
opera is speeding to its denouement, where we can hear in the fast pattering
parlando set against slowly moving harmonies the approach of the *secco*
recitative style of the eighteenth century. Some of what were to become the
standard modulatory strategies of that style also appear (see Ex.II.19). But
in the following scene, as Alidoro swoons in despair, a superbly graphic use
of chromaticism and silence shows that Cesti had lost little of the early-

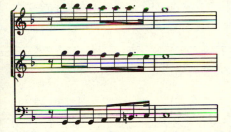

Ex.II.18a Cesti, *L'Orontea* (1666), Prologue

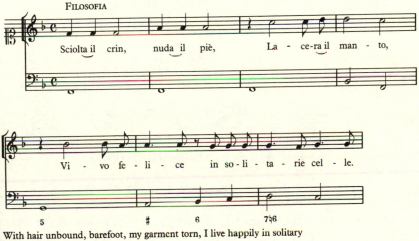

FILOSOFIA

Sciolta il crin, nuda il piè, La - ce-ra il man - to,

Vi - vo fe - li - ce in so - li - ta - rie cel - le.

With hair unbound, barefoot, my garment torn, I live happily in solitary
cells.

Ex.II.18b Cesti, *L'Orontea* (1666), Prologue

seventeenth-century zest for richly rhetorical declamation (Ex.II.20).
Often the recitatives are wrought up to a level of real sustained eloquence:
by the shaping and proportion of the phrases, by spasms of cantabile, and
hints of word-painting.

175

Accursed pair, accursed portrait, prodigious brushes, monstrous colours,
cruel agents of wanton warfare, yes, I tear you, I break you, yes, I rip you,
I shatter you, to the ground, to the ground!

Ex.II.19 Cesti, *L'Orontea* (1666), Act II scene 13

The real joy of Cesti's recitative-scenes lies in the profusion, the variety
and the aptness of the arioso episodes. Over and over again, for an effect of
comedy, to highlight a crucial incident – like the handing over of the golden
medallion (Act III scenes 10 and 12) on which the denouement will turn –
to portray more searchingly the emotional upheavals his characters are
undergoing, he will pluck critical lines from Cicognini's recitative texts and
transform them into fleeting episodes of song. The supreme example is
Orontea's big solo scene, Act II scene 17, which Cicognini designed, in
characteristic fashion, as an opening strophic aria followed by a long
soliloquy in recitative. In this soliloquy Cesti perceived two moments that

he felt needed to be transfigured in song: one when Orontea resolves to reveal her love for Alidoro – 'Ma nel mio cor sepolto' – the other when she bids him sleep on – 'Dormi, dormi, mio ben'. The shape, musical and emotional, of Cicognini's scene is consequently altered out of all recognition: it is framed by two $\frac{3}{2}$ lullabies; these enclose a central soliloquy in recitative at the heart of which stands a brisk arioso of resolution. In terms of the musical richness of the opera, these ariosi largely compensate for arias lost when Cesti sets lyrical texts as recitatives. The interesting point is that he so often saw fit to differ from his librettist in choosing how to pace, how to emphasize, the flow of the drama.

But alas! and does that torment assail my soul, oh God? To what tyrannous grief is my heart the prey? Alas, I can no more; my limbs tremble, my eyes are blinded, I expire, I swoon.

Ex.II.20 Cesti, *L'Orontea* (1666), Act II scene 14

Part III
Opera seria

10 · The *dramma per musica*

Enlightenment

As the seventeenth century draws to a close, we come to the moment identified by Croce as Italy's 'crisis of decadence . . . the beginning of the national renewal' (Croce 1949: 5). Social and political life was still completely dominated by the combined authority of the Papacy and Spain; religious and intellectual ideals remained those of the age of the Counter-reformation, except that they had become weary and unfervent. The great mass of the people appear to have been woefully ignorant and superstitious; they were kept docile by a rigorously authoritarian social structure, and some measure of emotional serenity was ensured by the ostentatious baroque pomp of religious and public life. If was not until the liberal papacy of Benedict XIV (1740–58) that the Jesuits lost their dominant role in education: meanwhile the syllabus in schools and universities was under strict ecclesiastical control, and every effort was made to ensure that intellectual life was not contaminated by the infiltration of heretical ideas from the North. Even in the eighteenth century not only had a very high proportion of the pre-eminent figures in Italian cultural life been educated by the Church – that was inevitable – but they were themselves in Holy Orders; the great music conservatories in Venice and Naples were Church institutions. But already with the ending of Spanish hegemony in the first decade of the new century, and the gradual shift of the political control of Italy to a more liberal regime in Vienna, the country began to change. It was subject to more cosmopolitan and progressive influences, particularly those emanating from France. And this in turn meant that Italians were able to claim a full share in the ideas and achievements of the Enlightenment. A joyful sense of awareness that Italy was 'rejoining the mainstream of European civilization' (Woolf 1979: 81) irradiated the country's intellectual life.

In this new situation, the story of Italian opera becomes more complicated. For the greater part of the seventeenth century Venice was so completely pre-eminent in the production of opera that only the most fleeting allusions have needed to be made to enterprises in Rome or Florence or other cities. But the enthusiasm of the Habsburg dynasty for opera encouraged the cultivation of the form in such centres of Habsburg influence as Milan and Naples, and made Vienna, the capital city of the Habsburg empire, one of the most productive and, by the very nature of the case, influential of all centres of Italian opera. The Spanish priest Stefano Arteaga, in his classic study of Italian opera written in the 1780s, still looked back on Charles VI, Emperor of Austria from 1711 to 1740, as the man 'to whom in large part Italy owes her dramatic glory' (Arteaga 1785, I: 74). The librettos of Charles's court poets, Silvio Stampiglia, Apostolo Zeno and Pietro Metastasio, served as models of taste and were set not only in Vienna, but all over Italy. And this interest was reciprocated; in Vienna was built up a substantial library of scores of the latest works produced in the Habsburg lands in Italy (Strohm 1979: 75).

It soon became clear that a very perceptible change in taste was affecting Italian drama, whether spoken or sung. Without exception, eighteenth-century critics and scholars looked back on the productions of the previous century with contempt. Quadrio, referring to spoken theatre, writes of 'the retreat of a pestilence' (Croce 1926: 127); Arteaga, referring specifically to opera, likens that of the previous era to 'an enormous chaos, a concoction of sacred and profane, of historical and fabulous, of mythology, ancient and modern, of true and allegorical, of natural and fantastic, all gathered together to the perpetual shame of Art' (Arteaga 1785, I: 248). Historically the most momentous aspect of the eighteenth-century determination to create order out of the inherited chaos was the separating off of heroic drama and comedy, and the bifurcation of the operatic tradition into two distinct genres, the *opera seria* and the *opera buffa*. Clearly something of a revolution had taken place; and the nature of the revolution can best be considered under three heads: didactic, pastoral and neo-classical.

'A school for the nation'

In the seventeenth century, the most cultivated Italians had worried their heads rather little about the popular theatrical forms of the day. One might find in the occasional court opera some faint echo of the humanist ideals of the founding fathers; but the operas performed in the public theatres of Venice, not to mention the comedies improvised in streets and squares all over Italy, were rarely touched by any exalted moral aim. During the first half of the eighteenth century, however, artists and intellectuals alike rapidly learned to appreciate the immense potential these popular forms had for instilling new cultural ideals. Goldoni's reform of the *commedia dell'arte* (discussed in Chapter 16 below) is the most famous example of this procedure; but, long before Goldoni, the opera had undergone a comparable 'enlightening' reform which in its day was regarded as at least equally momentous. The opera-house became a 'school for the nation': the phrase is Strohm's, and he explains it by remarking that it was in the opera-house that a wide spectrum of Italians found themselves exposed most consistently to the enlightened ideas that were permeating the country's intellectual life (Strohm 1979: 18–19). It was no longer sufficient for opera to be merely entertaining: characteristic of the early eighteenth century was a tone from which all elements of comedy and burlesque were banished, and in which erudition and philosophy combined to give an educative purpose to the opera-goer's delight.

This didactic note first becomes audible in a repertory of historical operas written by Stampiglia, Zeno and other like-minded men in the years around 1700. It was probably not an accidental vogue; for it was exactly in those closing years of the seventeenth century that there sprang up in Italy – in the wake of a visit in 1685 by a great French scholar, the Benedictine monk Jean Mabillon – a virtually new science of critical antiquarianism, particularly fruitful in the field of local history (Woolf 1979: 76). Beginning with *Il trionfo di Camilla* in 1696, Stampiglia produced a whole series of operas based largely on Livy's accounts of early Italian history. But it was Zeno who proved the most adept and erudite exponent of this new form. It was not of course the mere fact that his operas were historical that distinguished them, rather a new combination of scholarship and moral seriousness, the demonstration – in Metastasio's words (1767) – 'that our melodrama and Reason are not incompatible things' (Gallarati 1984: 19). Arteaga, having described Zeno as 'a man of tireless industry, a judicious journalist, a diligent collector, erudite without pedantry, an antiquarian without affectation [who] may properly be called the Pierre Corneille of the lyric theatre', continued:

Wherever he found in the vast field of history, in which he was so deeply versed, luminous examples of patriotism, or of a virtuous desire for glory, or of a generous constancy in friendship, or of nobleness and fidelity in love, or of compassion towards one's fellow men, or of grandeur of soul in adversity, or of prudence, or of fortitude, or of any other virtues, he took them up in order to adorn the theatre with them.

(1785, I: 326)

How far Zeno's concern for edification became the accepted norm in the heroic opera of the age is apparent in the chronological list of works which Dr Burney appended to his *Memoirs of the Life and Writings of the Abate Metastasio*. In this list of basic information, Burney sets out to specify 'the time, and place, where they were first performed, by whom set to music, *and the moral object of each*' (italics added) (Burney 1796, III: 316).

The Arcadians

These historical-didactic librettos that began to appear in the late 1690s did not monopolize the scene, at any rate not at first. They were accompanied by a scarcely less profuse production of pastoral librettos. And this is hardly surprising, for a major contribution to operatic reform was made by the ideals of the Arcadia, an academy supposedly of shepherds, but in fact, needless to say, of aristocrats, intellectuals and artists, founded in Rome in 1690, with the specific object of bringing about 'a complete revival of good taste in literature' (Crescimbeni, dedication of *Rime degli Arcadi*, 1716). By good taste, Crescimbeni meant a proper respect for the craftsmanlike control of form, a return to the aesthetics of imitation, and, above all, an abandoning of the extravagant virtuosity of the *stile metaforuto* (see p. 125). Stampiglia was a founder-member of Arcadia; in the following year Zeno founded a similar brotherhood – the Accademia degli animosi – in Venice, and this merged with the Arcadia a few years later.

The Arcadians acknowledged two primary sources of inspiration for their work: the neo-classical splendours of the great French dramatists of the seventeenth century, and the exquisite euphony of early Italian lyric poetry, especially of Petrarch. Their interest in opera, a form that combined drama and lyricism, was therefore quite natural, and pastoral returned briefly to favour as an operatic topic. Zeno's very first libretto, *Gl'inganni felici* (music by C. F. Pollarolo, Venice 1695), is actually set in 'Arcadia'; and his next two operas were both pastorals. The austere Girolamo Frigimelica-Roberti and various other librettists also cultivated the form. In the course of time it became all too easy to mock the affectations of the Arcadians – the rustic make-believe, the assumed names – for 'everybody who had the least knack for poetry, was metamorphosed into a shepherd, and fell directly upon composing rustic sonnets, eclogues, ydylliums and bucolics' (Baretti 1769, I: 251). But initially the Arcadians were inspired by a genuine idealism, a quest for a more natural and simple and heartfelt style that could serve as an antidote to the effusions of the baroque imagination. And if the pastoral could not, in the long run, of itself provide the variety of passions and the stirring action which opera really needed, something of this idealism lingered on. Whenever, in the heroic, didactic melodrama of the early eighteenth century duty or virtue or loyalty prompts a character to forswear his own inclinations, the pastoral dream returns. Arcadia became a metaphor for a world ruled by truth, sincerity and the promptings of the heart.

> Quanto mai felici siete
> Innocenti pastorelle.[1]   (Metastasio, *Ezio* Act I scene 5)

Aristotle revisited

Clearly there were neo-classical elements in the fashion for both historical and pastoral operas. But the dominant strain in the operatic reform of the early eighteenth century was a more explicitly neo-classical one. Not for the first time in the history of Italian opera, nor for the last, its most articulate practitioners decided that they could effectively redeem the theatre only by modelling it on Classical prototype. In a whole series of solemn and wordy prefaces to the librettos he produced in the 1690s and early 1700s, Frigimelica-Roberti attempted to re-educate his Venetian audiences in Aristotelian dramatic theory. A characteristic production was *Mitridate Eupatore* (set by Alessandro Scarlatti, Venice, Teatro S. Giovanni Grisostomo 1706) in which he explained that his aim was to imitate the type of drama described by Aristotle as having 'a double story . . . and an opposite issue for the good and the bad personages' (Grout 1979: 68). And it is worth quoting an extravagant and inaccurate tribute to Zeno's work from the second half of the century: it serves to show how educated men remembered his reputation at a time when they knew rather little of his actual writings:

Apostolo Zeno found the opera quite rude and imperfect, and he brought it within the jurisdiction of the Aristotelian precepts. As he was a great master of Greek, he endeavoured to give it a Greek cast, and crowded it with duos, trios and chorusses, imitating as much as he could the strophe, antistrophe, and epode of the ancient Greek tragedies. (Baretti 1769, I: 175)

Well, no, he didn't really do all those things; but that he endeavoured to give opera a 'Greek cast' cannot be denied. And he was surely encouraged in this ambition by the achievements of the great French tragedians, whose works he knew well. In 1704, we learn from a letter to Magliabecchi, his library contained the dramatic writings of Racine, both Corneilles, Molière, Prudon, Campistron, Quinault, Montfleury, Boursault, Palaprat and Passerat (Fehr 1912: 46). Zeno was often compared with Corneille – by Goldoni, for instance, who found him similarly 'serious, profound, and instructive' (1907, I, chapter XLI [1787]). And comparisons between Metastasio and the French tragedians, especially Racine, were also to be common. Recently Strohm has made stronger claims for Racine's influences on Metastasio (Strohm 1977: 902), but Metastasio himself denied any such specific indebtedness. In a letter to Belloy, written in April 1761, he says:

[I am] unworthy of the second praise which you have been so obliging as to bestow upon me, of having ingeniously and with wonderful art adapted French tragedies to the Italian stage; at least I can venture to say with truth, that this is what I never intended. Having perused the best dramatic productions of other countries, I always meant to write originally. And if the circumscribed condition of our natures or a memory too faithful in retaining such things as it has received with admiration and pleasure, has suggested to me beauties which I had read before upon similar occasions; supposing I was the inventor of them, I had taken the credit to myself. (Burney 1796, II: 250–1)

For Metastasio the proper parallel was between his work and that of the Greeks. Metastasio's claim is made in his commentary on Aristotle's *Poetics*. Starting from the firm conviction that Greek drama had been sung throughout – that, in Burney's words, 'in antiquity, there was no poetry without numbers, or without singing' (1796, III: 360) – Metastasio goes on to argue that the recitative of the modern opera performs the same function as the scenes of action of Greek drama; and that the arias of the modern opera are precisely comparable with the reflective choral commentaries of Greek drama: '. . . what else are the AIRS of our musical dramas, but the ancient *strophes*? And why such an out-cry against these visible relics of the Greek theatre?' (Burney 1796, III: 373–4). But the modern critic, even if he can accept this line of reasoning, will still wonder, as many eighteenth-century critics did, how the *lieto fine* – the 'happy ending' – of the eighteenth-century heroic opera, with its reconciliations and nuptials – its 'matrimoniale catastrofe' as Calzabigi was wittily to call it – is to be reconciled with the Classical view that pity and terror are the emotions proper to tragedy.

First it must be remarked that the *lieto fine* was by no means universal: that, particularly in the early years of the *opera seria*, a number of efforts were made to produce genuine operatic tragedy. Two of Metastasio's first three *drammi per musica* – *Didone abandonata* (Naples 1724) and *Catone in Utica* (Rome 1728) – belong in this group, and others were written by Salvi and Piovene, notably the latter's *Bajazet* (set by Gasparini, Reggio Emilia 1719, and, revised as *Tamerlano*, by Handel, London 1724). Nevertheless the *lieto fine* carried the day – according to Arteaga largely because Charles VI did not favour 'spettacoli sanguinarii' (Arteaga 1785, I: 73–4) – and in attempting to reconcile this with Classical precedent Metastasio fudged the issue. Clearly, when he speaks of 'admiration of virtue . . . the abhorrence of vice . . . fair means of affording delight and instruction without eternally condemning the spectator to tremble with horror, or weep with affliction' (Burney 1796, III: 376–7), Metastasio has shifted the aim of tragedy from 'purgation' – whatever Aristotle may have meant by that – to edification. As Burney drily observed, 'it is manifest, that Metastasio was no terrorist'. More persuasive, because it is more frank, and brimming over with all the self-confidence of the age, is Planelli's justification of the *lieto fine*.

The diminishing of the horrors of tragedy, whatever Misanthropes may say, is a certain proof of the progress which urbanity, clemency, and benevolence have made in modern times . . . Modern tragedy cultivated by a people many ages civilized, friends to commerce, hospitable to strangers, and professing a religion which inspires charity, mildness, peace, compassion, and beneficence, if it did not diminish atrocity, would disgust, beyond the power of poetry and music to suppress.

(*Dell'opera in musica* [1772], in Burney 1796, III: 382–3)

So while opera had certainly become serious, it had not – except in the few cases mentioned earlier – become genuinely tragic. In place of tragedy, audiences were offered a quality sometimes referred to as 'sospensione', a tension that arose out of some conflict in the mind of the protagonist –

between virtue and passion; or duty and expediency, perhaps – and which was often sustained at truly excruciating length.

The new libretto

In fact the generic term for the reformed opera libretto was not 'tragedy' but '*dramma per musica*', 'in which "dramma" is the basic definition and "per musica" a qualifying specification' (Strohm 1979: 23). As far as Zeno, the most admired architect of the new form, was concerned, it was a qualification to be regretted; he could have wished it otherwise, but in the opera-house tragedy was obliged to make concessions 'to modern taste, to spectacle and to music' (letter of 1720, cited in Fehr 1912: 32). The nature of Zeno's achievement, the manner of his reconciliation of the claims of drama and the claims of music, have been judiciously described in Fehr's monograph. For present purposes, it will be sufficient to emphasize just four things. First, Zeno's real interest was drama, not music: indeed he seems to have been largely indifferent to music. Music was therefore quite literally to be kept in its place. He did this by shifting it to the end of the scene (unless it was required naturalistically, as, for instance, when the cast is assembling for some great festive occasion): there, when the dramatic action was over, the aria could become 'a pure poetic abstraction, projecting the individual characters into an idealized sphere of universal expression' (Gallarati 1984: 13). At the same time Zeno enlarged enormously the scale of the recitatives between each of the musical numbers, so as to accommodate all the literary, philosophical and moral graces for which they might be admired by *cognoscenti*. Several references in his letters make it clear that one of the advantages of his format was that it allowed for performances in the form of spoken drama, 'without the interruption of ariettas' (Fehr 1912: 59); there are also records of Metastasio's *drammi per musica* being performed as spoken plays, with the arias paraphrased into recitative verse or omitted altogether (e.g. Goldoni 1907, I, chapter 21 [1787]).

Second, despite his lack of real interest in the art, Zeno did recognize that, if music had to be admitted to the theatre at all, then it was essential that the drama should be of a rather special type. It needed a *lieto fine*, of course, and plenty of spectacle (though Zeno did discipline this considerably in comparison with the seventeenth-century writers); above all it required a wider range of emotions than regular tragedy, particularly emotions of the softer type – *effeminatezze* as they were scathingly called by the severer critics of the day.

Third, if characters had frequently to be leaving the stage (because they could sing arias only when their part in the scene was finished), and if a wide variety of emotions was required, clearly the plot needed to be much more complicated and fast-moving than that of a real tragedy, whether Greek or French. Indeed the devising of plots for *drammi per musica* brought authors closer to the traditions of comedy than of tragedy, for the basic ingredients came to be such elements as 'intrigue, disguise, mistaken identity, *peripateia* . . .' (Monelle 1976: 267; Monelle is describing Metastasio but the description fits Zeno too).

Fourth – and this was a factor whose profound importance was recognized only slowly – the fact that music was confined to the close of the scene, and that Zeno developed his dramas as fully as possible without reference to the needs of the composer, meant that composers were rarely called upon to exercise their finer skills in illuminating the dramatic climaxes, or intensifying the dramatic crises. The dawning sense that in the *dramma per musica* poet and composer were avoiding one another as much as they were collaborating was an important factor in the innovations and reforms that took place later in the century.

Whatever its shortcomings, the *dramma per musica* that resulted from these considerations was intellectually more coherent than any other form opera had assumed since its earliest days. It was also, for that very reason, far more rigorously schematic. Reason and art combined to create an artefact in which poetry and music were held in a supremely mannered equilibrium. In Scarlatti's early operas, such as *Pompeo* (Rome 1683) or *La Rosaura* (Rome 1690), the individual scenes have no predictable structure: arias may be *escite*, *medie*, or *ingressi* (that is to say, entrance-arias, arias sung in the middle of the scene, or exit-arias: the terminology is Martello's, *Della tragedia antica e moderna* (Rome 1714)), and they may be action pieces, expressions of mood, or more generalized observations on the course of the drama. By the 1690s *ingressi* had already become more popular than *escite* and *medie*, and as Zeno (and those men who shared his ideals) gained a clearer impression of the musico-dramatic compromise they were aiming at, this trend was intensified. By 1700 Zeno was already being praised by Crescimbeni for eliminating superfluous ariettas (that is *escite* and *medie*), and by 1706 even Scarlatti, the most accomplished, experienced and old-fashioned opera composer in Italy, was ready to compose a score – *Mitridate Eupatore* – monopolized by *ingressi*.

With a substantial decline in the number of arias, and an almost complete standardization of their placing, the basic unit of the opera had become a scene which comprised dialogue or soliloquy in *recitativo semplice*, followed by exit-aria. And once the aria regularly followed the action rather than forming part of it, it was natural that it should begin to be treated as a largely independent form. Poets began to prefer, to the direct expression of feeling, a generalization, a philosophical reflection, a metaphor; composers began to cultivate more fully developed and rounded forms – to be specific, the most rounded form of all, the *da capo* aria. (I leave to one side for the moment the fact that this nomenclature is at most periods and for most levels of musical structure more misleading than enlightening; for the 1690s it describes the form well enough.)

Despite the apparent rigidity of this scheme, it would be wrong to make facile generalizations about the relationship between recitative and aria. Most moderns, being primarily interested in the music, are inclined to regard the aria as the climax – in a sense as the point of the scene. There is no shortage of justification for this view in the eighteenth-century theorists: C. G. Krause, for example, writes, 'sometimes the feelings become so strong and the affection so great that we cannot be happy till we have unburdened ourselves of them and opened our hearts' (*Von der musikalischen Poesie* [1752], cited in Robinson 1972: 57). Arteaga, on the other hand, spoke of the resolution of uncertainty, seeing the aria as 'from the philosophical point of view the conclusion, the epilogue or the epiphonema of passion' (Arteaga 1785, I: 50). The tendency to think of the arias as standing outside the action of the opera, as objective comments on it, was particularly prevalent among those who looked for parallels with the chorus of Classical tragedy. And we should remember that the eighteenth century – unlike ourselves – was as enthralled by the voice of reason as by that of passion, and admired the accomplished artifice of metaphor or apophthegm as much as the spontaneous cry of the heart. At very least we may be sure that there was no need for the operatic aria to be an overpowering explosion of human passion, as Mattei's tribute to Metastasio shows: 'What philosophy! What maxims! What truths! And everything so easily and delightfully explained! What field is not present on which music may spread its treasure?' (Robinson 1972: 60).

11 · 'Perfection and public favour'

A Golden Age of opera

If one consults a representative bibliography of eighteenth-century Italian music, one cannot but be struck by the fact that the great majority of critics and theorists who wrote on opera were active either at the beginning of the century or from the 1750s onwards. There is little or nothing from the 1720s or 1730s. This is at once exasperating and suggestive, because from the mid-century these years were looked back on as a Golden Age in the history of opera. And one cannot altogether suppress the suspicion that the period would have found it more difficult to maintain that image if the querulous breed of critics had been as active then as they were later – praising the glorious dead, and deploring the decadence of the modern age.

However, it is certainly the case that that great connoisseur of Italian opera, Dr Burney, saw the period in a roseate, idealizing light, and it is from him that I borrow my chapter title.

Between the years 1725 and 1740, the musical drama in Italy seems to have attained a degree of perfection and public favour, which perhaps has never been since surpassed. The opera stage from that period being in possession of the *poetry* of Apostolo Zeno and Metastasio; the *compositions* of Leo, Vinci, Hasse, Porpora, and Pergolesi; the *performances* of Farinelli, Carestini, Caffarelli, Bernacchi, Babbi, la Tesi, la Romanina, Faustina and Cuzzoni; and the elegant *scenes* and *decorations* of the two Bibienas, which had superseded the expensive and childish machinery of the last century.

(Burney 1776–89, IV: 561)

Earlier in the same chapter he had told us that Vinci's vocal compositions 'form an aera in dramatic Music', and that Pergolesi, 'the child of taste and elegance, and nurstling of the Graces . . . [marks] . . . a very important period of musical history' (Burney 1776–89, IV: 547, 551). Many of Burney's contemporaries and near-contemporaries likewise associated these composers with some kind of revolution in taste – fellow-composers like Jommelli and Grétry, men of letters like Rousseau and Heinse, critics like Arteaga. But I stay with Burney a little longer, who in his eulogy of Pergolesi wrote of his entitlement

to a niche in the temple of Fame, among the great improvers of the Art . . . if not the founder, [he was] the principal polisher of a style of composition both for the church and stage which has been constantly cultivated by his successors, and which, at the distance

190

of half a century from the short period in which he flourished, still reigns throughout Europe. (Burney 1776–89, IV: 557)

Vinci and Pergolesi in particular became quasi-legendary figures: the Amphion and Arion of the Age of Improvement; and they haunted the imagination of music lovers to the end of the century. There were good reasons for this, at least in Vinci's case: his association with Metastasio in the radiant Neapolitan years of the poet's youth; and with Farinelli and the group of great singers trained by Porpora; and he was the first real master of what came to be the most admired musical form of the age. But the early death of Pergolesi and the mysterious death of Vinci also appealed to the sentimentality of the times; both became the heroes of a number of apocryphal incidents, and were credited with the invention of much that was not theirs.

To understand the nature of the 'revolution' brought about by this generation of Neapolitans, one must appreciate the detestation which, in the second quarter of the century, men of taste felt for counterpoint, irregular or ambiguous phrasing and all other manifestations of the baroque imagination. Here, for instance, is the Count Benvenuto di San Raffaele, purporting to describe the state of music in Tartini's youth – *c.* 1710 presumably:

There still prevailed among writers that barbarous taste for fugues, canons, and in short, all the most complicated interweavings of a hispid counterpoint. This deplorable ostentation of harmonic skill, this gothic taste for conundrums and musical logogriphs: this music pleasing to the eyes and cruel to the ears, full of harmony and noise, and empty of taste and melody, manufactured according to the rules, if indeed the rules are so cruel as to permit the making of anything so displeasing, cold, confused, expressionless, tuneless and graceless [etc.]. (Arteaga 1785, I: 311)

What, one wonders, can the Count have been listening to to make him so very choleric: a Scarlatti cantata? a Corelli sonata? a Palestrina motet? However that may be, the important thing is that, in enlightened eighteenth-century eyes, this Gothic gloom was dispelled in a moment of blinding revelation, when musicians stood back from their contrapuntal 'conundrums and logogriphs' and for a moment contemplated Nature. 'Ecco il momento della rivoluzione'[1] exclaimed Arteaga; for it was of the very essence of Nature that no sooner did men take the trouble to look at Her, than they were instantly enamoured (Arteaga 1785, I: 276). And the man who was deemed to have experienced this 'momento della rivoluzione' most vividly was Leonardo Vinci, the composer who, to return to famous words of Burney, 'without degrading his art, rendered it the friend, though not the slave to poetry, by simplifying and polishing melody, and calling the attention of the audience chiefly to the voice-part, by disentangling it from fugue, complication, and laboured contrivance' (Burney 1776–89, IV: 547).

A development which the modern musician tends to regard as a deplorable impoverishment of the resources of musical art, the eighteenth century experienced as a genuine achievement of illumination, a break through to elegance, reason and sensibility. If challenged it was prepared to justify its preferences with philosophical arguments, as Rousseau did when he added to the long-familiar Aristotelian unities another unity of melody and expression (Radiciotti 1935: 13). No one expressed the impact of the new style more vividly – or with more reckless disregard of history – than Grétry: 'Pergolèse naquit et la vérité fut connue' (Radiciotti 1935: 82).

The art of Metastasio

In fact neither Vinci nor Pergolesi, nor any other of the composers I have mentioned, was the central figure of the perfected *dramma in musica*. That position belonged to Pietro Metastasio; so obviously and indisputably that some scholars who object to the use of the old term 'Neapolitan Opera' to describe the *opera seria* of the eighteenth century have suggested 'Metastasian Opera' instead. I have no objection to either, though I cannot see that anything is to be gained by the substitution. For Metastasio's rise to fame coincided with the rise to fame of the Neapolitan school of composers; until he moved to Vienna all his operas were first set by Neapolitans (details in Robinson 1972: 47–8); and it was therefore thanks to their music and the performances of the largely Neapolitan-trained singers for whom they wrote that the new type of opera impressed itself on European sensibility.

Metastasio's unique role in this tradition was not due to any extraordinary productivity, nor to the prestige he enjoyed from 1731 as 'poeta cesareo' at the Habsburg court in Vienna, though that surely helped. Most important was the fact that, for the first time in history, a major poet had turned his attention to musical drama; composers were so enthralled by the eloquence and beauty of Metastasio's verse that they found it irresistible, indispensable and unforgettable. His more popular texts were set dozens of times – the favourite *Artaserse* more than eighty times – by composers in every corner of Europe where Italian opera had taken a footing. That was why 'the lovers of Italian Poetry, as well as vocal Music . . . regard Metastasio as the primary source of their most exquisite delight in the union of these arts' (Burney 1796, I: iii). A more precise explanation of Metastasio's impact on eighteenth-century opera is offered by some of the Italian memorialists of the age. In his *Elogio di P. Metastasio* Michele Torcia describes him as the 'inspiring genius of the Bibbienas and Vanvitellis and Servandonis, of the Porporas and Vincis and Pergolesis, of the Farinellis and Caffarellis and Tesis' (Surian 1978: 344); and Saverio Mattei, scholar and friend of Jommelli, identified Metastasio as the true source of the operatic revolution of the 1720s:

A new revolution was preparing in theatre music by means of the poetry which was being cultivated by Metastasio. It is to Metastasio that we owe the fluidity and melodiousness of our arias: his metres inspired the composer's musical figures and ideas; and the clarity of sentiment and of expression combined with the sweetness of its outer form enchanted everyone, indeed ravished them, so that within a few years theatre music had reached its summit.   (Surian 1978: 350)

Whether this was strictly true or not, Metastasio was certainly a poet who enjoyed a very close association with musicians and who understood music probably better than any earlier theatre poet had done. In his Neapolitan days he had frequented the salon of the great dramatic soprano Marianna Bulgarelli (la Romanina), where he was on terms of cordial friendship with many of the leading musicians of the day; Carlo Broschi (Farinelli) became his closest friend, and from Porpora he learned singing and composition. Unlike Zeno, he loved music, and always strove to envisage the effect it might have on his dramas when the aria-texts were composed: indeed he apparently improvised at the harpsichord as a stimulus to his poetic fancy, a fact that can hardly fail to remind us of Metastasio's youthful precocity as an *improvvisatore* – a public performer of impromptu verse; for all accounts of the arts of the *improvvisatore* confirm that the poetry was declaimed in incantatory style against a simple musical accompaniment. Celebrity did not spoil him; he was always happy to collaborate with composers, advising and assisting in the most various ways: revising the text of *Didone abbandonata* for Vinci (Strohm 1979: 179), counselling Hasse on the use of *accompagnato* in *Attilio Regolo* (Burney 1796, I: 316), coaching the young Salieri in the arts of declamation (H. Abert 1978, I: 180). According to Mattei, Jommelli 'claimed to have learned much more from the conversation of Metastasio than from the lessons of Feo, Leo, and Padre Martini' (Surian 1978: 346).

In the previous chapter I have suggested some of the reasons why it no longer seems possible to accept the eighteenth-century view of Metastasio as a major tragedian. In an influential paragraph on *Didone abbandonata* the nineteenth-century critic De Sanctis coined the phrase 'a superficie tragico, a fondo comico'.[2]

The comic is to be found in that 'yes and no' of passion, in those sudden irresistible movements, which break out unforeseen and against expectation; in the irrational, pushed to the absurd; in the intrigues and low cunning, more worthy of a common woman than a queen; and all so apposite, so natural, so vital, that the public laughs and applauds as though to say: it is true!   (Translated in Monelle 1976: 274)

If at its most impassioned, Metastasio's art is closer to the spirit of comedy than of tragedy, at its ripest and most opulent – for instance in *L'Olimpiade* (Vienna 1733) – it veers between elegy and idyll, tears and smiles, with so easy an artfulness that one scarcely knows which is which; but again, of tragedy in the usual acceptance of the term, there is no trace. To quote another influential Metastasio critic, Walter Binni, the 'graph' ('diagramma') of the Metastasian melodrama records 'a continuous fluctuating vibration of the characters between hopes and fears . . . under the thrust of a destiny which alternately flatters and threatens and reveals only at the last its rational providential face' (Binni 1968d: 4). However different one work may be from another, Metastasio's dramas, through their whole range, achieved a synthesis of ecstatically lyrical tone and Classically rigorous form that was uniquely attractive to the age. Dionysos and Apollo were reconciled, sensibility and reason alike gratified in his work. Metastasio's notes on Horace's *Ars poetica* show how important to his own understanding of poetry this dichotomy was:

[The poet's mind] must be inflamed by that kind of burning agitation which is called *inspiration, enthusiasm,* or *poetic frenzy* . . . But lest that fruitful and most useful impulse . . . should exceed the bounds . . . it is essential always to bear in mind the golden words of Horace . . . 'Good judgement is the principal asset of a fine writer' and accordingly to take care that the transports of inspiration should never disturb the equilibrium of reason, but always be controlled by it.
(Binni 1968d: 476)

As the poles of Metastasio's own sensibility were 'poetic frenzy' and a rigorous Classicism learned partly from the example of Zeno, but more from the rigorous upbringing of his teacher Gravina, so the poles of his dramatic art are love and self-sacrificial heroism. This is true not only of individual works, but of the whole arc of his production, at least until the comparatively unproductive years after 1740. The explosion of youthful passion in *Didone abbandonata* (Naples 1724) was followed by a series of more austerely Classical works produced in Rome – *Catone in Utica* and *Ezio*, both 1728, show the trend most clearly; the exquisitely lyrical works of the last Italian and first Viennese years – notably *Artaserse* (Rome and Venice 1730), *L'Olimpiade* and *Demofoonte* (both Vienna 1733) – were followed by a series of more heroically Classical, determinedly didactic dramas – beginning with *La clemenza di Tito* (Vienna 1734) – which were seen by his contemporaries as the peak of his achievement, but which modern critics tend to regard as the beginning of his decline; for they detect a drying-up of the lyrical vein, a heavier hand with the sententiousness, a repetitiousness in the structure.

The poet as dramatist

In another of the classic pronouncements that are scattered through the pages of De Sanctis's *Storia della letteratura italiana*, the critic declares: 'Zeno was the architect of the *dramma per musica*, Metastasio was its poet.' Little then need be added here to what has been said in the previous chapter of the structure of the new kind of libretto. In Metastasio as in Zeno we find a strict separation of dramatic action and music; the same complex pattern of entrances and exits, the same ever-changing interrelations between the characters, the same multiple peripateias – *orologeria* (clock-making or clockwork) is a favourite term among Italian critics – are designed to produce an array of fluctuating atmospheres, moods and passions; common to both authors is the preoccupation with moral philosophy, the conviction that a primary function of drama is to instil truth. Metastasio only did these things much more beguilingly. The most rebarbative philosophical topics blossomed at his touch, thought Arteaga (Arteaga 1785, I: 352); Burney too found him the perfect embodiment of that Horatian precept that 'a true poet . . . unites the sweetness of verse with the utility of his precepts' (Burney 1796, III: 299).

The fact that Metastasio's range of accomplishments made him the great representative figure of eighteenth-century *opera seria* does not endear him to the modern opera-lover; for the style of opera he represents is profoundly alien to all modern principles of music drama. Yet every detail of his art formed part of a coherent aesthetic system. He pondered his work deeply himself, and his cultivated contemporaries experienced it as a supreme dramatic embodiment of their most human impulses and most enlightened aspirations. Those ideals inspired not only the fundamental principles of the operatic form but its finer stylistic details too. For example, that sententiousness which the modern sensibility finds so repellent was, in the eighteenth century, the natural cast of a reflective, well educated mind. Metastasio himself, in his letters, often speaks like a character out of one of the more solemn episodes of his own operas. Sententiousness seemed not only educationally desirable, but apt and natural dramatically, provided only, as Arteaga observed, it was not applied to those passions that tended to undermine reason, like love (Arteaga 1785, I: 55).

Metastasio's style of characterization is also, to our way of thinking, disconcerting; for the characters veer and grope their ways through the plot in a condition of continual perplexity. They do that, obviously, so that the complexity of their personalities may be broken down into a multitude of single facets expressible in solo arias. Attempts have been made to connect this 'perplexity' with a tradition of psychological self-analysis in Italian lyrical poetry extending back to Petrarch. Metastasio himself, as we might foresee, interpreted the problem in terms of a battle between passion and reason. In a letter to Bettinelli written in 1734, and prompted by criticism of *Demofoonte*, he argued,

I believe that a person may act differently in different situations without inconsistency of character. *Timanthes*, is a valiant young man, subject to the emotions of youth, though naturally reasonable, and furnished by education with maxims suitable to persons of his rank. When assaulted by passion, he is impetuous, violent and inconsiderate. But when he has time to reflect, or any object present, reminds him of his duty, he is just, moderate, and rational . . .
     . . . From the contrast of these two universal principles, reason and passion, arises the diversity in the characters of men, as each of these, or both prevail.

(Burney 1796, I: 148–50)

But the deepest problem of Metastasian opera, the issue that creates the seemingly unbridgeable gulf between his understanding of the art and our own, is the question of what constitutes dramatic music. The separating out of drama and music in Zeno had stemmed from the belief that music in its own right, as an autonomous art, could not be dramatic, or even expressive, at all. It might please the ear, or engage the intellect; but it could move the passions, and speak the language of reason and nature, only in so far as it served as an adjunct to, or a reinforcement of, or an imitation of, a poetic text. And for all that Metastasio understood music so much better than Zeno, acknowledging not simply its hedonistic charm, but its power to enchant, and to illuminate the hidden recesses of the heart, still these powers depended – as he put it in his reflections on Aristotle's poetics – on its 'keeping company with the poetry' (Gallarati 1984: 21). In the opera of the 1720s and 1730s such a belief led to an attitude diametrically opposed to our own. Because of developments in the later eighteenth century – especially in Gluck and Mozart – and thanks to those widenings of the orchestral and harmonic horizons associated with the 'German hegemony' from Haydn to Wagner, we have come to think of the composer as the man whose art realizes or embodies the drama; it is his melodic invention, his harmonic and orchestral imagination that conjures into theatrical life the thoughts and feelings of the characters; for us it is axiomatic that, potentially at least, an elaborately scored aria is more dramatic than one accompanied only by a small group of strings and continuo, that *recitativo accompagnato* is more dramatic than *recitativo semplice*, that an ensemble finale is more dramatic than a sequence of recitatives and arias. Metastasio's view was quite different. In *opera seria* during this classic phase *he* was the dramatist – far more so than the poets who worked with Gluck in his 'reform-operas' were ever to be. The composers (and singers) offered nothing more than an individual slant or colouring of a drama that was essentially Metastasio's, their role – as has been remarked – not altogether unlike that of the modern producer. 'Believe me', wrote Metastasio to the Chevalier de Chastellux in 1765, 'whenever music aspires at the pre-eminence over poetry in a drama, she destroys both that and herself . . . I know by daily experience, that my own dramas are much more certain of success in Italy, when declaimed by comedians [i.e. actors], than when sung by musicians' (Burney 1796, II: 318). For Metastasio, therefore, that music was most dramatic which allowed his own voice to be heard most clearly and unencumbered: the recitative and the so-called *aria parlante*. Conversely a more elaborate musical setting, a virtuoso *aria di bravura*, a sumptuous choral scene or a richly contrived orchestral texture generally showed that the piece in question served a non-dramatic or decorative function: hence their conspicuousness in the 'occasional' forms of *serenata* and *festa teatrale*, and – in opera – in scenes in which the singer stands back

196

from the action, drawing a moral or pointing an analogy in vivid and fanciful metaphor. Room was always found in the *dramma per musica* for such scenes, since without them music could display only half her charms. The essential point, however, remains; these were episodes of musical self-indulgence, to be countenanced only as the drama receded.

Strictly, then, it becomes difficult to avoid the conclusion that the crucial part of an *opera seria* was the *recitativo semplice* (cf. Monelle 1978). But that is only another way of saying what I have said already, that the drama is the creation not of the composer but of the poet. Of course the best composers wrote their recitatives carefully, vividly, even imaginatively; but in doing so they abdicated all personality, all fancy and inventiveness. The object was to give a scrupulously accurate delivery of the text according to formulae that were already completely standardized, and which were to endure as long again, so that Burney, at the end of the century, could describe them as 'fixed and permanent as a dead language' (Burney 1796, III: 344).

Naples and Venice

As has perhaps already become clear, I continue to believe in what has been called 'the fairy-tale of Neapolitan opera', as most eighteenth-century writers clearly did. The Neapolitan conservatories educated the most admired composers and singers of the age. Metastasio spent his formative years there, made his name as Italy's leading melodramatic poet there, and always preferred to work with Neapolitan-trained composers. The San Carlo theatre, built on to the Royal Palace of the Bourbon monarchy in 1737, rapidly became the most prestigious opera-house in Italy, and from the 1720s virtually to the end of the century Neapolitan composers were coveted in Rome and Venice, in Dresden, Stuttgart, Paris, London and St Petersburg. But it would be too reckless an oversimplification to suggest that the first fifty years of the history of the *dramma per musica* could be disposed of with a summary account of Zeno's reform and the revolution in musical taste accomplished by Metastasio, Vinci and his Neapolitan fellows.

For a start, some resolutely declined to reform themselves, and their number included the greatest of all the composers to set the dramas of Zeno and Frigimelica-Roberti, Alessandro Scarlatti. The contrapuntal tensions of his music, the seamless rhythms, the sophisticated harmonies – often in the minor key, which was very sparingly used by the new generation – made few concessions to modern style, even though this meant a gradual falling-off of popular enthusiasm for his music in the later part of his career. Indeed to the very end, despite a breadth of operatic experience unrivalled in the seventeenth century and equalled by few even in the eighteenth,

Scarlatti gives the impression that he was less at home in the thronging public theatres of Naples, than among a select audience of *cognoscenti* gathered in some Roman palace – the kind of environment, in fact, in which he had first made his name as a composer of opera.

But a contrast between old-fashioned, subtle Romans and innovatory, simplifying Neapolitans (most of whom, significantly, gained their spurs in comic opera) does not do either. For in point of fact many aspects of the new musical language of the Neapolitans were borrowed, particularly from Venice. As far back as Pollarolo, and still more decisively in Lotti and Gasparini (who nearly became Metastasio's father-in-law), the Venetians had been feeling their way towards new ideals of clarity, conciseness and simplicity. And well before Vinci and Leo, composers like Vivaldi and Orlandini had abandoned the *obbligato* and 'concertizing' use of instruments in favour of an orchestral texture of homogeneous flatness, quite frankly a background to the singing voice. The Neapolitans may have had more genius – their contemporaries certainly thought so; but it has been suggested that the only point at which they significantly departed from the style of the slightly older Venetians was in their more intimate dependence on the rhythms of the verse. And so the autonomous rhythm of the dance, still conspicuous in Venetian music, plays little part in the Neapolitan (Strohm 1978: 244).

The role of music in the *dramma per musica*

Eighteenth-century aesthetics taught that music imitates nature with the means proper to it. That meant not so much musical pictorialism, though that clearly had a role to play, but rather – in Metastasio's own words – 'to imitate the speech of men, with numbers and harmony' (Burney 1796, II: 135). It is possible that the Naples conservatories provided some kind of systematic training in this problematic art: an article in the *Giornale del regno delle Due Sicilie* for 24 October 1821 describes the Neapolitan composers of the previous century as having reduced 'melody to rules analogous to those constituting the grammar of every spoken language . . . The principle of their system lay in the rediscovery of the melodic shape (concetto melodico) and the rhythmic movement best suited to express the sense of the words' (Robinson 1972: 114–15). In an age of rapidly changing taste, the 1720–30 generation of Neapolitans set standards of word-setting that were admired for decades. In the 1780s Johann Friedrich Reichardt was still pointing to 'Non sò con dolce moto' from Leo's *Ciro riconosciuto* (Turin 1739) as a model of expressive declamation, and when the Italian scholar Radiciotti began exploring this repertory in the 1930s he was so impressed by the declamatory fidelity of Pergolesi's settings in *L'Olimpiade* (Rome 1735) as to speak of a 'Gluck prima di Gluck'[3] (Radiciotti 1935: 50): he found the same disdain for vulgar appeal, the same absence of concessions to mere virtuosity. But the composer who surpassed all others in his ability to wed voice and verse was Vinci; he, more clearly than any of his contemporaries, saw that the composer's task in the *dramma per musica* was not the emotional or atmospheric interpretation of a text, but the shaping into melody of the character's speech and gesture. 'Metastasio's verses are made to resonate, by that means discovering their real selves for the first time . . . [in some arias] the music is as natural as if it were not there' (Strohm 1979: 185). Strohm goes on to speak of the final pages of *Didone abbandonata* with – to the modern ear – their astonishing sparseness of means, and finds their haunting power the result not of any literary or musical conception but of a 'theatrical vision' inspired by a great singing actress (Marianna Bulgarelli).

An excerpt from the middle section of Jarba's 'Chiamami pur così' (*Didone abbandonata*, Act II scene 14) will show the extraordinary vividness of Vinci's declamatory style (Ex.III.1). Vinci incorporates snarling semi-quavers and menacing chromaticism; he punctuates the line with exclama-tory 'nò, nò's which give extra vehemence to Jarba's mood; there is even a recurrence of a line from the first part of the aria – 'chiamami pur così' – in the second, a tiny poignant detail which brings to operatic life all his festering resentment at being regarded as a 'barbarian'. But all this expressive and psychological and gestic vividness does not obliterate the verse: clearly, the music's rhythm arises from the poem's metre, and the rhetorical emphasis of word-repetition or coloratura is used only when the phrase of text has been heard at least once, plain and clear. Even in the *furioso* style composers aimed for this kind of clarity: often it is the orchestra that does the raging, and against that the voice gives a distinct syllabic account of the text (Ex.III.2). Other composers tended to be freer than Vinci with word repetitions, especially if they served some expressive purpose; and all composers of the period had a more nervously sensitive variant on the declamatory type of aria, a basically syllabic melody all a-tremble with grace-notes (Ex.III.3).

The examples I have quoted so far certainly illustrate the Neapolitan composers' preoccupation with 'imitating the speech of men, with numbers and harmony'. But even in this 'speaking' style of song, coloratura could be used to good expressive purpose. In addition to the kind found in Jarba's aria, which illustrates Rousseau's point that 'violent passion tends to choak the voice' (via John Brown, in Monelle 1979: 179), it may be used as a symbol of heroic virtue, a transmutation into sound of mighty deeds masterfully accomplished; or – on a small scale – to give rhetorical emphasis – almost 'madrigalian' emphasis – to an individual word. The full-scale *aria di bravura* however (and the elaborate orchestral apparatus that generally went with it) served not primarily an expressive or dramatic function, but a decorative one.

When, at the start of his book, Arteaga laid down the basic principles of

199

JARBA

Quel bar - ba - ro che sprez - zi non pla - che - ran - no i vezzi nò,

str

nò ne sof - fri - rà l'in - gan - no, nò, nò, quel

bar - ba - ro da te, chia - ma - mi, chia - ma - mi pur co - sì, non

sof - fri - rà l'in - gan - no, nò, nò - - -

That barbarian whom you scorn will not be appeased by flatteries, no, no,
nor will he allow himself to be deceived by you; no, no, that barbarian –
call me so if you will – will not allow himself to be deceived.

Ex.III.1 Vinci, *Didone abbandonata* (1726), Act II scene 14

All, all you enemies and evil-doers must tremble; treacherous ones,
you know it, and still you insult me?

Ex.III.2 Pergolesi, *Adriano in Siria* (1734), Act II scene 8

the opera as he understood them, he wrote that, while the poet had three
objects – to move, to depict, to instruct – the composer had only two: 'the
principal object is to move, the subsidiary to depict' (Arteaga 1785, I:
32–5). That is obviously not the whole story, but it does perhaps help
clarify one fundamental fact about the *opera seria*, particularly in this early
phase. Behind all the eighteenth-century attempts to classify and draw up

... That that heart, that haughty brow should feel love, should rejoice to
look upon me...

Ex.III.3 Porpora, *Semiramide riconosciuta* (1729), Act I scene 5

typologies of arias – Goldoni's *aria patetica, aria di bravura, aria parlante, aria di mezzo carattere* and *aria brillante* is one of the best known – there were, very broadly, two types of aria text, with two distinct functions and two distinct musical styles: 'the declamatory dramatic text, basis of the *aria parlante*, and the picturesque text – simile or otherwise – which is set either with special instrumental effects or as an *aria di bravura*' (Monelle 1979: 201).

In the 1720s and 1730s virtually all the more extravagant flights of bravura and all the more ostentatious examples of rhythmic and colouristic tone-painting arise from metaphor texts. A particularly interesting case is Pergolesi's *Adriano in Siria* (Naples 1734) where the most flamboyant pieces are settings of substitute texts, apparently added to the opera to provide a higher density of the picturesque than is to be found in Metastasio's originals. The effect of all these essays in tone-painting is, in the most literal sense, superficial. It is not quite true that Italians failed to recognize that instrumental music could be expressive: for example, in the famous letter to Hasse about *Attilio Regolo* Metastasio speaks of the 'character of the symphony [being] majestic, slow, and sometimes interrupted; expressing as it were the state of Regulus's mind in reflecting upon his entering that place as a slave, in which he formerly presided as consul' (Burney 1796, I: 323). Nevertheless in the fields of harmony and instrumental colour the imagination of Italian composers was still exceedingly inhibited, and their tone-painting sounds curiously remote, more like the metaphor of a metaphor than a direct impression of any experienced reality. The decorative effect of the *aria di bravura* is often heightened by

202

the actual style of the coloratura: tuneful, sequentially formed, neatly articulated.

The music of the *opera seria* was virtually monopolized by the solo aria; ensembles were limited to one or two duets per opera; the chorus was reintroduced by Leo, but none of his Neapolitan contemporaries showed much interest in it. Of the arias, a very few were in free forms motivated by their dramatic function, but the vast majority employed a basically similar, standard form that had evolved out of the *da capo* aria of the late seventeenth century. With the separation of the aria from the dramatic action, and the consequent temptation to think of arias as discrete works of art, the sophistication of their architecture had developed apace. In fact, by the second quarter of the eighteenth century, the vocal aria was the most highly developed of contemporary musical structures, employing a pattern of ritornellos and vocal sections as follows:

	ritornello 1	tonic
	A1	
	first vocal section (setting of first half of text)	tonic→dominant
principal section	ritornello 2	
	A2	
	second vocal section (first half of text repeated)	dominant→tonic (or all tonic)
	ritornello 3	tonic (*fine*)
	B	
middle section	third vocal section (setting of second half of text)	related keys, especially subdominant and relative minor
		(*Da capo*)

The ritornello was understood to give a résumé of the central idea or ideas of the aria. Heinichen, in his *Anweisung . . . des Generalbasses* (Hamburg 1711), advises composers to begin the writing of an aria by seizing on some *locos topicos* in the text, and letting the whole aria grow from the musical figure suggested by that. But in Italy, by the 1720s, that ideal of organic unity had been superseded by one of balanced, complementary or sometimes contrasting phrases: so that each of the sections A1, A2 and B were articulated into several subdivisions.

This practice was particularly common in the straggling design of the *aria di bravura*, but it took its most interesting form when it was prompted by some quality in the verse. In Metastasio it happened often, apparently inspired by the harmonious simplicity of his rhymes and rhythms, by the modern 'French' lucidity of his syntax, and the seemingly artless structure of his lyrics, which contained few enjambements, and tended to an epigrammatic conciseness in the closing lines of each half. Such verses as the following, from *Adriano in Siria*, contain the seeds not only of the short, balanced musical phrases of the new Neapolitan style, but also of its fleeting minor-key episodes, and its pungent cadence phrases:

Digli ch'è un infedele,
Digli che mi tradì.
Senti, non dir così,
Digli che partirò,
Digli che l'amo.[4]

Ex.III.4 Pergolesi, *Adriano in Siria* (1734), Act III scene 1

di - gli   che l'a - mo

Tell him he is a faithless one; tell him he betrayed me. No, listen; don't
say that. Tell him I shall go away, tell him I love him.

Ex.III.4 *continued*

A few bars of the principal section will show what Pergolesi made of it
(Ex.III.4). The transitional episodes of minor-key harmony and the
sharply contoured cadence phrases of the operatic aria were primary
sources of the Scarlatti sonata. Indeed the sonata style as a whole was deeply
indebted to the kind of thematic articulation found in these arias.

In Naples in the late 1720s and early 1730s Vinci, Leo, Pergolesi and
Hasse, not to mention a host of lesser composers, were all producing operas
inspired by the new ideals that have been the subject of these last two
chapters. But all the leaders of that generation disappeared with tragic
rapidity: Vinci, not yet forty years old, died mysteriously in 1730;
Pergolesi, having barely reached maturity, in 1736; Leo, still in his prime,
in 1744. Also in 1744, after several years of peregrination over much of
Europe, Hasse finally left Italy to settle in Dresden. But he alone survived
of the great representatives of what soon came to be seen as the Golden Age
of *opera seria*. And while he certainly developed beyond the limits of the
style he had cultivated in the 1720s and 1730s, he continued to enjoy
Metastasio's friendship and unqualified enthusiasm into the final quarter of
the century. Back in Naples leadership passed to a new generation, who
soon began to call into question the perfectly controlled equilibrium of the
Metastasian *dramma per musica*.

12 · The performance of *opera seria*

The social function of opera

If *opera seria* sounds a little daunting to modern taste, as it assuredly does, nevertheless, during the ascendancy of this form, opera became more popular than ever before. Venice continued to cultivate it with the same enthusiasm as in the seventeenth century; Florence, Rome, Naples and most other large cities were immensely more productive than they had been; and it spread to many new centres, for instance to the Tuscan provincial cities – Siena, Livorno, Pisa, Lucca, Pistoia – under the encouragement of the Grand Duke Ferdinando (Weaver and Weaver 1978: 34). Opera became so popular for two apparently distinct if not mutually exclusive reasons: in the first place as a public entertainment on the Venetian model; in the second, as the most spectacular of the art-forms appropriate to the representative courtly life of a royal or ducal capital. The two great court theatres of Italy were both opened within the space of a few years in the very heyday of Metastasian opera – the San Carlo at Naples in 1737, the Teatro Regio at Turin in 1740.

In fact the two aims of public entertainment and courtly representation were by no means mutually exclusive. Gala night at the San Carlo was a pageant contrived with the most ostentatious magnificence, involving the elite of the nation, ranked in symbolic order about the figure of the sovereign. Something of its effect as a public spectacle may be imagined from Burney's account of such an evening:

It is not easy to imagine or describe the grandeur and magnificence of this spectacle . . . It being the great festival of St Charles and the King of Spain's name-day, the court was in grand gala, and the house was not only doubly illuminated, but amazingly crowded with well-dressed company. In the front of each box there is a mirror, three or four feet long, by two or three wide, before which are two large wax tapers; these, by reflection, being multiplied, and added to the lights of the stage and to those within the boxes, make the splendour too much for the aching sight . . . as a spectacle [it] surpasses all that poetry or romance have painted . . .   (Burney 1771: 335–6, 339)

The court theatres, and such provincial theatres as those in Tuscany that had evolved out of the Academies of an earlier age, normally staged opera as a kind of seasonal ritual. It was particularly linked with the Carnival season – 26 December to the beginning of Lent – but with local variations. Thus in

Turin in the 1770s 'the serious opera begins . . . the sixth of January, the king's name-day, and continues every day except Friday till Lent' (Burney 1771: 63). On the other hand 'the opera at Naples acts from St Charles's day [4 November] to Lent' (there was a pause during Advent) 'and three times a week' (Grosley 1769, II: 235). Public theatres needed a more continuous round of activity, and usually offered more varied fare: comic opera, spoken plays, *commedia dell'arte* performances by visiting groups.

The explosion of operatic activity all over the peninsula led to a sharp increase in the demand for performers – particularly, of course, for solo singers; and the financial rewards for those who succeeded in establishing themselves at the top of the profession were alluring indeed. The consequences were manifold. Standards in church music seem generally to have declined: Burney reported that 'all the *musici* [*castrati*] in the churches at present are made up of the refuse of the opera-houses' (Burney 1771: 303–4). Fewer singers were now retained as court musicians, the vast majority being free-lance artists travelling wherever their engagements called them. The somewhat precarious character of the professional singers' career under these new circumstances encouraged the formation of travelling companies who took opera to provincial centres in Italy and beyond. In the process havoc was frequently wrought on the emotions and sensibilities of the inhabitants of these dead-and-alive spots. In 1768 a petition was presented to the King of Naples on behalf of the wives and mothers of Trani, where Maria Cecilia Coletti's attractions had destroyed the peace of several households, by bewitching husbands into 'scandaloso amoreggiamento',[1] and seducing young men from their studies (Croce 1926: 256). By the second half of the century some critics felt that opera had become too popular. What should have been an educative and ennobling experience had, thought Arteaga, degenerated into a mere pastime, an antidote to *noia*, sweetening the existence of a people which had been deprived of its ancient liberty. As a result, vulgar taste predominated over educated taste and the degradation of the operatic art was inevitable (Arteaga 1785, II: 5–6, 84). Algarotti shared this vision: the opera-house ought to be a Temple of Art, where the intellectual elite of civilized humanity – 'the Addisons, the Drydens, the Daciers, the Muratori's, the Gravinas, the Marcellos' – could sit in 'solemn audience' (Algarotti 1969: 473 [1755]).

How essential the box-system was to the financial well-being of an Italian opera-house has already been suggested in an earlier chapter (Chapter 6 above, p. 119). In court theatres and cities with a large diplomatic corps it was also important in the symbolism of social hierarchy: a box's desirability had nothing to do with visibility and acoustics; everything to do with its position in relation to the royal box. As in seventeenth-century Venice so now in Naples, Rome and innumerable other Italian cities, the opera-house

Plate 6 A scene from the 1729 production of Leonardo Vinci's *La contesa dei Numi*

Plate 7 A *spettacolo* in the Teatro San Benedetto, Venice, 1782

became the focus of social life. It was the most convenient place to meet, talk and take refreshment with friends; it provided facilities for cards, chess and gambling; even if you were old, disillusioned and bibulous, like Charles Edward Stuart, the Young Pretender, it was worth going, for your slumbers would perhaps be that little bit sweeter in the opera-house than at home (cf. Kelly 1975: 55–6). Burney describes the accommodation at Milan, which was typical of the better theatres:

The theatre here is very large and splendid; it has five rows of boxes on each side, one hundred in each row; and parallel to these runs a broad gallery, round the house, as an avenue to every row of boxes: each box will contain six persons, who sit at the sides, facing each other. Across the gallery of communication is a complete room to every box, with a fireplace in it, and all conveniences for refreshments and cards. In the fourth row is a *pharo* table, on each side of the house, which is much used during the performance of the opera . . .   (Burney 1771: 81)

Like Stendhal a hundred years later, Edward Wright, in Venice in 1720, found that those who wished to listen closely to the opera went into the pit. It would seem they had to, for reports are unanimous that, except during the performance of favourite numbers, the noise created by the audience was abominable; at a court theatre it was appreciably restrained when the sovereign was present, though still not enough to enable Burney to hear the singers clearly at the San Carlo. Wright uses a surprising period simile, remarking that the audience (at Reggio Emilia) 'minded the Opera no more (though Faustina sang) than if it had been . . . a sermon' (Wright 1730, I: 30). We have seen from Kelly's remarks on Roman audiences quoted in the Introduction (p. 14) that the intermittent attention paid to the spectacle did not blunt critical acerbity, nor conversely were the ecstasies of Glinka and his companions (cited at p. 398) a merely Romantic phenomenon. 'The refinements of vocal art were', reported Grosley, '[relished] with a delight, which in Italy is called the *foretaste of the joys of Paradise*, where, we may hope, there will be others equivalent, for those nations whose organs are less sensible to the powers of harmony' (Grosley 1769, II: 234).

To an outsider the spectacle afforded by an eighteenth-century Italian theatre – I do not speak yet of the performance – often appeared one of confusion, even pandemonium. But in fact behaviour was strictly regulated by protocol, in at least all court and civic theatres. A single example must suffice: at Florence the deputy in charge of theatre protocol was empowered to intervene

if there is 'extraordinary applause that might be found indecent to the dignity of a theatre qualified by the protection of this Sovereignty'. Further, if the audience divides itself into claques in favour of this or that actor or ballet dancer, he must use his authority to the point of calling out the soldiers to remove the obstreperous members of the audience and, if he thinks it wise, to arrest and remove also the actor or dancer who occasions such behaviour.   (Weaver and Weaver 1978: 55)

Opera as spectacle

We should have found the spectacle on stage no less astonishing. Burney was scathing about the seventeenth-century delight in 'expensive and childish machinery' (Burney 1776–89, IV: 561), but this certainly did not disappear overnight with Zeno's reforms. Edward Wright was still impressed with the 'dextrous managing [of] the Machinery' in Venice:

The Emperor with the Empress appear in a Triumphal Chariot, drawn by an Elephant. The Head, Trunk, and Eyes of the great Beast move as if alive, and *Tiridates* believes he is so. When, all of a sudden, as soon as the Emperor and Empress are dismounted and have taken their Seats, the Triumphal Chariot is transform'd into an Amphitheatre, and fill'd with Spectators. The Elephant falls all in pieces, and out of his Belly come a great number of Gladiators, arm'd with Bucklers, which were so many parts of the Elephant's Sides, so that he seems in a moment to be transform'd into a Company of arm'd Men, who make a Skirmish, all in time to the Musick. (Wright 1730, I: 84)

Zeno and Metastasio certainly encouraged a more moderate and rational use of spectacle. But with the vogue for the emulation of French opera that came to a climax in the 1760s, splendid visual effects returned, though not usually in the 'marvellous' style of the seventeenth century. Grosley was thrilled with an opera at Naples in 1758 which involved 'battles . . . fought between numerous bodies of dancing masters in rich uniforms . . . [and] cavalry . . . mounted on horses from the King's stables, or those of the first nobility' (Grosley 1769, II: 233).

Tastes in décor and design changed only slowly. Ferdinando Bibiena introduced angle-perspective at Bologna in 1703, and during the first half of the century this came to oust the earlier kind of perspective set completely: that 'now seemed boring' reported Algarotti in 1755. With its combination of seeming naturalness (for the spectator, as it were, *over-looked* the scene instead of being posed at the central viewing point) and real virtuosity (for the low vanishing points of both perspectives gave the set an immense looming height), the angle-perspective set was a typical product of the age. In the latter part of the century both set-designs and costumes began to show a growing awareness of historical authenticity. This has sometimes been attributed to the interest in the 'real life' of the Ancient World which had been stimulated by the excavations at Pompeii from 1748. The movement towards theatrical naturalism emanating from Garrick in London will also have contributed.

Acting and singing

The vividness, naturalness and spontaneity of the actors in the *opera buffa* were often the subject of admiring comment. It was very different with *opera seria*, in which a considerable portion of the acting was in fact a decorous ritual rotating round the principal singers, the luminaries to whom lesser figures served simply as 'candeglieri' – the expression is borrowed from Gaetano Berenstadt, one of Handel's singers in London (Lindgren 1981: 341). A fundamental issue was the respective rank and dignity of the characters, which was made manifest by such accessories as train-bearers, and by the positioning of the singers on stage. Metastasio was once consulted by the Abate Pasquini to resolve a dispute that had arisen at a rehearsal of *Demofoonte*. While his reply affects to place considerations of drama and common sense above anything else, it shows in fact that he for one did not question the importance of such stage decorum at all – simply felt that it might be interpreted a little more flexibly than some *prima donna*s did:

If you ask me who should be placed on the right hand, and who on the left, I must tell you I never meant to regulate that by the dignity of the personages, but by the convenience and necessity of the action. And if, in favour of such convenience and necessity, the superior personages chance to be on the left of the inferior, they may be respected and distinguished in various ways; for example: by being a little forwarder on the stage and facing the audience, while the subaltern characters are further on the stage, with their sides to the audience and faces towards the principal personages. And indeed by a thousand other expedients they may be distinguished, without having the right side of the stage assigned to them. (Burney 1796, I: 225–6)

Clearly, from this description, the greater part of the music of the opera would have been sung from a position at the front and centre of the scene. The stage was 'dressed' by a harmonious grouping of the performers, and the individual singer addressed himself to the audience from a 'composed stance' with 'rhetorically eloquent gesture and expressive face-play' (Savage 1989: 143). But the decade in which Pasquini was involved in this dispute with his *prima donna* was also the decade in which Garrick was revolutionizing the English theatre. There, too, in heroic or tragic drama, posed declamation and decorous processional had prevailed, until he ousted it with new ideals of naturalness and total illusion. 'If this young fellow be right, then we have all been wrong', exclaimed James Quin, the doyen of the senior tragedians (Heartz 1967–68: 111); and if that was the effect on someone brought up on English drama, one can only conjecture what might have been the impact on an Italian singer brought up on Zeno and Metastasio. One does not invoke Garrick casually, for his ideals spread rapidly to the Continent. 'Mr Garrick, the celebrated English actor, is the model I wish to put forward', wrote Noverre in his epoch-making *Lettres sur la danse et les ballets* of 1760 (Heartz 1967–68: 120); and Noverre at the time was a colleague of Jommelli at Stuttgart. Moreover, according to Burney, it was from Garrick that Gaetano Guadagni, Gluck's original Orpheus, acquired his ideas of acting.

While such foreign centres of Italian opera as Stuttgart and Vienna soon felt the influence of Garrick's new theatrical ideals, it was much fainter in Italy itself. There the older styles of acting survived, with singers jerking from mincing movements and gestures in the recitative into statuesque poses for the arias. Perhaps the growing fondness for accompanied recitative in the second half of the century was not unconnected with the desire to break down this particular dichotomy, for it was generally recognized that *accompagnato* required the most lifelike and characterful kind of acting. If to the end of the century audiences contrived to be overwhelmed by the pathos and beauty of the *opera seria* composed by such men as Paisiello and Cimarosa it was with a growing awareness that too often this state was achieved in despite of the spectacle presented by the actors.

It was achieved above all because of the stupendous vocal arts mastered during the course of the century. And it is the absolutely central and fundamental role of the singer *as singer* that makes *opera seria* the most mysterious and inaccessible of all operatic repertories; for the singer of whom we speak is not the *prima donna* or the lyric tenor or the *basso profondo*, but the *castrato*. And with the *castrato* we come to an aspect of the Age of Enlightenment that is surely very dark indeed. It is no doubt the case that every age has its own peculiar forms of humbug, hypocrisy and perversion, but few of them, one feels, can surpass those the eighteenth century indulged in over its opera singers in general and its *castrati* in particular. For what are we to make of an age that worshipped Reason, Nature and Truth, yet in music could conceive of heroism only in terms of the high soprano voice; or of the cultivated man who, if Burney is to be believed, regarded castration with revulsion as a disgrace to the Italian people, yet who built their most idealistic art-form round the products of that procedure; or of the ecclesiastic government of the Papal States which, regarding female opera singers as so morally reprehensible that they were banned from appearing on the public stage, supplied their place with male sopranos acquired by a process of mutilation clearly contrary to Canon Law, and the perpetrators of which were liable to excommunication (the clause in question is quoted in Milner 1973: 251); or of the gentlemen and ladies of quality who, affecting to regard the whole race of *castrati* with disdain and contempt, yet heaped riches on them in their eagerness to purchase their beguiling vocal arts and hazardless amatory ones? One does not wish to embark upon a homily; but it is scarcely to be wondered at if a group of men that was alternately pampered and scorned, lusted after and spat upon, idealized as the deities of musical art and railed at as its worst abusers, became wilful, capricious and egoistic.

The eighteenth century had its share of great tenors and basses and (female) sopranos, but it was chiefly owing to the *castrati* that vocal skills were more highly developed then than at any time before or since. There were physiological reasons for this – the singer retained the clarity of a boy's voice while developing the strength, lung capacity and breath-control of a man's. 'Say what one will', exclaimed Wilhelm Heinse, as he found himself falling under the spell of Pacchierotti in Venice in 1781, 'no woman has so many pure and perfect vocal chords and *such a chest*. There is a strength in the tone and a sustaining power such that the soul cannot but be swept away, as by a torrent' (Heinse 1857: 270).[2] Besides, the *castrati* benefited from a long period of uninterrupted vocal training, whereas natural male voices broke at what was, educationally, the most critical age.

The finest *castrati* had a brilliance, a flexibility, a haunting unearthly beauty of tone, a promptitude of fancy in the arts of ornamentation that have not been heard in the opera-house since Rossini's youth, and the sheer task of imagining which defeats the mind. Yet because of their status in the opera it is not surprising that, with all but the most fastidious, their art gradually tended to be dominated by that one quality in which they most obviously surpassed all other types of singer: brilliance. As early as 1723 Tosi felt that the modern style of singing was inclined to emphasize the brilliant at the expense of the pathetic and the cantabile, but this tendency became critical only in the middle decades of the century. One reason was the influence of Farinelli. By universal assent of all who heard him, Farinelli was the most phenomenally brilliant singer ever to have trod the operatic stage; and though he was himself cultivated and tasteful enough to retain the lifelong friendship of Metastasio, his effect on those who attempted to imitate him was almost certainly deleterious. What one might call the Problem of Virtuosity was worsened by a less obvious factor: the growing habit in the 1740s and 1750s of resetting again and again the same Metastasio (and to a lesser extent Zeno) librettos. As with the endless resettings of Petrarch sonnets in the sixteenth-century madrigal, a situation arose in which music underwent a forced development, because there was the continual need for composers to 'trump' all earlier settings of the same words. Virtuosity was one of the most convenient ways of doing this. As Metastasio himself put it in a letter of August 1755,

The singers of the present times . . . believe themselves more perfect, in proportion as their performance is remote from human nature. Their models are Nightingales, Flageolets, Crickets and Grasshoppers; not the personages they represent or their affections. When they have played their Symphony with the Throat, they believe they have fulfilled all the duties of their art.   (Burney 1796, II: 135)

In the second half of the century the tensions became progressively more acute between the formidable accomplishments of vocal virtuosity (often admirable, useful and desirable) and the quest for the natural, the true and the expressive. One may cite, as a single illustration of this tension, Arteaga's urging that impromptu ornamentation be restricted to those arias where it was expressively apt: joyful and festive arias, graceful ariettas, and songs that serve a naturalistic function within the drama (Arteaga 1785, II: 117f.).

The opera orchestra

The orchestra may be dealt with briefly. For some twenty or thirty years at the start of the century, the textural variety and those strands of distinctive *obbligato* colouring that had distinguished the orchestral style of the generation of Pollarolo and Scarlatti were gradually pared away. Orchestras did not necessarily become smaller, but, if we think of them in their own right for a moment, they did become poor things, drab and subservient, compared with Scarlattian, let alone Handelian orchestras. But no sooner had this deathly plainness been achieved than composers began to fan the orchestra back to life, adding new colours, enlarging the range of dynamic and expressive nuance with which the instruments played. In Vinci's *La caduta dei decemviri* (Naples 1727) we already find the composer relishing the effect of a carefully controlled orchestral crescendo (for full details see Robinson 1972: 121); and in the 1740s composers such as Perez and Jommelli marked the instrumental parts with increasingly refined nuances. During the second half of the century orchestras grew significantly in size: flutes appeared regularly, not simply as alternatives to oboes; clarinets were added, and horns and trumpets assumed a more regular role.

All this was perfectly normal for the period. But the Italian opera orchestra was nevertheless peculiarly different in constitution from the orchestras of northern Europe. At Milan in 1770, Leopold Mozart reported that there were fourteen first violins, fourteen seconds, six violas, two 'cellos, six double-basses, four flutes (two doubling oboes), two clarinets, two bassoons and four horns (Carse 1940: 24). At the end of the century at the San Carlo in Naples there were twenty-five violins, four violas, two 'cellos, six double-basses, two oboes, two clarinets, four bassoons, four horns, two harpsichords (Robinson 1972: 161). The oddities are at once apparent: an immense mass of violins, which must surely have endowed the orchestra's lyrical playing with an almost strident emphasis; and a heavy outnumbering of 'cellos by double-basses. Given the fact that the double-bass was 'played so coarsely throughout Italy, that it produces a sound no more musical than the stroke of a hammer' (Burney 1771: 353), and that two continuo harpsichords were in action as well, the orchestral sound must also have been distinguished by a percussive throbbing beat. The performance was directed jointly by the first harpsichordist, normally the composer, and the leader of the first violins. If the former was responsible for basic *tempi*, and for liaison between stage and pit, the ensemble within the orchestra was really the responsibility of the latter. To those used to the discipline of the best German orchestras, the orchestra of an Italian opera-house could seem rough. Dittersdorf reported that not even Gluck could achieve real finesse from the Bologna orchestra at the première of his *Trionfo di Clelia* in 1763 (Carse 1940: 84). But at its best this chamber-music type of orchestral playing, dependent upon the spontaneous inter-action of the performers, could be thrilling – even too thrilling. Other travellers confirm Burney's report that the Naples orchestra had

an energy and fire, not to be met with perhaps in the whole universe: it is so ardent as to border upon fury; and from this impetuosity of genius, it is common for a Neapolitan composer, in a movement which begins in a mild and sober manner, to set the orchestra in flames before it is finished. (Burney 1771: 378–8)

13 · The collapse of the Metastasian ideal

The undermining of Metastasian aesthetics

In the middle decades of the century the *opera seria* moved into a critical phase. A convenient symptom of the crisis was Metastasio's growing displeasure with the younger generation of composers: he judged Galuppi to be 'a good composer for violins, violoncellos, and for singers: but a very bad workman for poets'; Gluck 'has surprising fire, but is mad . . . [his] spirit, noise and extravagance, have supplied the place of merit in many theatres of Europe'.[1] In fact, complaints of extravagance, noise, 'vocal symphonies', 'graceless shriekings', become an obsession in the poet's correspondence from the late 1740s onwards. This is not simply to be dismissed as the middle-aged querulousness of someone who no longer comprehended what younger men of genius were doing. On the contrary, Metastasio comprehended all too well: the centre of gravity in the *opera seria* was shifting from the drama (in the Metastasian sense) to the music. This development was clearest when Zeno's texts were reset: the recitatives were drastically reduced in length, and the arias were, more often than not, rewritten to provide more euphonious verses that could be worked up into more elaborate musical forms. But resettings of Metastasio showed similar trends: the recitatives trimmed; the arias swelling to ever mightier proportions; the orchestral apparatus becoming continually more sumptuous and obtrusive.

Some of the reasons for this development have been touched upon in the previous chapter. If the *opera seria* repertory consisted largely of resettings of Zeno and Metastasio, the music (apart from the staging – and we have seen how constrained that was) was the only novel element; and therefore the composer's expressive powers, his fancy, the scope he provided for the virtuoso singer were factors bound to weight more heavily in the success of a new work. Metastasio's complaints about the mischief younger composers wrought on his *drammi* in fact provide an eighteenth-century parallel to the complaints about perverse productions of operatic classics in our own day. There may also be some truth in the claim of those critics who thought that audiences were hearing too much opera; they were 'satiated with beauty', their sensibilities blunted to the simple and natural (Arteaga 1785, II: 83–4). And it is surely significant, as Strohm has pointed out, that Rome had become a major centre of production (1979: 240). A city whose spasmodic seventeenth-century operatic tradition had come to a fitting symbolic close in 1697 when the Teatro Tordinona was demolished in the interests of public morality, experienced a phenomenal upsurge of enthusiasm for opera in the first half of the eighteenth century: between 1711 and 1733 five opera-houses were opened or reopened in the city.

The flourishing of opera in Rome affected the development of musical style in a rather roundabout manner. Female singers, it will be recalled, were not permitted to appear on the public stage there; and all-male casts obviously made it more difficult to realize the drama by any other than highly stylized means, which is to say, by any other than primarily musical means. To bring to dramatic life the contrast between the heroic and the treacherous prince, the spunky and the languorous *innamorata*, composers were bound to take their expressive and technical resources to extremes, sometimes to consider whether instrumental music or even the language of the *opera buffa* might not help the task of dramatic clarification. Of course it is true that, however perfect the musico-dramatic equilibrium achieved by the finest *opera seria* of the 1720s and 1730s, creative musical minds could not have remained contentedly within the confines of the Vinci idiom for decades on end. But that does not affect the real problem, which was a dispute – at first largely tacit – between *literati* and musicians as to whether music that was becoming increasingly subtle, complex and brilliant was undermining the established ideals of the *dramma per musica*: the imitation of nature, the expression of the passions of the human heart.

Niccolò Jommelli

Outstandingly the most talented and interesting of the Italians working through these critical decades, indeed one of the greatest figures of the whole century, was Niccolò Jommelli, whose productive career extended from 1737 to 1772. If I dwell for a little longer than usual on the impact that he made on his contemporaries, it is because one can think of no great opera composer whose work is less likely ever to be given the chance to make an impact on us. Jommelli's admiration for Metastasio has already been mentioned (cf. above, p. 193). The feeling was mutual: the 'spherical' and 'pacific' Jommelli 'has surprised me', Metastasio reported to Farinelli in October 1749. 'I have found in him all the harmony of Hasse, with all the grace, expression and invention of Vinci' (Burney 1796, I: 292–3). And, with qualifications, this esteem survived. Yet Jommelli was far from being the paragon of simplicity that the poet's tribute might lead us to expect. Indeed so subtle was his musical mind that by the end of his career he had left Italian musical taste far behind. 'A learned and ingenious Music, like that of Jomelli', declared Mattei in his funeral tribute, 'full of harmony and contrivance, which requires a careful execution, and the utmost stillness and attention in the audience, could not satisfy the frivolous and depraved taste of the Italians . . .' (Burney 1776–89, IV: 568). And no less a musician than Paisiello seemed to confirm this, when he spoke of an oversophistication of art (which he blamed on Jommelli's study of counterpoint with Padre Martini) leading to a downfall in his popular reputation (*MGG*, s.v. 'Jommelli'). Even German musicians found Jommelli's musical gifts formidable. In 1770 the young Mozart enthused over the beauty and craftsmanship of *Armida abbandonata* (Naples 1770), but found that it was 'too serious' for the theatre (Einstein 1946: 396); while C. F. D. Schubart in his *Aesthetik der Tonkunst*, written in the 1780s, actually judged him 'the first composer in the world' (Carse 1940: 5). All these are interesting and remarkable testimonies; but the most interesting of all comes again from Metastasio, this time in a much later letter written to Jommelli himself in April 1765:

> I regard the two masterly airs with which you have kindly favoured me, as precious gifts: and as far as the limits of my musical knowledge extends, I have admired the new and harmonious texture of the voice and accompaniment, the elegance of the one, and the contrivance of the other; and the uncommon unity of the whole, which renders them worthy of your abilities. I must confess, however, my dear Jomelli, that though this style impresses me with respect for the writer, you have, when you please, another which instantly seizes on the heart, without giving the mind the trouble of reflection . . . Ah, my dear *Jomelli*, do not abandon a faculty in which you have not, nor ever will have, a rival. In masterly airs, there may be composers, perhaps, who by dint of pains and labour, will approach you; but in finding the road to the hearts of others, their own must be formed of fibres as delicate and sensitive as yours.   (Burney 1796, II: 375–7)

Metastasio's reservations bring us to the nub of the matter. For Jommelli was simply one, the most richly talented, of a whole generation of composers who were wrestling with the problem of reconciling the claims of natural expressiveness with the possibilities of virtuosity.

By virtuosity I do not mean simply the brilliance of the singers, though that had become increasingly important and was stimulating a profusion of coloratura and word-repetition in most arias: a development that Metastasio, it need hardly be said, beheld with dismay. But just as often the virtuosity was the composer's own; when, for example, Jommelli becomes absorbed in a dextrous working out of the musical ideas, or revels in unexpected or extreme effects of expression. In quite early works we find excitingly eccentric handling of the musical forms for dramatic purposes and dense spasms of sophisticated chromaticism, worthy of Durante's almost legendary chamber-duets (Ex.III.5). Especially prophetic are those pages in which Jommelli tries to break down the dichotomy between 'full music' and 'half music' – the recitative and the aria – by punctuating *accompagnati* with eloquent orchestral 'symphonies', and by absorbing recitative into the arias.

ARTASERSE

che in o - gni mia for - tu - na se - co fi - nor pro -

vla 8 or higher

va - i se - co fi - nor pro - va - i o - gni pia - cer di -

vi - so, di - vi - so o - gni do - lor, di -

(vla)

vi - so o - gni do - lor.

. . .that in every shift of fortune I have hitherto shared every pleasant
experience with him, every sorrow, too.

Ex. III.5 Jommelli, *Artaserse* (1749), Act II scene 1

219

But it was the virtuosity of the orchestral writing that most deeply disturbed those connoisseurs who loved the music of the 1720s and 1730s. The concerto-like expansion of the aria-form necessitated ever huger ritornellos; so the orchestra was thrust more conspicuously on the audience's attention and, as Algarotti and Gluck were to complain, the stylized fracturing of the *opera seria* into acted recitative and posed song became more flagrantly unnatural than before. Orchestras grew larger and the scoring thicker and more complicated – Arteaga saw Jommelli as the source of this development, and Schubart confirmed that it was a common complaint about his music (Abert 1907: xiii). There had always been a place for elaborate orchestral numbers in the *opera seria*; to be specific, in those dramatically non-essential metaphor-arias. But, in Jommelli's music, orchestral tone-painting is no less characteristic of the dramatic arias. Even in the earliest works (and those contrapuntal proclivities that Paisiello was to deplore clearly contributed to this), his music is remarkable for the independence from the voice that the orchestra enjoys. There is little slavish doubling for the first violin, and very little padding out of the harmonies for second violin and viola. Every strand of the instrumental texture is animated and cunningly wrought. And the reason for this was that Jommelli was bent upon persuading opera-goers that, despite the scepticism of philosophers and *literati*, the orchestra could be made to 'speak', could play a major role in enhancing dramatic effect. As the Abbé Vogler wrote of him: 'he spoke without words, and allowed the instruments to continue to declaim even when the poet was silent' (McClymonds 1980: 329).

For it is certain that what Metastasio feared was mere compositional virtuosity, Jommelli intended as an enhancing of dramatic expression. Absolute fidelity to the poetic text was a cardinal principle of his work, as he explained to the librettist Gaetano Martinotti in 1769: 'it is my absolute duty not to betray the words, but to express them well; it is not my duty, indeed it is not in my power, to be able to give them an acuteness of sensibility and passion which of themselves, by their own nature, they do not have' (McClymonds 1980: 328). The elaborately contrived orchestral accompaniment was, then, not simply gratuitous complication: it was designed to provide an expressive enhancement of the text by orchestral means. And those little instrumental figures that animate the texture (particularly in the second violin) are not the arbitrary decorations of a self-indulgent contrapuntalist but an illuminating commentary on the song. Jommelli has borrowed from the *recitativo accompagnato* the idea of expressively significant figures, and by transferring these to the aria accompaniments he loads them with meaning. Sometimes we can hear the process in action, as in the recitative and aria 'Spargerò d'amare piante' from *Fetonte* (Stuttgart 1768). In this scene the sighing 'Lombard' rhythms

Ex.III.6a Jommelli, *Fetonte* (1768), Act I scene 7

of the introductory bars (Ex.III.6a) evolve during the course of the recitative into a more regular orchestral figuration (Ex.III.6b), which becomes in turn the material of ritornello and accompaniment in the following aria (Exx.III.6c and d).

Jommelli appears often to be aiming at a *ne plus ultra* of expressiveness: he is, in fact, a virtuoso of expression. The vocal brilliance he demands is quite astonishing; he requires a large orchestra and keeps it busily and meaningfully employed; his scores are heavily marked with dynamic and

Now let free rein be given to my groans. . .

Ex.III.6b Jommelli, *Fetonte* (1768), Act I scene 7

222

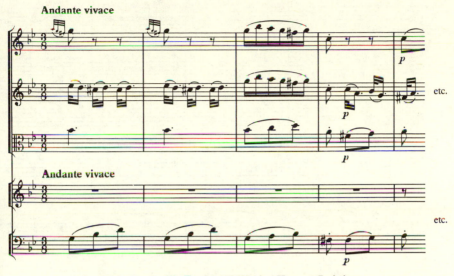

Ex.III.6c Jommelli, *Fetonte* (1768), Act II scene 7: Aria

expressive nuances; he has far more contrapuntal and harmonic resource than any Italian contemporary. But while all these things are without question applied to the illumination of the text, Jommelli seems singularly impervious to considerations of proportion and theatrical pace. To speak of dramatic time being suspended in the arias of an *opera seria* is a critical commonplace, and basically a sound one. But Jommelli's arias – almost everyone of them a 'Martern aller Arten' in scale and difficulty – make it clear why the credibility of this suspense was beginning to be lost. The following is a brief excerpt from the first half of the principal section of 'Fra cento affanni e cento' in *Artaserse* (Rome 1749). There has already been a long ritornello, and a complete sing-through, with considerable word-repetition, of the first part of the text:

> Fra cento affanni, fra cento affanni e cento,
> Palpito, tremo, palpito, tremo e sento
> Che freddo dalle vene, dalle vene
> Fugge, fugge il mio sangue al cor.[2]

During this the music modulates from tonic to dominant. The passage I quote follows: it is a kind of 'second subject', incorporating formidable virtuosity and a continual fluctuation of colour, texture and dynamics, all designed to heighten the emotional impact of the words. At the close of the extract the central dominant ritornello begins, and we are halfway through the principal section of a *da capo* aria! (See Ex.III.7.)

Ex.III.6d Jommelli, *Fetonte* (1768), Act I scene 7: Start of vocal section

Italian court opera: the French influence

Hasse, as has been remarked, finally settled in Dresden in the mid-1740s, staying there until the dissolution of the royal Saxon court music in 1760. In 1753 Jommelli accepted a post as Kapellmeister to the Duke of Württemberg at Stuttgart, returning to Italy only in 1770. Gluck, who had produced

Ex.III.7 Jommelli, *Artaserse* (1749), Act I scene 1

[Amidst hundreds and hundreds of troubles] I shake and tremble and feel the blood run cold from my veins to my heart. . .

Ex.III.7 *continued*

nearly a dozen operas in north Italy in the 1740s, became director of music to the Habsburg court in Vienna between 1754 and 1764. At the Imperial Court of St Petersburg, between the 1750s and 1790s, a whole series of distinguished Italians were employed: Manfredini, Galuppi, Traetta,

Paisiello, Sarti, Cimarosa. The point one is making is not that Italy was being drained of all its best operatic talent, but that by the third quarter of the century many of the most accomplished composers who had made their name in the 1740s (in Hasse's case earlier) had found employment outwith Italy, in royal or ducal courts that were centres of French cultural influence. It will also be appropriate to mention one francophile court – that at Parma – which was on Italian soil: Traetta did his most distinguished work in Parma, where he was director of music between 1758 and 1765.

Gluck's period of employment at the Viennese court is certainly the most famous of these associations and historically the most momentous, though a few words of caution may not come amiss. During his directorship, there was no resident Italian opera company in Vienna, and the crucial work of his 'reform' of Italian opera, *Alceste*, was performed only in 1767, two years after he had resigned his official appointment. To be sure, Gluck moved in a circle of cultured Italians in Vienna – the Intendant Durazzo, the ballet-master Angiolini, and (from 1761) the man of letters Calzabigi; but the theatrical life in which he was involved was predominantly French. Since 1752 a French theatre company under the impresario Hébert had delighted Viennese audiences with performances not only of the spoken classics – Molière, Racine, Voltaire – but with ballet and *opéra comique* beside. Durazzo himself soon began to take an active interest in the *opéra comique*. He established contact with Favart, the director of the Opéra comique in Paris, and, presumably through Favart's good offices, acquired for Vienna a regular supply of the latest and most successful specimens. It was Gluck's task to direct performances of these at court; from the first he added new airs of his own composition, and gradually his share in the work increased, until the later *opéras comiques* were entirely his own.

Opera seria was on the other hand hardly a major concern of Gluck's in these years. Most of his energy was channelled into French opera, and into a number of court *serenate* and *feste teatrali*. He also continued to write conventionally Metastasian *opera seria* in response to commissions from Rome and Bologna. Of his 'reformed' Italian works, only the *azione teatrale Orfeo ed Euridice* belongs to the period of his court appointment. But it is hardly surprising that when it came, Gluck's reform – achieved (under Metastasio's very nose) in conjunction with Durazzo, the master-mind of the whole operation; Angiolini, the disciple of Noverre, and one of the most accomplished exponents of the new ideal of dramatic ballet; and Calzabigi, once a devotee of Metastasio but now slowly evolving into his most formidable opponent – should take a form that involved the merging of the best features of both Italian and French traditions.

Gluck's reform was only the most radical and far-reaching example of a general tendency in Italian opera at this time. Much of what he achieved was also to be found in the work of Jommelli and his colleagues at Stuttgart.

And for our purposes there was an even better parallel in Italy; as Grimm observed in his *Correspondance littéraire*, the work of Gluck and Calzabigi in Vienna was matched in Parma by that of Traetta and the poet Carlo Innocenzo Frugoni (Yorke-Long 1954: 36).

During the 1750s Philip, the Bourbon Duke of Parma, and his chief minister Guillaume du Tillot transformed what had become a very run-down provincial city into an intellectual centre of real distinction. It acquired this distinction by means of a determined emulation of French cultural life. Though a Spaniard, Duke Philip was an ardent francophile; du Tillot's background was Parisian; the French *philosophe* Condillac was put in charge of the education of the young prince; a French *maestro di cappella*, Jacques-Simon Mangot, was appointed in 1756, and a ballet-school was opened in the same year. The principal diversion of the household was provided by a French theatre company – Goldoni was very impressed with it when he came to Parma to supply the theatre with some *opera buffa* texts.

But du Tillot was also anxious to create an Italian theatre in Parma, an Italian theatre enhanced by French elegance and magnificence; and clearly *opera seria* must play a central part in establishing any such tradition. He had a poet to hand: for Frugoni, one of the best and most versatile of the Arcadians, had resided mostly in Parma since 1724, and had served an operatic apprenticeship in those distant days by adapting librettos for Vinci and others.[3] In 1756 du Tillot appointed him *Revisore degli spettacoli*, and it was he who provided Italian translations for the French operas that began to be performed in Parma after Mangot's appointment. During 1757–58 the Parma court was treated to the second *entrée* of Rameau's *Les Indes galantes*, and complete performances of the same composer's *Castor et Pollux*, Rebel and Francoeur's *Zélindor, Roi des sylphes* and Mondonville's *Titon et l'Aurore*. In the autumn of 1758 Traetta arrived in Parma to prepare his *Solimano* for the forthcoming Carnival season, and during the next few years he and Frugoni collaborated in a series of operas that very clearly reflected du Tillot's Frenchifying ambitions; for they were modelled on Rameau.

During the 1750s and 60s court opera became more centrally important to the development of the Italian tradition than at any time since the early seventeenth century. But the repertory in question represents not so much a further step in the evolution of *opera seria* as a distinct genre within the tradition. We should not, for instance, imagine Traetta as a radical iconoclast burning with zeal to tear down the edifice of the Metastasian *dramma per musica*. Away from the company of du Tillot and Frugoni he continued to compose opera in the traditional style, just as, away from the company of Durazzo and his team, even Gluck composed the Metastasian *Antigono* for Rome, and *Il trionfo di Clelia* for Bologna. Nevertheless, in the

1750s and 60s francophile court opera contained many of the seeds of the future.

Algarotti and the reform of *opera seria*

Italian court opera took the form it did not merely out of a vainglorious desire to ape the magnificence of Versailles. The crisis of style which I described earlier in this chapter had persuaded many intellectuals and *litterati* that the days of Metastasian opera were numbered, that the style was in fact in chronic decline. The most influential of these critical assessment was a *Saggio sopra l'opera in musica* published at Livorno (Leghorn) in 1755. It was the work of Francesco Algarotti, a man one is tempted to describe as emblematic of eighteenth-century Italian cultural life. Widely travelled, something of a polymath, at various times a close associate of Lord Hervey, Voltaire and Frederick the Great, Algarotti had already published treatises on Newtonian optics, Russia, the *Aeneid* in translation, and the Empire of the Incas, when he turned his attention to opera, and provided a shrewd and cultivated assessment of the symptoms of its decline. He instanced the breakdown between the constituent parts of poetry and music; the overcomplexity of many of the arias; an insufficient scrupulousness in matching the musical style to its dramatic or expressive function; the arrogant and irresponsible virtuosity of too many singers; their carelessness in putting across the words, and their negligence in maintaining the stage illusion.

I have not quoted Algarotti directly (a substantial excerpt is in Strunk 1950: 657–72), because the reach of his influence – or, to put it a little more cautiously, the extent to which his ideas were shared – can best be demonstrated by quoting something else. The dedication of Gluck's *Alceste*, inscribed to the Grand Duke of Tuscany in 1769, provides a succinct and forceful summary of Algarotti's main points, all the more eloquent for appearing above the signature of a great composer.[4]

YOUR ROYAL HIGHNESS:

When I undertook to write the music for *Alceste*, I resolved to divest it entirely of all those abuses, introduced into it either by the mistaken vanity of singers or by the too great complaisance of composers, which have so long disfigured Italian opera and made of the most splendid and most beautiful of spectacles the most ridiculous and wearisome. I have striven to restrict music to its true office of serving poetry by means of expression and by following the situations of the story, without interrupting the action or stifling it with a useless superfluity of ornaments; and I believed that it should do this in the same way as telling colours affect a correct and well-ordered drawing, by a well-assorted contrast of light and shade which serves to animate the figures without altering their contours. Thus I did not wish to arrest an actor in the greatest heat of dialogue in order to wait for a tiresome *ritornello*, nor to hold him up in the middle of a word on a vowel favorable to his voice, nor to make display of the agility of his fine voice in some long-drawn passage, nor to wait while the orchestra gives him time to recover his breath for a cadenza. I did not think it my duty to pass quickly over the second section of an aria of which the words are perhaps the most impassioned and important, in order to repeat regularly four times over those of the first part, and to finish the aria where its sense may perhaps not end for the convenience of the singer who wishes to show that he can capriciously vary a passage in a number of guises; in short, I have sought to abolish all the abuses against which good sense and reason have long cried out in vain.

I have felt that the overture ought to apprise the spectators of the nature of the action that is to be represented and to form, so to speak, its argument; that the concerted instruments should be introduced in proportion to the interest and the intensity of the words, and not leave that sharp contrast between the aria and the recitative in the dialogue, so as not to break a period unreasonably nor wantonly disturb the force and heat of the action.

Furthermore, I believed that my greatest labor should be devoted to seeking a beautiful simplicity, and I have avoided making displays of difficulty at the expense of clearness; nor did I judge it desirable to discover novelties if it was not naturally suggested by the situation and the expression; and there is no rule which I have not thought it right to set aside willingly for the sake of an intended effect.

Such are my principles. By good fortune my designs were wonderfully furthered by the libretto, in which the celebrated author, devising a new dramatic scheme, for florid descriptions, unnatural paragons, and sententious, cold morality, had substituted heartfelt language, strong passions, interesting situations and an endlessly varied spectacle . . .   (Strunk 1950: 673–5)

It was not only in the work of Durazzo and his clique in Vienna that Algarotti's inspiration was recognized. He maintained a regular correspondence with Krause in Berlin (where under King Frederick flourished yet another Italian opera based in a francophile court), and in Parma his influence was still more direct; for he seems to have acted as a kind of artistic adviser or father-confessor figure, sustaining close links with Frugoni throughout the period of the latter's collaboration with Traetta.

The weakness that Algarotti and his disciples diagnosed in the *dramma per musica* had been inherent from the start, when Zeno so carefully separated off the music from the drama. But the downfall of Metastasian opera was, *pace* the reformers, not really the result of any irresponsibility on the part of the composers; on the contrary, it was rather due to their attempt to assume too much responsibility. For the more expressive and the more dramatic music became, the more intolerably the primeval flaw of the genre obtruded itself. The poetry (which was originally intended to provide the dramatic element) and the music (which was originally intended to function as expressive enhancement, as decoration and colouring, but which was now struggling to achieve dramatic expression in its own right) no longer recognized one another's proper stations. The task was to reconstitute the *Gesamtkunstwerk* in such a way that all its elements came under the control of a single co-ordinating mind.

At Stuttgart this mind was Jommelli's. Once the Duke had chosen the subject for the opera, Jommelli's control over proceedings was apparently absolute, not only in the pit, but on stage and even in the poet's study. But the most articulate critics tended to be men of letters, and it is no wonder if at most courts it was the poet that came to be regarded as 'the chief engineer of the undertaking', and if the first prerequisite of reform was to persuade the composer 'that he ought to be in a subordinate station' (Algarotti, in Strunk 1950: 667). It is ironic that the man who expressed the reformers' view most trenchantly was Metastasio himself:

The production of a drama, in which all the fine arts concur, is an extreme difficult enterprise. These, as much as possible to secure success, agree to elect a Dictator. Does music aspire at this supreme magistrature? Let it by all means be granted to her. But in that case, she must take upon herself the choice of the subject; conduct of the fable; must determine the number of personages to be introduced; the characters, and situations, must likewise imagine the decorations, and then invent her melodies; and lastly, appoint poetry to write verses that shall suit all these designs . . . If in this lyric theatre, an action is represented, if a fable is interwoven and unravelled, if there are personages and characters to be supported, music is in the house of another, and cannot be called the mistress . . .   (Letter of July 1765, Burney 1796, II: 325–7)

Obviously Metastasio saw the solution to the crisis that had arisen in terms of simpler, more modest arias – a return-to-Vinci movement. The younger reformers, on the other hand, aimed at a fusion of poetry, music and spectacle that brought Italian opera stylistically closer to French opera than it had ever been before.

Reform elements in Gluck, Jommelli and Traetta

In the operas of Gluck, Jommelli and Traetta, a profusion of French elements adorn the spectacle. Jommelli's Stuttgart operas, for example, tend to abandon the alternation of intrigue-laden recitative dialogues and solo arias typical of Metastasian opera in favour of a dramatic structure built of tableau-like scenes far more densely filled with music; ensembles and choruses abound; above all the spectacular and balletic elements are fully integrated into the opera. A striking example is found in the treatment of the traditional three-movement sinfonia at the start of *Fetonte* (1768). In the words of the libretto,

The scene opens towards the end of the first allegro of the sinfonia, which serves as an introduction to a ballet of priests, who dancing around the altar, with burning torches in their hands, light the sacred flame; then disperse to left and right of the altar.

Climene advances, accompanied by another group of priests, and singing the following invocation which is designed to take the place of the andante of the sinfonia. ['De'liquidi regni' is a larghetto for soprano solo and chorus of divided tenors.] While the sacred ministers accompany this chorus with the most solemn dances, Climene pours sweet-smelling perfumes on the altar. Hardly is the chorus finished when the subterranean roar of a sudden, terrifying earthquake, which takes the place of the second allegro of the sinfonia, astonishes, puts to flight and confusion the sacred ministers.

More familiar and more restrained examples of such a fusion of dramatic ballet and opera are to be found in Acts I and II of Gluck's *Orfeo ed Euridice*

(Vienna 1762). But the most unmistakable and extraordinary attempts to refashion Italian opera in the image of the *tragédie lyrique* were those of Traetta and Frugoni at Parma.

After the successful production of *Solimano* during the 1758–59 Carnival, Traetta and Frugoni collaborated in three operas staged at Parma in the next two years, all of them 'after Rameau': *Ippolito ed Aricia* 1759 (*Hippolyte et Aricie* 1733), *I Tintaridi* 1760 (*Castor et Pollux* 1737) and *Le feste d'Imeneo* 1760 (*Les fêtes d'Hébé* 1739). When Rameau's original *Castor et Pollux* had been produced in Parma in 1758, it had prompted the comment that, delighted as audiences were with the spectacular elements of the performance, they 'only desired to hear so grand a spectacle translated into their own tongue and *their own music*' (italics added) (Rezzonico's *Memorie di Frugoni*, in Yorke-Long 1954: 27). In the *rifacimenti* made for Traetta, Frugoni could not, then, content himself with a simple translation of the French originals; they needed to be refashioned to provide opportunities for Traetta to compose music in the Italian style – which is to say arias. *Ippolito* shows the process most interestingly, for in that case Frugoni cut back somewhat on 'le merveilleux' in Pellegrin's original text, and amplified the purely human aspects of the story – the aspects that justified reflective and impassioned arias – by recourse to Racine's *Phèdre*. Even so, the format of the Italian *opera seria* was transformed. The basis of the dramatic structure here, as in Jommelli, is no longer the pattern of recitative dialogue/solo aria/exit – that indeed is reserved for the more peripheral scenes. Instead Traetta and Frugoni build up the action from tableau: arias, often with a chorus of attendance, are fused into the surrounding recitatives; the recitative in all the more important scenes is *accompagnato* and frequently merges into sections of arioso. A fuller use of the accompanied recitative so that 'the heart and mind at once would be stormed, as it were, by all the powers of music' was one of Algarotti's dearest aims (Strunk 1950: 667). He held up the last act of Vinci's *Didone abbandonata* as a model for the style, but, curiously, the technique came to be indelibly associated with the 'uso di Francia'[5] well into the nineteenth century.

One aspect of French opera which Italian composers were not interested in imitating was its avoidance of substantial, distinct arias. All the same, as the dedication of *Alceste* shows, even in Italian opera the solo aria was coming under severe critical scrutiny. Typical complaints were that it had become disproportionate to its dramatic function, or that the over-liberal application of ornamentation by singers made all arias sound much alike. It was Gluck who attacked the problem most radically. In *Orfeo ed Euridice* and the Italian operas that followed it, he reduced the scale of the arias drastically, trimming off the greater part of the ritornellos, restraining coloratura and often eliminating it altogether, dispensing with those effusive word-repetitions that had become so typical of the Italian aria in mid-century. Seemingly coached by Calzabigi in the refinements of expressive declamation, Gluck evolved an aria style which, without for a moment sacrificing elevation of tone or lyric beauty, nevertheless seemed to be aiming at something beyond them, an austere, 'speaking' kind of melody in which music, verse and gesture found an indissoluble unity. Did he not claim, in the dedication of *Paride ed Elena* (Vienna 1770), that 'song in an opera is nothing else than a substitute for declamation' (Einstein 1964: 118)?

This was where Gluck differed most fundamentally from his Italian contemporaries. With Traetta and Jommelli there was no decline at all in the scale and brilliance of the aria. What did happen was that the old grand *da capo* form was abandoned in all but a small number of scenes. Elsewhere the aria was refashioned to make it more theatrically vivid, or a more precise reflexion of changing mood or psychological nuance. A good example is Oreste's 'Qual destra omicida' at the start of Traetta's *Ifigenia in Tauride* (Vienna 1763), which is a setting of the following text:

(i)   Qual destra omicida   — la morte m'appresta,
(ii) Ah ferma! t'arresta   — la madre m'uccida,
(iii) La madre spietata   — se sazia l'ingrata   — di sangue non è.
(iv) Oh Dio, non senti   — gl'ululati, i lamenti?
(v)   Ah! Barbara affretta — l'acerba ferita,
(vi) Qual dono è la vita   — se l'ebbi da te?[6]

Traetta sets this text in a kind of sonata-form, without ritornellos and without development, but with extensive episodes between exposition and recapitulation, and between recapitulation and coda. By this stage in the evolution of the aria the various phrases of text have become more exclusively identified with distinct members of the musical structure, and these can consequently be more distinctly expressive than in earlier years. In the present case, in both exposition and recapitulation, line (i) matches first subject, (iia) transition and (iib)–(iiic) second subject. Line (iv) is accommodated in the first episode, lines (v) and (vi) in the second: in both episodes the oboes are added to the string orchestra – indeed dominate it – so that much of the time Orestes seems to be *listening*, and the wailing semitones become audible images of the 'ululati' and 'lamenti' by which he is haunted. In the coda Traetta draws scraps of text from every section of the verse, tossing them together in nightmarish confusion. Though the aria is well-shaped – supremely so – the declamatory, broken-phrased singing, the relentless turmoil in the instruments, and a form that seems to parallel the mood of the singer rather than embodying some abstract ideal, combine to give the music an almost graphic theatricality new in Italian opera (Ex.III.8). But that is only one side of Traetta's work. Unlike Gluck, both he and Jommelli held firm to the belief that one legitimate aspiration of

Ex.III.8 Traetta, *Ifigenia in Tauride* (1763), Act I scene 1

san-gue di san-gue non è, di san - gue non è, di san-gue non è

. . .my implacable mother. . .my murderous mother. . .the barbarous
woman hastens to kill me. . .is she not yet sated with blood. . .

Ex.III.8 *continued*

opera was to provide the purely musical delight afforded by beautiful music
beautifully sung: that the composer (and even the singer) did have some
right to creative autonomy. This remained a strand in the Italian tradition
until the Romantic age.

History versus mythology

The reader will have noticed that, with the operas of Gluck, Jommelli and
Traetta, we have returned from Metastasio's predominantly historical
world to the world of Classical mythology. There were various motives for
the partial disillusion with historical themes that had set in. The most
obvious was the difficulty of accommodating the spectacular and balletic
elements that were so central to the French ideal of opera; Algarotti also
professed to find it implausible that such men as Cato or Julius Caesar
should express themselves in 'warbling'. A less obvious consideration,
which may nonetheless have been the most fundamental, was the fact that
History had come to seem inseparable from the drama of intrigue practised
by Zeno and Metastasio. Croce tells us that eighteenth-century Italians – in
this they were surely not alone – had no coherent philosophy of history;
rather they regarded it as a series of bad jokes, or mishaps undergone by
Reason and Nature, which only now, in the eighteenth century, were being
given their due in a programme of enlightened reform. As long as it was felt
that man 'did not carry his history in himself, but suffered it as a result of
the oppression of his rulers and the deceit of his priests, or of the
temperament that ruled his mind' (Croce 1949: 218–19), then the Metastasian drama of intrigue, in which the protagonists were the playthings of
passion, was a faithful image of the perceptions of the age. But in the third
quarter of the century the feeling was growing that the proper subject of
drama ought not to be the fleeting passions of the moment, but the abiding

ethos that informed the character; that character was most meaningful not as the butt of an intrigue, but, in Algarotti's words, as the 'main spring and activating spirit' of the drama. The Classical ideal of unity in diversity also encouraged a shift from a historical drama of intrigue to a type of drama that permitted more distinct, individual and steadfast figures. An illustration is furnished by Gluck's *Paride ed Elena* (Vienna 1770) in which, in the composer's own words, he was 'obliged to exert [himself] in order to find some variety of colour, seeking it in the different characters of the two nations, Phrygia and Sparta, by contrasting the rude and savage nature of the one with all that is delicate and soft in the other' ('Dedication' in Einstein 1964: 118).

Algarotti conceded that there were dangers with mythological subjects. The opera might degenerate into a mere show for the eyes, in which 'the principal action [was] whelmed under a heap of accessories' (Strunk 1950: 660). But well handled, he believed that mythology was the thing: the best subjects (those such as Dido, or Iphigenia in Aulis) combined distance and marvellousness (thus legitimizing music and spectacle) with familiarity and simplicity (thus eliminating wordiness and intrigue), and they provided the dramatist with characters whose passions were no longer accidents but the 'main spring and activating spirit' of the action. For the passions of the characters of Classical myth differed from those of Metastasian opera in being occasioned not by intrigue but by destiny. Dahlhaus suggests that Hegel's distinction of Pathos and Passion will help illuminate this shift:

> Those universal powers . . . which do not only appear autonomously in their own right (that is as Gods [Dahlhaus]), but equally are alive in the human breast and move the depths of the human soul, can be distinguished in the manner of the Ancients, as Pathos. The word is difficult to translate, for 'Passion' carries with it a derogatory connotation of baseness, since we demand that men should not be carried away by their passions . . . Pathos in this sense is an autonomous spiritual force, a vital constituent of reason and of free will. For example, Orestes kills his mother not out of any inner movement of the soul which we would describe as Passion, rather the Pathos that drives him to the deed is well-considered and circumspect. (Dahlhaus 1974: 295)

Mythology was, then, something that seemed to make a Classical ideal of art more easily realizable than History had made it. In the 1750s and 60s calls for the simplification and purification of art were again echoing and re-echoing across Europe. Algarotti's *Saggio* was, for opera, the most momentous of these manifestos; but Diderot's *De la poésie dramatique* (1758) with its proclamation of a new ideal of dramatic starkness – no intrigue, no secondary characters, no prettification – and Noverre's *Lettres sur la danse* . . . (1760) were hardly less influential. In Rome Winckelmann delivered the most long-resonating of all definitions of classicism in art: 'eine edle Einfalt und eine stille Grösse'.[7] Gluck made the acquaintance of Winckelmann when he was in Rome in 1756, though the extent to which he was influenced by him cannot really be established. But if in Jommelli and Traetta it is the multifarious splendour of the *Gesamtkunstwerk* ideal that predominates, it may surely be said of Gluck's *Orfeo ed Euridice*, *Alceste* and *Paride ed Elena* that no operatic music more fully and nobly embodies Winckelmann's Classic ideal.

Neither the move towards a more French style of *opera seria*, nor that towards Classical simplicity, went unopposed. Arteaga, for instance, regarded Calzabigi not as a reformer, but as 'one of the principal corrupters of the modern musical theatre'. He deplored the ease with which the 'brilliant sophistries . . . of the inhabitants of the Seine' had persuaded Italians to renounce that rationalizing of the opera that had been achieved by Zeno and Metastasio (Arteaga 1785, II: 174, 164–5). Metastasio too was at his most mordant when reflecting how spectacle had usurped the prerogatives of eloquence. But the most effective opposition did not come from the intellectuals: it was due to the fact that, outside Vienna and Parma and Stuttgart and the other great court theatres of the age, *opera seria* continued to flourish as a popular art. And while the impresarios of public theatres were all for spectacle (in so far as it could be afforded), they were nervous of the effect of Gluck's 'noble simplicity'. The revival of *Orfeo ed Euridice* at Naples in 1774 may be taken as symptomatic of their reserve. In place of the three soloists of the original it employed seven; and to Gluck's austere tableaux of declamation, song and dance, were added innumerable solo arias by J. C. Bach and others, in the most sensuous and brilliant modern style (Robinson 1972: 66f.).

14 · *Opera seria* in an age of ferment

Gluckian versus Metastasian aesthetics

The heroes of the last chapter had only a modest influence on the development of Italian opera outside the centres where they did their best work. Away from the elevating influence of the Parma court, Traetta did little to distinguish himself from the general run of opera composers of the age. Returned to Naples from Stuttgart, Jommelli produced works that were too 'operose' (Burney) for the taste of Italian opera-goers. Gluck acknowledged that the reforms he had instigated in Vienna were making little progress in Italy (Preface to *Paride ed Elena*, in Einstein 1964: 114). And though Calzabigi himself settled in Naples in 1780 and remained there until his death fifteen years later, neither composers nor theatre authorities were over-eager to avail themselves of his talents. Only at the very end of his life were Paisiello's settings of two of his librettos – *Elfrida* (1792) and *Elvira* (1794) – performed at the San Carlo. On the whole composers in the mainstream of Italian opera remained remarkably self-sufficient; not persuaded that what was happening in Vienna or St Petersburg was of greater interest than what was happening in Venice or Rome or Naples, and not over-impressed by the mighty *oltremontani*, Gluck and Mozart. Dean points out that *Idomeneo* (Munich 1784), by our lights surely the greatest *opera seria* of the age, had its first Italian performance in 1947 (Dean 1982: 378).

All the same, the reformers did have some impact. The Naples performances of *Orfeo ed Euridice* in 1774 may have perverted the composer's ideals deplorably, but they created a sufficiently singular impression for Paisiello to feel it was worth parodying the scene between Orpheus and the Furies in *Socrate immaginario* the following year. Two years later, in 1777, a newly established Nobile Accademia di Musica, founded by the Marchese di Corleto, began its inaugural season with a performance of *Paride ed Elena*, designed to 'demonstrate the decadence of Neapolitan opera' (Einstein 1964: 122). Simon Mayr learned to revere Gluck during his studies with Bertoni in Venice in the early 1790s, and the inspiration he drew from him is evident in many of his *opera seria* scores from *Saffo* (Venice 1794) onwards. If no real tradition of Gluck performance developed in Italy, his mere name sufficed to evoke powerful associations for decades, and his reputation as an uncompromising idealist survived into the 1820s. Pacini regarded him as the very embodiment of dramatic 'truth' (1865: 15), while Carpani in his little book on Rossini still sees the 'infuocato Gluckista'[1] as a rabid doctrinaire threatening the beauty of the musical art by his preoccupation with dramatic expression (1824: 69).

Gluck, then, was approached with reserve; conversely the view that the Metastasian *dramma per musica* was a thing of the past was by no means universal. Mercadante and Pacini were still setting Metastasio in the 1820s. But after *c*. 1770 these revivals were rarely unaffected by more progressive elements of taste. The 'rearranging of Metastasio to make a real opera' – to borrow the form of words Mozart used of *La clemenza di Tito* (Prague 1791) – describes equally well what happens in most of the Italian revivals. The sententious arias are quietly dropped; long scenes of recitative are trimmed drastically or paraphrased in such a way as to enable the composer to take a fuller share in the proceedings; scenes of reported action tend to be replaced by scenes of direct representation; most distinctive of all, the crisis of the dramatic action is sometimes shifted to the end of the act (or section of act) where an ensemble replaces the series of exit-arias in which, in Metastasio's originals, the action had tapered away.

If Gluck inspired respect – even awe – more readily than enthusiasm, Italian composers did during the last twenty years of the century slowly come round to paralleling many of his achievements. Italy even had its own 'Dedication to *Alceste*' – the dedication to Cimarosa's *Oreste*, written by Luigi Serio (Naples 1783):

The dramas of our day provide little interest, not for the lack of merit in the poetry, but because of the great void existing between the recitatives and the arias . . . because of the wilfulness of the singers . . . and because of the negligence and ignorance of the same, who utter the words without art and without the right expressiveness. Thinking to put a stop to such disorders, I have tried to reduce the recitatives to the minimum number possible, and have put choruses into the drama to regain the listener's attention. So that these [choruses] do not become mere ephemeral, noisy pieces, I have tried to unite them to the action . . . Usually, arias are nothing but an insipid warbling . . . I have managed to place the arias, especially those belonging to the chief characters, in such positions that the composer is forced to relate [the music] to the poetry and the singers to explain the passions.

(Robinson 1972: 69)

Many of the best operas abandoned the drama of intrigue in favour of a simple austere tale, in which, especially after 1790, a fully dramatic role is allotted to the chorus. The basic dramatic unit of the Metastasian age – *recitativo semplice*, aria, exit – gradually gave way to a more tableau-like structure, in which the dramatic focus was shifted from the recitative to the various sections of 'full music'. Sometimes this development was prompted by an external stimulus: Piccinni adopted it more regularly after encounters with Gluck in Paris; it first became prevalent in Cimarosa during his years in St Petersburg (1787–91). The trend of the time was to engage the composer more and more fully as the dramatic crisis intensified – quite the reverse of the Metastasian principle, in which the poet is the dramatist. The pattern recitative, *accompagnato*, arioso, aria – found for instance in Cimarosa's *Gli Orazi ed i Curiazi*, Act I, scene 5 (Venice 1796) – had come to represent a gradual dramatic or psychological intensification. There was correspondingly a radical reduction in the amount of *recitativo semplice*: the whole of the last act of Paisiello's *Catone in Utica* (Naples 1789) – which is, after all, a Metastasian opera – contained barely half a dozen bars of it.

Even the musical language was affected by ideals comparable to Gluck's. The quantity of coloratura was conspicuously reduced in Paisiello's later operas, and a corresponding gain in concentration was made: musical forms became more concise and urgent. The ideal of impassioned declamation sublimated into song inspired some of Cimarosa's noblest pages, and at many an emotional crux one is surprised by an almost hymnic simplicity and fervour, a quality still occasionally to be heard in some of Rossini's early works. The use of the orchestra to provide a complementary exegesis of the text became more frequent and more ambitious: and, as Jommelli had already done, composers drew freely on the symbolic and expressive figures coined in *accompagnato* recitative to make their accompaniments as explicitly meaningful as possible (Ex.III.9).

I have suggested that the aesthetics of the Metastasian opera were fatally undermined both by the elaboration and dramatizing of the musical forms typical of Jommelli, and by the *Gesamtkunstwerk* vision invoked by Algarotti and put into practice by Calzabigi and Gluck. That negative process was complete by the 1770s; but no coherent alternative philosophy of opera emerged from the clash of loyalties, the counter-currents of idealism and hedonism, of 'philosophical' taste and commercial imperatives. One has the impression that, although Gluck put the music back at the heart of the drama in a way that Metastasio could never have approved, nevertheless it was for musical reasons that a post-Metastasian – or sub-Metastasian – type of opera was clung to so tenaciously. Especially was it clung to for love of the solo aria. And no wonder: for in entrancing lyrical beauty, in sheer gorgeousness of sound, the aria ripened from year to year, from Piccinni through J. C. Bach and Paisiello to Cimarosa.

A further disruptive factor in *opera seria* of the period was the attempt to absorb various techniques that had evolved originally in *opera buffa*. Abert puts this development as far back as the late 1750s, when Piccinni began to accompany certain arias with pervasive, repetitive figures, and to adopt a freer, more spontaneous-sounding give and take between voice and orchestra (H. Abert 1978, I: 207). In Paisiello's mature works the fully fledged *parlante* technique is applied to *opera seria*. And once an ensemble is propelled by the orchestral momentum the voices are free to engage in truly theatrical declamation; the dramatic scene can vibrate with confrontational

MARCO ORAZIO

spe - me la spe - me l'a - mor

(str)   *f*   *p*

(+ob, cor sustain)

tuo - ni il cie - lo, mi - nac - ci la   sorte,

p (str)

L'au - ra e -cheg - gi   di quer - ru - li la - i   e-

ob

cl

ob

cor

cheg - gi   di que - ru - li la - i   etc.

etc.

etc.

. . .hope and love, let the heavens thunder, let destiny threaten, let the air
resound with mournful lamentations. . .

Ex.III.9 Cimarosa, *Gli Orazi ed i Curiazi* (1796), Act II scene 9

Change your mind. I must not. Consider. I did already. The throne. I did
desire it.

Ex.III.10 Paisiello, *Elfrida* (1792), Act II scene 8

tensions (Ex.III.10). During the 1780s the full-scale dramatic ensemble
finale emerged; by the time of Paisiello's *Pirro* (Naples 1787, text G. De
Gamerra) it yielded little or nothing in eventfulness to the finale of the *opera
buffa*. These were all developments surely desirable in the long run, but
certainly not unproblematic. For such *buffo* techniques tended to bring

with them an air of smiling, dancing exuberance which accorded ill with the elevated tone of the *opera seria*. Even the climax of *Gli Orazi ed i Curiazi*, the most grandly tragic Italian opera of the age, is marred by the disharmony between musical charm and dramatic horror. But if none of the operas of the period quite lives up to its heroic aspirations, *opera seria* had discovered in the *opera buffa* a way of co-ordinating music and drama which was less ponderous than Gluck's, and it had tapped a source of vital physical energy. Add to this the purely musical enrichments of the form achieved by such men as J. C. Bach and Paisiello, and the integrated use of chorus and ballet, and one has an *opera seria* which, whatever its aesthetic ambiguities and shortcomings, was far richer-textured and far more wide-ranging in its expressive and dramatic potential.

Foreshadowings of Romanticism

The earliest foreshadowings of Romanticism came, not in any aspects of musical technique, but in subject matter. For the first time in the history of Italian art, *literati* and musicians turned their eyes with real curiosity to the barbarian North; and what they saw fascinated them, for it represented a quite new world of feeling. In 1762 Dr Johnson sent his old friend Giuseppe Baretti his edition of Shakespeare, suggesting that he use his position as one of Italy's most estimable essayists to expound the poet 'to the ladies of Italy'. Which, in *La Frusta* for January 1764, Baretti duly did, declaring Shakespeare 'both as a tragic and as a comic poet to stand quite, quite alone, above all the Corneilles, all the Racines and all the Molières of Gaul' (Graf 1911: 317). A few years later, we find Metastasio savouring with reluctant and quizzical admiration the delights of Edward Young:

I have perused with avidity, and infinite pleasure, which I never expected to receive from excess of melancholy, the first six *Night Thoughts* of the celebrated poet Young, in your elegant version; and am extremely grateful to you for enabling me to have a knowledge of the English Muses, in spite of my involuntary ignorance of this excellent language . . . notwithstanding the want of order and connexion, his frequent repetitions, determined obstinacy in always shewing the dark side of every object, and unwillingness to conduct us to virtue by any other way, than that of despair; in spite (I say) of these oppressive circumstances, he seizes the reader, and transports him just whither he pleases.

(To Giuseppe Bottoni, 1771, in Burney 1796, III: 107–8)

But no Northern literature rivalled in popularity that of Ossian. For half a century, the 'Homer of the North' was the most admired of all British artists in any medium, and it was he who was the chief means by which, in the words of Matthew Arnold, 'this soul of the Celtic genius [was brought] into contact with the genius of the nations of modern Europe' (Fiske 1983: 41).

Extraordinarily, Italy was the first European country to experience the

Ossianic fever. The bulk of Macpherson's 'translations' were published in three volumes between 1760 and 1763; and already in the latter year an Italian version of a substantial selection from them – the work of Melchiorre Cesarotti – appeared in Padua. Cesarotti aimed to offer Italian readers a representative sample of the whole range of the bardic poems: he began with the epic of Fingal, followed with the drama of Comala, and concluded with the lyrical hymns. For our purposes *Comala* is the interesting piece. Macpherson had added an accompanying note to the effect that 'the variety of metres [indicate] that the poem was originally sung to music', and in his Italian version Cesarotti elaborates on this:

The chorus, and the variety of metre make it entirely similar to the *melodramas* of the Greeks. Adapted to music by a learned maestro, and embellished with suitable decorations, it could be an opera in a new style, and create a tremendous effect even in our times.   (Folena 1982: 239)

In short Cesarotti's *Comala* translation was a potential opera-libretto, and leading theatre poets of the day were in due course attracted by the challenge he had issued. Calzabigi himself produced a *Comala* as early as 1770, and of the younger librettists both Sografi and Rossi were in some measure followers of Cesarotti. The 'Ossianic' libretto introduced a new ethos, at once martial and elegiac, into Italian opera: and if the inspiration for this ethos was found in a remote legendary past, its full significance would become apparent only in the approaching Napoleonic age. For Ossian provided a store of themes, motifs, imagery and experiences by means of which the classical heritage of Italian opera was gradually transformed into a Romantic one: marches and war-songs; images of death, mourning and nostalgia; such typical fates as exile and death in a patriotic cause; awe before natural phenomena; the moonlit ruin in a wild, 'sublime' landscape; the harp-playing heroine. Perhaps the most momentous innovation that may be attributed to the Ossianic vision is the daring to write a tragic close of desolating bleakness, as in Calzabigi's *Elfrida* (though that is not strictly an Ossianic opera). The Metastasian dramatic method had long since succumbed; here the whole enlightened Metastasian world-picture is shattered: after the experience of Ossian the passions and conflicts that rend humanity are no longer to be reconciled in the sweet light of reason.

The growing popularity of the *opera semiseria*, which drew extensively on the dramatic themes and various of the musical forms of *opéra comique*, must also be reckoned a trait that anticipated Romantic taste; its great exponent at this period was Ferdinando Paer, who, from *Griselda* (Parma 1798) to *Agnese* (Parma 1809), composed seven such pieces. The mingling of the comic and the horrible, the aristocratic and the plebeian, disgusted some connoisseurs of the old school like Lord Mount-Edgcumbe, but provided composers with irresistible opportunities for more startling, colourful and piquant juxtapositions. Particularly congenial to the sentimentality of the age was the possibility of toying with the pathetic and the appalling – notoriously in the mad-scenes of *Agnese* – without having to follow them through to a tragic conclusion.

The politicizing of opera

What artist would normally bother himself with politics? asked Kapell-meister Kreisler; 'but a fatefully difficult age has grasped humanity with an iron fist, and anguish forces sounds from him which would normally be alien to him' (E. T. A. Hoffmann, *Kreisleriana* I-5). In the third quarter of the century, all the arguments about the reform of opera had been purely artistic ones. As we move into the Revolutionary period such arguments no longer carry absolute or even sufficient authority. The Seven Years War (1756–63) had dealt a severe blow to the cosmopolitan and apolitical ideals of the Enlightenment; and in the following decades artistic, intellectual and social life had become more politicized in most parts of Europe. Italy was no exception. The clearest symptom was probably the transformation in the late 1780s of the masonic lodges into hotbeds of Jacobinism. But the politicizing of the theatre was hardly less spectacular, particularly after the dramatic debut in 1777 of Count Vittorio Alfieri, the most forceful new voice in Italian literature, and an ardent republican. 'It was one of the merits of that noble spirit', declared Massimo d'Azeglio, 'to have found a Metastasian Italy and to have left it Alfierian. What is more, his first and greatest merit was to have discovered Italy, as Columbus discovered America, and to have started the idea of Italy a Nation' (1966, Chapter 4).

Alfieri's ideal theatre, even more explicitly than Zeno's and Metastasio's, was to be a 'school for the nation': but what the pupils now had to learn was 'to be free'. Alfieri's creed is found in a letter addressed to our old friend Calzabigi:

I firmly believe that men must learn in the theatre to be free, strong, generous, inspired by true virtue, intolerant of all violence, lovers of their country, fully conscious of their proper rights, and in all their passions, ardent, honest and magnanimous. Such was the theatre in Athens: and such a theatre can never be if it grows in the shadow of a prince . . .   (Angermüller 1982: 203)

In their meeker and more modest ways many librettists of the period shared Alfieri's ideals. Cimarosa's collaborators in the 1780s and 1790s included at least three such men: Giovanni Pindemonte (collaborator on *Giunio Bruto*, Verona 1781), S. A. Sografi (*Gli Orazi ed i Curiazi*) and Luigi Serio (*Oreste* 1783), who, despite his background as Bourbon court poet and university professor in Naples, eventually died in 1799 fighting for the Republican forces against the Sanfedisti. As late as the 1840s Salvatore Cammarano, the resident poet at the San Carlo theatre in Naples, was turning to Alfieri for inspiration – and running into trouble with the censors

245

for his pains. As opera became more politically tendentious, Algarotti's hope that mythological themes would return to favour was clearly doomed. From Alfieri, like-minded librettists learned that their aims could be realized most effectively by a glorification of the republican spirit of Ancient Rome, such as we find in Sografi's *Gli Orazi ed i Curiazi*. We return to Classical history in fact, but now with a pronounced political slant.

No one handled such librettos more interestingly than Vincenzo Monti. In his hands the libretto became what it had once been in seventeenth-century Vienna, a political allegory (cf. p. 136 above). He makes this quite explicit in the *licenza* to *Teseo* (composed Vincenzo Federici, Milan 1804):

> Greche imprese son ombra
> di vicende fra noi
> più famose, e d'eroi
> che per opre di spada e di consiglio
> maravigliose e nuove
> dell'antica virtù vinser le prove.
> Suona il labbro Teseo
> ma Bonaparte il cor.[2]   (Folena 1982: 256)

In Naples, four years later, Monti collaborated with Paisiello in *I Pitagorici*, a similar kind of political allegory in memory of those killed in the Neapolitan revolution of 1799. 'I have named no one', said Monti, 'leaving it to the audience to make the application' (*ibidem*: 260). With Monti begins a species of libretto writing in which the ostensible theme is transformed into the real theme by topical substitutions applied by the audience. It was a device against which censorship was helpless and with the aid of which, in the 1840s, Verdi was to do potent work in the political cause of Italian nationalism.

Music and drama

Italian composers were not so easily weaned from the sheer joy of making music as Alfieri might have wished. Neither Ossianic gloom nor Republican highmindedness were quite sufficient to dispel their hedonistic delight in the beautiful and the sensuous, their love of glorious melody, their admiration for the consummate art of the great performer. In the finest works of the period, the late *opere serie* of Cimarosa, this ambiguity has been seen as the source of a singularly rich and resonant art (Lippmann 1982: 56–9): the high seriousness of Cimarosa's intentions is not in doubt, and when bent on his dramatic theme he sustains the tension over long stretches of an act with a variety of resource that yields nothing to Gluck or Mozart. But within this frame he finds room for the purely musical too: for arias of exquisite gracefulness whose *raison d'être* is to rejoice the music-lover's heart.

246

Though a fervent commitment to the dramatic themes of the age was not always in evidence, the musical language did not stagnate. Changes were particularly striking in the fields of sonority and timbre, which became on the whole denser and darker. The emphasis placed on the chorus, the decline of the practice of castration during the Napoleonic years and the consequent shift to natural male voices, the continual enrichment of the orchestral resources all contributed to this. In the matter of orchestral practice, the Bavarian-born Mayr was particularly influential. 'His peculiar gift', wrote Stendhal, 'lay in scoring his orchestral passages, together with the *ritornelli* and the accompaniments of his arias, with all the new richness of harmonic effect which his contemporaries Haydn and Mozart were perfecting in Germany at that very time' (Stendhal 1956: 17). And he went on to compare his effect on Italian opera with that of Dr Johnson on English prose! For he created a 'style which was heavy, turgid and a thousand removes from the natural beauty of simple speech, but which, nevertheless, had a certain quality of its own, particularly when one had struggled and struggled and eventually got used to it' (*ibidem*: 23).

The woodwind instruments which Paisiello had begun to use thematically (particularly in the 'second subject' of his sonata arias) are now regularly featured in an *obbligato* capacity. New instruments are added to the opera orchestra for specific dramatic, or evocative, tasks: the cor anglais in *Lodoiska* (Milan 1800), trombones and serpent in *Medea in Corinto* (Naples 1813). To Mayr is also due the custom of highlighting certain pathetic or intimate numbers in an opera by means of a very distinctive chamber-music scoring: a device of which Donizetti and Verdi were both to make much use. In his *Trattatello sopra agli stromenti ed istromentazione* included in his *Zibaldone* of 1825 Mayr left some interesting reflections on the Italian art of orchestration in the pre-Romantic age. Rossini, he tells us, preferred the clarinet to the oboe because he found it had a less weak tone; Mayr himself deplored this development: he had learnt to regard the oboe as the 'King of the woodwind', marvellously apt to evoke grief, irony and rustic joviality. He warns against the abuse of the trombones, citing *Semiramide* as a particularly deplorable example, and Rossini is taken to task again over his indulgence in the effects of 'Turkish music', i.e. bass drum, cymbal, triangle. If Mayr had his way, these would be confined to the ballet (Witzenmann 1982: 304–5).

The other great development in musical style may be described as the dramatization of the aria. In the time of Paisiello this tendency was found in any number of forms. The fully fledged sonata aria gave Paisiello at his best an almost Mozartian finesse in exploring the contrasting facets of a basic mood. Arias were commonly fused into the surrounding dramatic action: by the already mentioned scheme of expressive intensification – recitative, *accompagnato*, arioso, aria; by commencing the aria with recitative-like

247

phrases; by avoiding the exit-convention at the close in favour of a cadence which projects the mind forward into the following recitative. One of the varieties of aria favoured by Piccinni – and indeed by many others – in the years after the abandoning of the grand *da capo* aria proved particularly prophetic: the aria in two sections, slow followed by fast, familiar from a dozen examples in Mozart's mature operas. Of all the aria types of the period this was the most dynamic; moreover, the thrust of the progression from slow to fast was generally prompted by some slight shift of mood in the text. In *Gli Orazi*, for example, Marco Orazio sings a two-movement aria in which the Largo 'Se alla patria ognor donai' and the Allegro non tanto 'Ah di giubilo quest'alma' are separated by the arrival of a chorus, and it is their telling him that he has been chosen to fight for Rome that prompts the switch from slow to fast. By the time of Mayr the sections of the aria are often separated by such linking transitional passages.

All these developments show that the *buffo* ideal of co-ordinating the dramatic action with continuous musical structures was becoming increasingly important in the *opera seria*. The climax of these tendencies towards the psychological, dramatic and theatrical enlivening of the aria comes with the minor figures between Cimarosa and Rossini; men like Guglielmi, whose arias are often fragmented into three or four parts.

The myriad and tumultuous variety of form and style in Italian opera at the beginning of the nineteenth century was at last brought under the control of a real master once more as Rossini came to his precocious maturity. His early reputation had been established in comedy, notably in the five one-act *farse* produced at the Teatro San Moisè in Venice between 1810 and 1813. But within a week or two of the last of these, he had produced at the Teatro La Fenice in the same city *Tancredi*, a '*melodramma eroico*', that was to have no less signal an impact on the evolution of serious opera.

There are perhaps three things to remark as contributing to the extraordinary success this opera enjoyed. One, without doubt, was the clarity and effectiveness of the musical forms. Nothing is lost of the tendencies of the last half-century to dramatize the individual numbers; but in many movements of *Tancredi* Rossini finds a way of making this dramatization simpler and more elegant. Henceforth, very rapidly, the structural variety of the previous period was to give way to a new kind of *sistemazione*, the standard double-aria form of the Romantic age, built on the progression from a slow, introspective cantabile to a fast cabaletta, sung twice. A second factor was the verve and skill of the orchestral writing. Much of the vitality with which Rossini was to revivify the *opera seria* and make it fitter to face the new expressive tasks of the Romantic age came from his instrumental inventiveness – the sparkle of the colours, the profusion of the rhythms, the dance of the 'gossiping themelets' (Rognoni) on which his *parlante* episodes are propelled. But one should not overlook the poetic evocativeness of certain pages either; Stendhal was to compare the prelude set by the seashore in Act I scene 5 with the descriptive passages in the novels of Scott, praising it for its psychological suggestiveness:

Tancred *must* not speak; but while he is contained in a silence so perfectly expressive of the feelings raging within him, the sighing horns of the orchestra conjure up a new portrait of his spirit, and echo emotions which, perhaps, he hardly dare acknowledge to himself, and which certainly will never find form in words. (Stendhal 1956: 56)

Finally, what surely played a major part in the success of the opera was the effortless, hedonistic charm of the young Rossini's lyricism. After more than a decade during which the fortunes of Italian opera had been in the hands of men of mediocre talent with perhaps over-solemn ambitions, Rossini brought back to *opera seria* something of that sense of joy that he so loved in the best music of the eighteenth century. In 1818, Carpani explained the secret of *Tancredi* to a Berlin journalist: 'There is cantilena and always cantilena and beautiful cantilena and magic cantilena and rare cantilena . . . Nature, which had created a Pergolesi, a Sacchini, a Cimarosa, now has created a Rossini' (Weinstock 1968: 38).

15 · A half-century of *L'Olimpiade*

Metastasio's *L'Olimpiade* (Vienna 1733)

No single composer occupies a really central role in the *opera seria* tradition; that distinction belongs to a poet, to Pietro Metastasio who, during a productive career of almost fifty years, enjoyed a reputation and an ascendancy over the lyric theatre which in its exclusiveness and longevity has never been matched. And so the threads of this section of the book will be drawn together, not in the study of a single opera, but of a text, one of Metastasio's subtlest and most beguiling: *Olimpiade*, by order of the Emperor Charles VI first composed by Caldara and performed in Vienna 'in the garden of the Imperial Favorita, in the presence of the august rulers, on 28 August 1733, to celebrate the birthday of the Empress Elisabeth'. Like all Metastasio's dramas, *Olimpiade* was reset again and again during the course of the eighteenth century: by Pergolesi and Leo; by Hasse, Galuppi and Jommelli; by Cimarosa and Paisiello and innumerable others. A comparative study of scenes from some of these settings should shed light both on the artificial yet poignant perfection of the *dramma per musica* in its heyday in the 1730s, and on the gradual transformation of the Metastasian ideal during the next fifty years.

Improbable as it may seem, the title of Metastasio's drama does indeed mean 'Olympiad' or 'Olympic Games'. The scene is set in the country of Elis, close to the city of Olympia, on the banks of the river Alpheus.

DRAMATIS PERSONAE
> CLISTENE, King of Sicyonia, father of Aristea.
> ARISTEA, his daughter, in love with Megacle.
> ARGENE, a lady of Crete disguised as a shepherdess under the name of Licori, in love with Licida.
> LICIDA, supposed son of the King of Crete, in love with Aristea, and friend of Megacle.
> MEGACLE, in love with Aristea and friend of Licida.
> AMINTA, tutor to Licida.
> ALCANDRO, counsellor to Clistene.

One had best begin with Metastasio's own Argument:

Clistene, King of Sicyonia, was father of twin children, Filinto and Aristea; but, warned by the Delphic oracle that he ran the risk of being killed by his own son, he had the former exposed – on the advice of the same oracle – and preserved the latter. She growing in years and in beauty was loved by Megacle, a noble and valiant Athenian youth, several times a victor at the Olympic Games. But unable to obtain the hand of Aristea from her father, to whom the very name of Athens was hateful, the despairing Megacle went to Crete. There he was attacked and almost overcome by brigands, but his life was saved by Licida, supposedly the son of the king of the island; and he became bound to his saviour in a tender and indissoluble friendship. Licida had for long loved Argene, a noble lady of Crete, and was secretly betrothed to her. But when the king heard of his love, being determined not to permit so unequal a match, he so persecuted the unfortunate Argene, that she was obliged to abandon her homeland and take flight secretly to the countryside of Elis where, under the name of Licori and disguised as a shepherdess, she lived hidden from the resentment of her family and the violence of her sovereign. Licida was left inconsolable at the flight of his Argene; and after some time, as a distraction from sorrow, he decided to betake himself to Elis and attend the celebration of the Olympic Games which took place there, with the participation of the whole of Greece, every fourth year. Leaving Megacle in Crete he went there and found that King Clistene, who had been elected to preside over the games and who had therefore transferred himself from Sicyonia to Elis, was offering his own daughter Aristea as the victor's prize. Licida saw her, admired her, and forgetful of the misfortunes of his first love, was ardently enamoured of her; but, being not at all skilled in the athletic exercises which were to be tested at the games, he despaired of being able to win her, and conceived a plan for supplying with cunning the defects of experience. He remembered that his friend had been several times the victor in similar contests; and knowing nothing of the ancient love of Megacle and Aristea, decided to make use of him, by making him compete under the assumed name of Licida. And so Megacle too came to Elis, at the vehement urging of his friend; but his arrival was so long delayed that the impatient Licida already despaired of it. It is from this point that the action of the present dramatic composition takes its commencement. Its object, or principal action, is the rediscovery of that Filinto who, because of the threats of the oracle, had been exposed as a baby by order of his own father Clistene, and to that end the loving frenzy of Aristea, the heroic friendship of Megacle, the inconstancy and the rages of Licida, and the generous compassion of the most faithful Argene all imperceptibly lead.

Metastasio names as his primary sources Herodotus, Pausanias and Natale Conti.

Metastasio as dramatist

Act I, scenes 1–3

This scene might be subtitled 'the arrival of Megacle in Elis'. It is set in a narrow, gloomy valley overshadowed with trees, which we may surely see as an emblem of the secretive and dishonourable action Licida is bent upon.

Within the first ten lines his character, Aminta's and that of the still absent Megacle are all vividly depicted: Licida violent and impulsive, Aminta the voice of moderation and restraint, Megacle – as Licida's despairing cry, 'Megacle istesso, / Megacle m'abbandona / nel bisogno maggiore',[1] shows – the very idea of loyalty. But the greater part of Act I scene 1 is given over to a descriptive evocation of the Olympic atmosphere: the temple rituals; the mass excitement; the sports cultivated; the prize. As Megacle has not arrived in time to compete, Licida must try on his own behalf.

But Megacle does arrive; and being willing to do anything to help or gratify his friend, accedes unquestioningly to his curious request. The appearance of Megacle in fact brings about a first peripeteia, a peripeteia that is significant in terms of psychology rather than plot. For as soon as Megacle has left again, Metastasio rounds off his picture of the self-centred, impetuous Licida by making Act I scene 3 an ironic mirror-image of Act I scene 1. Now he is all optimism, all gratitude, all unreasoning rapture. And as the sequence had begun with Licida dismissing Aminta's words of encouragement, so it ends with a more emphatic dismissal of his words of caution. Licida's impatience with his tutor accelerates from *ad hominem* reproach, through metaphor, to close in a simile aria.

> Oh! sei pure importuno
> con questo tuo noioso
> perpetuo dubitar. Vicino al porto
> vuoi ch'io tema il naufragio? A'dubbi tuoi
> chi presta fede intera
> non sa mai quando è l'alba o quando è sera.

> (Aria) Quel destrier, che all'albergo è vicino,
>   più veloce s'affretta nel corso:
>   non l'arresta l'angustia del morso,
>   non la voce che legge gli dá . . .[2]

Very signally this aria is an expression of that mood of impulsive eagerness that has driven Licida throughout this short sequence of scenes. The choice of the simile aria has been prepared for by the increasingly metaphorical tone of his closing speech, and the galloping rhythm – anapaestic *decasillabi* – reflects both the simile and the mood of the character, which perhaps do not coincide as often as they should in the eighteenth-century metaphor aria.

The only other aria here is sung by Megacle at the end of Act I scene 2 as he goes off to the temple to fulfil Licida's commission.

> Superbo di me stesso
> andrò portando in fronte
> quel caro nome impresso,
> come mi sta nel cor.
> Dirà la Grecia poi
> che fur comuni a noi
> l'opre, i pensier, gli affetti,
> e alfine i nomi ancor.[3]

This lyric expresses what is really the cardinal motive of the whole drama, Megacle's selfless devotion to Licida. Its style reflects the rather unusual preparation it has been given. For Megacle has barely appeared before he is hurried off on an unexplained mission. His comparative speechlessness (he has only five lines of recitative before singing his aria) suggests his unquestioning loyalty and his naivety, and of course underlines the urgency that pervades the scene. The aria-text consequently becomes a part of the action, Megacle's response to Licida's urging, and to this fact it perhaps owes its metre (recitative-like *settenari*) and its conversational tone (it is full of enjambements). It is a speaking and acting aria, with little of the sing-song phraseology that so often distinguishes Metastasio's aria-texts.

Act I, scenes 4–7

Each of the three acts has its choral scene. This one, set amid shepherds' huts on the riverside, is an eulogy of the pastoral life where love – in pointed contrast to the previous scene – knows no discontent and no deceit. 'Oh care selve! oh cara / felice libertà' is a refrain chorus with solo couplets for Argene-Licori that draws out all the poignancy of that contrast: here are love and loyalty, simplicity and satisfaction, peace and innocence.

Where the first scene was predominantly one of preparation and anticipated action, this is predominantly one of reminiscence. Argene is joined by Aristea, who, it seems, has already struck up acquaintance with the 'shepherdess'. And as they confide in one another the stories of their past, they provide the spectator with the whole sentimental history of the four principals – themselves, Licida and Megacle. The fantastic coincidences in this story, with which we are already acquainted from the argument, bring it close to the world of fairy-tale, and Metastasio is too fine an ironist not to offer the chance of the occasional wry smile:

> Ah! se [Megacle] sapesse
> ch'oggi per me qui si combatte.[4]

At the end of this long dialogue one notices, as at the end of Act I scene 1, the way the author prepares for the arrival of a new character. I suspect that these transitional dialogues may have been added to the main business of the scene partly to facilitate a regrouping of the characters on the stage. But certainly they were also designed to heighten the effect of 'reversal' when the new character did arrive. Here Aristea is about to go off to request her father to delay the start of the games when he arrives to announce, 'Figlia, tutto è compito.'[5] And the suspense and emotional turmoil of the drama really begin when he goes on to announce that, among the suitors, is a certain Licida, from Crete. That revelation, placed in masterly fashion at the climax of a piece of news that Clistene imagines must be making Aristea's heart swell with proud satisfaction –

> Ragion d'esser superba
> io ti darei, se ti dicessi tutti
> quei che a pugnar per te vengono a gara.
> V'è Olinto di Megara,
> v'è Clearco di Sparta, Ati di Tebe,

Erilo di Corinto, e fin di Creta
Licida venne.[6]

– is the charge which sparks off the emotional reactions that fill the rest of the scene and provide the material for its three arias: Clistene's own paternal words of advice, Aristea's plea to Argene to find out something of Megacle's fate, Argene's bitter indignation.

The first of the opera's moralizing arias comes very well from the royal father as he tries to cure what he takes to be a simple case of dumps.

> Del destin non vi lagnate,
> se vi rese a noi soggette:
> siete serve, ma regnate
> nella vostra servitù.
> Forti noi, voi belle siete,
> e vincete in ogn'impresa,
> quando vengono a contesa
> la bellezza e la virtù.[7]

Like all such arias it is essentially a hymn to the received order of things: the complementariness of beauty and valour, of serving and reigning, and therefore of the powers of love as co-ordinated in the institution of matrimony.

The king's departure leaves the women to continue their talk, now more bitterly and urgently. Though beautifully laden with a sense of lost love, Aristea's aria is another dramatic aria addressed directly to Argene and in effect continuing the conversation:

> Tu di saper procura
> dove il mio ben s'aggira;
> se più di me si cura,
> se parla più di me.
> Chiedi se mai sospira,
> quando il mio nome ascolta;
> se il profferí talvolta
> nel ragionar fra sé.[8]

It is noteworthy that, like 'Superbo di me stesso', the dramatic aria in Act I scene 2, this too is in *settenari*.

After Aristea's elegiac regret Argene's reaction is far more violent. So violent in fact that it is easy to take a piece of moralizing for a straightforward explosion of passion. The point is that the moralizing has been prepared with consummate skill; for in her fury Argene feels she has words of wisdom to offer her sex at large: 'Imparate, imparate, / inesperte donzelle'.[9] Argene is a more energetic young lady than Aristea – as her very liberated behaviour in taking flight from Crete shows – and her romantic disillusionment becomes a missionary cause. The metre matches the message: short lines and springing rhythms bear witness to the flaming impatience of her mood.

> Più non si trovano
> fra mille amanti
> sol due bell'anime
> che sian costanti,
> e tutti parlano
> di fedeltà . . .[10]

'Più non si trovano' is one of several arias in the opera which prove to be difficult to categorize in pigeon-holing fashion – as emotional outburst, metaphor, moralization etc. And that is a tribute to Metastasio's art, for at his best the arias tend to operate on several levels simultaneously, co-ordinating the language of the heart and the language of reason with the language of the imagination.

Act I, scenes 8–10

The third scene brings enlightenment to Megacle as to the nature of the 'tragic' dilemma that faces him, the undertaking he has given to win on behalf of his friend Licida the hand of the Aristea who is his own beloved. Its three constituent numbered 'scenes' bring in turn the recognition of this dilemma, Megacle's steeling of his soul in meditation, and what we might describe as the first ordeal – his meeting with Aristea.

The moment of recognition is made as telling as possible by virtue of Licida's garrulous happiness, for the young man quite revels in his anticipation of Megacle's victory. Hence, the decidedly comic effect of the revelation that it is for Aristea that his friend is to compete; an effect that is sustained at great length by his insistence that Megacle share in anticipation in every detail of his joy:

Licida	Oh! se tu vinci
	chi più lieto di me? Megacle istesso
	quanto mai ne godrà! Di': non avrai
	piacer del piacer mio?
Megacle	Grande.
Licida	Il momento
	che ad Aristea m'annodi,
	Megacle di', non ti parrà felice?
Megacle	Felicissimo. (Oh dei!)
Licida	Tu non vorrai
	pronubo accompagnarmi
	al talamo nuzial?
Megacle	(Che pena!)
Licida	Parla.
Megacle	Si, come vuoi. (Qual nuova specie è questa
	di martirio e d'inferno!)[11]

The whole scene is a charming example of that quasi-comic 'sospensione' that so often in Metastasio takes the place of tragic pity or terror. And that tone is the more prevalent because of his partiality for giving every new arrival of character and every new piece of information the effect of a peripeteia. A good example comes at the close of Megacle's eloquent and noble-minded soliloquy. He has resolved that he must do everything in his power to avoid the 'formidabile incontro'[12] with Aristea, when she just strolls in.

This first ordeal is rendered the more painful for Megacle by Aristea's joy at seeing him, the full-hearted expressions of love and loyalty that she pours out to him. There is a danger that, as Megacle stands downcast and inarticulate, modern taste will find the scene arbitrary and absurd beyond endurance; but think of it strictly as an ordeal, a purification of character according to rules self-imposed by a sense of honour, and its exotic poetry may begin to be felt. For Calzabigi it was Metastasio's finest achievement, a scene which 'if it alone survived of all the works of our poet, would be sufficient to assign him one of the most sublime positions in our literature' (Gallarati 1980: 505).

Irony is so often a keynote in Metastasio's scenes that his aria lyrics are often quite remote from any sense of transporting emotional élan. At the close of Act I scene 8 Licida in his supreme happiness prays to Cupid, brooklet and zephyr to conspire to lull Megacle into easeful sleep:

> Mentre dormi, Amor fomenti
> il piacer de' sonni tuoi
> con l'idea del mio piacer . . .[13]

The language is singularly apt in a drama which so far has passed entirely in the open air, but singularly remote from the true state of anguished consternation in Megacle's mind. In the duet for him and Aristea too there is irony with a vengeance. For in their most extended scene together they are so racked by the 'sospensione' of the moment that their duet becomes an agonized non-meeting of minds. It is a dramatic, almost conversational duet, and it may be noted that Metastasio again uses *settenari* for the purpose.

Megacle	Ne' giorni tuoi felici
	ricordati di me.
Aristea	Perché così mi dici,
	anima mia, perché?
Megacle	Taci, bell'idol mio.
Aristea	Parla, mio dolce amor.
Megacle	Ah! che, parlando, ⎫ oh Dio!
Aristea	Ah! che, tacendo, ⎭
à 2	tu mi trafiggi il cor.
Aristea	(Veggio languir chi adoro,
	né intendo il suo languir.)
Megacle	(Di gelosia mi moro,
	e non lo posso dir.)

à 2   Chi mai provò di questo
affanno più funesto,
più barbaro dolor![14]

Since our principal aim in this chapter is to understand how some of the most distinguished masters of the *opera seria* rose to the challenge of setting Metastasio, we need pursue this detailed examination of the text no further. Acts II and III may be briefly summarized.

Megacle, still masquerading as Licida, gains the victory in the Olympic Games and with it the hand of Aristea. But on the pretext of sharing his joy with his father he is granted permission to leave Elis briefly, entrusting Aristea to the care of his dearest friend, the real Licida, whom he introduces as 'Egisto'. From what follows it is clear that Megacle intends to kill himself, thus leaving Aristea and Licida to one another, his obligation to his friend repaid, and his vows of friendship fulfilled. But Licida's deceit is exposed; worse ignominy follows when despair drives him to make an attempt on King Clistene's life. Catastrophe is averted when Licida is recognized as the supposed long-dead Filinto, Clistene's son and Aristea's twin brother. And so the opera ends happily, with the pairing off of Filinto with Argene, and Megacle with Aristea.

Pergolesi's setting (Rome 1735)

What came to be probably the most admired of all settings of *Olimpiade* followed the Viennese première by approximately sixteen months. Pergolesi's setting was commissioned for the Teatro Tordinona in Rome and first performed there early in January 1737. A few alterations had already been made to Metastasio's text, the most significant of which reflect a balance of resources in the Roman theatre slightly different from that which obtained in Vienna. At the Teatro Tordinona there was no chorus; two of Metastasio's choral movements, in Act II and Act III, are therefore cut; the closing chorus of Act III becomes an ensemble of soloists and the Act I chorus 'Oh care selve', originally designed as a dialogue between Argene-Licori and her nymph and shepherd companions, becomes a solo aria. As if to compensate for these omissions a number of additional arias are provided, two for Alcandro, who had none at all in Metastasio's original, and an extra one for Aminta, 'Talor guerriero invitto' in Act I scene 3, which so to speak raises his dignity from the very start of the opera. In Act III Megacle's aria 'Lo seguitai felice' is replaced by 'Torbido in volto e nero', a metaphor text far less constrained by conversational naturalness than 'Lo seguitai felice', and therefore better able to serve as a truly dazzling display piece for the opera's hero.

Pergolesi's *Olimpiade* provides a characteristic example of *opera seria* vocal typology. All four principals – Licida and Argene, Megacle and

257

Aristea – are sopranos, which in Rome in the 1730s is tantamount to saying that each of them is a soprano *castrato*. Alcandro, alto, is another *castrato*, and natural voices are restricted to the two father figures, the king Clistene and the tutor Aminta, both of whom are tenors. This casting seemed to the eighteenth century self-evidently correct. It is – with minor alterations in the case of Alcandro – to be found again in all the settings discussed in this chapter.

The orchestra of strings is rarely written for in more than three parts. For when the viola part is independent – normally in ritornellos – the violins are in unison; and where first and second violins are independent of one another – as they often are while accompanying the voice – the violas double the bass. Two or three times an act the string orchestra is enriched with the addition of wind and/or brass. Of the Act I arias discussed above three are composed for such an enlarged orchestra. Oboes and horns are added to Licida's 'Mentre dormi', and oboes, horns and trumpets to the same character's 'Qual destrier'; the additional aria for Aminta, 'Talor guerriero invitto', is scored for strings, oboes and what the Brussels MS of the opera describes as 'trombe di caccia' – their part is in the bass clef and presumably they are horns. All these arias are either metaphor or simile arias, or – in the case of 'Mentre dormi' – replete with imagery; the association of metaphor and enlarged orchestra, made by so many composers of the period, goes far to explain the popularity of the type.

With the exception of the closing duet, the music of Act I consists entirely of solo arias – in that it is typical of the genre. All these movements, including the duet, are essentially similar in form, examples of what has often been described as the grand *da capo* aria. They are the products of an aesthetic that encouraged composers to think of arias as things of beauty in their own right, musical artefacts which – for all the slenderness of their texture and the almost exclusive focusing of their expressive power in the singing voice – are as sophisticated in design as any music of the period. Monuments of musical architecture, monuments of musical rhetoric and expression, cunningly fashioned as vehicles for great singing, such arias are the only tangible relics we have of what one is tempted to describe as the most irretrievably lost of music's golden ages.

The *da capo* after which the aria is named is only the most superficial feature of its design. It provided the symmetrical rounding-out of the form; it offered the ideal pretext for more generous helpings of the impromptu or quasi-impromptu ornamentation with which a fine singer could achieve a climax of brilliance or pathos; no doubt, in some measure, it was a helpful economy for hard-worked composers to be spared the labour of writing out approximately two-fifths of the music. Of course it required of Metastasio and his fellow poets texts of which the opening stanza could sensibly be repeated after the second stanza had been sung.

In fact the first stanza of a *da capo* aria was normally sung at least four

LICIDA (Voice only)

Men - tre dor-mi a - mor fo - men-ta.

il pia - cer de' son - ni tuo - i coll' i -

dea del mio pia - cer coll' i - dea del mio pia

cer _____ del mio pia - cer, del mio pia -

cer. Men - tre dor-mi a - mor fo - men-ta

il pia - cer de' sonni tuoi coll' i - dea del

mio pia - cer _____

___ col - l'i - dea del mio pia - cer _____

Fine

___ del mio pia - cer, del mio pia - cer.

etc.

While you sleep, may Love inspire with the thought of my content, the
content of your own slumbers.

Ex.III.11 Pergolesi, *L'Olimpiade* (1735), Act I scene 8

259

times, since its principal section fell into two balancing halves. The text was sung once as the music modulated from the tonic to, usually, the dominant, and a second time firmly in the tonic key but coloured by incidental touches of modulation – and that is to leave out of account the many examples of word-repetition and repetition of shorter phrases that are commonly to be found. In both these sections the lucidity of Metastasio's verse and Pergolesi's tender concern that it should be sung clearly, simply and expressively results in a series of short phrases – often given structural firmness by repetition or sequence – which mark out the flow of the music in a way which shows how vital the aria of this period was as a source of the sonata style (Ex.III.11). A final element of sophistication is provided by the ritornellos that frame the singing and mark more emphatically the salient points in the tonal design:

Ritornello	I
Stanza I	I→V
Ritornello (abbreviated)	V
Stanza I	I (but coloured by passing modulation)
Ritornello	I
(*Fine*)	
Stanza II	Related keys
(*Da capo*)	

Usually the opening ritornello provided the principal motif for the aria; a florid, often sequential extension which was the source of much of its virtuosity and energy; and a piquant cadence phrase, commonly repeated (Ex.III.12).

Any discussion of the expressive and rhetorical force which Pergolesi's music gives to Metastasio's verse must begin with a somewhat technical point. Metastasio used a comparatively small range of verse types in his lyrics; all of them display an exquisitely crafted smoothness; of the limping and confused metrics of the seventeenth-century aria text there is no trace. His favourite aria metre was the *settenario*, of which there were thirteen examples in the original form of *Olimpiade*. Other metrical types trail well behind, four *ottonari*, three each of *quinari* and *decasillabi*, two *senari*.

Given the care that Pergolesi took to clothe the verses in melody without obscuring them, it naturally followed that much of the rhythmic character of the music was a direct reflection of the metric character of the words. *Settenari*, for example, prompted two standard rhythmic responses: in duple or quadruple time ♩ | ♩ ♩ ♩ ♩ | ♩ ♩ (Ex.III.13a) or in triple time or compound time ♪| ♩ ♩♩ ♪| ♩♪ (Ex.III.13b); *quinari* suggested a ♩ ♪♪| ♩ ♩ rhythm (Ex.III.13c).

But such patterns provided only the barest framework for a rhythmic art of supreme finesse and suppleness. In some measure this suppleness is due to an inherent characteristic of Italian verse. The reason Italian poetic

Ex.III.12 Pergolesi, *L'Olimpiade* (1735), Act I scene 10

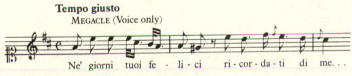

Tempo giusto
MEGACLE (Voice only)

Ne' giorni tuoi fe - li - ci ri - cor - da - ti di me. . .

In the days of your happiness remember me. . .

Ex.III.13a Pergolesi, *L'Olimpiade* (1735), Act I scene 10

Amoroso
ARGENE (Voice only)

O ca - re sel-ve o ca - ra fe - li - ce li-ber - tà, fe - li - ce li - ber - tà. . .

Oh dear woods, happy liberty. . .

Ex.III.13b Pergolesi, *L'Olimpiade* (1735), Act I scene 4

261

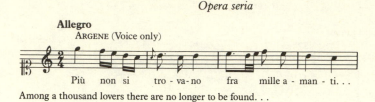

Più non si tro - va - no fra mille a - man - ti. . .

Among a thousand lovers there are no longer to be found. . .

Ex.III.13c Pergolesi, *L'Olimpiade* (1735), Act I scene 7

terminology emphasizes the number of syllables rather than the pattern of stress (*settenari* or *ottonari* rather than iambics or trochaics) is that the pattern of stress is in fact likely to vary considerably from line to line within a single stanza, in, say, *settenari*. Hence such variants on the schemes quoted above as ♩ ♪♪♩ ♩ | ♩ ♩ ♩ or ♩ ♩ ♩ | ♩ ♩ | ♩ ♩ (Ex.III.14). Furthermore, Pergolesi will sometimes wish, for rhetorical emphasis, to open up the caesura in mid-line. In general the rhythmic variants arise from the urge to express the sense of the words as vividly as possible.

Tu di sa - per pro - cura do - ve il mio ben s'ag - gi - ra

Take care to find out where my love is wandering. . .

Ex.III.14 Pergolesi, *L'Olimpiade* (1735), Act I scene 6

The opening aria, Megacle's 'Superbo di me stesso', furnishes an excellent example. Setting the basic scheme ♩ | ♩ ♩ ♩ ♩ | ♩ ♩ against the opening three lines of text:

(i) Superbo di me stesso
(ii) andrò portando in fronte
(iii) quel caro nome impresso . . .

we see that, in (i), Pergolesi highlights the idea of pride, obviously in terms of melody, but also rhythmically, by swaggering augmentation immediately followed by courtier-like flouncings as the underlying rhythmic pulse is resumed (Ex.III.15a). In (ii) the idea of urgent movement is clearly in the front of the composer's mind: the rhythmic pulse is diminished from crotchets to quavers and these subdivided into pairs of semiquavers (Ex.III.15b). The third phrase emphasizes the tenderness of Megacle's feelings for Licida with caressing grace-notes and word-repetition that extends the phrase (Ex.III.15c). These phrases alone suffice to show that Pergolesi's rhetorical priorities resulted in a style more variegated and discontinuous than that of earlier generations of serious opera composers. And this discontinuity opened the way to bold and fanciful expressive flights unforeseeable from the material presented at the start of the aria. A little later in this same aria Megacle's love for Licida is underlined in a totally unexpected way, a sudden pang of emotion prompting a passage of poignant *sostenuto* that breaks down the general briskness of the style (Ex.III.15d).

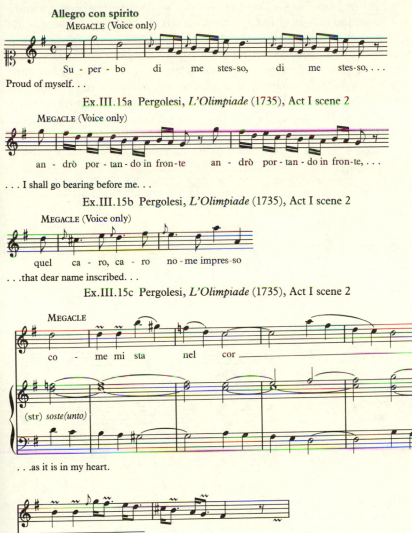

Ex.III.15a Pergolesi, *L'Olimpiade* (1735), Act I scene 2

Ex.III.15b Pergolesi, *L'Olimpiade* (1735), Act I scene 2

Ex.III.15c Pergolesi, *L'Olimpiade* (1735), Act I scene 2

Ex.III.15d Pergolesi, *L'Olimpiade* (1735), Act I scene 2

Pergolesi's scrupulous attention to the delivery of the words results in a melodic style best described as *parlando*. The text, especially in such moralizing arias as 'Del destin non vi lagnate', is likely to be perfectly audible throughout, for the florid brilliance that has so often been regarded as the be-all and end-all of the *opera seria* is largely confined to codetta-like extensions where the mood established by the fusion of words and music relaxes into a sheer pretty songfulness. But in other contexts the virtuosity can itself be powerfully suggestive. Of 'Superbo di me stesso' it has been remarked that 'the coloratura is pervaded by emphatic repetitions and really is at this tempo extremely difficult to sing, which is a positive not a negative factor if a young hero is being impersonated and if the person taking the role can sing it . . .' (Strohm 1979: 218–19).

It would be wrong to give the impression that Pergolesi was a musical

Oh dear woods, happy liberty. . .

Ex.III.16 Pergolesi, *L'Olimpiade* (1735), Act I scene 4

264

dramatist who thought only in the one dimension of expressive vocal melody. No composer trained by Durante in the environment where the Scarlattis were at home is likely to have been deaf to the expressive potential of harmony. He makes particularly effective use of that flux of major and minor to which all Neapolitans seem to have been partial. An exquisite example is Aristea's 'Oh care selve', where the customary modulation to the dominant in fact turns to the minor, and the harmonies seem to flood the song with a deeper significance, already perhaps hinted at in the siciliano rhythm: we are reminded that – though the words may be in the blandest pastoral style – Pergolesi has had to put them in the mouth of a girl who envies rather than shares the 'felice libertà' of the pastoral convention, and the aria becomes one not of escape but of poignant nostalgia (Ex.III.16).

In metaphor and image-laden arias Pergolesi's orchestra can also speak meaningfully. In the middle section of 'Mentre dormi', at the words 'e sospenda i moti suoi / ogni zeffiro leggier', one really is given a picture of zephyrs beating their wings with such infinite gentleness that all motion is suspended (Ex.III.17).

The suggestion of underlying sadness in Argene's idyllic song 'Oh care selve', and the blend of pride and tenderness in 'Superbo di me stesso', have already introduced us to one of the outstanding qualities of Pergolesi's

. . .and let every gentle zephyr cease to move. . .

Ex.III.17 Pergolesi, *L'Olimpiade* (1735), Act I scene 8

setting. It will surprise no one who is familiar with *La serva padrona*, for it is the sharpness of his dramatic imagination. It would be difficult to imagine an aria in any musical idiom that combines more effectively the merits of musical charm, fidelity to the text, and vivid and perceptive characterization than Argene's 'Più non si trovano'. The short lines in which Metastasio couches his apophthegm are punched out in a series of bright and breezy musical epigrams; 'Metastasio has tried to put in words a piece of collective wisdom . . . and Pergolesi has tried to give the formulation a melody that will put it back on every lip' (Strohm 1979: 221). And how beautifully apt it is to the spirited character of Argene that when the underlying sorrow in her heart threatens to well up, she drives it out with the sheer energy of her indignation (Ex.III.18). That Pergolesi was a musical dramatist to the finger tips, not merely an effective setter of words, is shown on a more ample scale in the duet that closes the first act. Here the tenderly 'speaking' melody that bears the true current of feeling backwards and forwards between Aristea and Megacle, is periodically racked by spasms of angular chromaticism that depict them on the verge of losing self-control, or broken down into dialogue of *opera-buffa*-like verisimilitude.

Leo's setting (Naples 1737)

How far these virtues are personal to Pergolesi rather than simply commonplaces of the tradition within which he worked becomes clear when we compare his setting with that of one of the most distinguished of his senior Neapolitan contemporaries, Leonardo Leo. His *Olimpiade* was the second opera to be performed in the new San Carlo theatre, in December 1737. In virtually all the qualities that make a musical dramatist, Leo's setting falls

Among a thousand lovers there are no longer to be found even so much as two souls that are constant; and everyone talks about fidelity.

Ex.III.18 Pergolesi, *L'Olimpiade* (1735), Act I scene 7

Proud of myself I shall go bearing that dear name before me. . .

Ex.III.19 Leo, *L'Olimpiade* (1737), Act I scene 2

delivery of the text, and often he impairs the clarity of the declamation by introducing melisma at an early stage in the aria; when he conspicuously varies the metric/rhythmic correspondences it is not easy to sense any expressive or rhetorical point in the variation. The fitting together of text and melody at the start of 'Superbo di me stesso' seems gauche and rather aimlessly contrary compared with Pergolesi's (Ex.III.19). Nor are any of the characters limned with the kind of musical distinctiveness that, for example, makes the strong-feeling, impetuous Argene leap from the pages of Pergolesi's score.

The virtues of Leo's opera are more purely musicianly ones, its most memorable pages due to the sheer musical conceptions and their execution. His setting of the duet 'Ne' giorni tuoi felici' is in effect an unbroken flow of impassioned melody with nothing of those dramatic effects of suspense or dialectic that mark Pergolesi's. But harmonically and expressively it is in many respects a richer movement, not least by virtue of its remarkable tonal scheme, which follows the emotional contour of the verse to the extent of closing all sections in the minor key:

Ritornello	Stanza 1	Ritornello (abbrev.)	Stanza 1	Ritornello	Stanza 2
I	I→ii	ii→V	I→i	I	vi→iii

Where Pergolesi is likely to bring each half of his aria designs to a climax by means of simple florid vocal writing, Leo is more likely to use skilfully crafted sequential passages exploiting rich suspension-laden harmony or neatly woven vocal-cum-instrumental textures. Altogether – though his metaphor arias are less ostentatious than Pergolesi's – he uses the orchestra more resourcefully, confining it less to the ritornellos, engaging it in echo and dialogue with the voice. Among the more innovatory of his orchestral textures are some that anticipate the simple, chordal accompaniment figurations of a later generation.

Superficially Leo's setting of the text is closer to the Metastasian original than is Pergolesi's. At the San Carlo there was no problem about recruiting a chorus, so all the choral scenes that Pergolesi had had to omit could be restored. This in turn meant that there was less pressure on Leo to provide additional arias. In fact there are two: one, Alcandro's 'Apportator son io' borrows its text from the *addenda* of the Pergolesi version; a second replaces the reprise of the chorus 'I tuoi strali' in Act III scene 7. In Naples it had been noticed that Licida has no Act III aria, and this piece, 'Deh s'hai pietade in seno', was added to provide one. Earlier in the act the genuine Metastasian text 'Lo seguitai felice' was restored in lieu of Pergolesi's 'Torbido in volto'. But the semblance of a greater fidelity to the poet is largely illusory. For while Pergolesi sets the recitative virtually complete, Leo cuts in freely, sometimes in ways which suggest a certain indifference to its literary and dramatic merits, or to the finer nuances of characterization. An extreme example is Act I scene 3 where, of Metastasio's twenty lines of dialogue, only six survive.

Galuppi's setting (Milan 1747)

Ten years later another distinguished and successful setting of *Olimpiade* was made by the Venetian composer Baldassare Galuppi for performance at the Ducal Theatre in Milan. As yet we can detect no fundamental change in the artistic values of the *opera seria*. Galuppi's vocal casting of four sopranos, two tenors and an alto is identical to Pergolesi's, and the design of the opera is still wholly dependent on an alternation of recitatives and solo arias in grand *da capo* form. Since Milan, like Rome, had no chorus, the handful of choral movements Metastasio had written for the Viennese première were omitted.

But, far more decisively than Leo's setting, Galuppi's betrays a dwindling interest in the eloquence and high artistry of Metastasio's original text. The more profusely florid scenes of recitative are hacked back ruthlessly, with little sign of any higher purpose than impatience. Sometimes quite important elements of the plot are sacrificed, as in Act I scene 4, where the lines that tell of Licida rescuing Megacle from the brigands who attacked him on his arrival in Crete are cut. It is perhaps more surprising, in what is still pure aria opera, to find that even Metastasio's provision of aria lyrics is beginning to be meddled with. As in Pergolesi and Leo, arias are provided for Alcandro; more interestingly, five of Metastasio's original aria-texts have been replaced by substitutes. While it is not altogether easy to detect any pattern in these substitutions, it is possible that *pasticcio* practice is involved here, or that some of the new arias are *arie di baule*. The new arias for Aminta, 'Tigre che sdegno ed ira' in Act II scene 5 and 'Si sprezzi il periglio' in Act III scene 5 (III.6 in Galuppi's numbering), are particularly suspicious, replacing the marine metaphors that came so aptly to the lips of a Cretan schoolmaster with verses that offered no gain in terms of musical stimulation.

The other three arias to be dropped were Argene's 'No, la speranza' in Act II scene 12, Megacle's 'Lo seguitai felice' in Act III scene 3 and Clistene's 'Non so donde viene' in Act III scene 6. And these are the most suggestive alterations, for all these movements might be described as conversational or ruminative arias, arias during which the dramatic or psychological action is rationally pursued. Galuppi's substitutions suggest that interest in this type of aria may have been waning, for all were replaced by texts that were more effusively emotional, or more colourful in imagery: 'Lo seguitai felice' for example, a Metastasian rendering of Ovid's maxim: 'Scilicet ut fulvum spectatur in ignibus aurum / tempore sic duro est inspicienda fides'[15] concerning Megacle's relation to the absent Licida, is replaced by an impassioned love-song addressed directly to Aristea.

> Per momenti a vagheggiare
> Tornerò pupille care,
> Quel seren che nel mio seno
> Infiammò col primo sguardo.
> Più valor trarrò da quelle
> Dolci labbra, luci belle,
> Che il momento del contento
> Al mio cor faran men tardo.[16]

An examination of the music may perhaps shed some light on the already quoted remark of Metastasio to the effect that Galuppi was 'a good composer for violins, violoncellos, and for singers; but a very bad workman for poets' (Burney 1796, I: 297). First, compared particularly with Pergolesi, he preserves much less of the music of the verse: his aria incipits, which is to say the seeds from which the musical designs grow, often show a quite cavalier unconcern for any natural relationship between poetic metre and musical rhythm. Sometimes such correspondences are hidden under clouds of *fioritura* or emerge only incidentally at a later stage in the aria. Regardless of the mood of the aria, the voice is likely to break into extensive coloratura passages at appointed places in both halves of the principal section, just as if Galuppi thought of the aria primarily as a vocal concerto. In the second place, the emancipation of the orchestra continues apace. Between the ritornellos it is no longer confined to a subsidiary accompanying role; not even to the echoes and antiphonies we have found in Leo. In Galuppi, occasionally and still modestly, the instruments will actually take the lead in the presentation of the themes, while the voices are momentarily reduced to declamatory interjections (Ex.III.20).

The greater musical elaboration of Galuppi's arias pushes the language of Italian opera even more clearly in the direction of the emergent sonata style. His opening themes tend to be clearly rounded off in the tonic key;

. . .you pierce my heart. . .be silent. . .why?. . .ah. . .

Ex.III.20 Galuppi, *L'Olimpiade* (1747), Act I scene 10

transitional themes to prepare the shift to the dominant in a far more thoroughgoing way – typically with bars of coloratura; each half of the principal section will be concluded with a distinctive cadence theme, a more than embryonic second subject which, having been heard in the dominant at the end of the first half, recurs in the tonic at the end of the second.

What Metastasio could not have been expected to appreciate was the fact that by the time of Galuppi composers were beginning to find in the very complexity and sophistication of the musical design the means of expressing dramatic, psychological or emotional ideas. The profusion and contrast of theme, the cunningly articulated tonal schemes in which the harmony is asserted, undermined, obfuscated, clarified anew, become dramatic tools in the hands of a good composer, and enable him increasingly to assume the leading role in the musico-poetic enterprise, even when his partner is Metastasio. The expressive burden of 'Superbo di mi stesso' – the coexistence in Megacle's own heart of heroic pride and tenderness for Licida – is beautifully captured by such means: the former in the bold plain intervals of the main theme and in the long passages of energetic coloratura, the latter by such textural and harmonic events in the unfolding of the design as the dreamy lingering and etherealized scoring at the start of the 'transition theme' (Ex.III.21).

. . . I shall go bearing that dear name before me as I bear it inscribed in my heart.

Ex.III.21 Galuppi, *L'Olimpiade* (1747), Act I scene 2

Jommelli's setting (Stuttgart 1761)

After Pergolesi's 1735 setting, Jommelli's of 1761 was probably the most admired of all *Olimpiades*. It was one of the very small group of Italian operas of the eighteenth century to be published in full score (*accompagnato* recitatives, arias and ensembles only), as the first, and in the event the only, number of a projected collected edition of Jommelli's operas (Stuttgart 1783).

Typically for Jommelli's mature work, the relationship of his *Olimpiade* to the Metastasian ideal of *opera seria* was uniquely ambiguous. In a sense the composer was more faithful to the poet than any of his predecessors since Caldara. If the printed libretto is to be trusted, he made few cuts in the recitative scenes compared with Galuppi, or even with Leo. And while a number of arias were omitted – 'Mentre dormi' in Act I scene 8, 'Siam navi' in Act II scene 5 and 'No, la speranza' in Act II scene 12 – there are no additional arias at all. The high literary distinction of Metastasio's dramatic poem is unimpaired by impatience or by concessions to singers in the form of interpolated arias that assort ill with the complexion of the rest.

Other features of the score tell a very different story, however. No fewer than eight of the recitative scenes, including almost all the dramatic monologues, such as that in Act I scene 9 in which Megacle steels himself to sacrifice his love to his friend, are set entirely or in part in *accompagnato* style. And at the dramatic climax of the opera in Act III scene 7 we find a momentous innovation that would surely have dismayed Metastasio profoundly. This is the scene in which Licida, condemned to death for his attempt on the king's life, is permitted, still in the presence of King Clistene, to see and embrace Megacle and bid him a final farewell. At this juncture Jommelli adds a dramatic ensemble, a trio which brings the emotional anguish to a head in a complex musical form.

Licida	Dolce amico ai giorni tuoi
	Giunga, giunga il ciel pietoso
	Che il destino invola a me.
Megacle	Ah! di Leto il guado ombroso
	Voglio anch'io passar con te.
Clistene	Che momento tormentoso
	Pena, oh Dio, maggior non v'è.
Licida	Viver dei.
Megacle	Che cenno è questo.
Clistene	Che spettacolo funesto!
Licida	Dammi ⎫
Megacle	Rendi ⎬ un altro amplesso
Tutti	Non resisto al fiero eccesso
	Del tiranno affanno mio.
Megalce	Prence, ⎫
Licida	Amico, ⎬ oh stelle, addio.[17]

... Prince. . . Friend. . . Oh stars!. . . Farewell. . .what anguish. . .

Ex.III.22 Jommelli, *L'Olimpiade* (1761), Act III scene 7

As Strohm has observed of these accompanied recitatives, 'the composer cannot say more clearly how very little he trusts the ability of language by itself to kindle emotions' (Strohm 1979: 299).

One of the reasons for the smaller number of arias in Jommelli's score is that his movements are even more monumental in conception. Their structure is not in essence much different from that of Galuppi's, but the scale is grander: the exposition of material in the orchestral introductions are concerto-like in amplitude, the passages of virtuoso coloratura are protracted at greater length, the middle sections are more often than not distinct episodes in contrasting tempo, almost all the themes are presented in the form of a more complex weave of voice and instruments. Indeed, there are in Jommelli many themes that are essentially orchestral – especially the 'second subject' themes – and during which the voice is reduced to the role of modestly intoning a few words. His orchestra was not in fact larger than that of his predecessors (strings, two flutes, two oboes, two horns are specified), but his operas gave a far more Germanic and 'learned' impression to his Italian contemporaries, because he always aimed at a cunningly wrought and finely detailed texture.

All this musical elaboration was not, as Algarotti and Gluck – not to

Proud of myself. . .

Ex.III.23 Jommelli, *L'Olimpiade* (1761), Act I scene 2

mention Metastasio himself – suggested, a symptom of the decline of the *opera seria* into a concert in costume; rather of Jommelli's determination and resource in exploring to the full music's powers of dramatic, rhetorical and emotional expression. It is his unwillingness to let the eloquence of Metastasio's verse (clothed in simple expressive melody) speak for itself that makes him so representative a figure in the third quarter of the eighteenth century. Where earlier composers were likely simply to double a vocal melody in the violins, Jommelli inclines to amplify it with instrumental detail that suggest an energy of feeling the voice itself is incapable of (Ex.III.23). Sometimes the orchestra takes up the chief expressive burden, and the voice is simply swept along on a symphony of evocative or pictorial figures, such as the galloping dactyllic rhythms (all that is left of Metastasio's poetic metre in this aria), the scurrying scale-passages, the impatiently tossing and snatching gestures that so vividly image the impetuous steed of 'Quel destrier'. Even at the start of an aria, Jommelli is inclined to break up, and reiterate and reorganize the phrases of the verse, and at later junctures adopts an even more sovereign indifference to its integrity. A striking example is provided by Clistene's 'Del destin non vi lagnate', the text of which has been quoted on p. 254. In readiness for the *dal segno* Jommelli tears the elegant lyric to shreds, creating out of it a sequence of rhetorical gestures, reducing it in fact to something not far remote from Verdi's ideal of the *parola scenica* (see p. 548).

Cimarosa's setting (Vicenza 1784)

Twenty years on, and the progressive refashioning of the Metastasian *dramma per musica* is assuming more radical forms. The trimming back of the recitative continues; Jommelli's fondness for modulating into *accompagnato* recitative at every great emotional crisis becomes standard practice. But by now not even Metastasio's beautifully structured intrigue is sacrosanct. Cimarosa's 1784 setting of *L'Olimpiade* is a two-act opera; Acts II and III of the original have been fused into a single act, and that necessarily entails some simplification and reorganization of the action.

Three details may be mentioned. First, in order to make a more direct and theatrical appeal to the audience, Licida's attempt on the life of King Clistene, hitherto reported in a messenger scene, becomes part of the onstage action. In the original *dramma* this messenger scene was Alcandro's chief *raison d'être*; deprived of it, he can easily be dispensed with altogether and disappears from the cast-list. In the second place, for Cimarosa's generation, the *opera buffa* has become the forcing ground for all the most exciting developments in opera; and he, like Mozart, was keen to introduce to *opera seria* some of the new musico-dramatic resources of the comic genre. There is nothing in *Olimpiade* quite so drastic or thoroughgoing as we find in Mozart and Mazzolà's transformation of *La clemenza di Tito* (Prague 1791), but the ensemble finale does make its appearance. Once Clistene has recognized Licida as his long-lost son, Filinto, the rest of the denouement and all the various reactions of the assembled characters to the benevolent provisions of destiny are subsumed into a continuous ensemble finale in several movements. Finally, as a small contribution to the necessary shortening of Cimarosa's conflated Act III, one of Aminta's arias (originally Act II scene 5) is transferred to the opening scene of Act I; it therefore becomes the first aria in the opera:

> Siam navi all'onde algenti
> lasciate in abbandono:
> impetuosi venti
> i nostri affetti sono:
> ogni diletto è scoglio:
> tutta la vita è mar.[18]

[A further quatrain in Metastasio's original lyric is omitted.]

This is an arresting and not ineffective modification; critics have often remarked that 'Siam navi all'onde algenti' is one of those lyrics that seem to sum up Metastasio's whole dramatic philosophy, suggesting how the bemusement of his characters, and the fantastical turmoils in which they are swept up, have their origin in the very nature of human existence. A reflection which in Metastasio's original had been cried out from the agitated heart of the drama becomes, in Cimarosa's opera, a kind of motto symbolically inscribed over the threshold.

That addition apart, Act I is less fundamentally altered. Two aria texts – 'Quel destrier, che all'albergo è vicino' (Act I scene 3) and 'Più non si trovano' (Act I scene 7) – are replaced by alternatives, 'S'affretta il passeggiero' and 'Fra mille amanti un core', which seem to have no advantage over the originals save perhaps their more commonplace *ottonario* metre. Throughout the act the classic alternation of recitatives and arias is preserved, and what Cimarosa makes one most aware of is the fact that year by year the operatic aria has grown more beautiful, more expressive, more sophisticated and sumptuous as composers took up into it more and more of the resources of their art. When, in 'Superbo di me stesso', he wishes to express the duality of Megacle's emotion – the pride in what he can himself achieve, and the tender affection with which he places this in the service of Licida – there seems none of the dimensions of music that is not brought into play: contrast of melodic line and rhythmic flow, of texture, harmony and even dynamics (Ex.III.24).

And something else more ominous for the future of the Metastasian ideal can sometimes be sensed. Cimarosa was one of the greatest masters of the *opera buffa*, and he was growing impatient with a state of affairs that in *opera seria* permitted arias and duets to be sung only during a suspension of dramatic time. His tendency to make them part of the forward momentum

276

Proud of myself, I shall go bearing that dear name before me as I bear it inscribed in my heart.

Ex.III.24 Cimarosa, *L'Olimpiade* (1784), Act I scene 2

of the dramatic action is seen in various apparently casual features: the occasional replacement of the standard sonata-form aria by examples of two-movement (slow–fast) arias of the kind familiar from Mozart ('Grandi è ver, son le tue pene'); the recitative-like incidents that sometimes interrupt the arias (Ex.III.25).

This new habit of thought is most strikingly manifest in the Act I finale – for that is what Cimarosa turns the duet 'Ne' giorni tuoi felici' into. Without altering Metastasio's text in any way (cf. pp. 256–7 above) he subdivides it into four segments: the tender, lingering, sorrowful and bewildered farewell (lines 1–8); an exclamation of anguish (9); an episode of soliloquy in which both agonize over their own dilemma (10–13); a final explosion of despair and reproach (14–16); and each of these segments provides the material for a new movement, linked to its neighbour in a continuous chain. Just occasionally – despite the aesthetics of the *dramma per musica* – some of Metastasio's more conversational lyrics did offer scope for genuinely dramatic music. This duet is a case in point – a provocation for any experienced *opera buffa* composer – and Cimarosa uses the technique of the ensemble finale in order to co-ordinate a series of musical incidents with the psychological development of the scene. Henceforth for a century, in *opera seria* no less than in *opera buffa*, the co-ordination of dramatic action and musical continuity was to be one of the major challenges to a composer's mastery.

Do not complain of destiny.

Ex.III.25 Cimarosa, *L'Olimpiade* (1784), Act I scene 5

Part IV
The tradition of comedy

16 · The *commedia dell'arte*

Aspects of Italian comedy

Few things could be more rash than to lay claim to an understanding of another nation's sense of humour. I therefore start from the comparative security of a received British point of view: that the greatest Italian humorist was the eighteenth-century Venetian playwright, Carlo Goldoni. I do not know that Italians would necessarily dissent from this. The gloss they might perhaps add is that Goldoni was a not entirely typical embodiment of the Italian comic genius – and that for several reasons. It was, for example, he who, by his reform of comedy in the mid-eighteenth century, hastened the demise of the 200-year-old tradition of the *commedia dell'arte* – next to opera, probably Italy's most brilliant and distinctive contribution to world theatre; the civic and moral virtues he celebrated in so many of his comedies, though ostensibly drawn from contemporary Venetian life, were in large measure a reflection of qualities he admired in the commercial milieu of the Protestant North-west of Europe, particularly England and Holland: above all un-Italian is the serenely smiling good humour that permeates his best plays. The dash and sparkle of the dialogue, the dazzling manipulation of the intrigue have the effect – to use Goldoni's own phrase – of 'una tempesta in mezzo alla calma',[1] and it is precisely this calm that is so rare in Italian comedy. It emanates from an enlightened optimism, from a cheerful faith in human nature and in its capacity for improving the human condition.

The laughter of the Italians has usually been more frenzied than it is in Goldoni – perhaps 'festive' is the word. For their comedy is rarely a play on the smiling surface of an agreeable and settled way of life; it tends rather to be an escape, a Carnival, even an antidote to despair. The subtler commentators on the Italian way of life have often remarked on a profound melancholy that lurks not far beneath the surface of animation and gaiety. Luigi Barzini described his fellow countrymen as 'pessimistic, realistic, resigned and frightened people', saw in their prodigal talents as artists and entertainers manifestations of a ruse 'to lull man's *Angst* to sleep and comfort him in his solitude', and went on to call as witness the novelist Ignazio Silone:

There is an intimate sadness which comes to chosen souls simply from the consciousness of man's fate . . . This sort of sadness has always prevailed among intelligent Italians, but most of them, to evade suicide or madness, have taken to every known means of escape: they feign exaggerated gaity . . . a passion for women . . . for fine-sounding words . . . I think there has never been a race of men so fundamentally desolate and desperate as these gay Italians.
(Barzini 1964: 75, 338)

Not the rounded human portrait, but the disguise of mask and puppet and caricature have been typical of Italian comedy; and not good-humoured naturalism, but clowning and charlatanry, slapstick and illusion. Generations after such a taste had been lost in most parts of Europe, Italians remained attached to a lusty, physical mirth inherited from the old Latin comedy. In short, farce, not comedy, was the form more characteristic of the Italian theatre, and the style of farce that demonstrated the Italian comic genius most comprehensively was the *commedia dell'arte*.

Commedia dell'arte

Despite attempts to establish rival definitions of the term, *commedia dell'arte* is best defined in the standard way, as comedy performed by professional players (*arte* = craft or guild). The point of the term was that the *commedia* developed in an age – the sixteenth century – when most drama was in the hands of amateurs, in schools, academies and courts. From time to time amateurs did try their hand at *commedia dell'arte* too, but more than other dramatic forms it depended upon a measure of virtuosity that could be achieved only by professionals – virtuoso clowning, virtuoso miming, virtuoso facility with the tongue. What most of all made it dependent upon the regularly constituted professional troupe was the fact that it was not performed from a written script, but improvised.

As a dramatic form, *commedia dell'arte* came to greatness in an age of intellectual and literary decadence. As Renaissance humanism yielded to Counter-reformation dogmatism, and as political liberty declined and absolutism spread, it became the best-loved form of entertainment throughout Italy. Indeed the verve and inventiveness of the comedians soon came to be admired through much of Western Europe. Can it have been coincidence that *commedia dell'arte* came to flourish at the time it did? Most critics have thought not. After all, in an age of rigid dogmatism what could be more delightful than abandoning oneself to the pleasures of unreason; and in an age of hierarchical absolutism what could occasion a more delicious thrill than the overthrow of taboo? Children defying their parents, servants outmanoeuvring their masters; wives cuckolding their husbands; the grey eminences of society breaking out into lewd caperings; such is the stuff of which *commedia*, at least in its mainstream, was made.

Aggressive and anarchic as it may sound, the *commedia dell'arte* intended no socio-political satire and occasioned little serious offence. Its apparently lethal contents were in large measure neutralized by the style of perform- ance. The action of the comedy seemed remote from any real world, thanks to the type-casting of the characters – many of whom wore masks. A rigidly patterned structure acted as a corrective to the anarchic impulses of the subject-matter. The characters tended to come in pairs – two old men, two comic servants, two romantic lovers – and their positioning and movement on the stage appears to have had an almost geometrical formality; the whole course of the intrigue depended upon a systematic series of reversals of fortune in which parallel scenes played a conspicuous part; within the individual scene speech prompted counter-speech, practical joke prompted counter-attack. All these features tended to exclude the possibility of empathy on the part of the watching audience, and with it the possibility of any wholehearted socio-political 'engagement'. Those who watched it did so not to be moved, but because they took delight in the playing out of a strategy; *commedia dell'arte* was ritual or festivity as much as it was drama.

The *commedia* fascinated and delighted much of Western Europe for centuries, and ever since its demise has haunted the imagination of all who take an interest in the theatre. But it is a difficult art-form to come to grips with, simply because the records of it are so incomplete. Its strength and its glory, its whole *raison d'être*, was its spontaneity, the scope which it offered for improvisation by virtuoso performers. Its uniqueness as an art-form was that it existed only in the inspired moment of creation. Those who devised and performed these plays left no scripts, nothing but a fair amount of iconographical evidence and the so-called *scenari* or *canovacci* – skeleton plots, listing the names of the characters, outlining the sequence of scenes, providing a few stage-directions and the gist of the major speeches. Everything else, everything that is to say that gave life and movement and real substance to the play – the details of the dialogue, the wit and repartee, the timing of the incidents, the elaboration of the 'turns', the practical jokes, the horseplay – depended upon improvisation. For music historians the poignant elusiveness of long-vanished performance traditions has always been a fact of life – what were Caccini's *sprezzatura*, or Handel's figured-bass playing, or Malibran's impromptu ornamentation *really* like? But with *commedia dell'arte* the problem for the imagination is that much greater, because the improvisation involved a whole team of artists and spread into several dimensions of the performance simultaneously.

The masks

'Pantaloon', 'Punch', 'Zany', 'Harlequinade' – even in English we have a whole series of terms which testify to the hold on the imagination of the stock characters of the *commedia*. Normally an Italian improvised comedy would have had between six and eight principals, most of them grouped in pairs, and each played by an actor who specialized in the improvisation of that one role. To begin with, the two old men: Pantalone, the prosperous Venetian merchant, was usually the butt of the intrigue. His prosperity did not exempt him from avarice, nor did his age spare him from ludicrous spasms of youthful lust. Periodically, individual actors and individual commentators made attempts to retrieve for Pantalone a measure of gravity and decorum. But the surviving image is Perrucci's, of a 'puer centum annorum'[2] (*Dell'arte rappresentativa* 1699, in Oreglia 1968: 78). His crony, the Doctor, was a pedant from Bologna, the seat of Italy's most venerable university. Whether his erudition was legal, medical or academic, the Doctor was a bore of inexhaustible garrulousness, proffering advice and furnishing information in interminable Latinate sentences, which tended to be punctuated by maxims of crushing banality. One of the standard jokes between these two worthies was that the Doctor found it difficult to get Pantalone's name right: he called him Piatlon, Piantalimon, Petulon, Pultrunzon, Pianzamelon, Padelon, Panieron (Lea 1934, I: 18–19). One supposes that the joke was particularly timely in the classic age of the *commedia dell'arte* because the Council of Trent, by its insistence on the maintenance of proper parish registers, had made names something about which people had become acutely self-conscious. And one remarks on this apparently small detail because it is obviously the source of the joke in *The Barber of Seville*, where Almaviva, disguised as a soldier, has precisely the same problem with Bartolo's name.

The second pair were the two 'zanni', or comic servants. Traditionally – though in fact the tradition was often ignored – one of them was cunning, one simple: Colombina, in Goldoni's *Il teatro comico* (Venice 1750), is still weighing up the respective merits of her two suitors, the 'shrewd one', Brighella, and the 'ignorant one', Arlecchino. Historically the two types were supposed to have derived from the inhabitants of, respectively, the upper and lower cities of Bergamo, which remained the homeland of the *zanni* throughout the history of the *commedia dell'arte*. These comic servants between them had a multitude of names, including in the early years Zanni – a dialectal corruption of Giovanni – which only later came to be a generic term rather than a proper name. But a handful of names gradually came to predominate, and the characters associated with them to cultivate a number of familiar recurring traits. The best-loved was Arlecchino, in principle the stupid one of the pair, with his patched costume, his stick, and his dreamy, strutting walk. But Arlecchino compensated for his dull wits by his phenomenal agility – 'he is able to scale palaces and fall from the highest balconies . . . to walk on stilts, to skip, pirouette, dance, somersault and walk on his hands' (Oreglia 1968: 58). Arlecchino was an innocent of the purest naivety, living wholly for the present moment, blithely oblivious of the likely consequences of his behaviour, though happily adroit at extricating himself from the pickles into which his lack of foresight led him. Goldoni has left us a superb literary example of a traditional Arlecchino in his *Servitore di due padroni* (Venice 1756), though, confusingly, he has renamed him Truffaldino. Arlecchino's only rival in popularity and longevity was Pulcinella. A comparatively primitive figure with no marked individuality, Pulcinella was a witty dolt whose personal traits tended to be fleshed out according to local taste. As a result, 'Croce studies him as a symbol of the Neapolitan populace . . . Magnin insists that in spite of his foreign name, "Polichinelle me paraît un type entièrement naturel, et une des créations les plus spontanées et les plus vivaces de la fantaisie française." We are convinced that Pulcinella naturalized to "Punch" stands for a peculiarly English sense of humour' (Lea 1934, I: 88–9). Two of the more active and scheming *zanni*, Brighella and Scapino, were often musicians. Francesco Gabrielli, one of the great Scapinos of the early seventeenth century, played the violin, various viols, the guitar, the harp, the spinet, the trombone, the mandolin, the theorbo, the lute and 'other instruments' (Nicoll 1963: 156).

Two young lovers form the final pair in the list of characters. Their successful union is the main point of the intrigue. Generally the desired consummation is brought about thanks to the good offices of one or both of the *zanni*, and often it involves the frustration of the plans of the two oldsters.

Of the multitude of figures who occasionally appeared to add spice to the central intrigue of old men, comic servants and lovers – Tartaglia, the stammerer; the braggart Capitano Spavento, and so on – only one was indispensable, the *servetta*. This serving-maid generally lacked the distinct personal traits of the *zanni*, but she too tended to have one of a standardized stock of names – Franceschina and Colombina were particularly popular. What is notable about the *servetta* is her growing prominence and refinement. Many of the early *servetta* performers were men; some are likely to have been harlots. It is hardly to be wondered at, then, that crude burlesque was at first the keynote of her scenes. As more professional actresses addressed themselves to the *servetta* roles, the emphasis shifted to quickwittedness and coquetry. The *servetta* of the *commedia* is the prototype of Serpina and Despina and Rosina and all the other soubrette charmers of the *opera buffa*. In fact the whole history of the development of the *servetta* was paralleled in the opera-house between Monteverdi and Cavalli in the mid-seventeenth century, and Cimarosa and Paisiello in the late eighteenth.

Except for the young lovers, the principal characters in the *commedia dell'arte* commonly wore masks and traditional costumes in traditional colours, and each spoke a distinct dialect – Venetian for Pantalone,

Bolognese for the Doctor, Bergamask for the *zanni*. The lovers went unmasked and spoke pure Tuscan. From the beginning the *commedia* thus divided its casts into two distinct types of character, which we may crudely distinguish as 'caricatured' and 'realistic', and which were surely reflected in that differentiation between 'parti serie' and 'parti buffe' that was to be so important in eighteenth-century comic opera. All the characters of the *commedia*, but especially the masks, were cumulative personalities, well-loved types who appeared again and again in ever-changing situations, their characters slowly transformed and enriched (or debased) as the decades passed. The appeal of this kind of dramatic characterization was beautifully underlined by Croce:

> Those actors were not simply themselves giving an individual performance, but the *semper florentes* Arlecchino and Brighella and Pulcinella and Pantalone and Doctor: species of genii and demiurges of merriment, who came down to bestow their kinds of blessings on mankind . . . and mankind awaited them eagerly, and their mood turned to one of joy simply to see them appear. (Croce 1946b: 510)

The skills of the comedians

The good *commedia* performer needed an imagination and inventiveness that was never at rest, a promptitude that enabled him to respond to his fellow performers both sharply and sensitively. The teamwork that was demanded by, for instance, the great duologues of scorn and reconciliation, led the best companies to acquire a refinement of ensemble that one is tempted to describe as operatic. But individual virtuosity was equally indispensable, particularly in those two features of the *commedia dell'arte* style which provide an even closer analogy with the opera – the *tirata* and the *lazzo*.

A *tirata* was simply a tirade, a long speech. For obvious reasons it was a hall-mark of the roles of the Doctor, the lover, and the braggart Captain. The mastery of the improvised *tirata* required long study, rigorous discipline and wide reading, the style of the reading and of the study depending on the character in question. For example, Andrea Perrucci, writing in 1699, advised the lover to read only books written in the best Tuscan, and to make a particular study of all 'the figures of speech and tropes used in rhetoric . . . metaphor, metonymy, synecdoche, autono-masy, catachresis, metathesis, allegory and irony – protasis, aphorism, syncope, comparison, apocope, antithesis, systole' (Nicholl 1963: 33). (Perrucci's advice is itself something of a *tirata*.) Several of the most accomplished performers published model *tirate*, and there is no doubt that actors did often memorize chosen passages, especially the rhyming peror-ations, or *chiusure*. Carlo Gozzi was still composing specimens for Antonio Sacchi's company in the latter half of the eighteenth century. The *tirate* that were printed remind the musician irresistibly of the texts of certain *opera buffa* arias. Here, for example, is a *tirata* delivered by the Doctor to a friend who is contemplating marriage:

Ah, so you want to take a wife, you want to form a matrimonial couple, you wish to make conjunction of male with female, which, however, should be called: Matrimonium est maris et foemina coniunctio, with good will on both sides, since ad contrahendum matrimonium requiritur consensus utriusque partis: thus we have in the article: De nuptiis, capite De matrimoniis, Codice tertio.

But first tell me one thing: this woman whom you wish to take to wife, is she beautiful, gay, fecund, robust, virtuous, noble, rich, wise, ripe for marriage, young, ugly, melancholy, good, bad, ignorant, erudite, sterile, slatternly, shameless, common, poor, crazy, a widow or an old woman? Don't be surprised if I speak to you thus, for you should know that if she is beautiful she will not be yours alone; if she is ugly you will come to hate her; if she is gay there will always be uproar in your house; if she is melancholy she will bore you to death with her tears . . .   (Oreglia 1968: 89)

The linguistic virtuosity of the *tirata* was matched by the mimic virtuosity of the *lazzo*: the word, whose etymology is still disputed, is probably best translated as 'turn'. Sometimes these turns were musical – a song or a dance; sometimes they took the form of an elaborate pantomime – characters groping around in the dark, mad-scenes, one person pretending to be two. But typically the *lazzo* was little more than a piece of stylized buffoonery – the *lazzo* of eating, the *lazzo* of beating, the *lazzo* with the fly. We may think of them as feats of virtuoso inanity, slapstick turns that were quite remote from reality and from the necessary development of the plot.

Commedia dell'arte and music

From the beginning music played a major role in the performances of *commedia dell'arte*: and the *commedia* in turn exerted a profound influence on certain forms of music. It is a happy coincidence that the earliest really detailed description of a *commedia* performance should have been written by a musician, Massimo Troiano, who was employed at the Bavarian court. And what makes his account of this performance – given during the festivities for the wedding of Duke Wilhelm and Renate of Lorraine in 1568 – quite exceptionally interesting is the fact that the Duke's great director of music, the composer of the sublime Penitential Psalms, Orlando di Lasso (for Troiano gives his name in its Italianized form), played a starring role as Pantalone! It is worth quoting from Troiano's description in some detail:

After the prologue Messer Orlando arranged for a madrigal in five parts to be sung while Massimo, who now played the lover, changed his clothes and dressed up in crimson velvet heavily trimmed with gold lace, with a cloak of black velvet lined with the finest sable . . .
. . . From the other side of the stage appeared Messer Orlando dressed as a Magnifico in a crimson satin tunic, Venetian hose of scarlet, a long black mantle reaching to the ground and a mask that drew roars of laughter at first sight.

He touched his lute and sang: 'Whoever passes down this street, and sighs not, happy man is he', and after repeating this twice he left the lute and began to complain of love, saying: 'O poor Pantalone, you cannot go down this street without filling the air with sighs and watering the ground with tears . . .'

. . . And Camilla fell in love with Zanni and took him into the house which is no marvel, since women so often leave the better for the worse.

Then there was music by five viols-da-gamba, and as many voices. Now tell me was not this a ridiculous act? . . .

. . . Peace made, Camilla was given to Zanni as his wife, and in honour of the marriage they joined in a dance after the Italian fashion, and Massimo, on behalf of Messer Orlando, craved pardon of the princely audience for so unworthy an entertainment and with due reverence wished them good-night . . .   (Lea 1934, I: 7–11)

Troiano's report suggests that Lassus introduced music into the *commedia* on three pretexts: in the intervals between one act and another, to provide a decorative framework for the play and suggest the passing of time; for naturalistic purposes, as in the wedding dance at the close; and for heightening the pathos of the more emotional and impassioned speeches, such as Pantalone's lament. The *commedia*-inspired madrigal-comedies composed by Vecchi and Banchieri at the end of the century seem to confirm this impression. Both *L'Amfiparnasso* and *La pazzia senile* take the form of a series of musical vignettes based on episodes from the *commedia dell'arte*; and in both, the composers associate music with the decorative framework of the play (prologues and interludes), with naturalistic dances and serenades, and with aria-like confessions of overpowering emotion.

While music was helping to give form and substance to the *commedia dell'arte*, it was in turn being affected by it. The influence of *commedia* on musical practice and musical style is clearest in the popular and pseudo-popular branches of the madrigal repertory. The *villanella alla napoletana*, with its ungrammatical, parallel-fifth-filled harmonic progressions, is likely to have originated in solo-song performances, in which the harmonies were improvised by the singer upon an instrument; and it is a striking fact that the vogue for the *villanella* began to spread through Italy at precisely the time that Neapolitans began to take an active role in the development of the *commedia dell'arte*. As the repertory of *villanelle* became more variegated, its reflections of the world of the *commedia* became clearer. The *bergamasche* reflect the habit of associating the barbarous vulgar dialect of Bergamo with the antics of the *zanni*; the *giustiniani*, commonly written in Venetian, often deal with 'sprightly and enterprising old men who have many points of resemblance with the mask of Pantalone' (Pirrotta 1955: 314).

Our real concern, though, is how *commedia dell'arte* influenced opera. In the masterly article from which I have just quoted, Pirrotta addresses himself to precisely that question, and argues that the *commedia* influence was crucial in three ways. First, it provided something of the subject matter of seventeenth-century opera, though not a great deal, as it happens, in the form of farcical comedy. True, Rospigliosi's *Chi soffre, speri*, composed by Marco Marazzoli and Virgilio Mazzocchi and performed in the Palazzo Barberini in Rome in 1639, included a complete set of masked characters modelled on those of the *commedia*. But that precedent was not much imitated. Only the comic servants became a fixed and permanent institution, the *servetta*, as has already been remarked, undergoing precisely the same transformation in opera as she did in the *commedia dell'arte*, from burlesque ancient with nymphomaniac tendencies and a tenor voice, to winsome soprano soubrette. More influential than the farces were the plays known as *opere regie*. The *scenari* so entitled were tragi-comedies strongly coloured by Spanish taste, and became particularly popular after *c*.1620. Picaresque adventures with a cast of romantic lovers, comic servants, magicians and spirits, and personified allegorical figures; the excruciating conflict of love and honour; an episodic and disintegrative structure – in all these qualities the *opera regia* provided one very significant source for the operatic subjects favoured by seventeenth-century Venetian composers. A powerful influence was also exerted by the *commedia* in the mundane matter of the organization of theatre troupes: having already been described in Chapter 6 it need delay us no further. But the third of the influences Pirrotta discerns – the stylistic – does require closer examination, for it was here that the mutual interaction of *commedia dell'arte* and opera had the profoundest effect. On the one hand the *commedia* became more musical; songs and dances played a more conspicuous part in the entertainment, and the better-organized troupes of comedians also tried to cater for the taste for splendid décor and ingenious machines on which early opera depended so heavily. On the other hand, the opera was, by the middle decades of the century, throwing much more emphasis on what, in *commedia* terms, we might think of as virtuoso 'turns': for did not the solo arias of the Venetian repertory begin to resemble the *tirate* or *lazzi* of the *commedia dell'arte*? Pirrotta suggests that the alternation of 'natural' dialogue and stylized solo *tirate* and *lazzi* prepared audiences for the alternation of conversational recitative and virtuoso, time-suspending aria in seventeenth-century opera. It is certainly true that by the second quarter of the century not all composers felt that the use of arias need depend upon lofty considerations of dramatic or psychological motivation: in the published score of *La catena d'Adone* (Rome 1626) Mazzocchi spoke frankly of their being introduced simply 'to alleviate the tedium of the recitatives'. A generation later, the librettist of Cesti's *Alessandro vincitor di se stesso*, Francesco Sbarra, expresses the same idea in language that implies far more clearly the analogy with the *lazzi* of the *commedia dell'arte*: speaking of the 'ariettas' he had introduced in the opera he remarked, 'if the recitative style were not intermingled with such a kind of *scherzi*, it would give more annoyance than pleasure' (Pirrotta 1955: 321). The parallel between the aria and the *tirata* is closer still. We might almost think of the commonplace books in which the actors collected material to incorporate into their *tirate* as anthologies for arias: for, to cite as an example Perrucci's advice to the lover, these materials tend to be organized according to some basic 'affect' – 'Love reciprocal, rejected, importuning, disdainful'; 'Jealousy, Friendship, Reconciliation, Reward, Leave-taking', and so forth (Lea 1934, I: 105); they incorporate examples of the appropriate rhetorical devices, particularly conceit and metaphor, and they provide a quasi-musical climax in the form of the rhyming *chiusette*. In style and function, the lover's *tirata* approached the operatic aria closely.

Commedia dell'arte in the Age of Enlightenment

Commedia dell'arte was omnipresent in Italy in the second half of the sixteenth century and throughout the seventeenth. It certainly had its opponents – more often on moral than artistic grounds – but one's impression is that it was performed everywhere and relished by virtually everyone. But with the founding of the Arcadian movement in the 1690s we move into a more fastidious age. One of the symptoms of the new critical temper was the appearance of a profusion of plays about plays; the line of them stretched from Gigli's *Dirindina* of 1712, through Goldoni's *Il teatro comico* of 1750, to Sografi's *Le convenienze teatrali* of 1794. More clearly than any other type of theatre piece, the play within a play proclaims its critical intention: it holds the theatrical world up for scrutiny; demands that the audience look hard at the theatre as an institution; and, implicitly at very least, proposes reform.

Sometimes the opera was the object of these critical examinations, sometimes the Spanish-influenced tragi-comedy; but the *commedia dell'arte* did not escape either. For the leading exponents of the ideals of Arcadia were, with some few exceptions, deeply hostile to it. The grotesque stylizations on which it depended made it remote from Nature and Reason – the two guiding principles of the new literary age; its language was undeniably vulgar, indeed in its exploitation of dialect made a point of flaunting its vulgarity; its plot, its humour and its practical jokes were often tasteless and obscene. While some authors aimed to reform the *commedia* by issuing treatises and essays, and composing improved *scenari*, the general view of arbiters of taste was that the task was hopeless. Their dismissive attitude was expressed with uncompromising bleakness by Muratori:

Today no small part of these comedies consists of buffooneries and lewd intrigue, in fact a tangle of absurd actions, in which we find not the smallest trace of that verisimilitude which is so necessary to the drama. The theatre has delivered itself into the hands of ignorant folk whose only concern is to make people laugh, and who have no other way

. . . of doing that than by using obscene and indecent equivocations, by assuming humorous poses, with practical jokes, disguises and similar kinds of nonsense, which they call *lazzi*, and which, not infrequently, are cold, insipid and stale, and, in most cases, improbable, disconnected and impossibly remote from reality.

(Binni 1968c: 427)

Despite the favour which the *commedia dell'arte* continued to enjoy with popular audiences, and despite a continuing royal line of great performers, the eighteenth century sees the decline and fall of its traditions. Alongside and gradually overshadowing the declining *commedia* there grew up a literary comedy, a substantial repertory of written works more in tune with the tastes of the age, and better fitted for the tasks of the age. Its model was not the traditional Italian comedy of masks but Molière (Gigli's *Don Pilone*, for example, originated as a *rifacimento* of *Tartuffe*). Its watchwords were Nature and Reason, and its aim was to help Italian society mature: to proclaim the ideals of good taste, integrity, and sociability; and, conversely, to satirize the vices of affectation, hypocrisy and selfishness. Nelli, one of the most versatile and productive comic authors before Goldoni, speaks of his work as being 'learned in the school of respectable men', his concern is 'honest laughter'. While the *commedia dell'arte* had transported its audiences into an imaginary world of pure illusion, the literary comedy of the Age of Enlightenment aimed to hold up a quizzical mirror to the realities of life.

Goldoni and Gozzi

The greatest of these reforming comic dramatists of the eighteenth century was the Venetian, Carlo Goldoni. He had much in common with his predecessors: a taste for the natural and the reasonable; the Enlightenment conviction that comedy could and should perform an educative function by mirroring nature, scourging vice, lending charm to the moral and social virtues, encouraging all men of good will to share fully in the life of the community. But more obviously than his predecessors Goldoni took an unashamed delight in the real world that was the object of his attentions: in the colour and vitality of daily life in the city square, on the canals, in the home. Gradually, at his hands, the Venetian scene was transfigured into an 'illuminist myth of the *cité parfaite*, where the industriousness and the happiness of the citizens are found in optimistic causal rapport' (Fido 1977: 9).

These concerns made Goldoni in principle hostile to the *commedia dell'arte*, though in fact he loved and admired much about the tradition: the pace, the sense of fun, the knife-edge excitement achieved by the great improvisers. But as long as the Italian sense of humour was conditioned by the domination of the *commedia*, Goldoni could not realize his aim of creating a comedy that reflected the reforming ideals of his age. There is therefore in his plays no lack of sharp satire directed at the *commedia*. He deplores the staleness and monotony of the plots, in which 'the audience know what Arlecchino is going to say even before he opens his mouth' (*Il teatro comico*, Act I scene 2). He urges the abandoning of the artificial acting styles of the day: direct addresses to the audience should cease; let there be no sing-song or false rhetoric in the delivery of the words, for 'the comedy is an imitation of nature, and must in every way reflect what is life-like' (*ibidem*, Act III scene 3). He castigates the unseemly and unintelligent laughter that accompanied the performance: in *Pamela fanciulla*, the young English gentleman Ernold has just returned from a Grand Tour, scattily enraptured with everything he has seen: he enthuses over Arlecchino's mask and costume, he finds his malapropisms a triumph of inventive wit, and concludes:

'I've just remembered a magnificent jest; you can't help laughing at it. Harlequin one evening in a comedy wanted to cheat an old man called Pantalone, so he disguised himself as a Moor, then as a moving statue, then as a skeleton, and at the end of his tricks he beat the good old man with his stick . . .' 'Sir', replies Bonfil, 'if such things make you laugh, I do not know what to think of you. Surely you do not want me to believe that in Italy intelligent men, men of spirit, laugh at stupidities of this sort. Laughter is proper to man, but all men do not laugh at the same thing. There is a noble form of laughter which arises from a skilful use of words, from clever conceits, from brilliant witticisms. There is also a debased kind of laughter which comes from scurrilities, from stupidities . . .'

(Nicoll 1963: 215)

And finally Goldoni dismisses all the rhetorical apparatus of the common-place books of earlier generations of *comici* and so much stultifying lumber: 'these similes, these allegories are not used any more . . . What diabolical nonsense! To compare a man in love with a pilot who is at sea, and then to say *The sailors of my thoughts!*' (*Il teatro comico*, Act II scene 9). In another scene Placida explains to Lelio, 'I have burned all my books containing such conceits, and all the actors with a modern, enlightened taste have done the same' (*ibidem*, Act II scene 2).

There was no real sense of disgust in Goldoni's reform of the *commedia dell'arte*, rather a tender-hearted solicitude; and there was no violence either, rather a process of educative collaboration. Men of letters had occasionally in the past provided new *scenari* for the *commedia*, and now, beginning with *Momolo cortesan* in 1738, Goldoni went a little further. This *scenario* had one part, that of the protagonist Momolo himself, written out in full, so that all the improvisation took place round a fixed and individually characterized focus. In the pieces that followed *Momolo cortesan* more written roles were added, the scope for improvisation correspondingly reduced, until with *Donna di garbo* (1743) Goldoni produced his first fully composed comedy. Even then the leading characters continued to wear the traditional masks of the *commedia dell'arte*; these were not abandoned until 1750, in the *Pamela fanciulla* which has already been quoted, and which was – it need hardly be said – based on Samuel Richardson's epoch-making novel.

Until the early 1750s Goldoni enjoyed a triumphant theatrical career, and *La Locandiera* of 1751 was its climax. But then he seemed to stumble and for some years to lose his sense of direction. In the plays that followed *La Locandiera*, his concern for the little world of Venetian society is dissipated: he turns to country life, to the gracious ease of the *villeggiatura* and to agriculture; a rival comic playwright, Pietro Chiari, pioneers a taste for more romantic, exotic and fantastic themes, and Goldoni cannot resist the urge to follow the fashion; he begins to be distracted by the scathing attacks on his work by Carlo Gozzi, nominally a supporter of the traditions of the *commedia dell'arte*, and the founder of an Accademia dei Granelleschi which was sworn to uphold linguistic purity in the face of the plebeian and dialectal debasements that ran riot in Goldoni's popular comedies.

But such distractions could not long deflect him from his true vocation. His love of the real Venice triumphed over the desire to pursue ephemeral trends, or to consume his energies in answering Gozzi. In his later works he returned to the homes and streets and squares and canals of Venice, chronicling the humdrum and everyday with the same kind of delight as his painter-friend, Pietro Longhi – 'Longhi, whose brush calls on my sister muse to seek out the truth', as Goldoni apostrophized him (Binni 1968a: 735). And so the playwright's theatrical career came to a climax in what Italian critics have called his 'choral dramas', dramas which Gozzi found scandalously plebeian, and of which Goldoni himself gave the best account in his preface to *Le baruffe chiozzotte* of 1762:

The theatres of Italy are frequented by all ranks of person; and the charge is so modest that the shopkeeper, the servant and the poor fisherman can all share in this public entertainment . . . I had deprived the simple folk of the visits of Arlecchino; they heard speak of the Reform of the Comedy and wanted to sample it; but not all characters were suited to their understanding; and it was only right that, for the pleasure of this rank of person, who pays just as the nobles and wealthy do, I should write some comedies in which they could recognize their own customs, their own defects and, if I may be permitted to say so, their own virtues.

Had Goldoni been nothing more than the most brilliant and prolific comic dramatist in eighteenth-century Italy his influence on the course of *opera buffa* would already have been pronounced. In fact, though, he was a practising librettist besides, the author of more than a dozen *intermezzi*, and of more than fifty comic operas. His work in this medium parallels that which he did in spoken comedy. Basically he was determined to make a more dramatically serious form out of it, to allot a more central role to the controlling intelligence of the librettist, and to discipline the individualistic virtuosity of the musicians. In the comic opera librettos, too, Goldoni broadened the range of subject in the 1750s, and, with more success perhaps than in his written plays, ventured into fantasy – as in *Il mondo della luna* (1750) – and into romantic sentimentality – as in *La buona figliuola* (1756). But more of all this in the appropriate place. (Cf. Chapter 19 below.)

Both as man and as artist Goldoni had, one would have thought, a charm winning enough to disarm all hostility. Much of his work was indeed immensely popular, but it incurred the undeviating detestation of Carlo Gozzi, a political and artistic reactionary, who saw in it every symptom of a debased civilization – incongruities of style, the undermining of traditional values, plebeian sympathies, a flabby illuminist tolerance. Gozzi, on the contrary, possessed all the wit, acrimoniousness and fanaticism of the best eighteenth-century controversialists. And some twenty years after the founding of the Accademia dei Granelleschi, between 1761 and 1765, he produced his own series of plays, ten 'fables' to set up against the deplorable Goldoni, and to exemplify his own undebased conception of comedy.

Gozzi's fables are the second great literary monument to the *commedia* tradition. In his *Memorie inutile* he declared that his intention had been to take under his protection the noble art which Goldoni was destroying. But in fact Gozzi's dealings with the *commedia* were hardly less ambivalent than Goldoni's own. Like his rival's early comedies Gozzi's fables effect a transition from a *scenario* with just a few written-out parts (*L'amore di tre melarance*) to composed plays with brief improvised episodes. The combination of satire and fairy-tale is hardly characteristic of the *commedia dell'arte*, and the masks in fact play a very minor role. In *Turandot*, for example, they appear as four of the servants of the Emperor of Peking; Pantalone is his Secretary, Tartaglia his Grand Chancellor, Brighella the Master of the Pages, and Truffaldino the Chief of the Eunuchs.

17 · *Contrascene* and *intermezzi*

The transformation of the *intermedi*

It is not at first sight easy to see any connection between the sixteenth-century *intermedio* – blended of allegory and spectacle, declamation, madrigal and dance – and the comic *intermezzo* of the eighteenth century, with its knockabout humour, its fast-moving naturalistic recitative and its vivacious arias and duets. In function, theme and every conceivable aspect of literary and musical style the Florentine *Intermedi* of 1589 are worlds away from Pergolesi's *Serva padrona* of 1733. There is, nevertheless, a direct, if tenuous, link between them; the practice of the *intermedio* ran as an unbroken thread in the Italian theatre from the Renaissance not merely until Pergolesi, but until the latter half of the nineteenth century. Of the multifarious forms it assumed during that period, the Bardian and the Pergolesian are, for the opera historian, only the most interesting.

In fact the Renaissance type of allegorical, spectacular *intermedio* survived much longer than is commonly appreciated. Maggi was still writing them in the eighteenth century. But their role was a more limited one; they were confined to a small number of functions in which their antiquated and elevated tone was felt to be appropriate, in the school dramas of the Jesuits, or as *pièces d'occasion* in celebration of political, dynastic or social events. In other forms of drama, the nature of the *intermedio* underwent a change, a change which we may describe – borrowing English theatrical terminology – as a growing preoccupation with antimasque: poets, choreographers and designers took an ever keener interest in the absurd, the grotesque, and the anarchic. The first opera to be publicly performed in Venice, Manelli's *Andromeda* of 1637, already shows this characteristic. While the first *intermedio* took the form of 'a madrigal . . . sung backstage by several voices in concert with various instruments, and . . . a most graceful dance', the second featured 'twelve savages [who] emerged to do a most extravagant and savoury dance of movements and gestures' (Troy 1979: 10). By the middle decades of the century such antimasque episodes had become commonplace, established and popular items in the public opera-houses of the Most Serene Republic.

At the same time the opera itself was beginning to find a role for minor characters from the lower social classes. As long as music drama had felt its proper home to be the Arcadian Golden Age of the pastoral convention, there was no scope for such 'realism'; but with the move from an imaginary world of pure poetry to a historical world with some clear basis in the everyday, serving girls, page-boys, nurse-maids became an established part of the operatic apparatus. Their purpose is clear in Monteverdi's *L'incoronazione di Poppea*: it is, first, to help give substance to the protagonists, to scrutinize their character from different angles, to evoke their world more fully and roundedly; and, second, to provide certain pleasures that the opera would otherwise lack, notably comic diversions. Such scenes came to be known as *contrascene*.

As the antimasque qualities of the *intermedi* became more pronounced, the comic servants began to meddle in them. Sometimes they acted as Masters of Ceremonies, introducing the dancers; and sometimes they got swept up into the dancing themselves. Dent quotes a typical example from Alessandro Scarlatti's *Clearco in Negroponte* (Naples 1686). After an aria in which the opera's heroine has invoked 'the horrid spectres of Cocytus', the hag Filocla parodies it. During the course of this parody aria – the final number of Act II of the opera – a pavilion rises up from the underworld, which Filocla takes to be inhabited by the young man on whom she dotes. When she investigates, however,

[there] comes forth a phantom, and *Filocla* wishing to escape from one of the wings, there appears a Moor, and the same thing happens at the other [exits]. Finally, she hides in the pavilion, whence she peeps out, while the said Moors dance with the phantom. *Filocla*, after the dance is finished, thinks that they have gone away, and comes out. The phantom, who is hidden, takes hold of her by her dress; she tries to escape, leaves her dress behind, and runs away. The phantom follows her.   (Dent 1960: 50 [1905])

As this connection between the comic servants and the *intermedio* became customary, there was, inevitably, a tendency for the *contrascene* to gravitate to the ends of the act; there the page-boys and nurses and so on could be ready at hand for the antics in which the dancers were going to involve them. But it was not until the early years of the eighteenth century that this pattern became exclusive; in the seventeenth, the comic characters usually made several other appearances during the course of an act.

In the earlier *contrascene* the travesty character was pronounced: the nurse was often sung by a tenor, the page-boy by a soprano or alto. The humour was of the crudest, a matter of the exchange of insults, of clubbings and kickings, of eroticism and *double-entendre* of abysmal tastelessness. But during the latter part of the century, the characters and consequently the style of the comedy underwent a transformation. The 'women' lose their inverted commas, become youthful, witty and resourceful; while the men age, become more pompous and gullible. By the early eighteenth century the most popular figures for *contrascene* are scarcely distinguishable from the old man (generally Pantalone, rather than the Doctor) and the *servetta* of the *commedia dell'arte*.

The comic *intermezzo* of the eighteenth century fuses the materials and style of the *contrascene* – its plots, its personalities and its poetic and musical idioms – with the principle of the *intermedio*. Given the tendency to concentrate the *contrascene* at the act's end, it was a natural enough step and it was made once two related dramaturgical developments had been completed. One was that the links connecting the comic characters with the main plot of the opera became increasingly tenuous, and finally broke altogether; the other that the *intermedio* abandoned its inheritance of spectacle and ballet in order to concentrate on miniature comedies in dialogue and song between two, or more rarely three, characters. This evolution was accomplished in the years 1685–1710 and can best be studied in the operas of Alessandro Scarlatti.[1]

Scarlatti's *contrascene*

In Scarlatti's earlier operas the comic characters often play an integral part in the main action. Gilbo, in *Massimo Puppieno* (Naples 1695), is the servant of the heroine Sulpizia, a noble Roman maiden; and he takes an active if unsuccessful part in assisting her romantic schemes. In one typically grotesque episode he is disguised as a girl, trembling for her virginity at the approach of the tyrant Massimino and his soldiers. But the days of such dramatic integration were numbered. In *La caduta de' decemviri* (Naples 1697), the comic servants Servilia and Flacco engage in some lighthearted banter on the breakdown of traditional decorum:

Servilia	Devi alla mia ragazza
	Portar qualche imbasciata?
Flacco	Oh, sei pur pazza;
	Oggi in alcuna parte
	Mezzano più non v'è,
	Questa in amore è un arte
	Che oggi un la fa da se . . .
Servilia	Questa in amar filosofia moderna
	Più libera s'interna
	E a trattarne da norma
	La materia d'amore in miglior forma.
	Ceremonie io non pratico.
	Al costume dogmatico
	Della presente età cede l'antico.[2]　　　　　(Act I scene 8)

If there is social satire in this scene, there is also a little operatic history. Servants were indeed becoming obsolete as go-betweens; hero and heroine did their own wooing, and the involvement of such as Servilia and Flacco with the main business of the drama was becoming more and more casual.

In *La principessa fedele* (Naples 1710) there are still *contrascene* episodes at various points in the opera, but the main comic scenes are at the close of Acts I and II, and midway through Act III. And by the time of *Marco Attilio Regolo* (Rome 1719) this development has reached its penultimate form. For the comic characters are limited to a few bars of recitative during the main course of the action, and fully fledged *contrascene* are introduced only at the act ends and in the middle of Act III. Indeed the *contrascene* of *Marco Attilio Regolo* are indistinguishable from *intermezzi*, except that they are performed by characters already familiar from the main *opera seria* plot.

The style of much of the comedy in these Scarlattian *contrascene* is familiar from the *commedia dell'arte*. Insult and the exchange of insult are well loved features, and with them goes the exploitation of that power of the Italian language to express its concepts as it were in a distorting mirror. In the final scene of Act I of *Marco Attilio Regolo*, Eurilla protests at being described as a 'ragazza'; but Leonzio presses on: 'Sì, sì, sei un ragazza, anzi una ragazzaccia, ragazzissima, furbetta insolentissima'.[3] Like the men of the *commedia*, the librettists of the day did a good line in ludicrous metaphor: 'Tu per i denti miei, cara mia gioja, / Sei giusto un biscottino di Savoia', says the tutor Alfeo to the beauteous Lilla (a page-boy in disguise); to which the youth retorts, 'Tu per farmi satolla / Un gran pasticcio sei di pasta frolla';[4] and so the images continue throughout the scene (*Eraclea* (Naples 1700), Act II scene 11). Silvio Stampiglia, the librettist of this opera, was adept at excruciatingly banal lyrics, often dependent upon some form of word play, or at least on some way of larking with the character-istics of the language. Earlier in the opera, 'Lilla' had been making a pass at Alfeo; the climax of this seduction scene was marked by the typical lyric:

> Son donzelletta amabile
> E son concupiscibile.
> Son svelta, ma palpabile,
> Son nubile, son abile:
> Ergo son appetibile.[5]

Such scenes of drag burlesque, and the literary style to go with them, are regular features of the repertory. *Commedia dell'arte*-like, too, are the snatches of incongruous erudition – *La principessa fedele* boasts a Muslim jailor who can swap Ariosto allusions with the heroine's lady-in-waiting.

In Scarlatti's music a favourite comic device is parody. Stampiglia's incongruous metaphors in *Eraclea* prompt a series of mock-lyrical numbers, of which the duet 'Decrepito Adone / Lilletta, Lilletta/ (Act III scene 2) takes the palm for absurdity. Alfeo is so overcome with emotion that he swoons, and has to be revived with vinegar. Each period of the music closes in languishing cadences, and the mood of languorous eroti-cism is enhanced by the addition of recorders to the basic orchestra of strings and continuo. Several scenes in Scarlatti – the duet 'Dal cupo

Averno' (*Marco Attilio Regolo*, Act III scene 7) for instance – confirm that the parody of invocation scenes had not yet lost its savour. And over and over again Scarlatti shows his resourcefulness in what one might describe as comic madrigalisms – Flacco's laughing song 'Certe terrestri Furie' (*La caduta de'decemviri*, Act II scene 9); the mocking shivers in Gorina's 'Suvvia, ben mio' (*La principessa fedele*, Act II scene 16).

Intrinsically the most arresting and historically the most momentous of the comic resources of the *contrascena* may be described as the mutual assimilation of acting and singing, the opening up of the lyrical set piece to movement and gesture. A vivid example of such an aria is 'È pur strano veder' (*Eraclea*, Act I scene 8), the middle section of which provides endless scope for comic histrionics: slow plagal cadences for bowing, mannered coloratura for 'smorfie', a pause for elegant spitting, and a change of metre and the striking in of the violins for a dance (see Ex.IV.1). At the slightest prompting of his comic imagination Scarlatti is prepared to switch pace from *allegro* to *adagio* and back again, to plunge from aria to recitative, and from recitative to aria, suggesting vividly and economically the inflections, the gestures and even much of the comic business demanded of the performer. A good example is 'Bisogna con giudizio' (*Eraclea*, Act I scene 5), the comic point of which is the tutor Alfeo's attempt to maintain an unruffled Stoic countenance in the face of the unfamiliar stirrings of passion. His continuo song is nothing but a string of morals delivered in impassively diatonic style, while the sensual spasms that so disturb him prompt a series of recitative asides, chromatic in harmony and erratically agitated in rhythm (see Ex.IV.2). The future resources of the *opera buffa* are glimpsed most suggestively in the often tiny, but nonetheless keenly characterized ensembles, such as the duet 'Io da te bramo' (*La caduta de'decemviri*, Act I scene 8), in which two comic servants strike up a provisional romantic relationship. The movement is a splendidly animated dialogue with phrases of sharp interrogation, vigorous avowals of fidelity, and a sensuous passage of interwoven and parallel duetting at the close of the middle section.

All the resources of comic style described so far are particular pleasantries, stimulated by a specific dramatic situation, or a specific aria text. But Scarlatti's *contrascene* also contributed in more general ways to the evolution of a musical idiom which was slowly honed to perfection to express the sparkling wit and the dancing joie-de-vivre of the great age of *opera buffa*.

Its outstanding characteristic is its dependence on syllabic word-setting – a drably academic formulation, in all conscience, which gives really no impression of the scope of the style; so one must particularize a little. The syllabically set aria may be in a vigorously expostulatory *concitato* style ('Tanta alterigia', *La principessa fedele*, Act II scene 8); it may hover on the verge of recitative, with all the flexibility of delivery which that implies

('Farò quanto poss'io', *Massimo Puppieno*, Act I scene 7); in giving declamation precedence over line it may anticipate the 'patter' of a later age ('È la voglia', *Massimo Puppieno*, Act III scene 19); in its pungency and conciseness and its avoidance of development or digression it may strike us

Ex.IV.1 A. Scarlatti, *Eraclea* (1700), Act I scene 8

I have to understand how to bow, how to simper, how to spit elegantly,
how to dance in the latest fashion.

Ex.IV.1 *continued*

One always needs to escape from danger by using one's discretion.
(What a mouth, oh God, what eyes! Alfeo, stand firm.)

Ex.IV.2 A. Scarlatti, *Eraclea* (1700), Act I scene 5

as a perfect musical analogy to the epigram ('Son gl'uomini più instabili',
La caduta de'decemviri, Act II scene 6); word repetition may serve as a
device of comic exuberance ('Poveri amanti', *Massimo Puppieno*, Act II
scene 9). Hardly less impressive than Scarlatti's ability to take fire from the
unvarnished, rhythmic delivery of the text is the extent to which he found
in the cadence a resource for comic characterization. Two arias from the
comic scene (11) in Act II of *Eraclea* provide a good impression of this
inventive variety: in Alfeo's 'Precipitata filosofia' there is a hemiola
broadening on 'filosofia' at the end of both phrases of the principal section,
as if the pedant were trying to hold fast to the dignity that so precipitately
trickles away in the main theme of the aria; in Livio's 'Io so che non son
cosa', on the other hand, there is a harmonically intensified repetition of the
cadence phrase of each part, which gives to the comedy a sudden pang of

301

teasing sensuousness. More often it is simply the exuberance of the cadences, frequently heightened by repetition, that distinguishes the comic style. Is it perhaps an underlying kinship between a firm and well fashioned cadence and a tart piece of repartee, that makes such cadences so important a resource of comic style?

The emergence of the *intermezzo* at Venice and at Naples

As Venice was the leading Italian operatic centre for the greater part of the seventeenth century, it was also the place where comic *contrascene* were first cultivated. But in the last quarter of the century, earlier than elsewhere, such scenes began to come under attack in Venice. In the preface to his libretto *Epulone* (1675), Francesco Frugoni was already expressing a critical distaste for the 'indiscriminate admixture of heroes, royalty and buffoons' (Troy 1979: 66). And by 1700 comic characters had been very largely eliminated from Venetian librettos, a purification of style which contemporary chroniclers such as Crescimbeni attributed to Domenico David and particularly to Apostolo Zeno. This development did not of course mean that the Venetian theatre had acquired an austere and elevated tone unknown in other cities; simply that the comedy was separated off from the drama proper rather earlier here than elsewhere. Ties between opera and *contrascene* were severed only to enable the latter to assume their independence as *intermezzi* – comic interludes of recitative and song performed by characters who no longer had any connection with the main plot, and set in a contemporary bourgeois world quite remote from the heroic, historical world of the opera. The independence of the Venetian *intermezzo* was confirmed by the habit of publishing its text in a separate libretto; and that in turn made it possible to perform the *intermezzo* whenever one pleased, and without reference to the opera with which it was at first associated. The earliest of these booklets with independent *intermezzo* texts date from 1706 and were produced for the Teatro Sant'Angelo and the Teatro San Cassiano.

At Naples there was no comparable decline in the popularity of the *contrascene*; well into the eighteenth century they remained virtually obligatory in any production in the Southern metropolis. Operas originating in other cities, such as Agostino Piovene's *Principessa fedele* (Venice 1709 – reset by Scarlatti, Naples 1710), were invariably fitted out with comic scenes to accommodate them to 'the custom of the city'.[6] Conversely the *contrascene* of Neapolitan operas were often removed when they were revived in the North, to be replaced by comic *intermezzi* or grotesque spectacular *intermedi*; this happened, for example, with the revivals of *Eraclea* at Parma in 1700. It was not until the 1720s that the characters of the Neapolitan *contrascene* finally lost all connection with the main opera. Even so, as our examination of Scarlatti's *contrascene* will have suggested, Venetian developments found some parallel in Neapolitan practice. By the early eighteenth century the number of *contrascene* was normally reduced to three, and these three scenes were normally placed exactly where the parts of a three-act *intermezzo* such as Albinoni's *Pimpinone* would be placed – at the end of Act I, at the end of Act II, and roughly halfway through Act III. It was with the phasing out of the third *contrascena* in the 1720s that the great, if brief age of the Neapolitan *intermezzo* began.

Given this history, the closeness in form and style of the *contrascene* and the *intermezzi* is hardly to be wondered at. They were placed at similar points in the opera; the great majority of them limited themselves to two singing characters, and employed the dramatic stereotype of the battle of the sexes, normally old man versus young woman; each of the two or three *intermezzi* normally comprised a single scene, the form of which consisted of a sequence of recitative dialogues and solo arias, and came to a climax in a concluding duet.

Between 1700 and 1750 the *intermezzo* was so popular that virtually any form of drama was unthinkable without it. Not only operas, but sacred music dramas and spoken plays too had their *intermezzi*. Pergolesi's earliest recorded compositions were in fact *intermezzi buffi* for *San Guglielmo*, a *dramma sacro* performed in the cloisters of a Neapolitan monastery (Walker 1949: 317). The universal popularity of the *intermezzo* and a general consistency of practice are to some extent disguised by a wide variety of terminology. The dividing line between *contrascene* and *intermezzo* is blurred enough; but apart from that, *intermezzi* were still sometimes described as *intermedi*, and already sometimes described as *farse in musica*; *divertimenti musicali* and *scherzi musicali* were other terms used (Troy 1979: 3); in Venice a terminological distinction was made between *intermezzi comici*, performed between the acts of spoken plays, and *intermezzi drammatici* performed between the acts of operas. As in the sixteenth century, there was no shortage of complaints from authors who felt that what should have been an incidental diversion was attracting a quite inordinate share of the audience's attention. According to Antonio Groppo, the Venetian to whom we owe the distinction between *intermezzo comico* and *intermezzo drammatico*, 'at present [1740] the operas are paid the least attention. Audiences are attracted only by the ballets and intermedi, and consider the opera, which should be the principal attraction, as an interpolation and relief from the dancers and buffoons' (Troy 1979: 3).

Despite this fever of enthusiasm for the *intermezzo* the repertory was dominated by a comparatively small number of works: Pietro Pariati's *Pimpinone* (first set by Albinoni, Venice 1708); Antonio Salvi's *Serpilla e Bacocco* (or *Il marito giogatore*, first set by ?Orlandini, Venice 1719);

Metastasio's *L'impresario delle Canarie* (or *Dorina e Nibbio*, first set by Sarri, Naples 1724); Gennaro Antonio Federico's *La serva padrona* (first set by Pergolesi, Naples 1733), and a handful of others.[7] The perennial freshness of these pieces was in part due to the fact that their form gradually changed over the years. New settings were made by different composers, and thanks to the widespread practice of 'pasticcio' – the compiling of operas from the pre-existent works of several different composers – and of 'substitution' – the replacement of the original arias by more popular or more fashionable settings of the same words – *intermezzo* performers had it in their power to transform and innovate every time they revived an old favourite.

Intermezzo and *commedia dell'arte*

Most of the dramatic themes employed in this repertory are recognizably related to the world of the *commedia dell'arte*. Their brief span, their tiny cast lists, with rarely more than two singing roles, inevitably means that most *intermezzi* are essentially amorous debates. The two acts of Goldoni's *Il gondoliere veneziano* furnish us with a typical story. Buleghin, the gondolier of the title, is nervous about returning to his 'putta di campiello', Bettina, because he has squandered all his money at cards. Bettina is indeed incensed, but after an exchange of insults, and a threat of suicide from Buleghin, the first *intermezzo* ends with the pair making it up. But Bettina does not entirely trust Buleghin's resolution to reform himself, and in the second *intermezzo* dresses herself up as a gondolier to be able to observe him more closely. Sure enough, Buleghin has again been gambling; this time he has lost everything – even Bettina's ring. But now at last his remorse is genuine, and he scorns the temptation, offered him by the pretended gondolier, his new friend – 'keep gambling till your luck changes'; 'look for another girl'. Overjoyed at Buleghin's loyalty, Bettina reveals herself and the *intermezzo* ends with a rapid succession of repentance, reconciliation and forgiveness, and matrimony. It will be noticed from this synopsis how even such a master of intrigue as Goldoni still tends to treat the *intermezzi* as two discrete and largely independent scenes. It is comparatively seldom that the first *intermezzo* ends in a condition of suspense which positively demands resolution in the second. No less common than such a love story as that of Buleghin and Bettina, is the story of an ill-matched marriage, generally one in which a high-born, wealthy but decrepit gentleman is tricked into matrimony with a low-born, young and sexy wench. *La serva padrona* is the classic specimen of this particular theme. Over and over again, under a variety of different names, the *intermezzi* poets brought on to the operatic stage Arlecchino and Colombina, or Pantalone and his *servetta*.

But while *commedia*-like themes dominated the *intermezzo* repertory there were several popular alternatives. Like the spoken drama of the period, the *intermezzo* sometimes satirized the contemporary world. The most poetically distinguished of *intermezzi*, Metastasio's *Impresario delle canarie*, is a burlesque depiction of the world of heroic opera; *Vespetta e Lesbo* (Venice 1708) and *Il pastor fido ridicolo* (1739) are, as the title of the latter makes clear, parodies of that pastoral preciosity associated with the Arcadian movement; the aping of French manners, which so disgusted Gozzi, and of Spanish cicisbeism, was the target of other *intermezzi* satires, among them Goldoni's *Monsieur Petiton*. In his *intermezzi* as in his plays, Goldoni sometimes abandoned caricature in favour of the lifelike representation of the real world. In the preface to *La birba*, he wrote

Stopping from time to time in St Mark's Square, in the place called the 'Piazzetta', and contemplating attentively the prodigious quantity of vagabonds who, singing, gambling, and begging for alms, earn their living thanks to the sweet profession of 'birba', it occurred to me to take them as the subject for a comic intermezzo . . .

(Mamczarz 1972: 140)

More surprising was the popularity of Molière as a model: at least half a dozen *intermezzi* were based on plays by the great French comedian. Troy's discussion of Salvi's *L'artigiano gentiluomo* details the kinds of reworking and transformation that were inevitable in the process of reducing psychological comedies to brief farces (1979: 80).

The character types that were to serve the *intermezzo* throughout its fifty years of glory were already well established when the form emerged from the *contrascene* in the early years of the century. By that time the *vecchia* – the hag – had already become the soubrette, the page-boy had become the *vecchio* – the old man – or the *zanni*. And in the battle of the sexes the advantage had therefore switched from male to female, for in any tradition of comedy youth always has the better of age. Most of the men and women we meet in this repertory will be recognizable as the 'demi-urges of merriment' from the *commedia dell'arte*. What is Goldoni's Buleghin, if not a charming example of a *zanni*; who are Uberto in *La serva padrona* or Pimpinone, if not reincarnations of Pantalone? The pedant doctor and the bragging captain appear too. But the central character, not only in any individual *intermezzo*, but in the whole repertory, is the youthful, emancipated, winsome and resourceful soubrette. Indeed it was in the *intermezzo* that she assumed her classic form and became at once the essential prop and the chief ornament of the whole comic opera tradition.

The *intermezzo* shares common ground with the *opera seria* in its fondness for sententious maxims. But obviously these lack the elevated moral tone of Zeno's and Metastasio's: quite often they are rather travesties than imitations, witty formulations of dubious morality, or assertions of plain commonsense made in defiance of the high-falutin' axioms of polite society. Others again have their origin in popular proverbs, like the opening aria of *La serva padrona*, 'Aspettare, e non venire.'[8] The *intermezzo* poets continue to quote and misquote classic authors, as the *commedia* performers had done: says Buleghin, at the close of his first scene of reconciliation with the long-suffering Bettina:

> Ogni trista memoria ormai se tasa,
> E so ponga in obrio le andate cose:
> M'insegna a dir cussì Torquato Tasso.
> T'obbedirò, Bettina, a cao basso.[9]

of which the first two lines are indeed a Venetianized quotation from Canto XVIII of *Gerusalemme liberata*. *Commedia*-like too are the ludicrously mannered metaphors that frequently adorn the form. 'La farfalla' from *L'impresario delle canarie* shows that Metastasio could parody himself as well as John Gay could.

In the fully fledged *intermezzo* the influence of the *commedia dell'arte* remained all-pervasive. One sees it in the dependence upon the traditional character types, upon slapstick and disguise. The opening sililoquy of Uberto in *La serva padrona* must be very like a *commedia* monologue, with its starting-point in a traditional proverb (the already mentioned 'Aspettare e non venire'), its bluster, its ineffectualness, the absurdity of its situation – he has been waiting for three hours for a servant to bring a cup of chocolate so that he can get fully dressed to go out. It proceeds though crude insults heaped on the head of the mute and stupid Vespone (who would presumably have been an adept mimer), to culminate in a preliminary verbal portrait – with hints of physical intimacies – of the *servetta* 'superbona', who 'alfin di serva diverrà padrona'.[10] Numerous are the arias which attempt to create something of the effect of a *lazzo*. One of the wittiest is certainly Albinoni's setting of 'So quel che si dice' in the third *intermezzo* of *Pimpinone*. Pimpinone, his eyes by now fully opened to the realities of life with the once bashful maiden he has made his bride, vainly attempts to prevent her from going to visit her friends. He is appalled to imagine himself the topic of conversation at such a gathering

> So quel che si dice, e quel che si fa:
> 'Sustrissima, Sustrissima, come si sta?'
> 'Bene.' E poi subito: 'Quel mio marito
> È pur stravagante, è pur indiscreto.
> Pretende che in casa io stia tutto il dì.'
> E l'altra risponde: 'Gran bestia ch'egli è.
> Prendete comare, l'esempio da me . . .'[11]

As can be seen, Pimpinone acts out his own vision of a ladies' tea-party at which tiresome husbands are the chief topic of conversation; the scope for such *lazzo*-like devices as falsetto singing and mincing feminine gestures are clear. Like the *commedia*, the *intermezzo* relished the kind of humour that arose from a garbling of foreign tongues or from uncouth dialects:

Troy quotes a splendid example from one of the earliest Venetian *intermezzi*, ?Gasparini's setting of the anonymous *Brunetta e Burlotto* (1708):

Brunetta	Sen Mussulmansin?
Burlotto	Non Sennor.
Brunetta	Non Sennor? Sarà Spagnuolo.
	Digame Cavallero
	Es Espagnol V.M.?
Burlotto	Nain, Nain.
Brunetta	Tedesco esso sarà.
	Vasfor ein Landasman bist du.
	Bist ein Taicer?
Burlotto	Non Monsieur.
Brunetta	Ah, Ah, questo è Francese,
	La lingua ancora so di quel Paese.
	Feites moy le plaisir Monsieur
	De me dire si vous etes Francois?
Burlotto	No Sar.
Brunetta	O Inglese è questo:
	Tu tell mi ifu aran Inghlis menn?
Burlotto	Minime, Nequaquam.
Brunetta	Tal linguaggio
	Ora non intend'io.

(Troy 1979: 86)

The music of the *intermezzo*

Thanks to the long history of the *contrascene*, composers had a comic musical style ready to hand for the *intermezzo*. That style was to be developed, polished and made more versatile before being transferred to the emergent *opera buffa*, but in essentials it changed little; it was already fully formed in the early Venetian *intermezzi* of Albinoni and Orlandini. Its hallmarks were simplicity, a restrained use of technical virtuosity, a very modest orchestral apparatus. But composers' sobriety in these musical dimensions was compensated for by their flamboyance in others: the witty zest with which they handled the text, and a truly inexhaustible rhythmic vivacity.

'There is no evidence that an exodus from the orchestra pit occurred when the intermezzo singers replaced those of the serious opera on stage', writes Troy (1979: 123). But if the full orchestra was retained, the scoring of the *intermezzo* was generally light. In *La serva padrona*, for example, the second violins are rarely independent of the first, and the violas rarely independent of the continuo. The continuo aria, rapidly falling into disuse in the *opera seria*, retained its popularity – for obvious reasons: for one thing it had long been associated with lower-class and comic characters, and for another it had the great advantage over arias with *obbligato* string or woodwind accompaniments of allowing the performer to enunciate the text with maximum clarity and flexibility. While woodwind instruments were sometimes employed, most effects of instrumental comedy and colour were achieved with the string group: onomatopoeic pizzicatos and tremolos, and whining glissandos, such as those in Hasse's *La serva scaltra* (quoted in Troy 1979: 123). Purely instrumental movements are very rare. But a few *intermezzi* close with dances, which remind us of the link with the seventeenth-century tradition. Introductory sinfonias or overtures are never employed, except in the case of *intermezzi comici* where the *intermezzo* emerges from the background of spoken rather than sung drama.

Much of the quiddity of the comic style comes from the continuing preoccupation of composers with the delivery of the text. Their concern for vivid word-setting resulted in a style that was not merely syllabic, but syllabic in a precisely imagined, almost gestic way. A good example is found in 'Stizzoso mio stizzoso' from the first *intermezzo* of *La serva padrona*, where the long, low notes on 'star cheto' and the detached, almost finger-wagging whisper that follows at 'e non parlare', guide the singer's delivery with graphic realism (Ex.IV.3). In almost all this music it is a natural but vivacious pronunciation of the words which dictates the length and rhythm of the phrase. Once these sharply articulated phrases have been coined from the inflections of speech, they become the substance of the play and pattern of the music. The fluctuations of tempo with which seventeenth-century composers like Alessandro Scarlatti had often underlined the comedy of the *contrascene* remains a common feature of style; but in the mature *intermezzo* comic contrast does not necessarily depend upon changes of tempo: juxtapositions of high and low, loud and soft, long and short, are all laid under contribution in forming the droll whimsy of the style. Most *intermezzi* included at least one tender and sentimental aria to set off the boisterousness of the prevailing idiom: in such pieces the whole musical apparatus of the age of sensibility was brought into play, grace-notes and ornaments – especially appoggiaturas – subtly differentiated rhythms and chromatic harmonic nuances. Recitatives tend to be far more lively than in the contemporary *opera seria*. In the opening scene of *Pimpinone*, Vespetta's mention of the importance to good breeding of a musical education prompts Albinoni to incorporate a snatch of solmization and a wisp of song; in the closing recitative of the first *intermezzo* of *La serva padrona*, Uberto's *tirata*-like eloquence reaches a ludicrous climax when he drops into a lower octave to underline 'ch'io cheto mi starò'.[12]

Melody and harmony, texture and colour were the first priorities of the *opera seria* aria; in the *intermezzo* on the other hand, where composers were seeking comedy and character, the emphasis tended to shift to rhythm, or, to be more precise, to timing – perhaps the most essential ingredient of the comedian's art. A fine example is found in the closing duet of the first *intermezzo* of *Pimpinone*; Pimpinone seems to have rounded off the principal section of the duet with an emphatic cadence, when Vespetta tosses in

308

star che - to, che - to e non par - la - re!

Be silent, and don't speak!

Ex.IV.3 Pergolesi, *La serva padrona* (1733), Act I

Never mind the compliments. Be content. I'm on my way. You're right.
My most illustrious master!

Ex.IV.4 Albinoni, *Pimpinone* (1708), Act I

an ironic 'illustrissimo padron',[13] which really does sound like a quick
mocking aside, a brief lyrical phrase without emphatic cadence, which
teasingly delays the ritornello (Ex.IV.4). The comic effect of repetition,
especially threefold repetition, was well understood by the *commedia*
artists, and – transferred with whole-hearted relish to the opera-house –
became a favourite mannerism of the *intermezzo* style: the bumbling frenzy

309

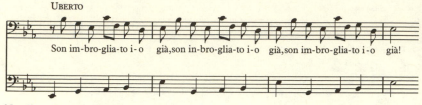

UBERTO

Son im-bro-glia-to i-o già, son in-bro-glia-to i-o già, son in-bro-glia-to i-o già!

Now I'm really in a muddle!

Ex.IV.5 Pergolesi, *La serva padrona* (1733), Act II

in which Uberto begins his aria 'Son imbrogliato io già' is simply one example of the myriad forms of mirthfulness which composers extracted from the procedure (Ex.IV.5). Above all it is their delight in cadences that makes us to sit up and mark the *intermezzo* masters' sense of rhythmic fun. All the best composers produced patterns of amazing variety and vivacity: a handful of characteristic specimens are cited by Lazarevich (1971: 312). Most musicians will have learned to appreciate the cadential revellings of this generation of Italians from the harpsichord sonatas of Domenico Scarlatti.

Broader comic effects are not uncommon. Literary parody has its musical counterpart in burlesque accompanied recitatives, such as that preceding Uberto's 'Son imbrogliato io già', or in the grotesque coloratura found in Sarri's *Dorinda e Nibbio* (quoted in Robinson 1972: 206). In some numbers a musical stylization of a detail in the text – a sigh or the pit-a-pat of a loving heart – becomes part of the composer's raw material: as in the substitute duet 'Per te io ho nel core' at the end of *La serva padrona*; to others an indulgence in onomatopoeic musical comedy gives a *lazzo*-like farcicality. The English traveller Edward Wright described how the *intermezzo* performers he had heard in Venice 'laugh, scold, imitate other Sounds, as the cracking of a Whip, the rumbling of Chariot Wheels' (Wright 1730, I: 85). And Wilhelm Friedrich Marpurg speculated that before long one might look forward to 'hearing fleas sneezing and grass growing' (Troy 1979: 92).

Troy warns us not to press too far the analogy between the ensembles of the *intermezzo* and those of the mature *opera buffa*, particularly on the grounds that the former make little if any provision for the advance of the dramatic action (Troy 1979: 118). Many of the *intermezzo* duets are in fact little more than divided arias, culminating in a few phrases of parallel sixths or tenths. Nevertheless the duets of *La serva padrona*, to look no further, show that the best composers were already adept at making their duets pieces of vivacious dramatic dialectic, if not of dramatic action. Did any master of *opera buffa* ever bring a dramatic confrontation more vividly to life in music than Pergolesi does the closing scene of *Intermezzo* I? The first half of the duet begins with the usual solos. Serpina's is echoed by Uberto's, even though he disagrees with everything she says – a kind of contradiction in parallel that was to become a favourite device of the *opera buffa* style. Serpina's second verse is more obviously characterized, particularly the mordant appeal of 'ma perchè?' and the bosomy thrust of 'che maestà'.[14] It is followed not by another solo for Uberto, but by a duet section in which, while Serpina presses him ever more winningly, he fluctuates between uneasy soliloquy and bluster, each expressed with an incomparable blend of simplicity and immediacy; the voices come together only for the dominant cadence phrase. In the second section of the duet (bar 57 onwards) Serpina dominates. She sings almost without interruption, producing an unbroken stream of musical ideas of the most apt and personable charm, while Uberto is reduced to short and ineffectual interruptions – 'Signorina, v'ingannate'[15] – or attempts to ignore her – 'La ra la'.

Later history of the *intermezzo*

Venice and Naples were the chief centres of production. In Venice the vogue tended to be erratic: there were years when few were performed; there were theatres, such as the San Giovanni Grisostomo, where they were frowned upon; by 1730 Bonlini was speaking of them as a thing of the past (Mamczarz 1972: 53). Nevertheless they revived, and in the long run Venice proved the city most productive of *intermezzi*. In the early years they were composed by the same men as were the *opera seria* which they adorned, especially by Gasparini. But Venice also produced the first specialist, Giuseppe Maria Orlandini, who was, in Quadrio's words, 'singular for his time in setting music to comic subjects' (Troy 1979: 44). For a period of some thirty years, from *c*.1712, Orlandini produced new *intermezzi* all over Italy, and his *Il marito giogatore*, also known as *Serpilla e Bacocco* (Venice 1719), was one of the most long-lived hits of the whole century.

Though Venice pioneered the *intermezzo* and produced specimens in greater numbers than any other city, Naples was ultimately the more important centre. The first big Neapolitan success was Sarri's *Brunetta e Burlotto* of 1720; thereafter the *intermezzo* flourished there until it was abruptly terminated in 1735, when King Charles III decided to replace *intermezzi* with ballets. As in Venice the repertory was dominated by the same composers as produced *opera seria*: Sarri, Leo, Mancini and Hasse were the most successful exponents. But among the Neapolitans was one composer who has virtually monopolized posterity's awareness of the *intermezzo*, not only in Naples but anywhere. The irony of Giovanni Battista Pergolesi's prepotency in the history of the *intermezzo* has been

311

revealed by modern scholarship. The extent of his work in this form proves to be modest in the extreme: not more than two *intermezzi* are certainly left by him, *La contadina astuta* (*Livietta e Tracollo*, Naples 1734) and *La serva padrona*. But there is nothing new in the misrepresentation that sees Pergolesi as the major figure of operatic comedy in the 1730s, and a man who did his best work in the comic style. Burney ranked him with Orlandini as one of the two great masters of the *intermezzo* (Burney 1776–89, IV: 535), and it was on the strength of little more than *La serva padrona* that Rameau paid his remarkable tribute: 'If I were thirty years younger, I would go to Italy and Pergolesi would be my model' (Girdlestone 1957: 440). For his own part Pergolesi seems almost to have resented the favour he won with his handful of comic pieces, complaining to Egidio Duni that he considered 'his serious works infinitely superior to the bagatelles that had gained him some reputation' (Walker 1949: 297). The soaring musical prestige of Naples in the 1720s and 1730s, and the spread of Neapolitan musicians all over Europe which accompanied this, coincided with the great age of the *intermezzo*. It was therefore the Neapolitan *vis comica* rather than the Venetian that stamped itself on European consciousness, and became a principal source of the early classical style.

The *intermezzo* repertory was performed by specialists who needed something of the same kind of versatility as the *commedia dell'arte* teams: singing, acting, dancing, acrobatics were all called for. The only Italian theatre with a permanent set of performers, however, was the San Bartolomeo in Naples, where Gioacchino Corrado played with a number of different partners between 1700 and 1735. Elsewhere the repertory was disseminated, like the *commedia*, by travelling companies, of which the peerless Rosa Ungarelli–Antonio Ristorini team was most admired. It was they who first introduced *intermezzi* to Munich (1722), Brussels (1728) and Paris (1729). A permanent company was established at Dresden from 1724, and this group actually gave the very first performances of Italian opera in Russia in 1731. Almost the last place to be colonized by the *intermezzo* troupes was London, where they appeared only in 1736–37; it was vainly hoped that they might restore the ailing fortunes of the Opera of the Nobility.

The final stages in the history of the *intermezzo* can be briefly told. Following the abrupt termination of Neapolitan *intermezzo* performances in 1735, the form went into a rapid decline in other cities too, particularly under the impact of the growing taste for full-scale *opera buffa*. Milan witnessed its last *opera seria* with *intermezzi* in 1738, Rome in 1740, Florence in 1746, Venice in 1750 (Troy 1979: 133). Thereafter the form survived only in the prose theatre in the form of the *intermezzo comico*. In this environment cast lists and orchestra lists began to grow, and the *intermezzo* slowly evolved into the *farsa*, the miniature *opera buffa* in the composition of which the young Rossini was to win his spurs. Among the greater figures who essayed the *intermezzo* in this late phase may be mentioned Jommelli, who laid particular weight on the aria, and Paisiello, who was so bold as to produce a new setting of *La serva padrona*.

After mid-century the *intermezzo*'s most glorious hour – indeed it lasted for a year and a half – came in 1752–54 in Paris. The touring company that settled there in those years was, by all accounts, an unspectacular one; the repertory it performed was entirely typical, including Pergolesi's *La serva padrona* and Orlandini's *Serpilla e Bacocco*, known in Paris as *Il giocatore*.[16] Yet it set passions aflame and struck some of the keenest minds of the age with the force of a revelation, for the *intermezzo* showed them that, even in an operatic medium, it was possible, in Algarotti's words, 'to cultivate simplicity and follow nature' (Strunk 1950: 671). The *Querelle des Bouffons*, one of the fiercest and longest-lasting aesthetic controversies of the eighteenth century, engaged almost everyone of distinction in French intellectual life. On the departure of the troupe in March 1754, Baron Grimm observed ironically: 'The Buffons, the Diderots, the d'Alemberts, all the men of letters of some reputation; artists of every kind, painters, sculptors, architects, whom this music has as-it-were, bewitched, will no longer go to the Opéra, and will have so much the more leisure to devote to their work' (Reichenburg 1937: 95).

The *intermezzo* and the *opera buffa* were not successive stages of a single development. They served rather different purposes, had different priorities, and flourished, in some measure, simultaneously. But it is not wrong to emphasize the extent to which the *opera buffa* was indebted to and influenced by the *intermezzo*. In subject-matter they were often close, indeed *intermezzi* librettos were sometimes reworked into *opere buffe* and vice versa, and certain qualities of form and style in the mature *opera buffa* almost certainly reflect the influence of the more modest form. It is at least suggestive that the 'new' *opera buffa* of Goldoni and Galuppi, the kind of *opera buffa*, that is to say, which used *parti serie* as well as the traditional types of role, emerged in Venice at exactly the time when the old conjunction of *opera seria* with *intermezzo* was abandoned. As for the musical language of the *opera buffa*, that was a medium that owed virtually everything to the experiments and achievements of *contrascena* and *intermezzo*.

18 · The flowering of comic opera in Naples and Venice

The Neapolitan *commedeja pe mmuseca*

It will be as well to commence this discussion by reiterating that the *opera buffa* grew up quite independently of the comic *intermezzo*. The two genres shared many traits of musical language; the structure of both comprised an alternation of *recitativo semplice* and solo arias (mostly in some kind of *da capo* form), with ensembles at the act ends; otherwise they formed two distinct theatrical traditions. While the *intermezzo* – until about 1750 at any rate – consisted of two or three short scenes for two or three characters, the *opera buffa* was a full-length, three-act opera with six or seven principal roles. And unlike the drastically parodied character types of the *intermezzo*, those of the comic opera at first represented quite normal people – the prosperous bourgeoisie and their servants, the lower orders of the aristocracy. Further, the *intermezzo* employed only natural voices, usually soprano and bass, while the voice classification of the comic opera had more in common with that of the *opera seria*: in Vinci's *Li zite 'ngalera* (Naples 1722), for example, both the romantic heroes have high voices – Carlo Celmino, the 'Gentleman from Sorrento', was a soprano, sung originally by a woman, while Titta Castagna was an alto, sung by a man. Finally, because the *intermezzo* was performed in the major Italian opera-houses (in conjunction with *opera seria*), it normally employed Tuscan – that is literary Italian; while the comic opera, normally performed in smaller theatres, perhaps for more popular audiences, tended – especially in Naples – to make extensive, if not exclusive use of the local dialect.

Full-length operatic comedy can be traced in various Italian cities in the first half of the eighteenth century. But at the risk of being over-schematic I shall confine my discussion of this period to Naples, where culturally the most interesting type evolved and where the best opera composers of the age – Alessandro Scarlatti, Vinci, Leo and Pergolesi – played a leading part in giving it its distinctive character. To begin with it was called not *opera buffa*, but in Neapolitan dialect, *commedeja pe mmuseca*, a terminology which perhaps alludes to the spoken theatre of the time and indicates that the role of the music is essentially decorative (Gallarati 1984: 113). But first a point must be conceded to such 'anti-Neapolitans' as Wolff, namely that, because it was predominantly in dialect, Neapolitan *opera buffa* did not travel well (Wolff 1975: 51–2). Even after Bernardo Saddumene had introduced Tuscan roles, specifically with the object of broadening its appeal to include non-Neapolitans (Preface to *Le noce de Veneviente*, in Strohm 1979: 160), it remained less influential in the world at large than the *intermezzo*. All this may be true, but Naples was after all no mere provincial city; it was in the eighteenth century the greatest metropolis in the peninsula and together with Venice the most vital centre of its cultural life. And in Naples an idiosyncratic form of operatic comedy was cultivated with a fervour of enthusiasm which flared up quite suddenly in the first decade of the century and never flagged until the Napoleonic age. 'The Neapolitans', wrote Francesco Maria Zambeccari censoriously at the end of December 1709, 'who all have the worst taste, are deserting the San Bartolomeo Theatre, where *Astarte* by Zeno and Pariati is being excellently performed, and filling the Teatro dei Fiorentini, where they are performing a really disgusting piece not fit to be looked at, in Neapolitan' (Croce 1926: 136–7). The Teatro dei Fiorentini had traditionally been the theatre for Spanish drama. It began to stage opera in 1706, and finding a profitable niche for itself in Neapolitan theatre life with its comic opera performances, devoted itself entirely to that form from the 1714–15 season onward. During the 1720s two further theatres, the Teatro della Pace and the Teatro Nuovo sopra Toledo, were opened expressly for *opera buffa*.

The 'really disgusting piece' for which the Neapolitans at the end of 1709 were so deplorably abandoning *Astarte* was an opera called *Patrò Calienno de la Costa*. With a text by 'Agasippo Mercotellis' – a *nom-de-plume* perhaps belonging to Nicolò Corvo (Croce 1926: 135) – and music by Antonio Orefice, *Patrò Calienno* had had its première in October; it was to be the prototype of a whole repertory of distinctly Neapolitan comic operas.

The cultural source of this epoch-making work – of which only the text survives – are obscure. But perhaps three things deserve to be kept in mind, which, while they certainly cannot 'explain' the opera, do serve to reduce its apparent isolation a little. First, dialect-opera was not without precedent: at least one earlier example (*La Cilla* 1707) had been performed privately in Naples, and a certain amount had been produced in the seventeenth century, particularly in Florence, where Jacopo Melani had composed a number of operas of everyday life in conjunction with the librettist G. A. Moniglia. Second, the beginnings of Neapolitan *opera buffa* coincide almost exactly with the beginnings of spoken dialect comedy, and this can hardly be fortuitous. The first of these dialect plays, an anonymous *Mezzotte* performed in the Castel dell'Ovo in 1701, was, thought Croce, a quite natural outcome of the rich dialect literature of seventeenth-century Naples, and of the growing taste of the times for simplicity and naturalness (Croce 1926: 132). The early *commedeja pe mmuseca* too occupies a comfortable middle ground between the stylized solemnity of the reformed *opera seria* and the stylized caricature of the *commedia dell'arte*. Third, though Scherillo's claim that the *opera buffa* is 'but an off-shoot of the [*commedia dell'arte*]' seems extravagant (1916: 3), the influence of *commedia* on certain scenes and certain types of characterization is unmistakable.

Whatever its sources, *Patrò Calienno* became the model for early operatic comedy. A microcosm of contemporary Neapolitan life, the opera presented a picture of its everyday joys and sorrows, the squabbles and scuffles and reconcilitions and celebrations of its volatile populace, vignettes of family life set in the best-loved quarters of the city among its most familiar landmarks. The 'democratic muse of dialect' had demonstrated that she could hold even the lyric theatre in her command.

Realism and stylization

Pane amava Eco vicina
Eco Fauno saltellante
Fauno Lidia, e il proprio amante
Era in odio a ognun di lor.[1]

Scherillo quotes Leopardi's charming translation of a Moschus idyll and suggests that it might serve as a synopsis of most of the plots of Neapolitan comic opera in the first decades of its history (1916: 55). From *Patrò Calienno* onwards the unravelling of a tortuous tangle of amorous relationships was to be the favourite theme. But between Orefice's opera and those of Logroscino, Naples' most popular composer of *opera buffa* in the years around 1750, there did occur some few new developments in the local tradition.

One of the most disturbing came in the mid-1720s when Metastasio – at the time still resident in Naples – began writing serenatas and *drammi per musica* which set new standards of natural eloquence and lyric beauty. The perfection of Metastasio's style had a disconcerting effect on some comic librettists, particularly on Saddumene and, in the 1730s, on Federico, Pergolesi's closest collaborator. Their young lovers tended to become Metastasianized – more refined and sensitive, prone to eloquent metaphor, Tuscan rather than Neapolitan in speech. The result of that development was to give to the Neapolitan speakers in the cast something of the apartness of the ghetto; their patois at once marked them out as being more boorish or stupid than the other characters. Comedy became more artificial and stylized, and the sense of being at ease in the real world, which *Patrò Calienno* had conveyed, was lost.

All the same, like 'Mercotellis' before them and like Goldoni in Venice later, this generation of Neapolitan librettists did remain for the most part firmly in touch with real life. Naturalistic street-corner scenes for instance are as typical of their work as they are of Goldoni's Venetian comedies. At the start of Saddumene's libretto for *Li zite 'ngalera* four of the characters are introduced like this:

Masto Col-Agnolo affellano Rasola nnanze a la Poteca soja, Ciccariello, che scopa, e canta, Ciomma nnanze a la porta, che fa pezzille, Carlo da lontano, che passeja.[2]

(Act I scene 1)

And some of the figures in this repertory remain as prosaic, as unprettified, as if they had stepped from the pages of Verga. In the same opera Col'Agnolo declare his love to Ciomma in far-from-Metastasian terms:

Sient'a mmè; tengo rrobba: aggio denare:
E tant'aggio da fare,
Ch'aje da essere mia.[3]

(Act I scene 6)

The librettist who best sustained this realistic tradition was Pietro Trinchera, whose artistic credo is found in the preface to *Il finto cieco*:

My style is to copy direct from nature (scrivere'ncoppa a lo naturale), and not to loot ancient comedies and . . . romances (de i'revotanno romanze). I have woven together a very, very slight affair, the sort of thing that could happen in your own house.

(Scherillo 1916: 274)

It was perhaps Trinchera too who kept clearest in mind the moral scope ascribed to comedy by the theorists of the age – the correction of human behaviour by the mockery of such foibles and vices as meanness and avarice, pomposity and hypocrisy: Planelli's list is 'una donna vana, un saccentino, une salamistra, un tagliacantoni, un affettato'[4] (Monaco 1968: 29). At any rate certain of the popular character types of *opera buffa* – the charlatan doctor for example, and especially the notary, 'a blend of mumbo-jumbo and Latin, of low cunning and common sense' (Scherillo 1916: 237) – were given their classic formulation in Trinchera's works. A satirical note is heard more clearly than in most of the repertory, and it may have been this which made him fall foul of the censors (for *La tavernola abentorosa*), and which led ultimately to his imprisonment and suicide.

By Logroscino's time, the splitting of the operatic cast into serious Tuscan roles and comic Neapolitan ones was encouraging the cultivation of a more grossly farcical tone in the dialect scenes. A near-contemporary chronicler, P. Napoli-Signorelli, attributed this development particularly to the influence exerted by Antonio Catalano, one of the great *buffo* basses of the day, on the librettist Antonio Palomba:

The foolishness of Palomba's verses found a kind of justification in the laughter which Catalano provoked. In token of which the poet and author [?actor] subsequently abandoned themselves to eccentricities. And what happened? The public was charmed with the most trivial scurrility, to such an extent that when it was intended to revive some dramas by Federico, they seemed lifeless and languid; those authors who did not feel inclined to gross buffooneries disdained to exercise their skills in a medium thus abandoned to monstrosities.

(Scherillo 1916: 287)

The inheritance of popular song and *commedia dell'arte*

Given dramatic themes of the kind I have described, it would be unsurprising if early Neapolitan *opera buffa* were found to be impregnated with elements from popular music. But in the very nature of the case, and especially because of the disdainful indifference to popular music shown by most eighteenth-century savants, these elements are not easily identified. Contemporary accounts of Neapolitan popular music never seem to have advanced beyond the ill-focused generalizations of Mattheson and Burney (quoted in Robinson 1972: 219–21). Both these authors emphasize the use of traditional instruments – guitar and, more specifically in Burney's case, *colascione*;[5] Mattheson appears to allude to compound time as a distinctive feature when he speaks of 'slow English jigs' and 'songs a la barquerole'; and Burney remarks on the slow movement of the voice, on the surprising modulations and sliding chromaticism. It seems possible, then, that the four arias entitled *barcarola* to be found in Leo's comic operas are related to popular traditions (Robinson 1972: 220), and Vinci's extraordinarily exotic aria at the start of *Li zite 'ngalera* surely resembles, in its sliding chromaticism at least, the kind of music Burney was trying to describe.[6]

As far as one can judge, the kinds of use which Neapolitan composers were to make of popular music were established by Orefice's example in *Patrò Calienno*. The opera begins and ends with what Scherillo called – on the evidence of textual concordances(?) – popular songs, and a third aria 'Anga Nicola' (Act II scene 8) he describes as being 'still in vogue' in 1883 (1916: 73–74). The other opera librettos of 'Mercotellis' employ popular music in similar ways: at the beginning of the third and last of them, *Patrò Tonno d'Ischia* (1714) for example, the eponymous hero, a master mariner from Ischia, comes with his *colascione* to sing under Menella's balcony. Starting the opera in this way gives the popular song an 'emblematic value': '"You are entering," says the canzonetta to the public, "the everyday world"' (Weiss 1986: 140). One deduces the use of popular music in Neapolitan *opera buffa* therefore from such criteria as the use of certain instruments (especially the *colascione*); allusions in the text to proverbs, children's games, songs known from spoken plays etc. (a good example from Auletta's *La locandiera* is in Robinson 1972: 210–12); and in certain cases from the dramatic context. On such criteria it would seem obvious that Logroscino is at very least imitating the style of popular music in *Il governatore*, Act I scene 8, where Don Crispino, having been mocked and scolded for his ponderous and affected manners, attempts a lighter style of wooing: he serenades Leonora with a fragmentary ditty in $\frac{12}{8}$ time, accompanied by a drone bass on the *colascione* (Ex.IV.6).

In the very earliest Neapolitan comic operas the concern to present on stage vignettes of 'real life' occasioned a turning away from the traditions of

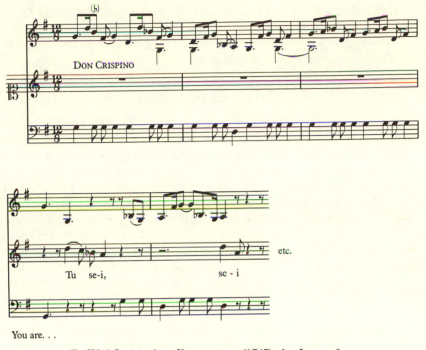

You are. . .

Ex.IV.6 Logroscino, *Il governatore* (1747), Act I scene 8

stylized farce represented by the *commedia dell'arte*. But the influence of the *commedia* was never entirely absent, and when the linguistic separating out of Neapolitan and Tuscan elements introduced a more mannered comic style in the 1720s, that influence began to grow stronger. Like the contemporary *intermezzi*, many an *opera buffa* has a plot which, in essence, simply elaborates a traditional *scenario*; many of the comic set-pieces are straight from the world of the *commedia*. There are several such in *Li zite 'ngalera*. Act I scene 14 is a shaving and shouting scene manipulated by the servant Ciccariello, who has – for the sheer fun of it ('Che bella burla che le vogli fare') – told both the barber Col'Agnolo and his customer Rapisto that the other is deaf; Act II scene 9 is built round a reading from Tasso's *Gerusalemme liberata* (in Tuscan of course) with jokes about pronunciation and unintelligibility.

Much of the musical comedy recalls the *commedia* too. Effects of of musical onomatopoeia are as popular in the *opera buffa* as in the *intermezzo*, as the examples from Leo cited by Robinson show (1972: 208). In some of the ensembles – that of Act II of Logroscino's *Il governatore*, for example – this naive kind of fun assumes a more elaborate form in which we may be forgiven for hearing anticipations of Rossini's delight in the sheer comicality of sound that can be extracted from a suitably absurd text (Ex.IV.7). Particularly *commedia*-like are those Act III finales *ad spectatores* in which the actors take leave of the audience – as they do at the close of *Li zite 'ngalera* – 'dancing, singing and playing'.

Arias and ensembles

From the time of Scarlatti's *Il trionfo dell'onore* (1718) at the latest, comic opera was written not merely by such minor figures as Orefice, but by the finest composers of the age. In sophistication, eloquence and beauty, its music yielded little to that of the *opera seria*, whose idioms and forms it in fact largely paralleled. As in *opera seria* the solo arias employed an expansive *da capo* form with ritornellos, and this was abandoned only for some clear dramatic purpose – for a popular song, or for an entrance aria. These, in the early days, tended to be set as continuo-accompanied ariosi, often with an 'open' tonal scheme: that is to say they closed in a key other than the tonic; by the middle of the century they were normally set as 'cavatinas' – in the eighteenth century a term meaning a song that lacked the middle section and *da capo* of the full-scale aria. Until the 1740s all the other solo arias still matched those of the *opera seria* in scale and complexity of design. Such a piece as Leonora's 'Se vuoi che per te amore' (*Il governatore*, Act I scene 2), like the most advanced arias of the *opera seria*, uses thematic contrasts to articulate the text of the principal section, and bears as a result the same strong resemblance to an exposition in the incipient sonata-style (Ex.IV.8).

But the subject-matter of the *opera buffa*, the importance of the audibility of its text, and the comparatively modest vocal skills of many of its performers meant that the *opera buffa* was less prone than *opera seria* to succumb to the temptations of virtuosity. Word setting continued on the whole to observe the principle of one syllable to a note, and to employ a more elaborate style only rarely and with due circumspection. Genuinely melismatic virtuosity could therefore be reserved for effects of poetic emphasis or dramatic characterization, such as the arrival of the swash-buckling galley-captain Federico to function as a kind of *deus ex machina* in Act III of *Li zite 'ngalera*. The style of the instrumental accompaniment remained lean and transparent; rarely are instruments other than strings mentioned, and rarely are the strings themselves divided into more than three parts. The combination of lucid word-setting and spare instrumentation on the one hand with lyrical charm and harmonic sophistication on the other gave a direct and vigorous quality to the expression, particularly perhaps in moods of pathos.

I have already compared the Act III finales of these early comedies with the *licenze* of the *commedia dell'arte*. The dramatic action is over before the

Il cer - vel - lo per le pos - te tù, tù, tù, tù, tù, tù, tù, tù, tù, tù, tù, S'ai man - da - to in ve - ri - tà, che ve- sparo zur - re, zur - re, zur - re, zur - re, zur - re, zur - re, zur

If you really have sent off your brains in the post. . .toot, toot, toot, What
a wasps' nest. . .buzz, buzz, buzz

Ex.IV.7 Logroscino, *Il governatore* (1747), Act II scene 15

LEONORA

Se vuoi che per te, che per te a - mo - re, che per

te a - mo - re il co - re, il co - re al fin, al fin mi

pungichi me-co tu allegro mostrati, la - scia la se-rie-

ta, o - ne - sto, sì, ma flu - vi - do l'u - so e'l trattar

mi pia-ce, ti rendi, ti rendi o no ca - pa-ce alle - gra

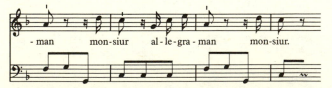

- man mon-siur al - le-gra - man mon-siur.

If you want love for you to pierce my heart one day, at least be a bit more
cheerful with me, away with this solemnity; I like a manner and
behaviour that is decent, certainly, but easy-going too; do you understand
or don't you? so cheerfully, monsieur.

Ex.IV.8 Logroscino, *Il governatore* (1747), Act I scene 2

music begins; and the finale takes the form of a celebration, or a drawing of the moral, during the course of which the actors retire from the stage. Such movements are very short and very simple, generally little more than a few phrases of block chords in dancing rhythms. But at the ends of the other acts of the opera we find the first modest beginnings of what was ultimately to develop into the most glorious achievement of the *buffo* style – the dramatic ensemble finale.

It is tantalizingly difficult to plot the first stages in the evolution of this form because so little music from the early years of the *commedeja* has survived. The librettos suggest that some finales may have been quite animated dramatically and scenically. But by the 1720s the influence of the *dramma per musica* was discouraging experiments in the co-ordination of ensemble music with stage action. Those early ensemble finales that survive are best described as *gliuòmmari* (tangles), a term apparently coined by the librettist Francesco Antonio Tullio (Scherillo 1916: 101). The intrigue comes to a climax in a scene of agitation and confusion, during which short, lively, indignant or aggressive snippets of song are tossed to and fro among the characters. A good example from Leo's *La semmeglianza di chi l'ha fatta* (Naples 1726) is quoted in full by Robinson (1972: 229–33). Better still is Vinci's Act I finale in *Li zite 'ngalera*, where to Leo's indiscriminate sprightliness is added a concern for characterization (cf. the droll, droning contributions of Rapisto), and a use of the orchestra which, if almost painfully functional, is prophetic in the way it sustains the inchoate patter of voices on the unbroken instrumental continuum (Ex.IV.9). But it must be emphasized that these are 'situation' pieces, not 'action' pieces. As early as Leo's *Lo matrimonio annascuso* (*c.* 1727) we can find a finale in two contrasting movements (Wolff 1975: 114), but for the first half of the century no real progress was made towards the genuine dramatic finale. Early this century extravagant claims for Logroscino's finales were made by Kretzschmar, and endorsed by other scholars. But the finales of *Il governatore*, the only Logroscino opera to survive in its entirety, are exactly the same kind of situation pieces as the *gliuòmmari* of the early Neapolitan *opere buffe*.

Goldoni and the *dramma giocoso*

As the middle of the eighteenth century approaches our attention must shift from Naples to Venice; for Goldoni was about to assume a leading part in the writing of *opera buffa*, and the results were to be epoch-making.[7] In his *Memoirs*, Goldoni unhesitatingly conceded Naples the primacy in the realm of *opera buffa*. He attributes its introduction in Venice to the initiative of the impresario Giuseppe Imer, to whose company he was himself attached for some years from 1734, and he claims his own

Fondazione di Venezia, performed at the Teatro San Samuele in 1736, as 'perhaps the first comic opera to appear in the state of Venice' (1907, I: xxxvii).

Goldoni's earliest essays as an opera librettist date from that eclectic and experimental phase in his career, in the mid-1730s, when he was still prepared to try his hand at anything, from heroic drama to comic *intermezzi*; and they are in fact in the latter modest form. At the time Imer

There, what a swindling rascal. . .goodness me, what a lot of blood. . .
blunderer, blunderer. . .come in, auntie. . . I'll make you sorry for it. . .

Ex.IV.9 Vinci, *Li zite 'ngalera* (1722), Act I scene 17

Ex.IV.9 *continued*

began to cultivate *opera buffa* in Venice, Goldoni's principal ambition as a dramatist was the reform of the spoken comedy, its transformation from the improvised farce of the *commedia dell'arte* into an urbane literary comedy of manners. He had found time to compose only four full-length *opera buffa* librettos by 1743, the year in which he left Venice to spend several years practising law in Tuscany. The vast bulk of his librettos – and there are more than fifty of them in all – was produced after his return to Venice in 1748. They began to appear, that is to say, at a time when his ideas on the reform of comedy had fully crystallized, and they were contemporary with the first and most productive phase of his mature spoken comedies. Historically most significant were the fifteen works written in collaboration with Galuppi. The first, *L'Arcadia in Brenta*, appeared in 1749; *Il mondo della luna* and three others followed in 1750; and they had produced ten more together by the end of the decade.

In view of their long and glorious operatic history, the slowness of the Venetians to take up the *opera buffa* is puzzling. There was certainly no problem temperamentally, as their mastery of the comic *intermezzo* showed; and Goldoni himself went out of his way to emphasize the musical gaiety of his fellow-citizens: 'There is singing in the squares, in the streets and on the canals. Merchants sing as they sell their wares, labourers sing as they leave their work, gondoliers sing as they wait for their masters. The foundation of the national character is gaity . . .' (1907, I: xxxv). Whatever the cause for their slow start, there was soon ample compensation. Goldoni became the seminal figure in the creation of a repertory which, for the sheer variousness of its delights, not even the Neapolitans could surpass. It is true that literary critics continue to complain – as they have done since the time of the controversies between Goldoni and Gozzi in the 1750s – of the unevenness of style in his librettos. But for the music historian exploring the operatic repertory of eighteenth-century Italy the particular joy of these pieces is that they bring into the opera-house virtually the full ambit of the dramatic world Goldoni had created in his spoken comedies – its teeming vitality, its irrresistible charm, its smiling and reasonable optimism.

It has been suggested that Goldoni preferred the term 'dramma giocoso' because he recognized that the spirit of comic opera was essentially playful and artificial (Gallarati 1984: 132); and that neither the ideological thrust nor the naturalism of his spoken plays is so marked in his libretti. It is certainly the case that the veto on the use of dialect that was, for some reason or other, in force in Venetian *opera buffa* inhibited his attempts to bring to the operatic stage the 'piccolo mondo' of the squares and alleys of the city as he had in some of his most triumphant spoken comedies, and as of course – *mutatis mutandis* – the early Neapolitan comic opera librettists had done. Stylization is also evident in the firm distinction he commonly makes between *parti serie* and *parti buffe*. Nonetheless the moral scope of his *drammi giocosi* is surely unmistakable. There are few of them in which some human weakness or foible is not deliciously satirized: the covetousness and gullibility of Don Poppone in *La diavolessa* who, having consulted cabbalistic signs and groped around in his cellar 'experiencing' the twitching of a hazel wand, spends much of the opera digging there for treasure; or, in *L'Arcadia in Brenta*, the absurd and ostentatious extravagance of those who starve themselves at home in order to be able to maintain villas in the countryside – a theme he was to return to in his exquisite *Villeggiatura*-trilogy of spoken plays a few years later. But in Goldoni far more than in the Neapolitan repertory we are aware of the optimistic obverse side of this satire. One of his most successful librettos, *La buona figliuola* (Parma 1757, music by Duni), was a reworking of *Pamela*, his 'model for virtuous lovers' (1907, II: ix). In other operas we meet with emancipated views on the relation between the sexes which, thanks to the idealism of their tone, strike a far deeper note than the traditional challenging sauciness of the *intermezzo* soubrette (cf. *La diavolessa*, Act I scene 3), or thought-provoking reflections on the simple life. A charming example is Nardo's apostrophe to his spade in *Il filosofo di campagna*:

> Vanga mia benedetta,
> Mio diletto conforto e mio sostegno,
> Tu sei lo scettro, e questi campi il regno . . .[8]   (Act I scene 5)

Of course, Goldoni is expecting us to laugh at Nardo, but as the soliloquy continues it becomes clear that he thinks we ought at the same time and in some measure to agree with him.

What is perhaps the single most individual trait of Goldonian comedy – the sublimation into gracious art of the stalest quibs and japes of the *commedia* – found ready acceptance in the *dramma giocoso*. The first act alone of *La calamita de'cuori* provides several examples. Its opening scene begins with an introduction clearly modelled on the '*parades*' of the *commedia*: the subject of the opera is suggested by a kind of tableau-cum-synopsis, a 'chorus' in which the four men in the opera (Armidoro 'the constant one', Giacinto 'the charming one', Saracea 'the swaggerer' and Pignone 'the miser') all avow their love for the mysterious stranger Bellarosa. When that lady appears, she proves to be – like *La donna di garbo* or Mirandolina in *La locandiera* – one of the several marvellous female roles which Goldoni modelled on the traditional *trasformazioni* of the *commedia* soubrette. The basic idea of the *trasformazioni* – Goldoni tells us, in words that set the opera-goer thinking of Despina – was that the soubrette 'appeared in different forms, changed her costume several times, played several different roles, and spoke in different languages' (1907, I: xliii). As far as Bellarosa is concerned, when she is with Pignone she manifests an earnest interest in the managing of her money; with Saracea, a quite piratical line in oaths and exclamations; with Armidoro, a fervent romantic ardour; with Giacinto, a foppish, pseudo-literary flirtatiousness. At the end of the act the same joke is developed further. The core of the finale is a guessing game, in which the four men try to imagine where she comes from. It provides excellent scope for those 'nationality jokes' which, as the traditional masks showed, were so deeply rooted in the *commedia*. Indeed, it might be said to provide a key to such jokes: where does she come from? Pignone, who assumes her to be 'l'economa vera', tries Florence, Genoa and Turin; Saracea, who assumes her to be a 'femina brava', tries Naples, Brescia and Bologna; and Giacinto, who assumes her to be a 'donna vezzosa',[9] tries Venice, Parma and Milan. (In fact she is from Ragusa (Dubrovnik).)

The dramatic finale

It was not merely the range of his dramatic themes that made Goldoni so interesting and influential a librettist. Structurally, too, his work introduced a quite new dimension into the genre, for it was to him – not to Logroscino or Piccinni or indeed any composer – that we owe the development of the dramatic finale, and hence the whole idea of an operatic ensemble packed with action;[10] as Gasparo Gozzi (brother of Goldoni's formidable adversary) wrote: 'he may call himself the first inventor of closing the acts with this novelty of pleasing and varied action' (Heartz 1977–78: 73). As far as one can see, it was not an innovation that resulted from any artistic programme or any philosophical preconception; it seems rather to have been a happy accident, an idea which once chanced upon proved irresistible. The dramatic finale plays no part in Goldoni's early librettos – though some of them were subsequently rewritten to incorporate such finales – and is only sketchily hinted at in two collaborations with Ciampi in 1748–49. But in the first of the Galuppi operas, *L'Arcadia in Brenta* – to be precise in its second act – the basic ingredients of the form are unmistakable. If one suspects serendipity it is because this ensemble finale is demanded by the plot: it is quite literally 'a kind of little comedy or play in itself', to borrow da Ponte's famous words; for five characters dress up in *commedia dell'arte* costumes and perform a masquerade, and it is the closing section of these theatricals that is set as a continuous dramatic ensemble.[11]

During the 1750s the dramatic finale spread all over Italy, and wherever it occurred it seems to be possible to identify it in some way with the influence of Goldoni. Piccinni – to whom some music historians have attributed the invention of the form – composed his first dramatic finale only in 1760; and the text of the work in question was by Goldoni (*La buona figliuola* once more). Late in the same year Piccinni introduced the dramatic finale to Naples, in *La furba burlata*, of which the chronicler Napoli-Signorelli wrote:

This opera introduced a novelty into our comic musical theatre. At Naples the act finales had been limited to a few lines at the moment of maximum action; but in the rest of Italy they were long and contained within many lines various incidents giving rise to variety of musical tempi and motives, as can be seen in Goldoni's *Buona figliuola* and *Filosofo di campagna* . . .   (Robinson 1972: 237)

In 1768 the young Mozart first came to grips with the composition of *opera buffa*, and again, as far as the finales were concerned, Goldoni was his mentor. For although his *Finta semplice* had been radically revised by Coltellini, the finales were untouched. Mozart was therefore confronted with a typical Goldonian scheme: each little incident in the chain of events is highlighted by a change of metre, which in turn points to a change in the style of the music. 'With such an experienced guide (and perhaps Leopold's advice as well?) his first finale could not help but become the resourceful and effective chain of contrasting little movements that it is' (Heartz 1977–78: 77).

Of the many composers who worked with Goldoni in the field of *opera buffa*, the one most closely identified with his innovatory achievements was Baldassare Galuppi, commonly known as 'Il Buranello' after his birthplace, the island of Burano. He was already an experienced hand in *opera buffa* when their collaboration began in 1749, for back in the early 1740s, when Imer first stimulated Venetian interest in the form, he had been employed to adapt Neapolitan opera to Venetian conditions. But the Goldoni operas made him an international celebrity – the first indeed to owe his reputation to the composition of *opera buffa*. It was on the strength of these that Burney ranked him second only to Jommelli among the opera composers of the age.

It fell to Galuppi to find an appropriate musical dress for Goldoni's dramatic finales. And very promptly he perceived that if they were to realize their full theatrical potential, they must be set in a way that was at once vivid and coherent. The Act I finale of *La diavolessa* shows a typical scheme:

i	Allegro C	E major	49 bars	Formal speeches for all three characters
ii	Andante $\frac{3}{8}$	E major	56 bars	Giannino and Dorina disagree about appropriate conduct towards Don Poppone
iii	Largo $\frac{2}{4}$	E minor	19 bars	Languorous flirting of Dorina and Don Poppone
	(flutes replace oboes for this movement)			
iv	Presto C	B major	38 bars	Giannino protests
	(closing half cadence)			
v	Recitative		2 bars	
vi	Largo $\frac{6}{8}$	E major	13 bars ⎫	The moral
	(Allegro) $\frac{3}{8}$	E major	48 bars ⎭	

In these finales the dramatic momentum is commonly sustained by the orchestra, for which Galuppi wrote with a far more sophisticated sense of

I look for her and can't find her; oh, what rage I feel in my breast; where the devil can she be?

Ex.IV.10 Galuppi, *Il filosofo di campagna* (1754), Act I scene 14

texture and colour than we find in the *gliuòmmari* of Vinci or Leo (Ex.IV.10). Contemporaries (when they were not complaining, like Metastasio) often paid tribute to the skill of his instrumental writing, and he was a legendary disciplinarian in the training of orchestras.

Galuppi and Piccinni

In arias and duets 'Goldonian' seems the fitting epithet for the smiling and humane quality of Galuppi's music. He is not a Rossini to set audiences rocking with laughter, nor a Mozart to bring them to the edge of their seats with excitement; both the effervescence of farce and the pungency of real wit are missing, and those who regard such things as the essence of *opera buffa* are likely to find Galuppi a shade lustreless. Even the most *tirata*-like arias are incorrigibly comfortable. But in the majority of his numbers the combination of suavity and liveliness, of good humour and elegance is an admirable match for Goldoni's own brand of humour.

The key to an appreciation of Galuppi's *opera buffa* remains an understanding of the manners of the eighteenth-century solo aria. Natural voices are still far from universal; most of Galuppi's operas make some use either of travesty sopranos (such as Rinaldo, the romantic hero of *Filosofo di campagna*) or of male altos (such as the constant Armidoro in *Calamita de'cuori*). Such roles as these – indeed all Galuppi's *parti serie* – preserved into the second half of the century something of those ideals of impassioned declamation and truthfulness of expression associated with *opera seria* in its radiant Metastasian dawn. The old grand *da capo* form was losing its poularity by 1750, and virtually disappeared from Galuppi's works after 1755. Its place was taken by arias that we may describe as sonata-like, provided it is clear that it is not the Mozartian sonata with which they are being compared, but the Scarlattian. The text is sung twice. The first time through, tonal articulation and contrasts of theme and rhythm resemble those of an exposition; the second time through – we may think of this as a counter-exposition – the music starts from the dominant and works its way slowly back to the tonic. It is only at this point – the cadence phrases – that there is close thematic parallelism between counter-exposition and exposition. Anyone who loves Domenico Scarlatti should in fact soon feel at home in Galuppi's musical world. We find the same absence of routine symmetry, the same fancifulness in underlining an expressive or rhetorical point, the same delicious inventiveness in the fashioning of cadence phrases.

A younger, non-Venetian composer who has already been mentioned several times deserves a short last word in this chapter. Niccolò Piccinni first gained a reputation as a master of *opera buffa* in Naples in the mid-1750s. Indeed it was the success of these works that toppled Logroscino from that pinnacle of popularity on which he had sunned himself since the death of Leo, and precipitated his disappearance into an obscurity from which he has never been retrieved. As his reputation spread beyond Naples, Piccinni embarked on a remarkable career: for some fifteen years after 1758 (his debut in Rome) and working mainly in Rome and Naples, he

If the mouse plays the fool and frolics with the cat, the cat itself. . .

Ex.IV.11 Piccinni, *Le finte gemelle* (1771)

proved to be one of the most prodigiously fertile talents in the whole history of opera. It was he who introduced the new Goldonian form of *opera buffa* to Rome and Naples; indeed the first of his Goldoni comedies, *La buona figliuola* (Rome 1760), enjoyed a success more sensational and more durable than almost any other eighteenth-century opera. With it the authors created a vogue for a more idyllic and sentimental branch of *opera buffa*, comparable with the French *comédie larmoyante*; it led, via Paisiello's *Nina*, to the *opera semiseria* of the nineteenth century.

So completely has *La buona figliuola* overshadowed the rest of Piccinni's vast output that, in the eyes of posterity, he came to be thought of as a composer whose talents were limited to the expression of 'the naive and the tender' (J. A. Hiller, quoted in *The New Grove*, s.v. 'Piccinni'). This is certainly unfair: he was a vigorous and versatile composer whose achievements parallel those of Galuppi in many ways: in the large-scale harmonic design of his ensembles, in the growing complexity of form and richness of detail in his solo arias, in the expressive eloquence with which he fused word and tone. In 1771 the Abbé Galiani paid Piccinni the highest of compliments when he wrote of him to Madame d'Epinay, 'il a atteint le but de la perfection de l'art. Il m'a appris que nous chantons tout et toujours quand nous parlons' (Monaco 1968: 91). The sophistication of his orchestral writing certainly surpasses that of Galuppi's. Abert thought him unparalleled among Italian composers of *opera buffa* for the imaginative way in which the instrumental figures were developed and sustained (1978, I: 255–6); even during the sung sections of an aria it is often the effervescence of instrumental detail that is the chief source of the music's wit (Ex.IV.11). Burney reported that Piccinni was 'accused of employing instruments to such excess, that in Italy no copyist will transcribe one of his operas without being paid a zecchin more than for one by any other composer' (1771: 306).

19 · Apogee and decline

Opera buffa after Goldoni

During the first half of the eighteenth century the spread of the *opera buffa* from Naples to Rome and to Venice had been slow, and the scope of the repertory remained modest. But in the 1750s it became a national rather than a merely local form, and this in turn meant that it soon became as popular in centres of Italian influence abroad as in Italy itself. By the 1760s *opera buffa* was warmly welcomed in Vienna and London, while, in Paris, Egidio Duni was transforming it into an idiosyncratically French form of *opéra comique*. The 'reform' of the *opera buffa* carried out by the great Venetians made these international conquests possible, because it had enriched incalculably both the dramatic and the musical qualities of the form. The range of Goldoni's dramatic style encouraged composers to recognize that none of the arts of great singing need any longer be excluded, and that all the sophistication of modern orchestral technique could very properly find a place; the technical innovations he had introduced – specifically the dramatic ensemble finale – opened up hitherto unimagined possibilities of musico-dramatic expression. Once Goldoni and Galuppi had demonstrated that dramatic action could be co-ordinated with musical continuity, librettists and composers were quick to apply the same principle at other points in the plot where a particular dramatic crux or comic situation could benefit from such spotlighting. This post-Goldonian era, when Piccinni, Paisiello and Cimarosa, not to mention a host of lesser composers, were composing *opera buffa* not only in Naples, their base-city, but all over Italy – indeed over much of Europe – was the most productive and artistically the pre-eminent era in the history of the genre.

One of the problems which the immense popularity of the new *opera buffa* brought was the need for what can only be described as mass production. And while there was no lack of men who could make at least a respectable job of composing the music, the thankless task of writing a libretto was a different matter. It was, as da Ponte's *Memoirs* will remind us, an undertaking that was difficult and unprofitable, both in financial terms and in terms of artistic glory. Apart from Goldoni – several of whose texts were reset by Neapolitan masters like Piccinni and Paisiello – there were few classic librettos that could be reset the way Zeno's and Metastasio's regularly were; even in Goldoni's case composers obviously felt that old jokes wore less well than old solemnities, and only his most popular pieces were set more than four or five times. Another possible source of comic librettos – in Italy as in the German-speaking world – was the inexhaustible French theatre. One of the most popular and influential operas in the whole repertory, Paisiello's *Nina* (Caserta 1789), was an adaptation from the French, and in its original form even retained the French feature of spoken dialogue. But the most telling symptom of the literary problems of the *opera buffa* at this time is surely the new phenomenon of the 'hack-librettist', who was to blight Italian opera until the middle of the nineteenth century. The prototype of this unhappy figure was perhaps the Neapolitan Giuseppe Palomba, credited in some sources with the composition of more than three hundred pieces, and of whom Cimaglia unkindly remarked that his librettos were infinite in form as well as number, 'since they have neither middle, nor beginning, nor end' (Scherillo 1916: 453). For the most part, only court poets (such as da Ponte) or amateurs (such as the Abbé Casti) could afford the immense investment of time, skill and wit that the craft of libretto writing demanded.

The Venetians had not only popularized *opera buffa*, they had made it respectable, intellectually and socially. In Naples a kind of official recognition of the form was granted in the 1767–68 season. The occasion was Paisiello's first major triumph, *L'idolo cinese*, to a text by the best of the Neapolitan librettists of the day, Giambattista Lorenzi. Tanucci, the Neapolitan prime minister, a man of severe tastes and certainly no enthusiastic patron of the theatre, was provoked by ecstatic reports of the opera to visit the Teatro Nuovo, incognito, to hear it for himself. So charmed was he, that he ordered a private performance to be given at Caserta for the Royal Family, who in turn also heard Paisiello's opera 'with the greatest of pleasure. At that time they did not honour *opera buffa* theatres with their presence, because of the detestable scurrilities that were found in such profusion in the greater part of them' (the editor of Lorenzi's *Opere teatrali*, quoted in Scherillo 1916: 345).

These developments coincided with a loosening of the links which had bound the early *commedeja* to the popular life of the streets. In a preface to a later libretto, *L'infedeltà fedele* of 1779, Lorenzi underlined his efforts to purge the *opera buffa* of grosser types of comedy in order to make it a more genteel form of theatre.

I have tried to find a way to distance myself from the usual popular and vulgar buffooneries which are so fashionable in our small theatres, contenting myself with using witticisms in moderation, sufficient to throw into relief the tragic elements I have introduced, and which hitherto have not been employed in musical comedies. My intention was that, between the wholly serious drama of the Royal Teatro di S. Carlo and the wholly comic drama of the aforementioned smaller theatres, this should serve as a middle-of-the-road kind of entertainment (un mezzano spettacolo), participating dis-

creetly in both manners, so that everyone should find in the capital a theatre corresponding to his taste.   (Scherillo 1916: 369)

This 'embourgeoisement' of the Neapolitan *opera buffa* led to further
changes in the use of dialect. Since Saddumene had first introduced
Tuscan-speaking roles in the 1720s the part played by dialect had slowly
been reduced. Lorenzi limited it further, to one or two characters in each
opera; moreover, the experts tell us that, in terms both of vocabulary and
syntax, it has been 'normalized' (Monaco 1968: 48–50). The object is
clearly to use dialect not to give the impression of a drama taken from real
life, but to spot-light a central comic figure, one of whose idiosyncrasies is
the use of an earthy patois. It is illustrative of this development that, while
in *L'idolo cinese* the *buffo* principal Tuberone speaks Neapolitan, his
servant Gilbo speaks literary Tuscan. The comic Neapolitan had become a
type, a grotesque, and the best-loved figures in the *opera buffa* repertory
acquired something of the almost mythical status of the *commedia* masks.
Such was the case with Barone di Trocchio, protagonist in an opera by
Gazzaniga to a text by Cerlone, first produced in 1769 (*DBI*, s.v.
'Cerlone').

These *personaggi napoletani* were introduced not with a view to corrective, satirical observation; their purpose was simply to make audiences
laugh. Their most necessary appurtenant was not one of the traditional
comic defects of character, rather some 'little everyday tic' (Monaco 1968:
29–30) that was at once idiosyncratic and ludicrous, such as Don Tammaro's barmy obsession with Ancient Greek philosophy in *Socrate immaginario*
(set by Paisiello 1775). After Goldoni, *opera buffa* began to lose sight of the
approved classic aims of comedy, to forget illuminist theories on the moral
scope of the theatre. Quite exceptional were the satirical inclinations of a
man like Casti (who in any case as a librettist worked outside Italy), whose
Cublai libretto, written for Salieri, was banned by the Austrian censor.[1]
Opera buffa in the last third of the eighteenth century took its tone from an
uncritical acceptance of the mores of contemporary society, and an attitude
of indulgence, indeed a positive relish, for individual follies and foibles. In
some comedies designed for performance at court, notably in *Nina*, we
seem close to an 'official' *ancien régime* art. 'Oh eccellenza', exclaims
Giorgio, 'mercè la vostra generosità, quella della cara Padroncina, non
manchiamo per nulla.' A little later the Count replies '. . . accettate tutto; il
Cielo esaudisce i voti dell'onesta povertà. Pregatelo per lei [the mad Nina],
questa è la vostra gratitudine'[2] (Act I scene 4).

The spirit of Carnival

Librettists held fast to the new thematic conquests made for the *opera buffa*
by Goldoni in the 1750s. The sentimental, idyllic strain introduced in *La*

buona figliuola is intensified in *Nina,* in which, prophetically, madness – a laughing matter earlier in the century – becomes a pathetic affliction, and in which comedy – insofar as it exists at all – is restricted to a Mark Tapley-like hearty, Giorgio, who remains faithful to his watchword 'allegramente' in the most dispiriting circumstances. Cerlone, a professed admirer of Gozzi as well as Goldoni – he adapted works by both of them for the Neapolitan stage – explored with special relish the realm of fantasy and exoticism, since, as he reported, 'I have seen that the further away from this Italy of ours I set the scene of action, the better pleased the spectators are' (Scherillo 1916: 297). But in general one may, I think, claim that the *opera buffa* in this age of mass production reverts to a condition that brings it, in many respects, closer than ever before to the *commedia dell'arte,* and to the spirit of Carnival.

Commedia had had an only marginal influence on the early *opera buffa,* where a realistic observation of everyday life had been the central inspiration; in Goldoni's time the links between *opera buffa* and his reformed comedy necessarily meant that the influence of *commedia* was a very indirect one. Now we enter a world in which the tone is predominantly farcical (though not ribaldly so); in which sensitive Tuscan lovers compete for the honours with a number of comic types, at least one of whom speaks dialect; and in which unproblematic laughter and the unconditional play of fantasy are far more important than either the correction of morals, or a truthful picture of real life. Cerlone and Lorenzi, the two leading Neapolitan librettists of the period, were both deeply versed in the arts of the *commedia*; indeed some of Cerlone's prose comedies still leave scope for improvisation. Lorenzi had served his theatrical apprenticeship as the 'amoroso' and as a writer of *scenarii* in a group of amateurs, who regularly performed *commedia* at the home of the Duca di Maddaloni; and his opera plots remain *scenario*-like, their chief *raison d'être* being to provide openings for *lazzi* and *tirate.* But the whole repertory, not just Lorenzi's, is full of *tirata*-like aria texts, of inane horse-play, and of dialogues modelled on those of the *commedia,* even if sometimes – like the burlesque Socratic dialogues in *Socrate immaginario* – they are wittily fashioned to fit the dramatic context.

Don Tammaro:	Dimmi insapiente simia, che cosa spinge l'asini?
Calandrino:	Il bastone.
Don Tammaro:	Quando il capo corpore o col pensiero comanda i membri, i membri cosa fanno?
Calandrino:	Si muovano.
Don Tammaro:	Va bene! Or dimmi, il capo chi è tra discepoli?
Calandrino:	Il maestro.
Don Tammaro:	E se capo è il maestro, li discepoli che cosa sono poi?
Calandrino:	Son tanti membri.
Don Tammaro:	Dunque muover ti dei giacchè membro di Socrate tu sei.
Calandrino:	Son convinto.[3] (Act I scene 4)

The conjunction of a farcical intrigue with the technical and musical resources of the fully mature *opera buffa* stimulated composers to explore the possibility of writing music that was, in its own right, comical. Perhaps the most striking single difference between *opera buffa* of this and of earlier periods is how much funnier the musical numbers have become. This is especially true with Paisiello, of whom Hermann Abert wrote, 'the mad and adventurous *buffo* spirit of the Italians here celebrates veritable orgies; the most impossible juxtapositions clash together, creating a confusion whose wild comedy was achieved only by Rossini among later composers, and which Mozart never even approached' (Abert 1978, I: 366). This comicality is particularly characteristic of the ensembles – the finales, the dramatic ensembles that transferred the technique of the finale to other turning points in the action, and the multitude of *gliuòmmaro*-like pieces which proliferated throughout the score, wherever librettist and composer felt that some ludicrously tangled situation could profitably be captured in a musical *lazzo*. Many of the comic resources developed with such inventive verve at this time sprang from seeds that were latent, indeed were sometimes growing healthily in Pergolesi or even in Alessandro Scarlatti. But thanks to the spread of the ensemble and to the freer use made of the orchestra, they could now be exploited in a denser and more riotous abandon.

A distinctive feature of the late-eighteenth-century *opera buffa* is the perfection of a technique referred to by contemporaries as 'nota e parola'. It will be recalled that some of Pergolesi's comic arias depended for their effect on a very busy, bustling and emphatic delivery of the words. But as long as the orchestra remained so subservient, the voice still had, in addition, to provide the theme and the rhythm of the music. By the 1760s the orchestra had come to take a fuller part, and Paisiello, quite early in his career, had mastered a style in which words could be delivered freer and faster, in a *parlato* that was sometimes tuneful, sometimes merely functional, but which in either case acquired a measure of musical poise thanks to antiphonal alternations of voice and orchestra (Ex.IV.12). The *nota e parola* style became even more *tirata*-like as a result of further technical developments later in the century: orchestral ritornellos that do not merely introduce the themes of the aria but which in their profusion of figures and their cumulative momentum seem – one might say – designed to build up a head of steam; sudden plunges into remote keys to give a fresh zest to a game that threatens to grow stale; orchestral themes against which the voice can patter away on reciting notes as fast as may be. All these features are well known from their classic formulation in Figaro's 'Largo al factotum', but before the end of the eighteenth century the *nota e parola* style was fully mature and already being applied to ensembles with masterly effect – in Cimarosa's *Matrimonio segreto* (Vienna 1792) for instance.

Another achievement of this period was the transformation of the

I forget I'm an idol, with smacks and slaps. . .

Ex.IV.12 Paisiello, *L'idolo cinese* (1767), Act I scene 7

gliuòmmaro, still much more common than the genuinely dramatic ensemble. A type of movement which had been written in an animated but rather featureless *parlato* was reshaped to form a witty and sometimes farcical musical *lazzo*. One may perhaps see the origin of this development in Pergolesi's fondness for various types of incongruous juxtapositions: high notes followed by low – quick-moving notes followed by slow-moving ones – the sharply profiled characterization in his *intermezzo* finales. The difference in the mature *opera buffa* ensemble is that such effects are no longer one-dimensional; the antithesis can be layered up in textures that create a full-bodied musical image of the dramatic situation. The result may be merely farcical, as in the trio for the raging Dr Bartolo and his two servants – one yawning and one sneezing – in Paisiello's *Il barbiere di Siviglia* (St Petersburg 1782); but the potential of this technique for poignant and searching dramatic irony – such as we are familiar with in Mozart – was well known in Italy too, as an excerpt from Simon Mayr will serve to illustrate (Ex.IV.13).

From the naive onomatopoeia of the *intermezzo*, the *opera buffa* devel-

Ex.IV.13 Mayr, *Che originali* (1798), Act I scene 6

What simperings, what poses. . . You are my idol. . .they are mad. . . You
are my soul. . . Where's the rope?. . . Ye benevolent gods, protect such
great love and faith.

Ex.IV.13 *continued*

oped another of its favourite comic resources. Composers found that
ensembles offered infinite possibilities for – to put it crudely – making
funny noises. The exploration of absurdity in sound had a long history
before the young Rossini embarked on his incomparably droll sallies. It was
especially popular in what da Ponte called the 'strepitoso, arcistrepitoso,
strepitosissimo' section of the finale, that scene of maximum pandemonium
that almost always immediately precedes the end of the act. Countless are

341

Ex.IV.14 Guglielmi, *La virtuosa di Mergellina* (1785), Act I scene 10

I hear a buzzing in my head. . .and a millwheel which forever spins me
round faster and faster. . .

Ex.IV.14 *continued*

the movements in which poetic metaphor and musical onomatopeia riot together in hilarious orgy. A good example closes Act I of Guglielmi's *La virtuosa di Mergellina* (Naples 1785); though when we look at the excerpts in Ex.IV.14, we can hardly fail to notice the absence of that orchestral resourcefulness that was to give Rossini's essays in the style so much of their matchless verve.

The crowning witticism of the mature *buffo* style is the accommodation of all these farcical, incongruous and anarchic elements into structures of immaculate symmetry, based on repetitions of almost clockwork regularity. These patterns can be very funny in themselves, as in 'Se fiato in corpo avete' (*Il matrimonio segreto* Act II scene 1), where two men who are squabbling violently sing identical music spaced out in the most deferential symmetry. More often, particularly perhaps in Cimarosa, we have the feeling that the drama is being transformed into a witty and sophisticated form of play, a manifestation of that *facultas ludendi* that flourished in so much eighteenth-century art (Huizinga 1949: 186–9). Stendhal was to define *opera buffa* (and Cimarosa was probably the composer he had in mind) as 'chaos organized and made perfect'.

As librettists and composers explored the wealth of new comic resources, their delight in older forms of fun did not fail. Many an opera has as its subject the parody of the conventions of *opera seria*, or the social customs of the opera-house. And more fleeting parodies of the heroic style and jokes at the expense of its great representative figure, Metastasio, are everywhere to be found. Scherillo quotes examples from Lorenzi's *Fra i due litiganti* text which presuppose an intimate familiarity with Metastasio's work (Scherillo 1916: 395); but a more casual acquaintance is sufficient to enjoy the jokes about Aristea's costume in *Che originali* – she is the singing daughter of a man crazily obsessed with music (Ex.IV.15). Of the composers, Paisiello was especially fond of parody: according to Abert, at least one example of parody is found in all his operas up to 1775 (Abert 1918–19: 407), and from that same year his celebrated send-up, in *Socrate immaginario*, of Gluck's *Orfeo* – very topical in Naples at the time – is one of the most sustained and still enjoyable specimens of parody in the history of opera (Ex.IV.16).

The musical language of late-eighteenth-century *opera buffa*

Paisiello, Cimarosa and their contemporaries were not only capable of being very funny; they commanded a musical language of great beauty too, at once sensuous and eloquent; for, to cope with the widening range of subject, composers had, from the middle of the century at least, drawn deeply on the *opera seria* and on the orchestral and chamber repertory of Central Europe. One clear sign of the growing sumptuousness of the later

(Voice parts only)

Here are flowers. . .alla Olimpiade. . .those feathers. . .alla Zenobia. . .
that garment of yours. . .alla Orazia. . .those little curls. . .alla Nitteti. . .
that wrap. . .alla Ipermestra. . .

Ex.IV.15 Mayr, *Che originali* (1798), Act I scene 7

buffo idiom was the gradual enlargement of the orchestra. In the 1750s
woodwind and brass instruments had supplemented the basic string group
only for certain numbers in the score. Flutes or clarinets or trumpets were
indeed rare enough to have still something of the effect of *obbligato*
instruments. By 1800 a 'classical' symphony orchestra was standard, even
in comparatively small theatres such as the San Benedetto at Venice. Some
critics saw this development as nothing more than a symptom of declining
taste, a source of gratuitous complexity and noisiness. But despite the
critics, composers were persuaded of the need for a larger orchestra because
they appreciated the scope it offered for dramatic colouring, or even
occasionally for poetic tone-painting. Paisiello's *L'idolo cinese* begins with
an exquisite example of such tone-painting, combined with simple,
expressive lyricism of a kind that was never forgotten, even in the most
voluptuous phase of the tradition (Ex.IV.17). Though orchestras grew,

. . . I return, dear furies. . . No! Must I then remain here? Yes! But at
least, beauteous furies, be less stubborn with me. . .

Ex.IV.16 Paisiello, *Socrate immaginario* (1775), Act II scene 10

there was no corresponding enlargement of the vocal resources: most
operas required some seven or eight soloists, and if a chorus was wanted,
'all the actors sing from off-stage', to borrow a phrase from the score of *La
grotta di Trofonio* (Naples 1785), Act I scene 5. (Similar rubrics are found in
other scores.) Paisiello led the way in abandoning the artificial high voices
of the *opera seria* in favour of the natural tenor for *parti serie*.

The solo aria reached a peak of expansiveness, refinement and expressiveness: if one were to seek for comparisons in the more familiar operatic repertory it would be to *Idomeneo* rather than *Le nozze di Figaro* that one would turn. Most of the characters in a Paisiello opera who are not broadly comic are kin to Don Ottavio or Fiordiligi. Rondo forms are

Ex.IV.17 Paisiello, *L'idolo cinese* (1767), Act I scene 1

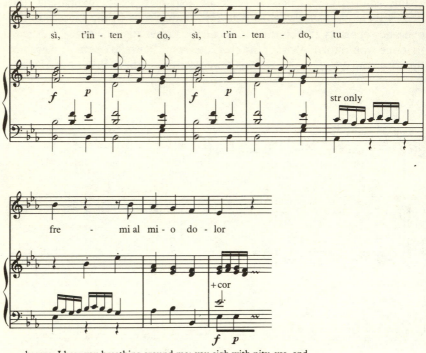

... breeze, I hear you breathing around me; you sigh with pity, yes, and
you tremble at my sorrow; yes, I hear you.

Ex.IV.17 *continued*

sometimes used (*Nina* Act I, scene 6); the shorter 'cavatina' continues to be
popular for entrance arias[4] and on rare occasions – as a device of dramatic
expression or characterization – elements of popular music seem still to be
drawn upon. A memorable example is the shepherd's song, accompanied
on the 'zampogne' (bagpipes), in Paisiello's *Nina* (Ex.IV.18). But in the
majority of cases the aria is a sonata-like or concerto-like structure: one
rather prefers the term 'concerto' because of the scale and the scope of the
ritornellos. The orchestra is highlighted not only here, but often in the
'second subjects' too, where, in Paisiello in particular, the thematic burden
is sometimes carried by the woodwind, or where voice and orchestra seem
to discourse together, or the orchestra to prompt or complement the
half-articulated feelings of the singer (Ex.IV.19).

   While the individual movements of the opera had become more
monumental than ever before, the structure of the opera as a whole had
become more flexible. It was no longer dominated by the pattern of
recitativo semplice and solo aria, for ensembles had become far more
numerous, particularly under the influence of the 'Viennese' librettists

Now the sun sets behind the mountain, and with its departure the
meadow becomes less beautiful.

Ex.IV.18 Paisiello, *Nina* (1790), Act I scene 9

Casti and da Ponte. Particularly interesting, because it marked a second
stage in the quest for musico-dramatic continuity, was the emergence of the
ensemble *introduzione*. One may postulate various motives for this development: to some extent, as we saw in the case of Goldoni's *La calamita
de'cuori*, it is a variation on an old *commedia dell'arte* feature, that of starting

But fondly in my heart some trace of love. . .

Ex.IV.19 Paisiello, *La grotta di Trofonio* (1785), Act II scene 5

the show by parading the characters in a kind of trailer; to some extent it may be the result of a spontaneous dramatic urge to pitch the spectacular *in medias res*, with a *gliuòmmaro* which would – by analogy with the finale – suggest a musical setting in ensemble form. But probably the crucial point is that the emergence of the fully fledged *introduzione* went hand in hand with the transformation of the traditional sinfonia. The standard Italian opera sinfonia – which furnished the crude prototype for the classical symphony – was a three-movement, fast–slow–fast, composition. In the 1760s Paisiello began to abandon this form in favour of one in a single movement, in 'sonata-form', except that a *concertino*-like episode tended to occupy the place of the development. But at the same time – perhaps looking back to an old *opera seria* custom of linking the close of the overture with the opening of the first scene (cf. p. 161 above) – Paisiello composed what he seems to have regarded as substitutes for the suppressed orchestral movements in the form of vocal tableaux. An interesting example is found in *Socrate immaginario*. At the end of the opening 'Allegro con spirito', inscribed 'Overtura', is written 'segue aperta di panno', and the opening vocal sextet is then actually entitled 'overtura di panno' – i.e. 'for the opening of the curtain'. Abert reports a nearly comparable case in Piccinni's *I viaggiatori* (Naples 1775), where the third movement of the sinfonia is replaced by a 'sung introduction' (Abert 1978, I: 357). Would it be making too much of a semantic detail to point out Paisiello's preference for the term 'Overtura' rather than 'Sinfonia'? Did he mean to suggest by this a change in function from the quite extraneous 'symphonic' entertainment that preceded the start of the opera in earlier days, to a movement that bridged the transition out of the social environment of the theatre into a world of make-believe as the curtains opened – at the 'overtura di panno'? The introductory vocal movement of *L'idolo cinese* (1767) was already a well developed dramatic ensemble in four linked movements. But the *introduzione* showed no decisive preference for such a scheme; other examples tended in quite the opposite direction, becoming statuesque settings of the scene. Such a solution was particularly tempting when a chorus was available, as in the original Caserta version of Paisiello's *Nina* – ultimately the model for the opening scenes of *La sonnambula* and *Luisa Miller* – where we hear an idealized peasantry singing of the joys of their simple life and in particular of their affection for the romantic heroine.

With Paisiello we have reached the composer to whom his successors, rightly or wrongly, attributed the invention of the *parlante* technique. This was one of the most seminal and influential techniques of the age, in Italy or anywhere else, for, elaborated and refined, it was to become the means by which – several generations later – was achieved the Romantic ideal of continuous music drama. The task Paisiello and his contemporaries set themselves was that of sustaining the cogency of the music even in those sections of the score where there was no scope for a lyrical, song-based continuity. And the technique they devised was that of entrusting the principal theme to the orchestra. There, safely in the background, it could be repeated, played in different keys, varied, even developed, without becoming oppressive; and while the orchestra thus guaranteed musical coherence, the voices were free to deliver the text in a declamatory,

Ex.IV.20 Paisiello, *La grotta di Trofonio* (1785), Act II scene 10

I wish, I command, and give order. . .that the noble Don Gasparone. . .
I draw near and still I wish. . . If they are not going to do this. . .

Ex.IV.20 *continued*

naturally paced manner, that required no intrinsic lyrical interest whatever
(Ex.IV.20). Rossini complained of the primitiveness of Paisiello's *parlante*,
regarding Cimarosa as its first real master; and it is true that Paisiello's
examples do suffer from a certain relentlessness and an apparent failure to
relate such musical incidents as modulation to the dramatic function. But,
following Abert, one may look at things in a more positive spirit, seeing

Paisiello's orchestral themes as being related to 'primitive noises' (and hence perhaps to the comic onomatopoeia of the *buffo* tradition) and to the improvisatory instrumental practices of folk music (Abert 1918–19: 412). This view, if it does not improve Paisiello's technique, at least suggests that the style was congruous and well rooted in the tradition. In any case, the crucial thing was that the *parlante* put into the composer's hands a matchless tool for controlling the dramatic pace of the opera – in some cases, one almost feels, of 'producing' the scene, in the modern sense – by purely musical means.

Rossini

The great age of *opera buffa* closed with Cimarosa's *Il matrimonio segreto* at Vienna in 1792. None of the later works of Cimarosa or Paisiello or any of their lesser contemporaries achieved the same classic status. Of the leading masters of the genre Anfossi died in 1797, Cimarosa himself in 1801, Guglielmi in 1804; Paisiello's later years were unproductively blighted in the turmoil of political faction. By the early years of the nineteenth century *opera buffa* was in full decline. Ideological and literary fashions provided nothing from which it could refresh itself; there were no distinctive and exciting new talents among the composers. In *La supplica di Melpomene e di Talia* (1804) Vincenzo Monti commented on the general bleakness of the scene:

> Del dramma comico
> Non dico niente
> V'avria pericolo
> D'un accidente.
> Goffo il soggetto
> Ladro il libretto
> Tutto un orribile
> Bestialità.[5]
> (Rinaldi 1965: 16)

It is easy to imagine that to the more strenuous idealists of the Napoleonic Age the charm of the *opera buffa* must have seemed insipid and trifling. Nevertheless, no sooner had a truly original voice made itself heard again, speaking the *buffa* language with verve and wit, than audiences flocked to the theatres as in the great days at Naples; once more a composer of *opera buffa* became a European sensation, his music stamped indelibly on the sensibility of every connoisseur on the continent.

Rossini was called by his teacher at the Bologna Liceo Musicale, Stanislao Mattei, *Il Tedeschino* – 'the little German'. It was not the first time such a reproach had been levelled at a young Italian composer, nor was it to be the last. From at least the time of Jommelli down to Verdi and even Puccini, the leading men of each new generation of Italian composers were charged with neglecting the truth and simplicity of their native tradition of song and worshipping the false, Gothic, idols of harmony and instrumentation. In Rossini's case, however, there is absolutely no doubt about his enthusiasm for German music, nor of its formative influence on him. Much of his craft of composition he acquired from Haydn, whose string quartets he spent long hours scoring; the 'always adorable' Mozart was, he told Felix Moscheles, 'my idol and my master'. Manifestly one of his own ambitions as a composer was to achieve, in his own modest, personal fashion, that fusion of Italian and German styles which he saw as the secret of Mozart's unapproachable perfection:

The Germans have always been at every time the greatest harmonists and the Italians the greatest melodists. But from the moment that the north produced a Mozart, we of the south were beaten on our own ground, because this man rises above both nations, uniting in himself all the charms of Italian melody and all the profundity of German harmony.   (to Naumann, 1867; in Toye 1954: 233)

With Haydn and Mozart as his idols, Rossini could not but set himself the highest standards, and early achieved mastery of his craft. Indeed, by the time he wrote *La cambiale di matrimonio* (Venice 1810) at the age of eighteen, he was, among Italians, in a class of his own. His command of contrapuntal artifice was effortless, as we see in the duet for the two basses, where he uses the scholastic device of augmentation to illuminate the ludicrous confrontation between the excitable Mill and the phlegmatic Slook (Ex.IV.21). The subtlety and breadth of the harmony in the slow introduction of the sinfonia and the variety and wit of the rhythms in the Allegro show how apt a pupil of Haydn the young Italian had been.

No doubt Rossini also learned much of the art of orchestration from his study of Haydn and Mozart. It was this aspect of his music that most often prompted the accusation that it was 'too German'. He liked to use a large orchestra (by the standards of the time); he took great care over the details of the scoring, and allotted a very full share in the proceedings to the woodwind and brass instruments. To some extent his 'Germanizing' of the Italian opera orchestra had been anticipated by Simon Mayr, a composer of Bavarian birth who had been resident in Italy since 1787. But what could be forgiven a 'barbarian' was less easily tolerated in a native Italian. In 1810 there were already protests from some of the cast of *La cambiale di matrimonio* that their singing was being drowned by the din of the accompanying instruments (Toye 1954: 20); and that became a never-ending refrain in the criticism of Rossini's music by his contemporaries. A characteristic specimen is found in a discussion of *La gazza ladra* (Milan 1817) in the Venetian *Giornale teatrale* in 1822:

the tempest of notes, not leaving you a moment to breathe, the timpani, the pipes, the trumpets, the horns and the entire family of the noisiest instruments assault you, transport you, trick you, intoxicate you, and many times transmute a sort of tragedy into a bacchanalia, a houses of mourning into a festivity . . .   (Weinstock 1968: 77)

When we read, as we often do in early-nineteenth-century criticism, of the singers being sacrificed by Rossini to the orchestra, it is tempting for the modern critic simply to dismiss the comment as the merest nonsense. But that will not quite do. The truth of the matter surely was that Rossini had a more developed sense of delight in the physical properties of music – texture and sonority, rhythm and dynamics, the colours of voices and instruments, the babble of words – than any earlier composer. And very early in his career he perceived the immense comic potential of these things. We can hear the unmistakable individuality of the Rossini sound at its simplest in the 'Misipípí, pípí, pípí' of Pacuvio's aria 'Ombretta sdegnosa' in *La pietra di paragone* (Milan 1812), and in its most riotous Bacchanalian ecstasy, in the Act I finale of *L'Italiana in Algeri* (Venice 1813), with its layering of 'din din', 'tac tac', 'cra cra', 'boum boum', its shimmering strings and skirling piccolos. The most sensational manifestation of the physicality of the composer's genius was, of course, the Rossini crescendo, in which he gave an authoritative personal stamp to a number of musical mannerisms that had long lurked inchoate in the *buffo* style. 'The author seems' – wrote Leigh Hunt – 'to delight in expressing a precipitate and multitudinous mirth; and sometimes works up and torments a passage, and pours in instrument upon instrument, till orchestra and singers all appear drunk with uproariousness, and ready to die on the spot' (Osborne 1986: 64).

Ex.IV.21 Rossini, *La cambiale di matrimonio* (1810)

This may be how an American behaves, but it's no good hoping to
swindle me. . . This is the way an honest man behaves: I'll pay you what
is owed and not expect any change.

Ex.IV.21 *continued*

These kinds of element had traditionally been regarded as the mere
superficies of music, having little to do with that quest for nature, truth and
beauty, that was so dear to the eighteenth century. With Rossini they
became essential and integral, part of the very quiddity of the music. This
was particularly true of rhythm. 'In rhythm resides all the power and
expressiveness of music', he once remarked (quoted Lippmann 1969a:
292), clearly expecting the comment to be received in the spirit of a mildly
improper *bon mot*. But Italian contemporaries seem to have believed him,
and dancing, strutting and swinging rhythms became one of the most
distinctive hallmarks of the repertory in the first half of the nineteenth

century. Few of Rossini's qualities are so individual as his brilliant handling of rhythm, on the small scale and on the large. Particularly characteristic are those juxtapositions in his large-scale ensembles, of stasis and momentum, of long freezes in which time stands still (often achieved by canonic writing for the voices), and explosions of zany, cavorting exuberance (in the form of *parlantes* or *strettas*). When one has once heard Rossini, the high spirits of Cimarosa and even Paisiello seems positively decorous. Geltrude Righetti-Giorgi, the alto who created the role of Rosina in *Il barbiere di Siviglia* (Rome 1816), recalled in her memoirs that among his contemporaries Rossini enjoyed the reputation (together with Mozart) of being a 'paladin of velocity' (Gallarati 1977: 257).

The contrived artifice of Rossini's rhythm is a major factor in the unique and individual flavour of his *opera buffa*, in its almost menacing vitality. It is as if the Carnival spirit that inspires Paisiello's most hilarious scenes had undergone a hypertrophic development, while those ideals of Nature and Humanity that inspired so much of the best comic opera between 1750 and 1790 had withered away. For despite the sentimental traits in *La Cenerentola*, and the further cultivation of rustic idyll in some pages of *La gazza ladra* (one of the most conspicuous milestones on the road from Paisiello's *Nina* to Bellini's *La sonnambula*), Rossini's work was quite remote from that humane and benign comedy at which the Enlightenment had aimed. By his time the librettos of *opera buffa* had lost their contemporaneity; the educative scope of the age of Goldoni had been abandoned. Unlike the *opera buffa* of that Golden Age, that of the nineteenth century looked back to the past, and in its most typical forms became a piece of exhilarating escapism – a fairy-tale fantasy, or an exotic dream of amorous encounters with moustache-twirling Turks. Even satire was largely aimless, a sending-up of human foibles which had no particular timeliness (as did those mocked by Goldoni) but which could be the source of a certain amount of preposterous fun, like the spirit of cool Anglo-Saxon mercantilism with which, in *La cambiale di matrimonio*, Mr Slook of Canada approaches matrimony: 'Sir, I have decided to form a matrimonial company. There is no suitable firm here, so kindly send me, on the first ship sailing for this colony, a wife of the following form and quality: . . .' (Act I scene 1). It has often been observed that Romani's text for *Il turco in Italia* (Milan 1814) is the perfect microcosm – one might almost say, parable – of the *opera buffa* of its period. No social foible, no issue of nature or humanity is at stake: Prosdocimo, the poet, simply roams the world looking for some incident that can be knocked into the shape of arias, trios, quartets and finales with the single aim of making an audience laugh.

Il turco possesses supremely and obviously a quality which is common to most, perhaps all, of Rossini's operatic comedies. It plays ironically and parodistically with the established conventions of the style; it is, to borrow a phrase of Stefan Kunze, 'ein Spiel mit dem *déjà vu*' (Kunze 1982: 76). Romani's libretto is a sparkling, witty example of the current type of *opera buffa* – consider, for example, the duet where the Turkish prince Selim and Don Geronio dispute their claims to Fiorilla, the Don's fickle and flirtatious wife:

Selim: D'un bell'uso in Turchia
          Forse avrai novella intesa;
          Della moglie che gli pesa
          Il marito è venditor.
Geronio: Sarà l'uso molto buono,
          Ma in Italia è più bell'uso:
          Il marito rompe il muso
          All'infame tentator.[6]   (Act II scene 2)

But the figure of the poet hovers about the scene, provides a distancing effect, makes of the ludicrous action, deliberately and avowedly, a spectacle and a game, to be enjoyed for the skill with which it is played:

Poeta [godendo dello spettacolo] Seguitate . . . via . . . bravissime!
                                   Qua . . . là . . . bene; in questo modo
                                   Azzuffatevi, stringetevi,
                                   Graffi, morsi . . . me lo godo . . .
                                   Che final! che finalone!
                                   Oh! che chiasso avrà da far.[7]   (Act I scene 17)

What is true of Romani's libretto for *Il turco* is true of Rossini's whole art of *buffo* composition. His operas are full of those same conventional structures that Prosdocimo was seeking, and their design is formalized and pre-fabricated to a degree. Quite accurately Wagner spoke of Rossini's 'quadratische Tonsatzkonstruktion'. But how inept such ponderous terminology sounds in the light of the scintillating dance of colour and rhythm, the verve and quirkiness of the musical ideas that play on the surface of these constructional blocks. Virtually all the elements of Rossini's musical language assume a 'ludic' character, which, far from aiming at any kind of imitation of life, sets it apart from life, and gives it the quality of ceremony or play. Many an aria or ensemble starts out from a close observation of character, or situation, or expressive truth; but such qualities are rapidly drowned out in the course of the song by the sparkling torrents of coloratura and the intoxicating dance of the rhythms. Rossini's celebrated 'canto fiorito' is, as Kunze very justly observes, clearly not intended either as parody or as the mere decoration of some simpler underlying melody (1982: 89). It is a sparkling and delicious essence in its own right, one of the ironic artifices by which Rossini's *opera buffa* is distanced from 'real life'.

The nearest thing to an artistic testament left by Rossini was the record of his conversation with Wagner in 1860 – though it is difficult to have much faith in the high-falutin' style in which Michotte transcribed it. He felt that the composer must, by the very nature of his art, claim some measure of independence from the words he was setting. It was not his task simply to declaim, or illustrate, or interpret the text; for, as he put it in a letter to Pacini in January 1866, 'this art . . . has as its only basis the Ideal and Emotion' (Weinstock 1968: 471). Apparently his aesthetics remained fundamentally those of the eighteenth century; and he aimed to give an ideal form to the impulses of the heart and the well-springs of character that lay behind and beyond the text. The novelty, indeed the sensation of the Rossini phenomenon, was due to the fact that – in comedy at any rate – these ideal forms unfolded not as decorous rituals but as madcap larkings. Such energy and such dynamism did Rossini's music possess that its powers seemed almost demonic; objective and aesthetically antiquated he may have been, and the librettos he set may have been mere escapist fantasies, but he swept the age of Napoleon off its feet. And in the soporific Age of Legitimacy that succeeded Napoleon in 1815, Rossini's operas still had the power, as in the case of Stendhal, to inspire the passion of a lifetime or, as Heine's testimony shows, to set the whole of Italy ablaze.

The decline of *opera buffa*

The last of Rossini's genuine and full-scale *opere buffe*, *La Cenerentola*, was composed as early as 1817. In his last active years in Italy he devoted himself to *opera seria*, setting a precedent that was followed by most of his younger contemporaries. Notwithstanding such delectable exceptions as Donizetti's *L'elisir d'amore* (Milan 1832) and *Don Pasquale* (Paris 1843), the repertory of the Romantic age was overwhelmingly heroic and tragic. The sentimental idyllic *semi-seria* genre, initiated by Piccinni's *Buona figliuola* and Paisiello's *Nina* and represented in the nineteenth century by such works as Bellini's *La sonnambula* (Milan 1831) and Donizetti's *Linda di Chamounix* (Vienna 1842), enjoyed some popularity, but the true *opera buffa* never recovered a central position in Italian musical life. A brief revival of the form in the 1850s produced a crop of pieces of which the best was probably *Crispino e la comare* by the Ricci brothers (Venice 1850); but this revival was illusory, perhaps the result of nothing more than a bout of escapism encouraged by the more stringent censorship which was imposed after the political upheavals of 1848–49. A shrewd observer such as Felice Romani, the master librettist of the age, and author of such *buffo* gems as *Il turco in Italia* and *L'elisir d'amore*, could already see in the 1830s that the genre was doomed. Writing in the *Gazzetta piemontese* in April 1839 he described it as a 'languishing, one might say chronic invalid, which the howlings and lamentings (piagnolona) of the new *opera seria* threaten every day to reduce to an extremity' (Rinaldi 1965: 422).

Thus it was that while Rossini's serious operas were slowly superseded in public favour by Bellini and Donizetti in the 1830s, and by Verdi in the 1840s, his comic operas remained unsurpassed – peerless models of style which any composer who wished to essay the *buffa* genre had to emulate. Their continued popularity in the theatre is charmingly testified by the same Romani: 'they fill the coffers of all the impresarios in the peninsula, exhilarate the ponderous Germans, inflame the frigid Britons, and make even the pensive Quakers of Pennsylvania dance with joy' (*Gazzetta piemontese*, 1 January 1840, in Rinaldi 1965: 373). There was, in technical terms, comparatively little to distinguish comic and serious opera in the post-Rossini age. The structures of *opera buffa* tended to be a little more concise and formal, the style a little simpler, the texture a little lighter. And a more conspicuous place was found for those operatic idioms that gave a good actor – particularly the *buffo* bass – the best opportunity to make the most of his words; *note e parole* arias remained popular, the old *recitativo semplice* with figured bass accompaniment survived into the second half of the century, and especially conspicuous was the *parlante*, the *sine qua non* of the mature *buffo* style since Paisiello. By this time the *parlante* had long become an established element in all types of opera, but its key role in *opera buffa* at once becomes clear if one looks at the conscientious, almost exhausting, way Donizetti handles it in such early comedies as *L'ajo nell'imbarazzo* (Rome 1824). Even Verdi first learned to handle the *parlante* in *opera buffa* – the ill-fated *Un giorno di regno* (Milan 1840).

Insofar as the *opera buffa* of the Romantic age could be said to have had a backbone, it was still provided by elements surviving from the *commedia dell'arte*. The four central figures of Donizetti's *Don Pasquale* – particularly Pasquale himself, 'an old bachelor set in old-fashioned ways, parsimonious, credulous, obstinate, but a good fellow at heart', as the libretto describes him – might easily have come from a seventeenth-century *scenario*. Generally the most forceful character in the opera is a masterful young lady who knows exactly how to get her man: clearly she descends from the eighteenth-century *soubrette*, though librettists are commendably resourceful in bringing her up to date. Ferretti's Gilda in *L'ajo nell'imbarazzo* is particularly delightful – a colonel's daughter whose glances, she complacently informs us, are like cannonshot knocking men off the battlements. Occasionally, as in Luigi Ricci's *Un avventura di Scaramuccia* – text by Romani (Milan 1834) – the traditional masks return. The evening's *pièces de résistance* tend still to be *tirate* of a classic cut: auto-biographical patter songs (e.g. 'Dapprima, figuratevi', *Crispino e la comare*, text Piave), spoof exhibitions of professional, especially medical, erudition (e.g. Donizetti's 'Mie Signore onorate', *La campanella* (Naples 1836)); and finale-*stretti* in the form of a crescendo of onomatopoeic and preposterous metaphors.

Parody and topical allusion remain favourite resources both for librettists and composers. Norina's *sortita* (entrance aria) in *Don Pasquale* purports to quote from a sentimental novel, prompting Donizetti to a simpering cantabile in which every phrase closes with mannered coloratura. Romani, translating and adapting Scribe's *Le philtre* to form the libretto of *L'elisir d'amore*, rewrites Belcore's (Jolicoeur's) *sortita* to turn it into a delicious piece of mock-classicism:

Je suis sargent,	Come Paride vezzoso
Brave et galant	Porse il pomo alla più bella
Et je mène tambour brillant	Mia diletta villanella
Et la gloire et le sentiment . . .	Io ti porgo questo fior . . .[8]

Crispino, at the start of the Ricci brothers' opera, sings a melancholy *canzone* in a quasi-popular § style, 'Una volta un ciabattino', which is surely intended as a droll allusion to Cenerentola's 'Un volta c'era un re'. Topicality must have been part of the fun with the galops and polkas in Luigi Ricci's operas, and in Donizetti's *Il campanello*.

The Ricci brothers' fondness for waltzes, polkas, and galops – Romani described it as an 'itch for monferrine and waltzes' (*Gazzetta piemontese*, 20 April 1839, in Rinaldi 1965: 437) – makes *Crispino e la comare* somewhat redolent of a Viennese operetta. Other operetta-like touches are not unknown in the repertory, notably at the close of *L'elisir d'amore*, where the final aria is set as a reprise of the 'barcarole' sung earlier in the act. There is no dramatic point to this; it is simply an enjoyable repetition of a number that Donizetti can be confident will have gone down well. But this same opera – an Italian reworking of an operetta-like French model – provided a splendid demonstration of the fact, that even in the days of its decline, the Italian *opera buffa* remained a properly dramatic form. Romani was not satisfied to treat the characters in the French style of Scribe, as a group of entertainers periodically breaking into musical numbers. In the traditional Italian way he exercised the dramatist's prerogative of empathy, entering into the dilemma of the characters, and fashioning his verse to depict the ebb and flow, the growth and development of their feelings. In *L'elisir d'amore* the operetta-like refrain-based ditties of *Le philtre* are replaced by multisectional forms in which the dramatic action is embodied in the succession of musical styles.

20 · *Il barbiere di Siviglia*: Paisiello's and Rossini's settings St Petersburg 1782, Rome 1816

Beaumarchais as a source of *opera buffa*

Our starting point should perhaps be the fact that, unlike the protagonists of the operas we have studied hitherto, all of whom were products of a Classical Mediterranean culture, Figaro derives from French literature. He is the hero of a trilogy of plays – *Le barbier de Séville*, *Le mariage de Figaro*, and *La mère coupable* – written and produced in Paris between 1772 and 1792 by Pierre-Augustin Caron de Beaumarchais. And the reason this is a good starting point is that the mutual influence during the eighteenth century of French comedy and Italian comedy was one of the determining factors in the literary history of both countries.

Commedia dell'arte troupes had performed in Paris as far back as the sixteenth century. Early in the reign of Louis XIV, in 1660, they had become so popular that an Italian theatre was established there. This survived, on and off, for a century until, in 1762, it was merged with the Opéra Comique. The influence of the *commedia dell'arte* on French culture was incalculable: Molière's comic art was rooted in it; some of Watteau's most haunting images were inspired by it; and even in its eighteenth-century decline it continued to fascinate and stimulate dramatists, especially Marivaux and Beaumarchais. But conversely, when Italians of the Age of Enlightenment looked to reform their own traditions of comedy, it was to France that they turned for guidance. Molière became the revered tutelary spirit of literary comedy, and a favoured source even for the operatic *intermezzo*.

Beaumarchais serves admirably as the representative figure of this fruitful interchange. A native Parisian born in 1732, he was a spectacular example of that distinctive eighteenth-century type, the adventurer. In addition to his literary activities he at various times enjoyed fame or notoriety as clock-maker, businessman, pamphleteer, courtier and diplomat. Of all these things it was, paradoxically, his connections with high society that contributed most to give his dramatic work so light a touch. A favourite pastime in the aristocratic French salons of the middle decades of the century was the *parade*. And it was in the writing of such *parades* that Beaumarchais served his dramatic apprenticeship. Four specimens survive from his pen, all of them composed for performance in the Château d'Etioles, the home of the financier Charles-Guillaume Le Normant, the indulgent husband of the lady best known to history as Madame de Pompadour. But while the environment in which the *parade* was performed was of the most opulent, the form itself was popular and earthy – indeed more earthy than any other type of written comedy cultivated in eighteenth-century France.

The *parades* originated in the popular theatres of the Parisian fairgrounds. Their purpose was explained in a three-volume collection of such works, *Théâtre des Boulevards ou Recueil de Parades* (1756): 'in order to attract people into their dens, the fairground actors used to appear on a balcony – very narrow and as long as possible – where they improvised farces on plans which had been preserved by tradition or which they themselves had written' (Scherer 1954: 14). It is not known who first had the whim of staging such pieces as entertainments for guests in the cultivated salons of the city; but by the 1730s they were well established there. From the *parades* of the fairground, those of high society inherited a slangy, jargon-ridden language, a relish for obscenity, and – most important for our purposes – a close kinship with the *commedia dell'arte*. Though these *parades* were composed rather than improvised, their plots were often based on the *scenari* of the Italian comedians, and the characters were related to those of the traditional masks.

Beaumarchais's *parades* were among the most Italianate of the whole repertory. He seems to have known Gherardi's collection of *scenari* well, borrowing from it not only plots but much repartee too; he left more to improvisation than most authors of literary *parades* (Larthomas 1977: 22). The indebtedness of *Le barbier* to this curious theatrical form has often been commented upon: indeed the comments began with Beaumarchais himself. For among two sheets of observations which he jotted down on the comedy is found the following remark on Act II scenes 5 and 6: 'They contain something of the *parade*. Is it not a simple form of gaiety (un petit moyen de gaieté), that la Jeunesse should be old and l'Eveillé imbecile?' (*ibidem*: 37). On the other hand, there seems to be no real evidence for a claim that has sometimes been made, that *Le barbier* is actually a reworking of an early Beaumarchais *parade*.

Even when we discount that possibility, the genesis of the work is sufficiently complicated. In 1772 it was offered to the *Théâtre Italien* as an *opéra comique* – that is to say as a spoken play with songs and other musical numbers. Beaumarchais himself is thought to have been largely responsible for the music, which he had based upon genuine Spanish songs collected during his residency in Madrid. It was refused. Traditionally the refusal is said to have been caused by fear of wounding the sensibilities of a leading singer who had been a barber; but in any case Beaumarchais himself may have had second thoughts. In the 'Lettre modérée sur la chute et la critique du Barbier de Séville', which he later published in the printed edition of the text, he spoke of his disillusion with French theatre music, complaining of its lack of passion and gaiety and dramatic verve – all qualities fundamental to the success of his play. *Le barbier* was therefore rewritten. The role of music was much reduced, the text was polished and adorned with literary graces, and in January 1773 it was offered to the Comédie-Française as a four-act play. This was accepted for performance, but the production was delayed when Beaumarchais found himself involved in a number of major political and legal scandals. In fact, it was February 1775 before it was finally produced, and by then Beaumarchais had rewritten it once again. Seemingly carried away by the combative zest that had sustained him through the last eighteen months, he had seen fit to load his text with topical allusions, and satirical sallies at the expense of his adversaries. The result was a bloated five-act drama which failed abjectly and was withdrawn after one performance. Three days later, Beaumarchais was ready with another revision, the four-act version with which we are familiar today, and which was presumably very close to the form of the play as originally presented to the Comédie-Française in 1773. Even this was not quite the end of the story. For the comedy still retained five musical numbers from the original *opéra comique*, and one at least of these, 'Quand, dans la pleine', prompted a typically Gallic brouhaha at the première. Why, one wonders? Was the quantity of music an infringement of the decorum of the genre? A footnote which Beaumarchais appended to this scene clearly suggests as much:

This arietta in the Spanish style was sung at the Paris première despite the hooting, the noise and racket, customary in the pit in those days of crisis and combat. The actress's timidity has since then prevented her from daring to repeat it, and the young rigorists of the theatre have praised her warmly for this reticence. But if the dignity of the Comédie-Française has thereby gained something, it must be acknowledged that *Le barbier de Séville* has lost a great deal. That is why, in theatres where a small quantity of music will not have such great consequences, we invite all directors to restore it, all actors to sing it, all spectators to listen to it, and all critics to forgive us for it, for the benefit of the style of the play and the pleasure which the piece will give them.

(Act III scene 4)

However often revised and however fundamentally transformed, *Le barbier de Séville* is unmistakably an offshoot of the *commedia dell'arte*. Its story – an elderly guardian's attempt to hold on to his pretty young ward as a bride, and the confounding of this scheme by a young admirer aided by a resourceful servant – was 'the well-worn plot of a thousand Italian *scenarii*' (Niklaus 1968: 36). Each of the principal characters is recognizably related to the stock figures of the *commedia*. Bartholo – though we are spared the characteristic tirades of incoherent pedantry – is the traditional *Dottore*: if he lacks a mask he does have a 'grande perruque', which identifies his values as those of a vanished age, a costume of black and a scarlet cloak.

Figaro, his principal adversary, is a magnificently humane and individual transformation of the *zanni*. Niklaus finds relics of Scapino and Arlecchino in his costume (*ibidem*: 11), and Blom recognizes him as a last glorious manifestation of the French type of Harlequin created by Domenico Biancolelli for the benefit of an audience 'who did not care to have a great actor's talent wasted on the parts of dunces and dullards, but liked to see him in more spirited, witty and adroit roles' (Blom 1927: 536). Of the lovers, Rosina at least is clearly a figure from the *commedia*. Especially characteristic is the issue of tutelage, and her success in evading its constraints thanks to a combination of seeming modesty and reserve with actual quickwittedness and ruthlessness. Blom finds a Brighella latent in Basilio (that 'pauvre hère qui montre la musique à sa pupille, infatué de son art, friponneau, besoigneux, à genoux devant un écu'), and a Pepe-nappa – the Sicilian narcolept – in l'Eveillé (*ibidem*: 539, 530).

Various features of style stem from *Le barbier*'s distant origins in the *commedia*. The characterization of such figures as Figaro and Bartholo is obviously far removed from the caricature of the masks, but does at least resemble that in the total absence of any ambiguity: a preference for crystal-clear portraiture had been declared by Beaumarchais at the outset of his literary career, in the preface to *Eugénie* (1767), where he speaks of the importance of making immediately manifest to an audience the nature and intention of the characters. Particularly noteworthy is the tremendous pace of the action, and the enormous number of twists of fortune that drive it on its way. While making a startling departure from French literary tradition, this again relates the play to those dazzling games of strategy which sustained the Italian *commedia*. A mannerism of Beaumarchais's is the bravura tirade, in which items are accumulated, with something of the preposterous fluency of the *commedia tirata*. A short but typical specimen is found in Bartholo's denunciation of the Age of Enlightenment: 'Siècle barbare! . . . qu'a-t-il produit pour qu'on le loue? Sottises de toutes espèces: la liberté de penser, l'attraction, l'électricité, le tolérantisme, l'inoculation, le quinquina, *l'Encyclopédie* et les drames' (Act I scene 3). Louis XVI at least had no doubts about the sources of Beaumarchais's comic style. When Mme Campan read to him and the queen the first version of *Le mariage de Figaro*, 'the King often interrupted me with exclamations which, whether of praise or blame, were always apt. Most often he cried out: "What bad taste; this man is continually introducing to the stage the habit of the Italian *concetti*"' (Scherer 1954: 117–18).

These *commedia*-related qualities are of course not the only noteworthy elements of Beaumarchais's dramatic style. I have singled them out partly because Italy is my theme, and partly because it is precisely these things that make his plays so congenial for operatic treatment. If the characterization is lucid and unproblematic, not too dependent upon wordy analysis, then it is the kind of characterization that can best be expressed in musical terms, in terms of line, tessitura and colour, of gesture and movement. If there is a profusion of twists of fortune, then the composer has ample scope for those veerings of pace and mood and style which Da Ponte and Mozart have taught us to regard as the quintessence of the mature *opera buffa*. If the characters periodically explode into tirades, then the chances are that not a few potential aria-texts lie embedded in the play. With the benefit of a hindsight inspired by Basilio's 'Calumny-aria' we might even venture to claim that the Rossini crescendo is latent in Beaumarchais's comic style!

But having said all that, I believe a more general point about the play needs to be emphasized if we are to see why Figaro was so attractive a figure to some of the greatest masters of *opera buffa*. It is a quality we have already come across in Goldoni, but Beaumarchais seems to me to surpass the Venetian in the verve, comic invention and universality with which it is expressed. *Le barbier* is a *locus classicus* for what was surely, as far as comedy was concerned, the great cultural experience of the age: the moment when human beings cast aside their masks, broke free from the constricting stereotypes of rank and caste, and discovered the fullness of their humanity. Of course this is still a formal world, but the decorum of that formality no longer imposes limits on man's vitality and passion and wit.

Thanks to the many operatic qualities of Beaumarchais's play, the task of Paisiello's librettist, Giuseppe Petrosellini, was simple: so simple in fact that his libretto requires no real discussion. Paisiello himself, in a letter to the Abbé Galiani, described it as 'the French comedy . . . translated into Italian verse' (Loewenberg 1939: 158) and that is accurate enough; no comic invention was required, nor did Petrosellini need to recast or reorganize the action in any way. Several scenes – notably the singing-lesson scene, but also Figaro's first appearance, in the throes of musical creativity, and the serenading of Rosina – were already operatic in the play and provided the librettist with everything he required. It was Beaumarchais too who prescribed an orchestral thunderstorm between Acts III and IV (Parts III and IV in the opera). Several tirades provided aria-texts – Figaro's account of his travels, 'Scorsi già molti paesi', or Basilio's 'La calumnia, mio signore', for example. Where Beaumarchais himself provided no such guidance, it was, we learn from another of Paisiello's letters, the composer and not the librettist who decided upon 'the distribution of the musical numbers' (Loewenberg 1939: 159); it was Paisiello, that is to say, who chose those sections of Beaumarchais's fast and naturalistic dialogue which were to be emphasized and lingered over in aria or ensemble. Obviously in turning the French prose into Italian verse that was designed to be set to music, Petrosellini had to abbreviate and simplify, and much of the verve of the original dialogue was lost in the process.

Nevertheless the degree of his fidelity is notable, nowhere more so than at the close of the second part of Act I. Contrary to Paisiello's usual practice in the 1780s there is no dramatic ensemble-finale at this point (though for the Neapolitan *première* in 1787 he revised it to provide one: see Scherliess 1982); instead there is a gradual tapering away of the action. The act, like Beaumarchais's, closes with a solo scene for Rosina.

Paisiello's *Barbiere di Siviglia*

Today Paisiello's *Barbiere di Siviglia* is his best-known opera. But it is not wholly representative of the type of *opera buffa* that had evolved in Naples in the 1760s and 1770s. For it was composed during his residence in Russia, for a theatre audience with different expectations, and no tried and trusted Neapolitan colleagues were at hand to assist him in the task. The finest operas of his earlier Neapolitan years had been fashioned in collaboration with the master craftsman Lorenzi; in St Petersburg Paisiello had to make do with the inexpert Petrosellini, who limited himself to the task of translating Beaumarchais's play into Italian verse with as little creative interference as possible. Marvellously vital as the dramatic theme of the opera is, it has no roots in the teeming popular life of the streets of Naples, and makes no use of dialect. Nevertheless *Il barbiere* is one of Paisiello's masterpieces, and the fact that nothing of its effect depended upon Neapolitan topography or Neapolitan dialect helped it to travel more widely than such gems as *L'idolo cinese* or *Socrate immaginario*.

The first essential quality of Paisiello's art is already familiar to us from the work of the eighteenth-century masters of *opera seria*. In *opera buffa* too, one of the composer's most fundamental skills was that of writing music which was expressive, characteristic, and intimately bound to the words of the libretto, yet which sublimated these qualities into harmonious musical forms. To modern ears the dramatic expressiveness will often seem overwhelmed by the stylistic decorum, with its symmetrical patterns of repeated and varied and counter-poised phrases, and with those spacious orchestral introductions in which all dramatic momentum is suspended in a concerto-like résumé of the principal themes. But as the ear attunes itself, one perceives that this formal and gracious art, these suave and polished melodies, are in fact full of poetic and scenic and psychological suggestiveness. Consider for example 'Già riede primavera', sung by Rosina during her 'singing lesson' (the text is borrowed from Metastasio's canzonetta 'La primavera' – one of Petrosellini's happier touches). The aria has an extended, concerto-like ritornello, and is laid out on the most ample scale, combining sonata-like elements with the contrasting middle section and reprise of the *da capo* form. But as soon as the voice begins to sing we hear that all the details of this elaborate, 'purely musical' structure have an admirable expressive aptness. The gentle dance of the dotted rhythms in the opening theme has its source in Metastasio's image of the smiling Spring; the timing of the appearance of clarinet and bassoon *obbligato* parts confirms that they are a musical metaphor for the 'grato zeffiretto'; and as we reach the line 'scherza fra l'erba e fior', the play of the breezes and blossoms is mirrored in the little touches of thematic play between instruments and voice, and among the instruments themselves. Paisiello's art is that of all the best eighteenth-century Italians: word and tone fit like hand and glove; but never does the aptness of the music to text or situation result in obtrusive 'illustration' or in any abuse of what is natural in musical terms. To borrow the terminology of Paisiello's own day, we may say that his music translates the Natural and True (those elements of expressiveness, of characterization, the intimate relationship of word and tone) into the Ideal (the harmonious musical form).

More proper to the *opera buffa* is a type of aria bearing little resemblance to those of *opera seria*, which we may describe as the tirade-aria. Three of the *commedia*-like tirades from Beaumarchais's play are turned into such arias: Figaro's autobiographical 'Scorsi già molti paesi' (Beaumarchais, Act I scene 2), Basilio's on the art of calumny, 'La calumnia, mio signore' (Beaumarchais, Act II scene 8) and Bartolo's 'Veramente, ho torto' (Beaumarchais, Act II scene 11). Basilio's aria is not a success, which is no doubt why Rossini felt called upon to show how it ought to be done. Paisiello is incapacitated by the feeble lyric – a shapeless text with no real wit or point in the climax – and can do nothing with it but set it in a conventional aria form. He goes through it twice over, once in a progression from tonic to dominant, once in a matching progression from dominant back to tonic; and that repetitive symmetry destroys the whole point of the piece which, as Rossini was to show, lies in the idea of a single, irresistible, unbroken crescendo.

But where the text gives him half a chance, Paisiello proves a redoubtable master of the style. What, for instance, could better parallel the effect of a tirade than the *allegro* of Figaro's aria? The casual opening (*sotto voce*, first violin only); the whispered motto-like phrase with which the voice begins; the gradual increment of energy and pace, as instruments are added to the orchestra, the violins become more animated, and the voice breaks into *parlato* figures; the rapid series of rising modulations – C major, D major, E minor, G major, A minor, C major – as Figaro sweeps on entranced with his own fluency; and finally the triumphant assertion 'ma però di buon umore d'ogni evento superior'[1] with its achievement of the new key centre, and the dash of martial colouring provided by oboes and horns. Rossini learnt a thing or two from this aria, and much of Leporello's 'catalogue aria' sounds almost like a recomposition of it.

Thanks to Mozart and Rossini we have learned to look upon the dramatic ensemble as the cornerstone of the *opera buffa*. To composers of an earlier generation its role was less crucial, and though there are several such dramatic ensembles in Paisiello, neither in number nor in artistry do they match those of his great successors. All the same it is worth spending a little time on them, because it was to Paisiello that contemporaries attributed the pioneering of the technique with which Mozart and Rossini achieved some of their greatest effects (e.g. Carpani 1824: 19–20). The nature of the task is clear if we look at, say, the second movement of the Rosina–Bartolo duet 'Lode al ciel' – the *allegro non tanto* section beginning 'Una carta? cos'è quella?' It is to find some way of driving the action forward while at the same time highlighting enough salient moments to make the form musically coherent. The *parlante* technique that Paisiello evolved for this purpose has been described in the previous chapter (p. 351 above). It was purely functional in character, making no attempt to give any real individuality to the instrumental figures, or to colour or harmonize the music imaginatively. But it did serve to make stand out all the clearer those moments when, by virtue of periodic phrase-structures, or word repetition, or emphatic cadential harmony, or changes of texture, the composer needed to underscore some dramatic incident: Bartolo's eagerness to retrieve Rosina's paper; his realization that he has been made a fool of; Rosina's little soliloquy, and so on. Rossini may have had no very high opinion of Paisiello's *parlante*s, but at their best, they did open the ears of his contemporaries to a new way of perceiving the relationship between music and drama. In the first movement of the quintet 'Don Basilio', the opening figure really does seem to watch and wait and hold its breath, and provides a perfect background for the whispered exclamations of dismay that punctuate the tense silence of the scene. And at the recapitulation, 'Oh che viso!', the way Paisiello uses the same theme to give an unanswerable emphasis to the dismissive 'andate a letto' is masterly (Ex.IV.22).

Dramatic ensembles are, however, less typical of Paisiello's art than what we might describe as 'situation ensembles'; ensembles, that is to say, which involve no genuine dramatic action, but which capture a single comic moment. Such pieces may, I think, be regarded as operatic *lazzi*. They are unconcerned with any question of dramatic necessity or even fitness, and they are totally remote from any sense of dramatic time; rather must they be regarded as *tours de force* of musical wit, sparked off by some incident in the drama, but essentially there for the sake of their own intrinsic absurdity. The prime example in *Il barbiere* is the terzetto for Bartolo, Giovinetto and Lo svegliato, in which the fuming doctor interrogates his two servants, one of whom is able to do nothing but yawn, the other nothing but sneeze. In such a piece the composer has no interest in generating a dynamic momentum (as in the tirade aria), nor in sustaining a naturalistic dramatic pace (as in the *parlante*). Such movements progress nowhere, but move in

Ex.IV.22 Paisiello, *Il barbiere di Siviglia* (1782), Act II scene 11

Rosina

(Don Basilio!) (Good heavens!) Oh what a face! Go to bed. [feeling his
pulse] This is a fever, go to bed. A fever! I tremble: go to bed.

Ex.IV.22 *continued*

372

circles, as the composer shuffles and reorders the blocks of music. Their particular delight is that they fill the harmony with hilarious contrasts and incongruous juxtapositions. Typically ludicrous in the terzetto and remote from any sense of dramatic purpose is the gradual evolution of a hilarious *buffo* texture of snapping *parlato*, yawns and sneezes (Ex.IV.23).

It is in these *lazzo*-like ensembles that Paisiello brings home most forcefully one of the most fundamental truths about the *opera buffa*; that the sheer craft of the musical composition can in its own right be a source of wit and high spirits. I am not talking here of music's power of enhancing the word or embodying the drama, but of its own inherent 'ludic' qualities. And these qualities do not of course need a whole formal number to display themselves. In the Finale there is a delicious small-scale example, where Paisiello picks up a tiny detail from the text (Basilio's inability to resist money) and makes *musical* fun out of it. Petrosellini provides a mere couplet:

> Questo è un peso che fa dir di sì
> Il danaro fa sempre così.[2]

Having set this charmingly as an epigram, Paisiello turns it into a musical joke, prolonging the cadences with slowly prancing reiterations of 'sì, sì', gracefully tossed between the voices.

One last quality of *Il barbiere di Siviglia* deserves consideration. The opera is a perfect model of eighteenth-century orchestration; to study it from that point of view helps make at any rate intelligible those contemporary complaints about the needless complexity of Mozart's scoring, or the wilful noisiness of Rossini's. Composers of Paisiello's generation were no longer content with an orchestral ensemble almost monopolized by the strings; regularly they included oboes and horns, and presumably bassoons – though they are rarely specified – and sometimes during the course of the opera they would employ flutes and clarinets. Occasionally the instrumentation of a particular movement will be programmatic, as is that of the Count's serenade, 'Saper bramate', where the guitar is represented by pizzicato violins and a mandolin.

Paisiello's use of the standard orchestra remains a model of simplicity and discretion, which yet manages to suggest the expressive characteristics of the wind instruments with an almost symbolic force. The string writing is utterly transparent – rarely in more than three parts: 'cellos are never independent of the double-basses, and the violas often double the same line at the upper octave; where the violas have their own line, first and second violins are usually in unison. To this string group the woodwinds are added with the very nicest sense of purpose. Usually the oboes and horns are employed to colour or thicken or sustain the underlying harmonies; flutes are conspicuous when the music moves into the open air, as in the

Ex.IV.23 Paisiello, *Il barbiere di Siviglia* (1782), Act I scene 5

374

What sort of a song is this! What? How? Speak up! Damn you!

Ex.IV.23 *continued*

Introduzione, in Rosina's 'Lode al ciel', or in the thunder-storm; and the clarinets are unmistakably the instruments of romance. They occur just four times in the score: in the Count's serenade, in Rosina's 'Giusto ciel', in her singing-lesson aria, and in the opening section – the love-duet section – of the Finale. A short passage in 'Già riede primavera' illustrates the poetic nuances of Paisiello's scoring admirably. After a richly scored, almost *concertato*-like opening ritornello, and a first aria section in which solo clarinet and solo bassoon have been conspicuous, we reach the lines

Tornan le fronde agli alberi,
L'erbette al prato tornano,
Ma non ritorna a me
La pace del mio cor.[3]

The romantic clarinet and the bassoon fall silent, leaving the theme to be coloured by the sharper, more melancholy timbre of the oboes; and at 'Ma non ritorna a me', all the woodwind withdraw, the singer in her loneliness abandoned by everything but the three-part string group.

Avoiding 'temerarious rivalry'

In 1816, when Rossini's opera had its première at the Teatro Argentina in Rome, Paisiello – a notoriously touchy man – was still alive, and his *Barbiere* was still a classic of the Italian repertory. Rossini therefore took the precaution of writing to the venerable old master, 'declaring to him that I had not wanted to enter into a contest with him, being aware of my inferiority, but had wanted only to treat a subject that had delighted me, while avoiding as much as possible the exact situations in his libretto' (to Scitivaux, 1860, in Weinstock 1968: 54). In the libretto printed for the first performances, Rossini's librettist, Cesare Sterbini, makes the same point in rather fuller detail:

M. Beaumarchais's comedy is performed in Rome arranged as a comic drama entitled *Almaviva*, or *L'inutile precauzione* . . . out of consideration for the feelings of respect and veneration which animate the composer of the music towards the so celebrated Paisiello, who has already treated this subject under its original title. Called upon to undertake this same difficult task, Maestro Gioacchino Rossini, so as not to incur the reproach of a temerarious rivalry with the immortal author who preceded him, has expressly requested that *The Barber of Seville* should be versified entirely anew and that a number of new situations should be added for musical pieces such as are required by modern theatrical taste, which has changed so much since the period in which the renowned Paisiello wrote his music.   (Loewenberg 1939: 162)

These two documents, Rossini's letter and Sterbini's 'Avvertimento al pubblico', really provide the key to, if not the whole story of, their reworking of Beaumarchais's play. They depart further from Beaumarchais's original, partly because Paisiello and Petrosellini had remained so faithful to it, partly because the conventions of early *ottocento* opera imposed certain requirements upon them; they tiptoe gingerly round some details in the drama, to avoid 'temerarious rivalry', only to pounce zestfully on others whose possibilities had gone unexploited by their predecessors; the whole design of the opera – which Sterbini surely planned in close co-operation with Rossini – is a fascinating amalgam of self-denial and creative criticism.

The clearest case of self-denial is found in Sterbini's treatment of a scene which Rossini would surely have handled brilliantly – that between Dr

Bartolo and his yawning and sneezing servants. In Sterbini's libretto the scene (Act I scene 11) never advances beyond a rather incoherent and – in operatic terms – pointless recitative, presumably because the same scene had occasioned one of Paisiello's most triumphant feats of musical wit. But on the whole Sterbini is conspicuously successful in the task Rossini set him. A case in point is the second scene of Act I – Figaro's cavatina. Sterbini makes no use of what had been the focuses of Paisiello's (and Beaumarchais's) scene – the picture of Figaro in the throes of musical composition, and his long narrative account of his adventures. Instead 'Largo al factotum' gives a picture of Figaro's status in Seville society, a virtuoso elaboration, brimming with vitality and self-dramatization, of what in the eighteenth-century versions had been a mere final detail in his autobiography. Conversely, where, for whatever reason, Petrosellini and Paisiello had not drawn full advantage from the original play, Sterbini moves in. His singing-lesson scene is, for example, much closer to Beaumarchais than Petrosellini's: it has much more of his informal naturalism, making the most of those moments where Bartolo dozes off, and interrupting his arietta just as Beaumarchais had done, to explain how Rosina's name has been substituted for that of the original nymph.

It is certain, though, that Sterbini and Rossini would hardly have needed to make so elaborate an apology for their new opera if it had not in many respects paralleled the early work rather closely – if it had not indeed, at several points, amounted to a creative criticism of it. Such pieces as Basilio's 'La calumnia è un venticello', Bartolo's 'A un dottor della mia sorte', and the quintet in Act II make no attempt whatever to avoid 'temerarious rivalry'. It is perhaps not fortuitous that Basilio's aria follows immediately the scene with the yawning and sneezing servants. Having allowed Paisiello an unchallenged triumph there, Rossini now does challenge him quite specifically; and trounces him so comprehensively that we cannot hear the older composer's work without being acutely conscious of the fact that neither musically nor dramatically is it as good as it might be. The seeds of Rossini's superiority here are carefully planted in Sterbini's text. Like Petrosellini, he models it on Beaumarchais's original tirade; but unlike Petrosellini he soars above merely literal fidelity. Each item from Beaumarchais is elaborated with a prodigality of duplicating detail,[4] which enables Rossini to linger over his musical description and make one single crescendo a sufficient theme for the whole aria: Paisiello, it will be recalled, had to tell the story twice.

In almost all those scenes in which Paisiello's work is challenged the later opera is far funnier: the comedy tends to be broadened, exaggerated and energized. A good example of this change of tone is found in the recitative and duetto No. 4 in Act I, in which, in the best Italian comedy tradition, the effect of money on the inventiveness of a servant's mind is, compared with Beaumarchais, ludicrously exaggerated. True, Beaumarchais's Figaro had spoken of gold as 'le nerf de l'intrigue': but in Sterbini – excellent work again! – this is hyperbolized into:

> All'idea di quel metallo
> portentoso, onnipossente
> un vulcano la mia mente
> incomincia a diventar.[5]

And all the details of the plan to get Almaviva into Bartolo's house – the disguise as a soldier, the billeting ticket, the pretended drunkenness – in short, all the resourcefulness that in the play had been the natural cast of Figaro's mind, becomes in Sterbini a result of the mental effervescence occasioned by Almaviva's money. What had been a small naturalistic detail of characterization is transformed into an occasion for laughter, its joking essence highlighted by the refrain, 'che invenzione prelibata / bella, bella, in verità!'[6] The 'natural' comedy of the play tends, in Sterbini's rewriting, to approach farce; those elements that were already farcical to be driven to the very verge of the grotesque. And sometimes Sterbini's comic imagination lures him into parody, a playing with the conventions of the operatic form in an ironic self-awareness of which eighteenth-century *opera buffa* had been largely innocent – as when, in the Act I *Introduzione*, he has Fiorello and the rest of Almaviva's minions literally making a song and dance about the need for silence.

Besides avoiding 'temerarious rivalry', Sterbini had, he tells us, to provide a number of pieces because they were demanded by modern taste. Often it is the demands of those newer operatic conventions that prompt his departure from Beaumarchais – as indeed it is in the *Introduzione* just mentioned: the scene is far removed from the almost casual naturalness of Paisiello partly at least because of the need to accommodate the chorus and a cavatina for one of the principals. Similarly at the end of Act I: Sterbini remains with Beaumarchais as long as he can; but for what had by this time become the two crucial movements of the dramatic ensemble finale, he could find nothing in the play and had to veer off independently: the Andante 'quadro di stupore' is engineered by bringing about a confrontation between Almaviva and the officers of the law; and the final *stretta* of confusion is developed out of this tableau in one of those ludicrous onomatopoeic metaphor verses which had been proving their usefulness to *opera buffa* composers for half a century:

> Mi par d'esser con la testa
> in un'orrida fucina,
> dove cresce e mai non resta
> delle incudini sonore
> l'importuno strepitar . . .[7]

Sterbini is sometimes constrained to provide aria-texts where there is, in Beaumarchais, no very obvious cue for them: an *aria del sorbetto* for Berta in Act II, and Rosina's cavatina in Act I. This latter is one of the librettist's best pieces of work, a brilliantly managed addition to the plain outline of the play: we might properly describe it as a piece of literary criticism, which spells out for us all the sparkle, wilfulness, and resource of Rosina's character. She is in love, and nothing is going to prevent her from getting her man:

> Il tutor ricuserà,
> io l'ingegno aguzzerò.
> Alla fin s'accheterà
> e contenta io resterò . . .
> Si, Lindoro mio sarà;
> lo giurai, la vincerò.[8]

Demure and submissive she is quite happy to appear: *but*

> Ma se mi toccano – dov'è il mio debole,
> sarò una vipera – e cento trappole
> prima di cedere – farò giocar.[9]

Rossini's *Barbiere di Siviglia*

Once the opposition of the Paisiello clique had been overcome, Rossini's *Barbiere di Siviglia* rapidly established itself as one of his best and most popular scores. And as the decades passed it became clear that it was proving still more durable than Paisiello's classic setting. Thirty years later, at a time when *opera buffa* was virtually extinct, Felice Romani, the finest Italian librettist of the Romantic age and one of its most eloquent music critics, remarked that it had lost nothing of its vernal freshness, and provided a perfect antidote to the spectres and night-owls of northern Romanticism (*Gazzetta piemontese*, 18 September 1846, in Rinaldi 1965: 371–2). Another fifty years on and it had become – despite *Il matrimonio segreto* and *Don Pasquale* and Rossini's other gems in the *buffo* form – quite simply the peerless classic of the genre; in Verdi's words it was 'for its wealth of original musical ideas, its comic verve and truth of declamation, the finest *opera buffa* in existence' (to Bellaigue, 1898, in Verdi 1913: 915). And this status it has never lost, even in an age as unsympathetic to the musical ideals of the *primo ottocento* as the 1920s when Ildebrando Pizzetti, in an essay entitled 'L'immortalità del Barbiere di Siviglia', described it as 'the most divinely graceful and entirely perfect comic opera that has ever been composed anywhere in the world'. And he went on to compare revivals of *Il barbiere* with the ever-recurring wonder of sunrise: 'Like the return of the light each morning, [this opera] fills our hearts with gladness and joy' (Bonaccorsi 1968: 117, 118).

To describe *Il barbiere di Siviglia* as being as nearly perfect an opera as any composer has ever achieved is not to dispute that, compared with, say, the masterpieces of Mozart, it has its limitations. Indeed its very perfection is in part achieved by Rossini's denying himself some of the riches of the late-eighteenth-century *opera buffa*. Critics have occasionally been troubled by this; Stendhal, in speaking of the Rosina–Figaro duet No. 7, 'Dunque io son', diagnosed 'a slight attack of *scepticism* in sentimental matters – which, for a young man of four and twenty represents no small advance along the hard road to philosophy and worldly wisdom. Rossini's peace of mind will benefit, unquestionably from this advance, but I suspect that his genius is liable to suffer proportionately' (Stendhal 1956: 184–5). Stendhal was troubled by the feeling that *Il barbiere* was a less humane work than the greatest *opere buffe* of an earlier generation, or indeed than Rossini's own earlier pieces. Certainly the emotional warmth, the sentimental empathy that had come to characterize many of the best examples of the form, is largely abandoned. Despite the protests of Alberto Zedda in the preface to his *edizione critica* (1969), it is difficult not to feel that in Rossini's opera the individual characters are closer to their origins in the *commedia dell'arte* than they had been in Paisiello's opera or in Beaumarchais's play. So that when Stendhal exclaims – of the same Rosina–Figaro duet, in which the heroine has learned that 'Lindoro' loves her – 'I refuse to believe that even in Rome, the love of such a creature as Rosina should be so utterly devoid of the slightest suggestion of melancholy . . . of certain finer shades of fastidiousness and hesitation' (1956: 183), he is really objecting that Rosina is not a fully rounded human being, but in very quintessence a soubrette. In the same way the opera's arias are not illuminations of character so much as *performances* – tirades of a musical virtuosity which in earlier *opera buffa* had been anticipated only by Leporello's 'catalogue aria', and the scale and tone of which are largely unrelated to any real dramatic function. Figaro's 'Largo al factotum' is the supreme example of such a 'performance', an aria addressed to the audience with no motivation in dramatic verisimilitude whatever; for 'make way for the city factotum' is hardly a life-like injunction in a deserted street at daybreak! The same caricatural distortion of the 'natural' is found in many a detail of the dramatic action too: at the departure of Basilio in the Act II quintet, for example, or – best of all – at that point in the Act I finale where the squabbling principals are interrupted by the arrival of the soldiers. The theatrical gesture of surprise is here driven far beyond any consideration of mere expressiveness. A very unremarkable knock at the door, of which the company has already been forewarned, prompts an episode (it is really the coda to the E♭ *allegro* section of the finale) of suspense, mystery, even terror, not far removed in spirit from *I Masnadieri*'s vision of the day of judgement. Manifestly,

Rossini's concern is not for a merely 'truthful' representation of surprise and dismay, but for a representation wrought up by hyperbole to a state of caricature.

From very few operas does one derive so vividly the impression of drama understood, not as an image of reality, or a mirror of life, but as a highly self-conscious work of art. Such eighteenth-century lode-stars as Truth, Simplicity, Nature and Humanity have yielded their place to Artifice, Virtuosity and Mask. Without partaking of those disconcerting changes of tone that characterize 'romantic irony' as it is generally understood, Rossini's opera does seem to have something in common with that quality – a detachment from its own emotional and psychological sources; an ironic delight in the composer's virtuosity, in his creation of harmonious forms, and his dazzling displays of rhythmic and colouristic wit. One of the clearest symptoms of this sovereign detachment is the profusion of sparkling *fioritura*, of which Stendhal so often complained. Even at their most lyrical, the melodies of *Il barbiere* are far removed from those traditional *buffo* ideals of simplicity and naturalness which Rossini indeed parodies in Bartolo's arietta No. 12, 'Quando mi sei vicina'. Nor do the roulades serve any very obvious expressive or rhetorical purpose. The crux of the matter is shrewdly identified by Kunze when he writes of 'the consummate elegance with which Rossini evades an emotional intensification of the melody . . . As the *parlando* is decked out to form a bubbling chatter that persiflages articulate speech, so the "*canto fiorito*" distances itself from any undisguised emotional revelation in the melody' (Kunze 1982: 91).

Towards the close of the *primo tempo* in the terzetto No. 16, 'Ah qual colpo', Figaro peers out of the window and sees two people approaching the door with a lantern; an interrupted cadence cuts short the florid duet of the two lovers. It seems a very obvious effect: but in *Il barbiere* it is in fact a rare example of a musical detail which illustrates the stage action, or – to put it the other way about – of the stage action commanding a detail in the musical design. For, as Rossini was to explain in his famous conversation with Wagner, he believed that music should not servilely follow and interpret the words, but be free to develop according to its own inherently musical laws. This Rossinian conviction had, long before that meeting, been one of the primary sources of Schopenhauer's philosophy of music: in Schopenhauer's own words, 'If you try to adapt music too closely to the words, or model it on the action, it is forced to speak an alien language. From this fault no one has distanced himself so much as Rossini . . .' (Bonaccorsi 1968: 116). And of Rossini's operas, we might add, none is so successful as *Il barbiere* in eliminating from the musical numbers anything that cannot be reconciled with a purely musical understanding of form:

recitativo accompagnato plays a negligible role, and virtually never are the arias and ensembles subject to 'extraneous interventions' (Gallarati 1977: 262) prompted by stage action.

In the previous chapter I have described Rossini's art in more general terms and suggested how the massive sectional blocks of his 'ideal' musical forms are galvanized into life by the flickering play of colour and texture on the surface, and the throbbing and driving rhythms that animate them from within. A marvellous demonstration of these characteristics is found in Figaro's cavatina No. 2, 'Largo al factotum'. Its block-like repetitive structure may be represented diagrammatically thus:

AB	A, C, A, cadences	link, D, D', cadences	C, B, free, B, E
prelude	predominantly tonic	new keys	predominantly tonic, elements of reprise and coda

Moreover all the sections represented by capitals in the diagram are themselves built on repetition patterns (to this is due much of their pounding energy): A is a *rosalia*-like sequence, B a crescendo, C a set of round-like overlappings, D an orchestral theme played thrice, etc. The control of pace throughout is masterly, giving the impression of gathering momentum and mounting excitement, despite the reality of an unchanging *allegro* §. The three crucial stages are A, B, and E. A is a perfectly regular eight-bar phrase, repeated sequentially; but the variety of pace within it – the rhetorical pause, the sudden spasms of activity, the pregnant silences – is hugely inventive, witty, and – as a way of arresting attention – theatrical; when Rossini wishes to whip up the excitement more rapidly – for the arrival of Figaro on stage, or for the break into the *stretto* at the close – he uses B, a driving orchestral crescendo-theme with vocal interjections; the climax of this process of mounting rhythmic exuberance comes with E, when, for the first time in the aria, the orchestra retreats into the background, leaving the voice to pursue a hectic *note e parole* style. The effect is electrifying: as if the music had suddenly increased its pace enormously and swept downstage to the footlights.

But the numbers of *Il barbiere* are not simply chunks of musical architecture propelled according to some principle of autonomous rhythmic vitalism. On the contrary, most of them demonstrate an extraordinarily happy gift for finding musical patterns that in various ways and at various levels function as analogies to the stage action. An excellent example of this typical blend of schematic structuralism and vivid theatricality is the first section of the Act I finale. We find here nothing really resembling the symphonic flux of Mozart's comparable movements. Instead Rossini uses a handful of highly distinctive, symmetrically phrased themes which periodically recur, essentially unaltered, to create a broadly ternary musical pattern:

A¹ (predominantly C major)	Alvaviva disguised as a drunken soldier bursts into Bartolo's house, claiming to be billeted there.
B (G major and other keys)	Rosina enters; whispered conversation of the lovers; Bartolo tries to get rid of Almaviva.
A² (predominantly C major)	Having swept aside Bartolo's document of exemption, Almaviva offers to fight him. Exchange of letters with Rosina.

Each of the three sections is dominated by an orchestral theme reiterated several times as the basis for *parlante*, and each of these themes has its appropriate expressive character. Theme I, heard five times in A^1 and twice in A^2, is a strutting march theme, clearly suggested by Almaviva's disguise (Ex.IV.24a); theme II, heard five times in B, is a rapid pattering theme, perhaps suggested by the quickening of Almaviva's pulse as he first espies Rosina (Ex.IV.24b). No fewer than 76 bars of music are provided by simple repetitions of these two themes (8×7, 4×5); they provide the tone of the scene, the sense of rigorous formal discipline, the almost Stravinskian mordancy of Rossini's wit.

But the dramatic vividness and the urgent theatricality are due to the other factors, of which I mention just a few. The A section has a subsidiary, gloomily sliding theme, heard three times in all (unchanged) which, besides acting as a foil to the march theme, is sensed as an embodiment of Bartolo's suspicion; there is a florid lyrical theme placed at the culmination of both A^1 and A^2, which surely, besides its structural function, acts as an expression of Almaviva's fervent hopes. And when we come to the main dramatic turning points or comic incidents, we find they are not so much composed into the music as vacated, so that the performer can do with them as he will. There is one such free quasi-recitative in each of the three sections: at the old *commedia dell'arte* joke over Bartolo's name; at the point where he produces his letter of exemption only for Almaviva to knock it out of his hand; at the business with the letter and handkerchief.

It is worth lingering briefly over these free interstices, for they are a crucial element in *Il barbiere*, the means by which the blocks of the musical construction are prised apart to accommodate little details of theatrical naturalism. If we return for a moment to 'Largo al factotum', we cannot fail to notice that Rossini strenuously resists any temptations to 'interpret' the text in his music; the physical élan of the rhythms and sonorities is a translation into musical terms of Figaro's *joie de vivre*, and that is that or, rather, that is almost that. For if the poetic text can be swept up into a purely musical structure, Figaro himself cannot. To have him dancing obediently to the pattern of the music would be to reduce him to a mere puppet; if he is to come to life as a dramatic character he must be able to

Ex.IV.24a Rossini, *Il barbiere di Siviglia* (1816), Act I scene 15

Ex.IV.24b Rossini, *Il barbiere di Siviglia* (1816), Act I scene 15

step out of these patterns, to perform, to act autonomously, to give the impression that he is in charge of them. That is where the free episodes and the extra-schematic cadences come in: the lingering over 'colla donnetta . . . col cavaliere', the La-la-ran-la-ing, above all the free section that leads into the coda (from 'Figaro, Figaro, Figaro'). Sterbini's text is torn to shreds here, and added to as well, to help Rossini project Figaro's self-dramatization.

The beautifully lucid and architectural musical patterns could not parallel and reflect the dramatic action half so well were it not for Rossini's wizardry in controlling his audience's sense of time. Nowhere has a composer played more skilfully with the tensions and contradictions between theatrical time and 'real' time. Rossini perceives that the stock of techniques he had inherited from the past gave him the means of expressing this relationship in three ways: employing recitatives, or those quasi-naturalistic effects of musical rhetoric to which Verdi was to give the name 'parola scenica', he could allow time to pass realistically; using the orchestra to carry the burden of the music and threading the voices on to this in *parlante* he could create an alternative sense of time, a theatrical or artificial one; allowing the voice to control the momentum whether in inward cantabile or brilliant coloratura he could suspend the sense of time altogether.[10] These three techniques had always tended to be associated with specific dramatic functions, with crises in the action (*parola scenica*), with direct speech and dialogue (*parlante*), with emotional effusion (lyricism) respectively. What was new in Rossini was only the precision of the stylization; his music was formally exquisite, but at the same time – according to the idiom chosen – keenly functional.

Rossini's musical patterns are then not purely or abstractly musical: nor when we attend to them closely are many of the finer musical details. Surprisingly often some feature of the musical design, some detail of technique, some refinement of texture or voice distribution proves to be – or at least is heard to be – not just an incident in the music-making, but a dramatic point of real aptness or wit. Gossett sees in the use of 'strict sonata form' in the Allegro vivace of Bartolo's aria No. 8, 'A un dottor della mia sorte', 'a wonderfully ironic comment on the pedantic character of the tutor' (*The New Grove*, s.v. 'Rossini'). That is a very attractive suggestion and exactly the kind of thing I mean, but the fact that there was no such thing as an academic stereotype of 'sonata-form' in 1816 does make it a little less plausible than one could wish. Less problematic is the Andante of the Act I *finale* where, as often happens in a 'quadro di stupore', motionless, dumbfounded astonishment is expressed in the slowly circulating patterns of a canon, while the slow-moving pizzicato string chords suggest that even heartbeats have almost come to a halt. A little earlier in the same finale – four bars after figure 86 – another canon had been used for very different, but no less dramatically apt purposes. Indeed this Vivace is one of the wittiest passages in the opera. What more perfect musical metaphor could there be for a scene of confused and contradictory explanations than a patter-song canon, in which every singer has to struggle valiantly to get his words out at all, but in which, despite this hard work, all the words are in fact unintelligible because of the clashing of consonants and dissonance of vowels? Or consider the moment in the quintet No. 13, where Rossini decides to make a glorious musical joke out of Basilio's departure, changes tempo and elaborates 'Buona sera, mio signore' into a separate movement. The very use of lyricism after the *parlante* of the preceding Andantino gives the words of Basilio's opponents a note of irresistible charm and courtesy;

but by distributing the theme between the voices the way he does, Rossini also suggests the conspiracy between them; and the suddenly loud cadence phrases with their wrenching modulations provide that glint of steel, that peremptory brusqueness that will not be denied.

One must note too that the most mannered forms of lyricism can become similarly meaningful. Rosina's cavatina No. 5, 'Una voce poco fà', provides a masterly demonstration of the possibilities of what one might call rhetorical expression. The object is not to interpret the words with harmonic or colouristic expressive devices, but to enable Rosina to put them across to an audience herself. Hence, a rhythm and sparseness of accompaniment that demands we attend to them, and a placing of the key syllables on notes which encourage her to colour her voice: 'risuonò' down in the chest register; and on 'Lindoro', once the poignant C♮ suggesting the wound of love, and many times high Es and G♯s suggesting love's triumph. At the far end of the spectrum are those coruscations of coloratura into which Almaviva is forever breaking. What, if we may put it so crudely, does the choice of style mean in such a piece as the aria No. 18, 'Cessa di più resistere'? Is it an expression of the effervescence of Almaviva's joy; or the nonchalant ostentation of the wondrous vocal art of Garcia the creator of the role; or the delicious glitter of Rossini's own musical exuberance; or the ironic distancing from sentimentality? Surely it is all these things. For when opera is so consciously an artefact as it is in Rossini, when song, spectacle and story-telling meet in so stylized a celebration of art, there can be no one-to-one relationship between the dramatic idea and the notes in which Rossini embodies it.

As I have described the characteristics of Paisiello's scoring, something must clearly be said about Rossini's; as we have seen, it was regarded by the more old-fashioned of his contemporaries as one of the most outrageously extravagant features of his musical language, and despite the distortions it suffered at the hands of 'tradition', and from which it was rescued only with the appearance of Zedda's edition in 1969, it has for long been admired as one of the most scintillating aspects of his musical wit.

In the time-honoured fashion of the *opera buffa*, *Il barbiere* affords one or two instances of programmatic scoring: a guitar for both Almaviva's serenades in the first scene and, more surprisingly, a piano for just a few bars – no more than a dash of naturalistic colour – in the singing-lesson scene. But most aspects of the eighteenth-century tradition of instrumentation have been quite transformed; in particular Rossini's fondness for a wide range of blended and contrasting colours leads to a complete break-down of the *obbligato*-like use of woodwind instruments found in Paisiello. Typical is the introduction to the cavatina 'Ecco ridente in cielo' in No. 1, where (to mention simply the woodwind instruments) the eight-bar period presenting the tune is divided: four bars clarinet, two bars flute and clarinet, two bars oboe and bassoon. But not entirely unrelated to earlier *obbligato*-scoring is the more romantic notion of characteristic scoring, of which the best example in *Il barbiere* is the duet No. 10. While in earlier movements in the opera Rossini has often left out the oboe (especially from the very fast movements), and while flutes have sometimes been replaced by piccolos, this is the only movement of the opera to have a quite distinctive woodwind tone-colour. It is provided by clarinets and bassoons, trilling and gliding oilily throughout the principal theme of the duet, and contributing to its ludicrously unctuous tone with eighteenth-century precision.

But the inimitable hallmark of Rossini's *opera buffa* orchestration is provided by those orgiastic revellings in the physical qualities of colour, texture, sonority and rhythm that are found in so many *stretti*. The *stretto* of the Act I finale is – together with the matching section in *L'Italiana in Algeri* – the *locus classicus* for sheer sonority used as a means of inducing raptures of comic delight. One may profitably cast an eye back to Guglielmi's essay in musical onomatopoeia in *La virtuosa di Mergellina* (Ex.IV.14), and then look at Rossini's score: a memorably rollicking theme sung in unison, *sotto voce*, set against a background of string harmonies over which the violins dance with unflagging joie-de-vivre, and into which trumpets, horns, clarinets, piccolos and sistrums scatter single notes and pairs of notes in a manic pointillist glee. And sonority and dynamics are by definition the whole point of the passage that follows, one of those incomparable crescendos in which the music, in Stendhal's words, 'flares up into a kind of brilliant bonfire, touched off by the sparks of his own wit' (1956: 178).

Part V
Romantic opera

21 · Italian Romanticism

A programme for art

To anyone brought up on north European manifestations of Romanticism with their indulgence of the play of fantasy, the premium they place on the cultivation of the subjective world of the inner self, their yearning for some distant or transcendental elsewhere, their partiality for the strange and supernatural, the most authoritative Italian definition of Romanticism will seem improbably mundane. It comes from Alessandro Manzoni, the Milanese poet and novelist, himself one of the most distinguished exponents of the movement he was defining. According to Manzoni, the Romantic writer should take 'L'utile per iscopo, il vero per soggetto, l'interessante per mezzo'[1] ('Lettera sul romanticismo' (1823), quoted in Rinaldi 1965: 362).

Manzoni defined a form of Romanticism which, in its humanist, utilitarian bias, had not yet rejected the inheritance of the Enlightenment. What was perhaps new was the choice of beneficiary: for this 'useful, truthful and interesting' art was written not simply for the betterment of those cultivated individuals to whom Metastasio had addressed himself; on the contrary, it aimed at nothing less than the regeneration of an entire society. The peculiar significance of the Romantic movement in Italy was a consequence of the fact that, during the Revolutionary and Napoleonic periods, art had become politicized, or, to use a more Mazzinian phrase, 'socialized'. It was able therefore to act as a potent force in Italian life during those decades of political, social and idealistic ferment known as the *risorgimento*. Indeed the Italian nation that emerged from the *risorgimento* was in no small measure the achievement of the intellectual and imaginative speculations of its artists. When the Congress of Vienna was convened in 1815 to discuss a new political dispensation for Europe following the downfall of Napoleon, the consequence for Italy was a 'Restoration', which, for the most part, reconstituted that multitude of kingdoms, duchies and grand-duchies, and provinces of the Austrian empire, that had existed in the peninsula before the Napoleonic conquests began; they had disparate histories and traditions, different assets and different problems. This condition of fragmentation lasted throughout the Romantic period; it was in the realms of the spirit and the imagination that unification first became a reality.

The primary motive of Italian Romantic art was a desire to express and form the new society that was emerging in the post-Napoleonic age. Artists addressed their work to the emergent Italy: they aimed to fashion and educate the nation, to sustain it emotionally and spiritually. 'The men of spirit and letters', Marshal Bellegarde wrote to Metternich in 1815, 'are trying to write with a common purpose, which under an academic form hides the political aim of making Italy its own master, an idea which is disturbing even as a Utopia' (Colquhoun 1954: 118). The poet Silvio Pellico remarked that, in Italy, to be a Romantic was to be a Liberal; 'and only ultras and spies dare call themselves classicists' (Rinaldi 1965: 363). Looking at the matter from the point of view of a nationalist philosopher, Mazzini strove, in everything he wrote about art and artists, to inculcate a sense of sacred mission:

The art which you practise is holy – he urged young composers – and you, if you would be its priests, must likewise be holy. The art which is entrusted to you is intimately connected with the progress of civilization, and can be its spirit, its soul, its sacred perfume, if you draw your inspiration from the affairs of progressive civilization, not from arbitrary laws. (*Filosofia di musica*, 1836)

Like Manzoni, Mazzini emphasized that 'truth' – by which he meant the reality of the everyday world – was the stuff of modern art, not the quest for some ideal of beauty enshrined in aesthetics. The time had come 'to substitute for fabled fictions descriptions of the Truth', wrote Giuseppe Montani in the influential Florentine periodical *Antologia*, during the controversy surrounding the appearance of Monti's *Sulla mitologia*. And *risorgimento* Italy's finest satirical poet, Giuseppe Giusti, was prompted by Verdi's *Macbeth* to formulate an antithesis of the fantastic and the true, that Verdi himself adopted as a motto, inscribing it in the album of his dear friend the Contessa Clara Maffei: 'the fantastic is something that can put the imagination to the test; the true puts to the test both the imagination and the heart' (Barbiera 1915: 102; Giusti's letter is in Verdi 1913: 450).

There were those, and Giacomo Leopardi, greatest of Italian nineteenth-century poets, was among them, who feared that a politicized art was a prostituted art. If Leopardi's fears were shared by rather few Italian Romantics, it was surely because politics was not in itself the ultimate aim of these men. On the contrary politics – even liberal-Italian-nationalist politics – was an inadequate ideal: if the new Italy that they longed to bring to birth was to be a worthy descendant of the Italy of the Renaissance, the Italy of the Communes, and the Italy of Classical Antiquity, then a transfigured humanity was the real objective. It was this task – the fashioning of hearts, souls and minds – to which artists addressed themselves. In Massimo d'Azeglio's famous words, 'once we have made true Italians, Italy will make itself' (1966, II: 12). So while, of course, *risorgimento* Italy had its heroic soldiers and politicians, its Garibaldi and its Cavour, it was more dependent than resurgent nations have generally been on those we might describe as 'patriots of intellect and imagination' – a phrase used by Romani in his obituary tribute to Donizetti in the *Gazzetta piemontese* in April 1848. Alongside Garibaldi and Cavour we must set such men as Mazzini, instilling into his countrymen a profound philosophical awareness of the reality of nationhood: Manzoni, tirelessly revising his great novel *I promessi sposi* so as to help give Italians from every part of the peninsula a contemporary national language; d'Azeglio – taking his cue perhaps from Foscolo's 'O italiani, io vi esorto alle storie'[2] – writing historical novels with the avowed aim of 'initiating a slow work of regeneration of the national character through a patriotically inspired literature' (1966, II: 12); Donizetti, Bellini and Verdi, uniting in emotional enthusiasm the citizens of Turin and Trieste, of Parma and Palermo.

The artist in society

Every aspect of Italian *risorgimento* culture shows the interaction between the timeless values of art and the urgent priorities of contemporary society. Among the more everyday manifestations I would mention the popular dramatic entertainments staged by Meneghino Moncalvo in the streets of Milan, which were spiced with such violently anti-Austrian allusions that he was 'regularly imprisoned twice weekly' (Ghislanzoni 1958: 270), or what we should now call the arts columns of the better newspapers, such as Romani's *Gazzetta piemontese* – particularly influential after the spread of coffee-houses and public reading-rooms in the 1840s.[3] At the further end of the scale one need think only of two great Italian novels of the age: Manzoni's *I promessi sposi* took as its theme 'the great age-old sorrow of his oppressed fatherland' ('il grande secolare dolore della sua patria oppressa' – an 'early critic', quoted in Whitfield 1960: 226); Ippolito Nievo's *Confessioni d'un italiano*, on the other hand, was the story – as its title suggests – of the making of an Italian. Its opening sentence (the elderly narrator is looking back over his life) is characteristic: 'I was born a Venetian on 18 October 1775 . . .; and with the grace of God I shall die an Italian when that Providence which mysteriously governs the world wills it.'

The effect of the work of these 'patriots of intellect and imagination' was profound. Ardent young men did find in art the inspiration to dedicate themselves to the forging of a new age. 'Do you remember', wrote Settembrini of Leopardi's early patriotic *canzoni*, 'the days of our youth, when the Austrian police were at our heels, and we created in our books a world in which we found life and liberty? . . . All that world, that excitement, those unfettered plans, those dreams, was represented by Leopardi in those Canzoni' (Leopardi 1966: 69). To study literature at a university – particularly at Milan, the capital of the Austrian provinces – was to enrol oneself in the ranks of liberalism. It was during the *risorgimento* that the Italian Faculties of Arts acquired that association with political activism that they have never since been able, or indeed sought, to cast off.

Those Romantic artists who could find the right tone occupied a central role in *risorgimento* society, a position of such fundamental importance to the people in whose midst they worked, as has rarely been paralleled in cultural history. Poets and novelists, great and small, strove to write with a simple eloquence that would be accessible to all, and often succeeded in breaking down the barriers between the intellectual world and the general public that had bedevilled Italian literature for so long. But no medium achieved this aim with so sure a touch as opera. The successful operas of the Romantic age obsessed Italian society at all levels: from the theatre which was its true home operatic music flooded over into the streets, where barrel-organs ground the best-loved strains; into the churches, where organ transcriptions adorned the divine service; into soirées and private drawing-rooms; opera was even a favourite pastime of the industrial labourer, as Dickens found when he visited the marble quarries at Carrara in 1846.

All this enthusiasm for opera was not a matter of a mere liking for music. Better than any other artistic form, opera articulated the deepest emotional needs of the Italians at this turning-point in their history: it expressed their common humanity, a passionate conviviality, their aspirations and ideals. At the crises of their existence they turned to the music of the operas they loved best as the most eloquent way of expressing themselves: one may cite the case of the patriot de Felici, incriminated in an attempt on the life of the Papal Secretary of State, Cardinal Antonelli, 1855, who sang Manrico's 'Ah! che la morte ognora' to the priest sent to him before his execution; or the service held in Palermo cathedral to celebrate the liberation of Sicily from the Neapolitan Bourbons in 1848, when, according to the report of Lord Mount-Edgcumbe, the blessing of the tricolour was accompanied by 'the stirring strains of "Guerra, guerra" from the *Norma* of Bellini', and 'the Committee advanced up the aisle preceded by a band of music playing the duet from the *Puritani*' (Acton 1961: 195).

The theatre became the focal symbolic building at the heart of all Italian cities. And the impact it achieved there might entitle us to regard it as a kind of spiritual Trojan Horse. For in the early days of the Restoration there is little doubt the opera-house continued to be regarded as an adjunct of the ruling dynasty. D'Azeglio's comment that the Austrians ruled Milan through La Scala has often been quoted; and the reasoning the Austrians may be presumed to have employed is spelt out in full in a memorandum drawn up by Monsignor Luigi Ciacchi in 1837 to encourage the Pope to support opera more enthusiastically in Rome:

The theatre, considered in the abstract, is and can only be an object of indifference to the government, an object to be tolerated, an object with no immediate connection with the heavy cares of the state.

But considered concretely, in view of the links it forges in society between the people and the government, it naturally changes its aspect, and necessarily takes its place among the beneficent concerns of the governing classes.

In order for a people to be more calm and content with the government to which it finds itself subjected, it is absolutely clear and confirmed by the experience of centuries that the means most fitting and conducive to this end is a suitably distracting theatre, decently entertaining and soberly diverting; and particularly at this time the distraction and entertainment of the people is the healthiest cure for the wounds that have been inflicted in almost every part of the world. (Cametti 1938: 245)

But opera composers did their work too well. What was thought of by such men as Ciacchi as a form of pleasurable and wool-pulling escapism became an education in nationhood. Increasingly during the 1840s theatres were chosen as the scene for political demonstrations; and well before then, if one was bent on the breeding of conspiracy, or the infiltration of society with subversive new ideals, no better starting place could be found than those hives of private boxes in which the casual coming and going of acquaintances was a social ritual of two hundred years' standing.

Style and matter in Italian Romanticism

The aesthete's delight in art for art's sake was superseded by a different kind of enthusiasm, an enthusiasm triggered off by those transfiguring educative ideals the art enshrined. The thought, the idea, that was captured in word or tone or image acquired a new importance, the manner mattered less. In poetry, for example, the rhyme, the lovingly fashioned strophes, all the graceful, sing-song elegance of the Arcadian tradition retreated before a harsher eloquence in which the poet aspired to speak as truthfully and as thoughtfully as he might. Already at the close of the eighteenth century Alfieri took pride in being 'pensato non cantato':

> Mi trovi duro?
> Anch'io lo so:
> Pensar li fo.
> Taccia ho d'oscuro?
> Mi schiarirà
> Poi libertà.[4]

One of the casualties of these new attitudes was the privileged position in Italian intellectual life of Classical Antiquity: the history of the Ancient World, Graeco-Roman mythology, the artistic forms and styles sanctioned by Classical, especially Aristotelian, aesthetics. Manzoni felt that this negative achievement, the rejection of 'mythology, the servile imitation of the classics, [and] rules based on . . . the authority of the rhetoricians', was the most distinctive mark of Italian Romanticism in its early years ('Lettera sul romanticismo', in Manzoni 1970: 317–18). In the opera-house, during the 1820s, Metastasio, whose dramas had survived all changes of taste for a hundred years, at last dropped out of the repertory: composers making their debut at that time had no interest in the 'genere classico' which he had represented with such beguiling eloquence. In 1828 Bellini scornfully rejected the idea of an opera on *Cesare in Egitto*, 'because the subject is as old as Noah' (letter to Florimo, in Bellini 1943: 177). It was also in the 1820s that the literary journal *Antologia* acted as the forum for a lively controversy, sparked off by Monti's *Sulla mitologia*, between the defenders and the opponents of the traditional Classical styles. Three lines from Monti's poem provide a touchstone:

> Spenti gli dei, che del piacere ai dolci
> Fonti i mortali conducean, velando
> Di vaghe forme amabilmente il vero.[5]

For Monti himself and for many of his readers the note of nostalgia here was overwhelming. For the full-blooded Romantic generation the lines might almost have been an enemy battle-cry. They did not wish truth to be 'amiably veiled with beauteous forms', they wished it to be expressed naturally and directly in a way that was in tune with the times.

In this aspiration they elected to follow new heroes, men who explored worlds of feeling and modes of expression startlingly different from those of the Classical traditions. Exemplary for the most wholehearted Italian Romantics were the novels of Scott and Dumas; the poetry of Ossian, Goethe and Byron; the plays of Schiller and Hugo and above all Shakespeare. Italian Romantic critics of Shakespeare admired two qualities in particular. Manzoni emphasized its naturalness and spontaneity, the free flow of idea and expression, uninhibited by such rules and formalities as were characteristic of the French dramatic tradition. Mazzini on the other hand highlighted his incomparable art of characterization: 'Shakespeare's characters have life and movement as if they came from the hands of God . . . they bring to the stage life and character in the most real, the most true, and the most perfect way that it has ever been granted a man to achieve' (Mazzini 1910: 186). But it was the unsystematic enthusiasms of the poets that best expressed the effect of Shakespeare on the Romantic imagination. 'Do you remember', Silvio Pellico wrote to his brother in 1815, 'the effect which reading Shakespeare and Schiller had on us? It was as if the horizon expanded itself before our very eyes' (Nulli 1918: 170). A few years later, in 1818 in the *Conciliatore*, he made the characteristically Romantic observation: 'If Shakespeare's *Othello*, with all its numerous characters and with no unity of place or time, nevertheless excites pity and terror, it is a true tragedy, an absolutely true tragedy, just as much as if it produced the same effects with three characters and an adherence to all the most venerable authorities' (Nulli 1918: 170). The prodigality of Shakespeare's imagination created an extraordinary effect on the Italian Romantics, and earned for him a prestige such that by himself he was 'authority enough to counter the whole of Antiquity, of the Renaissance, of the eighteenth century' (*ibidem*).

If Shakespeare, not to mention Schiller and Hugo and others of the period's heroes, taught Italians to see 'truth' more clearly, and to speak the language of the heart more directly than ever before, another influence, no less potent and in some ways more specifically relevant to *risorgimento* art, emanated from the great German clergyman-scholar, Johann Gottfried Herder. It was Herder who formulated an idea that was to become the central *Leitmotiv* of Mazzini's writing: that each truly constituted nation had its own genius, which was expressed in its language and its culture – particularly its popular culture – in its social behaviour and its traditions, in the experiences of its history and its religious life. And what Herder and Mazzini preached, many an Italian Romantic artist aimed to put into practice. A primary task was to teach the emerging nation its own history, to help it understand the deepest sources of its own identity. In Italy, of course, as in many other parts of Europe, the Romantics re-discovered and explored the Middle Ages, uncovering the country's roots, investigating its claims to nationhood, seeking paradigms for the modern world. One episode thrilled them more than any other: the founding of the Lombard League, the oath of Pontida and the battle of Legnano. Historians expounded its significance, poets and novelists from Berchet to Carducci exercised their eloquence in glorifying it, Verdi – in collaboration with Cammarano – made it the subject of his most flagrantly politicized opera. The clamant topicality of that phase of Italian history that culminated in the Battle of Legnano was that it showed how once, by putting behind them their traditional rivalries and resentments and uniting in a common cause, the Italian communes had been able to conquer and drive from their land the German emperor, the mighty Barbarossa himself.

In origin, Romanticism was a north European phenomenon, and the influence of Northern taste remained a potent one even on the very distinctive dialect of Romanticism that evolved in Italy. As early as the 1760s some Italians had begun to thrill to the mysterious vibrations emanating from Ossian (cf. pp. 243–4 above). And after Ossian a growing appetite for unfamiliar worlds of feeling, for images of an 'elsewhere' remote from the sun-drenched Classical, Mediterranean world was fed by further translations, from Gray and Young, and from the German poets. The strange allure that Italians had discovered in Ossian – in his bleak Northern landscapes, in his moods of nostalgia and wild desolation – remained fresh throughout the Revolutionary period and into the Romantic age. And this enthusiasm for Ossian helped predispose Italian minds in favour of other Northern products, notably the verse narratives and historical novels of Sir Walter Scott. If Stendhal is to be trusted, even

Rossini's version of *The Lady of the Lake – La donna del lago* (Naples 1819) – was experienced as Ossianic: 'La musique a vraiment une couleur ossianique et une certaine énergie sauvage et piquante', he wrote of a Paris revival in 1824 (Ambrose 1981: 66). By then the Scott influence, without which, on Manzoni's own confession, *I promessi sposi* would have been unimaginable, was approaching its climax in Italy (Colquhoun 1954: 187). It reached a peak in the later 1820s and 1830s, and formed an essential part of the spiritual landscape against which Bellini and Donizetti produced their most characteristic work.

Sensibility and subjectivity

In the second volume of his *Conversazioni critiche* Benedetto Croce published a review of a study by Gina Martegiani entitled *Il romanticismo italiano non esiste* (Florence 1908). He concludes that

The fundamental thesis championed by the author is not new, but is substantially accurate. Romanticism in the psychological or moral significance of the word, such as it possessed in Germany especially, did not exist in Italy in the period called Romantic. It did not exist and could not exist, not only because the Italian spirit was at that time occupied with other problems (national, political and social) but because in Italy its historical presuppositions were lacking: the religious reform, the mysticism, the philosophy, the poetic Middle Ages, the myth and the legend. There were even lacking those weaknesses, those negative elements, that quality of turbidity, vagueness and disharmony, which afflicts the Germanic peoples. Even our national virtues prevented the flourishing of genuine Romanticism. (Croce 1942: 216)

Croce is surely right: the finest and most characteristic form of Italian Romanticism is that type defined and exemplified in Manzoni. There is something both superficial and second-hand about the imitation of Scott and Byron and the other Northern Romantics so admired in Italy at this time. Nevertheless Northern Romanticism did strike deep enough to have a profoundly disturbing effect on Italian traditions of art, to create new ways of thinking and feeling about it, to place sensibility and subjectivity at the heart of artistic perception. Sensibilities were often overwrought, and the reader of verse and, especially, the spectator in the theatre dissolved into tears with remarkable promptitude. Reactions to the operas of Bellini provide a typical illustration: 'In the second act [of *La sonnambula*] the singers themselves wept and carried the audience along with them', reported Glinka in Milan in 1830–31, 'so that in the happy days of Carnival, tears were continually being wiped away in boxes and parquet alike. Embracing Shterich in the Ambassador's box, I, too, shed tears of emotion and ecstasy' (Glinka 1963: 61). Verdi's ideas of audience behaviour remained very much like that to the end of his life. What he hoped for was not the respectful silence typical of German opera-houses but an atmosphere in which the spectators 'carried away by a single emotion, participated in the action that unfolded before their eyes, and followed it trembling, quivering and weeping' (Conati 1984: 346). We find among Italian Romantics a new awareness of the beauty and mystery of Nature, indeed we find that same post-Rousseau tendency to discover in Nature an image of the divine harmony that is so characteristic of the early German Romantics. In *Le ultime lettere di Jacopo Ortis*, under the date 20 November 1797, Foscolo describes a visit to Petrarch's last home in Arqua. After a long rapturous account of the landscape bathed in early morning light he concludes:

You might have heard diffuse itself a solemn harmony, blending among the woods, the birds, the flocks, the rivers, the toil of men; and meanwhile the air was perfumed with the exhalations which the earth in the exultation of its joy sent up from the valleys and the mountains to the Sun, the principal minister of nature. – I pity that wretch who can awake silently and coldly, and look upon such blessings without feeling his eyes bathed with tears of gratitude.

That sense of the sacredness of art, which Mazzini expressed so forcefully, perhaps tended to lead to another form of subjectivity: the cult of the artistic personality, the obsession with self and the inner life, the 'convulsions or swoonings . . . the analysing, foretelling, and distinguishing of every most minute emotion' which so disgusted Leopardi (Leopardi 1966: 74). No better musical example could be cited than Mercadante's symphonic poem *Il lamento del bardo*, composed after the onset of his blindness. This piece, Florimo reported, 'is nothing but the expression of his grief at his new state of suffering . . . in this sad and grand composition he depicts himself, the anxious state of his soul, and the *idée fixe* (fisso pensiero) of his true misfortune' (de Napoli 1931: 213).

Such traces of the cult of the artist as hero were, in a European context, modest indeed. Nevertheless they contributed to a growing conviction, particularly important in the world of opera, that he should be less ready to allow his vision to be compromised by the forces of convention. Most composers of Romantic opera were involved in the assertion of this principle: Rossini in his elimination of the custom of impromptu ornamentation; Mercadante demanding that his scores 'should not be altered in the slightest, whether by additions or cuts or transpositions' (letter to Florimo apropos *Elena da Feltre*, January 1838, Naples Conservatory Library); Verdi by his gradual abandoning of *puntature*, a convention according to which, at revivals of an opera, the music might be revised to suit more precisely the vocal capabilities of the new cast. Ultimately, though this step was far less common in Italy than in other parts of Europe – and indeed it flatly contradicted the Manzonian creed outlined at the beginning of his chapter – the view of art as the expression of a superior vision or sensibility could lead to the feeling that the artist and his work were beyond good or evil, to be judged by purely aesthetic criteria regardless of morality or usefulness. Guerrazzi's rapturous acclaim of Byron, for example, expresses the conviction that, at its most powerful, the artistic impulse was an eruptive, devastating power; that Apollonian restraints must, if need be, break down in honour of Dionysus.

I have not seen the Niagara falls, nor the Alpine avalanche, I do not know what a volcano is like; but I have witnessed the most furious tempests, the thunderbolt has exploded close by me; and yet I think that all these spectacles, known and unknown, are not by a long way to be compared with the awe inspired in me by that immense spirit.

(Simhart 1909: 30)

The new explosive force represented by such Northern Romantics as Byron was particularly momentous for the evolution of opera. The unharmonious world picture that had already been introduced in a small number of Ossianic operas in the late eighteenth century now came to prevail, sweeping away for ever the reasonable, optimistic and idealistic vision of Metastasian opera. Composers had to come to terms with dramas conditioned by violence, madness and perversion; and they had to brace themselves to square up to the tragic ending.

The Catholic revival

A religious revival accompanied the spread of Romantic ideals. The surrender of sceptical reason to the claims of the inner life, and the rediscovery of the Middle Ages, both encouraged this revival. So too, as Manzoni observed, did 'the emancipation of literature from pagan traditions' which accompanied the rejection of Classical authority ('Lettera sul romanticismo', in Manzoni 1970: 341). At the close of the Napoleonic age the prestige of Catholicism had been low. The Church had been quite unable to prevent Napoleon from exploiting it in the most cynical manner; the papacy had been humiliated over and over again; and in bringing about the downfall of Napoleon the leading role had been played by non-Catholic powers, either Protestant (Britain and Prussia) or Orthodox (Russia). Yet immediately after the Restoration an astonishing revival of prestige authority and genuine faith occurred.

The Catholic revival stemmed from France, in particular from the writings of Lamennais, a priest, and of de Maistre, a civil servant and polemicist. Led by Lamennais, Catholics were taught to regard the protestant, liberal and sceptical assaults that had threatened their faith in recent centuries as unequivocal errors, not as symptoms of human progress that might be countenanced with a benign, 'enlightened' tolerance. Led by de Maistre they learned to view the Pope as the only credible authority in ethical and spiritual matters, and hence as the only guarantor of the social and moral order against those anarchic forces which had erupted so terrifyingly during the Revolutionary period. But while Italians were happy to have their religious faith fanned into new fervour by Lamennais and de Maistre, they did not emulate the French by associating revived Catholicism with political reaction. In Italy Catholicism had to come to terms with progressive ideals: de Sanctis defined the tone of Italian religion in the Romantic age memorably when he wrote of 'the famous trio liberty, equality, fraternity evangelized' (de Sanctis 1870–71, chapter 20). De Sanctis's trio, duly evangelized, is indeed found to permeate much that is most distinctive in the culture of the age. Manzoni's writings from the '*Inni sacri*' to *I promessi sposi* proclaimed a Catholic faith united with an egalitarian sympathy and compassion. Mazzini's programme for dramatic reform envisaged a fusion and superseding of what he saw as the two supreme types of drama of earlier ages – the blindly religious 'Drama of Fate', represented at its finest by Aeschylus, and the self-assertingly humanist 'Drama of Individualism', represented at its finest by Shakespeare – in a new and higher form of drama, 'the Drama of Providence'; and the spiritual function of this would be 'to form a brotherhood between earth and heaven . . . and give to human history [by which Mazzini seems to have meant political and social progress] the consecration of God' (Mazzini 1910: 194). Of the more specifically polemic writings produced by the 'Neo-Guelphism' set off by de Maistre, Gioberti's *Il primato morale e civile degli italiani* (1843) was outstandingly important. It 'introduced into Italy the national question under the papal banner' (Adolfo Omodeo, quoted in Hearder 1983: 197), arguing that the well-being of the nation depended upon a crusade led jointly by the Holy City (Rome) and the Warrior Province (Piedmont).

Neo-classical nostalgia

The point will by now have been taken that because of the social, educative and political ideals of so many Italians the anarchic and subjective strains in Romanticism were far less conspicuous in Italy than in France or Germany or Britain. The majority shared Manzoni's contempt for that style of Romanticism that he described as 'a mishmash of witches and ghosts, a systematic disorder, a recherché extravagance, an abdication of common sense' ('Lettera sul romanticismo', in Manzoni 1970: 344). And there was a further factor that restrained Romantic excess. Despite Manzoni's assertion that the rejection of the Classical past had been one of the decisive achievements of Italian Romanticism, a strong vein of neo-classical nostalgia ran through the intellectual life of the time. Many Italians still saw themselves as the uniquely privileged heirs of the Classical tradition. '[I thank] heaven that I was born an Italian', wrote Leopardi in 1817, 'for after all our literature, even if it is little cultivated, is the only legitimate daughter of the two truly great ancient ones' (Leopardi 1966: 56). And even while they were intoxicated by the heady brews of the new Romanticism not a few artists, in all mediums, continued to yearn for the untendentious and unproblematic beauty of an earlier age.

These nostalgic counter-currents in the prevailing Romanticism assumed many different forms. One extreme manifestation was provided by that group of poets, headed by Quintilio Guanciali at Naples and Diego Vitrioli at Reggio Calabria, who chose to compose their work in Latin rather than Italian.[6] But less peripheral figures were also affected. Foscolo's last major work *Le grazie* was, in de Sanctis's words, 'hurled like a challenge at the new age' (de Sanctis 1870–71, chapter 20), which Foscolo felt had, in rejecting Classical mythology, rejected one of its most precious inheritances. Even Felice Romani, the best and most influential librettist of the period, whose collaboration with Bellini and Donizetti provided Italian opera with some of its most quintessentially Romantic monuments, was torn between the conviction that opera should incorporate 'everything that imagination can conceive or passion suggest', and altogether more retrospective inclinations:

For myself, I confess, when I am most bored by the reveries of our Hugos and our Scotts, when I am most afflicted by the depressing philosophism that discolours and turns every flower of this life pale, I take refuge in the past centuries, I warm myself in the sun of ancient wisdom, and console myself for the turpitude of the present with the virtue of the past.   (Quoted in Lippmann 1969b: 34)

Nor were composers unaffected by this ambivalence. Despite the 'revolutionary' works of the 1830s for which he is best remembered, Mercadante remained a life-long devotee of the traditional aesthetic principles of an earlier age – 'the intimate and affective expression of the words sublimated in simple melodies', the revelation of 'the idea of the *Beautiful* and the *True*' (Mercadante 1867: 34–5). Pacini's finest opera, *Saffo* (Naples 1840), was inspired, according to his own account, by his reflections on the musical theory of the Ancient Greeks and his attempts to 'approximate to their Melopea' (Pacini 1865: 95). Mercadante and Pacini were not, of course, the giants of Italian Romantic opera. But they were distinguished enough and popular enough in their day to encourage us to recognize that Italian Romanticism, even in its operatic forms, was not a monolithic movement obsessed with Ossianic strangeness, Hugoesque horror and the multifarious delights of mediaevalism.

22 · Dramatic themes: the libretto

The librettist and his responsibilities

The librettists who wrote the texts for Italian Romantic opera were faced with momentous tasks. Opera was Italy's most popular art form; it needed to come to grips with the new artistic and spiritual ideals thrown up in the debates about Romanticism, and in due course to arm itself for new social and educative tasks.

It must be said that librettists rose to these challenges rather uncertainly: it was not a vintage age for dramatic poets. The poet-patriot Niccolò Tommaseo once wrily observed, 'As a truly appalling alternative to the dungeon, princes could condemn their rebellious subjects to the daily reading of opera librettos' (Rinaldi 1965: 445). Hardly more flattering was the view of Rossini, who dismissed as 'robaccia pessima' – the most awful rubbish – virtually everything since Metastasio (*ibidem*: 421). But if there was no new Metastasio or Goldoni to give irresistible eloquence to the perceptions and sensibilities of the new age, there were some elegant versifiers and conscientious craftsmen. Rossini himself excepted from his strictures Felice Romani, and Romani was indeed almost universally admired for the sweetness and harmoniousness of his verses. The librettos he wrote for Bellini – actually he preferred the term 'melo-tragedies' – were probably the finest of the age. But the leading Neapolitan librettist Salvatore Cammarano was a no less fastidious worker, acutely conscious of the dignity of his task:

. . . if I don't hurry my work it is because I have too much pride in it, and too much zeal for your management, and immense respect for the public – and you, better than any other person, know that I decline tempting offers so as not to betray my principles . . .
(Letter to Barbaia, 16 June 1838; quoted in Black 1984: 47)

Romani and Cammarano were both resident poets attached to particular opera-houses: Romani to La Scala, Milan, from 1813 to 1834, Cammarano to the Royal Theatres of Naples from 1834 to 1852. Cammarano's actual title was 'poeta drammatico e concertatore de' Reali Teatri', which we might translate 'librettist and stage-manager . . .', for at that time a theatre poet had a far wider responsibility than that of simply writing the libretto. He had, at an early stage in the planning of the opera, to supply the impresario with detailed notes on costumes and properties. And when the

403

text was finished and the music composed and learnt, such production skills as the period demanded were likewise his affair. In the memoirs of Romani's widow we read of the poet's exertions at the early rehearsals of *Il pirata* (Milan 1827) as he tried to teach Rubini to act: 'Get up, move back, stir yourself, gesticulate . . . No, no, not like that . . . you're angry now . . . a step backwards . . . clear words . . . with an agitated voice . . . Good Lord, don't talk rubbish . . . make a gesture of contempt . . . now forward threateningly . . . no, not like that' (Rinaldi 1965: 196). The librettist's role in blocking the big tableaux for chorus and the full ensemble of soloists actually involved him in the musical conception. For it was apparently customary to keep each group of choral voices as intact as possible on the stage – women at the front, tenors on one side, basses on the other, for example[1] – and that is why we find Cammarano during his collaboration with Verdi on *Luisa Miller* (Naples 1849) telling the composer which voices are to sing what: 'the basses of the chorus will be the archers; the tenors and women the villagers' (Verdi 1913: 472).

Censorship

Few of the librettist's tasks were more important and none was more trying than that of dealing with censorship. Despite the popular image, in which there is much truth, of Verdi as a mighty router of censors, it was normally the librettist who had the primary role – strategically and artistically – in this fricative affair. As soon as a subject had been chosen, he had to submit a synopsis to the censor's office for approval; and if the subject was deemed to be of a dangerous kind, it was normally at this stage that it was forbidden – as Dumas *père*'s *Catherine Howard* was forbidden when proposed for Verdi's Venetian debut in 1843. Versification went ahead only after this preliminary clearance, though the librettist might in fact already have begun providing the composer with the texts of a few numbers while the censors were still mulling over his synopsis. Once the versification was complete, the libretto was resubmitted to the censors, and it was at this stage that they criticized it in detail and gave instructions for emendations. Because the composer normally had so short a time to complete his score, he would be at work on it virtually from the moment the librettist began to versify the synopsis; and rarely was it finished until a few days before the première. That is why there are frequently discrepancies between the words he set to music and the words approved for performance and therefore printed in the libretto. (Black 1984: 232–4 describes these procedures in detail.)

Severity of censorship varied startlingly from one part of Italy to another, as Stendhal's comments on a performance of Alfieri's *Saul* in Naples show:

This tragedy must exert some power over the *secret nationalism* of the Italians. It rouses them to transports . . . My friend the marquis tells me that only three of Alfieri's tragedies are permitted here; four in Rome; five in Bologna; seven in Milan; none in Turin. Consequently to applaud them is a point of honour, and to find fault with them is the mark of an *ultra*. (Stendhal 1817, entry for 2 April)

But the kinds of inhibition, vexation and complexity of thought involved in dealing with censorship in any part of Italy soon become apparent if one considers for a moment some of the official guidelines drawn up for the censors in the comparatively liberal Grand Duchy of Tuscany:

Dramas based on subjects taken from the Old Testament are permitted when written by celebrated authors and in a sublime style worthy of the subject, and when the theatre and the means of the impresario provide the necessary facilities for presenting them in a dignified and fitting manner.

No performance can be permitted of a drama based on subjects taken from the history and the affairs of the Church.

It will be necessary to take the most scrupulous care to see that in the ballets, even the serious ones, nothing should be permitted which could relate to the history of the Old Testament or to that of the Church.

The general rules for the censorship of printed works in which are disseminated religious principles or principles that are politically subversive, or of works based on a malicious plan threatening to weaken or destroy veneration for Religion or for the Throne and which awaken in people's minds emotions hostile to either of these, will be applied more strictly to theatrical performances.

Equally to be banned from the stage are all those comedies which could offend morals and good manners and at which every class of person could not properly be present, especially those representing sinful love affairs, faithless husbands and wives, scandalous intrigues with young girls who marry or even become mothers clandestinely, before finally forcing from their parents consent for what they have done; all those, in short, in which insubordination and lack of respect in the children is seen to triumph over paternal authority.

Also to be excluded from the theatre are all those tasteless pieces in which are exhibited only crimes and atrocious deeds, such as assassination, premeditated murder, despairing suicides, and such other topics as are rendered interesting only by the singular difficulty or the barbarous circumstances attending the crime . . .

The judgement of the censor will be very sharp on performances based on stories from Italian history, and prohibit absolutely performances of a kind which could in any way offend the conscience and the principles of modern times. He should also forbid under all circumstances performances in which appear members of the royal families of Europe who lived in ages not far distant from our own.

The so-called 'dramas of feeling' generally translated from the German or the French, in which dangerous and exalted passions appear on the stage, may be tolerated, but not encouraged, and the censor will forbid absolutely those which give clear evidence of tending to corrupt the heart and deprave morals . . . (di Stefano 1964: 60–2)

Clearly the primary concerns were to spare the political establishment any embarrassment, to avoid any possible offence to the perhaps over-delicate religious susceptibilities of the age, and to do the utmost to prevent errors of morality or taste. An Italian censor's idea of the perfect operatic subject is ironically underlined by Bellini in commending *I Puritani* to his Neapolitan friend Florimo: 'it contains *no religion, no nefarious love-affairs, no politics whatsoever*' (Bellini 1943: 479).

But political history, religion and new conceptions of morality and taste were precisely the burning issues of the age, the things about which the most serious-minded Italian Romantics cared most deeply. Censorship made it difficult for the librettist to handle them except gingerly, indirectly, even surreptitiously.

Religion in the sense of Christian religion was indeed a non-starter in the opera-house, though a few operas were produced based on Old Testament subjects – Rossini's *Mosè in Egitto* (Naples 1818) and Verdi's *Nabucco* (Milan 1842) among them. When in 1838 Donizetti and Cammarano made so bold as to prepare a work based on the life of the third-century Armenian saint Polyeucte, King Ferdinand himself intervened to ban it, 'deigning with his own sacred hand to declare that the histories of the Martyrs are venerated in the Church and are not presented on the stage' (Black 1984: 48). The sacred texts of the Christian church, biblical and liturgical, were protected with a still more scrupulous piety. It was the last-minute qualms of the ecclesiastical censor over the biblical reading at the climax of Verdi's *Stiffelio* (Trieste 1850) that to all intents and purposes destroyed that opera. In some cities the very vocabulary of religious discourse was banned: in 1851 the Archbishop of Ferrara forbade performances of *Luisa Miller* because of the over-frequent use of such words as 'angelo', 'inferno', 'cielo' and 'Iddio'. Elsewhere these irreverences were more tenderly corrected, by means of a censor's 'dictionary of synonyms' which provided 'cielo' for 'Dio', 'genio' for 'angelo', 'abisso' for 'inferno', 'eliso' for 'paradiso', 'prodigio' for 'miracolo', and so forth (Rolandi 1951: 145).

Clearly there could be no question of subjecting historical themes to such blanket condemnation, and in this librettists and censors engaged in subtler fencings and parryings. To be sure the situation was difficult enough for authors: history was the very stuff of Romantic drama, yet whole regions of it were inaccessible. The royal families of Europe were as untouchable as the early saints of Armenia, and the history of Italy was taboo no less than the history of the Christian church. This is the burden of the famous exchange of letters between Giuseppe Giusti and Verdi at the time of *Macbeth*. But a high proportion of Italian opera was composed for production in the Austrian territories, or indeed in France, and under those circumstances librettists and composers were often tempted by the comparatively liberal laws of censorship to tackle historical themes that would not have been countenanced for a moment in Bologna or Rome or Naples. The censors in these latter cities were then posed with a real problem. Simply to forbid the performance of operas by such national celebrities as Rossini or Donizetti or Verdi would have been dangerously provocative, and they soon became adepts at what was intended to be a more subtle way of defusing the explosive potential. The title of the opera and the names of the characters would be changed, and the action removed to some place remote temporally and geographically: in Rome Verdi's *Giovanna d'Arco* became *Orietta di Lesbo*; Rossini's *Guillaume Tell* became *Rudolfo di Stirling*. One wonders how much difference it really made. As we have seen, the long tradition of operatic allegory in Italy was still alive in the nineteenth century. And there is no doubt that audiences were just as well able to play the game of substitution as the censors themselves; that if the censors could transform *La battaglia di Legnano* into an *Assedio d'Harlem*, the audiences could as readily transform *L'assedio d'Harlem* into a *Battaglia di Legnano*. Whoever the characters on stage purported to be, the emotions that moved them, the ideals that inspired them, belonged to the here and now of nineteenth-century Italy.

Many, perhaps most, librettists and composers were eager to explore a new repertory of dramatic themes, to escape from too close a dependence on the traditions of the Classical Mediterranean world into those new realms of feeling opened up by English, French and German Romanticism. In fact, French Romantic drama became the favourite source for Italian Romantic opera; and that is why, in the censor's office, taste and morals became an issue hardly less sensitive than politics and religion. For the ethos of much French Romantic drama was deeply offensive to the harmony-seeking moralists and old-fashioned humanists who supervised Italian official taste. One welcomes the insistence of John Black that the censors were frequently cultivated and caring men, not necessarily philistine at all; but all the same it cannot have been easy for the more fervently Romantic spirits to coexist with them. Reading a paternalistic effusion like the Neapolitan censor's report on *Roberto Devereux* one ceases to be surprised that librettists so rarely rose to the artistic challenges that faced them.

[The censorship] as far as it is in its power has kept on encouraging young authors, approving their output when it has discerned in them signs of talent which provide hope for better things: and it has noticed with pleasure that it has not been unsuccessful in its attempts to direct their steps away from the present fashion of contaminating the stage with representations of atrocious misdeeds, coldly premeditated. Already, thanks to its watchfulness, more than five young men can be counted, all capable of weaving together a melodrama with melodious verses based on a well constructed plot . . .

(Quoted in Black 1984: 52–3)

A new repertory of dramatic themes

One should probably begin with Sir Walter Scott, a taste for whose writings was acquired very easily by a generation nourished on Ossian. The earliest Scott opera in Italy was *La donna del lago* (Naples 1819), the text of which

407

was written for Rossini by Leone Andrea Tottola at a time when none of Scott's works had yet been translated into Italian. It has been suggested that this particular subject was chosen because, with its bard (in the opera he becomes a chorus of bards), its evocative descriptions of wild scenery and its spasms of balladesque melancholy, it was of all Scott's works the most Ossianic (Ambrose 1981: 65–6). Scott was to be a primary source of much that was most representative of the new era: of Manzoni's great historical novel *I promessi sposi*, and its many imitations; of Tommaso Grossi's epic of the crusades, *I Lombardi alla prima crociata* (the source of Verdi's opera); and of many strands in the historical dramas of Victor Hugo and his epigones. It is no coincidence that the high tide of Scott's popularity in Italy arrived in the late 1820s at exactly the time when Bellini and Romani were producing Italy's first full-blooded, uncompromisingly Romantic operas.

In a telling phrase Robert Louis Stevenson defined Romanticism as 'the movement of an extended curiosity and an enfranchised imagination' (Schmidgall 1977: 114), and placed Scott at the head of it. The Waverley Novels came to be seen as 'the scenic and historical wonders of the Romantic era' (*ibidem*); and that far, at least, critical perceptions in Italy matched those in Britain. It is true that Scott was imperfectly understood, sometimes flagrantly misrepresented, often ineptly imitated. Some saw in his books little but 'ghosts, ruined castles and ancestral curses', and therefore placed him among the manifestations of Gothic Horror (Ambrose 1981: 59); some distorted his meaning for political ends; in dramatic adaptations, especially in opera librettos, little trouble was taken to build up the all-important historical background that might have given some deeper perspective to the Romantic agonies holding the centre of the stage. But when all is said, Scott's books provided Italian opera with some kind of model for dramatic themes in which were blended history – in the sense of a distant past that could be upheld as exemplary in faith, or ethics or valour – and bizarre and terrible happenings, which attacked the nerves and emotions of the spectator as much as they spoke to the mind. This blend proved uniquely appealing to theatre audiences of the second quarter of the century.

The mood of opera grew more sombre; the tragic close became more general. As the full tide of Romanticism flooded in over Italy from the North, it was increasingly difficult for even the most nostalgic enthusiasts for Enlightenment optimism to evade this issue. There was of course resistance to the tragic mode, and spasmodic efforts to mitigate its effect. A notorious case was the re-writing of the final scenes of Rossini's *Otello* for Rome in 1816. But once accepted, the closing death-scene became a cherished ingredient of Romantic opera. In *Il pirata* and the other 'melo-tragedies' he wrote for Bellini, Romani took particular care over the culminating 'tableau of terror', establishing a pattern for those scenes of death, devastation and despair which, a few years later, Verdi was to make so peculiarly his own. And at least one great singer of the period, *il tenore della bella morte* – Napoleone Moriani – owed much of his reputation to his prowess in such scenes: 'the extinction of life is expressed by singing that has the tints, the shuddering, of death itself; it is like a trampled narcissus that bows its head, and in whose bosom the transient echo weeps and laments' (a review in *La fama*, 1844, quoted in Walker 1962: 88).

Librettists usually found their subjects in the repertory of the prose theatres of the larger cities: the Teatro Fiorentini in Naples, for instance, supplied most of Cammarano's (Black 1984: 160). A few of these plays were Italian, a few German or English, at least in origin, but the overwhelming majority came from France, where the playwrights of the period poured forth well made plays with inexhaustible facility. To a large extent this theatrical profusion amounted to the playing of resourceful variations on a common stock of themes; but this was no disadvantage as far as operatic adaptation was concerned. Librettists and composers had few qualms about repeating subjects that were already familiar: a tragic and sanguinary love-triangle in a pseudo-historical setting, for instance, rarely failed to fire Donizetti's muse. The first Romantic generation in Italy was too enthralled with the expressive potential of the new fashion to worry much about repetitiousness within the fashion. They sought intoxicated states of soul, passions driven to violent extremes, tangles of character which sped the protagonists to an irrational doom. For no longer was there any question of the dictates of the heart being qualified by virtue and reason, no longer could every intrigue, every conflict be finally resolved in a harmonious denouement.

Though many Italian librettists might now have cried with Werther: 'Ossian hat in meinem Herzen den Homer verdrängt',[2] ultramontane fashions did not quite monopolize the Italian stage. Romani was ambivalent in his attitude to Romanticism from the first (cf. p. 402 above), and ultimately, after he had abandoned his career as a theatre-poet for one in journalism, he became deeply hostile to many aspects of the new movement. Even Cammarano, a younger man by more than a decade, was sometimes prompted to distance himself from the more extreme manifestations of Romantic taste. Of *Maria di Rudenz* (Venice 1838), based on Anicet-Bourgeois and Maillan's *La nonne sanglante*, he was to write, 'those who know the crude and gloomy happenings in that play will readily appreciate that I wanted to tone down its outlandish horrors, and if I hadn't been able to succeed in my purpose (and perhaps no one could) these few words will serve to indicate how much I abhor this bloodstained northern genre' (Black 1984: 44). And Bellini did not speak for quite all composers in his scorn for Classical historical subjects. Mercadante seems to have been reluctant to abandon Metastasio: even as Romani and Bellini were revealing the brave new world of uncompromising Romanticism in the years 1827–28, he was still setting *Ezio* and *Adriano in Siria* (admittedly in much altered form); and he returned to Classical sources with every appearance of satisfaction after barely a decade dabbling with more fashionable types of theme: for, reported Florimo, 'in subjects taken from Roman history, Mercadante felt at ease, and his imagination had ample space to roam. He seemed to envisage with surprising clarity those severe customs, those virile sentiments, those robust practices which made the Roman people conquerors and governors of the world' (Florimo 1880–84, III: 16).

The staging of Romantic opera

New dramatic themes and new aesthetic ideals inevitably led to a new type of spectacle. Traditional neo-classical perspective sets remained popular into the 1820s, and particularly in Milan made the opera of the age of Rossini a spectacle of monumental grandiosity: 'in Milan, everything is sacrificed to mass effects of form and colour, and to the general impression. It is [Jacques-Louis] David's own special genius transposed into the medium of decor' (Stendhal 1956: 439). But during that decade sets became more modest, and a greater premium was set on the suggestive and the individual. The vogue for Romantic historicism brought in new iconographical motifs: the ruined Gothic castle, graveyards, moonlight scenes, and scenes of wild nature which surely echo contemporary developments toward a more natural style of landscape painting (Ambrose 1981: 76–7). New effects of lighting became possible. As a matter of fact gas-lighting was often felt to be more prosaic and less flexible than the oil lights and prisms of the past – Ricci indeed goes so far as to call it a 'mortal blow to scenography' (1930: 28) – but Daguerre's invention of the diorama in Paris in 1822, and such new resources as the phantasmagoria, which Verdi learned about from Sanquirico at the time he was planning *Macbeth*, put extra poetic and evocative powers into the hands of stage designers.[3]

It remained a prime consideration in Italian opera to present an enchanting visual composition on stage. A cultivated pictorial allusiveness was still common. Moses' costume in Rossini's *Mosè* was copied from Michelangelo's statue in the church of San Pietro in Vincoli (Stendhal 1956: 310); Verdi intended to model the spectacle of the Act I finale of *Attila* on the Raphael 'tapestries or frescoes' in the Vatican (Verdi 1913: 441). But an interest in visual authenticity was slowly gaining ground – Stendhal tells us that for the première of Rossini's *Elisabetta* in 1816 the Naples management sent to England for historically accurate costume sketches; and Lady Morgan witnessed a production of Spontini's *La Vestale* at La Scala in (?)1820 in which

the chariots, moulded upon that splendid relic of antiquity, the *Biga* at Rome, are drawn
by fiery and impatient horses, and driven by impetuous charioteers, exactly as they are
represented in the ancient bas-reliefs . . . The living groups are formed after the finest
sculptures, and down to the bronze vase in the Consul's festive board, the lamp, tripod,
and consular chair, all seemed borrowed from *Herculaneum* or *Pompeii*.

(Morgan 1821, I:99)

Above all librettists and scenographers were becoming sensitive to the need
for a more intimate harmony between the action, the characters and their
visual setting. A good example of this scenographic pathetic fallacy is to be
found in Cammarano's synopsis for *Lucia di Lammermoor*, where he
remarks of the Act II duet between Edgardo and Ashton, '. . . The storm
howls terribly and reflects the rage which invests the two cruel enemies'
(Black 1984: 244).

Performers too were affected by these developments. Malibran, under
the influence of Talma, 'wished to introduce in the theatre artistic and
archeological truth and, with this in view, she had copies made of a quantity
of costumes from the archives of Venice, and from the miniatures in some
old manuscripts' (Sterling-Mackinlay 1908: 118). Authentic and truthful
impersonation became the aspiration of many of the finest singers, and
Cammarano's production notes for Naples show that the librettists of the
period were eager to encourage these naturalistic tendencies (Black 1984:
283). One could, however, go too far; in London Giuseppe Ambrogetti
had, while learning the role of the father in Paer's *Agnese*, sought 'to qualify
himself for this part [by studying] the various forms of insanity in the cells
of Bedlam; but unfortunately, in seeking to render his impersonation true,
he made it too dreadful to be borne. Females actually fainted, while others
endeavoured to escape from so appalling a spectacle' (Hogarth 1851, II:
299).

A new ideology

The kind of nostalgia which Mercadante felt for a more familiar, humane
world was not a major creative force in the opera of the age. More vital was
an aspiration, which we find clearly articulated only by philosophers and
critics, but which some creative artists certainly shared, towards a quite
new type of drama, more in tune with the political and social aspirations of
the age. And in this context, we must first invoke the name of Mazzini. He
too, like the later Romani or the later Mercadante, rejected the idea that the
delirious, ego-centred effusions of Romantic melodrama provided a sound
basis for modern opera. But he rejected it not in order to regress into an
outdated eighteenth-century world view. Mazzini saw, or believed that he
saw, that mankind was on the verge of a new stage in its evolution, which he
defined as the age of 'socialized humanity'. This new age needed its own

411

archetypal dramatic form. It would be a 'profoundly religious, profoundly educative social drama . . . greater than Shakespeare by as much as the idea of Humanity is greater than the idea of the individual' (Mazzini 1910: 196). Mazzini's prescription, clearly, is a left-wing programme for *risorgimento* art.

Ideologically tendentious opera had occasionally made its appearance in the productions of the revolutionary period at the close of the eighteenth century, but at the Restoration this note falls silent. The *bel canto* of Rossini and his epigones was largely innocent of extra-musical ideas – 'who would seek in an opera for an idea?' enquired Mazzini witheringly (1910 127); though that was not to prevent audiences at a later date from reading their own ideology into Rossini (cf. Chapter 25, p. 453 below). If there were, in Rossini's time, considerations other than those of making music, they were more likely to be ones of practicality or expediency. Dramatic and musical ideals were constrained by the financial realities imposed on or by impresarios; the singers in the company had to be flatteringly catered for, the *convenienze* of the tradition had to be observed. A turning point came in the late 1820s with the beginning of the partnership of Bellini and Romani. Opera could become a vehicle for ideas in the sense that Mazzini intended only if singers were persuaded to forgo their claims to be regarded as creative artists in their own right, and to subordinate themselves to the overall conception of librettists and composer. By some mysterious alchemy of personality, intelligence and intuition, Romani and Bellini, as soon as they met and began to work together, recognized that they were in a position to demand exactly that. Count Barbò witnessed an illuminating scene between Bellini and the great tenor Rubini at an early rehearsal of *Il pirata*: 'Admit it', said Bellini, 'the real reason you don't like my music is that it doesn't leave you the usual opportunities; but if I have got it into my head to introduce a new style, a type of music which expresses the words very precisely, and forms a single unified conception of song and drama, come now, must you be the one to refuse to help me?' (Adamo and Lippmann 1981: 455–6).

Once the primacy of librettist and composer had been re-established, opera could become the vehicle for the spiritual and moral values of Romanticism and, by a natural association of ideas, of Liberalism. The dramatic themes taken in hand displayed their liberal colours in various ways, ways which it is perhaps legitimate to see as either Mazzinian or Manzonian. These ideological overtones are clearest in the works of the young Verdi.

Most obviously Mazzinian are those operas in which the action has been designed to highlight the national and religious dimensions of the theme, and the choric and 'democratic' resources of the medium. Mazzini's yearning for a type of drama worthy of the age of 'socialized humanity' was to be clearly answered in the group of pieces beginning with *Nabucco* and *I Lombardi* in which the fates of the individual protagonists are inextricably tangled up with the fates of whole nations: in which history and religion, the foundations on which nationhood most vitally depends, are an integral part of the dramatic theme. In such operas the protagonists themselves hardly function like real people at all; they are simply types, exemplars of the qualities of fortitude and faith on which the new Italy was to be built.

The social values of the new age could, however, be proclaimed less publicly, in a fashion it is tempting to see as Manzonian. Verdi critics have often emphasized how crucial to his dramaturgy are loving but tortured relationships between father and daughter. In fact one can go further, as Luigi Baldacci has done in a distinguished essay, and assert that even the most private-looking of Verdi's operas – *Oberto*, or *Luisa Miller* or *Rigoletto* – are social dramas in the sense that their action is rooted in family relationships. The passions aroused by the Romantic exaltation of the ego are 'vigilantly supervised by social conscience'; the loss of virtue is a tragic haunting nemesis; and while the father functions as the heaven-ordained guarantor of divine law, the mother, often dead, becomes a kind of Mary-figure, watching, praying and interceding in heaven. This kind of dramatic scheme, suggests Baldacci, has the effect of immersing all the characters and saturating the action in a 'totalitarian religiosity' (1974: 183).

The structure of the libretto

In his *Filosofia della musica* of 1836, Mazzini, the philosopher who did more than anyone to urge Italian opera towards a new ideology, complained of the state of the art in his own day. Since it was not inspired by any grand overriding idea, it was impossible for it to add up to more than the sum of its parts:

An opera cannot be defined except by the enumeration of its parts – a series of cavatinas, choruses, duets, trios and finales, interrupted – not joined together – by any old recitative, which is not listened to: a mosaic, a gallery, an accumulation, or more often a clash of different ideas, independent and disconnected, which swirl about like spirits in a magic circle . . .   (Mazzini 1910: 128)

Mazzini wrote as if he knew exactly how libretti were prepared. If he didn't, he made a shrewd critical diagnosis, for it was indeed the case that to carve up a dramatic plot into a sequence of discrete parts was the most basic of the librettist's tasks.

When the librettist drew up a synopsis, it was not merely to provide a guide for the censors. It formed the basis of the operatic structure too, by articulating the action in a series of 'numbers'. Furthermore, the synopsis was accompanied by a so-called 'distribuzione', which showed which characters were involved in which ways in which numbers. It served as a guide for the impresario and the composer, to help them assess the workload, and therefore the status, of each singer. Was a tenor *di cartello* required for such and such a role, or would a good *comprimario* be able to manage it? Was this a part for a *comprimario* or would it be wiser to eliminate it from some of the more complex scenes and give it to a singer of the secondary rank?[4]

This scheme of 'numbers' created an operatic structure quite different from the smoothly flowing intrigue of Metastasian opera. It resulted in a series of tableaux, each focused on one or two primary incidents, and each observing an essentially identical pattern. The exposition of the dramatic issue would take place in recitative, still employing the traditional *versi a selva* mixture of non-rhyming or casually rhyming *settenari* and *endecasillabi*; and the first, more static half of the tableau would then culminate in a reflective lyrical verse which provided the composer with material for an aria in slow-moving cantabile style. After this a *tempo di mezzo* brought about a transition from reflection to resolution, from retrospection to anticipation and led to a second lyrical verse, the cabaletta, the brilliant climax to the scene, which, with an explosion of physical energy, propelled the drama forward into its next stage. Such, essentially, was the pattern for virtually all numbers: duets and larger ensembles were inclined to extend it backwards with a *primo tempo* preceding the cantabile: a more fluid type of movement normally carried along on orchestral themes or figurations. But only a handful of single-movement arias (generally distinguished by such titles as *romanza* or *canzone*) and choruses made no reference to the standard pattern.

The grandest feature of this structural scheme was the 'finale', the finale, that is to say, not of the opera, but of Act I (or Act II in a three- or four-act piece). This finale was the 'keystone' of an arch-like structure, and after it there followed, not so much an anticlimax, as a shift towards a more intimate style of theatre – a pattern that was still very evident in *Aida* or *Otello*. It contained the opera's central dramatic incident, which usually took the form of some tremendous confrontation or clash of personalities, a thrilling peripeteia, or blood-curdling *coup de théâtre* – the meeting of the two queens in *Maria Stuarda*; Edgardo's interruption of the wedding ceremony in *Lucia di Lammermoor*; Germont's arrival at the party and denunciation of his son's behaviour in *La traviata*. We know from Verdi's correspondence how important such confrontations were to his sense of theatre. In fact the choice and placing of this central happening was probably the most crucial of the librettist's choices in planning the opera, and there is some evidence to suggest that the 'distribuzione' was planned outwards from it (Black 1984: 179–80).

The librettist as poet

No less important to the composer than the librettist's skill at devising a sound structure for the drama was his eloquence as a poet. Certainly the quality of a poet's verses was less exposed in Romantic melodrama than it had been in the days of Metastasian *opera seria*. But still clarity, mellifluousness and an easy rhythmic flow remained ideals. Few librettists – very few – passed this test; but Romani did: 'When one sings Romani's verses', exclaimed Giuditta Pasta – 'creator' of the roles of Norma, Amina and Beatrice di Tenda – 'so flowing, so expressive, the lineaments of mouth and face compose themselves in such a way that they just feel beautiful' (Rinaldi 1965: 419). Cammarano was likewise admired for the flow of his verses: it contained comparatively little in the way of syntactical convolution, the composer's task was rarely made more difficult by awkward breaks in the sense in mid-line, or by clumsy enjambements. And, as Budden has remarked, 'no librettist showed a greater flair for precipitating the atmosphere of a scene through a carefully constructed nucleus of words', and he goes on to quote 'Viva Italia forte ed una /colla spada e col pensier' (for heroic patriotism); 'Il pallor, funesto, orrendo / che ricopre il volto mio' (for romantic horror) (1973–81, II: 60). In a famous essay, 'Words and music in Italian nineteenth-century opera', Luigi Dallapiccola suggested that there were finer musical points too which might depend on the understanding of the poet: that, for example, his help was needed if the composer was to get a really effective 'take-off' for his arias and ensembles. For by Dallapiccola's Law of the Third Line some kind of 'emotional crescendo is always found in the third line or in the third couplet. It is brought about through rhythmic animation or through a surprise of a harmonic nature or else through an upward movement of the vocal line' (Dallapiccola 1980: 202); and without some motivation in the verse that 'emotional crescendo' would be unlikely to work effectively.[5]

It has been estimated that at the time of the unification of Italy in 1870 fewer than 10 per cent of its inhabitants spoke what would today be recognized as the national language – those that inhabited the area of Tuscany between Florence and Siena.[6] Elsewhere a wide range of local dialects was used for most everyday purposes; many of these dialects had their own literature and not a few were mutually unintelligible. When at the early sessions of the national parliament in Turin the deputies struggled to express themselves in Italian, 'they were speaking a dead language in which none of them were accustomed to converse' (Migliorini and Baldelli 1964: 249). Since the literary achievements of Dante, Petrarch and Boccaccio in the fourteenth century the Tuscan dialect had enjoyed a unique prestige; that is why it became the basis of modern Italian. But with the passing of the years the convention of using Tuscan as Italy's literary language encouraged a style which became increasingly archaic and unrealistic in flavour. It was no easy task for nineteenth-century novelists or dramatists to fashion a pan-Italian style that was artistic, eloquent and direct.

The complexity of the issue was exacerbated by the fact that, for centuries, Italians had prided themselves on having two distinct literary styles, one for prose, another – more Latinate, orotund and periphrastic – for verse. The poet Cesare Cantù left an illuminating account of his training in rhetoric in the 1820s:

In poetry . . . the further you can distance yourself from the speech of the vulgar mob the better. First of all there is the choice of words: you will not say *abbrucia, affligge, cava, innalze, è lecito, spada, patria, la morte, la poesia*; but *addugge, ange, elice, estolle, lice, brando, terra natia, fato, musa* . . . And, my boy, you must abhor base ideas which recall things too everyday. For proper names, substitute an elegant circumlocution; you will not say *amore*, but *bendato arciero*; not *vino* but *liquor di Bacco*, not *leone, aquila*, but *regina de'volanti*, and *bionda imperator della foresta* . . .

(Migliorini and Baldelli 1964: 252)

This artificial poetic language was of course the language of the opera libretto, and to dismiss it as preposterous fustian is beside the point. For we are dealing not with a realistic or conversational dramatic idiom, but with drama in the highest of high styles. Well set to music such verse is not merely redeemed; it plays a modest but far from negligible role in helping Romantic opera achieve its own distinctive type of eloquence: elevated, grandiloquent and unmistakably coherent.

23 · The life of the theatre

Administration

The number of theatres in which opera was performed remained very large. There were some local areas, for example the city of Venice, where for special reasons there was a contraction of theatrical activity compared with the eighteenth century, and there was during the Napoleonic period a typical attempt to rationalize the number of the theatres in proportion to the population available to support them.[1] But there was no overall decline in the popularity of opera, the productivity of composers, the number of places, large and small, or theatres magnificent and humble, where opera could be heard. There were court theatres as in Turin and Naples, and municipal theatres as at Trieste; there were theatres such as La Fenice at Venice that were owned by companies of predominantly noble share-holders, and others that were privately owned – which is why when Mendelssohn went to the redecorated Teatro Argentina in Rome in 1831 he was amused to hear the audience greeting the youthful Prince Torlonia with cries of 'Bravo Torlonia, grazie, grazie' (Mendelssohn-Bartholdy 1899: 80).

But whoever owned the theatre, the ordinary day-to-day administration was almost everywhere now in the hands of an impresario. It was his task to choose a repertory of works for the season, to commission new operas, to engage the artists, and to balance the books. Some exceptional impresarios, men like Alessandro Lanari, also busied themselves with artistic matters, insisting on the quality and stylishness of the sets and costumes, and ensuring that the staging was managed in such a way as to help the singers come across well to the audience. Much of the work of organization was still carried out according to customs and conventions established over gener-ations of 'fixing' and string-pulling, bullying, bribery and opportunism. John Rosselli, in his magnificent exposition of the lifestyle of the im-presario, quotes some examples of these conventions from Giovanni Valle's theatre manual of 1823: leading singers must not have sung during the previous season within sixty miles of the theatre for which they were not engaged; the 'first days of the month' meant 'up to the tenth'; even if singers had agreed to sing whatever roles the impresario might assign to them, they could not be forced to undertake parts that would damage their voices, etc. (Rosselli 1984: 110). But during the first half of the nineteenth century these received customs gradually gave way to practices that were more strictly professional and legalistic, and which were enshrined in increasingly comprehensive contracts – like those that Verdi scrutinized so remorselessly and held to so meticulously.

It need hardly be said that the impresario was not a free and independent agent answerable to nothing beyond his own professional conscience and the constraints of funding. He was responsible for a form of entertainment occupying a position at the very heart of Italian public and social life, whose power over people's minds it would not be extravagant to compare with that of television today. And as the society in which he worked was an authoritarian and sometimes despotic one, rulers and governments took a close interest in what he was up to. After all the theatre, as Count Strassoldo, President of the government of Lombardy-Venetia, pointed out to the viceroy in 1825, 'attracts to a place open to observation during the hours of darkness a large part of the educated population (Rosselli 1984: 82).

Supervision was particularly suffocating in the court theatres. In Turin, the Queen took it upon herself to allocate the boxes and fix the prices. 'Her list decides the number of quarterings requisite to occupy the aristocratic rows of the first and second circles, and determines the point of *roture*, which banishes to the higher tiers the *piccoli nobili*' (Morgan 1821, I: 45). At the far end of the peninsula, in Naples, Queen Maria Cristina was more exercised by moral issues. It was her threat to withdraw her patronage from the San Carlo theatre that prompted the drawing up of a new set of regulations which, among other matters of moment, required ballerinas' tights to be coloured green above the knee 'so as not to inflame young blood' (Acton 1961: 76). At Parma in 1837 the start of the Carnival season was jeopardized when the director general of police and other governmental dignitaries discovered the female chorus for *Lucia di Lammermoor* wearing white costumes adorned with red and green ribbons: an allusion, it was suspected, to the tricolour of the Napoleonic Kingdom of Italy. Hasty atonement for this indiscretion was encouraged by the threat of imprisonment for the impresario and his assistants in the local fortress (Rosselli 1984: 94). Audience behaviour was another matter that governments attempted strictly to control, posting police regulations in the theatres to that purpose. Stendhal was both amused and appalled by the barbarity of the penalties threatened in Rome: 'One hundred blows with a stick administered instantly on the scaffolding permanently erected in the Piazza Navona . . . for any spectator who takes another's place; five years in the galleys for anyone who raises his voice against the theatre doorman etc.' (Stendhal 1817, entry for 30 August 1817). Sometimes the impresarios took the initiative in this uneasy relationship between themselves and their overlords. Particularly resourceful in his attempts to squeeze extra funds out of the Papal Treasury was the Roman impresario Vincenzo Jacovacci. One of his favourite expedients, we read, 'was to arrange for twenty or so ballerinas to sing hymns of praise to the Pontiff as he crossed Sant'Angelo bridge in his carriage. The Pope, who was not insensible to these displays, would smile and bless the beautiful girls, and the following day, [Jacovacci's] request for a special subsidy of ten thousand crowns was accepted' (Conati 1984: 35–6).

Despite such examples of direct regal or governmental intervention, the routine supervision of the impresario and his theatre was generally in the hands of a committee of noblemen and/or well-to-do citizens. Valle's manual details the supervisory board's responsibilities: they breathed down the impresario's neck incessantly, enforcing discipline at rehearsals, settling questions of etiquette such as the relative status of the singers, enforcing fire regulations, ensuring that costumes were clean, decent and historically accurate, approving posters and printed announcements, summoning the armed forces to arrest theatre personnel who were insubordinate during rehearsals, etc. (Rosselli 1984: 85–6).

Theatres remained heavily dependent financially upon their box-holders who, in theory at least, provided a dependable capital sum for the impresario to work with at the start of each season. In fact, particularly during the political upheavals in the early years of the century, some theatres came close to ruin because of the failure of box-holders to honour their obligations. In addition to the capital supplied from the boxes, the impresario could count on a fairly regular income at the door. For in most theatres it was still the custom that box-holders had to pay again, an admission charge, each time they entered the theatre. This *ingresso* was a very modest sum: paid by subscribers and occasional customers alike, it entitled non-box-holders to standing room in the theatre; but if they wanted to make themselves really comfortable there was an additional hire charge for seats, 'benches furnished with backrests', in such elegant theatres as La Scala (Stendhal 1956: 429).

No impresario could run opera as a profitable business on the basis of admission charges alone. Various schemes were tried for supplementing income: lotteries, balls, benefit nights. But quite the most promising during the Napoleonic period had seemed to be persuading governments to restore to theatres the gambling monopolies of which they had gradually been stripped in the second half of the eighteenth century. By recovering this monopoly theatres were able to make a start winning back customers from cafés and private gambling salons for their own faro, rouge-et-noir and roulette tables. But the privilege did not survive the Restoration, except in Naples, and even there it lasted only until 1820, prompting Stendhal to the gloomy prognosis that Italy's two greatest theatres, La

Scala and the San Carlo, were doomed (*ibidem*: 435). What certainly did happen was that governments had to provide very much more substantial sums in the forms of direct subsidies if they wished their theatres to flourish. Rents for boxes also rose steeply.

What exacerbated the impresario's financial problems was the steadily rising cost of staging opera. In an age of more excitingly individual talents, certain composers – notably Rossini, Bellini and Verdi – could gradually push up their fees. But the most exorbitant expenses involved the principal singers, the cost of whom began to rocket in the late 1820s and 1830s. It is true that Italian opera-houses could not attempt to match the kinds of fee commanded by the best singers in Paris or London. Still, even in Italy, fees were two or three times higher than anything paid in the eighteenth century (Rosselli 1984: 59–65). When the Neapolitan journalist Vincenzo Torelli drew up a scheme for the reform of theatre management in Naples in 1848, his detailed financial calculations assume that the three leading soloists, soprano, tenor and bass, will between them cost more than all the other performers put together, including a chorus of fifty and an orchestra of eighty (Black 1984: 112–13).

These more modestly rewarded performers caused difficulties of another kind. While principals were paid in four large instalments – *quartali* – stage-crews, and usually choruses and orchestras too, were paid a daily wage (Rosselli 1984: 12). A steady supply of cash was essential, which is why there was no room in the early nineteenth-century repertory for operas that proved not to be popular successes. An unsuccessful opera meant a decline in admission takings, raising for the impresario the spectre of bankruptcy and for the singers that of no pay. More than one impresario took flight in the middle of a failing season leaving his performers unprovided for.

The company

At Naples in the 1830s and 1840s the two royal theatres, the San Carlo and the Fondo, generally employed between them a company of about fifteen to twenty soloists, a chorus of fifty plus fifty non-singing extras, an orchestra of eighty, twelve principal dancers and a corps de ballet of eighty-four (Black 1984: 11–12). These are the resources of exceptionally well endowed theatres: in Italy only La Scala could have matched them, and there obviously the figures would have been much lower because one would be talking of one theatre rather than two. Conditions were tolerably good in such theatres, and singers tended to stay there, particularly at the San Carlo, for extended periods. But that is not to say that they had permanent companies. In theatres all over Italy the only real permanence was provided by the chorus and the orchestra; principal singers were engaged for a season only, and between seasons most of them were on the move, the successful ones making for wherever they could command the highest fees, the less successful for anywhere that was prepared to engage them.

One can see obvious advantages in a system which enabled a theatre to engage a singer full time, but only for the current season. But there were drawbacks too. If the two royal theatres of Naples had to share a maximum of twenty soloists between them, it is easy to imagine the length of the roster in the smaller houses: it amounted to little more than the cast for a single opera. There were rarely any understudies, the same cast was required to perform the entire repertory for the season, and one or two of the operas were likely to be newly composed, needing to be learned and rehearsed from scratch. As performances were commonly given four or five times a week, singers were driven to the very limits, sometimes beyond the limits, of what was physically possible. The strain was particularly severe on the aristocrats of the lyric stage, the singers 'di cartello'. To sing five William Tells or Normas in the space of a week is something no singer could attempt with impunity, even with the superior technique and easier delivery of an early-nineteenth-century singer. Yet to resist the temptation to oversing, as Nozzari did as early as 1809, refusing to perform more than three of four times a week, was to expose oneself to the charge of capriciousness (Rosselli 1984: 127). Nothing shows more poignantly the intolerable pressures that the finest singers could be under than the career of Giuseppina Strepponi, who had lost her voice for good by the time she was twenty-seven. In Florence, early in November 1838 she found herself singing six performances of *La straniera* within the week, to compensate for the fact that she had been ill and unable to perform the week before. 'Last night the opera went very well', reported Pietro Romani, director of the orchestra, 'but in her aria in the first act la Strepponi was overcome by such a cough that she had to retire behind the scenes without finishing' (Walker 1962: 63). Under such circumstances the frequent reports of singers being exhausted or losing their voice, sometimes, as in Strepponi's case, permanently, is scarcely to be wondered at.

If Berlioz is to be believed, the large numbers involved in the choruses of the royal theatres of Naples did not guarantee a strong and disciplined ensemble:

The chorus was indescribably feeble. A composer who writes for the San Carlo assured me that it is extremely difficult if not impossible to get a decent performance of music written in four parts. The sopranos find it very hard to keep a separate line from the tenors, so one is more or less obliged to write the two parts in octaves. (1969: 196)

He was politer about the levels of accomplishment achieved by opera choruses in more northerly cities, but nowhere were genuinely professional standards to be anticipated. In the words of a paper prepared by A. Carcano on the organization of the Teatro Comunale of Rome in 1872, the chorus was made up of 'the pariahs of art' (Rosselli 1984: 118). For most of them, singing in opera was a form of 'moonlighting': a way of eking out the precarious livings they earned as street vendors or humble artisans by 'laying by their leather aprons, [to] assume the costume of the dramatic wardrobe' (Morgan 1821, I: 269). Lady Morgan was reporting from Parma, where she found that the chorus 'executes the music of Rossini, Mozart &c. coarsely indeed, and vociferously, but not inaccurately'. Needless to say wages were very low: but they were supplemented by certain time-honoured privileges, such as borrowing costumes to wear in street carnivals (Rosselli 1984: 119). No doubt genuine enthusiasts were to be found in their ranks, and they would surely have responded to inspired direction. But the average opera chorus seems to have been a troublesome and unruly crew.

Except in the greatest theatres the orchestras shared some of the same characteristics. At Palermo, for instance, only the principal violinist, principal flautist and principal trumpet were treated like real professionals and paid a monthly salary; the rest were in effect day labourers, collecting their pay after each performance (Tiby 1957: 90). In most theatres the 'professors' were augmented by a motley collection of auxiliaries, like the solitary cellist Berlioz heard at the Teatro Valle in Rome in 1831, 'a goldsmith by trade' (1969: 186). In the 1850s one of the best-organized orchestras in Italy, that of the Teatro Comunale in Bologna, consisted of 'an inner core of officially appointed lifetime members . . . a surrounding ring of officially temporary but often long-serving players who hoped to be taken on one day as permanent, and an outer ring of students who played for nothing' (Rosselli 1984: 115). In plenty of theatres indiscipline was as endemic in orchestras as in choruses. 'At the Valle', reported the Roman *Rivista teatrale* in 1834, '[the orchestra] is permitted to chatter in a loud voice, to applaud the singers when the audience disapproves of them, to leave and resume their seats from time to time straddling across the partition which separates the orchestra from the pit' (Radiciotti 1905: 160).

Roman orchestras, it would be fair to say, were notorious, until the impresario Lanari began to lick them into some sort of shape in the mid-1830s. Spohr left a scathing account of them in the early years of the Restoration, as did Berlioz and Mendelssohn in 1831. And it was not simply the view of foreigners: as late as 1843 Mercadante found them intolerably provincial (letter to Persico, 24 September 1843, Naples Conservatory Library). Provincial Italian orchestras could, it is true, have their charm; at least they could for an enthusiast like Stendhal: 'They make mistakes, . . . there are certain notes which their fingers just do not possess the necessary dexterity to strike correctly. Yet what fire! What delicacy! What soul! What a feeling for music' (1956: 289). But the only orchestras to meet with the almost unanimous admiration of musicians were those of La Scala and the San Carlo.

Throughout this period the old custom remained in force according to which the first three performances of a new opera were directed from the piano by the composer. By all accounts he would have actually played the instrument only in an emergency (except of course in the *secco* recitatives still to be found in *opera buffa*), otherwise controlling the performances more in the manner of a conductor than of a continuo-player in an earlier age, 'giving the leader, by word and gesture, the indication of the tempo he desired' (Donizetti to Duke Visconti, 17 January 1834, in Zavadini 1948: 343). Once the opera was launched the composer's seat at the piano was taken by the 'maestro al cembalo', but the directing of the performance now passed to the leader – the 'primo violino, capo e direttore d'orchestra', who, reported Spohr, 'conducted from the first violin desk. Apart from him there is no further direction, either from the piano or with a baton, but simply a prompter with the score, who whispers the text to the singers and gives the chorus a beat where necessary' (1860–61, I: 276). The leader's responsibilities included the correction of the instrumental parts, the rehearsing of the orchestra, the control of tempo at the performance, taking the initiative in putting right any mishaps. Because he was, in Lichtenthal's words, 'the depositary of the composer's secrets', he played from a *spartitino* which provided details of all his particular responsibilities (1826, s.v. 'Esecuzione'). The best leaders also displayed the genuine interpretative flair we expect today from a conductor. It was reported of Giuseppe Festa at Naples that 'once he had understood the composer's intentions he thought of ways of achieving such effects as the composer himself had never imagined' (Pacini 1865: 42).

The idea of sinking the orchestra in a pit rather than simply partitioning it off from the stalls gained favour only later in the century. Throughout the Romantic period the arrangement of the orchestra remained that of an age that knew nothing of conductors in the modern sense:

The first violins sit turned towards the stage, with the second violins facing them; the viola players are also situated in these two rows; the other row is occupied by the wind and percussion instruments, then the double-basses and 'cellos which take up the two extremities of the orchestra.   (Lichtenthal 1826, s.v. 'Posizione d'orchestra')

But even as Lichtenthal wrote a new arrangement was gaining favour, that which we have already seen Donizetti commending to Duke Visconti. In this arrangement, 'the principal quartet of the orchestra, being gathered together in the middle, can at will lead the rest of the instruments' (Zavadini 1948: 343). Later in the century, coinciding probably with the demise of the 'primo violino, capo e direttore d'orchestra' that began in the 1860s,

Italian theatres adopted a third seating plan, of which a good description is given by Verdi:

At the front of the orchestra are grouped those instruments which form the harmony – flutes, clarinets, oboes – which we call the concerto. Behind them are arrayed the horns, trumpets, and trombones, and behind them, forming a circle to enclose the other instruments, come the first violins, 'cellos and double-basses. In this way, the brass never drowns the quieter instruments, and one achieves a better, and at the same time, clearer ensemble [than in French orchestras].   (Conati 1984: 268)

Spohr pays a backhanded tribute to the thoroughness with which performances were rehearsed when he describes the première of his Concerto No. 8 at La Scala in 1816. The orchestra played well, he writes, but not without mistakes: '[it] is accustomed to have too many rehearsals for it to be able to perform something quite faultlessly after only one' (1860–61, I: 282). For an opera, the schedule of rehearsals in fact went through four stages: piano rehearsals (those for the soloists in the early part of the century still customarily being held in the *prima donna*'s lodgings); 'after that are held the so-called *provette*, or quartet rehearsals, that is with the [two] violins, viola and bass; then follow the *prove a grand'orchestra*, and finally two dress rehearsals (Lichtenthal 1826, s.v. 'Prova'). This seems a generous allowance, but was certainly not excessive considering that the performances were conductorless and a chamber-music-like initiative was required from many members of the orchestra.

Theatres and audiences

When Lady Blessington visited La Scala for the first time she was, like most visitors, very taken with it: 'It is a very fine theatre . . . What did strike me, was the superiority of its decorations and cleanliness over ours' (1839–40, entry for ?1828). Almost all important Italian theatres were transformed during the early decades of the nineteenth-century. Any schemes for redecoration or improving the facilities of a theatre were matters of immense public interest, described in minute detail in the press. They were particularly important in a city like Venice where several opera-houses were competing for patrons and customers. More comfortable seating was provided in the stalls; as early as the 1830s some theatres began to replace the old lighting systems of wax candles and oil lamps by gas lighting,[2] which was more economical and must have improved the air too; though perhaps not more than the improvements in toilet facilities introduced during the Napoleonic period, which meant that it was no longer necessary for corridors or retiring rooms to be adorned with malodorous buckets. The disgust that could be occasioned by an 'unimproved' theatre that had survived the Restoration is vividly recorded by Lady Morgan in Rome:

The Roman theatres . . . are dark, dirty and paltry in their decorations; but what is infinitely worse, they are so offensive to the senses, so disgusting in the details of their arrangement, that to particularize would be impossible: suffice it to say, that the corridors of the Argentino exemplify the nastiness of Roman habits and manners more forcibly than volumes could describe. It is in this *immondezzaio* that one is taught to feel how closely purity in externals is connected with virtue in morals . . .

(Morgan 1821, II: 235–6)

By contrast, the magnificence of the new San Carlo, rebuilt after destruction by fire in 1816, could be described by Stendhal as a '*coup d'état*'.

I believed I was transported into the palace of some oriental emperor. My eyes are dazzled, my soul ravished . . . this room, reconstructed in three hundred days, is a *coup d'état*: it attaches the people to the King more than that constitution Sicily has been granted . . . All Naples is drunk with joy. (1817, entry for 12 and 13 February)

Unhappily the new San Carlo was less sympathetic acoustically than the earlier theatre had been; vast in size, it also helped make fashionable the building of larger auditoriums. Given the very special prestige the San Carlo enjoyed, it played no small part in encouraging that new style of singing in which 'either one hears the singers shout, or one doesn't hear them at all' (Spohr 1860–61, II: 13).

On 4 November 1819 the *Gazzetta privilegiata di Venezia* announced a number of alterations to the Teatro San Giovanni Grisostomo that had been undertaken by the proprietors Giovanni Gallo and Luigi Facchini, among them 'the shrewd contrivance of transforming the topmost row of boxes into a gallery with a separate entrance, in order to facilitate access to the performances for the *minuto popolo*' (Mangini 1974: 205). Though Gallo and Facchini were the first theatre owners in Venice to make this move, there were certainly precedents for what they had done in other Italian theatres. The interesting point about this particular announcement is that it makes quite explicit the fact that such rebuilding was linked with an expansion of the popular audience for opera. It marks in fact the final refinement of the idea of the theatre as a microcosm of Italian society.[3]

The distribution of the boxes in an Italian theatre had always had a strongly hierarchic symbolic significance. The desirability and prestige of a particular box had little to do with acoustics or the view of the stage it afforded, much more with its proximity to a royal or ducal box. Most desirable were those in the second row, but in the best theatres boxes in the first row and even the third would also be occupied almost exclusively by aristocratic owners. Above that one found a thicker and thicker sprinkling of owners from the professional classes; in a second-class theatre or a theatre in a smaller town such people would of course have been able to stake their claims on boxes lower down. The pit was the resort of a more middle-class audience – of those professional men who could not afford boxes, trademen, students, visitors passing through the town, perhaps still, as in the eighteenth century, some servants of boxholders; in many theatres the front rows were reserved for the military. It was also the place where were gathered those rare melomanes who actually wished 'to concentrate on watching the opera right through from beginning to end' (Stendhal 1956: 429). The *popolo minuto* who occupied the gallery are vividly described in a Milanese dialect poem by Carlo Porta, 'Olter desgrazzi de Giovannin Bongee': they include 'a fireman, a lamplighter, several soldiers, and a tailor employed as assistant to an old clothes dealer' (Rosselli 1984: 45).

In some respects the opera-house still belonged to the old, pre-Romantic Italy. It was only after 1848 that it lost its central position in civic life; until then it continued to be thought of as 'the city's salon', to quote Stendhal's description of La Scala. In a principal theatre, thanks to the box-system, all the best society of the town had its own private rooms, to which it repaired as a matter of course each evening during the season. An habitué might hear perhaps twenty or thirty consecutive performances of the same opera.

Under such circumstance a consecrated, undivided attention to the music was not to be expected. Visiting La Scala for a performance of Soliva's *Statua di bronzo* in October 1816 Spohr was exasperated:

During the powerful overture, several very expressive accompanied recitatives and all the ensemble pieces there was such a noise that one heard hardly anything of the music. In most boxes cards were being played and in every part of the theatre there was loud talking. For a visitor who would like to listen attentively, nothing could be imagined more intolerable than this infamous din; however, from people who see the same opera perhaps thirty to forty times and who visit the opera only for the society no attentiveness can be expected.   (1860–61, I: 276)

Lady Morgan observed the same scene with a more sympathetic, feminine eye:

The fronts of the boxes almost uniformly exhibit a tête-à-tête; sometimes a lady and gentleman, sometimes two ladies: for only two appear in front, though the back of the box may be crowded. The ladies take off their large bonnets and hang them on the box, exactly as at Paris; and the elegant *demi-toilette* prevalent in the Scala would not have shamed the inventive genius of Mademoiselle Victorine of Bourbonite memory. The most scrupulous ladies of the highest ranks come alone in their carriage to the opera. As soon as they enter their box, and have glanced their eye along the circles, giving or returning the Italian salutation, which has something at once infantine and coquettish in its beckoning gesture, they turn their back to the scene, and for the rest of the night, hear and see nothing out of their own society, except when apprized by the orchestra that some scene in the ballet, or some *aria* or *duo* in the opera is about to be performed, which it is good taste or good fashion to listen to and admire. Then indeed the most rapturous attention is lent; but the scene over, the 'Crocchio ristretto', as they call it, (or private chit-chat) is resumed, and is only interrupted by the ingress and egress of visitors. Every box has its *habitués*, its privileged guests; and it is a tiresome rule that the last arrival is always a signal for the first to depart . . . The observance of this rule is so strict, that it sometimes leaves a passion half declared, a plot half revealed, a confidence the most critical, or an opinion the most important unfinished. Nothing can be less enjoyable, though more decent, than this etiquette of the opera . . .   (1821, I: 96)

An opera-house attached to a court was less of a social amenity. The San Carlo, for instance, always brightly illuminated and with no curtains to screen the boxes, was a much more public kind of place than the 'gorgeous and gloomy' (Hazlitt 1826) La Scala, and a more formal style of dress was therefore obligatory. If the monarch was himself present, theatre etiquette automatically became much stiffer. Dearly as an Italian audience loved to pass judgement on every detail of the performance as it progressed, applause or whistling, or indeed any noisy manifestation of pleasure or displeasure, was out of the question in the Royal Presence. There were of course degrees of formality. Lady Blessington reported that at Genoa the King and Queen of Piedmont-Sardinia were allowed to enter and leave the theatre 'without any of those uproarious acclamations which with us await the sovereign', that indeed 'no notice whatever is taken of the King and Queen's presence', beyond the observation of silence (1839–40, entry for 3 May 1823). It was very different in the Kingdom of the Two Sicilies. A ludicrous incident is recorded from Lecce when King Ferdinand was visiting the city – and therefore the opera-house – in the mid-1850s. 'Ever and anon, as was his wont, he rose to pull up his breeches. Each time this happened, presuming he was about to retire, the audience rose with him in unison' (Acton 1961: 376).

Noisy as theatres surely were, there appears to have been some recognized decibel threshold which it was improper to transgress. We read of pit audiences in Milan crying 'zitti, zitti' to card-players in the boxes whose games became unduly contentious (Stendhal 1817, entry for 25 October 1816); and at Turin of '"a gentle usher, Authority by name", who every five seconds hissed some lady of quality and high breeding whose voice was heard with an éclat above the rest' (Hazlitt 1826). But audiences showed no capacity whatever for a sustained attention to music. A delicious illustration of the fact is provided by Meyerbeer, who in Venice in Holy Week 1818 attended performances of *Messiah* and other sacred works in the Teatro San Benedetto:

. . . the only really enjoyable part of the spectacle was the sight of the elegantly dressed ladies and gentlemen in their illuminated boxes. They sat there quite crushed with boredom, but didn't dare either to yawn or to talk, since a few days before the performance [Cavaliere] Grizzo had explained, with his usual courtesy, that these compositions were masterpieces of the human spirit, that anyone who didn't enjoy them was an ass; and that anyone who was disposed to chatter during such music, the way one does during an Italian opera, could only be an ill-educated peasant.

(Meyerbeer 1960, I: 576)

But that is not to say that audiences had lost their critical faculties. On the contrary, they were demanding and opinionated; but on the whole – to judge from the composers they acclaimed and the operas they singled out for particular approbation – shrewd too, with a very keen sense of quality within the conventions they knew and understood. No doubt they were sometimes factional, obstreperous or unjust: 'All the anger, the contumely, the calumnies which today erupt in political conflict, gathered at that time [before 1848] around the heads of poets and artists; and they used to fall upon them fiercely and with deadly effect' (Ghislanzoni 1958). But at least they made up their own mind about things, and rarely allowed themselves to be manipulated by a *claque*, as they did in Paris. And there was another side to the picture painted by Ghislanzoni; for when they heard beautiful music beautifully sung, their feelings erupted no less powerfully. The result was a warmth of enthusiasm, a shared rapture with few parallels in the modern history of music.[4]

The repertory

At a flourishing theatre in a large city, patrons could hope to have opera during three seasons each year: the Carnival season which began on St Stephen's Day (26 December) and continued until the beginning of Lent; the Spring season beginning after Easter and extending into June; and the Autumn season beginning in September and ending with the start of Advent. During the Restoration period some theatres extended their seasons, particularly by running on the Carnival season into the early weeks of Lent. In making this move, one concession was granted to religious scruples, namely that Lenten operas should be performed without ballets.

Not all cities could support theatres which provided opera in such quantities. Under those circumstances they concentrated on Carnival. It was the longest season, socially the most brilliant, musically the most exciting. Then at least, a theatre would aim to put on an impressive repertory of pieces, even if financial or other problems meant that it had to close for the rest of the year, as La Fenice did for a few years after 1814, and as even La Scala did in the 1850s. The opening and closing nights of the Carnival season were the most dazzling social occasions of the year:

Since the day when *Religion* stalked back into the land to reclaim its birthright, there is no opera performed during Advent . . . with the result that, now, the old, tense anticipation of novelty is increased a thousandfold by deprivation of the foremost requirement of life . . . Not a woman in the whole theatre, on that evening, but is decked out in the gayest and most gorgeous of her gala-dresses . . . I should merely be wasting my time if I were to attempt a description of the wild extravagance of these carnival premières.　　　　　　　　　　　　　　　　　　　　　　　(Stendhal 1956: 435–6)

In many theatres the close of the season was marked by banquets and masked balls.

Small as the companies of singers were, they were commonly required during the course of the season to give something between fifty and eighty performances of perhaps half a dozen operas. Stendhal's estimate, eighty to one hundred (1956: 435), seems on the high side, in the light of the detailed chronology of performances drawn up for La Scala, a very active theatre, by Giampiero Tintori (Gatti 1964, II). But in one respect life was easier than it is for the modern opera company: they were not expected to perform operas in different styles and from different periods every night of the week. The repertory was almost exclusively modern and almost exclusively Italian. At La Scala during the 1830s, for example, the occasional performances of Auber and Boieldieu alone broke the Italian monopoly. Operas composed earlier than Rossini were, if anything, even rarer: *Don Giovanni* which appeared briefly during the Carnival/Lent season 1836 was the only example to be seen at La Scala during the decade. The repertory was narrowed still more by the tendency to delegate *opera buffa* to smaller, more popular theatres, such as the Valle in Rome, while the grander theatres concentrated more exclusively on heroic opera. At La Scala between 1790 and 1796, thirty-six comic operas had been performed compared with sixteen heroic operas. Forty years later the position was reversed, and at least twice as many serious as comic operas were being performed there, even if such works as *Don Giovanni* and *La sonnambula* are counted among the comedies.

The custom which Charles III had established at Naples in 1735 of performing ballets as interludes and epilogues to the opera remained current in all the better theatres, providing a densely packed evening's programme. A typical night at La Scala in 1816 is described by Spohr:

After the first act of the opera [Soliva's *Statua di bronza*] a grand heroic ballet was given which likewise rose to imposing dramatic heights by virtue of the artistry of some of the dancers, and the splendour of the sets and costumes. As it lasted nearly an hour one had entirely forgotten the first half of the opera. After the second act of the opera yet another ballet was performed, a comic one, hardly any shorter, so that the whole performance lasted from eight o'clock until twelve o'clock. What hard work for the poor musicians!

(1860–61, I: 277)

24 · The musical language of Italian Romantic opera

Operatic structure

If there were pockets of resistance to Romanticism, fits of half-heartedness in the Italian adoption of its thematic, scenic and emotional habits, it was perhaps because there was no natural affinity between the new mode and the musical language Italians had inherited from the eighteenth century. The style of Italian music – its melodic and rhythmic character, its harmonic vocabulary, the patterns and textures into which composers had learned to weave voices and instruments – was frankly ill adapted to many of the challenges posed by the new movement. Over the centuries Italian opera had acquired a magnificent eloquence in situations that called for heroic, impassioned utterance, but it was a lucid, self-confident, self-knowing kind of eloquence that found itself at a loss when faced with the murky shadows, the tremulous, intangible nuances of feeling, the mysterious dreams, the nightmares and ecstatic visions evoked by the Romantic imagination.

For some decades Romantic subject-matter coexisted with a manner of musico-dramatic articulation that, in principle, had changed little for more than a hundred and fifty years. As late as the 1840s, after the death of Bellini and with Verdi already launched on his operatic career, theorists wrote about the aesthetics of opera in terms that were still essentially Metastasian.

The arias are like gems joined together in a piece of jewellery, and the metal which joins them is the recitative. This can be considered as the path along which the action progresses; the *cantabile* is the place where it stops and dwells upon a peroration of the passions . . . They are by nature such different things, that one must be careful not to dress the one in the attributes of the other, and to ensure that a clear line separates them. (Ritorni 1841, I: xlvi)

But if the time-honoured distinction between 'full' music and 'half' music was still observed, the contrasts that resulted were now fashioned into structures that, on the surface at least, were more complex than in the eighteenth century. This complexity was made possible by a shift from a drama of intrigue (on the Metastasian pattern) to a drama of pictures or tableaux. There was no attempt to treat the dramatic subject in consistent depth; instead, as the previous chapter has shown, the action was concentrated in a number of focal incidents. And each of these, from the time of Rossini down to the 1850s, was articulated in an essentially similar way which it will be helpful to recapitulate. First, there would commonly be a short instrumental prelude, setting the mood, or perhaps suggesting the way in which the characters gather on stage – eagerly, reluctantly, in anguish of mind, in an intoxicated romantic daze. Then the dramatic matter of the scene would be introduced, argued and elaborated upon in a recitative. This first part of the scene, generally static, even retrospective in character, culminated in the cantabile, a reflective aria or ensemble in a composer's richest lyrical vein. After the cantabile there was generally an abrupt change of tone: sometimes it was brought about by a switch from reflection to decision in the mind of the protagonist; sometimes the arrival of a new character or group of characters served as catalyst. In either case the cantabile was followed by a transitional movement, the *tempo di mezzo*, during which the momentum of the scene was re-established, often in music the burden of which was carried by the orchestra; this *tempo di mezzo* surged forward to culminate in the cabaletta or stretta, a fast, often brilliant vocal movement, sung twice to bring the scene to a close.

When all due cognizance has been taken of the occasional movements in which the scheme is varied or elaborated upon, there is no escaping the fact that the overall structure of Italian Romantic opera was schematic in the highest degree. And there is some justice in the remarks of those critics, like Ritorni, who complained of 'the boring uniformity of every opera . . . each of them composed of parts with a predetermined structure, and from the very same situations and words . . . so that all operas are like identical twins. When you have seen one you have seen them all' (Ritorni 1841, I: lxi).

This was a complaint which most of the leading composers and librettists of the period were to echo at some stage in their careers. All the same, for a variety of reasons, some good, some bad, the trend to standardization was difficult to resist. In an age when the economics of the opera-house made mass-production unavoidable, a reliable blueprint that predetermined at any rate the formal scheme of the music made life a little less frantic for composers and singers alike. If, as was assuredly the case, the impression created by the singers as singers was a major contributory factor in the success of an opera, then an operatic structure that enabled the principals at each of their main appearances on stage to regale the audience with the full range of their art – declamatory in the recitative, lyrical in the cantabile, brilliant in the cabaletta – had much to recommend it. Nor should the sheer musical effectiveness of the plan be underrated; for with its wide expressive range, the quasi-architectural balance of its constituent parts, and the exhilarating, theatrical thrust set up by its gathering momentum it could be – as countless scenes in Rossini, Donizetti, Bellini and Verdi demonstrate – the perfect operatic scheme.

There were, however, complicating or, perhaps more strictly correct, diluting factors that also came into play. In Italy Romantic opera was not and could not be a purely, ideally expressive type of dramatic art. It was composed for a society that consumed opera at an astonishing rate, and, in the sense that this meant there was a virtually limitless demand for new operas, composers had it easier than their modern counterparts. In 1846 the Italian correspondent of the *Allgemeine Musikalische Zeitung* reported that, during the previous eight years, 1838–45, 342 new operas had been staged in Italy, and 130 new maestros had made their debut. On the other hand, their work came under all the pressures that a consumer-society brings in the form of commercialization and competition. The competition was truly formidable. Italy teemed with maestros trained to compose opera and eager for the commissions which theatres all over the country issued each year. And a factor which they could never allow themselves to forget was that they were addressing themselves to an audience of connoisseurs; an audience which, thanks to the box-system, attended opera regularly and knew every note of the popular successes of the day. Audiences were in effect the paymasters of the impresario and their indifference or hostility could not be disguised or compensated for by state subsidies; they saw it as their right and duty to act as arbiters in determining the success or failure of every opera presented to them. Of the typical opera audience of Restoration Italy Stendhal wrote:

These are men possessed of seven devils, determined at all costs, by dint of shrieking, stamping and battering with their canes against the backs of the seats in front, to enforce the triumph of their opinion, and above all to prove that, come what may, *none but their opinion is correct.* (1956: 112)

Such audiences expected to pass judgement on every aspect of an opera – on its music, on the performance, on the costume and décor. And they did this during the performance. The success of an opera was determined by the frequency and the enthusiasm of the acclamations it received in the theatre: if audiences did not like it, it cut little ice to read in the newspapers the next day that, in the considered opinion of the critics, maestro so-and-so showed a refreshing charm in his melodies, or that his harmony and instrumentation were deeply scientific.

Under these circumstances it was impossible for a composer to concern himself exclusively with vivid drama or beautiful music. In every scene in the opera the composer did his utmost to thrill, to delight, to move the audience by the power of his art, but having done that he submitted himself to their judgement. This ritual of audience participation had to be accommodated within the musical form. That is why it would have been pointless, indeed inept, to sustain the musical argument with the kind of continuous expressive density that is characteristic of German Romantic opera. The perfectly rational and artistically defensible structure of Italian opera as outlined at the start of this chapter came to be adorned with a number of features that serve no other purpose than that of making room for the passing of judgement. These features cluster round the two lyrical movements, the cantabile, and the cabaletta.

In the first case the idea is innocuous enough. Each cantabile closes with a cadenza, after which there is a pause, a break in the musical continuity which can be prolonged *ad libitum*. Clearly there need be nothing meretricious in such a cadenza, particularly in view of the generally florid character of the cantabile. But its function in the theatre ritual of the period was to act as a cue for applause, while the point of the break was to make room for that applause. To modern taste the treatment of the cabaletta is more problematic. As practised by Rossini, the cabaletta had generally been a single fast and brilliant movement which incorporated extensive stretches of repetition. If all was going well it would have the effect of whipping up the theatrical excitement, and with it the audience's enthusiasm, for the close of the scene. In some cabalettas, particularly in his later works, Rossini devised a variant of this scheme which manipulated the audience's enthusiasm with much adroitness, and was to be the model for the cabalettas of all young composers. The cabaletta was broken off by loud orchestral cadences at its first climax of brilliance; then, after some moments of this orchestral din, it was repeated in its entirety. The repetition would be brought to a more emphatic close and rounded off by more orchestral cadences still more extensive and vehement in style. Clearly the intention was that audiences should be encouraged to applaud between the two statements of the cabaletta as well as at the end. If they did applaud the repeat had the effect of an encore, which could be rendered even more brilliant by the addition of some spontaneous vocal ornament; if they didn't, they got the repeat anyway, and it might be hoped that at a second hearing in a still more dazzling form it might please better. But for our purpose the point is that the loud orchestral tuttis in which the cabalettas of the period are embedded served no dramatic or expressive purpose. Indeed it was music designed not to be heard at all; it was, in the words of one German observer, 'a mere invitation to applause . . . the enthusiasm of the audience set to music' (*AMZ*, vol. 48, 1846, col.433f.). I cannot, in this context, resist quoting Spohr again, whose account of the reception of his Concerto No. 8 at La Scala, Milan, in September 1816 illuminates Italian audience habits charmingly.

I had the pleasure of seeing that my new concerto . . . appealed very strongly to the taste of the Italians, and especially all the lyrical passages were received with the greatest enthusiasm. [Clearly, what happened was that he was loudly applauded at the end of each solo section of the work. And this he regarded as a very mixed blessing] . . . This noisy applause, welcome and encouraging as it is for the soloist, remains nevertheless an intense annoyance to the composer. As a result of it all continuity is destroyed, the painstakingly elaborated tuttis go quite unnoticed, and one hears the soloist recommence in a new key, without knowing how the orchestra effected the modulation.   (1860–61, I: 281–2)

Spohr's Italian contemporaries knew better than to waste their time with the 'painstaking elaboration' of their tuttis; but what they provided instead – those 'mere invitations to applause' – have become senseless and ugly relics in an age that expects to pay attention to all that is sung and played in the opera-house.

Romantic opera in Italy remained 'number' opera. All who were involved in its production conspired to ensure that that was so. Librettists wrote texts that clearly differentiated between recitative and song sections, as such theorists as Ritorni urged; composers on the whole liked to work in clearly articulated musical forms, concise enough to be sustained as song, without too much need for symphonic device, and obviously the need to provide scope for audiences to have their say only exaggerated these sectionalizing tendencies. All the same, between Rossini and Verdi there is no mistaking the fact that Italian opera was gradually moving towards a greater degree of musico-dramatic continuity.

An early symptom of this tendency was the abandoning in heroic opera of the old *recitativo semplice*, and its total replacement by recitative accompanied either by strings or by the full orchestra. Rossini has generally been credited with this innovation in *Elisabetta* (Naples 1815) and *Otello* (Naples 1816); though in fact Mayr had anticipated him by two years in *Medea in Corinto* (Naples 1813). During the 1820s the expressive and dramatic significance of the recitative was further enhanced by flowerings of arioso. It was a development which gained momentum from the first Milanese operas of Bellini. 'What pleased above all in *Il pirata*', wrote Ritorni, 'was the extending of musical significance to the recitatives, which were elevated to the richness of the arias, while the latter were humbled somewhat, contrary to the common practice, so that the transition should be natural' (1841, I: lxvii). Donizetti was quick to learn the lesson. In *Anna Bolena*, his first mature masterpiece, there is a similar profusion of ariosi: what is more, the autograph score shows that as he worked on it Donizetti was continually on the look-out for ways of breaking down the clear-cut frontiers between recitative and aria, worrying away at such demarcation points as orchestral introductions or reiterated cadences, and whittling them down, smoothing them over or eliminating them altogether (Gossett 1985, Chapter 6).

The lyrical forms themselves gradually became less sacrosanct. Some stimuli towards a freer handling of them came from outside Italy. There was, for example, a growing awareness of the splendours of the German tradition of instrumental music and a tentative interest in the possibility of adapting symphonic skills to operatic purposes. Many Italian composers received commissions to compose for the Théâtre Italien or even for the Opéra in Paris. And familiarity with French traditions encouraged them to essay a wider variety of lyrical forms, and to handle solo, choral and orchestral resources more ambitiously in the building up of the theatrical tableau. A sense that the inheritance of Rossini did not need to be viewed like the Mosaic Tablets of the Law, that renewal, reform and revitalization of the tradition was essential if opera was to come to terms with the Romantic age, affected all who worked thoughtfully in Italian opera. It affected even Saverio Mercadante, the most old-fashioned of the major composers of the period. Indeed for a few years in the late 1830s Mercadante became of all Italian composers the boldest in his quest for new ways of interpreting the traditional operatic structures. Few of the formal innovations generally associated with Verdi's operas of ten or fifteen years later are not somewhere adumbrated here. Conventional schemes are always liable to be overturned: in Foscari's aria in Act I of *Il bravo* (Milan 1839) an off-stage romanza is heard between the two statements of the cabaletta; while Ubaldo's aria in Act III of *Elena da Feltre* (Naples 1838) merges cantabile, declamation, cabaletta and chorus into a single flexible *scena* that takes singularly little note of the layout of Cammarano's text. As Verdi was to do, Mercadante also reduced radically the number of full-scale arias: there is none in Act I of *La Vestale* (Naples 1840) and only a one-movement *preghiera* in the second; in all acts of this opera the music is composed in one virtually unbroken sweep, each number being smoothly dovetailed into the next.

If the Romantic reform of the structure of Italian opera was gradual, hesitant, deferential, it was largely because of the composers' need to carry singers and audiences with them. The stories of Donizetti's and Verdi's arguments with two *prima donnas* who resented the sacrifice of their prerogative to close the opera with a brilliant solo 'rondo' – Henriette Méric-Lalande in the case of *Lucrezia Borgia*, Sophie Loewe in the case of *Ernani* – are well known. Less well known is the resistance of audiences to such innovations. As one example of many one may cite the reception at Venice in 1818 of Rossini's *Armida*, which the composer had ventured to close with a chorus, reducing the protagonist Armida to isolated cries for vengeance and havoc. This, the *Nuovo osservatore veneto* reported, was taken to represent 'the very image of negligence . . . so that the curtain fell amid a universal silence and the Rossinians left the theatre with slow steps, pensively' (Radiciotti 1921: 31). Discouraging as such reactions must have been, all the major composers of the period played their part in seeing that the pattern of Italian opera never became too much of a strait-jacket, that it became gradually more varied, more fluent, and flexible, more responsive to the dramatic needs of theme and character.

The primacy of song

Most Italian composers saw little need for any fundamental shift of priorities within the musical language that filled these structures. Conservative critics regularly complained about the Teutonic complexity of Rossini's scoring or the intolerable brassy din of Verdi's, but in fact the supremacy of the solo singing voice was uncontroversial and unchallenged. 'The melodic voice part (la parte melodica vocale) . . . must form the principal aim of the art of Euterpe', wrote Pacini to a would-be reformer, Achille Castagnoli, in 1841 (MS letter, Biblioteca Communale, Pescia). And never were the traditional values more drastically asserted than by Bellini, in a heated letter to Carlo Pepoli, librettist of *I Puritani*, which I have quoted in my Introduction (p. 7 above).

The effect of this unequivocal emphasis on the expressive and rhetorical powers of the human voice was that Italian operatic music continued, throughout the Romantic period, to preserve something of that two-dimensionality that had characterized it ever since the 'reform' of the 1720s. No shadow of contrapuntal sophistication darkened its pages, and those new expressive resources that were being discovered by the German Romantics in an extended harmonic vocabulary and an enlarged palette of instrumental colours were viewed by Italians with a kind of admiring awe, not unmixed with suspicion. For the time being they continued to invest their confidence in those elements of the musical language that reinforced the supremacy of the voice – in melody and in rhythm. As Rossini put it to Antonio Zanolini, 'musical expression rests in the rhythm, in rhythm is all power of music' (Lippmann 1969a: 292).

If we believe, as Stendhal did, that 'the fundamental quality of some of Rossini's finest compositions is not true *emotion*, but *physical excitement*', we may feel that he is a special case (1956: 382). Certainly the rhythmic character of his music, with its floridly rhetorical *ad libitum*s and its progressive dissolution of rhythmic feature into a giddy play of coloratura, is not entirely typical of the period. But of the central importance of the rhythmic dimension in Italian Romantic music there can be no question.

Of this repertory as a whole a cardinal feature is the close dependence of the musical rhythm on the text. Particularly after Bellini and Donizetti had simplified the melodic style of opera, there developed a close and systematic correspondence between verse metre and musical rhythm. The musical phrase corresponded with the line of verse; the various standard metres commonly used in aria-texts were matched by a variety of characteristic rhythmic schemes within the phrase; hence Verdi's ostensibly puzzling comment to Boito when they were working on the revision of *Simon Boccanegra*: 'I don't much like *ottonario* metre because of those damned notes on the upbeat ▦ ' (Medici and Conati 1978, I: 25). Given these metric–rhythmic correspondences there was so little scope for genuine rhythmic variety during the course of an aria that the typical aria style of the period has been described as 'isorhythmic' (Lippmann 1973–75).

These correspondences had been inherited in large measure from the eighteenth century, when, however, the characteristic rhythms had been used in far more varied and sophisticated overall rhythmic designs. In the nineteenth century they were presented directly and relentlessly, undisguised by word-repetition and uncomplicated by such refinements as the shift of the melodic line from voice to instruments and back again. Lippmann suggests that this policy of drastic rhythmic simplification was part of a conscious attempt to make Romantic opera penetrate more memorably into the minds of an audience, to make it more popular and democratic in tone. The inherited rhythmic types also came to be distorted by new expressive aims. The force and fervour of so much music of this period encouraged, for example, a new emphasis on dotted rhythms, or on rhythms in which one or more of the accented notes within the phrase are extended (Ex.V.1).

Perhaps there was some lingering eighteenth-century sense of decorum in these metric–rhythmic correspondences. But composers were certainly not rigidly bound to them. Indeed a comment in Pacini's *Memoirs* suggests that his reputation as the 'maestro delle cabalette' was in part due to his willingness to experiment rhythmically: 'My cabalettas did not' – he wrote – 'gush forth like limpid waters from a pure spring. On the contrary, they were the fruit of some reflection, since I studied ways of giving a different emphasis (accento) to the metres of the poetry, so as not to fall into

Cursed be the moment which made me your lover. . .

Ex.V.1 Donizetti, *Lucia di Lammermoor* (1835), Act II scene 5

melodies that recalled other ideas' (1865: 84).

The rhythmic idiosyncrasies of Italian Romantic opera were just one aspect of a melodic style which, in the broadest terms, was becoming more declamatory. Rossini's melodies, at their most expansive, had depended for their execution upon skills inherited from the great *castrati* of the late eighteenth century: ease of delivery, the brilliantly pointed articulation of coloratura, phenomenal breath-control, the creative application of embellishment. It was a style that did not lend itself well to the dramatic ambitions of Romanticism. But Rossini himself had pointed the way to an alternative when in, for example, *La Cenerentola*, or Act III of *Otello*, he had made use of simple melodies, almost folk-like in tone, as a way of expressing the most sincere and deeply felt aspects of character. Composers continued to draw on this *popolaresco* style for purposes of dramatic characterization, as Donizetti did for Gennaro in *Lucrezia Borgia* (Milan 1837), or for Pierotto in *Linda di Chamounix* (Vienna 1842). But popular song becomes a more general ideal for all those composers who, in response to the feeling of the times, aspired to 'inform their work with truthfulness' (Pacini 1865: 93).

As a result, simpler and plainer melodies became a hallmark of Italian opera in the late 1820s and 1830s. The profuse word-repetitions of an earlier age were abandoned, at least until the closing sections of a song; and the *fioritura*-laden lyricism of Rossini was succeeded by a style that was predominantly syllabic, thus highlighting those rhythmic–metric correspondences already discussed. In some extreme cases these tendencies brought song back once more to the Renaissance ideal of elevated declamation. The first operas composed by Bellini in conjunction with Romani, especially the second of them, *La straniera* (Milan 1829), prompted the critic of *L'eco* to write: 'he has adopted a method, which we do not well know whether to describe as sung declamation, or declamatory song' (Bellini 1943: 196). In the late 1820s Pacini too claimed to be 'making some progress in the declamatory style' in connection with his opera *Il talismano*. Perhaps the most radical manifestation of the trend is found in those 'reform operas' of Mercadante – *Il giuramento*, *Elena da Feltre* and *La Vestale* – in which the composer transforms, far more radically than Bellini or Donizetti had ever done, the convention of a brilliant concluding 'rondo' for the *prima donna*. In all these operas the cabaletta is replaced by a tiny cantabile which breaks down into graphic declamatory gasps as the hand of death takes firmer hold of the character. *Il giuramento* serves as an example (Ex.V.2).

The design of arias evolved to match this changing lyrical style. Rossini's arias had tended to have an open-ended, chain-like structure in which each musical idea in turn found its momentary equilibrium by virtue of the balanced symmetries and repetitions in which it was set, before making

Ex.V.2 Mercadante, *Il giuramento* (1837), Act III scene 2

For me there is no hope, and I leave love to you; ah, do not weep, smile at me. . .your hand. . .here on my heart. . .happy, yet happy I die. . .

Ex.V.2 *continued*

way for another idea usually more animated or exuberant, to be handled in the same way. For some years this principle continued much in use by younger composers. But from *Il pirata* Bellini popularized a tighter form with pronounced elements of reprise, and this became the most widely favoured aria-design in the 1830s and 1840s. 'È gettata la mia sorte' from Verdi's *Attila* (Venice 1846) serves as an example of a structure found over and over again in this repertory:

È gettata la mia sorte,	A		
Pronto sono ad ogni guerra;	B	Tonic	(But this pattern of tonal relationships is only one of several possibilities)
S'io cadrò, cadrò da forte,	A¹		
E'il mio nome resterà.	C		
Non vedrò l'amata terra	D	Relative minor	
Svenir lenta e farsi a brano . . .	E		
Sopra l'ultimo romano	A¹	Tonic	
Tutta Italia piangerà.	C¹		

The final two lines of text are then repeated to a new coda theme, which in turn leads to free cadential material (see Ex.V.3). It should be added that during the 1840s Verdi tended increasingly to convert the largely formal reprise of such an aria as this into a climactic phrase in which the initial lyrical idea returns intensified and transformed.

German influences

It will be recalled that Rossini's Bolognese teacher Padre Mattei nick-named him 'il Tedeschino', not least because of his absorbing interest in the music of Haydn and Mozart. And his first distinguished critic, Stendhal, always wrote as if the 'heavy Germanic' character of the later operas, from *Elisabetta* onwards, was a self-evident fact for all audiences and critics.

My fate is cast, I am ready for every battle; if I die, I shall die the death of
a hero, and my name will endure. I shall not see my beloved land slowly
waste away and be torn to pieces. . . .over the last Roman all Italy will weep.

Ex.V.3 Verdi, *Attila* (1846), Act II scene 4

But they surely misrepresented the situation. As Budden has pointed out, there is little common ground between the orchestral writing of Beethoven or Weber and Rossini's 'slightly fantastic manner of scoring, with a hint of parody in it' (1973–81, I: 10). With its clearly separated strands of colour and its fondness for the solo treatment of the woodwind, Rossini's orchestral style was certainly brilliant and inventive, but hardly Germanic; and Italian contemporaries might have been less startled by it had their native instrumental tradition not declined so abysmally during the previous quarter-century. Rossini himself was quite clear that it would not be a good thing for Italian opera if composers were tempted to lay too much emphasis on orchestral writing, or to put too much faith in the expressive power of harmony. As he is reported to have instructed Filippo Santocanale with regard to *Il Puritani*, 'Do daily urge Bellini not to allow himself to be seduced by German harmony, and always to rely on his happy way of organizing by means of simple harmony, full of feeling' (Lippmann 1969a: 288).

Nevertheless, the fact remains that there was, during the first half of the century, a gradual but total transformation of the sound-world of Italian opera. And this transformation was associated, not only by unsympathetic or old-fashioned critics, but by the composers themselves, with their curiosity about German instrumental music: with Rossini's devotion to Haydn and Mozart; with Pacini's 'setting ever greater store by the supreme German musicians' (1865: 41); with Donizetti's study of the quartets of 'Haydn, Beethoven, Mozart, Reicha, Mayseder', to which he attributed his knack of 'economizing on imagination and working out a piece from few ideas' (letter of 15 May 1842, in Zavadini 1948: 602).

The first step in this transformation took place during the Napoleonic period and had little or nothing to do with German influence. There was a renewed interest in choral writing in opera (some of the reasons have been discussed in Chapter 14); at the same time some effort was made to eliminate the custom of castration, so that composers came to rely more heavily on the natural male voices. Both these factors contributed towards a darkening of the colours and a thickening of the textures of Italian music compared with the aria-based, soprano-dominated opera of the eighteenth century.

By contrast, German influence was pronounced in a second development – the use of an enlarged and more imaginatively deployed orchestra. The Bavarian-born Simon Mayr, who settled in Italy and became probably the most influential composer of opera there in the twelve or fifteen years before the debut of Rossini, did more than anyone to encourage Italian musicians to open their ears to the dramatic and evocative powers of instrumental timbre. A full account of his orchestral innovations is not required here; but it may be noted that in addition to introducing 'new' instruments to the operatic instrumentarium – cor anglais in *Lodoiska* (1800), trombone and serpent in *Medea in Corinto* – it was Mayr too who popularized the use of chamber-music-like ensembles to accompany scenes of peculiar intimacy or poignancy, a custom that Verdi was still observing in the 1840s. A later German immigrant who produced a number of influential operas in Italy was Meyerbeer. His Italian operas already show that uncanny sense of atmosphere, achieved largely by instrumental means, for which he was to be so much admired by Berlioz. Italian composers were glad to avail themselves of these enlarged orchestral resources, but tended to handle them in a curiously old-fashioned way – concertante or *obbligato*-like – rather as an eighteenth-century composer might have done. This is particularly true of Mercadante, something of a grey eminence among Italians of the period, who was much revered by contemporaries for what Donizetti was to call his 'happy fusion of Italian song and German accompaniment' (MS 'Scritti e pensieri', Museo Donizettiano, Bergamo). His vocal numbers are not merely introduced, but punctuated and decorated too by elaborate woodwind solos: on occasion he even applies the same principle to recitative.

A third stage in this development was the attempt to adopt something of the substance of German music to the purposes of the Italian dramatic tradition, especially perhaps its more wide-ranging and imaginative sense of harmony, and its 'symphonic dialectic', that art of coaxing out of a simple musical idea a long, unbroken process of growth, evolution, development and change. It was an uncomfortable legacy for composers whose sensibilities had been formed in so different a school; and frequently they made heavy weather of it. In the mature scores of Mercadante, for instance, one finds the composer weaving more and more instrumental detail into the accompaniment patterns, with results that are sometimes fascinating, sometimes merely oppressive and clogged. And the composer's harmonic and modulatory resources, much admired as they were at the time, remain strangely anachronistic in effect. Instead of opening up new worlds of feeling, as Weber or Schubert were doing, Mercadante wrote a style of harmony that was still conditioned by Corellian habits of thought: he merely elaborates the traditional procedures to the point of abstruseness.

More nimble-minded craftsmen like Rossini and Donizetti sensed that symphonic techniques could best be employed to enrich the old *parlante* technique in those parts of an opera where an eager thrusting momentum was required – as indeed the *opera buffa* had already suggested. When Rossini began to naturalize these techniques in heroic opera it was in the *primo tempo* and the *tempo di mezzo* that they found their most natural home. There they provided an unbroken musical argument, which carried along the singers unresisting, but which at the same time could be responsive to fleeting nuances of feelings. As for 'Romantic' harmony, that was not a

443

craft to be mastered, but a new way of feeling; and it is to be doubted if any Italian composer before Verdi had it. At any rate it is difficult to think of any operatic scene earlier than *Rigoletto* in which the dramatic potential of chromatic harmony is fully and masterfully apprehended. There we certainly have it, in the Sparafucile scene Act I scene 7. With a few eerie chords – in which harmony, colour, dramatic function are absolutely one, absolutely inseparable – Verdi evokes the sinister scene: then he threads the muttered conversation of the two basses on to a kind of orchestral aria, in which the ghastly glint of the colours and the furtive patter of the rhythms brings all the suppressed horror of the encounter marvellously to life. At the close of the scene Verdi again demonstrates his feeling for the new type of harmony, underlining the words in which Sparafucile reveals his identity with a series of chords such as to make the imagination quake. The scene is not remotely Teutonic in feeling, or indeed in technique; but it would, I think, be fair to regard it as a magnificent theatrical naturalization of those elements that Italians particularly revered in German music of the Classical and early Romantic age.

The art of singing

The transformation of the musical language of opera carried in its train a transformation in the style of performance, particularly of the art of singing. It was a change that one should not exaggerate, for it was retarded and its effect was softened by the formidable status that the singer enjoyed as a creative artist in his own right.[1] There is little doubt that a performance of one of the young Verdi's operas given by a team of 'Early Music' practitioners would bring us much closer to the effects imagined and heard by the composer than one given by modern opera singers trained in *verismo* and 'music theatre'. For all that, in the ears of contemporary audiences there was a revolution in the performance of opera between Rossini and Verdi.

No one who has lived to experience the Age of the Producer will be much moved by laments about the Bad Old Days when opera was dominated by singers. But it should be understood that the status of star singers in opera was an elevated one, and to our way of thinking accorded them a thoroughly exaggerated importance. They were not seen as being servants of the composer, faithfully seeking to realize as accurately as possible his vision. In a sense the boot was on the other foot: an opera was bespoke for a specific company of singers and it was the composer's task to tailor his music to their capabilities as finely as possible, exploring their virtues to the full, disguising their shortcomings. A phrase of Donizetti's is definitive: 'to serve the situation and to give the artists scope to shine' (letter of 24 October 1841, in Zavadini 1948: 558). When an opera was revived in another theatre with a different cast it was normal for the music to be adapted to suit – sometimes by the composer, more often by another musician engaged by the theatre that was staging the revival. Those *puntature*, as they were called, might involve transposition, the replacement of types of coloratura that were ill suited to the new singer's voice by coloratura that was suited, even the wholesale refashioning of the melody. It was not the least of the innovations of *Macbeth* that it marked Verdi's break with this custom.

We get a vivid account of singing in the old style in Michotte's pamphlet describing an evening at Rossini's villa at Passy in 1858: Marietta Alboni is performing Arsace's scena from *Semiramide* Act I scene 5.

Our ears were not used [any longer] to that masterly diction, to such solid *sostenuto* in that largo with its lapidary structure 'Ah, quel giorno', which ten cellos (Prince Poniatowski's remark was just) could not equal! I should add the impression made by the feverish vigor of the allegro: 'Oh! come da quel dì' in which, despite the fast tempo of the writing and the multiplicity of the notes, not one of them was slighted, not one but emerged without shock, without violence, in its full sonorous value! (Michotte 1968: 105)

Rossini himself is prompted by this performance to outline to his guests the principles of bel canto, which, he asserts, depend upon three things: '1. The instrument – the voice – the Stradivarius, if you like. 2. Technique – that is to say, the manner of using it. 3. Style, the ingredients of which are taste and feeling' (*ibidem*: 108). During the course of further conversation he makes clear how infinitely painstaking and slow the earlier stages of mastering the art were. It is abundantly clear from his remarks that his music required, and that he himself could enjoy, only a style of singing that was more relaxed, less forceful, than what was fashionable by the middle of the century. Indeed the delicate filigree work of his *canto fiorito* obliged singers to maintain a light, airy, almost playful delivery, distancing the music somewhat from the crisis of the action and the passions of the character. Yet Rossini was by no means a straightforward conservative, maintaining the values of eighteenth-century singing into the Romantic age. Indeed he was himself charged with bringing about a 'terrible revolution' in the art by these who – like Stendhal – believed that singing was not a merely reproductive but an impulsively creative art: that 'the subtler nuances of emotion . . . can be expressed by the human voice alone, which treats them [in part at least] as a matter of spontaneous improvisation in immediate response to a direct relationship with the audience' (1956: 335).

The grounds for Stendhal's disapproval was that Rossini had seen fit to restrict the liberty singers had traditionally enjoyed to embellish and vary their music. In this respect, if in no other, his views on singing looked to the future rather than the past. It was an essential part of Mercadante's 'reform-operas' that the performers should learn to think of themselves as faithful servants of the composer with no licence to alter the score in the slightest, 'whether by additions or cuts or transpositions . . .'; moreover it should be performed with wholehearted enthusiasm, 'without any arbitrariness in tempo or in the addition of *fioritura*' (letter to Florimo, January 1838, Naples Conservatory Library). And these restrictions were not affected by the fact that composers such as Bellini and Donizetti had already gone a long way towards eliminating written-out coloratura and were cultivating an altogether plainer melodic style. By the 1840s the centuries-old vocal art of spontaneous embellishment, with which Jenny Lind was still enrapturing audiences in distant London, had been abandoned altogether in Italy. We get a clear indication of Verdi's views on the matter in a letter written by his pupil and assistant Muzio in 1847.

[Lind] has an unsurpassable agility, and to show off her virtuosity she is inclined to err in using excessive *fioritura*, turns and trills, things which pleased in the last century, but not in 1847. We Italians are not used to things of this sort, and if [she] came to Italy she would have to abandon her mania for embellishments and sing simply, having a voice uniform and flexible enough to sustain a phrase in Frezzolini's manner

(Garibaldi 1931: 329)

These developments were simply one sign of the fact that during the late 1820s and 1830s, as composers pursued more original and idiosyncratic dramatic visions, the traditional musical skills of opera singers ceased to be all-sufficient. Beauty of tone and virtuosity of execution yielded pride of place to expressiveness and dramatic perception. The demonstration of the art of the *prima donna* was less important than the impersonation of character. There is of course no absolutely clear-cut dividing line between the two conceptions, but a crucial stage in the transition is certainly marked by the beginning of the epoch-making collaboration between Bellini and Romani. 'In this opera', wrote Romani of *La straniera*, 'it is not just a matter of singing, it is a matter of passion, of soul, of imagination' (Rinaldi 1965: 218). The demands that Verdi made on his singers were still more radical.[2]

What was seen as a more truthful style of acting, the increasingly sensational and violent tone of the dramas themselves, the use of heavier orchestral textures – all these things combined with the plainer lyrical style of the period to encourage a louder and more impassioned style of singing. The extension of the chest-range of the tenor voice from about G upwards to the notorious 'ut-de-poitrine' of Gilbert Duprez, a development of the 1830s, was the most sensational symptom of this trend. Connoisseurs of the older style of singing could not but deplore what they heard as a 'coarse and stentorian bawling' – the phrase is from the critic of the London *Athenaeum*, Henry Fothergill Chorley (1862, I: 297). And they deplored it the more because it was accompanied by a continual and undiscriminating application of vibrato, a vibrato which Rossini compared with the buzzing in his ears produced by the shaking of the floor at the approach of his brewer's dray (Michotte 1968: 106). Indeed no one expressed more scathingly than Rossini his outrage at the loss of the grand old art of *bel canto*.

These days the art of singing is on the barricades; the old florid style is replaced by a nervous style, the solemn style by that kind of shouting we used to describe as being in the French manner; and finally the tender, sentimental style by the rabidly passionate! As you see, my dear Florimo, today it is simply a question of lung-power; the kind of singing one feels in the soul, and sheer splendour of voice have been banned.

(Lippmann 1969a: 290)

25 · Rossini in Naples

Rossini comes to Naples

Among the more colourful personalities of Restoration Italy must be counted the Neapolitan impresario, Domenico Barbaia. Semi-literate and foul-mouthed, Barbaia had amassed a vast fortune which he spent flamboyantly in indulging his passions for racehorses, diamonds and paintings. He had begun to make a name for himself during the Napoleonic period, when he ran a gambling syndicate; this, based at first in Milan, rapidly took over much of the Italian theatre. By 1809 Barbaia was in Naples, controlling the gambling rooms attached to the theatres there, and conducting with immense entrepreneurial flair a business empire that, during the remainder of the Napoleonic period, dealt in army contracts, and after 1815 in building (Rosselli 1984: 31). He was also Italy's outstanding impresario, running the Royal theatres of Naples with only brief interruptions from 1809 to 1840.

By Barbaia's time, Naples could look back on a theatrical tradition that not even Venice could surpass, an unbroken operatic Golden Age stretching from Alessandro Scarlatti in the closing decades of the seventeenth century to Paisiello, still active in the early years of the nineteenth. The city took a proper, dignified pride in these traditions, and was less disposed than the more northerly cities of the peninsula to be bowled over by any young *parvenu*, even one so startlingly talented as Rossini; Naples was indeed of all the operatic centres of Italy the most reluctant to capitulate to his charms. Nevertheless, by 1815 Barbaia had decided that indigenous musical traditions were in danger of stagnating, and that the verve and brashness of Rossini were exactly the things to revivify them. He was brought to Naples in that year, and he stayed there as artistic director of the city's musical life until 1822. These six years represent both the core and the climax of his work in the Italian theatre, and the operas he produced during this period, particularly the eight serious ones, can be regarded as the deepest and firmest of the foundation stones of Italian Romantic opera.

Some Neapolitans, especially the older *cognoscenti*, gave Rossini a cool welcome. Stendhal reported that while they were prepared to give him full credit for the panache and stylishness with which he composed in a manner '*characteristically entertaining to the present generation*, [they were of the view that] as to ideas, as to anything really fundamental, there was no comparison . . . between this modern upstart and those fine old composers of days gone by' (Stendhal 1956: 308). As late as 1818 there was still a clique of anti-Rossinians prepared to exalt Morlacchi's 'old-time simplicity and nobility' at the expense of Rossini's 'vain and false ornaments' (Toye 1954: 78–9). But gradually Rossini overcame this reserve, and became the Neapolitans' 'adopted favourite son' (Gossett 1983: 33). He began cautiously, testing out his new audiences, as he was later to do in Paris, with two operas, *Elisabetta, regina d'Inghilterra* and *La gazzetta*, of which a high proportion of the music was adapted from earlier works. He found that the Neapolitans' taste was cultivated and sophisticated: they were more familiar than most audiences with foreign, especially French opera, and led the way in accepting certain stylistic innovations modelled on French practice – orchestrally accompanied recitative, for example, and a prominent role for chorus; they enjoyed the services of one of the best orchestras in Europe (the comments of Spohr and Stendhal on the San Carlo orchestra date from Rossini's years in Naples); and they were far more open-minded towards dramatic and musical experimentation than were audiences in most Italian cities, prepared to accept tragic endings in *Otello* and *Maometto II* (which had to be changed into happy endings for revivals in Rome and Venice respectively), prepared even to forgo the full-scale independent overtures which had proved such delicious ornaments to the earlier Rossini operas. Rossini soon decided that for as long as he was in Naples, it was well worthwhile taking quite unprecedented time and trouble over the composition of his new scores.

In many ways the circumstances in which he now found himself were ideal. He was very comfortably off personally and his impresario, Barbaia, maintained a superb company, the key members of which remained in Naples throughout Rossini's residence there. For posterity that is precisely the problem: these Neapolitan operas were tailored to the skills of one of the most brilliant teams of singers ever assembled in one place, and for that very reason present hair-raising difficulties for anyone who attempts to revive them. Rossini was following an age-old tradition in seeking inspiration in the qualities of his singers, composing music that challenged, stimulated, publicly proclaimed the finest facets of their art. But thanks to some whimsy or effervescence in his own character he derived particular pleasure from driving his artists to the very limit in their mastery of what we may describe generically as florid song. In earlier years, working with such consummate vocalists as Maria Marcolini and the last of the operatic *castrati*, Giovanni Battista Velluti, Rossini had already begun to develop a manner in which the vocal lines were dissolved into vertiginously rearing and plunging runs and coruscating divisions. The prowess of the Naples company prompted him to develop this tendency to a *ne plus ultra* of virtuosity.

Among this company were three principal tenors, two of whom, Giovanni David and Andrea Nozzari, ranked among the finest artists of the age. As their voices were interestingly distinct in quality – David was a *tenore di grazia*, a consummate artist at the floating of high-pitched florid lines; Nozzari had a wider tessitura and a darker and more robust timbre – Rossini took particular delight in exploring the dramatic and characterizing potential of the tenor voice – Roderigo versus Otello; James V versus Roderick Dhu in *La donna del lago*, etc. Stendhal suggests the kind of delight Naples audiences could look forward to from such juxtapositions in his account of a passage in the Act I finale of *Otello*: 'but . . . to hear a performance barren of the glorious rivalry of some Nozzari and Davide striving to outdo each other in perfection, goaded higher and ever higher in achievement by the spur of emulation, is to hear nothing' (1956: 222).

The weight laid on the tenor voice in these operas brought about a distinct shift in the tessitura of Italian opera. The days of the dominance of high voices, whether *castrato* or female, were numbered, and operatic composers began systematically to explore the potential of the natural male voice. Apparently still more striking to Rossini's contemporaries than his formidable tenor roles was what has sometimes been described as his emancipation of the bass voice (from its confinement to *opera buffa* that is to say, and to a restricted range of venerable character types in *opera seria*). Such old-fashioned habitués of the opera as Lord Mount-Edgcumbe found this a startling, indeed perverse development, deeming that basses 'take the lead in opera with almost as much propriety as if the double bass were to do so in the orchestra' (Mount-Edgcumbe 1824: 122). But the talents of such artists as Filippo Galli and Michele Benedetti were not to be overlooked, and inspired Rossini to write a series of superb bass-roles culminating in the title-role of the original *Mosè in Egitto*, which astonish us today only because Rossini wrote for the bass with much the same florid abandon as he did for tenor or female voices.

Rossini's leading ladies were Rosmunda Pesaroni, a spectacular contralto, with a sufficiently modern artistic conscience to be prepared to undertake so modest a role as that of Pippo in the Naples revivals of *La gazza ladra*,[1] and, most famously of all, the Spanish-born soprano, Isabella Colbran. 'Perfect in method and in style . . . with a prodigious range . . . of almost three octaves, from low g to top e . . . which she delivers with complete evenness of softness and energy' (*Il redattore del Reno*, April 1807, quoted in *DBI*, s.v. 'Colbran'), Colbran was also a celebrated beauty with a magnificent stage presence. At the time of Rossini's arrival in Naples she was reputed to be Barbaia's mistress, though she expeditiously abandoned the impresario's bed for that of the young composer, and in due course became his first wife. It was therefore presumably for political reasons that Colbran, closely linked through Barbaia to the Neapolitan court, was so scurvily handled by liberal critics like Stendhal. Stendhal's denunciations are deliciously witty:

If I have sat once in the San Carlo theatre, I have sat a score of times, and listened to Signora Colbran embark upon an aria, which after the first few bars, would tail off into the most excruciating, the most insupportable cacophony; and one by one I have watched my neighbours creep out of their seats, shaking, neurotic, their patience frayed and their endurance exhausted – yet all in dead silence, without a word. And after *that*, let anyone deny that terror be the principle of despotic government . . . (1956: 150)

but there is little enough reason to suppose what he writes to be true. A competent critic, hearing Colbran sing in Vienna in 1822 in a series of performances of *Zelmira*, Rossini's last Neapolitan opera, wrote of 'the fine *portamento* of her voice, perfect intonation, highly polished method. And then the Graces sprinkle with nectar her every syllable, her every *fioritura*, every *gruppetto*, every trill. Runs of almost two octaves through clearly articulated and pearl-like semitones and the other choice artifices of her singing show her to be an artist of the first rate' (*DBI*, s.v. Colbran'); and Rossini himself, at a time when any erstwhile romantic attachment had long ceased to colour his judgement, remembered her as 'the greatest' singer of her age; which put her second only to Malibran, 'the unique' (Michotte 1968: 121).

Subject-matter and aesthetics

The subjects of Rossini's Neapolitan operas were drawn from a mixed array of sources. Given his very reserved enthusiasm for the tastes of the new age, it is no surprise to find him continuing to make some use of traditional types of theme. *Armida* (1817) and *Ricciardo e Zoraide* (1818) were based on Italian epic poems: Tasso's *Gerusalemme liberata* and Forteguerri's *Ricciardetto* respectively. When he and his librettists turned to the French theatre for their materials, it was not to the contemporary repertory, as it was to be with Donizetti, Bellini and Verdi, but to the Classical and neo-classical, to Racine's *Andromaque* in *Ermione* (1819), to Belloy in *Zelmira* (1882), and later to Voltaire in *Semiramide* (Venice 1823). But two of his Neapolitan operas did show Rossini at least tentatively in touch with newer fashions: *Otello* (1816) was, in a manner of speaking, based on Shakespeare's tragedy, whlie *La donna del lago* (1819) was the earliest Italian opera inspired by the immense enthusiasm for Sir Walter Scott that was just sweeping Europe.

How far this made them genuinely Romantic operas is another question. Certainly the blending in the first tableau of *La donna del lago* of hunting party and barcarolle is in the highest degree picturesque; and the use of six on-stage hunting horns, spatially distributed to facilitate echo effects, seems a direct attempt to translate one of Scott's couplets into theatrical terms: 'faint, from further distance borne / were heard the clanging hoof and horn'. But this opening scene apart, there is little else in the music of the opera either in the way of musical characterization or of picturesque tone-painting to evidence a Romantic sensibility. In *Otello* too, for the greater part of the time, the 'Romantic' literary source is of little or no importance to the character of the opera. The plot has been described as one of 'archetypical situations' and 'familiar melodramatic formulas' (Gossett 1979–80), and for two acts nothing but the most casual and fleeting coincidences of action, characterization and language suggest that it has anything to do with *Othello* at all. Such contemporaries as had any real love and understanding of Shakespeare were withering in their contempt for the libretto. Byron, after viewing the opera in Venice, wrote that 'they have been crucifying *Othello* into an opera . . . all the real scenes with Iago cut out and the greatest nonsense inserted; the handkerchief turned into a billet doux, and the first singer would not *black* his face, for some exquisite reasons assigned to the preface' (letter of 3 March 1818). More telling still were Stendhal's strictures on the opera's moral incoherence:

If the passion of jealousy is to be effectively conveyed through the medium of art, it must first be rooted in a soul possessed of a love as desperate as that of Werther himself – of a love which may be *sanctified* by self-inflicted death. Any love which fails to rise to this degree of intensity has, in my opinion, no right to be jealous; where love is tepid, jealousy is an impertinence . . . (1956: 206)

and he went on to offer a critical insight of a remarkably modern kind, to the effect that 'in *Otello*, we are so electrified by the magnificent musical quality of the songs, so spellbound, so overwhelmed by the incomparable beauty of the theme, that we invent our own libretto to match' (*ibidem*: 212).

Yet the 'wretched librettist' of Stendhal's strictures was the Marchese Francesco Berio di Salsa, a Neapolitan nobleman of wide culture and immense erudition, whose 'literary . . . acquaintance extends itself to the utmost verge of the philosophy and belles-lettres of England, France, Germany and his native country. He has read every thing, and continues to read every thing' (Morgan 1821, III: 278). Indeed he was reputed to know much of Homer, Sophocles, Terence, Corneille, Alfieri and Shakespeare by heart. What appalled Byron and Stendhal earned the gratitude of many of Berio's Italian contemporaries as a demonstration of the kind of tact necessary if 'the tremendous catastrophes of the ferocious Shakespeare'[2] were to be made palatable to fastidious tastes. Furthermore Berio did produce a final act which, by its concentration, its fidelity to the Shake-spearean sources and, ultimately, its astonishing theatrical boldness, enabled Rossini to produce one of the most famous and incontrovertibly Romantic acts in all nineteenth-century opera. Meyerbeer's tribute is notable: 'this third act really is god-like, and what is extraordinary is that its beauties are absolutely anti-Rossini-ish. First-rate declamation, ever-impassioned recitative, mysterious accompaniment full of local colour and, particularly, the style of the old-time romance at its highest perfection' (Weinstock 1968: 59).

The retuning of Italian operatic sensibility can be felt not only in such overtly Romantic scenes as these. During his visit to Naples in 1817 Spohr reported on a new theatrical dispensation for the weeks of Lent: 'in place of the traditional oratorios, operas are to be given this year as usual, but without ballets, which are forbidden at this season' (1860–61, II: 16). Two of Rossini's Neapolitan operas, *Mosè in Egitto* (1818), based on the tragedy *L'Osiride* by the Olivetan monk Francesco Ringhieri, and *Ermione* (1819), based on Racine's *Andromaque*, described by the composer as *azione tragico-sacra* and *azione tragica* respectively, were designed to supply this new need for operas of a biblical, oratorio-like grandeur, which could be staged as part of a Lenten opera season without danger of provoking a reactionary or clerical backlash. *Mosè* in particular, where whole scenes were handled in an oratorio-like manner, as massive tableaux of choral drama sullied by no trace of secular intrigue, provided Italian theatres with a new type of spectacle. By placing a religious and national community at the centre of the drama and using the chorus to express that community's aspirations and hopes, *Mosè* was to provide Verdi with the most helpful and distinguished model for his risorgimental manner. And we know from Balzac's *Massimilla Doni* (1839) that Italian audiences were already disposed to interpret such a score in a topical sense before Verdi had even started his career. 'Il me semble avoir assisté à la libération de l'Italie, pensait un Milanais. – Cette musique relève les têtes courbées, et donne de l'espérance aux cœurs les plus endormis, s'écriait un Romagnol.'

In Rome and Milan during this period, but not in Naples, Rossini offered another timely alternative to the traditional ethos of the *opera seria*. *Torvaldo e Dorliska* (Rome 1815), *Matilde di Shabran* (Rome 1821) and *La gazza ladra* (Milan 1817) are all *opere semiserie*, *La gazza ladra* the most distinguished and influential example of the genre.

For all the breadth and novelty of Rossini's subject matter there is no gainsaying a deep scepticism in his attitude to the new Romanticism. Never does one feel that complete identification with new areas of experience and a new type of sensibility that one finds in the most characteristic works of Donizetti and Bellini. His reaction to a libretto sent him by Count Carlo Donà in April 1853 is wholly in character:

I have always been the firm friend of natural and spontaneous situations . . . and if I had any advice to give you it would be to return within the bounds of the natural, instead of adventuring into the world of absurdity and diabolism from which . . . modern philosophers have laboured so hard to deliver a too credulous humanity.

(Radiciotti 1921: 20)

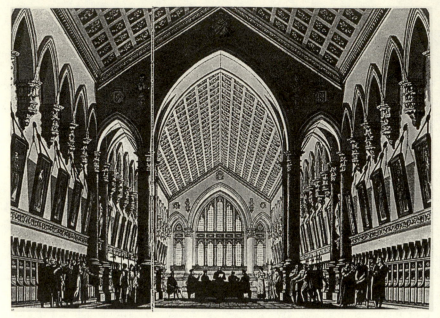

Plate 8 Set design for *La gazza ladra*, La Scala, Milan, 1817

Rossini's clear-eyed, critical stance is shown too in the *scenario* he sketched in 1830 for an opera based on Goethe's *Faust*. According to his own account of this, he subjected the German poet's metaphysical apparatus to a Mediterraneanizing process, 'leaving out the spectres, demons and lugubrious fantasms [and] having the fates and genii sing instead' (Weinstock 1968: 171).

The paradoxical Romanticism of Rossini's opera texts reflects a similar paradox in his musical character: for the composer who was to be revered as the *fons et origo* of Italian Romantic opera was more an anachronism than a pathbreaker, a musician whose wit, whose sovereign stylishness and keen intellectual joy in music-making mark him as a great eighteenth-century master. When Giuseppe Carpani heard *Zelmira* in Vienna in 1822, the appreciative essay which he was moved to write expresses his admiration entirely in terms of the illustrious dead: 'at times you seem to hear Gluck, at others Mozart and Handel; the gravity, the learning, the naturalness and the suavity of their conceptions live and blossom again in the score of *Zelmira*' (Toye 1954: 101). No doubt critics always tend to express themselves in this way, but in the case of Rossini it matches the man; for if anything is clear about his perception of his own art it is his sense of indebtedness to, and kinship with, the eighteenth-century operatic traditions that had reached their final glory in Mozart and Cimarosa. He had, asserted Stendhal, 'no conception whatsoever of the emergence of a *new ideal of beauty*', and insisted that 'no one can hope to propose any new aesthetic ideals, since, in the short period which has elapsed between Guglielmi's day and our own, the nature of man has had too little time for development' (1956: 327–8). It was a view he maintained to the end. His last surviving letter, to Tito Ricordi, complains that Boito, in his *Mefistofele* libretto, was 'trying to do in one day what can only be achieved in years' (21 April 1868, in Gál 1965: 241).

The heresy, as he saw it, that most offended him was the conviction of many nineteenth-century composers that music could be 'a literary art, an imitative art, a philosophical melopoeia' (letter to Lauro Rossi, 1868, in Lippmann 1969a: 293), which clung servilely to the text, taking the cue for its own behaviour from the promptings of the poet. Rossini, on the contrary, believed that music was an art 'in principle wholly imaginative, and in purpose stimulating and expressive' (tutta ideal quanto al suo principio, e quanto allo scopo, incitativa ed espressiva) (*ibidem*: 291). 'Music', he continued, 'is . . . the moral atmosphere filling the space in which the characters of the drama play out their parts.' And the task of the composer was therefore not to imitate what the words were already saying sufficiently clearly, but by the resources of his own art to render the hearts and minds of the listeners more susceptible, to attune them to the situations of the story and the passions and destiny of the characters. There are times when Rossini's views on the aesthetics of opera sound almost like Debussy's.

How far Rossini's own music was free from any servile, imitative dependence on text or dramatic situation is clear from the ease with which it lent itself to being transferred from one context to another – the kind of thing that, twenty years later, was to be wholly repugnant to Verdi's conception of dramatic music. Not only did Rossini regularly transfer music from one opera to another in the time-honoured fashion of the *aria di baule*; on occasion it was re-used in connection with new texts the sense of which was quite remote from that of the original. Lippmann quotes a striking example from *Mosè* (my Ex.V.4). The music which in the original version of the opera was sung by Elcia, the young romantic lover, to the words:

> Tormenti, affanni, smanie!
> Voi fate a brani il core!
> Tutto di Averno o Furie
> Versate in me il furore.
> Straziate voi quest'anima,
> Che regge al duolo ancor![3]

reappears in the second version sung by Pharaoh's wife, Sinaide:

> Che ascolto . . . oh! qual nell'alma
> Piacer mi scende ancor
> All'amor suo la calma

Love! Torments, troubles, frenzies! You tear my heart to shreds! Furies,
you pour out in me all the rage of Avernus. You torment this soul, which
yet has the power to feel pity.

Ex.V.4 Rossini, *Mosè in Egitto* (1818), Act III

Io deggio del mio cor.
Ventura, onor e gloria
Gli sian propizj ognor.[4] (Adamo and Lippmann 1981: 443)

In such a case one can scarcely even speak of a 'moral atmosphere'; the secret of the music's effectiveness in both contexts is almost entirely 'incitativo', a matter of the listener's sensibility being wrought up to an unusual degree of susceptibility by its sensuous charm and throbbing vitality, plus, of course, such expressive nuances as the singer herself was able to provide.

The conviction informing all Rossini's art, that the autonomy of music must be preserved, made it impossible for him to warm to the idea of 'irreproachable diction' and 'masterly declamation' as commended to him by Wagner during their memorable conversation in 1860. For all the wit and graciousness of his manner he did not disguise his belief that such aims signalled 'L'oraison funèbre de la mélodie' (Lippmann 1969a: 292). On a larger scale, too, Rossini could not see how it was possible for musical forms, dependent on their own intrinsic principles of repetition, symmetry, variation and contrast, to be fashioned to suit the requirements of a different, poetic or dramatic, art. His unwillingness to concede that music might content itself with being merely dramatically functional is illustrated in dozens of episodes in all his scores. A simple example is provided by the march embedded in the *Introduzione* of *Otello*. In style it is less like a stage march than a movement from a wind-band serenade, for as Otello and his attendants advance towards the Doge the music does not simply grow louder, it is subjected to a series of florid variations: composers, in Rossini's view, should always be making music.

Balzac's novel *Massimilla Doni* is of course a work of imaginative fiction rather than of music criticism. But it contains at least one *aperçu* of the first order which may fittingly be quoted here: the idea that the floridity of Rossini's mature music (which for many modern opera lovers gives it a distance and coolness very alien to their image of Italian Romantic opera) is, in part at least, an assertion of purely musical values, that is to say of imagination, of expression and of enchantment. And Capraja, the character whose words I quote, finishes, perhaps a little unexpectedly, by placing Rossini in the company of E. T. A. Hoffmann:

La roulade est la plus haute expression de l'art . . . Chargée de réveiller dans votre âme mille idées endormies, elle s'élance, elle traverse l'espace en semant dans l'air ses germes qui ramassés par les oreilles, fleurissent au fond du cœur . . . Il est déplorable que le vulgaire ait forcé les musiciens à plaquer leurs expressions sur les paroles, sur des intérêts factices; mais il est vrai qu'ils ne seraient plus compris par la foule. La roulade est donc l'unique point laissé aux amis de la musique pure, aux amoureux de l'art tout nu. En entendant ce soir la dernière cavatine, je me suis cru convié par une belle fille qui par un seul regard m'a rendu jeune: l'enchanteresse m'a mis une couronne sur la tête et m'a conduit à cette porte d'ivoire par où l'on entre dans le pays mystérieux de la Rêverie . . .

457

Rossini's musical language

Despite what has been said of the retrospective character of much of Rossini's aesthetics, the years he spent in Naples were, from the musical point of view, a time of innovation and experiment. The overall design of the opera, the shaping of the individual movements, the deployment of the orchestral and vocal forces, in all such particulars – after a rather cautious start with *Elisabetta* – Rossini innovated more and more boldly during the four years between *Otello* and *Maometto II*. Thereafter there was something of a consolidation, and *Semiramide* (Venice 1823) became 'a *summa* of the values of the entire preceding tradition' (Zedda 1979: xxi). To some extent the formal innovation of these years may have been inspired by the more international tastes of the Neapolitan opera public; Rossini himself was involved in the direction of Spontini's *Fernand Cortez* (Paris 1809) at the San Carlo in 1820. It is no accident that two of his finest works from these years, *Mosè* and *Maometto II*, were to prove ideally suited for adaptation as Parisian grand operas.

Some aspects of the originality of structure are related to a matter already discussed: the enlargement of the range of subject-matter. It was the opportunity to transform the traditional Lenten oratorio into a solemn and spiritually edifying kind of opera that prompted Rossini to place unprecedented structural weight on the choral tableaux of *Mosè*. In operas of every kind, however, there was a gradual reduction in the number of solo arias, as he became more interested in architecturally and texturally richer musical forms, forms within which a wider range of mood and dramatic action could be accommodated. Even the *sortita* of the *prima donna* was occasionally sacrificed in favour of an ensemble, as Desdemona's is in Act I of *Otello*. An extreme example of the boldness of Rossini's formal innovations, characteristically and ironically belittled by the whimsical title, is the 'terzettone' (big fat trio) from *Maometto II*, where a finale-like conglomeration of short movements sucks up into itself much of the main action of the first act. Act III of *Otello* surpasses all earlier Italian operas, at least since Monteverdi, in being conceived as a single, dramatically inspired musical entity. The opening recitative is interrupted by the off-stage *canzone* of the gondolier; the principal number, Desdemona's *romanza* 'Assisa al pie d'un salice', is interrupted and finally cut short by recitatives; and of the songs, both the *canzone* (twenty-seven bars of $\frac{2}{4}$) and the *preghiera*, 'Deh, calma, o ciel' (twenty-seven bars of $\frac{6}{8}$), are so compressed as to impede as little as possible the thrust of the drama towards the final catastrophe.

Nothing shows the innovatory character of the Naples operas more clearly than Rossini's treatment of the overture. Despite the effort of such reformers as Gluck and Jommelli, the overture had in Italy remained part of the social frame of the opera, a movement quite extraneous to the main dramatic business. The overtures of Rossini's early operas had been in this tradition; but thanks to the wit and flair of their instrumental writing and the electrifying vitality of their rhythms they proved to be, not mere gratuitous incidentals, but key factors in his popular success. Newly arrived in Naples, all too aware of the independence of Neapolitan taste, desperately anxious to please in the southern metropolis as well as he had in the cities of the north, Rossini began in 1815–16 with a number of operas in which he, as it were, exhibited some of the choicer wares on which his reputation was based. The high proportion of borrowed and reworked music in his first Neapolitan operas includes two overtures, that for *Elisabetta* reworked from *Aureliano in Palmira* (1813) (and used again for *Il barbiere di Siviglia*) and that for *Otello* from *Sigismondo*. Thereafter, having got the measure of his new audience, Rossini abandoned the traditional type of overture, except in the operas he composed for other cities (*La gazza ladra*, *Semiramide* etc). In its place he devised a new style of *Introduzione*, heard at its most impressive in *Mosè* and *Maometto II*, a grand tableau of orchestral, choral and ensemble music that plunges the spectator straight into the thick of the dramatic action. Such overtures as are to be found in the later Neapolitan operas treat the form in a quite new way, though they may perhaps owe something to the experiments of such late-eighteenth-century masters as Paisiello. The most interesting is that to *Ermione*, which is from time to time interrupted by an off-stage chorus lamenting the destruction of Troy.

It was during the years Rossini spent in Naples that the standardization of the operatic structure (as described in Chapter 24) was brought about. But while the double-aria *scena*, containing both cantabile and cabaletta, is the preferred pattern, Rossini, unlike some of his followers, is not afraid to cast his numbers into new forms, or to experiment with the structure of the individual movement if a different scheme seems more appropriate to the idea that is to be expressed. Not even the *prima donna* is immune to such initiatives: in Desdemona's aria from the close of Act II of *Otello* Rossini creates an effect of distraught incoherence by a very odd aria structure in which the whole weight of the design is carried by a *primo tempo* and a *tempo di mezzo* (the latter propelled by an orchestral theme almost caricaturally grotesque in instrumental colouring); there is but a single phrase of cantabile and that leads directly to the brilliant cabaletta-like cadences with which the number closes. Among the wide range of aria types in these operas are some which preserve eighteenth-century elements: a sonata-like presentation of the themes is found in some more old-worldly or regal contexts – in Douglas's aria from Act I of *La donna del lago*, for instance, or in Uberto's (King James's) cavatina in the second act. Even the *da capo* principle is not entirely extinct. A characteristic and fascinating balancing-act between the old world and the new is provided by Rodrigo's 'Ah come mai non senti' (*Otello*, Act II). The asymmetrical lyric of 3 + 7 *ottonari* is set in a *da capo* pattern, the seven lines 4–10 providing the material for a *tempo di mezzo* between the two lyrical settings of lines 1–3. But while the first appearance of 1–3 is a very beautiful broad cantabile, they return as a cabaletta-like allegro, sung twice. Rossini has superimposed the thrusting physical momentum of the Romantic scena upon the statuesque psychological obsessiveness of the *opera seria*. *La donna del lago* ends with one of the few examples in the nineteenth-century repertory of a genuine rondo, with three returns of the brilliant theme decked out with ever more dazzling coruscations of coloratura; while of the several strophic songs, Desdemona's 'Assisa al pie d'un salice' is a beautiful example of genuinely expressive variation writing.

Although they were written for the greatest singers of the age, the arias of Rossini's Neapolitan operas are already beginning to yield pride of place to ensemble scenes. And here one finds a range of styles and techniques which, for thirty years, was to provide Italian composers with patterns for all their musico-dramatic needs. Commonly the duet, or at any rate any single movement of the duet, represents a frozen moment of heightened perception, and for such a situation Rossini found an ideal form, succinctly demonstrated in 'Vorrei che il tuo pensiero' (*Otello*, Act I). It may be described as a phase of antiphony (Ex.V.5a), yielding to a phase of free imitation (Ex.V.5b), yielding to a phase of parallel singing (Ex.V.5c): a scheme that in turn gives, or may give, characterization, musical artifice, and sheer sensuous delight their due. But one can also find in Rossini that type of 'dissimilar' duet from which Donizetti and Verdi were to generate such theatrical electricity: in the Elena–Uberto duet within the Act II terzetto from *La donna del lago*, for example, he juxtaposes the cantabile phrases of the soprano against more *parlando*-like, minor-key ejaculations in the tenor in an effort to recreate within the closed form dramatic tension and the conflict of character.

Among the more extraordinary episodes in these operas one must certainly include the many 'canonic' Adagios and Andantes to be found in the larger-scale ensembles. These movements commonly occur at the most acute dramatic crises. They are literally moments of enchantment, ensemble soliloquies during which time stands still as some moment of high emotional tension is transpeciated into a tableau of sheer sonorous magic. Rossini likes to present his principal canonic theme in a series of variations, shedding new colours on it by moving it from key to key, and fashioning new melodic shapes out of it in the process.

Except for the unsuccessful and soon forgotten *La gazzetta*, composed for the Teatro Fiorentini in 1816, Rossini wrote no comic operas for Naples. But the absorption into the musical language of *opera seria* of a whole range of musical characteristics that had once been proper to *opera buffa* was a major factor in the development of his personal style. Notable hallmarks of this style are an orchestral brio that seems always on the verge of gesture or onomatopoeia, a verve and piquancy in the themes that propel the *primo tempo* and *tempo di mezzo* sections of the scene, and, perhaps above all, an unprecedented emphasis on the emotional and theatrical power of rhythm. In the march and chorus at the start of the Act I finale of *Otello*, for example, the music so throbs and reverberates with inner life that one has

I would wish your thoughts might tell me the truth. They are always frank with you: no, you have no cause to fear.

Ex.V.5a Rossini, *Otello* (1816), Act I

How fierce are the throbbings which love awakens in us. . .

Ex.V.5b Rossini, *Otello* (1816), Act I

How fierce are the throbbings. . .

Ex.V.5c Rossini, *Otello* (1816), Act I

the impression of a piece moving at twice its real pace. The outcome of this extraordinary rhythmic vitality is, as Stendhal wrote of *Elisabetta*, a style which 'offered all the great emotional tension and drama of the *opera seria*, without exacting the usual toll of dreariness and boredom' (1956: 155).

Quite early in the Naples period this fusion of the genres also came to embrace the various types of coloratura singing that had hitherto been regarded as proper to the one or the other. The years 1816–17 mark, in Celletti's formulation, the fusion of *agilità di grazia* (from the *opera buffa*) with *agilità di forza* (from the *opera seria*), of *canto di garbo* (*opera buffa*) with *canto di bravura* (*opera seria*); and he cites *Otello* as the opera in which this fusion is first achieved.

Brilliant vocal writing was not lacking in even his earliest works. But it was brilliance of a conventional and systematic kind, entailing a smooth-flowing semi-syllabic delivery of the text in regular patterns of triplet quavers or semiquavers, and designed in such a way as to accommodate further improvised virtuosity by the singer, particularly at cadences. By the time of *L'inganno felice* (Venice 1812), a freer, more fanciful type of embellishment is to be found, one that suggests that 'Rossini was beginning cautiously to introduce himself into the performers' sacred precincts' (Celletti 1968: 881) and gave to certain of his cantilenas what we might anachronistically describe as a Chopinesque elegance. And from then up to the time of *Elisabetta* and *Otello*, often stimulated by the skills of a particular performer – Maria Marcolini in several of his earliest operas, or Giovanni Battista Velluti in *Aureliano in Palmira* (Milan 1813), or Isabella Colbran in Naples – Rossini continues to enlarge the scope of his coloratura effects and pack his numbers more and more densely with them. Characteristic of his mature style are soaring and plunging runs of spectacular rapidity, sometimes fashioned into periods of seemingly nonchalant symmetry, suggestive of a new ideal of *sprezzatura*. In this context, simplicity of melody, sustained in long phrases free from the encrustations of *fioritura*, became, as Stendhal observed, a symbol of 'deep emotional sincerity' (1956: 264).

Some sensitive musicians and critics did not care for the amassing of coloratura that distinguishes Rossini's Neapolitan operas. Stendhal's strictures are well known, and some of them have been quoted earlier. Spohr too felt that the singing voice lost much of its peculiar charm, that it was perhaps even 'debased, when [Rossini] forces it into passages and roulades which any mediocre instrumentalist can deliver far more accurately and coherently' (1860–61, I: 336). But when it is performed with the truly masterful execution that he surely expected of his Neapolitan singers it gives his music a 'beauty without heaviness' (Lippmann) that is like nothing else in opera: a unique amalgam of air-borne grace, and reckless verve.

From what has been said of Rossini's aesthetics it will be understood that some of the expressive and dramatic resources bequeathed by him to Italian Romantic opera were equivocal, and not easily described. He belonged to a generation which still held the view that 'the composer's first duty is that of giving *musical* delight. [Dramatic] expression is only the second aim' (Carpani 1824: 69). But Goethe's famous description of the art of the German singer, Wilhelm Ehlers,[5] reminds us that in the age of strophic song, audiences were much more sensitive than they are today to the expressive effects that the performer himself could achieve through the nuances of his art: through phrasing, through dynamic gradation, through variation in vocal timbre. And there can be little doubt that, in this sense, Rossini's florid song would, when sympathetically performed, have struck contemporary audiences as being much more expressive and much more dramatic than it can seem to those of us brought up on Verdi and Puccini.

But many of the explicitly expressive resources of the Romantic age also have their origins in Rossini's art. Occasionally one finds in his operas pages that are as pointedly expressive or as laden with dramatic significance as anything from Donizetti or Verdi twenty or thirty years later. Act III of *Otello* provides several famous instances. Everything about the gondolier's song, for instance, is expressively and dramatically to the point: the balladesque melody set against an atmospheric tremolo; the very fact of its being sung off-stage, which gives it something of the significance of a portent; the extreme brevity which at once symbolizes and sharpens our sense of the transitoriness of human affairs. Later in the act the Desdemona–Otello duet co-ordinates the human cataclysm of Desdemona's murder and the natural cataclysm of the tempest with a theatrical flair that yields little to the last act of *Rigoletto*.

But in more general senses, too, Rossini's Neapolitan operas did prove a source of dramatic inspiration to a younger generation. With their tremendous tenor and bass roles they provided such a composer as Verdi with a good starting-point for that much keener sense of vocal characterization that was to be typical of Romantic opera. Furthermore, Rossini mastered his craft by means of what seems to have been a uniquely enthusiastic study of Haydn and especially of Mozart, the composer he was ever after to revere: 'the admiration of my youth, the desperation of my mature years, the consolation of my old age' (Gossett 1983: 5). Frequently his music was attacked by his Italian contemporaries as being too Germanic and erudite, for overwhelming the melody in a tumult of harmony, for 'preferring the intelligence which contrives and calculates to the divine fire . . . which creates and perfects', as the *Giornale delle due Sicilie* wrote of *Armida* (quoted in Radiciotti 1921: 21). But by taking an intelligent and creative interest in German instrumental music Rossini was in fact giving the decisive stamp of his personal approval to a tendency that was to have incalculable consequences for Italian opera. The great French Romantic painter Eugène Delacroix was to single out the orchestral introductions and interludes and epilogues as the most genuinely Romantic part of Rossini's operas: 'only in him does one find those pathetic introductions and those passages which, though often very fast, summarize a whole situation for the soul and do it outside all the conventions' (Weinstock 1968: 147). He was writing of *Guillaume Tell*, but there is virtually nothing in that late masterpiece which is not clearly foreshadowed in the Neapolitan operas.

Though he can hardly be regarded as a true Romantic himself, no other composer did half as much as Rossini to provide Italian Romantic opera with a form and style of its own. Sometimes his influence on his successors can be seen in some specific work or even scene: Act III of *Otello* surely provided a model for the scene of Gilda's murder in *Rigoletto*, and returned to haunt Verdi as late as his own version of Shakespeare's tragedy, and the risorgimental manner of *Nabucco* and *I Lombardi* obviously drew much of its inspiration from *Mosè*. That same opera, together with *Maometto II*, was recognized by Rossini as having a special affinity with the monumental pieces that Spontini had produced at the Paris Opéra between 1807 (*La Vestale*) and 1819 (*Olympie*). On settling in Paris, he adapted both of them for his new home, *Maometto II* as *La siège de Corinth* (1826), *Mosè* as *Moïse et Pharaon* (1827): and in these forms both operas served as foundation stones for the massive edifice of Parisian grand opera, which was to assume its definitive form in the next decade.

But obviously Rossini's influence was deepest and furthest reaching in

Italy itself. It has never been easy for non-Italian critics to see Rossini as an altogether appropriate father-figure for Italian Romantic opera: his own position with regard to Romanticism has seemed too equivocal, his style too precariously poised between the past and the future, between high comedy, frigid formalism and flagrant melodrama. Was that perhaps the secret? At any rate I know of no evidence that Italian composers themselves sensed any inadequacy in the way Rossini came to terms with and naturalized what was, after all, a spiritual movement profoundly alien to the traditions of Italian art. In recent years, a few half-decent performances of Rossini's Neapolitan operas (probably the first for well over a century) have begun to reveal that he did indeed bring off the improbable amalgam triumphantly, and that his successors were not deceiving themselves in seeing this repertory as constituting 'a tradition to which [they] could only look back in awe' (Gossett n.d.: 3). The new types of subject-matter that he had gingerly essayed were explored more fully and whole-heartedly; the formal conventions he had established served all Italian composers for another thirty years and more; and every mannerism of his musical language – the *canto fiorito*, the crescendo, the driving rhythms and the brash instrumentation – was imitated, often *ad nauseam*, and rarely with even a modicum of Rossini's own elegance and panache.

26 · A franker Romanticism

Epigones of Rossini

For fully a decade after the Restoration Rossini indeed bestrode the narrow world of Italian opera like a colossus. The 'great reformer', as Pacini was to call him (1865: 8), bequeathed to his younger contemporaries a dramatic format and a musical language which they found irresistible and inescapable. Later in his memoirs Pacini went on, 'my contemporaries . . . all followed the same school, the same style, and consequently all were imitators, just as I was, of the *Great Luminary*. But, good heavens, what else was there to do if that was the only way of earning a living?' (*ibidem*: 64). That Rossini's palpable superiority over all his rivals left Italian opera, on his departure for Paris in 1824, in a state of lustreless epigonism was the opinion both of those in the thick of Italian operatic life, like Pacini, and of those who observed the scene with the detachment of distance. Donizetti best expressed the indebtedness of his generation in some manuscript 'Scritti e pensieri sulla musica' jotted down probably in 1843:

Rossini was a genius, and as such he opened up the imagination of his contemporaries – to effect revolutions like that one has to be a genius. After him (I speak for Italy) every other composer lived and continues to live with the knowledge, or with the taste, or with the skills born of the style created by that genius.

(MS 'Scritti . . .', Museo Donizettiano, Bergamo)

Rossini's own *obiter dicta* on the subject of his younger contemporaries are less illuminating than one could wish. Perhaps, finding himself universally regarded as a species of Olympian, he decided it behoved him to give utterance in the manner of a benign oracle, sometimes spicing the utterance with his wicked sense of humour: Vaccai was a composer 'in whom sentiment was allied to philosophy' (*The New Grove*, s.v. 'Vaccai'); 'the composer in Italy with the most genius is Pacini' (Bellini 1943: 443) – 'Heaven help us if he knew music' (*The New Grove*, s.v. 'Pacini'). But Pacini did know enough music for Rossini, urgently pressed for time, to entrust him with the composition of three movements for *Matilde Shabran* (Rome 1821), and for Pacini to carry off the commission with sufficient panache for the deception to go unobserved. Of the dozens of composers who made their debut in the opera-house between 1815 and 1825 only one was regarded as potentially a serious rival to Rossini, and that was

Mercadante, particularly after the triumph of his seventh opera *Elisa e Claudio* at La Scala in 1821. 'If we have two Rossinis', remarked Carpani, 'so much the better' (Mooney 1970: 8–9).

Carpani's comment need not be taken to imply that Mercadante made a better job of imitating Rossini than the rest did. It is more likely that audiences and critics sensed in his music a certain personal quality, an idiosyncrasy of sound, that raised it above competent anonymity. This quest for some modest individuality of voice within the Rossinian *lingua franca* was one Mercadante shared with all the better Italian composers of the day. Pacini devoted his particular care to the cabaletta, trying to break free from the traditional rhythmic formulae, and succeeding at his best in achieving a quality of spontaneity, elegance and wit which earned for him the soubriquet 'il maestro della cabaletta' (Pacini 1865: 84). Example V.6 from *Giovanna d'Arco* demonstrates these qualities. Donizetti's individuality was first sensed in a certain 'learned' quality, which contemporaries often attributed to the training he had received at the hands of Simon Mayr: the Act II septet of *La zingara* (Naples 1822) was, opined Carlo Conti, an ensemble 'that only a pupil of Mayr would have the capability and knowledge to create' (Ashbrook and Budden 1983: 219). As for Mercadante himself, it is tempting to describe the most individual feature of his style as a kind of laborious conscientiousness. Even in his early works it was the style of the orchestral accompaniment that most impressed his hearers. Of *I Normanni a Parigi* (Turin 1831) the *Gazzetta piemontese* wrote, '[in instrumentation] he is superior to them all, not even excepting the Pesarese' (Mooney 1970: 13).

There is a certain irony in the fact that several of this group of younger composers most obviously succeeded in asserting their individuality against the composer who had once been known as 'Il Tedeschino' by the increased prominence their musical style accorded to Germanic elements. If Mercadante and Donizetti 'Germanized' most successfully, it was a very

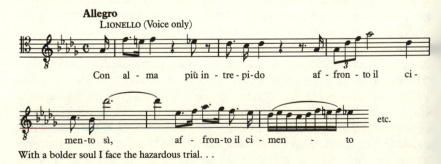

With a bolder soul I face the hazardous trial. . .

Ex.V.6 Pacini, *Giovanna d'Arco* (1830), Act II

general tendency in the opera of the age. The contrapuntal *jeux d'esprit* of Raimondi and Vaccai, the experiments in chromatic harmony of Donizetti and Federico Ricci, the use of unusual combinations of instruments in Vaccai all bear witness to the Italian desire, as Pacini puts it, 'to capitalize on the great German musicians' (1865: 41).

The other conspicuous development in the musical style of 1820s was a purely national affair. Several times in his memoirs Pacini tells us that, in addition to new types of cabaletta, he was seeking for a simpler melodic style. In later years (1839–40) he was to explore the repertory of popular song 'in order to inform my work with that truth that is so difficult to capture in our art' (1865: 93). This was a search in which Pacini was not alone. Donizetti's early operas, for all his easy competence with the forms and the florid manner of Rossini's heroic style, contain a significant number of melodies which seem to be laden with a much heavier burden of dramatic truth'. Simpler, sometimes almost folk-song-like in character, they cling much more closely to the verses than Rossini's melodies, allowing the singer to declaim the words with an empathetic rhetoric that was no part of the older composer's aesthetic.

This slowly changing musical language was the result of a changing ethos in the theatre. Composers were interested in the possibility of bringing about a more intimate fusion of verse and music; they were more wholehearted in their enthusiasm for Romantic taste; they were ready to make a commitment, of a kind that Rossini would never be able to reconcile himself to, towards a more literary conception of opera. These tendencies are clearest in the operas Donizetti wrote in the later 1820s.

Donizetti brought to Italian opera much of that quality of urgent emotional vehemence that in the hands of the young Verdi was to reach an almost brutal degree of intensity. As early as 1826 when, 'for my diversion', he reset Tottola's notorious libretto for Carafa's *Gemma di Vergy* (Naples 1816), he discovered that he had a natural aptitude for dealing with the most violent and sanguinary tales. 'I want love, violent love', he was to write to the impresario Giuseppe Consul in 1833, 'because without that subjects are cold' (Zavadini 1948: 379). Demands for 'brevity – for pity's sake – brevity' run through his correspondence with his librettists as they do through Verdi's. At the same time, Donizetti, who was later to be described by Giuseppina Strepponi as a man of 'goodness and vast culture . . . a truly superior artist and gentleman' (Weinstock 1964: 162), seems to have been the first of the Italian Romantics to make a habit of steeping himself in what one might describe as the cultural atmosphere of his subjects. While working on *Il diluvio universale* in January 1830 he reported to his brother Andrea that he had 'read the writings of Sassy, of Calmet, Lord Byron's "Heaven and earth", and Father Ringhieri's tragedy *Il diluvio* . . . From these authors, and cribbing and botching bits from various tragedies, I have brought forth a synopsis, which the poet quite likes . . .' (Zavadini 1948: 271). The self-deprecating tone is typical of Donizetti. But the fact of the matter is that by such exercises he was getting deeper into his subjects, attuning himself to the atmosphere that he had to recreate musically in his operas. It is no accident that Mazzini saw in Donizetti the first signs of a new kind of dramatic seriousness, of an opera of ideas such as he felt Italy needed to help usher in the new age:

The individuality of the characters, so barbarously neglected by the servile imitators of Rossini's lyricism, is printed with rare energy and religiously observed in many of Donizetti's works. Who has not felt in the musical expression of Henry VIII the language, severe, tyrannical and artificial at the same time, that history assigns to him? And when Lablache fulminates these words:
　　Salirà d'Inghilterra sul trono
　　Altra donna più degno d'affetto, etc.
who has not felt his spirit shrink, who has not understood all of tyranny in that moment, who has not seen all the trickery of that Court, which has condemned Anne Boleyn to die?
　　　　　　　　　　　　　　　　　　　　　　　　　　　　　　(Gossett 1985: 9)

Bellini

It was the greatest of the group of composers active in the 1820s and 1830s who was least over-awed by the dominating personality of Rossini. Vincenzo Bellini was a pupil at the Real Collegio di Musica in Naples from 1819 to 1825 at a time when it was directed by Niccolò Zingarelli, a distinguished composer of opera, whose own theatre career had, however, come to a close as early as 1811 with a setting of *Berenice, regina d'Armenia*, an updated version of a libretto by Zeno. Zingarelli was an avowed anti-Rossinian; he frankly admitted to Rossini that he regarded him as a corrupter of youth, and seemed to view him as a charming but irresponsible vandal, who had played the leading part in destroying the true art of expressive song; allegedly he kept Rossini's scores locked up in an inaccessible part of the college library where they could do no harm (Orrey 1969: 13). It was of course a hopeless undertaking to attempt to isolate the best young musicians of southern Italy from the influence of a composer who completely dominated the repertory of the city's opera-houses. There can be no question but that Bellini knew Rossini's operas intimately, particularly during his last two years at the college when, as a senior pupil, he was entitled to attend performances at the San Carlo Theatre twice a week. Nonetheless, Bellini enjoyed a very close relationship with Zingarelli, and the old man's creed, as reported by Francesco Florimo, a fellow pupil who became Bellini's closest friend, obviously sounded a sympathetic chord in his own musical personality.

If you sing in your compositions, you may be sure that your music will please. If on the other hand you amass harmonies, double-counterpoint, fugues, canons, notes and further notes etc., maybe the musical world will applaud you after half a century, maybe it won't, but certainly the public will disapprove. The public wants melodies, melodies, always melodies. If your heart knows how to dictate them to you, make it your study to set them out in the simplest way possible, and your success will be sure, you will be a composer. (Adamo and Lippmann 1981: 445)

Almost certainly one of the things that made it possible for Bellini to react sympathetically rather than scornfully to this kind of exhortation was his deep interest in popular song. Like Pacini, he was one of those young Romantic musicians who had learned to regard popular song with something approaching reverence, as a source of unparalleled expressive directness. Given the lack of scholarly interest in Italian folk music at that time it is not possible to demonstrate how and in what measure Bellini drew on this repertory in fashioning his own melodic style. But the kinship between his operas and Neapolitan popular song of a slightly later date has at least been demonstrated in a contrary sense, since Scherillo showed how phrases from some of Bellini's best-loved pieces were absorbed into such *canzoni* as 'Fenesta ca lucive' (Adamo and Lippmann: 449). It was Scherillo too who reported, via Florimo, that Bellini as a student had compiled for himself an anthology of Sicilian verses, from which 'he was often humming and strumming' (*ibidem*).

Simple, impassioned song became and remained the highest ideal of Bellini's art. Indeed in the famous letter to Pepoli written towards the end of his career as they worked together on *I Puritani* (Paris 1835), we surely hear Zingarelli's teaching still, reformulated by a more vehement personality:

Carve in your head in letters of adamant: *the music drama must make people weep, shudder, die by means of singing* . . . Musical artifices kill the effect of the drama, still worse in music drama are poetic artifices; poetry and music, to be effective, demand naturalness and nothing more. (Bellini 1943: 400)

It is no surprise to learn that old Zingarelli took a particular pride and delight in the achievement of this favourite pupil. The Milanese theatre-journal *I teatri* reported of the Neapolitan première of *Il pirata* in June 1828 that 'during the entire performance, tears of joy flowed from the eyes of this illustrious veteran of song' (Bellini 1943: 106).

Compared with the brilliant, extrovert public style of Rossini, Bellini's art of song was more sentimental, more ecstatic, and more inward. Again and again in his best operas he produces cantilenas in which are distilled an extraordinary force and depth of feeling, and which even musicians basically unsympathetic to the idiom find irresistible. In Florence in 1831, Berlioz attended a performance of *I Capuleti e i Montecchi*: contemptuous of the style, out of humour with the mediocrity of the performance, seething inwardly at what he took to be a travesty of his beloved Shakespeare, he suddenly found himself, in the stretto of the Act I Finale, overwhelmed by a phrase of wonderful élan and intensity . . . The two voices singing as one, as though in perfect union, give the melody an extraordinary force and bold impetus; and whether it was the context in which the phrase occurred and the manner in which it was then brought back and repeated, or the sudden effect of the unison, so unexpected and so apt, or the beauty of the tune itself, I was carried away in spite of myself and applauded enthusiastically.

(Berlioz 1969: 161–2)

But there is rather more to Bellini's melodic art than I have so far suggested. For one is dealing with a phenomenon not simply of aesthetic beauty, with a gift for a sublime simplicity of utterance that makes Bellini at his best one of the company of Purcell and Handel, of Mozart and Schubert; nor simply with what one might call the timeliness of his melody, that quality whereby, for example, the dissonant drooping appoggiaturas of a particular type of Bellinian cantabile, that 'tenderness of tears' admired by Zingarelli, prove to be a perfect mirror of the pathos and despair with which so many Romantic librettos are laden. As usual, Verdi sums up the fuller truth penetratingly and succinctly: 'It's true that Bellini is poor in harmony and orchestration . . . but rich in feeling and in a melancholy entirely his own. Even in his less known operas, in *Straniera* and *Pirata* there are long, long, long melodies such as no one wrote before him. And how much truth and power of declamation there is, especially in the duet between Pollione and Norma . . .' (1913: 415–16).

'Truth and power of declamation': very early in his career Bellini came to recognize that the simplicity and emotional force he had learned to give his melodies were uniquely dramatic attributes, for they made possible a fusion of verse and music that had not been attempted in Italian opera for generations. Singers, finding certain of their prerogatives curtailed, did not always take kindly to the style. At rehearsals for the Genoa *rifacimento* of *Bianca e Fernando* in 1828, the *prima donna* Tosi demanded a new cavatina, because the one Bellini had composed 'was without any passages of agility, music fit for children'. Even Rubini, at his first encounter with Bellini at the time of *Il pirata*, was vexed and mystified by the plainness he was cultivating. But once converted, by the passion of the music and the force of Bellini's exhortations, Rubini became the most persuasive exponent of this 'new genre . . . a style of music which expresses the words scrupulously, and forms of song and drama one single concept' (Bellini as quoted by Cicconetti, in Adamo and Lippmann 1981: 456).

As they tried to describe this new style, contemporary musicians and critics frequently spoke of Bellini's 'philosophy', a term we first hear being used by Serra, leader of the opera orchestra at Genoa. Serra was, in Bellini's own words, a 'bravissimo contrapuntista' and a 'criticone' – a formidable critic; he could not abide Rossini's music (which must have made his profession a trying one in the 1820s), but was enraptured by Bellini's *Il pirata* and *Bianca e Fernando*, because they were 'full of philosophy'

(Bellini 1943: 71). This attribute is conveniently described in a review of *La straniera* in *I teatri*, 16 February 1829, which speaks of 'that philosophy, constant in Bellini, whereby he always follows with his music the poetic phrases and the situations' (Bellini 1943: 193). Romani put it perhaps more tellingly himself, when he wrote of 'the indissolutely firm union of verse and music'.

The achievement of this style, in which melodies of exquisite beauty and profound expressiveness seem to blossom from an almost naturalistic declamation of the words, marks not only Bellini's own maturity, but the real beginning of a full-blooded Romanticism in Italian opera. It came in the late 1820s with Bellini's removal from Naples to Milan to work on the commission for *Il pirata*. One of its necessary consequences was that it led the composer to attach a new degree of importance to the libretto. Obviously Bellini acknowledged the truism that 'the libretto is the foundation of an opera' (1943: 397); and obviously he recognized that the intelligent collaboration of the librettist was required if he was to achieve the 'brevity, fire and action' that were the hallmarks of his style as they were to be of Verdi's. But Bellini needed more from his librettist. If one of his music's aims was, by some mysterious alchemy, to transmute verse into a sublimely singing eloquence, then that verse had to be worthy of the treatment it was to receive. This consideration became a real worry in the case of *I Puritani* (Paris 1835) when, following his disastrous squabble with Romani over *Beatrice di Tenda* (Venice 1833), Bellini found himself lavishing his most mature and luxuriant music on a mediocre libretto by Count Carlo Pepoli:

The book has the major defect of poor dialogue: the situations are beautiful, the expression repetitive, commonplace, sometimes stupid, in a word one sees that the author is someone who has no heart and does not understand how to express well the feelings of his characters: this defect detracted nothing from the success in Paris, because they don't understand the words here; but it will impair the effect a great deal in Italian theatres. (1943: 554)

With Romani, Bellini's collaborator on *Il pirata* and all his subsequent operas save *I Puritani*, there was no such danger. Not only was he the author of much of the most harmonious, expressive and finely crafted verse to be found in the nineteenth-century libretto; he was also immediately charmed by the young Sicilian, and felt a deep and instantaneous sympathy with what he sensed to be his aims. He divined in Bellini, he was later to claim, 'a passionate heart, a mind ambitious to soar beyond the sphere in which it was restrained by academic rules and the servility of imitation . . . [From the first] we understood one another, and we struggled united against the vicious conventions of the musical theatre, girding ourselves to eradicate them little by little, by dint of courage, and loving perseverance' (*Gazzetta piemontese*, 1 October 1835, in Rinaldi 1965: 195). In no time

Romani's talents had become the very life blood of Bellini's art: 'for me Romani is essential', he declared to Florimo in 1828 (Bellini 1943: 158).

Romani was to find Bellini a demanding collaborator. Ten times the poet had to rewrite the final cabaletta of *La sonnambula*, eight times Norma's great prayer 'Casta diva'. The story is told that while they were working on the final scene of *La straniera*, Romani became so exasperated that he finally exploded: 'For goodness' sake, what do you want?' Bellini replied: 'I want something that is at the same time a prayer, an invocation, a threat, a delirium', and rushing to the piano he improvised to show the librettist how he felt the scene. The poet responded with the eight lines beginning 'Or sei pago, o ciel tremendo', and the final result was one of the most thrillingly dramatic cabalettas of the whole era (Rinaldi 1965: 216). 'That boy does what he wants with me', Romani once ruefully complained; 'but his manner is so fascinating, and he knows how to make his wishes sink so deep into my heart that it is impossible to resist' (*ibidem*: 246). It may be said that, between them, Romani and Bellini made heavy demands on their performers too, for these new 'philosophical' operas, these 'melotragedies', as Romani himself liked to call them, rendered anachronistic certain of the most highly-prized of the singers' arts.[1] How even the greatest composer among Bellini's seniors could fail utterly to see the point of what he was doing is curiously illustrated by Rossini's attempt – at the behest of Giulia Grisi – to embellish the cabaletta 'La tremenda ultrice spada' from *I Capuleti e i Montecchi*, to dissolve the declamatory contours of 'philosophi-cal' song back into his own language of florid song, and replace by his own quite different enchantments Bellini's 'truth' (Adamo and Lippmann 1981: 458; Ex.V.7).

Many of the features of Bellini's musical language were of course shared in common with other opera composers of the day. We find a decline in the number of arias relative to the number of ensembles; and we find a tendency to dissolve the frontiers between the various constituent parts of which an opera is made up. Recitatives are pervaded by ariosi; the arias themselves frequently absorb ensemble elements – snatches of dialogue, or reflections from bystanders – so that the song becomes richer, perhaps more 'truthful', since the dramatic function of the aria is not lost from sight. Sometimes, as in the opening of *Norma*, Bellini follows in the footsteps of Spontini and Rossini by building up a sequence of scenes into a single massive tableau, a complex formed of chorus, ensemble and instru-mental music and unified by recurring themes. Altogether recurring themes are becoming more conspicuous, sometimes with a quite simple reminiscing purpose, sometimes in subtle and indirect evocation – as when 'Suoni la tromba' in Part II of *I Puritani* alludes back to the off-stage military choruses at the very start of the opera.

Other aspects of his musical style were more peculiarly his own. First,

Romeo prepares to brandish the terrible avenging sword. . .

Ex.V.7a Bellini, *I Capuleti e i Montecchi* (1830), Act I scene 3

Romeo prepares to brandish the terrible avenging sword. . .

Ex.V.7b Bellini, *I Capuleti e i Montecchi* (1830), Act I scene 3, as embellished by Rossini

despite all the unequivocal evidence that Bellini knew a lot of German instrumental music and admired it deeply, he was, of all his Italian contemporaries, the one least obviously affected by it. His orchestration is exceptionally simple, often to the point of bareness, allowing the voices to stand out in high relief. And compared with Rossini or Mercadante or Donizetti he is little interested in using the orchestra to sustain a quasi-symphonic momentum through *parlantes* or *tempi di mezzo*. Secondly, it is in Bellini's music that a new narcotic sensuousness begins to creep into Italian opera. In 'Casta diva' or the Act II finale of *Norma* we hear the voice of a composer who, for all his lack of a developed orchestral imagination, manifestly 'luxuriates in sound', revels in 'the ecstatic unfolding of sonorities'. The phrases are Lippmann's, who goes on to suggest that the rising chromatic sequences which often contribute to these effects surely influenced the idiom of Wagner's own curiously stirring ecstasies (1983: 171–2).

It is worth noting, finally, a trait of Bellini's character that is not at first sight obviously an artistic matter at all: his insistence on being paid for his operas more than any other composer among his predecessors or contemporaries. After the triumph of *Il pirata* he was able to demand fees substantially higher than Vaccai or Donizetti or Mercadante had ever received. But this was not simply a matter of greed or vanity. Several passages in his letters confirm that Bellini was determined to take all the time he needed to write beautiful operas. His rate of production was indeed low for the period; he was not prepared to diversify his activities and provide himself with a regular salary by taking on a teaching post in a conservatory or an administrative one in a theatre; nor, after the Genoa *Bianca e Fernando*, was he interested in supplementing his income by supervising revivals and making *puntature*[2] for his established successes. John Rosselli, whose observations these are, describes him as 'a new type of autonomous artist' (Rosselli 1983: 20). No longer content to act as a hired artisan purveying a commodity to his audiences, Bellini represented a new phenomenon in Italian opera, a composer who demands recognition as a divinely inspired artist.

A time for the examination of conscience

When Donizetti first heard a Bellini opera – it was a rehearsal of *Bianca e Gernando*[3] in May 1826 – he wrote to his old teacher Simon Mayr, 'This evening there will be given at the San Carlo the *Bianca e Gernando* . . . of our Bellini, his first production – beautiful, beautiful, beautiful, and especially because it is the first time that he writes. It is unhappily beautiful, as I shall find out with my [opera] two weeks from now' (Weinstock 1964: 48). With his characteristic warmth and openness Donizetti spoke for an entire generation of Italian composers: the chorus of acclaim that greeted Bellini's operas included even Mercadante, a man not over-generous to his rivals. And the signs of his influence soon became apparent. Federico Ricci was to judge that Bellini 'brought infinite progress in the art [of opera], especially in the dramatic sense' (letter of 28 April 1837, Naples Conservatory Library). By 1829 even the facile Pacini was beginning to set his sights higher. In *Il talismano* 'I made some progress in the declamatory genus, and strove to identify myself with the subject, so as to give some sense of unity to the style of the composition' (Pacini 1865: 68). But within a few years he gave up the unequal struggle. After three failures in Naples in 1833, 'I began to understand that I must withdraw from the arena: Bellini, the divine Bellini, and Donizetti had surpassed me' (*The New Grove*, s.v. 'Pacini'). The impact of Bellini was obviously a major factor in making the 1830s 'a time for the examination of conscience' (Ballola 1977: 375).

No one examined his conscience quite so diligently as Mercadante, nor struggled so heroically, as we can see in some of his autographs, with its artistic dictates. It is probably fair to say that he was particularly well placed to embark on an objective reappraisal of the tradition, for twice during this crucial period he withdrew from the hurly-burly of Italian operatic life to pursue a career in a different environment. From 1827 to 1831 he was in Spain, while from 1835 to 1840 he worked in Novara – 'a provincial city, where no one talks about anything but rice, wheat, wine and maize' (letter to Florimo, 10 July 1835, Naples Conservatory library) – as director of music at the cathedral.

His Spanish years, it will be noted, were those that witnessed Bellini's meteoric rise to glory. But that did not mean that the Bellini phenomenon was something that Mercadante missed. On the contrary, he came to know Bellini's scores almost as soon as they appeared, and was himself responsible for the staging of several of them in Spain. That his Spanish years prompted him to reflect more on his aims as a composer is suggested by the first operas composed after his return, especially *I Normanni a Parigi* (Turin 1832) where one finds a music less brilliant in style, less conventional in form and with some traces of that Bellinian ideal of 'philosophy'. And it was during his years as a church musician at Novara that he produced the series of 'reform operas' for which he is still dimly remembered: *Il giuramento* (Milan 1837), *Le due illustri rivali* (Venice 1838), *Elena da Feltre* (Naples 1838), *Il bravo* (Milan 1839) and *La Vestale* (Naples 1840). His status in Italian music by the close of the decade is suggested by a note in a Neapolitan newspaper in October 1839 announcing his imminent arrival in the city: 'this illustrious maestro, supreme in art, most supreme in character, is the champion (sostegno) of Italian music since Donizetti has succumbed to foreign enticements' (*L'Omnibus*, 12 October 1839). But once he settled again in Naples as director of the Conservatory (from 1840) his vision of the reform of Italian opera in a Romantic spirit seemed to fade.

At first sight, the reform that Mercadante attempted to carry through in the late 1830s is entirely typical of the period, very much in the spirit of what Bellini had been doing a few years earlier, and indeed of what Verdi was to do a decade later. There was to be no complacent reliance on formal stereotypes, the music was to be more responsive to the text, the performers were to be disciplined to carry out meticulously the intentions of the composer. A letter Mercadante wrote to Florimo while at work on *Elena da Feltre* has often been quoted:

I have continued the revolution begun in *Il giuramento*: the forms varied – trivial cabalettas banished, crescendos eliminated – concise working-out – fewer repetitions – some novelty in the cadences – proper attention paid to the drama: the orchestra rich without covering the voices – the long solos in the ensembles, which compel the other parts to stand coldly by and damage the action, removed – little bass drum and very little *banda*[4] . . .

But the most important thing is . . . not to allow my score to be altered in the slightest, whether by additions or cuts or transpositions. The singers should study it carefully and neglect nothing in the ensembles, putting their whole heart into declaiming and accentuating it, without any arbitrariness in tempo or in the addition of *fioritura*.

(Letter of January 1838, Naples Conservatory Library)

The orchestral sophistication which critics had noted even in Mercadante's early scores became more pronounced, in part, one may conjecture, stimulated by the example of Meyerbeer, whose *Les Huguenots* he heard in Paris in 1836. There is at any rate a distinct whiff of the Paris Opéra in several movements which Mercadante scores for small and somewhat recherché combinations of instruments: for example in the duet 'Cielo di grazia' in Act II of *Il bravo*, the greater part of which is scored for two harps, pizzicato solo 'cello and pizzicato solo double-bass.

More startling than the orchestral innovations, however, is the unprecedented freedom with which Mercadante handles Rossini's structural legacy. Something of this has already been described (cf. Chapter 24 above, p. 435). But its most personal feature was Mercadante's transformation of the cabaletta. It was not that he found anything amiss in the idea of rounding off the scene with a fast or vigorous movement. But in place of the gaily dancing rhythms, the vocal virtuosity and the repetitive design typical of cabalettas in the 1830s, he tended to compose them in a declamatory style, clearly differentiating the voices in duets or trios, and avoiding stereotyped 'vamping' accompaniments. Mention has already been made of what is probably Mercadante's most startling formal innovation: the death-scene cantabiles of *Il giuramento*, *Elena da Feltre* and *La Vestale*, which he is not afraid to conclude in a stark minor tonality (cf. p. 438 above). Altogether one feels that the Mercadante of these years fully deserved Liszt's tribute, in the context of a thoroughly derogatory survey of the Italian scene: 'Exception must be made for Mercadante. He has the wisdom to write slowly, and revise his compositions with care . . . The latest works of Mercadante are without question the most seriously thought out of the contemporary repertory' (*The New Grove*, s.v. 'Mercadante').

While we may concede that in the late 1830s, with Rossini retired, Bellini dead and Donizetti usually abroad, Mercadante was the nearest thing to a great composer regularly working in the Italian opera-house, he was certainly not a Romantic to the manner born; even in his reform-operas one is struck by features which suggest he was no natural progressive. For all his concern for musico-dramatic continuity, the design of the component parts of his scores tends still to be elaborated with a loving care more typical of the eighteenth than of the nineteenth century. Where most of his contemporaries were content to write instrumental introductions for their arias that quoted just a few bars of the melody, almost in the manner of a prompt, Mercadante was fond of long elaborate preludes that included florid cadences as well as thematic material; he often rounded off his arias with carefully wrought postludes too. This ritornello-like treatment of the orchestra gives the music a spacious, leisurely quality which accords ill with the sensational and violent action which accompanies it. And while his harmonic resource was much admired by his Italian contemporaries it betrays a strangely old-fashioned sensibility, not really far removed from that of Corelli or Durante.

In fact it is difficult to believe that Mercadante's reform welled up from any deep and passionate commitment to the refashioning of Italian opera at all. I would be inclined to see it rather as something that he was prompted to – one might even say, that was thrust upon him – at a stage in his career when he was suffering an acute crisis of confidence. One factor in this crisis was that – whatever incidental benefits it may have brought – separation from his spiritual home, Naples, had torn up the very roots of Mercadante's art. His letters show how ardently he longed to return to the southern metropolis, but it was not until 1840 that he found a suitable position there. Then in Paris in 1836 his *Briganti* was produced: for any Italian composer the challenge to win over the cool, critical French public, was the acid test of mastery. Rossini, Bellini and Donizetti had triumphed gloriously; Mercadante failed. Perhaps most alarming of all, since the early 1830s he had felt a drying up of his youthful inspiration, especially when it came to the writing of cabalettas. In November 1831 while at work on *I Normanni a Parigi* he wrote to Florimo:

As usual I am very displeased with myself, and while it would be tolerable if I had you close at hand to help with your advice, here on the contrary I am at my own mercy and everything seems awful to me. If you should have any beautiful and new cabalettas you could send me you would be doing me a kindness, because the first movement – the Adagio – I can compose that, but these accursed cabalettas ruin everything, and the more I strive to be original, the more I see they are as stale as can be.

(Letter of 23 November 1831, Naples Conservatory Library)

Other letters show that it was actually Florimo's counsel that played a major part in setting Mercadante on the road to reform: in a letter to his friend describing the success of *Il giuramento* he actually quotes the advice Florimo had given him: 'short movements, variety of texture (tessitura diversa), some extravagances to break out of the common rut of things etc.', and he continued: 'so thank you, thank you, for what you have done, and I beg you never to deprive me of your advice' (27 April 1837, Naples Conservatory Library). A later letter provides confirmation: 'If I had not followed your advice, I should still have been stuck with accursed cabalettas, repetitions, longueurs etc. I owe this new career of mine to you, who have shaken me out of my lethargy, restoring me to new musical life' (7 January 1839, Naples Conservatory Library).

For a time he made a tolerably convincing job of his reform, but deep down Mercadante was no more in tune with the values of the new age than Rossini had been. His lifelong idealization of the old Neapolitans is clear from his letters, and even more, from a curious lecture delivered to the Neapolitan Royal Academy of Archaeology, Literature and Fine Arts in 1867, entitled 'A brief, historical account of theatrical music from Pergolesi to Cimarosa'.[5] He commends Pergolesi's aesthetic principles, which he sees as entailing 'the intimate and affective expression of the words, sublimated in simple melodies', while in more general terms he sees the task of the composer as that of revealing 'the idea of the *Beautiful* and the *True*'. On the other hand, of the composers most in tune with the new Romanticism, he was contemptuous of Donizetti and detested Verdi. He took no pleasure in contemporary literature, a fact which surely explains his frequently ana-chronistic choice of dramatic theme. Where a composer like Verdi was always on the look-out for new types of drama, Mercadante was quit happy to rework well tried ones. He persevered in setting Metastasio longer than any other composer known to me – *Ezio* in 1827, *Adriano in Siria* in 1828 – and after barely a decade conforming with Romantic literary fashion, he returned to the Ancient World with *La Vestale* in 1840. Thereafter Graeco-Roman themes outweigh all others. Nor did he show anything like the critical acumen of Bellini or Donizetti or Verdi in getting to grips with the dramatic challenge of a new text. Can one imagine any of them empowering a friend (Florimo once more) to act on their behalf in having some changes made in a libretto? (Cammarano had provided too many arias in *Elena da Feltre*.) 'I am too far away to go into such details, and you know the game better than anyone – I shall approve everything . . .' (letter of 27 April 1837, Naples Conservatory Library).

It is hardly surprising that, back in Naples after 1840, Mercadante turned his back on reform. But by then it was too late to be old-fashioned with an easy conscience. Much as he might have wished to take refuge in a crepuscular world of 'sweet Cimarosan memories' (Ballola 1977: 369), the modern age could not be shut out. For Mercadante had seen and heard Meyerbeer in Paris, and could not resist the temptation to embellish his own scores with more elaborate orchestral textures and more recondite harmonies. He knew that audiences of the 1830s and 40s demanded of opera a more thrilling theatricality, and within the old-fashioned frame-work he attempted to provide it, galvanizing his music with hectoring, double-dotted rhythms and eliciting from the orchestra that increasingly 'deafening clamour' that Florimo was to censure (Florimo 1880–84, III: 118). He was embarrassed by the naive exuberance of the old-fashioned cabaletta and was driven into ever more factitious contrivance as he sought 'some extravagance to break out of the common rut'.

The later works of Pacini are also those of a man who had examined his conscience. He had returned to the opera-house in 1839, after an interlude of five years during which he had been involved primarily in musical education in Viareggio and Lucca; but now he was giving more time and thought to his music and promptly found himself 'baptized by public opinion as no longer the composer of facile cabalettas, but rather of elaborate works, the product of much meditation' (Pacini 1865: 98–9). *Saffo* (Naples 1840) was indeed one of the most high-minded operas of the period, a worthy companion to the reform-operas of Mercadante. Here too the structures are notably flexible, and in many scenes, conventional recitative is abandoned in favour of a profusion of arioso or *parlante* passages that reflect the dramatic action with scrupulous care. The orchestration is resourceful, the chorus plays a major part in the working out of the drama, and there is no lack of harmonic invention: in his 'Memoirs' Pacini tells us that Aristides' reflections on the diatonic, chromatic and enharmonic *genera* were ever present in his mind as he worked on it (*ibidem*: 95).

But like Mercadante the reformed Pacini could not always resist the temptation to overload his scores, to try to make the style do more than it had ever been designed to do. The scoring does not always avoid meaningless complication, the *scene* tend to be fraught with a fuss of illustrative detail, and the straining for the characteristic sometimes leads to results that are more odd than convincing. In *Maria, regina d'Inghilterra* he attempts a cabaletta in which the characters are differentiated thematically and metrically (Ex.V.8).

The mature works of Donizetti

The most exciting of the developments that followed in the wake of the Bellini phenomenon of the late 1820s was the emergence from the teeming ranks of maestros of Donizetti as a major creative talent. He shared many of the concerns of the other leading innovators of the 1830s: his scenes became more continuously musical and expressive as a result of the increasing density of arioso packed into them; he made more extensive and more dramatically pointed use of recurring themes; in seeking to maximize the melodramatic tensions in his operas, he came to place more of the weight of the design on the ensemble, especially on the duet of confrontation, less on the solo aria; he showed a keener interest in atmospheric or suggestive orchestral colour (a remarkable example, subsequently abandoned, was an *obbligato* for glass harmonica in the mad-scene of *Lucia di Lammermoor*); and he achieved, in a quite different sense from Bellini, some remarkable fusions of declamation and lyricism. In the cantabile of the Act II duet from *Roberto Devereux* (Naples 1837), for example, lyrical song gives way to arioso, and arioso to recitative, so that the climax – Nottingham's appeal for mercy – becomes a starkly dramatic one, not one that has been transfigured into song (Ex.V.9). From his performers he had come to demand the most scrupulous attention to the expressive nuances in his scores, for it was 'the

Ah! give me a dagger, that at least I may shed his blood. . . Abandon
yourself to your grief, to your cowardly rage. . .

Ex.V.8 Pacini, *Maria, regina d'Inghilterra* (1843), Act I

*ritardando*s, the *crescendo*s, the *accelerando*s etc. that give rise to the colours;
the light; the shade' of the drama (Zavadini 1948: 672).

Donizetti was so entirely lacking in self-importance, so sovereign in his
command of his *métier*, and he renovated and innovated with so little
suggestion of portentousness that his works have, to the best of my
knowledge, never earned the ominous tribute of being described as
'reform-operas'. The economy of means and directness of effect which he
had inherited from the tradition were little affected by the complicating
tendencies of the 1830s. 'Put any score of Donizetti's beside one of
Mercadante's or Pacini's and what leaps to the eye is its sparseness'
(Ashbrook and Budden 1983: 123). But, as Donizetti himself insisted,
simplicity should not be confused with trash. Nor was the functional
economy of his mature style necessarily more indolently achieved than
Mercadante's laborious plenitude. From *Anna Bolena* onwards there is
scarcely an opera in which the inherited structures and the inherited
musical language are not submitted to shrewd and critical reappraisal.

This reappraisal cost him much labour. Like all composers whose early
career was spent in the shadow of Rossini, Donizetti tended automatically
to fall into the elegantly balanced structures, the patterns of symmetry and

Ex.V.9 Donizetti, *Roberto Devereux* (1837), Act II

I never came so sadly into the royal presence. I carry out a grievous duty.
It is the sentence on Essex. [He gives her a paper.] The minister is silent,
now the friend speaks in his favour. Mercy! mercy! What! What! [Turning
on him a proud glance] Could Elizabeth's heart deny it?

Ex.V.9 *continued*

repetition that distinguish Rossini's own work. But, increasingly, dramatic intelligence rebelled against facile habit. As he worked on a score many of the repetitions were eliminated, many symmetries disguised; and the clear-cut frontiers between one movement or section and another were often dissolved so as to impair the flow or thrust of the dramatic action as little as possible. Donizetti, like Bellini, was bringing to the Rossinian scheme of opera a more contemporary type of sensibility, which gave 'proportion and balance lower priority than directness of utterance, avoidance of formal repetition and . . . dramatic continuity' (Gossett 1985: 59).

Of all the inherited conventions of style it was the cabaletta about which Donizetti became most self-conscious, in this resembling Pacini and Mercadante. As early as 1830 he had eliminated cabalettas from *Il diluvio universale* because he found them incongruous in a sacred drama. In his mature operas there are of course dozens of effective and well written cabalettas in a conventional style. But the high priority he placed on 'serving the text' prompted him to adapt the form to dramatic circumstance more resourcefully than most of his contemporaries. The usual exuberant release of energy might be replaced by a slow, plain kind of melody more appropriate to a scene of tragedy – Edgardo's 'Tu che a Dio spiegasti l'ali' from *Lucia di Lammermoor* is the *locus classicus*; the second statement might be rewritten, as it is in the closing cabaletta of *Maria Stuarda*, where the fleeting glimpse of the major key is like a smile through the tears; in the Giovanna–Enrico duet from Act I of *Anna Bolena*, Romani's text varies the normal pattern of feeling, introducing anticipations into the cantabile and memories into the cabaletta, a procedure which prompts Donizetti to link them thematically (Ex.V.10).

When all this has been said, Donizetti gives the impression of a composer more deeply rooted in, more at ease with the practices of, the contemporary theatre than any major composer after Rossini – a brilliant talent, but a mainstream, unproblematic talent. If we compare Bellini's remark to Rubini, 'admit it . . . You do not like my music because it does not allow you the customary opportunities' (Adamo and Lippmann 1981: 455), with Donizetti's to the effect that his music aspired 'to serve the situation and give the artists scope to shine' (Zavadini 1948: 558) we note the latter's more relaxed attitude to the *convenienze*. Unlike Bellini, he was always agreeable to the idea that new singers undertaking roles in revivals of established operas should be provided with *puntature* that accommodated the music to the particular qualities of their voice. He was less intransigent than Bellini, or later Verdi, in resisting singers' claims for their 'rights'. A notorious example is provided by *Lucrezia Borgia* (Milan 1833). Having given his *prima donna* Henriette Méric-Lalande a mere one-movement *sortita* in the prologue, he felt unable to hold out against her demand for a brilliant aria finale to end the opera; when in 1840 he at last succeeded in finding a singer (Erminia Frezzolini) prepared to drop this brilliant finale and allow the reinstatement of a tragic finale, he compensated her by turning her *sortita* into a full-scale two-movement aria. Once he had agreed to write the cabaletta finale for Méric-Lalande, Donizetti strove to match it to the situation and mood of the drama. But 'Era desso il figlio mio' is only one of many arias and ensembles in which Donizetti's desire to serve the text never caused him to suppress completely those elements of virtuosity and sheer pleasurable music-making that had been basic to Rossini's understanding of operatic song. Donizetti was as responsive to the views of his audiences as of his singers. When news reached him of the failure of *Caterina Cornaro* (Naples 1844), he was anxious to do all he could to emend what he recognized must be its shortcomings: 'give me, as soon as possible, exact information on the pieces which were disliked and also of the ones that were least suited to la Goldberg's voice . . . I will see if I can rework the piece, for I confess to you I did not think it so horrible!' (Zavadini 1948: 726).

Donizetti's complaisant temperament is not to be accounted merely a weakness. He drew strength from it too, his musical imagination being challenged and enlarged by the qualities of the performers who worked with him. One example may be quoted. In the years around 1830 there is a

Ex.V.10 Donizetti, *Anna Bolena* (1830), Act I scene 5

I shall be more unhappy than Bolyn, more to be wept for. I shall have the
pain of being repudiated and it will not be a husband I have offended. . .
(Cause me) no more remorse, for pity's sake. . . Put your mind to rest in
the king. Let him see you happier now in the love that makes you his own.

Ex.V.10 *continued*

marked falling out of favour of the kind of brilliant *canto fiorito* writing that
Rossini had used for his big bass roles. Soon afterwards Donizetti made
acquaintance with the art of a superb young baritone, Giorgio Ronconi,
who had been engaged as a principal for *Torquato Tasso* (Rome 1833). The
dramatic and lyrical emphasis on the baritone voice in this opera resulted in
a darkening of vocal colouring which was to remain typical of many of
Donizetti's later scores. It was an apt development, given the gloom and
violence of many of the subjects Donizetti handled, and it established the
dramatic baritone as a voice type that was absolutely central to the
expressive power of Italian Romantic opera.

Like all the best-established Italian composers Donizetti was invited to Paris when the Théâtre Italien commissioned *Marino Faliero* (1835). A few years later he followed in the footsteps of Rossini by adapting one of his Naples operas to form a Parisian grand opera. And in describing to Mayr how he was going about transforming *Poliuto* into *Les martyrs*, he provided some illuminating insights into the distinctiveness of the French style:

> I have had to rewrite all the recitatives, compose a new finale for Act I, add arias, trios, and such related ballets as they use here, so that the public may not complain that the facture is Italian . . . French music and dramatic verse have a *cachet* all their own, with which every composer must conform; whether in the recitatives or in the lyrical pieces. For example, a ban on crescendos, etc., a ban on the usual cadences, *joy, joy, joy*; then between one statement of the cabaletta and the other there is always poetry that intensifies the action without the usual repetition of lines which our poets use.
>
> (Zavadini 1948: 494–5)

Thereafter, during his last three years as an active theatre composer, Donizetti produced a further five operas for various Paris theatres. In bulk his French operas surpass those of any other Italian of the Romantic age, and in historical and artistic importance they rival those of Rossini and Verdi.

During his 1835 visit he had his first taste of Parisian grand opera, catching some of the early performances of Halévy's *La Juive*. On him, as on many newcomers to Paris, it was the spectacle that created the deepest impression: 'it isn't illusion any more, it's truth . . . They burn the Jewess alive. It seems real, you know, – it makes you ill – it makes you ill like the music they sing in the meantime' (Zavadini 1948: 369). Next year, back in Italy, he attempted an Italian opera in the French style, *L'assedio di Calais* (Naples 1836), a historical drama, with ballet as an integral part of the spectacle, numerous large-scale ensembles and rather fewer arias in the standard cantabile/cabaletta form.

But while Donizetti obviously admired much about French opera, and certainly did not attempt to evade its influence, he mistrusted its tendency to emphasize spectacle at the expense of feeling and dramatic urgency. In his appetite for brevity, speed and an unflagging fierceness of passion Donizetti was a kindred spirit to Verdi. *L'assedio di Calais* was hardly into production before he was deciding that the third act – that with the ballet – was too slow-moving and less successful than he had hoped.

Donizetti was never a composer to be venerated as Rossini and Bellini had been. He was commonly swept up in the blanket condemnations of Italian opera periodically indulged in by French and German observers – Schumann's description of *Lucrezia Borgia* as 'music for a marionette theatre' particularly hurt him (Zavadini 1948: 502). Nevertheless the sequence of operas he wrote between 1830 and 1843 made him in many respects the most fully representative figure in Italian opera at the height of the Romantic movement. Like Bellini, if less exclusively, the mature Donizetti concentrated on tragic opera. But his dramatic tastes, perhaps because he was less closely associated with Romani, were more genuinely innovatory and more unequivocally melodramatic. In several operas, including *Sancia di Castiglia* (Naples 1832) and *Belisario* (Venice 1836), he dispenses with anything resembling a conventional love interest; while *Torquato Tasso*, *Maria di Rohan* (Vienna 1843) and especially *Lucrezia Borgia* show a highly developed partiality for the reckless mixing of the tragic and the comic, the festive and the macabre, commended by Victor Hugo in the preface to the play from which the last-named opera is adapted:

Le poète . . . fera toujours apparaître le cercueil dans la salle du banquet, la prière des morts à travers les refrains de l'orgie, la cagoule à côté du masque. Il laissera quelquefois le carneval débraillé chanter à tuetête sur l'avant-scène; mais il lui criera du fond du théâtre: *Memento quia pulvis es* . . .

And if few fellow-composers explicitly paid homage to Donizetti, they found that he was so consummate a master within the conventions of form, style and taste of the period that his best operas carried a conviction that not infrequently astonished them. Berlioz, Bizet, and many another composer sooner or later found themselves uttering more or less personal variations of an amusing remark that the young Hugo Wolf was to make: 'I must say that, although I am a great opponent of Italian music, yet the opera rather pleased me' (F. Walker 1968: 32). Even from Verdi, compliments to Donizetti are hard to find. Yet he carried imprinted on his memory many a Donizetti scene where situation, character, mood and musical idea are fused in an extraordinarily telling way, and drew on these scenes in his own work, particularly in the years after 1847 as his own manner became more personal (Dean 1974). Though much Donizetti fast vanished from the repertory, one opera at least, *Lucia di Lammermoor*, was to prove a touchstone of Romantic sensibility through much of Europe for most of the century. It was *Lucia* that conquered Berlioz's distaste, as it was *Lucia* that surprised the idealistic young Wolf with a poetry and power to which he had persuaded himself it could have no claim. And the role which *Lucia* played in two of the greatest nineteenth-century novels, Flaubert's *Madame Bovary* and Tolstoy's *Anna Karenina*, shows that it had become 'a symbol of ill-starred love, of human relationships interfered with and destroyed by practical, social considerations' (Weinstock 1964: 112), a work which the most cultured men of the age would not have been embarrassed to set beside *Romeo and Juliet*.

27 · The young Verdi

At the centre of Italian Romanticism

Old-fashioned music lovers frequently complained of a decline in craftsmanship, and a coarsening of taste in the music of Italian Romantic opera.
Such foreign musicians as Berlioz and Mendelssohn, who travelled in Italy
at the height of the Romantic enthusiasm, left scathing accounts of musical
culture in the peninsula, and created an image of the musical world
inherited by the young Verdi which still conditions our reactions to the
repertory. It will be well to remind ourselves that, notwithstanding this
image, the Romantic composer in Italy was typically a man of wide culture,
just like the Romantic composer in other parts of Europe. One might, for
instance, cite the case of Vaccai, a modestly successful composer of opera
between 1815 and 1839, author of four verse tragedies in the style of Alfieri,
and translator of Méhul's *Joseph* and Bach's *St Matthew Passion* (un-
completed). Donizetti's interest in reading up the literary background to
his operas has already been mentioned. His own skills as an author enabled
him to write, or to contribute significantly to the writing of, several of his
own librettos in both the comic and the tragic vein, including *Fausta*
(Naples 1832) and *Don Pasquale* (Paris 1843).

The wide culture of the young Verdi needs particularly to be insisted
upon. For the music he wrote in his early years is not perhaps altogether of
the kind one would expect from a man of cultivated tastes. But he was in
fact the first composer to be totally steeped in the ethos of Italian
Romanticism.

Based from his student days onwards in Milan he was, for a start, at the
geographical heart of the movement. The city of Manzoni (whom Verdi
revered above all living authors, and in whose memory he was to compose
his *Requiem*); of Grossi (whose epic poem *I Lombardi alla prima crociata* was
the only entirely and unqualifiedly Italian source ever to provide the theme
for a Verdi opera); of Hayez (whose historical paintings so often draw on
the same repertory of themes as Verdi's operas: *Conte di Carmagnola*, *Vespri
siciliani*, *Ezzelino da Romano*, *Francesco Foscari*, *La sete dei crociati*, etc.).
And Verdi himself moved in these circles at least from 1842, when he was
first introduced into the salon of Clarina and Andrea Maffei (Barbiera 1915:
101). Soon he became one of the most intimate members of the circle. Of

the many friends he made there among the artistic leaders of the day, two are of particular interest for our purpose. One was Andrea Maffei himself, because in what has been called Italy's 'Age of Translation' Maffei was one of the most diligent of translators. It was his Italian rendering of Schiller, 'castrated and infamous' as it was subsequently judged to be, that revealed the splendours of the great German dramatist to Verdi and provided the source for at least three of his operas. Indeed for the first of these, *I masnadieri* (London 1847), Maffei himself wrote the libretto. Another intimate was Giulio Carcano, like Maffei a poet in his own right, and like Maffei best remembered as a translator, specifically for having accomplished the tremendous task of rendering the complete Shakespeare into Italian verse, an undertaking just begun when he and Verdi first met in the Maffei salon. Verdi's love and reverence for Shakespeare was to be one of the great formative and enduring experiences of his life; he was to describe him as 'a favourite poet of mine, whom I have had in my hands from earliest youth and whom I read and reread constantly' (letter to Leon Escudier, 28 April 1865, in Rosen and Porter 1984: 119). And Carcano played no small part in the growth of these feelings – 'by continually speaking and writing to Verdi about Shakespeare, by sending him his *King Lear* translation in 1843, by reading *Macbeth* to him at Clusone in 1847 [*recte* 1846], by dedicating *Anthony and Cleopatra* to him in 1875' (from an address by Giovanni Rizzi (1886), cited in Rosen and Porter 1984: 46).

Shakespeare, we have seen, was one of the touchstones of Romantic sensibility in Italy as in France and Germany. All the same, an enthusiasm for his work, particularly an enthusiasm as generous and unquibbling as Verdi's, remained the mark of a liberal, cultured elite; that there was no question of a wide popularity was shown by the 'laughter and howling' that greeted the Italian première of *Othello* in Milan in 1842 (Weiss 1982: 141). But it was an enthusiasm that was crucial for the development of Verdi's art. In fact virtually all his operas, from *Ernani* onwards, originate in his own literary enthusiasms, not just in Schiller and Shakespeare, obviously, for he rapidly became widely read in the dramatic literature of much of Western Europe. But this wide reading was undertaken not in the hope of acquiring topics for conversation at elegant society gatherings. Verdi was forming his taste, refining his sensibility, and above all seeking new perceptions of dramatic truth that might deepen and enrich contemporary opera.

The literary taste acquired in these years encouraged his propensity for boldness and originality of theme. He would certainly have endorsed Romani's comment that 'the patrimony of opera includes all that imagination can conceive or passion suggest'. But he followed through that conviction far more consequentially than Romani ever felt able to do. As far as the censors allowed, Verdi was prepared to be politically bold, as in *Attila*

(Venice 1846), or *La battaglia di Legnano* (Rome 1849); to be socially and ethically bold as in *Stiffelio* (Trieste 1850) or *La traviata* (Venice 1853); to be imaginatively bold, as in *Macbeth* (Florence 1847). In this work he attempted to open up Italian opera to the whole fantastic, supernatural and nightmarish world of Northern Romanticism at its bleakest and most uncanny. Florentine critics at the time felt that he failed, that 'all those pieces in which the supernatural powers intervene . . . lack that mysterious, *fantastic* character that the situation calls for', perhaps even that 'Italian talents, born under a warmer sun and a more splendid sky, lack in their palettes . . . colours suitable for representing supernatural objects in the manner that Northerners can' (*Ricoglitore*, 20 March 1847, quoted by Conati in Rosen and Porter 1984: 231). And modern critics on the whole have not felt disposed to disagree. But that is not the point. For better and for worse, Verdi was the complete musical representative of the Italy of the Romantic Age. For the first fifteen years of his operatic career, until *La traviata*, let us say, his music embodies Italian Romanticism entire – its tastes, its hopes and aspirations, even its errors and its follies.

Verdi the tribune

By the time Verdi entered these circles his commitment to the Italian nationalist cause was whole-hearted. I say 'by the time' because there is clear evidence that in earlier years he had cordial relationships with pro-Austrian groups in Milan (Parker 1981, Chapter 1). Later in life his sense of public duty made it easy for Cavour to persuade him to take an active part in Italian politics, and between 1861 and 1865 he sat as a parliamentary deputy in Turin. But he was never seriously tempted to enrol as a fighting man. In these early years he seems to have felt that there was a more important role for him to play as a 'tribune': his contribution was of course not to be compared with that of the fighting men who did the real work, but it was all he was capable of. When his librettist friend Piave joined up as a soldier for the Republic of Venice, Verdi wrote to him, 'You talk of music to me!! What are you thinking of? Do you think I want to concern myself now with notes and sounds? There is and should be only one kind of music pleasing to the ears of the Italians of 1848 – the music of the guns! . . . I too if I had enrolled would wish to be a common solidier, but now I can only be a tribune' (Budden 1985: 48–9). As Budden remarks, Verdi presumably used the term tribune in the sense of a popular orator, for he continues, 'a wretched tribune at that, as I am only eloquent by fits and starts'. The most specific contribution he made to the national cause in his capacity as Italy's musical tribune was a setting of Mameli's patriotic hymn 'Suona la tromba'. It was written at the request of Mazzini, in a style 'as popular and simple as possible', and despatched on 18 October 1848 with the hope that it might soon 'be sung amid the music of the cannon on the Lombardy plain' (Verdi 1913: 469). But the scope for this kind of work was limited. There was a far more significant role for Verdi in the opera-house, helping to make a present reality of the creed uttered by Alfieri sixty years before (cf. Chapter 14 above, p. 245).

It was on the strength of his operas, not for 'Suona la tromba', that Verdi acquired his unique status as the 'bard of the *risorgimento*'. For he learned to exploit much more deliberately than earlier composers had done the peculiar powers of opera to conjure communal emotions. It was an art that heightened the sensibilities, exalted the passions, caressed and jangled the nerve-ends until audiences were wrought up to a pitch of excitability. And it did this with people who were gathered together fraternally and convivially in theatres so designed as to permit fullest expression to both their public and their private selves. To function as a tribune in this environment one did not even need an explicitly political theme, as Heine's comments on an opera produced at La Scala in 1828 show. A British visitor has reproached a 'pale young Italian' with indifference to the great issues of the day:

The evening before, we had seen the production of a new opera at La Scala and listened to the scenes of slaughter, which as usual had formed part of the occasion. 'You Italians', said the Briton to the pale man, 'seem to be dead to everything except music; this is the only thing able to excite you.' 'You wrong us,' said the pale man . . . 'Ah', he sighed, 'Italy sits amid her ruins, dreaming elegiacally, and if sometimes, at the memory of some song, she awakens of a sudden and springs wildly up, this enthusiasm is not just for the song itself, but rather for the old memories and emotions which the song awakened, which Italy always carries in her heart, and which now pour out in a torrent – and that is the meaning of that mad uproar which you heard in La Scala.'

(Heine 1830: Chapter 27)

For a quarter of a century after the Restoration Italian audiences adopted increasingly the habit of interpreting opera in the light of their political aspirations, and conversely of expressing their civic and national ambitions through the music that most excited them. The biographies of Bellini, Donizetti and Mercadante all provide instances. A particularly good example was an incident at the production of Donizetti's *Otto mesi in due ore* at Modena in 1831. The performance coincided with the outbreak of an insurrection, and one evening during an interval the highly wrought audience clamoured for an Italian hymn. The orchestra, having no such piece in their repertory, broke into a rendering of the Act III march, which 'pleased the patriots so well that from that evening forward, Donizetti's *Otto mesi* march became a sort of local revolutionary symbol' (Weinstock 1964: 320). With Verdi the links between opera and the political ambitions of the *risorgimento* became stronger and more explicit. In the words of Luigi Dallapiccola, 'the phenomenon that is Verdi is unimaginable without the Risorgimento. Whether or not he played an active part in it is unimportant, he absorbed its air and its tone . . . formulated a style through which the Italian people found a key to their dramatic plight and vibrated in unison with it' (Porter 1983: 204). Quite how literally true Dallapiccola's observation is is shown by the extraordinary incident witnessed near Verdi's villa at Sant'Agata by the German journalist A. von Winterfeld, probably in 1883:

The fading day forced us to think of our return journey, and Verdi insisted on driving us to the station in his gig. On the way we met a party of field workers, who were returning in the sunset from their day's work. Catching sight of the Maestro, they stopped beside the path, doffed their caps and sang, with that innate vocal talent of Italians, the beautiful male chorus from *I Lombardi*, as we drove slowly past.   (Conati 1984: 152)

In playing his part as tribune Verdi had to solve the problems imposed by censorship. After all, the censors, even in the most liberal parts of Italy, could veto the choice of any theme they deemed inflammatory; they could wreak expurgatory havoc on a finished libretto; and they took a continuing interest in the effects operas produced in the theatre, so that it was possible, after a performance of *Nabucco* in 1847, for Angelo Mariani to be reprimanded by the Milan commissioner of police 'for having given to Verdi's music an expression too evidently rebellious and hostile to the Imperial Government' (F. Walker 1962: 151). It followed that flagrantly political operas were feasible only under the rarest and most exceptional circumstances. Nothing short of the demise of the Papal government in Rome and the impending establishment of a Roman Republic could have made possible the staging of *La battaglia di Legnano* in the city in January 1849. An opera on the same subject by Bozzi had been banned in 1846 (Rubsamen 1961: 101). Far more typical than *La battaglia di Legnano* are those operas in which Verdi follows the example set by Monti early in the century, expressing the concerns of the here and now through subjects that are apparently remote in time and space. The opera becomes, in some degree at least, an allegory: and the ostensible theme is transformed into the real theme by topical substitutions applied by the audience. This is certainly not how the composer would have wished it. 'How many subjects there are in our own history', he exclaimed in a letter to Giuseppe Giusti in 1847, 'but unfortunately . . . if we want something at all effective we have, to our shame, to resort to foreign things' (Abbiati 1959, I: 691).

For an opera to function effectively in terms of *risorgimento* ideology the crucial thing was not an Italian subject, but a subject that was not too private, the way, for example, that *Stiffelio* or *La traviata* were to be. Of course Verdi wanted idiosyncratic characters and stirring theatrical confrontations, for drama is a problematic genre without them; but the essential thing was that the dramatic theme should entail conflict on a national or international scale. A basic concern was the national identity, and the historical and religious foundations on which that identity was grounded. And so Verdi wrote operas about the conflict of Crusaders and

Saracens (*I Lombardi alla prima crociata*), about the English invasion of France in the time of Joan of Arc (*Giovanna d'Arco*, Milan 1845), and – the key work in this repertory – about the destruction of the Jewish state, and the Jewish exile in Babylon (*Nabucco*, Milan 1842). It was in *Nabucco* that he first discovered the formula and brought it to dramatic life with a magnificent idealistic fervour that the later *risorgimento* operas never quite managed to recapture. For all the superior sophistication, for all the greater musical richness and dramatic flair of such scores as *Macbeth*, *Luisa Miller*, and *Rigoletto*, *Nabucco* was *par excellence* the representative opera of *risorgimento* Italy. As Giosuè Carducci was to put it: 'With the first throbbings of his youthful art Giuseppe Verdi presaged and heralded the revival of the fatherland. Oh songs unforgettable and sacred to anyone born before the '48!'

In *Nabucco* and the other *risorgimento*-tinged operas that followed it, patriotism, religion, the idea of holy warfare, are pervading motifs. Corporate moods, prayerful, and militaristic, play a central part. Faced with dramatic themes of this kind, Verdi dug down deep into his earliest musical memories, of the hymns and liturgical music he had played in the village church at Le Roncole, of the raucous strains of the Busseto town-band. These operas, particularly *Nabucco* and *I Lombardi*, are saturated in an atmosphere of popular, indigenous music-making, a fact which must have accounted for no small part of their directness of address.

Verdi made no attempt to transfigure or sublimate this vulgar material; quite the contrary. In certain moods he was a peremptory kind of artist, impatient of lingering word-repetitions, scorning the floating *fioritura* clouds of *bel canto* song. His music has a thrusting forward momentum, propelled by strutting and stamping rhythms, coloured by the snarl of brass and the thud of percussion, punctuated from time to time by brutal explosions of noise. Such characteristics prompted a typical sally from Rossini: 'If the name of the composer had been kept hidden from me, I should have wagered that he could only be an artillery colonel' (Michotte 1968: 108).

The emphasis on the nation in the plot of the opera is matched in the music by an emphasis on the chorus. Indeed we know from Muzio that the Milanese were so thrilled with the choral writing in *Nabucco* and *I Lombardi* that they dubbed Verdi 'il padre del coro'. It was a development that must have gratified Mazzini, who, in his *Filosofia di musica* (in Mazzini 1910), had called for a larger role for the chorus to reflect democratic trends in contemporary society. 'The solemn and complete representation of the popular element' to which Mazzini looked forward was surely achieved, by eschewing any kind of contrapuntal artifice and writing with the greatest conceivable directness. In keeping with their popularist expressive task, some of the best choruses – 'Va pensiero' in *Nabucco*, 'O signore, dal tetto natio' in *I Lombardi* – are largely unison songs, the 'Jerusalems' of the Italian *risorgimento*. Beside these full-scale choral movements, Verdi has a thrilling way of introducing the unison chorus into certain types of aria: Zaccaria's 'Come notte al sol fulgente' (*Nabucco*, Act I), or Foresto's 'Cara patria, già madre e reina' (*Attila*, Prologue). Perhaps he borrowed from the prayer in *Mosè* the idea of a responsorial treatment of soloist and chorus, but he handles it more compactly and with a more spontaneous-seeming informality. These arias are invariably patriotic in character, and it is the function of the soloist to act as a popular leader, the person who provides the flash of perception, or the slogan that inspires his companions to identify themselves with the cause. The spread of the song from principal to chorus provides a thrillingly immediate image of the spread of inflammatory ideas in a democratic society, articulated first by a few ardent solitaries, acquiring irresistible force and momentum when embraced by a whole people: *vox populi, vox Dei*.

As with the choral writing, so too with the instrumentation: *Nabucco* provides a pattern by virtue of what Chorley was to call 'the utterly disproportionate predominance of the brazen instruments' (1862, II: 290). Four of the marches in the opera employ the *banda* – that on-stage military band occasionally recruited for the theatre from the ranks of a local regiment. In the orchestra, the brass is no less conspicuous. Tunes in instrumental marches and choruses alike tend to be reinforced with trumpet and trombone; horn, trombone and cimbasso give accompanying chordal patterns a glinting, thudding menace. Verdi borrowed from Rossini's Moses the idea of accompanying the prophet's most portentous recitative with brass instruments, but in the context of *Nabucco* the effect is rather different, suggesting perhaps that Zaccaria's Jehovah is a god of military solution. This brassiness of scoring; the all-pervasive march-rhythms, brisk and tingling with suppressed energy; the brusque force of many of the musical ideas; the urgent impatience that galvanizes the whole massive choral and scenic apparatus – all added up the sound of a distinctively new voice in Italian opera. No wonder that patriots heard in it a voice prophesying 'la patria risorgente'.

What *Nabucco* clearly is not, however, is a consistently worked-out political tract for the times, heavy with finger-wagging, Brechtian didacticism. Still less consistently allegorical are the *risorgimento*-inspired operas that follow. If there had been an Italian Thomas Mann on the scene in the 1840s to produce some 'Meditations of a non-political Italian' it is impossible to suppose that Verdi would not have recognized the force of his argument; and he shows that magnanimity in his treatment of character that Mann, borrowing from Schopenhauer, claimed as the prerequisite of an artist of integrity. Nabucco and Attila may be on the wrong side, but Verdi spares no pains to invest them with eloquence and to engage our sympathy for their version of the truth. Character, individual character in all its rich idiosyncratic diversity became the ruling passion of Verdi's life as an artist, and the *risorgimento* odes and military marches with which their story was punctuated came increasingly to sound like distractions, episodes introduced out of a sense of public duty rather than of artistic necessity. It is no accident that early critics, like Basevi, began to detect a weariness of spirit in Verdi's choruses after *I Lombardi*, and that Verdi himself admitted to having, for the time being, nothing further to say in the march style after *Giovanna d'Arco* (letter of November 1845 to Piave, cited in Abbiati 1959, I: 593–4). After *I Lombardi* risorgimental considerations impoverished Verdi's art rather than enriching it: that he nevertheless continued to grow in stature was due to other factors.

The inspiration of literature

In much Verdi, as in Bellini, one senses that the operatic song has taken shape as a kind of sublimated declamation.[1] But besides this direct Bellinian response to the words he was setting, Verdi depended on his texts in a more peculiar sense. He was keenly aware of the unique literary qualities of the sources he drew upon for his operas, and he insisted that his librettists should preserve as many as possible of them in their own work.

Widely read in the dramatic literature of much of Western Europe, sometimes guided in his reading by such friends as Carcano and Maffei, Verdi had an unerring eye for the operatic potential of what he read. Like Donizetti and Bellini he was thrilled by bizarre confrontations – the Roman general Aetius partitioning the world with Attila the Hun in Zacharias Werner's *Attila, König der Hunnen*; the adulterous Lina throwing herself at the feet of her husband, a Lutheran pastor, in the middle of a church service in Souvestre's and Bourgeois's *Le pasteur*. And he was uniquely susceptible to the thrill of character. A Lady Macbeth, a Triboulet or an Azucena would haunt his imagination for months, sometimes for years on end, making their stories irresistible.

But once the suitable model had been found, Verdi went further. He believed that the source play offered much more than a plot, a series of powerful situations and a handful of memorable characters. He came to see it as an inspiration and an ally in the task of enriching and rejuvenating the very musical language of Italian opera. A fine play had an atmosphere uniquely its own, which Verdi aimed to recreate: even the dramatist's language – the full, detailed sequence of ideas, the choice of imagery and metaphor, the sheer poetry – might, if faithfully imitated, inspire flights of musical fancy that were unimaginable as long as composers rested content with the standardized forms and the mannered diction of the conventional libretto. The Verdian ideal of fidelity to the literary source finds character-

istic expression in a letter he wrote to Marianna Barbieri-Nini, his first
Lady Macbeth, when she was about to start work learning the role:

The plot is taken from one of the greatest tragedies the theatre boasts, and I have tried to
have all the dramatic situations drawn from it faithfully, to have it well versified, and to
give it a new texture, and to compose music tied to far as possible to the text and to the
situations: and I wish this idea of mine to be well understood by the performers; indeed I
wish the performers to serve the poet better than they serve the composer.

(Rosen and Porter 1984: 29)

The consequences of this attitude are particularly momentous in the operas
which the young Verdi modelled on Victor Hugo, Shakespeare and
Schiller, three authors who profoundly interested and excited most of the
leaders of Italian Romanticism.

It was Hugo to whom Verdi turned first. *Ernani* (Venice 1844) was the
first of his operas to be composed after he had established a national
reputation with the risorgimental grand operas of his early years, *Nabucco*
and *I Lombardi*. He was aiming now for something less monumental in
style, something 'very fiery, packed with action, and concise' (letter of 11
June 1843, in Abbiati 1959, I: 469), and the perfervid leader of the French
Romantics seemed exactly the man to supply these desiderata. Verdi
turned to Hugo a second time in *Rigoletto* (from *Le roi s'amuse*), his earliest
unqualified masterpiece, and the first of his operas to have maintained a
place in the repertory from the day of its première until now. In both cases
Verdi seems to have perceived the opera latent within the play in a sudden
visionary intuition. Indeed he himself drew a parallel between them:

You know, six years ago, when Mocenigo suggested *Ernani* to me, I exclaimed: 'yes, by
God . . . that would be a winner'. Now I was going over several subjects again when *Le
roi* [*s'amuse*] came into my mind like a flash of lightning, an inspiration, and I said the
same thing: 'Yes, by God, that would be a winner.'

(Letter of 3 May 1850, in Abbiati 1959, II: 62–3)

These instantaneous perceptions surely came to Verdi because Hugo did
offer himself extraordinarily well to operatic adaptation. Indeed the
Viennese music critic Eduard Hanslick went so far as to suggest that his
plays needed to be so treated; that they were 'less tragedies to which music
would do violence, than librettos which have not yet been composed'
(1875: 222). Hugo's principal characters are melodramatically overdrawn,
and seem entirely at home in the emotional confessional of aria and
ensemble. The relationship between dramatic action and the outpourings
of eloquence is more akin to operatic techniques than to the best models of
poetic drama. For as in an opera, where the recitatives link and motivate
the arias and ensembles, so too in these plays, the plot seems contrived
chiefly with a view to providing openings for the poetic '*tirades*'. It is not the
dynamic of action nor the illumination of character that are Hugo's primary
concerns, but passion and eloquence; and the operatic aria and ensemble

Plate 9 The frontispiece from the first edition of the piano-vocal score of
Ernani, published by Ricordi

499

provide perfect vehicles for his sonorous grandiloquence. Finally, it is a typical trait that his acts should culminate in blood-tingling tableaux of confrontation: the exposure of the disguised Lucrezia at the Venetian Carnival in the prologue of *Lucrèce Borgia*; Don Carlos stepping from the tomb of Charlemagne to confound the conspirators in Act IV of *Hernani*. How much more convincing such scenes are when translated into the form of the operatic ensemble Hugo himself seems to have conceded when he remarked that he envied Verdi the medium that made possible the quartet in *Rigoletto*.

When talking about *Rigoletto*, Verdi returned again and again to the issue of the characters: Triboulet was a character 'worthy of Shakespeare . . . One of the greatest creations that the theatre in any country or period could boast . . . Putting on the stage a character grossly deformed and absurd, but inwardly passionate and full of love, is precisely what I find the beautiful thing' (letters to Piave, 28 April 1850, 8 May 1850, December 1850, in Verdi 1913). It was his recognition that Gilda was a heroine totally unlike the aristocratic *grandes dames* who normally took the principal roles in Romantic opera that prompted him to a radical refashioning of the form: 'I conceived *Rigoletto* [sc. the part of Gilda in *Rigoletto*] without arias, without finales, as an unbroken chain of duets, because I was convinced that that was most suitable' (letter of 8 September 1852, in Verdi 1913: 497). Characterization is not perhaps one of the qualities of Hugo best recognized today, but there can be no doubt that, together with Shakespeare, he was the catalyst for Verdi's own fascination with dramatic characterization, and his exploration of the musical means by which it could be attained. If *Rigoletto* was the work in which mastery was achieved, it was *Ernani* that set him on course. Neither *Nabucco* or *I Lombardi* had notably enlarged Verdi's grasp of the potential of musical characterization. But faced with a play in which three men – an addled and vindictive old aristocrat, a Romantic rebel, and a prince in whose breast private passions and public responsibilities compete for mastery – battle for the heart and mind of the Lady Elvira; and – a detail that should not be overlooked, though it has nothing to do with Hugo – embarrassed by a request from the Venetian management to write one of these roles for a popular mezzo-soprano, Verdi found himself thinking long and deeply about the vocal casting of his opera. Out of this reflection there emerged a definition of those male vocal archetypes that were to serve him for the rest of his career: 'the granite-like, monochrome bass (Silva) older than the roots of his family pride; the heroic tenor, lyrical, ardent, despairing (Ernani); and partaking of both natures, now zephyr, now hurricane, the Verdi baritone (Carlo), the greatest vehicle of power in Italian opera' (Budden 1973–81, I: 147). From *Ernani* onwards musical characterization became a central concern in virtually all his scores: as Mila has remarked, the opera 'initiated a whole series of character studies' (1958: 153).

Characterization was a crucial issue in Verdi's reverence for Shakespeare too. But here is is the truthfulness of characterization that was the particular source of admiration. Indeed, in later life, Verdi was to see in Shakespeare a model for a kind of 'verismo' that would surpass all other types of dramatic art.

To imitate truth may be a good thing, but to invent truth is better, far better. Perhaps there seems a contradiction in these three words – to invent truth – but ask Papà. It is possible that he may have met a Falstaff, but he is hardly likely to have met so villainous a villain as Iago, and never such angels as Cordelia, Imogen, Desdemona etc. etc., yet how true they are. (To Clarina Maffei, 20 October 1876, in Verdi 1913: 624)

In this perception of Shakespeare Verdi was echoing – not necessarily consciously – the words of Mazzini, who of all nineteenth-century Italian intellectuals produced the most substantial body of critical writing on Shakespeare.[2] Shakespeare's 'truthfulness' was emphasized in the writings of another distinguished Italian critic, Alessandro Manzoni. But here it is the formal freedom that was particularly admired, Shakespeare's sovereign disdain for the dramaturgical dogma by which French dramatists felt themselves to be bound, and the effects of spontaneity and naturalness which this enabled him to achieve. This admiration too was shared by Verdi. Indeed Verdi went further, relishing as peculiarly effective and peculiarly Shakespearian that blending of comic and tragic to which Manzoni could never quite reconcile himself. What Verdi, in a letter to Cammarano, once described as 'the mixture of the comic and the terrible (à la Shakespeare)' (Weiss 1982: 144), was something which on several occasions – in the unwritten *L'assedio di Firenze*, in *Luisa Miller*, in *Rigoletto* – he tried to introduce into his own work.

It should not surprise us to find that Verdi's view of Shakespeare was very much in line with that of the leading Italian intellectuals of the age. Shakespeare was an enthusiasm confined to an elite, and Verdi enjoyed his Shakespeare in full consciousness of what he stood for in the artistic and philosophical circles of Romantic Italy. It seems beyond doubt, for instance, that he had pondered A. W. Schlegel's commentary on *Macbeth*, which he would have found appended to the Rusconi translation he used in preparing his opera. The structure of Verdi's *Macbeth* is built round those scenes that Schlegel had highlighted as vital to an understanding of the play; his letters to Piave often echo Schlegel's views; and (probably at Verdi's request) reissues of the standard Ricordi libretto from 1848 onwards were furnished with a preface summarizing some of the cardinal points in Schlegel's essay (reprinted in Rosen and Porter 1984: 349–50). This preface was specifically aimed at disarming the kind of criticism the opera received at its Florentine première from 'those whose passion for reason blinds them' to the kinds of truth revealed in the 'fantastic genre'; it lays particular emphasis on the role of the witches.

Shakespeare's freedom of form and his life-like characterization were the most difficult of attributes to transpose into the profoundly stylized medium of Italian opera. Verdi's determination not to duck the issues posed by the witches exacerbated the problem. For there was next to nothing in the musical language of his predecessors to help him forge an idiom apt to the 'ignoble and vulgar instruments of hell . . . emblems of the hostile powers which ferment in nature's breast' (Schlegel). If he failed in this particular task – and I think we must concur to that extent with the early critics – *Macbeth* remains, unlike all earlier Italian operas on Shakespearian themes, a genuinely Shakespearian opera. It is Shakespearian by virtue of Verdi's ideal of fidelity to his literary model, even when – perhaps especially when – that entailed unprecedented technical and imaginative challenges.

The composer took a more than usually active part in the preparation of the libretto, as he was to explain to Tito Ricordi: 'I made the synopsis myself, indeed I did more than the synopsis, I wrote a full prose version of the drama, showing the distribution of the acts, the scenes, the musical numbers etc. . . . then I gave it to Piave to versify' (letter of 11 April 1857, in Verdi 1913: 444). Nor did Piave escape more minute prescriptions: how many lines there were to be in a particular cantabile, what metre was required for a particular chorus, and so on. Verdi occupied himself with the libretto to this exceptional degree, we may be sure, so that the amount of conventionalizing undergone by Shakespeare's tragedy should be reduced to a minimum. He was determined that its 'sublime' characters should not be watered down into stereotypes of Romantic melodrama, and that the evocative power of Shakespeare's language should not be sacrificed for the standardized vocabulary and circumscribed imagery of the professional librettist. The result of Verdi's involvement was a libretto in which all but a handful of phrases are modelled on Shakespeare's own.

This reverence of one great artist for another remote in time and working in an alien tradition was an unprecedented phenomenon in Italian opera. And it had a momentous impact on the growth of Verdi's musical imagination, as can be seen most clearly in those two movements that the composer himself described as 'the most important in the opera' (letter to Cammarano, 23 November 1848, *ibidem*: 62), the *gran scena e duetto* in Act I and the *gran scena del sonnambulismo* in Act IV.

The duet is a recreation of the dialogue between Macbeth and Lady Macbeth after the murder of Duncan in Act II scene 2 of Shakespeare's play. Verdi has retained virtually all the evocative details in which the original is so rich: the owl-cry, the perturbed dreams and prayer of

I heard the owl's shriek. . .what was it you said just now?

Ex.V.11a Verdi, *Macbeth* (1847), Act I scene 13

Donalbain and his attendant; the 'Amen' that stuck in Macbeth's throat; the voice that cried 'Sleep no more! Macbeth doth murder sleep'; and so on throughout the scene. And for each of these poetic images he fashions a musical analogy (Exx.V.11a–c). The result is that Shakespeare's poetic imagination, mediated through Verdi's musical imagination, begins to wreak havoc on the established forms of Italian opera. The ensemble no longer has space for fallow interludes and tame symmetries; it has become densely packed with significantly expressive music.

Like Shakespeare, Schiller was one of the great discoveries resulting from the cosmopolitan enthusiasms of the first generation of Italian Romantics. In the early years of the Restoration his plays and essays were a favourite topic of discussion in the pages of the *Conciliatore*,[3] and translations of the plays began to appear from 1813. Verdi's friendship with Maffei, ultimately the translator of Schiller's complete works, was probably instrumental in arousing the composer's interest in the great German dramatist. In 1845, Verdi had composed *Giovanna d'Arco* to a libretto by Temistocle Solera, apparently quite oblivious of its associations – admittedly vague – with *Die Jungfrau von Orleans*. But from the time

I heard the courtiers praying in their sleep: 'God be with us always',
they said; 'Amen', I wanted to say, too.

Ex.V.11b Verdi, *Macbeth* (1847), Act I scene 13

Maffei interested Verdi in making a setting of *Die Räuber* (*I masnadieri*, London 1847), Schiller became an enriching influence on his art.

Compared with Hugo-inspired and Shakespeare-inspired operas the number inspired by Schiller is small. The greatest of them, *Guillaume Tell* and *Don Carlos*, are not Italian operas at all, but grand operas written in French for Paris. The currency of another of the most distinguished, Donizetti's *Maria Stuarda*, was restricted by censorship. Mercadante, Pacini

MACBETH

a - vrai per guan - cia - li   sol ve - pri, o Mac-bet - - - - - -

ppp

to!   Il son - no per   sem - pre,   Gla - mis,   uc - ci -

de - - - - sti!

ppp

Oh Macbeth, you will have only thorns for your pillow! Glamis, you
murder sleep for ever.

Ex.V.11c Verdi, *Macbeth* (1847), Act I scene 13

and Vaccai all wrote operas more or less closely modelled on Schiller, and
the closing scene of Bellini's *Beatrice di Tenda* was inspired, to some extent,
by the matching scenes of *Maria Stuart*, the most popular of Schiller's plays
in Italy. But really the only Italian operas closely modelled on Schiller and

widely performed in Italy were *I masnadieri*, *Luisa Miller* (Naples 1850) and, much later, the Italian revision of *Don Carlos*. This is a modest harvest, considering the prestige Schiller enjoyed. It must have disappointed Mazzini; for he regarded Schiller as the ideal model for the young dramatists who were to help build the new Italy (cf. Chapter 22 above, pp. 411–12). But something of Mazzini's dream is certainly realized in those three Verdi scores, where the private emotional lives of the protagonists do become elaborately and significantly entangled in the larger world of social and political organization.

In 1846, after the production in Venice of *Attila*, Verdi suffered some kind of nervous breakdown. From the period of enforced repose that followed, he emerged mentally and imaginatively renewed. He put aside the styles of opera in which his earliest successes had been gained – whether Romantic melodramas like *Ernani*, or *risorgimento*-inspired pageants of national life like *Nabucco* – and addressed himself to more ambitious tasks. In particular he was preoccupied with two issues. The first was how to escape from the restrictions of conventional characterization, how to create characters who were as unique and as 'real' – to use Verdi's own favourite term of commendation – as those in the poetic drama he most admired. A second, complementary ambition was to set these 'real' characters in a 'real' world – to make society part of the subject of the drama. If Shakespeare was the principal source of inspiration in the first case, Schiller's example was certainly a contributory factor in the second.

In Verdi's first Schiller opera, *I masnadieri*, the relationship between the hero, Carlo, and society is still sketchy. But it is there, and it matters since Carlo is a classic early example of an outsider, tragically alienated from the world in which he finds himself. With *Luisa Miller* and *Don Carlos* the aim of setting 'real' characters in a 'real' world is more fully achieved: Verdi does recreate something of a life-like complexity in the relationship between the realm of personal feelings and that of social organization. To paraphrase one of his own remarks – and he was echoing Mazzini – he has moved on from the type of opera that is made of arias and duets to a new type made of ideas: ideas like the conflict of class-structure and humane feeling ('Mode' and 'Menschheit') in *Luisa Miller*, or of dogmatism and libertarianism in *Don Carlos*. Real characters in a real world, with the emphasis on the characters, was Verdi's diagnosis of what 'verismo' involved – or ought to involve. After *Luisa Miller* he was to carry this preoccupation into other kinds of real world where Schiller might have been ill at ease, notably in *La traviata*. But the three Schiller operas, *I masnadieri*, *Luisa Miller* and *Don Carlos*, are conspicuous landmarks on the road towards Verdi's very individual brand of realism.

Verdi's idealism

To point out how much of the innovatory character of Verdi's earlier operas was stimulated by his literary sources, is to show that Verdi's admiration for Hugo, Shakespeare and Schiller, and indeed others of the authors to whom he turned in the first fifteen years of his career, was one of the inspirations of his idealism, of that uncompromising firmness with which he pursued his dramatic vision regardless of the entrenched conventions and habits of the opera-house.

One may begin with the formal conventions, of which none, by 1850, was any longer sacred to him. In *Stiffelio* he dispenses with the *Introduzione*; there are no finales, properly speaking, in *Rigoletto*, and no full-scale aria for the *prima donna*. During the preliminary stages of work on *Il trovatore* he proclaimed: 'If in operas there were neither cavatinas, nor duets, nor trios, nor choruses, nor finales etc., etc., and if the whole opera was (if I might express it this way) one single piece, I should find it more reasonable and proper' (letter to Cammarano, 4 April 1851, in Abbiati 1959, II: 135). Where the subject demanded it, he was implacable in overthrowing the conventions of casting, deaf to the pleas of *prima donna*s, theatre poets and impresarios alike: the final scene of *Ernani* did not lend itself to a rondo-finale for Sophie Loewe and therefore Signora Loewe would have to do without a rondo, even if it did make her sing out of tune on the first night in pique; there were only and could be only three principal roles in *Macbeth* – Macbeth, Lady Macbeth and the witches, and he was not going to enlarge the role of Macduff to turn it into a plum tenor part to suit the Parisian management.

The tenacity with which Verdi held to his convictions caused him to make unprecedented demands on his singers. The shift away from beautiful singing to dramatically meaningful singing, which Romani commented on in Bellini's *La straniera*, is embraced far more radically by Verdi, particularly with *Macbeth*. The score has some extraordinary directions for interpretation: 'staccato a marcato assai: ne dimenticarsi che sono streghe che parlano';[4] the original Lady Macbeth, Marianna Barbieri-Nini, left an illuminating account of rehearsals for the opera, of how 'for three months, morning and evening, I tried to impersonate someone who speaks in her sleep, who (as the maestro put it) utters words . . . without moving her lips, the rest of the face motionless, the eyes shut'; the Act I duet 'was rehearsed, incredible as it may sound, one hundred and fifty times, so that as Verdi said, it should sound *more spoken than sung*' (Monaldi 1898: 83). Varesi was the only person who could manage Macbeth 'both because of his way of singing and because of his intelligence . . . Perhaps you will say he sings out of tune, but that doesn't matter, since the part would be almost totally declaimed, and he is very good at that' (Muzio to Barezzi, 27 August 1846, in Rosen and Porter 1984: 7). On the other hand Eugenia Tadolini was an unsuitable person to take the part of Lady Macbeth in a Naples revival in 1848 on the grounds that she had 'too great qualities'.

Tadolini is a fine-looking woman, and I should like Lady Macbeth to look ugly and evil. Tadolini sings to perfection, and I should like Lady not to sing at all. Tadolini has a marvellous voice, clear, limpid and powerful; and I should like Lady's voice to be harsh, choked and hollow. Tadolini's voice has something angelic about it, and I should like Lady's voice to have something devilish.

(To Cammarano, 23 November 1848, in Verdi 1913: 61–2)

Not surprisingly, the young Verdi seemed to many of his fellow artists a 'difficult' man, 'earnest and self-important', in the words of the correspondent of the *Allgemeine Musikalische Zeitung* in 1845 (perhaps Peter Lichtenthal; cited in Conati 1984: 12). Barbieri-Nini again, this time paraphrased by Checchi, provides a portrait that gives a feel of authenticity:

The implacable Verdi spared no thought for his artists: he tired and tormented them with the same number for hours on end, and he never moved to a different scene until they had managed to perform the piece in a manner which fell least short of his ideal. He was not much loved by the multitude [of performers], for no word of encouragement, no 'bravo' of conviction ever passed his lips, not even when orchestral players and members of the chorus believed they had done everything possible to content him; and those foul-mouthed, witty Florentines, quick to take offence, gave vent to their anger . . . (Conati 1984: 25)

Verdi as musician and craftsman

'In the Devil's name, since this is Italy, why do we go in for German art?' exploded Verdi in 1878. It is simply one of many similar expostulations in which he expressed his conviction that a flourishing art needed deep roots, long traditions, a fine tact in recognizing the limits within which it can be effective. But it was not the complaint of a narrow-minded man. Twenty years later Verdi was expressing to the Berlin novelist and journalist Felix Philippi the admiration and awe which he felt for *Tristan*, especially for Act II, 'one of the finest creations that has ever issued from a human mind . . . wonderful . . . quite wonderful' (Conati 1984: 329).

This admiration came from a musician of vast experience, and a very wide acquaintance with the world's music, old and new. His library contained much Bach and a representative selection of the best German music down to Brahms and Wagner; Berlioz and Liszt, Smetana and Dvořák, Bizet and Saint-Saëns were all to be found there, together with a fair sprinkling of early music. But the most revealing fact about his collection is revealed only in the bookcase in his bedroom: there in a place of honour alongside the works of Dante, Shakespeare and Schiller are scores of the string quartets of Haydn, Mozart and Beethoven. These, we must infer, were, for Verdi, the 'Classics', the works from which no musician could long absent himself, for in these was to be found the highest and best that the musical mind was capable of. This was not something that Verdi came to recognize only in the years of his maturity; already in 1845 when Emanuele Muzio came from Busseto to study with him in Milan, he treated the classical quartet as the epitome of taste and skill, the indispensible foundation for any musical education worthy the name (cf. Muzio's letter to Barezzi, 29 April 1845, in Garibaldi 1931: 198).

The relationship between Verdi's own musical education and the qualities of his early operas is not easily perceived. His student years in Milan coincided with a drastic decline of interest in classical music, instrumental and vocal, and a narrowing of public taste until it became preoccupied with contemporary Italian opera to the exclusion of virtually everything else. Opera supplied music for more than the theatres; the repertory of barrel-organs in the streets, of military bands at public or state occasions, of church organists at Mass, of pianists in their private houses, was for the most part operatic. Writing in the *Allgemeine Musikalische Zeitung* in 1842, Peter Lichtenthal lamented the fact that, while good performances of classical orchestral and chamber music had always been something of a rarity in Italy, they had 'declined significantly in recent years, so that there remained for the educated musician no other real musical enjoyment than that of reading the scores of those heroes' (Parker 1981: 46). And that is what not only the connoisseurs like Lichtenthal, but young students like Muzio, and Verdi before him, did. There is no reason to doubt that musical education was thorough and rigorous, but in a way that was remote from the actualities of contemporary musical life. You went to the opera-house to hear how contemporary maestros handled the problem of dramatic composition; but your compositional skills were based on a 'reading' of the classics – which 'illuminated the intellect of the observer in prodigious fashion' (Pacini 1865: 79) – and the solution of abstract musical problems – the 'canons and fugues, fugues and canons' that Verdi remembered from his lessons with Lavigna. Rather like Ciceronian prose in a nineteenth-century education in the humanities, or the vocalises and technical studies of the singing school at Bologna under Rossini, composition was studied as a pure rather than an applied skill: the composer acquired dexterity of hand, a facility in thinking musically. It was up to him to find out when and how, if indeed at all, these accomplishments were to be applied in the composition of real music.

In the melody-based, two-dimensional musical language of Italian opera the application did not come easily or naturally. There is in the Naples Conservatory a curious letter written by Federico Ricci to one F. de Villars in April 1857, in which he attempts to defend Bellini against the charge of an inadequate musical education, and prove that he had 'studied the classics' by showing, not how his harmony or instrumentation or powers

509

of development had benefited, but how many of his *melodic* ideas he had borrowed from Beethoven and Mozart. If the problem of applying one's musical education to the tasks of composing opera was a general one, the discrepancy between what he had studied and the kind of music he wrote was particularly startling in the early works of Verdi. Once in the theatre, pace and excitement became his musical priorities, 'don't be a bore' his watchword (Mila 1958: 36). He had nothing of the aesthete's concern for good taste, and hurled himself at the dramatic and expressive tasks he had assumed quite unconcerned by the dismay more fastidious ears felt at his battering rhythms, his raucous scoring, and the spasms of sheer noise with which he underlined theatrical points.

One thing however that even the most uncomfortable critics could not deny was Verdi's determination to compose characteristic music. A comment of his own about *Rigoletto* unconsciously echoes dozens of early reviews of his work: 'whether my music is beautiful or ugly I don't write it by chance, but always try to give it a definite character' (letter of December 1850, in Abbiati 1959, II: 87). Every new dramatic task undertaken by Verdi stimulated him in new ways. The theme of national and religious rejuvenation in *Nabucco* prompted him to investigate the operatic possibilities of choral writing, of march and hymnody. Faced by a drama that highlighted the monstrous egocentricity of human passions in *Ernani*, he was driven to explore to the limits the expressive potential of the various voice-types; the depth and density of the poetry of Macbeth moved him to question the binding force of the received forms of *ottocento* opera. Another of Verdi's own remarks, that he didn't like to start work composing an opera until the libretto was complete and that 'when I have a general conception of the whole poem the music always comes of its own accord' (letter to Piave, 19 August 1843, *ibidem*, I: 472), shows that he also had an early grasp of the elusive concept of *colorito*; which in Basevi's classic definition is that principle of unity which the music finds 'in the general concept of the drama . . . the centre on which converge the various pieces of the opera' (1859: 114).

But what must surely have most impressed Verdi's contemporaries was his insistence that the personality and the mood of his characters should be reflected as directly as possible in the music he wrote for them. This concern is evident at every level of the musical invention: in the choice of idiom – in the energetic, hard and icy glitter of Lady Macbeth's music, for example, or the sentimental old-world (that is Bellinian/Donizettian) *bel canto* of Germont; or in the very shaping of the melodic lines: Budden nicely draws out the psychologically illuminating contrast between the heroine's two cantabiles in *Il trovatore* – how in 'Tacea la notte' 'Leonora's hopes had been high, and the melody had worked towards a soaring climax with the melody opening out like a flower . . .' while in 'D'amor sull'ale rosee' 'her lyricial wings are drooping and her melody dissolves into a series of dying falls' (Budden 1973–81, II: 99). Even what appears to be a purely formal feature – the treatment of an orchestral introduction, for instance – is likely to be transfigured by Verdi's dramatic and psychological purpose-fulness. In 'Caro nome' in Act I of *Rigoletto*, where Gilda muses over the declaration of love made by 'Gualtier Maldè', the orchestra presents the theme in a trance-like *dolcissimo*, and this then becomes the topic of a series of blissful, ethereal variations – a perfect formal image of her tender musings. In 'Tutto le feste' on the other hand, after the words 'Ciel dammi coraggio', the solo oboe gives the uncanny impression that Gilda is trying over in her mind the words in which she is to explain to her father how she has been seduced; and when thoughts of love have quickened her pulse and brightened her voice too much, it is the solo oboe that returns as the admonishing voice of conscience.

Biographers have often remarked on Verdi's many friendships with sculptors. One of these sculptors, Giovanni Dupré, who saw a lot of Verdi during the weeks he spent in Florence for the production of *Macbeth*, assures us that the composer would discuss the art 'with rare perspicacity' (Conati 1984: 19). Is it purely fortuitous that the characters in his own early operas seem to have something tangible and sculptural about them, and that the dramatic excitement seems so often to arise, not from dialectic (however fashionable that word may have become in modern criticism), but from the contrast and juxtaposition of monumentally hewn figures? Budden succinctly defines this hallmark of Verdi's style as 'the conflict of personalities embodied in voice types' (1973–81, I: 34). Compared with his predecessors he shows little interest in the type of duet in which both characters share the same thematic material, and little in duets for similar voices (two sopranos, two tenors etc.), for in both these types there is little scope for the frictions of *character*, as opposed to such purely musical frictions as the play of dissonance and suspension.

The duet became the crucial formal element of Verdian opera. For it embodied in the most vivid and succinct way those juxtapositions, tensions and conflicts on which his dramatic style depended. It is entirely in keeping with the stark theatricality of his early manner that he often reduces more complicated situations to duet-like antitheses. A good example is found in Act I of *Il trovatore*, where at the *stretta* 'Di geloso amor', Cammarano had given each of the three characters a complete verse to sing. Verdi reduces this carefully proportioned scheme to a plain confrontation of Luna versus Leonora and Manrico, the latter two singing together in octaves. But conversely where an aria is addressed to someone on stage with the singer, Verdi liked to revert to a Rossinian and pre-Rossinian scheme, giving it an ensemble dimension which dramatically invigorates the form. In *Ernani* Silva reacts to Carlo's 'Lo vedremo' while he singing; in *Attila*, Attila passes comment on Odabella's 'Allor che i forti corrono' while she is singing. And the possibility arises that the style of the aria be gradually modified in response to these external stimuli. The most extraordinary example of this kind of thing comes in Act I of *Stiffelio*: 'Vidi dovunque gemere' ought to be a cantabile. But the effect is rather of a whole series of contrasting ariosi set of by Stiffelio's reactions to his reunion with Lina.

As a melodist Verdi drew freely on the common musical language that he had imbibed as a young man in Milan, where Rossini, Bellini and Donizetti, Mercadante, Pacini and the Ricci brothers furnished virtually the entire operatic repertory. But one individual trait began to emerge early in his career and has the profoundest importance for the dramatic character of his music: the cantabile melodies tend to grow in passion and beauty as they move towards their close; they give the effect not of the continuation or elaboration of an initial lyrical impulse, but of a masterfully controlled advance towards a final culminating climax which itself forms the illuminated focal point of the number. The thrusting, forward momentum of Verdi's music is therefore not something confined to the obviously energetic pages of *parlante* and cabaletta. Even the most formalized and sumptuous arias – comparatively primitive ones like 'Dagli immortali vertici' (*Attila*, Act II) and sophisticated ones like 'Ah, fors'è lui' (*La traviata*, Act I) – have an emotional momentum that make them much more theatrically urgent than comparable pieces by Rossini or Bellini. By the end of this period Verdi has already taken this tendency to its ultimate conclusion, and has mastered the art of summarizing and discharging in a single glorious cantabile phrase – unattached to any formal aria – the pent-up emotions of a whole scene: 'Amami Alfredo' (*La traviata*, Act II scene 6) is the *locus classicus*.

This quality in Verdi's melodies is simply one detail in a musical style of thrilling propulsive force. All Italian composers of the period were anxious to reconcile the demands of musical design with those of dramatic action, to make their music more continuous without impairing the momentum of the story; but none compared with Verdi for the energy with which he attacked the problem. From the start he was an exceptionally dynamic composer: he never let the pulse of an individual movement, even of a cantabile, slacken; never allowed the rhythm to vaporize in clouds of *fioritura*. And rarely did he relax his grip on the momentum of scenes between cantabile and cabaletta: freely rhythmical recitatives find no place there, everything is controlled and driven forward on orchestral themes or figurations.

By the time of *Rigoletto* this *velocità* – the term is from Rovani, the *scapigliato* novelist – is being sustained over whole scenes, even over whole acts at a time. Verdi tackles the problem in a variety of ways. The whole of the opening scene is propelled on a suite of dances, which are interrupted only when a significant dramatic point can be made by the interruption – the intervention and denunciation of the Duke by Monterone. Sometimes it is a matter of the dovetailing of the musical numbers: the dramatic action of the Act I finale has already started, and can already be heard to have started, in the coda of Gilda's 'Caro nome'. The amount of recitative, that is to say the amount of music during which Verdi relaxes his grip on the rhythmic thrust of the opera, is radically reduced. After the opening scene of Act II of *Rigoletto* there are only six bars of recitative for the rest of the act.

No aspect of Verdi's music was to develop and change so astonishingly as his use of the orchestra. In the operas he composed at the end of his career, particularly *Falstaff*, the instrumentation has a wit, a panache and refinement which was to enchant even that wizard of orchestral effect, the young Richard Strauss. But at first, Verdi showed little or no real interest in the orchestra as such: it was simply there to provide some extra colour and emphasis for a musical conception that was already complete in all essentials with the composition of the voice/accompaniment short score. Orchestration was a purely mechanical task which he normally began 'only after the piano rehearsals have started' (letter of 9 April 1843, in Abbiati 1959, I: 463).

There are perhaps a few pointers to future development even in the earliest scores. Verdi tends to work the accompaniment patterns harder than Bellini or Donizetti. Sometimes they have something of the fussing complexity of Mercadante (Pagano's aria in *I Lombardi*), and sometimes each element in the text is rhetorically underlined with orchestral figures, rather like the gestures that punctuate some particularly grandiose accompaniment recitatives (the Profezia in Act III of *Nabucco*). As in so many aspects of his art a change of attitude is perceptible after the breakdown he suffered in 1846, particularly with his work on *Macbeth*. From this point he starts to think of the orchestra as a group of instrumental families, rather than as a conglomerate of melody instruments, bass instruments and filling instruments; and he scores for colour and mood, not simply for emphasis. There is a telling comment in the letter to Cammarano about the Naples revival of *Macbeth*: 'The instruments under the stage must [for the large San Carlo theatre] be augmented, but take care that no trumpets or trombones are used. The sound must seem distant and muted, and so only bass clarinets, bassoons, and double bassoons should be used, nothing else' (23 November 1848, in Verdi 1913: 62).

At the same time, while many of his orchestral accompaniments become simpler and more transparent, Verdi begins to show a marvellous aptitude, when some rather special dramatic task faced him, for loading the orchestral figurations with expressive significance. The orchestral accompaniment of Lady Macbeth's sleepwalking-scene is of an expressive density unprecedented in Italian opera, with throbbings and syncopations, creeping chromaticisms and sighs in virtually every bar.

28 · Bellini's *Norma* (Milan 1831)

Aspects of the libretto

Of the seven operas that Bellini composed to texts by Felice Romani, the poet himself judged *Norma* to be 'la più bella rosa della ghirlanda'.[1] As was commonly the case at the time, the poet borrowed the names of his characters and much of the plot from the contemporary French theatre, from Alexandre Soumet's tragedy *Norma*, first performed and published in Paris in 1831, only shortly before he and Bellini began work on their opera. Soumet's play was in turn modelled on more distinguished literary works which Romani knew well, Euripides' *Medea* and Chateaubriand's prose epic *Les martyrs*. Soumet acknowledged the resemblance between his play and *Medea*, and something of the Euripides survives in the opera: the central female figure, a priestess (or enchantress) of profoundly passionate disposition who has been abandoned by the father of her children for a younger woman; both dramas depict a clash of cultures, which the leading male figure (Jason/Pollione) feels in some way justifies his contemptuous indifference to the anguish of his abandoned mistress; she either kills or attempts to bring herself to kill her two sons; in both, the dramatic form is severe, economical, revolving with obsessive single-mindedness round the central figure.

But the ethos of the opera comes from a different source. For Norma is surely Velleda, a legendary priestess of ancient Gaul whom we may properly regard as an archetypal figure for that tangling of Mediterranean and Northern worlds so characteristic of Italian Romanticism. Velleda appeared already in the Classical sources, Tacitus' *Germania* and Statius' *Silvae*, and she returned to the mainstream of European literature in the enthusiasm for 'bardic' literature stimulated by Ossian. Via Klopstock and Kretschmann, Velleda arrived in Italy with Pindemonte's *Arminio* of 1804, and Monti's 'Il bardo della selva nera' of 1806, where she is described as the

> . . . indovina vergine Veleda,
> Cui l'antica paura incensi offria
> Nelle selve Brutere, ove, implorata,
> L'aspra donzella con responsi orrendi
> del temuto avvenir apria l'arcano.[2]   (Rinaldi 1965: 258)

Plate 10 Giulia Grisi as Norma

The transformation of Velleda into a tragic Romantic heroine was the achievement of Chateaubriand, together with Soumet Romani's most important source. In the ninth and tenth books of *Les martyrs* he tells of how the young and beautiful priestess fell in love with and at last succeeded in seducing the Roman soldier Eudore, a Christian. Her story is set in a world of dark Northern forests into which the sun rarely penetrates. Its gloomy character is nowhere better shown than at one of its holy places:

A quelque distance du château, dans un de ces bois appelés chastes par les Druides, on voyait un arbre mort que le fer avait dépouillé de son écorce. Cet espèce de fantôme se faisait distinguer par sa pâleur au milieu des noirs enfoncements de la forêt. Adoré sous le nom d'Irminsul, il était devenu une divinité formidable pour des Barbares qui, dans leurs joies comme dans leur peines, ne savent invoquer que la mort. Autour de ce simulacre, quelques chênes, dont les racines avaient été arrosées de sang humain, portaient suspendues à leur branches les armes et les enseignes de guerre des Gaulois; le vent les agitait sur les rameaux, et elles rendaient, en s'entrechoquant, des murmures sinistres.

In this sombre world, profoundly alien from the values of Mediterranean civilization, women enjoy a peculiar moral and spiritual authority; none more so than the young priestess. But she, even more than Medea, is to be a victim of irreconcilable cultures, of the clash of Gaul and Roman, of Druid and Christian. Her liaison with Eudore sparks off an insurrection against the Roman occupying army, and finally she ritually cuts her own throat to expiate the crime.

An avowed admirer of Chateaubriand, and specifically of his success in bringing 'the bardic harp to resound' in *Les martyrs* (Rinaldi 1965: 262), Romani strove to preserve much of the atmosphere of his work in the opera. A high proportion of its scenes are night scenes. References to the 'selve' or 'boschi' in which the drama is set are ubiquitous, and on several occasions the conflict of Northern and Southern worlds is translated into the metaphors of his poetic imagery. But the racial and religious tensions of Chateaubriand are simplified by the elimination of the Christian element. As so often in drama of the *risorgimento* period the society for which our sympathy is engaged – that of the Gauls – is presented as a priestly-military coalition defending its belief and its traditions against an alien invader. Romani may well have had no ulterior motive in mind, but it is hardly surprising that some of his choral scenes seemed, at certain particularly inflammable stages of the 1830s and 1840s, as provocative as anything in Solera and Verdi:

> Dell'aura tua profetica
> Terribil Dio, l'informa;
> Sensi, o Irminsul, le ispira
> D'odio ai Romani e d'ira.
> Sensi che questa infrangano
> Pace per noi mortal.[3]

(Act I scene 1)

In one of his early essays (in *Perseveranza*, 13 September 1863), Boito recalls that *Norma* was still provoking outbursts of patriotic fervour when he was a student in Milan in 1858 (Nardi 1944: 49).

In the magnificent tragic figure of Norma, Romani has drawn on all his sources. A figure of immense authority in her society, divinely endowed with more than human powers, Norma has in the arms of Pollione succumbed to an all-too-human frailty. The anguish of conscience which she suffers at having betrayed both religious vows and patriotic duty is heightened by the very different anguish she feels as a deserted woman. Proud, aristocratic and autocratic by upbringing, Norma is humbled by love and grief to the point of abasing herself before a man who is unworthy of her, and enduring humiliation before the young girl who is her own protégée. But Romani strikes out on his own too, with stupendous operatic effect, by making his Norma more pathetic, more tender, and ultimately nobler. Unlike Soumet he does not end with a mad-scene, nor does Norma in her own death destroy her children, Medea-like, in order to torture her treacherous lover. More pathos can be wrung from the children by the self-assertion of her maternal love, which moves her ultimately to commend them to the protection of her elderly father Oroveso. And a nobler passion is manifested in a denouement in which she first ensures that Pollione shall die to expiate the wrongs he has committed against the Gauls, and then sacrifices herself on the same pyre.

Though he was the most admired Italian librettist of the Romantic age, Romani was in no sense a formal innovator. In time-honoured fashion he continued to differentiate between recitative verse – which he continued to write in the *versi a selva* style that had been employed for recitative from the very beginnings of opera – and lyrical verse – in which he employed a variety of more regular, rhyming metres. Compared with those of Metastasio, the last poet whose work we examined in any detail, these lyric verses occupy relatively more space. For they are no longer seen as reflections on, or lyrical or passionate appendices to, the phases of the dramatic action; rather do they embody virtually all the high-points of the drama, coinciding sometimes with crises in the action, sometimes with the most illuminating passages of self-revelation. Their metrical range is surprisingly restricted. The *settenari* and *ottonari* that were Metastasio's favourites are Romani's favourites too. He uses *quinari accoppiati* extensively in the closing scene, and that too was a Metastasian commonplace. Only in one respect does the librettist seem to be in the vanguard of fashion. In two choruses, 'Norma viene' (Act I scene 3) and 'Guerra, guerra' (Act II scene 7), he makes use of *decasillabi* in the anapaestic form that Manzoni, thanks to such poems as 'Marzo 1821', had brought into favour as a vehicle of patriotic exaltation.

Guerra, guerra! Le galliche selve
Quante han querce producon guerrier;
Qual sul gregge fameliche belve
Sui Romani van essi a cader . . .[4]

It has to be said that Bellini found little rhythmic stimulation in these galloping dithyrambs.

Poetic structure and musical structure

In the schemes of metre and rhyme employed by the poet there are very clear implications for the structure of the music. And as these implications were well understood by all opera composers, it is no surprise when the musical organization of the score turns out exactly as Romani must have anticipated. The second scene of Act I, Pollione's recitative and cavatina, 'Meco all'altar di Venere', is a case in point. Twenty-one lines of *versi a selva* are set as recitative, three eight-line stanzas of *settenari* as a cantabile; a further eight lines of *settenari* in dialogue were clearly designed to provide for a *tempo di mezzo*, which is how Bellini treats them, and a final eight-line stanza of *ottonari* supplies the cabaletta.

But such literal correspondences as these are in fact rather rare. In the hundred years since the heyday of Metastasian opera the composer had increasingly asserted his claim to be the real dramatist in the opera-house, and therefore the person who had the ultimate say in the fashioning of the operatic form. Even when he worked closely with his librettist, as Bellini did with Romani, he was likely to want to give certain dramatic ideas a more vivid embodiment than the librettist had necessarily envisaged, and this meant drawing structural implications from the libretto which its author had not foreseen.

A fine example is provided by Norma's great *aria di sortita* 'Casta Diva'. In the broadest outline the musical and poetic structures again correspond. But the cantabile in this scene is a *preghiera*, a prayer that accompanies the rituals associated with the cutting of the sacred mistletoe and the worship of the moon. Bellini therefore resolved that its scale must be grandly expanded. He split Romani's eight-line text into two four-line verses and set each to the same full-scale cantabile melody to form the outer pillars of a huge three-part structure. The central episode in the design is provided by the chorus, for whose contrasting strain Bellini repeated the complete first quatrain of Norma's text – Romani's libretto had simply provided two lines of endorsement at the very close of the cantabile. Furthermore, the greater part of Norma's cantabile is also played in the form of an orchestral prelude, a section of the design that is far more extended than usual because Bellini obviously conceived it not simply as the introduction to an aria, but as music for a solemn pantomine.

Often the freedoms which Bellini allows himself are prompted by what appears to have been a lack of interest in the *parlante* style, a reluctance to propel the drama on the symphonic momentum of the orchestra. For Bellini it was the poetic word, conjured into declamation or song, that was the determining factor in the pacing of the operatic action. In Act II scene 3 (*scena* and duet for Norma and Adalgisa) I think we must suppose that the switch from *versi a selva* to *ottonari* at 'Deh! con te, con te li prendi' was intended by Romani to mark the start of a *primo tempo*. What he surely would not have envisaged was that the composer would set most of the *ottonari* as a kind of premature cabaletta. For although in the libretto Adalgisa does have a long solo to follow Norma's, the layout and the rhyme-scheme of the verses do not suggest that they were intended to match 'Deh! con te'. Where Romani would have anticipated a freer, *parlante*-based continuity in the first part of the scene, breaking into formal aria only at the matching lyrics 'Mira, o Norma, a'tuoi ginocchi / Ah! perchè la mia costanza', Bellini has characteristically written a symmetrical, song-based form.

More commonly Bellini plays down the *parlante* style in favour of a more mercurial succession of figurations and textures, intent, it would seem, on expressing each fleeting element in the text in the way he feels matches it best. In the text of the *scena ultima*, the first aria section ('Qual cor tradisti'), in *quinari accoppiati*, is followed by some twenty lines of *settenari* in agitated dialogue form, which are clearly intended to function as a *tempo di mezzo*. Bellini breaks up their continuity into four distinct phases:

(i) an episode of urgent, agitated declamation ('Norma! . . . deh! Norma! scolpati . . .')
(ii) a brief *parlante* based on the reprise of an orchestral theme first heard in Act I in association with Norma's children ('Cielo! e i miei figli?')
(iii) a quite different slow lyrical *parlante* for Norma's confession ('Tu m'odi')
(iv) the start of a cantabile for her prayer to Oroveso ('Deh! non voler li vittime')

This last is perhaps the most quintessentially Bellinian touch, for he fuses the closing lines of these *settenari*, a six-line stanza of *quinari accoppiati*, and indeed a series of *ottonari* stanzas into one single musical form, drawing out the tears and pathos and despair of the catastrophe in one long, sustained ecstatic cantabile.

In all these scenes Bellini is approaching a conception of operatic structure that was to become increasingly important in the next thirty years, according to which the operatic forms are not merely conventional patterns of tried effectiveness, but may themselves function as an essential element in the dramatic expression. In a few superb scenes in *Norma*, notably the first of the Norma–Adalgisa duets, this aspiration is fully achieved.

The first movement of the duet is more correctly thought of as a solo cantabile for Adalgisa, 'Sola, furtiva, al tempio'. But Norma adds a commentary to her companion's song, is eventually caught up in it herself, and rounds out each verse by continuing Adalgisa's major-key cadence phrase in more exalted and lingering fashion. It is not difficult to see where the inspiration came from for Bellini's wonderful handling of the structure of this movement. It came both from the dramatic irony of the situation (Adalgisa is describing an experience that Norma, to her shame, has shared), and from Romani's masterly handling of the details of the versification. For even during the recitative Norma is beginning to comment 'aside' on Adalgisa's words, is already experiencing in recollection the emotions that her young friend is about to distil in song. That is why the aria actually starts while the recitative conversation is still continuing. The last phrases of recitative are superimposed on a long orchestral prelude which anticipates the theme of the aria; and this superimposition of recitative dialogue and aria introduction shows that 'Sola, furtiva, al tempio' is as much the music of Norma's heart as it is of Adalgisa's (see Ex.V.12).

Adalgisa's aria-text is in *settenari*. Romani had the happy inspiration of keeping Norma's occasional comments in *endecasillabi* – keeping them, that is, in recitative verse. He places them at the chief interstices of the design – after the first quatrain and at the close of the first verse, and at the close of the second verse, this last time no longer 'aside'. Bellini in fact distributes these asides rather more freely than Romani's verse structure implies, but surely does so only because the metre has suggested that they be set in *parlando* rather than in the same cantabile idiom as Adalgisa herself employs.

One last detail in this scene: Norma's last comment, that is to say the coda to the second verse, 'Ah tergi il pianto', is addressed to Adalgisa and prompts a moment of intimate dialogue. But Romani has provided no text for a *tempo di mezzo*, so Bellini himself appropriates a few words from the cabaletta text to transform the final stages of the *cantabile* into a transition into the cabaletta. The whole movement is thus a wonderful example of how in Bellini's hands a *bel canto* aria can materialize out of the action with uncompromising dramatic truthfulness and in due course evolve and flow on into the next phase of the action.

Resisting German influence

The testimony of both Florimo and Glinka confirms that Bellini knew and admired much German instrumental music. But the comparative dearth of orchestrally based *parlante* episodes in *Norma* suggests that he may have had doubts, despite the distinguished precedent of Rossini, about the desirability of adapting anything resembling a symphonic style to operatic

Ex.V.12 Bellini, *Norma* (1831), Act I scene 8

521

(Oh memory! [absent-mindedly] Exactly so was I entranced simply to
behold his face.) But. . .are you not listening to me? Carry on. . .
I'm listening. Alone, secretly, to the temple. . .

Ex.V.12 *continued*

use. When, further, we recall Verdi's comments on what he felt to be the
weakness of Bellini's harmony and orchestration (Verdi 1913: 415–16) we
may begin to suspect that, of all Italian opera composers of the Romantic
age, Bellini was most sceptical about the advisability of absorbing 'Germanic' features of style.

As a matter of fact, the scene that Verdi criticized – the opening of the
Act I *Introduzione* – is one of Bellini's most conscientious attempts at
atmospheric scoring. Set against the opening of the Nile scene in *Aida* it
will indeed seem a pedestrian essay in nocturnal tone-painting. But if
Bellini shows no very imaginative sense of what an orchestral fabric might
be, the instrumental colours themselves – low horns and bassoons, *divisi*
violas and 'cellos over a double-bass foundation – are selected with some
sense of gloomy decorum.

But not even within the accepted conventions of Italian operatic scoring is Bellini notably craftsmanlike or resourceful, as Donizetti or Mercadante are. The string writing in his aria accompaniments is, for example, almost startlingly functional; over and over again 'cellos and double-basses provide a bass line, violas sustain the harmony, and first and second violins march or dance or sway above them. Meanwhile the woodwind instruments either sustain the harmonies or they don't: only rarely – in 'Sola, furtiva, al tempio' for example – are they used to colour certain selected harmonic turns or progressions, as was to become standard practice with Verdi. When used as melody instruments the woodwinds are seldom chosen to lend a particular mood to the music – as the cool sacral flute is chosen for 'Casta Diva'. More often they are used generically, as in 'Meco all'altar di Venere', where the chattering descant is scored for clarinets, oboes, flute and piccolo more or less indiscriminately, depending rather on the volume or density required than on colour.

Bellini's instrumentation has its quirks, of which the most striking is surely a bizarrely reckless use of trombones, now as a means of accentuation, now to lend a suggestion of portentousness (even in recitatives), now as daubs of inspissated blackness (in the deranged coda of 'Meco all'altar di Venere'). It has its inspirations too, such as the ominous rumble of timpani punctuating the pure string sound in the see-sawing accompaniment of 'Qual cor tradisti'. But it may be asserted that compared with the scores of his Italian contemporaries, let alone of German or French contemporaries, Bellini's show a singular lack of concern for orchestral sophistication. It may also be asserted that this orchestral 'nudity' is better regarded as a deliberate reaction against the orchestral virtuosity of Rossini than as an incidental deficiency. For Bellini's mission was to lead Italian opera back away from the seductions of tone-painting, or virtuosity, or musical science, and to restore dramatic song as an art of incantation.

Bellini's harmony lends itself even less well to systematic description than does his orchestration. There are times when his grip on the very grammar of harmony seems precarious; in any event, during recitatives he is prepared to use startling or uncouth progressions as rhetorical gestures for dramatic effect, as at Pollione's interruption of Adalgisa's prayer in Act I scene 6 (Ex.V.13). The $\frac{6}{4}$ chords in another of these curious little progressions tempt us to surmise that Verdi may have found suggestions for his own wonderfully idiosyncratic harmony in Bellini (Ex.V.14). Conversely some of the sublimest pages in *Norma* are sustained on a vocabulary of four or five basic chords. The music in such instances acquires its high charge of expressiveness not from the harmony itself, but from the relationship of the melody to the harmony, and particularly from the multitude of dissonant appoggiaturas with which a Bellini melody tends to be laden: appoggiaturas down and appoggiaturas up, chromatic appoggiaturas and double appoggiaturas and irregularly resolved appoggiaturas.

There she is! Go, leave me, I will not hear reason. [Flavio exits]
[dismayed] Oh!. . .you here! What do I see!. . .

Ex.V.13 Bellini, *Norma* (1831), Act I scene 6

'Casta Diva' shows the potentialities of the style, not only in the glorious cantabile of the soloist, but, more unexpectedly, in the central interlude too, where the caressing thirds of the chorus sway along more or less ignoring the slowly moving harmonies that throb in the background (Ex.V.15).

As with the bareness of his orchestration, one suspects that Bellini's

già tur - ba - to è il se - re - no?...

. . .already the calm is disturbed?

Ex.V.14 Bellini, *Norma* (1831), Act I scene 8

harmonic language is in large measure a renunciation of distractions. For where the use of an extended harmonic vocabulary, including dense chromaticism, does not threaten the supremacy of song, he proves an adept. There is, for instance, much chromaticism in the orchestral prelude to the *Introduzione*, where it is used to sharpen up the sighing appoggiaturas, to make the cadences more emphatic, to give a more sombre expressive tone to some of the melodic lines. In the *scena* preceding 'Qual cor tradisti' in the Act II finale Bellini shows that he can sustain chromatic harmonic progressions at very considerable length as an instrument of tension. And the climaxes of 'Casta Diva' or of 'Deh! non volerli vittime' (Act II finale) show that he also appreciated the role that chromatic harmony might play in creating that sheer ecstasy of sound that is one of his most personal contributions to romantic opera. Lippmann hears in the rising sequences of the latter one of the sources of Wagner's '*Tristan*-chromaticism' (Adamo and Lippmann 1981: 488).

Drama, rhetoric and incantation

In the fifteen years preceding the composition of *Norma* the old *secco* recitative had given way entirely, in serious opera at least, to recitative accompanied by the orchestra. But the dissolution of the boundaries between recitative and song had not progressed far, and it is fully understandable that, outside the lyrical numbers, Bellini still draws heavily on the old traditions of the *recitativo accompagnato* for much of the dramatic force and the expressive eloquence of his scenes. It remains very generally the case that voice and instruments alternate, that the words are delivered into the silence, but that the mood of this silence has been prepared or the sense of the words will be reinforced by short orchestral interjections. Bellini does not disdain the most conventional eighteenth-century *topoi*, as where Pollione, in his first *scena*, imagines himself plunging into the abyss;

Ex. V.15 Bellini, *Norma* (1831), Act I scene 4

. . .beauteous visage without cloud and without veil. Chaste goddess, who
bathe in silver these ancient forests, turn on us your beauteous visage. . .

Ex.V.15 *continued*

but he fashions original ones too, as in the opening *scena* of Act II where at
'Non posso avvicinarmi' the musical movement is frozen in a hand-
wringing, sighing paralysis (Ex.V.16). And though the orchestra is allowed
no finery and is kept strictly in its place, it is, in some of the instrumental
preludes, learning to speak more vividly. Much is suggested, for example,

in the prelude to the Adalgisa–Pollione duet in Act I – the silence and stillness of the scene; Adalgisa's furtive tiptoeing entrance; perhaps, in the flute and clarinet cantilena, the voice of tender passion that keeps calling her back to this place 'dove a me s'offerse la prima volta quel fatal romano';[5] moral anguish in the chromatic cadence phrase.

The Rossinian days of carefree music-making are over; for with Bellini, as his contemporaries never ceased to insist, a 'philosopher' has entered the Italian opera-house. He is a composer who never adopts a particular manner, never aims to create a special effect, never takes up any musical idea unless he is satisfied that some dramatic or poetic truth is thereby illuminated. The coloratura that Rossini with his prodigious *joie de vivre* scattered broadcast all over an opera becomes, on its rare appearance in *Norma*, the vehicle by which woman transforms herself into fury (Ex.V.17). Despite the large number of duets, Bellini only once composes a cadenza à 2, and that is at the close of 'Ah sì, fa core, abbracciami', when it can serve as the symbol of the most complete and intimate mutual understanding. Not even the most seemingly conventional numbers betray

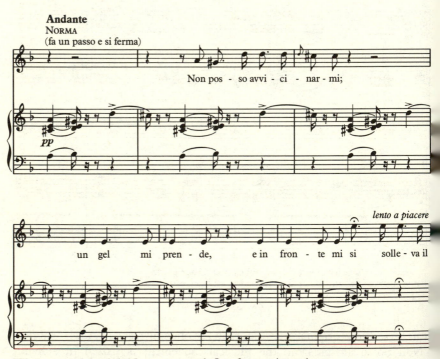

[Takes a step and then halts] I cannot approach; I am frozen to ice, and on my brow [my hair] stands on end.

Ex.V.16 Bellini, *Norma* (1831), Act II scene 1

NORMA (Voice only)
con tutta forza

Oh non tre - ma - re, oh non trema - re, o __

per - fi - do, no, non __ tre - ma - re, ah __

non tre - mar per le - i . . .

Oh, do not tremble, perjured man; no, do not tremble for her. . .

Ex.V.17 Bellini, *Norma* (1831), Act I scene 9

any lapse in Bellini's philosophical intentions, as we may see from the case of Pollione's cabaletta 'Me protegge, me difende'.

At the close of the *tempo di mezzo* Pollione collects himself, determined to defy all the supernatural powers that infest these Northern forests. This summoning of his inner resources is suggested by a thematic introduction, and the fact that he is explicitly defying the powers whose voice we have just heard off-stage is suggested by a cabaletta melody that seems intended to trump the march of Norma and the Druids. It has the same strutting rhythm, the same vaulting arpeggio shapes, but a more brilliant élan; in the second half, as in the second half of the march, the contours veer up again and again like a clenched fist. At the end of each quatrain Bellini breaks out from the march rhythm with great rhetorical effect, first with a fragrant and vulnerable turn to G minor at thoughts of love; then with an angry downsmashing cadence at 'L'empio altare abbatterò'.

For all these dramatically truthful elements one remains very aware of the fact that Pollione's cabaletta is a formal set-piece. In the finest movements of the opera this ceases to be the case: the music becomes an embodiment of the drama, responds to its needs with wondrous flexibility; situation, character, poetry all seem to have been conjured into song.

'In mia man' is one of the several movements where Bellini superimposes upon the structure of Romani's verses a rather different structure of his own, as the following diagram will make clear:

Verse	a b a b	c c d d	e f e f ‖ a b	a b c c	d d e f	e f
Music	a b c d	a b c d	E a b c d	F g g	H I	‖ *tempo di mezzo*
(Key)	I	I	V I	VI	I	

529

In performance one cannot fail to sense how absolutely right the composer's apparent high-handedness is. The stillness, the tension, the stalemate of wills mirrored in the motionless calm of no fewer than twenty-six bars without a hint of modulation; the sudden vision of freedom, of escape, as the music opens up to the dominant C major; the inexorable return to the tonic and the opening theme as Pollione declines the bargain; the turn to D minor and the gradual acceleration in the delivery of the words as Norma begins to realize that she must despair of conquering Pollione's will – all these things represent a perfect fusion of music and meaning. Moreover the text is presented with a wonderful vividness. The melody is sculpted round the words and loses nothing by being broken up into dialogue (Ex.V.18); crucial phrases are highlighted by tessitura ('Adalgisa fuggirai'), by 'madrigalisms' ('Ch'ei piombi attendo'), by rhetorical repetitions ('mai più, mai più'). In short, it is a magnificent example of that kind of music 'which we do not well know whether we should call sung declamation or declamatory song' (Bellini 1943: 196). And with the idea of 'speaking' melody we are close to the heart of Bellini's art.

These speaking melodies are everywhere. Yet Bellini's determination to give so many of his arias a declamatory character does not in the least impair their lyrical beauty. No more glorious melody ever graced an opera than that of the cantabile of the first Norma–Adalgisa duet; but it is full of these 'speaking' touches – the recitative-like, commaed-off fragments in the opening bar and at 'Vieni, ei dicea', the enjambement and turn to the major key at 'più fervida crebbe la fiamma ardente', and a tonal scheme that vividly underlines the urgent passion of Pollione's remembered words. Not infrequently, as in the arioso 'Teneri figli' at the start of Act II, the melody not only speaks, it gestures – one might almost say it acts. For in the opening phrase it seems to bow down over the sleeping children, while exactly at 'il cui sorriso' it takes a smiling turn to the major key, against which the voice tugs with a long, bitter-sweet appoggiatura.

Often Bellini likes to thicken out his melodies in parallel thirds or sixths. In some of the more declamatory pieces, such as 'Oh! di qual sei tu vittima', this may be felt to give the line a more emphatic density. But it has another effect: to give the music a solemn sweetness that has more to do with enchantment than with drama; and this element of enchantment plays no small part in Bellini's work. We remember his words to Pepoli: 'the music drama must make people weep, shudder with terror, and die, through singing' (1943: 400). Bellini was, I believe, the last composer of opera fully to recognize that song was not just a means to a dramatic end but a magical power. It is song as incantation – swaying rhythms, sensuously rising chromatic sequences, climactic melodic unisons – that transfigures the horrible catastrophe of the opera and has the power to dissolve performers and spectators alike into one of those communal ecstasies which Glinka

Bellini's *Norma*

At last you are in my hands; no one can break your bonds. I can do it.
You must not. I want to do it. And how? Listen. By your God. . .

Ex.V.18 Bellini, *Norma* (1831), Act II scene 10

witnessed (see p. 398). 'Casta Diva', one of those famous Bellinian 'melodie lunghe, lunghe, lunghe',[6] also has this power. This is not a 'speaking' melody at all; the delivery of the text is notably slow. And while the word-repetitions and ceremonious flourishes of the song may suggest the fervent ritual gestures and genuflections of a priestly celebrant it is not so much a staged action we are experiencing as a spell. The singing draws us up into an enchanted vision-world that resounds with harmony – the slow throbbing chords of the orchestra, the entranced murmuring of the chorus, the ethereal, incantatory ululations of Norma herself.

German Romantics like E. T. A. Hoffmann were inclined to believe that instrumental music served best as 'the language of the unknown Romantic spirit world', transporting the listener 'through the ivory gate into the kingdom of dreams'. We may feel that of the Italian opera composers of the *primo ottocento* Bellini must be counted the supreme Romantic, because he showed that song too had this mysterious, irrational power, a magic beyond the understanding of words.

Part VI
Cosmopolitanism and decadence

29 · Italian grand opera

The background to Verdi's later operas

The operatic activity described in this final section of my book took place against a backcloth of the most dramatic events in the modern history of Italy: national independence was achieved; Italy became a colonial power; she was sucked up into the First World War; Mussolini's Fascist state was established. While not a lot of this need concern us, some political and social developments certainly did bear upon the story of opera.

When Verdi composed *Rigoletto*, *Il trovatore* and *La traviata*, the three masterpieces that brought Romantic melodrama to its perfection in the early 1850s, the effects of all the revolutionary upheavals of the years 1848–49 had seemingly been eradicated. Italy remained 'a geographical expression', its political life fragmented and incoherent; for the legitimist status quo inherited from the Congress of Vienna in 1815 had been restored and reasserted.

But during the 1850s, under the brilliant leadership of Count Camillo Cavour, there emerged in Piedmont the first truly modern Italian state. Piedmont led all other regions of Italy in the scientific improvement of agriculture, in the building of railways, in the establishment of a capitalist economy under the aegis of a National Bank. When during this same decade, Mazzini's last attempt at republican revolution failed, Piedmont – the heartland of the Savoy monarchy – found itself the focus of virtually all unitive, nationalist aspirations. In September 1855 Daniel Manin, a Venetian republican, issued a proclamation in *The Times* of London and the Paris newspaper *Siècle* which captured nobly the spirit of the age:

Convinced that above all Italy must be made, that this is the first and most important question, we say to the Monarchy of Savoy: 'Make Italy and we are with you. – If not, not.'

And to the constitutionalists we say: 'Think about making Italy and not of enlarging Piedmont; be Italians and not municipalists, and we are with you. – If not, not.'

I think it is time to give up existing party divisions based on purely secondary differences; the principal, vital matter is whether we are of the unifying nationalist school of thought, or whether we belong to the separatist, municipalist school.

I, a republican, raise the banner of unity. If all those who want Italy gather round and defend it, then *Italy will be*.   (Mack-Smith 1968: 215)

Between the spring of 1859 and the spring of 1861, in a sudden tremendous surge of events prompted by the somewhat uneasy co-ordination of Cavour's political acumen and Garibaldi's charismatic military leadership, the unification of Italy was indeed achieved: each of its erstwhile kingdoms, duchies and provinces, excepting only Venetia and Rome, made fealty to the Savoy monarchy of Piedmont; and Venetia and Rome were acquired during the following decade. But even as the unification of Italy was being accomplished, a severe blow to the integrity of the new state came with the publication in 1864 of a papal Syllabus of Errors. Pius IX declared the Church's hostility to liberalism, and brought about an alienation between religious and political life that was not be be resolved until Mussolini's concordat with the Vatican in 1929.

Italy's first national government (1861–76) was in the hands of men of the most austere integrity. Since they were obsessed with financial rectitude, with paying off the nation's debts and balancing its budget, severe taxation was inevitable. In fact Italy rapidly became the most heavily taxed state in Europe. Altogether its problems were formidable. Some of its proudest spirits – the elderly Mazzini among them – found themselves profoundly disillusioned by the processes of compromise, opportunism and improvisation through which the new Italy had come into being. And with the best will in the world the task of fusing into a single civility the progressive and the backward, the prosperous and the poverty-stricken, the democratic republican and the quasi-feudal was bound to prove infinitely laborious; the more so as the various disparate regions had barely so much as a language in common.

New and vast burdens of responsibility devolved upon the Italian people. And this had a profound effect on the theatre as an institution: never again after 1848–49 was it to hold quite such a central place in national and civic life. As early as 1850 the owners of the Pergola theatre in Florence were bewailing the fact that politics was taking young people away from the theatre (Rosselli 1984: 169). There was as a result less interest, less excitement occasioned by new operas than in the past – unless they were by Verdi. Gradually the productivity of the operatic industry declined, and during the period 1850 to 1880 most theatres came to depend more and more heavily on an established repertory of classics.

During the same period one new development was healthy in at least one sense: the building in several cities of huge new theatres, of which the Teatro Dal Verme in Milan (1864) and the Teatro Costanzi in Rome (1880) were to be artistically the most noteworthy. These theatres were unsubsidized, and they offered – among much else – opera at cut prices to genuinely popular audiences. But while they played a part in diffusing still further the already widespread enthusiasm for Verdi, Donizetti, Bellini and Rossini, they did nothing to counteract the tendency towards a hardening and narrowing repertory, and nothing to encourage original and imaginative new scores.

By 1861 the omens were clear to Verdi: the Italian theatre was in a chronically unhealthy state. And when, early that year, he was elected parliamentary deputy for Borgo San Donnino (now Fidenza), he promptly presented Cavour with some radical proposals for its reorganization. What he wanted to see was opera-houses which, relieved of their financial worries by state subsidies, would be able to combine the highest artistic standards, the encouragement of new talent, and a kind of proselytizing social work. He recalled his scheme in a letter to Opprandino Arrivabene some fifteen years later:

I perfectly agree that the theatres of Italy must have regular orchestras and choruses, salaried by the government and the city halls. As early as '61 I proposed the following to Cavour for the three principal theatres of Italy [in the capital, Milan and Naples]: chorus and orchestra salaried by the government; evening classes in voice for the people (gratis) with the obligation that they lend their service to the local theatre; the three conservatories of the above-mentioned cities tied to the theatre, with mutual obligations between theatre and conservatory. The programme could have been realized, had Cavour lived, with other ministers it's impossible. (Busch 1978: 390)

As the Italian government struggled to solve its economic problems, there was indeed no hope of so idealistic a scheme being realized. In fact such subsidies as theatres did enjoy were withdrawn, not augmented; and new taxes were imposed on them. During the 1860s and 70s most opera-houses reeled from one financial crisis to another. Verdi was much struck by the irony of the situation when, on the death of Rossini in 1868, it was proposed that he should receive a state funeral and that a monument should be erected to him in Santa Croce in Florence, the national pantheon:

. . . the government's idea is a noble and fine one . . . And yet, when I recall that this same government has disclaimed responsibility for the conservatories, withdraws its subsidy from the theatres, imposes a tax on admission, another on contracts, so rendering impossible the practice of the art which Rossini represented, then these honours seem to me a mockery, an affectation of feeling, an hypocrisy and worse! (Verdi 1913: 206)

After Unification, responsibility for subsidizing opera-houses had shifted from the state to the local town councils. Their resources were quite unequal to the task, the more so as opera had become, and was continuing to become, steadily more grandiose, complex and expensive to stage. The story of Italian opera in the 1870s is a melancholy chronicle of curtailed seasons, bankruptcies and closures. Not even theatres with proud artistic records stretching back for generations were spared. Verdi was profoundly pessimistic: 'our theatre is sick unto death and it must be kept alive at all costs . . . If theatres close they won't open again' (Budden 1973–81, III: 270).

In December 1870 Mercadante died. For the previous thirty years he had been the deeply reactionary Director of the Conservatory in Naples, the most glorious of all Italy's institutions for advanced musical training. Only a few years earlier the government had seriously considered washing its hands of musical education altogether. But now it was persuaded that it would be opportune to set up a commission to investigate all the Italian conservatories of music and, where necessary, make proposals for reform.

Early in 1871 Verdi, in the thick of his work on *Aida*, received two invitations. One came from Florimo and the professors of the Naples Conservatory urging him to accept the directorship in succession to Mercadante; the other, from the Ministry of Education, asked him to serve as chairman of the investigating commission. Initially Verdi declined both; subsequently he was persuaded by his good friend Piroli – parliamentary deputy for Parma – that it would be very much in the public interest if he did involve himself in the discussions about the future of musical education. But even before he had reached the point of agreeing, the invitations prompted Verdi to examine afresh his views on this question; and he recorded them in letters to both Florimo and Piroli.

Verdi's attitude is interesting and predictably individual; indeed we might say that by the standards of the 1870s it is rather extraordinary, not notably more progressive than Mercadante's, which is not to say that it may not be wise. It remained his conviction that, whatever the case elsewhere, in Italy the musical health of the nation depended not upon conservatories but upon theatres, and he reiterated what he had told Cavour ten years earlier. Basically the conservatories should be left alone; government money should be invested rather in supporting the ailing opera-houses. When Florimo, on behalf of Naples, and Piroli, on behalf of the government, pressed him further, he elaborated on the topic of musical education. Both letters are deeply characteristic; I quote from that to Piroli:

. . . I shall speak only of the *composer* and the *singer*, because I believe that as far as instrumental performance is concerned (which has always given excellent results) there is little to reform.

For the young composer then, I would wish very long and strict studies in all branches of counterpoint.

Studies of old music, sacred and secular. But one should note that, even among the ancients, not everything is beautiful, so one has to be selective.

No study of the moderns! This will seem strange to many; but when I hear and see today so many works made as bad tailors make clothes after a pattern, I cannot change my opinion . . . When the young composer has completed strict studies, when he has found his style and has confidence in his own powers, then, if it is wished, he can very well study these (modern) pieces, with no danger of becoming an imitator. It could be objected: 'who will teach the young man to orchestrate? Who will teach him imaginative composition?' His head and his heart, if he has one.

For the *singer* I would wish: an extensive knowledge of music, exercises in voice production; a very long study of *solfeggio* as in the past; exercises in singing words with a clear and perfect pronunciation. Then, without any *maestro di perfezionamento* to teach him singers' affectations, I would like the youngster, thoroughly grounded in music and with a well trained and flexible throat, to sing guided by nothing but his own feelings. That would not be academic singing, but inspired singing. The artist would be an individual, he would be *himself* or, better still, he would be the character he has to represent in the opera.

I don't need to say that these musical studies must be combined with a wide literary culture . . .   (Verdi 1913: 249–50)

Needless to say, Verdi's views were too idiosyncratic to meet with general assent. The conservatories were reorganized, and they were brought up to date rather than, in Verdi's famous phrase to Florimo, 'progressing by returning to the past'. Nothing received higher priority than the acquisition of those orchestral skills that Verdi regarded as a private matter for the composer's own head. A new model conservatory was established at Pesaro with money left by Rossini.

Music publishers

During the 1840s a new factor had been introduced into the workings of the Italian opera industry by the publisher Francesco Lucca. Hitherto new works had normally been commissioned by an impresario for production in a particular theatre during a particular season. Lucca developed the habit of commissioning operas for his own publishing house. (Verdi's *Attila*, Venice 1846, and *Il corsaro*, Trieste 1848, are early examples.) He then made himself responsible for choosing the theatre, negotiating with the impresario and supervising the production. Rosselli discerns two factors that encouraged this practice. One was the trend toward repertory opera, 'which meant an increasing demand for the hire of orchestral scores', the other the introduction in 1840 of a measure of copyright protections, 'which in the end suppressed piracy and made exclusive rights in a score worth paying for' (Rosselli 1984: 174).

Lucca's initiative obviously tended to reduce the power and influence of the impresario, and to increase correspondingly that of the publisher. It was not long before Lucca's great rival, the House of Ricordi, followed suit. The third of the line, Giulio Ricordi (b. 1840), was to play a leading part in the preparation and production of all Verdi's later operas, and of all those of Puccini that appeared before his death in 1912. The time, energy and worry both Verdi and Puccini were spared by Ricordi is incalculable. But there was an obverse side to the picture. Without the enthusiastic support of a publisher, life could be more difficult for a composer – as Catalani was to find; for there was no longer the direct commissioning link between him and the theatre.

By the closing decades of the century Ricordi was exerting an influence on the course of Italian opera second to no one. He was a man of parts:

linguist, poet and critic, artist and composer (under the name of Burgmein) of drawing-room pieces, orchestral works, a ballet and an opera; soldier, businessman and negotiator of formidable energy and flair. The journalist Giuseppe Depanis left a vivid memoir of 'Sör Giüli' in his prime:

Small in stature, trim, spare, Giulio Ricordi . . . possessed a lively mind together with a vast culture . . . Firm in his likes and dislikes, tirelessly active, he was present everywhere and saw to everything. In his study there was a continual procession of composers, librettists, singers, conductors, agents and impresarios. His manner was somewhat reserved, with something of the aristocrat and the soldier in it; he would settle a business affair in a few words; from hearing a budding prima donna he would pass with a certain weary elegance to the sampling of a new score. First impressions were decisive; and he was rarely prepared to change his mind; artists and composers who were perfectly aware of this would solicit his judgement with a kind of holy terror . . . A valued friend – and a formidable opponent. (Budden 1973–81, III: 297)

After some youthful flirting with *scapigliatura* (see Chapter 30 below) and a certain amount of whoring after strange gods in the early 1860s, Giulio Ricordi – like his father Tito and his grandfather Giovanni before him – became a devoted admirer of Verdi; and not merely because, as Verdi had frankly put it to Tito, 'I am in large part the origin of your colossal fortune' (letter of 24 October 1855, in Verdi 1913: 168). Ricordi came, in fact, to feel a deep, atavistic reverence for the magnificent proclamation of *italianità* he heard in Verdi's music, and the nurture of his genius became the primary mission of his middle years. It is at the very least questionable whether *Otello* and *Falstaff* would ever have come into being without his patient, devoted and resourceful support. In later life he played the same crucial role in Puccini's career, becoming, in Puccini's own words, 'the only person who inspires me with trust, and to whom I can confide all that is going through my mind' (Carner 1974: 51).

One other publisher played a notable part in Italian operatic life in the second half of the century. Edoardo Sonzogno had also been a *scapigliato*. He came of a wealthy family of Milan industrialists, owned the Teatro Lirico in the same city, and published – as did Lucca and Ricordi – his own house journal. But his particular contribution was to have established a fashion for one-act operas by the introduction of the Sonzogno competition for young composers. Notable works occasioned by this venture include Puccini's first, *Le villi* (Milan 1884), and most famously and influentially Mascagni's *Cavalleria rusticana* (Rome 1890).

Relations with the Paris Opéra

A rapprochement with French grand opera was the crucial development in Italian music in the 1850s and 60s. From *Les vêpres siciliennes* (Paris 1855) – Verdi's most purely French work, written in collaboration with the old wizard of Parisian theatrical knowhow, Eugène Scribe – to *Aida* (Cairo

1871) – in which grand opera is exalted to an unprecedented sublimity and purity – the influence of the Opéra is unmistakable.

For Verdi, who had brought Italian Romantic melodrama to a thrilling perfection in the early 1850s, the attraction was understandable. He was not a composer who was happy to repeat himself. By 1852, when he signed the contract for *Les vêpres siciliennes*, he was certainly ready for wider horizons, for fresh ways of approaching the organization of musical form, for the stimulus of a chorus and orchestra used to working at levels of sophistication that were no part of the Italian tradition. Perhaps, too, he was dimly conscious of a wish to challenge Meyerbeer, the one contemporary (as yet!) he seriously recognized as a rival.

A rival, in Verdi's eyes, meant a composer whose works triumphed in the theatre – unlike those of the only dimly cognized Wagner. Meyerbeer's operas and those of his followers were doing that increasingly, even in Italy, which, until the 1850s, had contented itself with a repertory of almost exclusively native works. During the 1840s *Robert le diable* had been introduced to several leading theatres, including Florence, Venice, Parma and Milan. *Les Huguenots* followed it at a distance of a few years. Both operas became standard repertory items after Mariani took them up at Genoa, in 1852 and 1857 respectively. They were, far more than any Italian opera, magnificent vehicles for the country's first virtuoso conductor, and by the 1870s, together with Halévy's *La Juive*, they rivalled Verdi's best-loved works in popularity.

The rarity value of Meyerbeer's grand operas – he produced just four of them between 1831 and his death in 1864 – and the all-embracing sumptuousness of their format gave to performances of them a kind of festival solemnity hitherto rare in the Italian opera-house. But gradually Verdi's own operas began to acquire something of the same quality. He was successful and prosperous, able to relax the relentless routine of the 'galley years' a little, to compose what he wanted, when he wanted. By now, many of the commissions that most attracted him – on both artistic and financial grounds – were coming from abroad. *Les vêpres siciliennes* and *Don Carlos* (1867) were both for Paris; *La forza del destino* (1862) for St Petersburg, *Aida* (1871) for Cairo. Such operas had a solemnity of purpose and aspired to an international prestige in a way that reminds us of the old court operas of Vienna or Stuttgart; it was an attitude which encouraged the Meyerbeerian manner. Given Verdi's example, and given the fact that the rate at which new operas were commissioned was slowing down conspicuously by the end of the 1850s, such lesser contemporaries as Filippo Marchetti, the Brazilian A. Carlos Gomes – resident in Italy for many years from 1864 – and especially Amilcare Ponchielli likewise found the grand opera format irresistible.

None of these composers – Verdi least of all – was content with servile imitation of the splendour and sophistication of Parisian grand opera. Verdi's attitude to the Opéra was in fact deeply equivocal. No other theatre, he declared in 1852, had caused him such boredom and irritation (1913: 151); early in 1855, when Berlioz was the sympathetic witness of a 'terrible scene' made by Verdi at rehearsals of *Les vêpres siciliennes*, he was so wearied and exasperated by the musicians' condescension and lack of enthusiasm that he tried to call off the whole production (*ibidem*: 157–9); the 'Tortoises of the Opéra', as Giuseppina Strepponi called them (F. Walker 1962: 267), were still by their arrogance and long-windedness making rehearsals scarcely endurable during the preparations for *Don Carlos* in 1866. In 1869, years of frustration, exasperation and humiliation boiled over and poured out in a famous letter to his Parisian friend Camille du Locle, one of the two librettists of *Don Carlos*. Verdi's conclusion was that

I am not a composer for Paris. I don't know whether I have the talent, but I do know that my ideas on artistic matters are very different from yours.

I believe in inspiration: you on the other hand in manufacture; I admit your *criteria* as a topic for debate: but I want enthusiasm, which you lack both in feeling and in judging. I want Art in whatever manifestation it may be, not the *amusement*, the *artifice* and the *system* that you prefer. (1913: 221)

Nor did Verdi fail to notice the unhealthy influence the Opéra had on some of the composers he most revered. For all his admiration for Meyerbeer and his profound indebtedness to him, he could not hide his suspicion that the theatrical élan, the real dramatic fire of the best Italian opera eluded him; that what he called the 'mosaic effect' of Parisian opera, 'its discontinuity of style [is] in places so patent . . . as to make one believe that [Meyerbeer's masterpieces] were composed by two different people' (Budden 1982: 14–15). He was even prepared to utter the heresy that *Guillaume Tell* did not so much benefit as suffer from what he called 'the *ficelles* of GREAT ART' in a foreign style (Verdi 1913: 321).

Be that as it may, Italian composers were mesmerized by Parisian grand opera for decades: by the magnificence of the spectacle – 'ever before my eyes I have the many, many magnificent scenes to be found in your operas', Verdi told Scribe in 1852 (Porter 1978: 97); by the blatant theatricality; by the profusion of sharply profiled genre scenes; by the richness of the musical resources on which it could draw. And there is no escaping the fact that in certain purely musical respects it represented a liberation for an Italian composer. Its forms were more various, its rhythmic inventiveness was less beholden to the metrics of the libretto, and it showed a wilful, imaginative daring in appropriating 'German' effects of scoring and harmony to operatic purposes.

Verdi's creative interest in grand opera showed as early as *Nabucco* and, especially, *I Lombardi* which, with its vast, pageant-like succession of historical scenes, the flexibility of its forms and its harmonic and orchestral flamboyance, was painlessly translated into the Parisian *Jérusalem* in 1847. By the 1850s he was ready to learn more: how to clarify and dramatize the tensions in a tableau by giving to each constituent element its own melodic, rhythmic and tonal identity, as he does in the double-chorus at the start of Act I of *Les vêpres siciliennes* (Budden 1982: 15–18); how to give his melodies a more flexible and complex rhythmic articulation by freeing them from the traditional correspondences with poetic metre – Boito's reaction to this aspect of *Les vêpres siciliennes* has been recorded in the Introduction (cf. p. 10 above); this was a skill which, once acquired, was promptly transferred to Italian-language works. Verdi was enchanted by the delicious genre-scenes of French opera and began to introduce them regularly into his own works – in *Les vêpres siciliennes* and *Don Carlos*, of course, but in *Aroldo* too (Rimini 1857), and especially in *La forza del destino*.

Dramatic themes

As a musical dramatist Verdi had always craved the original, the bold, the startling. In the 1850s, the particular form this appetite took was that of a quest for complexity, for the mingling of the apparently irreconcilable. He confessed to preferring Ariosto's riotous muse to Tasso's; he ranked 'myriad-minded' Shakespeare above the severer Greek tragedians; he remembered bizarre Hugoesque inspirations like *Rigoletto* more fondly than operas of a classical cut like *I due Foscari* which lacked 'the variety my crazy brain would like' (Budden 1973–81, II: 361). To achieve a Shakespearian amalgam of light and dark, of comedy and tragedy became a cherished ambition, realized with something close to perfection in *Un ballo in maschera* (Rome 1859).

This complexity was not always so happily achieved; for Verdi showed no inclination to relax the pace or the concentration of his dramatic manner. His passion for brevity, for dispensing with the inessential, for ellipse, came to an unhappy climax in the first version of *Simon Boccanegra* (Venice 1857), of which Basevi complained that he needed to read it SIX TIMES (Basevi's emphasis) before understanding it; even then, as Budden notes, he didn't get the story quite right (1973–81, II: 250).

The scale, the scope and the sheer complication of that opera, of *La forza del destino* and of *Don Carlos* occasioned a new phenomenon in Verdi's work: an uncertainty as to whether he had succeeded in finding the right form for the dramatic idea. There were eventually to be two quite different versions of *Simon Boccanegra*; two or three less radically distinct workings of *Forza del destino*; and in the case of *Don Carlos* a whole multitude of alternatives for each of the five acts. Clearly these operas were problematic in a way that was new in Verdi's work. There have been, indeed there still are, critics who feel that he was getting too thoughtful, too self-conscious; that the magnificent spontaneity and 'naivety' of his native style was becoming sicklied o'er by a too Hamlet-like reflectiveness.

With *Aida*, on the other hand, he returned to a more traditional, indeed a surprisingly old-fashioned, and simply structured theme. And this very simplicity enabled him to achieve a classic perfection, a poise, a flawless address of musical means to dramatic ends that no other Verdi opera surpasses. In the vastness of its scale, however, *Aida* is typical of the period. For the drama of romantic passion that destroys Aida, Radames and Amneris is set against an epic panorama of warfare, dynastic ambition and religious bigotry. *Aida*, like *Don Carlos* and *Simon Boccanegra* before it, is in grand opera style, placing affairs of state at the very heart of the dramatic action. In all these operas individual passions are subject to political and religious pressures; the best and most spontaneous emotions of the heart are oppressed or poisoned by 'the grim arts of rulers, the tortuous secrets of government, the intrigues of the ambitious, by *force majeure* . . .' (Mila 1958: 246–7). Those 'real' characters that Verdi had laboured so hard to fashion in the first fifteen years of his career now came to be placed in a 'real' world.

But the setting was never allowed to usurp the prerogative of character. It is typical for Verdi that, even in the festival opera *Aida*, as the drama moves towards its climax our attention is focused more and more on a small group of vulnerable individuals, and all the pageantry of religion and state, all the pomp and circumstance of public life fades into the background. That is not to deny that Verdi's interest in getting the feel of the milieu intensified to an almost Puccinian degree during this phase of his career. At work on *Les vêpres siciliennes* he consulted a Neapolitan friend, de Sanctis, over Sicilian traditional customs and festivals. For *Aida* he demanded of various advisers a mass of miscellaneous information about religious rituals, ancient musical instruments, Egyptian geography, and much else. This opera, based on a story by Auguste Mariette, one of the great Egyptologists of the age, was, more than any other Verdi work, intended to have all the trappings of authenticity. Mariette himself took a keen supervisory interest:

I need not tell you that the editing [of the synopsis] is mine. If I have intervened, it is, in the first place, because of the Viceroy's order and, in the second place, because of my belief that I could give the work true local colour, which is the indispensable condition for an opera of this kind. Indeed I repeat to you that what the Viceroy wants is a purely ancient and Egyptian opera. The sets will be based on historical accounts; the costumes will be designed after the bas-reliefs of Upper Egypt. No effort will be spared in this respect, and the *mise-en-scène* will be as splendid as one can imagine. You know the Viceroy does things in a grand style. This care for preserving local colour in the *mise-en-scène* obliges us, by the same token, to preserve it in the outline itself. In fact, there is a special phraseology for this – a frame of mind, an inspired note which only a thorough acquaintance with Egypt can provide. It is in this capacity that I have intervened and continue to intervene.

(Letter of 27 April 1870, to Camille du Locle, in Busch 1978: 11)

In the event there was less 'authenticity' either in the spectacle or in the music than Mariette might have hoped. For Verdi the point of his enquiries was not any kind of theatrical archaeology; rather to fill his mind with colours and images that would stimulate his imagination, so that his musical conception of *Aida* would acquire individuality and integrity, a *colorito* unique to itself and appropriate to its dramatic theme.

In *La forza del destino* the 'real world' in which the tragedy of Alvaro and Leonora is set threatens to swamp the protagonists altogether: Baldini writes of the 'extraordinary perversity' of its dramatic structure (1980: 283). One can only wonder at the mysterious intuition by which Verdi chose this of all subjects for the city where Mussorgsky was soon to start work on *Boris Godunov*. For, as has often been noted, the panoramic view of society the opera provides, the tapestry-like chronicle of episodes set in palace, in monastery, in tavern, in army encampment, give *La forza del destino* a prophetically Russian flavour.

Hugo, Schiller and Shakespeare remained Verdi's heroes and all of them contribute to this singular opera. The bizarre dramatic conception, with its characters 'twice as large as life and half as life-like' (Budden 1973–81, II: 431), betray the abiding fascination of the Hugo school of dramatists. Schiller – to be precise, an episode from *Wallensteins Lager* which Verdi had admired for years – was freely plagiarized in the encampment scenes. Above all *Forza del destino*, in the vastness of its conception, in the breadth of its sympathies and in the variety of its registers, breathes much the same spirit as Shakespeare's chronicle plays.

There can be no doubt that, now more than ever, Shakespeare was the lodestar in Verdi's strivings for the 'real' and the 'true'. In the numerous tributes to the English poet which punctuated his conversation and his letters, that is the refrain: 'But that could well be true! But it is true! It is like that!' (conversation with Italo Pizzi, in Conati 1984: 341). Shakespeare was 'the dreamed-of goal' (Mila 1958: 78) as during the 1850s and 60s Verdi began really to stretch himself, to juxtapose and blend registers more daringly (*Ballo in maschera*, *Forza del destino*), to deepen his analysis of character (*Don Carlos*), to evoke in tone painting the power and the poetry of the forces of nature (*Aroldo*, *Simon Boccanegra*).

Character and ethics

Per quel destin che a gemere
Condanna ogni tenore
La moglie del baritono
Amo d'immenso amore.[1]   (Ghislanzoni 1870)

Ghislanzoni's parody of operatic stereotypes was in fact no longer quite on the mark. In the case of Verdi at least characterization was less likely to be conditioned by vocal archetypes; sometimes it had a refinement, a tremulous ambiguity quite new in Italian opera. Particularly was this true of *Don Carlos*, the only one of his Paris operas to be conceived from first principles with Verdi in total control. Knowing he could draw on a more subtle instrumental tradition, confident that he had mastered the problems of setting the French language to music, he was somehow inspired into what, remembering Gounod (cf. Introduction, p. 10), we might describe as the heliotrope, mignonette and violet shades of characterization. Never before had a tenor hero so ambiguous as Don Carlos, so flecked and muted with light and shadow, trod the boards in an Italian opera.

Increasingly Verdi's characters are the embodiment or the battle-ground of ideas; for we have reached an age when, to borrow an antithesis of Verdi's own, 'operas of cavatinas, duets etc.' have to give way to 'operas of ideas' (letter to de Sanctis, 21 May 1869, in Budden 1973–81, II: 442). *La forza del destino* is indeed unique among his operas in having an abstract idea for its title. In *Don Carlos* Verdi recognized that the crucial scenes were two tremendous encounters of the 'severe and terrible' King Philip, one with Rodrigo (the spokesman of liberty and human dignity), the other with the Grand Inquisitor (the spokesman of ecclesiastical obscurantism); for the heart and mind of Philip is the battlefield where these ideas come to the issue. *Un ballo in maschera* sets a very different monarch at the centre of the stage, the enlightened Riccardo (properly Gustavo, King of Sweden), through whom – the sweet solemn harmony of *Preludio* and *Introduzione* tells us – good governance is close to achieving a quite Arcadian *musica humana*. Riccardo-Gustavo, all generosity, all impetuosity, is destroyed by an enemy unknown to Philip. He is destroyed in fact by his own liberal virtues of tolerance and faith in the human heart, by his inability to take sufficiently seriously either the light or the dark forces that threaten him: the aerial frivolity and irresponsibility personified in Oscar, or the subconscious, irrational and instinctive urges personified in Ulrica.

During the 1850s, Verdi was still having trouble with the censors; indeed, their vexatiousness came to a climax in that decade, and the painful and absurd expedient of anatopism was an ever-present reality of operatic life, dimming the brightness of the composer's vision, confusing the clarity of his dramatic idea. *Stiffelio*, to quote the extreme example, was not rescued for the opera-house by conversion into *Aroldo*: it was simply rendered anachronistic and implausible in the highest degree. *Un ballo in maschera* is one of Verdi's most perfectly achieved operas; but despite that, it is impossible not to feel that its dramatic theme suffers in being removed from its proper setting at the sophisticated court of an absolute monarch of enlightened views. After 1861 censorship was relaxed in those parts of the peninsula that had become part of the united Italy. And this was timely. For as Verdi and his contemporaries handled bigger and more complex themes, engaging themselves with 'dramas of ideas', the simple moral imperatives of the *risorgimento* years became obsolete. Opera began to be more ambiguous and equivocal in its moral thrust.

The most conspicuous example of this 'transvaluation of values' was the original, St Petersburg 1862, version of *La forza del destino*. Following in the footsteps of the Duke of Rivas's play, Verdi had pursued the dramatic idea to its logical conclusion and closed in a mood of bleak and blasphemous nihilism: the despairing Alvaro commits suicide, having first fatally wounded Don Carlos, who, however, dies only after having stabbed to death his own sister Leonora. It was an ending which early audiences consistenty found repellent and which Verdi, who for all his love of boldness and originality never ignored the feelings of the public, eventually decided would have to be revised. The spirit of this revision – reconciliatory, confessional – which was carried out in 1869 in collaboration with Ghislanzoni, has often been described as Manzonian. It may have been in some measure inspired by the *Promessi sposi* of Petrella (Lecce 1869) for which Ghislanzoni has recently completed the text, and the original of which was for Verdi 'not only the greatest book of our time but one of the greatest books that ever came out of a human brain' (Martin 1965: 18).

The last years of the traditional libretto

The structure of the libretto changed more slowly than its content. When, in 1853, the Venetian lawyer and playwright Antonio Somma evinced an interest in libretto-writing – he was to produce both *Un ballo in maschera* and a *Re Lear* for Verdi – the tips the composer gave him were not only rudimentary but conventional in the extreme. 'For a musical setting you need verses for cantabili, verses for *pezzi concertati*, verses for *larghi, allegri*, etc. all alternating with one another so that nothing becomes dull or monotonous' (Budden 1973–81, II: 361). And Verdi didn't hesitate to demand 'correction' when Somma forgot to close a recitative with the traditional *endecasillabi* (*ibidem*: 367).

During the next twenty or thirty years such assumptions were increasingly called into question; Verdi's attitude to the libretto became progressively more radical. Even so, it was not until the early 1890s that the traditional structures and the traditional stylistic decorum commended to Somma in 1853 were quite abandoned. The libretti of *La Wally* (by Illica), of *Manon Lescaut* (by Illica, Giacosa and several others) and of *Falstaff* (by Boito) all demonstrated the final obsolescence of the old 'Code Rossini'.

It was the metrical regularity and the stanzaic forms of the libretto that were softened up first. A key document in the process is Ghislanzoni's *Aida* libretto, work on which is exceptionally fully documented. *Aida* was, we may say, a festival opera, designed among other things to provide a cornucopia of song, dance and spectacle; it had a plot of classic, old-fashioned simplicity. Yet even in this context Verdi was by now urging upon his collaborator every kind of theatrical boldness, exhorting him to cast off old habits and liberate himself from the formalism of the traditional libretto.

It was, for example, while working on *Aida* that Verdi defined his famous concept, the *parola scenica*. By *parole sceniche* he meant 'those [words] that carve out a situation or a character . . . I know well that sometimes it is difficult to give them a select and poetic form. But . . . (pardon the blasphemy) both the poet and the composer must have the talent and the courage, when necessary, *not* to write poetry or music' (Busch 1978: 31). Whatever the cost to rhyme or to metre, he insists in other letters, the characters must say what they have to say; the *parola scenica* must spring forth boldly, an integral part of the singer's impersonation of his role.

What Verdi does not yet demand is the total dissolution of the distinction between recitative and lyricism; that was something that came only with his Boito operas. In fact there was an unresolved struggle in Verdi's imagination between a yearning for the radical overhaul of all convention and a profoundly conservative sense of the values of Italian opera. It was sometimes rather amusingly illustrated in the correspondence with Ghislanzoni over *Aida*.

We are up to the fourth act . . . the duet between *Amneris* and *Radames* . . . Develop this situation as you see fit, and develop it well; and have the characters say what they must without preoccupying yourself in the least with musical form.

But no sooner is that said than it is qualified:

Obviously if you were to send me recitative from beginning to end, it would be impossible for me to write any rhythmic music; but if you were to begin immediately with any rhythm whatever and continue it up to the end, I would not complain at all. Perhaps, perhaps, it would be necessary to change it, just to write a tiny little *cabaletta* at the end.   (16 October 1870, in Busch 1978: 79)

A few days later Verdi is proposing that the scene should begin at once 'in lyric form', and that Ghislanzoni might try the *settenario doppio* metre.

As late as *Aida*, then, the conventions of libretto-writing were being not so much overthrown as disguised, cunningly refashioned. The refashioning owed much to Verdi's growing interest in metrical novelty. Two things particularly attracted him in this respect. He had become very partial to long lines for aria-texts. Both 'O cieli azzurri' in Act III – a late addition – and 'O terra addio' in Act IV were written in *endecasillabi* (a metre hitherto confined to recitative) at his specific request. And he was intrigued by the possibility of transferring to Italian verse the mixture of metres sometimes found in the lyrics of French opera. Again the closing scene of *Aida* furnishes the classic example.

The French even in their lyric verses sometimes lengthen or shorten the line. Why couldn't we do the same? . . . A somewhat unusual verse form for Radames would oblige me to look for a melody different from those usually written for *settenari* and *ottonari*.

Then he sketches such a lyric, and continues:

You cannot imagine what a beautiful melody can be written for such a strange form, and how much charm the *quinario* gives after the three lines of *settenari*, and how much variety the two *endecasillabi* that follow.   (13 November 1870, in Verdi 1913: 663–4)

One other thing is clear from the correspondence about *Aida*: there had been no change in the habits of thought acquired during the long years of collaboration with Piave. Anyone who worked with Verdi was expected to subject his literary skill unconditionally to the will of the composer. Verdi continued to intervene forcefully at every stage in the preparation of a libretto, dictating its overall strategy, the content and structure of the individual scenes, the choice of vocabulary and metre. It is amusing that this massive demonstration of the composer's tyranny over the librettist should involve Ghislanzoni, a poet who in his dealings with other composers entertained very different views on the relationship: 'liberty to the poet to make and dramatize the libretto as best it pleases him, liberty to the composer to accept it' (Brown, in John 1983: 42).

Musical structure

Between the 1850s and the 1880s composers became increasingly diligent in their search for some kind of musical unity – a singleness of conception which would match the unifying dramatic idea. The quest took various forms and affected musical structure at different levels. Verdi was fond of expressing the ideal in terms of composing 'in a single breath'. For him the crucial thing was the irresistible sweep of the musical argument. Towards the end of his life he offered some advice to the young Umberto Giordano: 'Compose the first act, without pausing, without corrections; when you have done this, put the sheets of music to one side and start the second act. Proceed with the second act in exactly the same way, and then continue with the third and fourth acts. Then rest. When you have recovered your strength, revise and correct everything; you can be sure that this is the only way of avoiding error' (Conati 1984: 374).

None of the manifestations of this quest for unity was more characteristic of the period than the interest in thematic economy, in the fuller use of a smaller number of dramatically significant themes, a procedure bearing a superficial resemblance to *Leitmotiv*. Working on *I Lituani* in 1873, Ponchielli remarked to Giulio Ricordi, 'in the past people didn't pay much attention to thematic unity; now on the other hand it's regarded as something absolutely essential, and indeed I would almost say that too much is made of it altogether' (Budden 1973–81, III: 282).

Verdi was comparatively little affected by the urge toward 'thematic unity' in the sense Ponchielli apparently intended. He belonged to a generation that had come to maturity when the aesthetics of the number opera had hardly begun to be regarded as problematic, and had shown in *Rigoletto*, *Il trovatore* and *La traviata* that a unified musical conception was perfectly achievable within that old form. In later operas the musical designs are more subtly responsive to situation and character, the recitatives more poetic and song-like, the transitions and links more cunning in their craftsmanship. Verdi's unity – as his remarks to Giordano suggest – was essentially a matter of the flow of the musical invention, of 'endless melody', one is tempted to say. And this musical continuity unfolds in perfect synchronism with the dramatic action.

To suggest that Verdi was not very concerned for 'thematic unity' is not to imply that he was in any danger of forgetting the dramatic potential of recurring themes. His use of them continues to be most effective when characters are themselves remembering the past, particularly when it is a case of 'Nessun maggior dolore . . .' There is a superb example in the Act III finale of *Ballo in maschera*: Riccardo, alone in his study, reflects on how he is to redeem Amelia's honour, and then prepares to see her for the last time. His aria 'La rivedrà' from early in Act I is gravely remembered, reluctantly put away, and finally – after the warning of the assassination attempt – recklessly embraced in a context of doom, with terrible clamorous emphasis on the minor-key harmony that had once been no more than a fleeting shadow.

Commonly it is the orchestra that takes over these thematic reminiscences. And at the close of the Act III trio in *Don Carlos* – where a passing cloud of mistrust between Carlos and Rodrigo is dispelled by memories of their oath of mutual loyalty – Verdi surely sowed the seeds of those notorious, ecstatic orchestral cantilenas with which the *veristi* were to be so prodigal. His use of such reminiscence themes was, it need hardly be said, always motivated by the dramatic idea. But their theatrical effectiveness did not go unmarked: 'Imagine', wrote Mariani to Verdi during a run of performances in Bologna; 'Last night and tonight we had to repeat *four times* the famous eight bars for orchestra that conclude the trio in the third act' (F. Walker 1962: 342). And it was as an effect rather than, necessarily, as an embodiment of some dramatic thought that the device was to become so threadbare by the end of the century.

When all is said, throughout the 1850s, 60s and 70s Italian opera remained a song-based structure, a design of arias, ensembles and choruses. It was the aria that changed most radically at first, in particular because by the end of the 1850s virtually all composers had become acutely self-conscious about the cabaletta. Indeed it came to be regarded as a kind of fetish, symbolizing with bewitching dreadfulness an antiquated conception of melodrama. For that very reason Verdi was prepared in due course to profess a deep attachment to it: 'if a young man should be born tomorrow who could write one as good as, for example, "Meco tu vieni o misera" or "Ah perchè non posso odiarti", I should go and hear it with all my heart and renounce all the harmonic fiddle-faddle and all the affectations of our learned orchestrators' (to Giulio Ricordi, 20 November 1880, Verdi 1913: 559). In practice he was rather less simplistic.

Already in 'Ah! m'abbraccia' in Act I of *La battaglia di Legnano*, an opera much affected by his absorption of French influences in the late 1840s, Verdi had composed a full-scale aria in ternary form, rather than in the customary two movements of cantabile plus cabaletta. Such tripartite structures became increasingly common during the 1850s, notably, as one might anticipate, in the Parisian *Vêpres siciliennes*, where both 'Et toi, Palerme' and 'Au sein de la puissance' adopt the ABA form. And in the original *Simon Boccanegra* the same type of design was incorporated as the cantabile of a complete cantabile–cabaletta scheme in Amelia's Act I *scena* 'Come in questa ora bruna'. In isolation the ternary aria lacked the theatrical verve of the traditional two-movement Italian aria. But it was more succinct and with its built-in element of contrast and reprise lent itself to more subtle reflection, and to a more analytical inwardness.

By the 1870s virtually all arias were single-movement cantabiles, 'romanzas', in the terminology of the period. The ternary form was still found, as it is in 'Celeste Aida', but other designs were more popular. Sometimes the central episode of a ternary form was pared away to insignificance, giving in effect a two-verse strophic aria, in which the second verse was often more richly scored, and perhaps more fully developed melodically. 'O cieli azzurri' (*Aida*, Act III) is a superb example of the kind of dream-like meditation often expressed in this form. The other type of aria is more complex, and would seem to take its point of departure, Budden suggests (1973–81, III: 208), from the duet. Such a piece as 'Ritorna vincitor – l'insana parola' (*Aida*, Act I) is an interior monologue, a sequence of short contrasting movements contributed in alternation by the two souls that Aida finds inhabiting her breast. As is commonly the case, the aria begins in a state of agitation with a quick movement in the minor key, and via a series of reconsiderations, a kind of inner dialectic, eventually achieves resolution in the final slow *maggiore* – 'Numi, pietà'.

The duet, which, at least since *Rigoletto*, had formed the backbone of Italian opera, took longer to break away from traditional patterns. And perhaps that is not surprising; for the juxtaposition of voices, of personalities, of emotions and attitudes gave – or could give – a riveting theatrical immediacy to the form. Even in *Aida*, where Verdi boasted of having composed the whole of Act III as 'a single piece', and where his vast correspondence with Ghislanzoni bears eloquent testimony to a desire to break with old habits, the traditional structures are unmistakable in no less than four of the duets: Aida–Amneris in Act II; Aida–Radames in Act III; Amneris–Radames and Aida–Radames in Act IV. It is the imaginative skill with which Verdi – and sometimes others – revitalize or modify these old forms that compels admiration, not any intrinsic novelty of conception. The cabaletta of the Aida–Amneris duet, for example, is superimposed upon the music of an off-stage chorus which provides a timely reminder of the political context of their private quarrel. In Act II of *La Gioconda*,

Ex. VI.1 Ponchielli, *La Gioconda* (1876), Act II scene 9

552

[Dragging him towards the bank] Do you see there, on the dead canal, a
vessel forcing its way?. . . Be silent! Alas! ever since I have noticed you. . .

Ex. VI.1 *continued*

Ponchielli lights upon a strikingly effective way of working a 'dissimilar'
cabaletta: as the second singer begins, the melody of the first is played as an
orchestral countermelody, creating an emotional effect of confrontation
even in a section of solo song (Ex. VI.1).

In a repertory which in so many ways aimed to emulate grand opera, it is
not surprising to find an even more massive traditional structure – the
concertato finale – surviving long as the keystone of the operatic design. It
had probably been the point of departure for Cammarano's dramatic
strategy back in the 1830s (see Chapter 22 above, p. 414); and ironically it
remained the real starting point for the collaboration between Verdi and
Boito on *Otello* in 1880 (F. Walker 1962: 477). During the 1870s Ponchielli
had become a redoubtable master of what Illica called the 'concertato a
tutta ribalta'[2] (Nicolaisen 1980: 39); and his example helped give the old
form a new lease of life into the 1890s. 'There are no move obvious
imitations in the early works of Catalani and Puccini than those large
ensembles in which they attempt to adopt Ponchiellian rhetoric' (*ibidem*:
40).

Meanwhile, as with so much else in Italian opera, while the principle had been retained it had undergone a great deal of dramatic enlivening. To Verdi at least, it was no longer acceptable simply to freeze the action at some supremely fraught turning-point in the drama for a feast of highly charged song. He abandoned that kind of finale after the first *Simon Boccanegra*, thereafter insisting on at least some kind of continuous dramatic process, even if – as in *Aida*, Act II – it was nothing more sophisticated than 'an emotional tug-of-war, one side pleading, the other resisting' (Budden 1973–81, II: 39). In the Act II finale of *Un ballo in maschera*, Verdi is more ambitious, and rises magnificently to the emotional complexity of his theme. As Amelia unmasks herself, the mounting tension of the whole tremendous act dissolves in sneering laughter. That moment of bathos sets off a fine piece of psychological portraiture. The noblest characters in the opera have been shamed and humiliated, the trash justified. And yet Amelia's tragic dignity redeems the squalid situation, her song floating with a sublime simplicity of grief above the mutter of cynicism and embitterment.

While the *Finale* survived long, the *Introduzione* didn't. A full-scale Introduction with *sortitas* for some of the principals, such as we find in *Un ballo in maschera*, was by now quite exceptional. Increasingly the tendency was to pitch the spectator *in medias res*, particularly into a scene of naturalistic casualness – Leonora and her father saying good-night in *La forza del destino*, Ramfis and Radames discussing the likelihood of war with Ethiopia in *Aida*. Operas tend to begin not with grandiose or picturesque tableaux, but with intimate conversations set against an atmospheric orchestral backcloth. Budden, whose knowledge of the repertory is un-surpassed, believes that such 'naturalism' was unheard of outside the prose theatre until Verdi introduced it to opera in his first *Simon Boccanegra*.

The musical language

In May 1868 in the midst of the brouhaha occasioned by the notorious Broglio letter to Rossini – the Minister of Education was seeking ways of extricating the Goverment from the financial burden of supporting musical education, and made a number of ignorant and insulting observations on the contemporary state of music – Verdi set down some of his own reflections on the decadence of modern opera in a letter to Piroli.

I am the last person to need to defend my own period or accuse others of the past, but it would be easy enough to point, even in certain operatic masterpieces of an earlier age, to the brainless conventionality of the numbers, the pedantry of the *pezzi concertati*, melody more often than not turning into singing exercises, false expression, a hard, heavy and monotonous scoring without poetry and above all without purpose. We too have our failings, and they are considerable, but there's less conventionality, more dramatic truth in the form; the ensembles speak a language proper to the passions expressed (an ugly language perhaps but it's a great step forward); the expression is more truthful; and above all the scoring has a meaning and a purpose which it didn't have before.

(Budden 1973–81, II: 32)

It will be helpful to use Verdi's diagnosis as a guide to the changes that took place in the musical language during the third quarter of the century.

Not everyone, even in the 1860s and 70s, shared Verdi's small regard for vocal pyrotechnics; there was no shortage of coloratura and *fioritura*, or of 'singing-exercise' arias in the works of his lesser contemporaries. All the same, Verdi's own example was gradually compelling a change of outlook, and his view, insisted upon with ever less inclination to compromise, was that 'the vocal writing had to provide an immediate reflection of the psychology of the character . . . [to] register feelings, conflicts and changes of mood, with a rapidity unknown to earlier opera composers' (Celletti 1980: 233). Even in his earliest works Verdi had shown little interest in brilliant vocal writing for male voices; by the time of *Simon Boccanegra* it had been largely abandoned even for the soprano.

Simon Boccanegra was indeed an extreme case. 'If there aren't many melismata in my music, there's no need to clutch at your hair and throw a mad fit', he told his first Boccanegra (Budden 1973–81, II: 254). By concentrating almost exclusively on declamatory song rather than on lyrical, let alone florid song, Verdi ensured that this opera promptly earned an unenviable reputation for severity and obscurity.

The warmth and the charm soon returned, in *Un ballo in maschera*; but thanks to the declamatory intention, his arias had also become more concentrated than ever before. They were also more lyrically prodigal. The full glory of Verdian song is achieved in what Budden calls his '*Aida* manner', though there are anticipations a-plenty in *Ballo* and *Don Carlos*. It entails 'a profusion of basically symmetrical melodic ideas so closely packed as to seem separate articulations of a single cantilena' (1973–81, III: 107). But the reason for this prodigality was that every segment within the cantilena had a precise expressive purpose, was finely attuned to text, character and situation.

The *canzone* 'Di' tu se fedele' sung by Riccardo in the character of a simple fisherman (*Un ballo in maschera*, Act I) provides a rather startling example. It begins with the genuine article as it were, a beguiling popular song of exotic and haunting allure. But then with the conventional 'rowing' accacciaturas and the grotesque defiant leap at the cadence Riccardo begins to ape the style; and finally, with the dancing staccatos and braying guffaws, it becomes clear that what he is engaged in is an irresponsible lark, and mockery is really his aim. In the arias at the start of Act III of the opera we hear Verdi applying the same principle with a more minute psychological finesse. There is scarcely a phrase in 'Eri tu che macchiavi' where the music does not colour or deepen the verbal nuance – the accusing, minatory gestures at the start; the pang of tenderness at 'delizia dell' anima mia'; the unhinging of the key at 'esecrabile',[3] and so on. Verdi's melodic language had reached a stage of meaningfulness where, even in a cantabile – if one may be paradoxical to make a point – every phrase has become a *parola scenica* (see Ex.VI.2).

Ex.VI.2 Verdi, *Un ballo in maschera* (1859), Act III scene 1

It was you who soiled that soul that was the joy of my soul, who win my trust and then with one execrable stroke poison the universe for me!

Ex. VI.2 *continued*

While 'horizontally' the distinctions between song and declamation, between aria, arioso and recitative begin to dissolve, so too do the 'vertical' distinctions between melody and accompaniment. The singing voice no longer moves in a different sphere from the instruments that accompany it. During the 1850s the orchestra matures to become a fully articulate partner, eager to echo, to respond to, to set its own countermelodies against those of the singer. And the melody comes to be a kind of golden thread winding its way through the total concentus of voices and instruments, a richly musical texture of lines, rhythms, harmonies and colours. While perhaps seeming to lose its autonomy and its primacy, Verdi's mature melodic style has in fact increased its expressive possibilities. I paraphrase Mila because no one, I think, has described Verdi's lyricism more eloquently: 'no longer constrained within the strict line of a melodic phrase, [the song] fragments itself, rummages among the words, seeking out and accentuating the most important of them, it has shy hesitations, sudden impulses, the peremptory dryness of spoken recitative, tender and fleeting melodic sallies' (Mila 1958: 121).

'Above all the scoring has a meaning and a purpose which it didn't have before'; it became more supple and chamber-music-like. No longer was the orchestra a more or less garishly coloured backcloth, its texture occasionally varied in a very formal manner by the *obbligato* use of solo instruments, or by movements for a reduced ensemble. Individual voices advance out of the orchestral texture and retreat into it again more flexibly; flecks of colour dapple the surface; light and shade, transparency and opacity wait on the more finely nuanced moods of the characters.

Until *Falstaff* one is rarely aware of Verdi – or indeed of any other Italian composer – as a virtuoso of the orchestra. But what he did do with increasing sureness of purpose was to draw from his instruments astonishingly original sounds, precisely imagined for particular dramatic ends. Were aridity of heart, grimness of purpose, the deadening effect of absolute power ever expressed in blacker shades of black than in the Grand Inquisitor scene of *Don Carlos*? Did moonlight ever flicker on water with more magical stillness than at the start of Act III of *Aida*? The role of the orchestra in *Aida* is outstandingly important in creating that unique sense of ambience – tropical, sensuous, mysterious – that so stirred Puccini.

Though Verdi expostulated much about the need to keep the orchestra in its place, he was interested in all kinds of new developments that affected it: in the different seating arrangements he came across in Paris or Vienna; in new instruments like the cornets of the Paris Opéra, which have a starring role in *Don Carlos*. For *Aida* he even experimented with new designs of trumpet and flute constructed to his own specifications. But he was independent minded in this as in so much else. He continued to write for the old Italian valve-trombones – there are passages in late Verdi that simply cannot be played on modern instruments – and, like Brahms, another composer with a healthy contempt for fashion, he never reconciled himself to the sound of valve-horns. The prelude at the start of Act II of *Don Carlos* is composed for natural horns crooked in four different keys, presumably so that the multitude of simultaneous open and stopped tones cancel one another out and create an overall smoothness and consistency.

One thing Verdi does not mention in his letter to Piroli is harmony, and that seems curious, for in no respect had his own musical imagination developed more prodigiously. By the time of *Simon Boccanegra* he was not nervous of the boldest ellipses, or the most flagrant spasms of chromaticism, provided always that they served an expressive or dramatic purpose. Particularly characteristic of his mature style was a freedom in the use of second inversion chords with few parallels in nineteenth-century music. By taking away the foundation tones that give stability to the harmony he imparts a sense of flux, of lability, to the phrase; and this helps sustain the momentum of the music in a highly personal way.

Nonetheless Verdi's feeling for harmony, and what one might call his philosophy of harmony, remained Italian and classical in the highest degree. Though he was to learn to admire *Tristan und Isolde*, continuous dissonance, even of a mild kind, had an intolerably irritating effect on his sensibility. The prologue to Boito's *Mefistofele*, Mascagni's *L'amico Fritz*, and Bruneau's *Le rêve* all exasperated him by their 'frightful excess of dissonance' (Budden 1873–81, II: 46). A compulsive feeling that harmonic tensions must be resolved affected Verdi's key-sense as much as his chord-sense. It was not until comparatively late in his career ('Morrò ma prima in grazia', *Ballo in maschera*, Act III) that he was prepared to close a lyrical movement in the minor key. On rare occasions we may hear this habitual tonal poise harnessed to a particular dramatic purpose. In the final scene of *Aida* 'each successive idea in the duet follows at the key a fifth below the one before, as though both singers were relaxing further and further into an atmosphere of peace' (Budden 1973–81, III: 253).

A more declamatory style of melody, a richer orchestral palette, a more expressive and sensuous harmonic language: all these things, in the third quarter of the nineteenth century, made the charge of Wagnerism inevitable. Lamenting of *Simon Boccanegra* how song had turned to declamation, and accompaniment to symphony, and how music had altogether become 'the shadow of the poetry', Basevi was moved to assert that 'not even Wagner would have ventured so far along this road' as the Verdi of the Simone–Fiesco duet 'Del mar sul lido' (Budden 1973–81, II: 286). *Don Carlos* prompted a distressingly obtuse outburst from Bizet: 'Verdi is no longer Italian. He wants to write like Wagner. He no longer has any of his own faults; but he also lacks a single one of his own virtues' (*ibidem*, III: 26). It took an altogether exceptional critic – one appreciative of the strengths of traditional Italian opera while at he same time sympathetic to the 'Wagnerian' ideals of the latter part of the nineteenth century – to give the Verdi of the 1850s and 60s his due. Fortunately Italy had at least one such in the person of Filippo Filippi of the Florence *Perseveranza*, who wrote of *Un ballo in maschera*:

having rejected convention and formula, having assigned to each character his own particular language and having rendered the dramatic situation with evident effectiveness, in fact having moulded the drama, Verdi can take his seat between the past and the future and turning round to each of the two sides can say to one party: 'Do you want tunes, ideas, proportions, a beginning, a middle, a continuation and an end? Do you want rhythm, phrasing, pure music? You have it and to spare. And you others, gentlemen of the future, do you want general colouring of the drama, faithful interpretation of the words, freedom from hackneyed and conventional forms? Do you want ideals, gracefulness, distinction of character? Do you want banality banished and in its place the new and the elegant? Do you want the orchestra and the stage to be like a single statue? and a kind of aesthetic pantheism to prevail everywhere? Help yourselves; there is plenty for all your needs. (Budden 1973–81, II: 423)

Changing ideals of performance

Operas like *La forza del destino*, *Don Carlos* and *Aida* made unprecedented demands on the performers. When so many theatres were in such a precarious financial situation it was no time to be embarking on idealistic reforms – or so it might appear. But Verdi believed that they could be revived if taken firmly in hand, and inspired with zeal for a new style of performance to match the new style of opera. As he put it to Arrivabene,

I have tried to revive some of our theatres and to give them productions that are somewhat suitable. Where for many years one fiasco followed another and the final quarter-salary could not be paid, in the four theatres, where I conducted or rather commandeered the performance, the crowds poured in and the profits were enormous. You will say: *'And what do you care about profits?'* Yes, I do care, because they prove that the production was interesting, and thus they show us how to do well in the future . . .
(Busch 1978: 320)

Finance was by no means the only difficulty. In many theatres there was still nothing resembling a professional standard of discipline. Preparing the first Padua performance of *Aida* in 1872, Faccio had had to have a back-stage bar nailed up since 'choristers and supers went [there] between acts to get indecently drunk' (letter to Verdi, 21 June 1872, in Busch 1978: 311). A profounder problem was the ingrained attitude of star singers and, perhaps worse, of old-fashioned impresarios, who simply could not understand that it no longer guaranteed success 'to put two or three well known names on the playbill' (Verdi).

It was particularly difficult to eradicate such attitudes in Rome and Naples. Their more conservative social fabric and their long and glorious operatic traditions were positive disadvantages in coming to terms with what was now needed: 'because they have had Palestrina, Scarlatti and Pergolesi, they think they know more than anyone else. Yet they have lost their bearings, and now they know very little. They are somewhat like the French: *Nous, nous, nous*, and they let themselves be applauded' (letter of Verdi to Arrivabene, 20 August 1872, in Busch 1978: 320). What the new style of opera demanded above all else was teamwork – a good chorus and orchestra, careful staging, a thorough rehearsing of the ensemble. If impresarios were not able to provide the time and insist on the discipline necessary for this 'they should stick to cabaletta operas' (letter of Verdi to Torelli, (?)30 January 1872, *ibidem*: 280).

Verdi had never been beholden to star singers. From very early in his career he had insisted on selecting his own casts – or at very least on vetting and endorsing them. No singer could be imposed on him, 'even if Malibran herself should return' (letter of 7 December 1856, Verdi 1913: 197). And this was because he refused to acknowledge the right of performers – whether singers or conductors (a breed of whose pretensions he was beginning to grow suspicious) – to function as autonomously creative artists. He was, he declared, 'content to hear simply and exactly what is written' (Busch 1978: 150). He did not need singers or conductors to discover new effects for him because as yet 'no one has ever, ever, ever been able, or known how, to draw out all the effects conceived by me . . . *Not one*!!!' (to G. Ricordi, 25 March 1875, *ibidem*: 380).

The ideal of a fully integrated performance by an ensemble of singers and players thoroughly rehearsed under the eye of the composer was achieved by Verdi in the years around 1870, notably in the first Italian stagings of *Aida* at Milan, Parma and Naples. As a philosophy of performance it was new, or perhaps one should say long forgotten, in Italy; but it created a profound impression on young Giulio Ricordi, who was in turn to pass on Verdi's creed to Puccini. 'Oh! yes, there was a time when everything depended on the virtuosity of the throat. For *Sonnambula* and *Norma* one had to have specialists. Today opera needs a homogeneous cast, the more intelligent the better! It is not the artist who is responsible for the success of the opera, but the opera itself' (letter of 12 October 1895, in Carner 1974: 91).

During the 1850s Angelo Mariani, who was *primo violino direttore d'orchestra* and *maestro concertatore* at Genoa from 1852, earned a reputation as the outstanding orchestral director in Italy. Perhaps towards the end of the decade, certainly by the 1860s, he had abandoned the traditional appurtenances of violin and bow in favour of the baton, and became Italy's first conductor in the modern sense of the word. Verdi first worked with Mariani at Rimini in 1857 during preparations for the première of *Aroldo*. And it can hardly be coincidence that this score contains his earliest essay in orchestral virtuosity, the Act IV *burrasca*, a flight of colouristic fancy which he 'would never have risked without the presence of an authoritative baton' (Budden 1973–81, II: 12).

The experience of *Aroldo* persuaded Verdi that the time had come for the conductor to take a fuller share of responsibility than heretofore, for him in fact to provide the controlling, co-ordinating musical intelligence to which singers, instrumentalists and stage crew should all be subject. By the time of *Aida* he was telling Ricordi that 'two-thirds of the success of an opera depends on the conductor' (letter of 7 January 1871, in Busch 1978: 128). A few weeks later he returned to the same theme: 'with the music of today, musical and dramatic direction is a real necessity.' And he urged Ricordi to use his house journal and 'get busy on this topic . . . Preach the vital need of capable men as conductors of theatrical music, show the impossibility of success without intelligent interpretation and flog the mob of asses who massacre one's operas' (5 February 1871, *ibidem*: 136).

How little Verdi allowed singers their head when he conducted is suggested in some contemporary German accounts of performances of the *Requiem* under his direction. Critics were struck by the pace, the rhythmic verve, and the comparative strictness of tempo. Solo voices were not indulged in the slightest, but 'used in the same way as orchestral instruments: singers and players are treated as one large orchestra'. At the same time expressive nuances were 'sharper, more strident . . . than is customary in Germany' (Conati 1984: 125–6). The new order was not yet reflected in fees. When performers were being selected for the Cairo première of *Aida*, the *prima donna* Teresa Stolz demanded payment at the rate of 30,000 francs a month; Mariani was to get 45,000 for the whole season.

As 'operas made of cabalettas' came to be superseded by 'operas of ideas', it was essential that singers should have a fuller intellectual grasp of what they were doing; in fact they needed to understand the ideas that inspired, motivated and sustained the characters they represented. A remark in the production book for *Don Carlos* (1884 edition) may be quoted: 'the artists should be recommended to pay great attention to this piece [the King Philip–Rodrigo duet in Act II] . . . The actors should thoroughly identify themselves with the two characters who stand face to face and who represent two great principles in the history of mankind' (Budden 1973–81, III: 97–8).

Polished or brilliant vocalism for its own sake now interested Verdi less than ever. What he demanded of his singers in the way of basic equipment was 'the voice . . . the soul . . . [and] that *je ne sais quoi* which would have to be called *spark*' (Verdi 1913: 263). Not surprisingly, in view of the complexity of opera as an art-form, the multitude of its dimensions, and the critical phase in its development we have now reached, Verdi's remarks on how he hopes singers so gifted will perform do not always say the same thing: his emphasis is likely to vary according to context. Thus (astonishingly) he writes to Ricordi that the role of Radames 'mainly requires *action, action, action*' (Busch 1978: 262). But a few years later, in an environment where acting was perhaps more likely to be taken for granted, he was shifting his position radically, telling a Viennese journalist:

Italian singers are often unjustifiably criticized for neglecting acting for the sake of *bel canto*. Yet how many singers are there who combine both, who can act and sing? In comic opera both are easily combined. But in tragic opera! A singer who is moved by the dramatic action, concentrates on it with every vibrant fibre of his body, and is utterly consumed by the role he is portraying, will not find the right tone. He might for a minute, but in the next thirty seconds he will sing in the wrong way or the voice will simply fail. A single lung is rarely strong enough for acting and singing. And yet I am of the opinion that in opera the voice has, above all, the right to be heard.

(*Signale für die musikalische Welt*, Leipzig, July 1875, in Conati 1984: 113)

And like Rossini himself Verdi assumed as the first prerequisite for good singing an effortless command of the voice as an instrument. It was the sense of strain that often troubled him with German singing; they tried to sing too loudly and their singing was therefore 'no poetic expression of the soul but a physical struggle' (*Neue freie Presse*, Vienna, June 1875, in Conati 1984: 110).

Italian admiration and emulation of Parisian grand opera led to the introduction, during the 1850s, of the so-called *disposizioni sceniche*, production books modelled on the *mises-en-scène* of the Paris Opéra. They provided minute descriptions of costumes and décor, detailed stage directions, and a great deal in the way of advice and exhortation as to how singers should interpret their roles.

These production books confirm the trend towards a repertory opera based on a comparatively small number of 'classics' which were likely often to be revived. Since they were published by the House of Ricordi – Giulio Ricordi wrote many of them himself – they underline the growing control of the publisher over theatre performances. And, most important of all, by providing a permanent record of a composer's original conception, they assert the primacy of the creative vision over the pressures exerted by local conditions or the idiosyncrasies of performing artists.

The production books show that the desire for a more natural style of acting was beginning to affect choruses as well as soloists. 'Take care', we read in the 1881 production book for *Simon Boccanegra*, 'that this movement of people across the square should not have the appearance of an organized procession' (Budden 1973–81, II: 282). And as the role of the chorus had become crucial again dramatically and musically, Verdi also insisted on pushing up the standards of choral singing. The sound he aimed at was 'full, robust and powerful', with resonant, open voice production – 'those Jewish voices that seem to scream "shoe laces and knitting needles" must not be heard at La Scala' (Busch 1978: 263; the allusion is to Isacco's aria in *La gazza ladra*).

One of the secrets of the desired choral sound was a large number of inner voices. It as a great mistake to reduce them, Verdi insisted, since it as the great wave of sound produced by them 'that tempers the high voices'. He went on to suggest for *Aida* a distribution of sixteen first and sixteen second tenors, sixteen bass baritones and sixteen low basses, twelve first and twelve second sopranos and twelve contraltos (24 May 1871, Busch 1978: 164). Chorus masters needed to be very strict about the rhythm of choral singing, and in particular 'to be very, very, very alert about the downbeat'. For it was a common defect among even the best Italian choruses – and Verdi specifies that at Bologna – 'to miss the attack or to attack weakly' (*ibidem*: 262).

Verdi continued to experiment with the arrangement of the orchestral seating. It was, he declared to Ricordi, as they prepared for the Italian première of *Aida*, 'of much greater importance than is commonly believed – for the *blending* of the instruments, for the sonority and for the effect' (*ibidem*: 183). He was to continue to experiment and to change his views down to the time of *Falstaff*, but in the late 1860s and 1870s his attitude was much affected by Viennese practice, as he explained to Florimo:

I would like your theatre – (I'm speaking to the Artist, not to the Neapolitan in you) – to adopt several modifications, which with modern scores have become indispensable, regarding the manner of production, the chorus and perhaps the orchestra itself. How can you 'just to mention one point', still put up with divided violas and divided 'cellos? How can you in that way achieve any *bow-attack*, *nuance*, *accent* etc. etc.? Besides which, you thus sacrifice the full sound of stringed instruments en masse. This is a remnant of the past, when violas and 'cellos played in unison with the double-basses. Accursed customs! And talking of customs, I must tell you of one. When I went to Vienna and saw all the double-basses massed together in the very middle of the pit, I (who had been *accustomed* to seeing them sprinkled here and there), I gave a great gesture of surprise and a little smile, which meant: 'these foolish Germans etc . . .' But when I went down into the orchestra pit and found myself sitting opposite these double-basses, and heard the powerful *attack, the accuracy, the cleanness of tone, the pianos, the fortes* etc. . . . I realized that I was the *fool*, and laughed no more. From this you will understand how I think the violas and 'cellos, which combine so often in modern operas, should be arranged.   (Conati 1984: 265–6).

One can only hope that, consolidated in this way, violas and 'cellos were able to improve Verdi's opinion of them as a 'race of hounds' and a principal source of havoc in the instrumental ranks (letter of 5 August 1857, in Budden 1973–81, II: 280).

The sound of the orchestra was not the only factor motivating these innovations. Like Wagner, Verdi was haunted by the dream of making opera a more totally absorbing experience, of creating on the stage an imaginary world less compromised by the exigencies of traditional theatre life. Among the innovations that would, he prophesied to Ricordi, 'surely come some day', were:

taking the spectators' boxes off the stage, bringing the curtain to the footlights . . . making the *orchestra invisible*. This is not my idea but Wagner's. It's excellent. It seems impossible that today we tolerate the sight of shabby tails and white ties . . . mixed with Egyptian, Assyrian and Druidic costumes . . . and, even more, the sight of the entire orchestra, which is part of the fictitious world, almost in the middle of the floor among the whistling or applauding crowd. Add to all this the indecency of seeing the tops of the harp, the necks of the double-basses, and the baton of the conductor all up in the air.
(letter of 10 July 1871, in Busch 1978: 183)

Amilcare Ponchielli

Never had Italian opera been so completely dominated by a single individual as it was by Verdi in the third quarter of the nineteenth century.

He did of course have some productive contemporaries, and some of them enjoyed the occasional success. Anyone with the appetite may read about them in Volume II of Budden's classic study, *The Operas of Verdi*. But at a time when individuality of utterance was at a premium and mere fluent competence interested no one, not one of them could be said to have made a truly distinctive contribution.

An exception should perhaps be made for Amilcare Ponchielli. And if one sounds doubtful even about that, it is because it is difficult not to agree with Verdi that, excellent musician as he was, he too lacked individuality. Verdi's explanation, typically, was that he had 'seen and *heard* too much' (letter of 5 February 1876, in Busch 1978: 387).

Ponchielli's philosophy of opera was profoundly though not rigidly conservative. He took an intelligent interest in the 'futurists' with their 'genere sinfonico orchestrale', and toyed with the idea of the *Leitmotiv* himself – I say 'toyed' because unless diabolism is an itch or a *tic*, nothing more incommensurate to its dramatic purpose than Barnaba's *Leitmotiv* in *La Gioconda* could well be imagined (Ex.VI.3). But he recognized that 'progress' and innovation could be only gradual in the theatre. As he put it in a letter to G. P. Galloni, 'if the management has to make money, one has to make oneself understood by all the public, including the clockmaker, the coal merchant and the sealing-wax vendor'. And he agreed with Verdi that the new style of music criticism, professional and addressed to the intelligentsia, made the composer's task appreciably more difficult. 'For them everything is conventional . . . that big-head Filippi is always talking about . . . the *inevitable* major after the minor, the *inevitable* move to the fifth or the minor, the *inevitable* accompaniment, the *inevitable* close (*comune*) etc.' (Nicolaisen 1980: 114).

It was only comparatively late in his career that Ponchielli became a respected public figure. He had made his debut at Cremona as early as 1856 with an operatic version of *I promessi sposi*. But the really successful phase of his career extended from the revised version of that same opera (Milan 1872) to *Marion Delorme* (Milan 1885) and thus belongs to the period of Verdi's temporary retirement from the theatre after *Aida*. In most of these

Poco più animato

Ex.VI.3 Ponchielli, *La Gioconda* (1876), Prelude

565

operas Ponchielli follows in the footsteps of *Don Carlos* and *Aida*, using a grand opera format in which the tragic human drama is set against a backcloth of momentous, or at least colourful historical events. He was the first Italian composer of opera to show, from the start of his career, a mastery of modern instrumentation. In his orchestral writing, which at its best is poetic, evocative and delicately nuanced, he evidenced a sensitivity to dramatic atmosphere – from the sombre Slav colouring of *I Lituani* (Milan 1872) to the garish orientalism of *Il figliuol prodigo* (Milan 1880) – which some critics have felt to rival the 'ambientism' of his most distinguished pupil, Puccini.

Unashamedly, however, Ponchielli attached the deepest importance to lyricism. And that meant, as a corollary, a certain reserve in the face of some developments of the 1860s and 70s. 'I believe', he wrote to Ricordi as he worked in *La Gioconda*, 'that where the Italian public is concerned it's vital not to make too much of the drama, otherwise you land yourself in rhythms that don't arrest the attention and you have to exploit the orchestra, and finally you need the kind of artist whom we don't have today and who perhaps didn't even exist in Rossini's time . . . Therefore in my opinion it's best to stick to the lyrical side' (Budden 1973–81, II: 283).

In his cult of melody Ponchielli still finds a place for the florid song that had long since disappeared from Verdi's scores. At the same time he cultivated a new style – slow-moving, ecstatic, self-proclaiming – that was to become one of the sources of *verismo* lyricism. A good example is the so-called 'rosary' theme from La Cieca's *romanza* 'Voce di donna' (*La Gioconda*, Act I), placed, almost like the refrain of an operetta number, as the culminating moment of the song (Ex. VI.4). It was a type of melody that lent itself well to thrilling orchestral restatements. If the original inspiration came from the Act III trio of *Don Carlos* (see pp. 550–1 above), Ponchielli, by his enthusiastic cultivation of such orchestral perorations, did much to create a fashion that was exploited *ad nauseam* by the *verismo* composers. In Cilea's *Adriana Lecouvreur*, for example, three of the four acts – not to mention most of the intervening ensembles – close in this way (Nicolaisen 1980: 98). The Ponchiellian prototype for such effects comes at the close of the third act of *La Gioconda*, where the theme which a few minutes earlier had expressed Enzo's fears for Laura is blared forth by the full orchestra after her apparently lifeless body has been discovered. Filippi left an admiring account of its impact on early audiences:

When the word, with the aid of cantilena or of declamation, has said everything it could, the orchestra comes to say the rest, and with a power, an effectiveness, an expressivenes that are to be wondered at. With this secret effect of his (con questo suo segreto) Ponchielli, the other evening, in the third finale, so original and terrible, made . . . the public leap into the air. (*La perseveranza*, 14 February 1880, in Nicolaisen 1980: 96)

If Ponchielli's total achievement in the field of opera was slight, it was not due to any lack of musical gifts but rather to an insufficiently urgent and

LA CIECA

affrett.

pure da me non par - ta - si, da me non

P a tempo

affrett.

rall.

par - ta - si senza un pie-to - so don, no!

col canto

(Si toglie il rosario dalla cintola) *a tempo*

no! A te que - sto ro - sa - rio

PP *leggerissimo*
a tempo

che le preghie - re a - du - na;

etc.

etc.

. . .but do not depart from me without a pious gift, no, no! [She takes the
rosary from her belt.] I give you this rosary which invokes prayers. . .

Ex. VI.4 Ponchielli, *La Gioconda* (1876), Act I scene 4

well-focused dramatic instinct. It has been argued that he further lacked 'the cultural or spiritual power necessary' to direct his gifts (*The New Grove*, s.v. 'Ponchielli'). Such shortcomings left him a prey to self-doubt and hesitancy, quite incapable of bending collaborators to his will in the service of a clearly perceived artistic vision.

30 · *Scapigliati* and bohemians

Scapigliatura

The group of artists and intellectuals, mostly Milanese, who during the 1860s and 70s came to be known as the *scapigliati* (the dishevelled ones) were not in any sense a regularly constituted society or fellowship. But during the first decade or so after Unification many young artists, several of them with a background of Mazzinian republicanism, found themselves disillusioned with the new Italy, impatient of the heroic rhetoric of public life and of *risorgimento* art, and scornful of the bourgeois philistinism which they believed they detected everywhere. In associating themselves with *scapigliatura* they became the earliest Italian exemplars of a typical nineteenth-century dilemma, the alienation between modern life and modern art.

Their unofficial guide was Giuseppe Rovani, a man who to the world at large was known as a historical novelist in an old-fashioned, Manzonian style. In fact Rovani was an altogether unlikely leader for a new artistic movement, being deeply conservative in many ways. One of his keenest followers, Carlo Dossi, reported of his musical tastes that they were 'like his taste in everything else, profoundly Italian. He hated the new school of composers which tried to compensate for its lack of ideas with its shattering din, and said of [those who] scorned the Italian muse, "who contemns Homer, will never be Virgil"' (Pestelli 1977: 607). In other respects Rovani's views were more radical; younger associates were particularly stimulated by his grandiose general ideas on the arts, by his Baudelairean sense of the affinities between them, and by his eagerness to see the clear-cut frontiers between them broken down. Dossi again: 'Colours, perfumes, forms have occult and intimate connections with music, and the time will come when people will sing and play life copies of a bunch of flowers, a tray of sweets, a statue, a building, just as today they do from the page of a *romanza*, or from a score on the music-stand' (Nardi 1949: 121).

Rovani drank himself to death at an early age. In fact, an aura of disrepute and depravity hangs about many of the group, notably two of its best poets, Emilio Praga and I. U. Tarchetti. How Praga impressed his contemporaries is vividly suggested by Croce:

Emilio Praga, drinker of absinth, blasphemer, depictor of orgies, bard of doubt and of tedium, inviting the elderly Manzoni to die, because there had now sounded 'the hour of the Antichrist', hymning the Seven Deadly Sins that were so dear to his heart, 'bow the knee, as in a temple'. A quarter of a century ago [before 1904] he gave us a sense of bewilderment and discomfort, a repugnance imperceptibly tinged with youthful curiosity for the unwholesome spectacle.   (Croce 1914: 241)

And Tarchetti ended his brief life in a state of lugubrious withdrawal from reality, 'strolling in cemeteries, meditating on tombs, a new Hamlet, conversing with grave-diggers and offering them cigars' (*ibidem*: 295).

The idea of the artist as a thorn in the flesh of bourgeois society helps emphasize the connection between the *scapigliati* and the Parisian bohemians of a generation earlier. Felice Camerone, one of the most committed of *scapigliati*, made a quite explicit identification of the two movements, shuffling the terms *scapigliatura* and *bohème* indiscriminately:

Scapigliatura is the denial of prejudice, the partisan of the Beautiful and True, the affirmation of individual initiative against quietism . . . Reactionaries persecute *la bohème* because it sounds the call to revolt; hedonists hate it, because it interferes with their digestion; the intelligentsia slander it, because they cannot understand it . . . *La bohème* is destined to pass from the purely artistic field to social conflict. After thought comes action . . . Political *scapigliatura* prepares the mine of revolution in the newspaper, primes it with the powder of agitation, and makes it explode at the barricade.
                                                                  (Groos and Parker 1986: 57)

These remarks come from the preface to his 1872 translation of Henri Murger's *Scènes de la vie de bohème*, the novel which was to inspire operas by both Puccini and Leoncavallo. If they seem unexpectedly and inappropriately fierce, it is because Camerone's politicized vision of *scapigliatura/ bohème* was not at all to Puccini's taste. His enchanting and disarming opera (Turin 1896) is drawn directly from the milder French original, and has shed a roseate and sweetly perfumed haze over everyone's conception of artistic bohemianism; but *La bohème* is far from telling the whole truth about *scapigliatura*.

That there was much high-spirited pose and much good fellowship among the *scapigliati* one has no reason to doubt. But there was a darker side too, which, even if it left no such single monument as *La bohème*, really affected opera more profoundly.

Italian Romanticism had, between *c.*1815 and *c.*1850, formed only a very imperfect analogy to transalpine Romanticism. As its primary task had been that of creating a national and popular art, apt to the forging of a new society, there had been little scope for the cult of individuality, or for the exploration of the subconscious and irrational forces that move the mind. That lacuna in the story of Italian Romanticism the *scapigliati* sought to fill. But they did so in an age of Darwinism, of Positivism, of Social Science and Psychology; and it is not to be wondered at if their intuitions and subjective visions were dark ones. Not infrequently it was chaos and old night that their explorations revealed, and the voices of Hell itself to which they gave utterance. The startling 'transvaluation of all values' that came about is revealed in the words of an early 'polemica letteraria' of Boito: 'our generation . . . shouts every day at the top of its voice that Catholicism is crumbling, that fetishism is in ruins . . . that a God has rotted away, that a Man has become divine . . . that Genius alone is the son of God, that the Eutychian heresy of eighteen centuries has become the sublime truth' (Nardi 1949: 150).

Boito was to become the greatest achiever among the *scapigliati*, not least because from *c*.1866 he rapidly outgrew its more negative manifestations. But the darkness remained. He was haunted by the antithesis of light and dark, beauty and ugliness, and obsessed with the problem of evil. These preoccupations were classically formulated in his early poem 'Dualismo'.

> Son luce ed ombra; angelica
> Farfalla e vermo immondo;
> Son un caduto chèrubo
> Dannato a errar pel mondo,
> O un demone che sale
> Per tortüose scale
> Verso un divino ostel . . .[1]

They were given their most powerful literary form in the legend, *Re Orso*, and, as critics noted from the first, they also informed his opera libretti, most obviously that of his own *Mefistofele* (Milan 1868; rev. Bologna 1875). Scarcely one of his libretti is without its Mefistofele-like villian: Barnaba in *La Gioconda*, Paolo in the revised *Simon Boccanegra*, Iago in *Otello*, each of them 'the embodiment of the everlasting "No!" addressed to the True, the Beautiful, the Good' (*Mefistofele* 1868: preface to libretto).

Scapigliati musicians: Arrigo Boito and Franco Faccio

Besides being a poet, Boito was one of the most notable musicians among the *scapigliati*. And alongside him one must place his bosom friend Franco Faccio, a fellow student at the Milan Conservatory in the late 1850s and early 1860s. Fervent adherents to the Italian nationalist cause, they had during their student years attracted much attention with two patriotic cantatas, 'Il quattro giugno' and 'Sorelle d'Italia', of which Boito wrote the verses while the music was shared between them. But for all their political and philosophical *italianità*, in musical matters both were devotees – feverish and exalted devotees – of German instrumental music; in the words of the report on Boito's work during the academic session 1857–58, 'he tends always to the ultramontane and the abstruse' (Nardi 1949: 43).

This tendency was surely encouraged by Boito's composition teacher at the Conservatory, Alberto Mazzucato, one of the most forward-looking of musical educationalists in Italy in the 1850s. Mazzucato's creed is conveniently summarized in an article in the *Gazzetta musicale* in 1858, in which he attacks the provincialism of those who claimed that Italian music could draw its strength only from national elements: '. . . practice and theory alike demonstrate so clearly that all the arts can acquire new life and benefit . . . from the exchange of ideas, from the assimilation of new aesthetic elements . . ., even though they may be of foreign provenance . . . for art today wishes to be cosmopolitan no less than national' (Nardi 1949: 45).

When they graduated from the Conservatory in 1862 the two friends were awarded a government travel scholarship to enable them to spend some time visiting musical centres in northern Europe: curiously they spent most of their time in Paris, and none in Germany. On Boito's return to Italy after this episode, he began his career as a journalist, and it was then that his musical tastes really became clear, though clarity is perhaps not the outstanding quality of his writing. The columns of *La perseveranza*, of the *Giornale della Società del Quartetto* and of *Figaro* swelled and resonated with his prose rhapsodies on Beethoven, Bach, Mendelssohn, Schumann and their 'spherical' music:

The Sublime is more simple than the Beautiful. The Beautiful can incarnate itself in all sorts of forms, the most strange, the most multiple, the most disparate; but for the Sublime only the one great form is fitting, the divine form, universal, eternal – the *spherical* form. The horizon is sublime, the sea is sublime, the sun is sublime. Shakespeare is spherical, Dante is spherical, Beethoven is spherical . . .

(F. Walker 1962: 455)

One composer who – perhaps surprisingly – was not spherical was Wagner. Boito at this stage, in the early 1860s, was not a Wagnerian, though at the time of the first Bologna performances of *Lohengrin* in 1871 he did briefly become an enthusiast: he is in fact the addressee of the master's 'Letter to a young Italian friend'. In the 1860s Boito showed, as far as modern opera was concerned, no more perception than most of his fellow-countrymen. Not Wagner but Meyerbeer was the supreme exponent of the form, the composer 'whose works, once appreciated, caused Italian operas to collapse by the hundreds like the bricks of the walls of Jericho: most of Bellini's, the greater part of Donizetti's, almost all of Rossini's . . . and some of Verdi's' (*Figaro*, 11 February 1864, in Budden 1973–81, II: 16).

As creative musicians neither Faccio nor Boito had talents commensurate with their aspirations, or – what was worse – with their powers of self-advertisement. Faccio's first opera, *I profughi fiamminghi* (Milan 1863), to a disappointingly conventional text by the outrageous Praga, was attended by all the clamorous publicity typical of the *scapigliati*. A celebratory dinner-party given for Faccio by a number of friends was the occasion for the notorious Boito ode 'All'arte italiana' that Verdi was to find so deeply offensive. Verdi's anger is understandable, for Boito affected to find in this not particularly brilliant opera, in which 'what is good . . . isn't new, and what is new is a little boring' (Mariani to Verdi 20 May 1865, in Budden 1973–81, II: 23), justification for the hope that

> Forse già nacque chi sovra l'altare
> Rizzerà l'arte, verecondo e puro,
> Su quell'altar bruttato come un muro
> Di lupanare.[2]

Neither it nor its successor *Amleto* (Genoa 1865), which Faccio composed to a libretto by Boito himself, lived up to the advance publicity. And in the long run both Faccio and Boito were too honest and too perceptive to pretend to themselves that they did.

Faccio's talents and idealism eventually found their proper outlet in conducting. He became the best Italian conductor of his generation, the natural successor to Mariani, two highlights of his career being the Italian première of *Aida* and the *prima assoluta* of *Otello*. He had exactly those qualities that Italian theatres in the 1870s most urgently needed: 'much energy, much musical memory. He is also very severe and reserved with the members of the orchestra who esteem and obey him without a whimper. He maintains the most perfect discipline. To this he adds a secure, calm and effective beat which brings about a truly commendable performance' (Ricordi to Verdi, 8 January 1871, in Busch 1978: 131).

Boito too composed two operas, *Mefistofele* (Milan 1868, rev. version Bologna 1875) and *Nerone* (posthumous, Milan 1924), both to his own texts. Despite the clamorous fiasco on the first night of *Mefistofele*, these have worn rather better than Faccio's; but both are deeply problematic pieces. When even Verdi was finding it difficult to turn Italian opera into a drama of ideas, it is scarcely surprising that the young Boito stumbled in trying to give adequate operatic form to the whole vast human and metaphysical panoply of Goethe's *Faust* – for unlike Gounod, he incorporated into his opera both parts of the tragedy. Nor was he ever able to bring to completion his epic depiction of the Roman Empire in disintegration. *Nerone* became a kind of Italian *Khovanshchina*, that was to prove performable only after the ministrations of Toscanini and Vincenzo Tommasini.

For sheer highmindedness *Mefistofele* had few equals in the whole tradition of Italian opera; at the same time it was a work of real, if not often persuasive originality. Its production, as everyone with even the slightest interest in art recognized, was one of the momentous events in the cultural life of nineteenth-century Milan. Francesco d'Arcais, music critic of the Florentine *Opinione*, testified to the fever of curiosity that raged in the city on the night of the première: 'that piazza . . . crowded with people anxiously awaiting news of the opera; those errand-boys who, at the end of each act, carried bulletins of the battle to the remotest quarters of the city; those scarcely parliamentary debates at the Café Martini, and the impatience, the challenges, the epigrams, and the satires' (Nardi 1949: 275).

If, in the last resort, *Mefistofele* simply will not do, it was not because Boito's dramatic conception was inadequate. As Nardi has written,

to have followed the action which culminates and concludes with the death of Margherita by a fourth act, which in a first episode makes reference to the exigency of gold and in a second to the aspiration towards artistic beauty, and then in a symphonic intermezzo to have made reference to the ideal of power; – all this was more than sufficient to give significance to the fifth act, in which Faust does indeed arrive at the point where the merciful grace of God can come to meet him. For he has been carried up thither through an entire gamut of experiences, bearing his thirst for knowledge and his thirst for life to ever loftier regions of error and struggle. (Nardi 1949: 303)

It was Boito's powers of musical invention, not his intelligence that failed him.

With the possible exception of the prologue, which, with a boldness of enharmonic modulation unprecedented in Italian opera, made a deep impression on certain types of sensibility – Saint-Saëns thought it 'the best piece of music to come from Italy in the late nineteenth century' (Nico-

. . .the dark one and his blonde girl swing around tightly embraced. . .

Ex.VI.5a Boito, *Mefistofele* (1875), Part I, Act I

574

Ex.VI.5b Boito, *Mefistofele* (1875), Prologue

laisen 1980: 138) – the music is more 'interesting' than beautiful, more curious than expressive or powerful. Nothing is more remarkable than Boito's independence of mind, but in a rather negative sense. The light, darting, *scherzoso* style that he uses in his portrayal of Mefistofele is arrestingly novel, an attempt to make tangible his belief that evil is best seen as nihilism rather than force. Much of the music is quite startlingly spare, as if Boito by a profound and unremitting contemplation of the most banal tags and scraps hoped somehow to rediscover their pristine magic: a circle of fifths stripped to barest essentials, to suggest the mystery of distance (Ex.VI.5a); infantile juxtapositions of major and minor to symbolize nihilistic malevolence (Ex.VI.5b); the most naively mechanical patterns of chromaticism to embody a satanic orgy (Ex.VI.5c).

Perhaps the most suggestive feature of the original 1868 *Mefistofele* is the paucity of traditional 'closed' lyrical forms. It has been proposed that this may reflect not only the obvious thing – Boito's impatience with the conventional 'formulae' of Italian opera (see below, p. 580) – but also 'the exaltation – wholly in the spirit of *scapigliatura* – of the criticial, reflective, polemical function of the spectacle at the expense of the sentimental' (Salvetti 1977: 602). In this context, the opera's one big aria, Mefistofele's 'Son lo spirito che nega', banally formalistic and punctuated with ribald

Ex.VI.5c Boito, *Mefistofele* (1875), Part I, Act II

Hurry up, you slender ones, hurry up, you strong ones, time may cheat us, our women are already up there. This is the tremendous night of the Sabbath. . .

whistling may be seen as 'an incarnation of the goliard derision with which the lucid intellectualism of the *scapigliati* regarded the bourgeoisie and its desire for a hedonistic operatic spectacle' (*ibidem*).

Wagnerism

Wagner was first brought to the notice of Italian musicians in February–March 1856, when Abramo Basevi, the Florentine doctor and music-lover who three years later was to publish the first and one of the most perceptive of monographs on Verdi, wrote a series of articles for the journal *L'armonia*.

But for a long time after Basevi's pioneering essays, even to the best informed and most progressive Italians, Wagner remained a man of mystery. Knowledge of his work was sketchy and piecemeal; it was difficult enough to see what exactly he aimed at, quite impossible to judge how far his operas were succeeding in realizing his aims. There was no more intelligent or alert young musician in Italy in the 1860s than Boito; his prevarications on the topic of Wagner perhaps show better than anything how precarious the level of understanding was.

In 1861 Camillo Boito jokingly referred to his brother's 'Wagnerian music'. But Arrigo's Wagnerism was ill grounded, and by the time he started to write as a music critic he was thoroughly disillusioned: Wagner was the Bar-jesus of contemporary opera, 'a false apostle . . . a false precursor, one of those dangerous propagators of truths ill said, ill thought, ill heard; one of those madmen who, with their thoughts on the light, diffuse darkness' (F. Walker 1962: 453). Some years later, at the time of the Bologna première of *Lohengrin* he got to know some of Wagner's music really well; he translated *Rienzi* into Italian and became something of an aficionado. But again the enthusiasm waned and soured.

One cause of the disillusion must surely have been the discrepancy between Wagner's announced programme of reform and such of his music as Boito knew. Reconciliation of the creative and polemic aspects of his work was difficult enough in any part of the world in the 1860s because, until the Munich production of *Tristan und Isolde* in 1865, nothing more mature than *Lohengrin* (1847) had been staged anywhere. In Italy no theatre ventured to perform any work of Wagner's, youthful or mature, before 1871. Wagnerism was essentially a theoretical and philosophical matter, at best fleshed out with some acquaintance with the published vocal scores. During the 1870s all this changed. The works of Wagner's early maturity were staged – after *Lohengrin* in 1871 came *Tannhäuser*, 1872; *Rienzi*, 1874; *Der fliegende Holländer*, 1877. 'Music-drama' in his later style was first heard in 1883, the year of Wagner's death, when Angelo Neumann's touring company brought the *Ring* (in German) to several Italian cities, though not to the Ricordi–Verdi stronghold of Milan.

The Wagner stronghold was Bologna. There were given the Italian premières of *Lohengrin* and *Der fliegende Holländer*, and later of *Tristan* (1888) and *Parsifal* (1914). In part this Bolognese tradition was due to commercial considerations. The Italian rights in Wagner's operas had been acquired by Ricordi's chief rival, Giovannina Lucca – which is not to say that Signora Lucca was a notably perceptive Wagnerian. In 1880 she was bold enough to attempt 'to persuade Wagner to reduce the tetralogy, if possible, and while preserving its grandiose character, shorten it so that it will last one single evening' (letter of 17 November 1880, in Carner 1974: 29). But since she owned the scores she was eager to see them staged, and the Bologna Teatro Comunale was the Lucca pocket-theatre as La Scala was Ricordi's. There was also the factor of Bologna's civic pride. In the newly unified Kingdom of Italy, Bologna was anxious to assert its cultural claims, perhaps 'to upstage Milan as a cultural centre', and, more specifically, 'to endow [itself] with a cosmopolitan image' (Miller 1984: 172–3). The immediate occasion of the *Lohengrin* production in 1871 was an international prehistory conference held in the city. As a leading Bologna music critic, A. Sangiorgi, wittily remarked, 'for a prehistory conference, music of the future is best' (*ibidem*).

During the last three decades of the century Wagner's influence was as manifold in its workings in Italy as elsewhere. If it was not quite so potent a force among composers as it was in some corners of Europe this may have been partly a case of temperamental disaffinity. It must also have been due to the glorious achievement of Verdi and to the uncompromising integrity and independence of his art.

Verdi, it should be understood, was, with reservations, an admirer. Echoes of his first impressions of Wagner – the Bologna *Lohengrin* – have been heard in many of his pages. And as he grew older he seemed to grasp the magnitude of Wagner's achievement ever more clearly.[3] But Italian composers' sense of the primacy of song, and therefore their commitment to finite lyrical structures, helped discourage too crass an epigonism. At the same time, Verdi's sophisticated development of the *parlante* technique – for example in the *congiura* scene in *Un ballo in maschera* – meant that it was but a small step to organizing scenes on the basis of a network of recurring orchestral themes. This was the nearest the better Italian composers came to Wagnerism; it was indeed the greater part of what would have been understood by Wagnerism in most parts of Europe at the time. Massenet, for example, the leading Parisian master, described his *Manon* (1884) in the following terms:

The whole work moves and develops upon some fifteen motifs which typify my characters. To each character a motif . . . These motifs run the length and breadth of the opera and are reproduced from act to act, shading off or coming into prominence, like the play of light in a picture, according to the situation. In this way my characters keep their personalities distinct until the end.   (Harding 1970: 78)

A comparable stage of development in Italian opera is reached in the 1890s with Puccini's first mature operas, *Manon Lescaut* (Turin 1893) and *La bohème* (Turin 1896), in Catalani's *La Wally* (Milan 1892) and Verdi's *Falstaff* (Milan 1893).

Grosser frenzies of Wagnerism manifested themselves only among non-musicians. By 1883, d'Arcais felt that it had become a substitute religion for certain types of intellectual. Like other religions it boasted its martyrs. Such, at any rate, was the glory claimed by Giovanni Papini – the later 'futurist' – when he was clapped in jail for too clamorous an expression of ecstasy at a Wagner concert (Miller 1984: 179). In 1873 Wagnerism had been a topic of debate in the Italian parliament; an attempt was made by some deputies to legislate against the corruption of the national conservatories by the infiltration of foreign art. At the end of the century the German master's influence on Italian politics was felt once more. He was one of Gabriele d'Annunzio's inspirations when, sickened by the liberal effeminacy of the new Italy, that disconcerting man of letters attempted to claim for the artist a right to shape the nation's destiny, to assert a more heroic and virile idealism, and 'abandoning the traditional image of the alienated victim . . . [preached] the need for intellectuals and artists to lead the politically dominant bourgeoisie to a revival of aristocratic spiritual values' (*ibidem*: 190).

The influence of French lyric opera

Italian composers continued to find a source of refreshment for their operatic tradition in the contemporary productions of the French lyric stage. One is, of course, no longer speaking of the grand opera that had proved so exasperating an influence during the previous decades. In the 1870s and 80s Meyerbeer remained as firmly entrenched in the Italian repertory as ever; but newer names began to rival the allure of his. Bizet's *Carmen* and Delibes' *Lakmé* became established favourites in the leading theatres during the 1880s. Following, as they did, in the wake of *Aida*, both operas helped enhance the prestige of local or exotic colour as a musico-dramatic resource, and *Carmen* played a far from negligible role in predisposing Italian audiences in favour of operatic realism.

In purely musical terms the most influential of the younger French voices was that of Massenet. He had been introduced to Italy with a production of his fifth stage work, *Le roi de Lahore*, at Milan in 1879. Ricordi was sufficiently impressed to imagine that he had found an answer to Lucca's Wagner, and promptly commissioned Massenet to compose a new opera for Italy. This, *Hérodiade*, was to be a setting of an Italian text by Angelo Zanardini. But in fact Massenet found that he could compose only in French. A French version therefore had to be made, by Louis Gallet, and in due course this was retranslated into Italian by Zanardini.

In the long run, this apparently cumbersome procedure may have been no bad thing, since it meant that the Italian repertory was infiltrated with something of that peculiarly intimate fusion of music and language at which Massenet excelled. The particular distinction of the French operatic tradition which he represented was its more chamber-music-like attitude to the medium. That is to say, the vocal and instrumental resources were employed more delicately, and the operatic manner was generally more informal, and casually conversational. I cite, as a beautiful example of this new French style, the first aria in *Werther*. The eponymous hero, who is making his way to the home of the local magistrate, strolls through a smiling countryside which entrances him by its burgeoning vernal freshness. At first the current of the music is borne by the orchestra, there is a snatch of recitative as Werther asks the way of a passing countryman, and only gradually as his musings become more ardent does the song become genuinely lyrical; even then there is much intimate give-and-take between voice and orchestra.

Massenet's informal aria style was emulated by several of the younger Italians, most obviously and most successfully by Puccini. Numerous Puccini arias begin 'in a slow hesitating manner, with the vocal theme, in some cases, first given to the orchestra while the voice glides in, chant-like, on soft reiterated notes' (Carner 1974: 290). Budden makes out a good case for Massenet's influence on the young Catalani too (1973–81, III: 275–6). He had actually studied at the Paris Conservatoire for a year in 1872–73 and heard at least two Massenet oratorios performed in the French capital, during his stay. When Boito provided him with an opera text (*La falce* 1875) brimming over with the deft metrical fluidity so typical of the *scapigliati* poets in general and his own verses in particular, Catalani seized with both hands the opportunity to imitate the flexible, conversational lyrical style of the French master.

Operatic aesthetics and the new style of libretto

The example of Rovani helped open the eyes of the *scapigliati* to the possibility of a more intimate kinship between the arts. It is not surprising to find that many of them were curious about the aesthetics of the Wagnerian *Gesamtkunstwerk* nor that they took a leading part in the debates about the future of Italian opera.

The young Boito invariably worked on the assumption that the anachronism of traditional opera had been demonstrated to the satisfaction of all but the indolent and the superficial. His mission was to drag and goad Italian music forward into the vanguard of contemporary European art. In one of his more scrutable essays, prompted by Cagnoni's *Il vecchio della montagna* (Turin 1860), he expounded to his readers a distinction between musical form and musical formula, the latter being the inadequate structural principle on which all Italian opera had hitherto been based:

There are in the language of men words and meanings which are easily confused, and which, especially in aesthetic matters, it is useful to disentangle; two of these words are *form* and *formula*. The Latins, who knew what's what, made of the second the diminutive of the first . . . And here it is necessary to state at once that since opera has existed in Italy, down to our own times, we have never had true operatic form, but always only the diminutive, the *formula* . . . The designations: aria, rondo, cabaletta, stretto, ritornello, *pezzo concertato*, are all there, drawn up for inspection, to confirm the truth of this assertion. The hour has come for a change of style; form, largely attained in the other arts, must develop, too, in our own; its time of maturity must have arrived; let it take off the *toga praetexta* and assume the *toga virilis*, let it change name and construction, and instead of saying *libretto*, the term of conventional art, say and write *tragedy*, as did the Greeks. (F. Walker 1962: 451)

Boito's prescriptions for cure were never as helpful as his diagnoses. Wagner's early operas failed to persuade him that Germanic music-drama was the answer, and his prophecies about Faccio's efforts were wildly overpitched without being specific or illuminating.

One thing, however, is perfectly clear. All the younger composers had become painfully self-conscious about the conventional song-based forms of opera. And in seeking some timely alternative principle of organization no composer – whether he was an intellectual like Boito, or a natural musician like Puccini – would henceforth fail to allot a far more central role to the orchestra. 'Let us exercise ourselves on the symphony and the quartet, so that we may be able to face up to the melodrama', wrote Boito in 1864 (Salvetti 1977: 572).

In the last third of the century instrumental music flourished in Italy as it had not done since the early eighteenth century. It has to be said that much of this activity was essentially a Germanic importation, sustained by quartet societies, by orchestral societies, and by the circles of pupils and admirers gathered around distinguished virtuosos resident in Italy – von Bülow in Florence, Liszt in Rome, Thalberg in Naples. But, despite Verdi's scepticism, it was also true that the conservatories were now providing a far more rigorous and imaginative training in instrumental composition. Few of the better pupils left them without having learned to delight in orchestral tone painting and tone poetry. One of the attractions for Puccini in Fontana's libretto for *Le villi* was that it offered 'ample scope . . . for the descriptive, symphonic kind of music, which attracts me particularly' (letter of July 1883, in Puccini 1974: 42).

When Boito began writing opera texts – *Amleto* for Faccio and *Mefistofele* for himself were the first – he confidently launched himself into a radical reappraisal of the whole question of what a libretto was. He recognized that the hidebound structures and the rhythmic stiffness of so much Italian opera arose inevitably from the metrical organization of the traditional libretto. And the most important of the technical innovations of his early libretti therefore took the form of a fundamental loosening-up of metrical structure: the centuries-old dichotomy of *versi a selva* and lyrical stanza (= recitative and lyrical number) was at last abandoned.[4] At the same time those tendencies that have earned Boito a reputation for preciosity – a fondness for arcane vocabulary, for extravagant imagery, for linguistic virtuosity of every kind – were already much in evidence. Such things betray the joy a real poet takes in his command of the *métier*. And Boito was indeed the chief figure in a historic movement that was to re-establish the opera libretto as a literary form. During the next generation Giacosa, Verga, d'Annunzio, Pirandello were all to be more or less seriously involved in the writing of texts for opera – which did not compensate for the lack of a real successor to Verdi!

If it was Boito who did most to assert the new degree of importance which the poet had in modern opera, no one took the point better than Giulio Ricordi; and none of the many shrewd decisions of that wily operator was more momentous than his determination to find a worthy poet for the young Puccini, the composer he had decided was Verdi's Crown Prince. The choice he alighted on was Giuseppe Giacosa, a leading figure in the Turin Dante Alighieri society, which was roughly the Piedmont equivalent of the Milan *scapigliati*.

By the 1870s and 80s Giacosa, an infinitely scrupulous artist, had established himself as the most successful playwright in Italy. His chosen medium was poetic drama, and in this medium he worked with a versatility so notable that it has often been taken to prove that he had nothing substantially or properly his own to say. Justice on that point need not concern us. But what is of interest is that Croce's essay on Giacosa – and it is he who leads for the prosecution – includes an account of his first great success, *Partita a scacchi*, which, while it shows no knowledge at all of his work for Puccini, describes the play in terms of a libretto *manqué*:

Giacosa's drama is a simple sketch (canovaccio); it is a libretto which serves as point of support for the aria, for the duet and for the cabaletta. The public to which it is ideally addressed is not one . . . that would pay attention to a line of verse which trembles and makes others tremble with aesthetic delight. It is a public to which one has to say and say again the simplest things, shouting them out and singing them over again
(Croce 1914: 217–18)

In *Mefistofele* Boito had tried to do everything himself in the truest *Gesamtkunstwerk* manner, to make of poetry and music one single conception. In fact, like the young Wagner, he had gone further and conducted the performance as well, an unhappy idea which had apparently originated with Filippi 'under the pretext of forming a complete trinity: poet, composer, and director' (Mazzucato to Mariani, 24 February 1868, in Nardi 1944: 250). After the failure of *Mefistofele* a very different procedure became fashionable. It was modelled on French practice: and involved setting two authors to work together on the libretto.

In the case of Giacosa the chosen collaborator was Luigi Illica. The two men were first called in together by Ricordi when two earlier librettists, Marco Praga and Domenico Oliva, had thrown up their hands in despair of ever satisfying Puccini with the text for *Manon Lescaut*. Later Giacosa and Illica produced the texts of all Puccini's most popular successes: *La bohème* (1896), *Tosca* (1900), *Madama Butterfly* (1904).

It was an extraordinary and difficult collaboration. To begin with the two men had diametrically opposed views of their task. Illica was an impetuous, improvisatory worker, frankly recognizing that a libretto was nothing more than the sketch for a work of art. As he put it in a letter to Puccini in 1907:

The form of a libretto is created by the music, only the music and nothing but the music . . . A libretto is nothing but a sketch. Méry puts it well when he says: 'The verses in an opera are only there for the convenience of the deaf.' I shall therefore continue to give in every libretto importance only to the treatment of the characters, to the cut of the scenes and to the verisimilitude . . . of the dialogue, of the passions and situations . . . That which has real value in a libretto is the word. The words should correspond to the truth of the moment (the situation) and of the passion (the character). Everything lies in that, the rest is *blague*. (Carner 1974: 80–1)

Often he was as good as his word, discarding the traditional proprieties of Italian verse to write those casually rhymed and irregularly scanning lines which Giacosa was to dub 'illicasillabi'.

Giacosa on the other hand was a perfectionist, concentrating and refining the versification, wrestling to find the *mot juste*, as if he were bent on the loftiest of literary tasks. A letter to Ricordi about the Café Momus scene of *La bohème* captures much of his tormented conscientiousness:

I don't feel it, I can't get inside it; it doesn't succeed in convincing me or in creating for me that fictitious reality without which one can accomplish nothing. I have messed up more paper on this scene and I have racked my brains more than for any of my dramatic works . . . I must have done it, redone it, and then gone back to do it again a hundred times. I haven't extracted one single line that I like. I have worked this evening from 11 to 3 in the morning; I started work again at 7.30; it's 5 p.m. now, and the scene has not moved ahead one step. (Groos and Parker 1986: 37)

To make things worse, few composers can have been more difficult to work with than Puccini, inexorable in his demands for a libretto 'that will move the world' (Puccini 1974: 29) but so much less able than Verdi to explain what he really wanted, and far more prone to self-doubt and paralysing vacillations. Posterity is again indebted to Giulio Ricordi that, despite Giacosa's periodic avowals never to be trapped into writing a libretto again, so much was achieved. It was Ricordi's adroit, imaginative and generous chairmanship of this difficult trinity that enabled wounded pride to be soothed, conflicting claims to be adjudicated, threatening impasses to be circumvented.

Alfredo Catalani

Another composer with direct links to *scapigliatura* was Catalani; in fact he was the model for one of the most famous of *scapigliato* paintings, Tranquillo Cremona's *L'edera*. Though he was certainly a more genuinely creative musician than either Faccio or Boito, his work too leaves a curiously pathetic overall impression.

In Catalani's case that impression is not unconnected with the circumstances of his brief life. He had an unusually wide musical training, at the Pacini Institute in his native Lucca; at the Paris Conservatoire, and finally at the Conservatory in Milan, where he was a pupil of Bazzini. Through Bazzini he was introduced to the salon of Verdi's old friend Clarina Maffei, and through her he got to know the leading *scapigliati* of yesteryear, reformed and unregenerate alike. It was Boito who provided the text for his graduation exercise, *La falce*, in 1875.

Perhaps neither Boito nor, what was worse, Ricordi were quite convinced of Catalani's distinction. Boito, normally the most generous of men, was desultory to the point of callousness in responding to pleas for further libretti, and Catalani was never to find the loyal, skilful, self-effacing literary collaborator that modern opera so urgently needed. Since Ricordi was not particularly interested in his work, he attached himself to the rival firm of Lucca, and it was a major blow to his ambitions, when, in 1888, Giovannina Lucca sold out to Ricordi's. Even now Ricordi was so little excited by Catalani's work that virtually all initiatives in furthering his career had to come from the composer himself, by now helped and encouraged by the brilliant young conductor Arturo Toscanini. It was the composer who had to commission and pay Zavadini to rewrite the libretto of *Elda* (Turin 1880), to turn it into a viable opera. And the revision, now known as *Loreley*, lay gathering dust at Ricordi's for two years until Catalani himself organized a performance in Turin (1890). If one recalls the energy, the patience and the cunning with which Ricordi cultivated old Verdi and groomed Puccini, it is no surprise to find that Catalani – frail, sick and seemingly without influential friends – came to be jealous of Puccini with a morbid, pathological jealousy that has been compared with that of Bellini for Donizetti (Klein 1967: 223). He felt little but contempt for the other musical heroes of the early 1890s, the first *veristi*: 'is it worth the trouble to write anything serious?' he exclaimed to Depanis on learning of the triumph of *I pagliacci* (Nicolaisen 1980: 176).

Catalani's qualities did make a deep impression on a few discriminating musicians. During his Hamburg years, Mahler was a warm admirer of *Dejanice* (Milan 1883); ultimately, though sadly too late to be of any help to Catalani, Verdi came to feel real esteem for his work. But it was Toscanini who responded most wholeheartedly to its blend of purity, idealism and fastidiousness. To the end of his life he was convinced that Catalani represented Italian opera more nobly and eloquently than any composer after Verdi. And it was he who was largely responsible for the limited vogue that some of the operas – *Dejanice*, *Loreley* and *La Wally* – have enjoyed since the composer's premature death.

Unlike his more successful contemporary and fellow-Lucchese Puccini, Catalani was out of step with the taste of the times. If the *scapigliati* were belated Romantics, he was a belated *scapigliato*, a dreamer and idealist totally at a loss in the new world of *verismo*. On the other hand Germanic myth and legend fascinated him, sometimes to the despair of his warmest admirers: 'how can one possibly interest the public in mermaids?' groaned Toscanini of *Elda* (Klein 1967: 217). He inclined too to the Germanic tendency to see his characters as symbolic abstractions; though Ashbrook attributes this to the *scapigliatura* conditioning of his early years and to a *scapigliato* fondness for 'a rather shallow irony rooted in an unresolved dualism' (*The New Grove*, s.v. 'Catalani').

Germanic features are not lacking in Catalani's music. This was probably one factor in Verdi's long-lasting coolness; in or around 1892 he described him 'as excellent musician, though he has an exaggerated idea of the importance of the orchestra' (Budden 1973–81, III: 274). Like Boito, Catalani saw tone poetry in the German sense as a resource that could much enrich the operatic medium. In fact he was one of the very few nineteenth-century Italians to have written a genuine tone-poem. *Ero e Leandro* (1885) was inspired by Boito's libretto of the same name, rather as Mendelssohn's *Die schöne Melusine* was by the libretto which Grillparzer wrote for Beethoven. Evocative orchestral interludes adorn all his works. His sense of values is perhaps suggested by the fact that his first stage work, *La falce*, begins with an extended symphonic prologue, very possibly inspired by the battle-symphony in the 1868 *Mefistofele*. It purports to depict the course of the battle of Bedr, beginning with the dawn, following the shifting fortunes of the fight, and ending with an epilogue evoking the silence of the corpse-strewn sands. Catalani's feeling for *Naturromantik*, a quality singularly lacking in most earlier Italian opera, has been compared with Weber's (Budden 1973–81, III: 290).

Early audiences found his harmonic style problematic or, a favourite term of scepticism at the time, 'futuristic'. Even in *La Wally*, his most mature and accomplished work, it is difficult not to sympathize with them. What one misses is that individuality of voice that would fuse all the intriguing details of his harmony – the naive diatonicism, the haunting late-Verdian-modality, the obsession with augmented triads, the flagrant parallelisms, the oddly incoherent transitional modulations, the *ad hoc* trouvailles – in a truly personal synthesis (such as Puccini was to achieve with every new sound poached during his wide-eared travels round the contemporary musical world).

For the rest, Catalani wrestled with the same issues as all his Italian contemporaries from Verdi downwards. He sought an alternative to the ponderous rhetorical apparatus of the grand opera, which he had eventually got out of his system with 'his Ponchiellian opera' *Dejanice* (Nicolaisen 1980: 154). An acute problem was musical continuity. His early works were pervaded by a sense of 'conventional arias and duets in search of a musico-dramatic format' (*ibidem*: 159). Manifestly he did not find it easy to sustain musical invention and theatrical vitality through the orchestral recitatives that linked them. He and Puccini 'crossed the great divide' (Budden 1973–81, III: 289) between disguised number opera and continuous music-drama simultaneously, arriving on the far side in the memorable winter 1892–93 which saw the premières of both *La Wally* and *Manon Lescaut*, not to mention *Falstaff*. The new style, in technical terms, was essentially that of *Otello*. The arias and ensembles were swept along on a seamless orchestral fabric woven out of significant *motifs*. Sometimes these *motifs* evolve from one lyrical movement and form a symphonic transition into the next; sometimes they serve something of the identifying or symbolic purpose of a *Leitmotiv*.

The young Puccini

No greater contrast is imaginable than that between the misty impersonality of Catalani and the unmistakable and inimitable individuality of Puccini, his junior by only four years. Puccini had suddenly discovered his vocation after the desultory studies of his youth, when a performance of *Aida* at Pisa in 1876 'opened a musical window' (Carner 1974: 19). Thereafter he devoted himself as exclusively to the cultivation of opera as any of his Italian predecessors: 'Almighty God touched me with His little finger and said: "Write for the theatre – mind, only for the theatre." And I have obeyed the supreme command.' (Puccini 1974: 29). He was also, as Gianandrea Gavazzeni noted, the last in the great line of Italian composers who all his life retained the most direct and intimate links with 'theatrical reality' (Martinotti 1977: 459).

It is no small part of the uniqueness of Puccini's status in the operatic world at the close of the nineteenth century that he was perfectly equipped, mentally, emotionally and musically to make his spiritual home at the very heart of its decadence, in that place 'where erotic passion, sensuality, tenderness, pathos and despair meet and fuse' (Carner 1974: 245). Those unsympathetic to his art have repeatedly asserted that he did not set his aims high, that it is informed by no idealism, no spirituality, no higher purpose. Pizzetti described his preferred type of theme as being the 'drammetto di piccole mediocri anime borghesi'[5] (Martinotti 1977: 453). It is certainly possible to belittle Puccinian opera – as it is that of Massenet or Richard Strauss – as something designed to serve as the frivolous pastime of a doomed bourgeois civilization. And it cannot be denied that in it the glorious humanist tradition of Italian art is *in extremis*. Nevertheless his work surely merits the place it holds in the affection and esteem of opera-goers for the consummate artistry and urgent eloquence with which it speaks of the only verities Puccini could be sure of – the passions that intoxicate, torment and destroy. These humanist relics were precious enough to inspire a tireless devotion to a style of art that was still 'written for all races of men' (Carner 1974: 251).

For all the sophistication of his musical technique, Puccini was an instinctive composer with, on his own admission, 'more heart than mind' (*ibidem*: 245). He had little of the intellectual in his make-up, and as a student had been bored to death by the classes in literature and aesthetics. The orchestral background of his operas may suggest an Impressionist refinement, an almost morbid sensibility, as it flickers and shimmers with suggestive half-lights and shades. But at their core there burns an impassioned song, ecstatic and in a sense naive, which makes Puccini one with all the greatest of his Italian predecessors.

So it was no *scapigliatura*-like ratiocination that put Puccini in the vanguard of operatic developments in the 1890s: rather an intuitive sixth sense from which he acquired an exceptionally acute feel for the musical world in which he lived. That gave him the confidence to emulate Boito and Catalani in the 'descriptive, symphonic kind of music' (see p. 581), and steered him unerringly away from the pomposity and rhetoric of grand opera towards the more intimate expressiveness and the more natural-seeming dramatic flow of French lyric opera. And it was his instinctive tenderness for small things – sentimental if one will – that gave him a realist's delight in turning the ambience of an opera, the surface and texture of its decor, into music, and appalled an old idealist like Hanslick because it seemed to mark 'the last step toward the naked, prosaic dissoluteness of our time' (Groos and Parker 1986: 133).

But for all the strength and acuity of Puccini's instincts he had only the most tremulous faith in them. Ricordi was unshakably confident that he had found Verdi's heir apparent, but Puccini rapidly became as unsure of himself as Catalani. In particular he suffered endless agonies of doubt over the question of whether he had found the right subject. He knew none of those flashes of intuition in which Verdi recognized, 'That's it!' After his earliest operas, *Le villi* (Milan 1884) and *Edgar* (Milan 1889), had foundered on the inept, anachronistically Gothic librettos of Ferdinando Fontana, he tended to choose 'guaranteed' subjects, subjects, that is to say, that had already proved themselves as spoken plays: Sardou's *Tosca*, David Belasco's *Madame Butterfly* and *Girl of the Golden West*, Didier Gold's *La houppelande*. And all these plays are of a common type, depending for their effect on an unmistakable, blatant and visible theatricality. He came to insist on 'what he called "*l'evidenza della situazione*"', which should enable the spectator to follow the drama even without understanding the actual words' (Carner 1974: 284).

La bohème (Turin 1896)

Given the spiritual identity of the Milanese *scapigliatura* of the 1860s and 70s and the Parisian *Bohème* of the 1830s and 40s, one can hardly fail to close this chapter with a few words on Puccini's best-loved opera. The composer was too young to have been closely associated with the original *scapigliati*, but the biography of his student days in Milan in the early 1880s records anecdotes enough to suggest that he lived very much in the 'bohemian' manner which they had brought into fashion (see Carner 1974: 27).

Puccini's opera is a sentimental, nostalgic idealization of the movement. In it the bewitching amalgam of rebellion and idealism, of crass follies and beautiful dreams which Murger's writings had already made the badge of the nineteenth-century student-artist, acquired a deeper poetry and pathos. What the opera conspicuously does not do is to reinforce Murger's moral warnings about the danger of lingering too long in Bohemia: 'c'est le préface de l'Académie, de l'Hôtel-Dieu ou de la Morgue'. Still less does it attempt to make his story a document in the cause of Socialist realism as the Italian translator Camerone urged (see p. 570 above) and as, in some measure, Leoncavallo does in his treatment of the same theme, *La bohème* (Venice 1897). All the same, the feel of Puccini's opera was authentic enough to have impressed Debussy, who is said to have remarked to Manuel de Falla, 'I know of no one who has described the Paris of that time as well as Puccini in *La bohème*' (Carner 1974: 336).

The librettists' clear understanding of what kind of drama they were aiming at is apparent in the preface to the libretto, where they speak of 'remaining faithful to the characters . . . being meticulous in reproducing some of the particulars of the ambience . . . going along with Murger in subdividing the libretto into distinct tableaux' (Ferrando 1984: 100). In fact, as they go on to acknowledge, one character, Mimi herself, has been transformed by mingling her attributes, as they are described by Murger, with those of Francine. The effect is to soften, to sweeten and to etherealize.

In its attention to ambience, *La bohème* shows its kinship with the new vogue of *verismo*. One detail which the librettists quote from Murger's own preface catches the eye: '*Bohème* has its own special way of talking, its own jargon . . . Its vocabulary is the hell of rhetoric and the paradise of the neologism' (*ibidem*). With *La bohème* the traditional high-flown poetic diction gave way to a slangy colloquialism that only at rare moments of exalted feeling returned to anything like the norms of operatic eloquence. It was one detail of that 'sensational break with the last romantic and artistic traditions of opera' deplored by Hanslick (Groos and Parker 1986: 134). Another was Puccini's delight in musical décor. Writing to Ricordi about what eventually became Act III, he exclaimed, 'I am exceedingly pleased with the first scene . . . I warn you that we shall need four bells. Matins are ringing from the Hospice of St. Thérèse and the nuns are coming down to pray. *Ensemble*: xylophone, bells, carillon, trumpets, drums, cart-bells, crackings of whips, carts, donkeys, tinkling of glasses, a veritable arsenal' (1974: 101–2). At rehearsals he insisted on the perfect co-ordination of music and spectacle: a curtain dropping too soon or too late could wreck an opera. 'When he composed he knew what he wanted', reported Luigi Ricci (1954); 'there was an inexorable cine-chronometer which followed all the action down to the smallest detail'. It was a feature that impressed the more discerning critics from the first, as we may see in a beautifully written review of the Paris première by Verdi's friend Camille Bellaigue.

M. Puccini's music willingly attaches itself to concrete, palpable reality, to the outward and to appearances, to its exterior and insignificant signs . . . This surface reality, which is to profound truth what décor or costume . . . are to thought or feeling, M. Puccini's music expresses marvellously, giving us its acute and constant sensation. And how does the music manage this? Sometimes by renouncing itself, by not fearing to sacrifice itself to word or to action, or to theatrical display and purely scenic effects . . .

(Groos and Parker 1986: 136)

As Giacosa and Illica suggest, the four acts of the opera are four distinct tableaux, only casually associated with one another. That too was a step of considerable boldness: the dramatic action has no more coherent a unity in the Classical sense than *Pelléas et Mélisande*, a fact which occasioned some part of the critical displeasure that greeted the première. Carner calls it 'the first opera in history to achieve an almost perfect fusion of romantic and realistic elements with impressionist features' (1974: 337).

Much of the Puccinian skill and much of the magic is found *in nuce* in the opening scene of the opera, the dialogue between Marcello and Rodolfo. Marcello is a robust humourist, Rodolfo a dreamy sentimentalist, and between them the two friends sum up much of Murger's *Bohème*: the verve and the high-spirited conquest of adversity on the one hand; the poetry, the pathos, the warming idealism on the other. The mood of the scene oscillates between these two facets, and each has its proper theme.

The first is commonly regarded as the bohemians' *Leitmotiv* (Ex.VI.6a).

Ex.VI.6a Puccini, *La bohème* (1896), Act I

589

...that I have no faith in the sweat of my brow.

Ex. VI.6b Puccini, *La bohème* (1896), Act I

Watch the stairs!

Ex. VI.6c Puccini, *La bohème* (1896), Act I

It is a 'symphonic' theme, borrowed in fact from Puccini's early *Capriccio sinfonico*, perhaps – it has often been suggested – as a symbolic memory of his own bohemian student years. This theme is the source of much of the *Kleinkunst* pictorialism later in the act – Marcello's shivering with cold (Ex.VI.6b); the flickering of the fire; the friends' clattering descent of the stairs (Ex.VI.6c). The second theme is that of Rodolfo's aria 'Nei cieli bigi', the music of his dreaming aspirations (Ex.VI.7a). It is sung rather than played, lyrical rather than symphonic; and by its means Puccini links together and bathes in an idealistic glow a whole range of related ideas – the warmth of the fire when Rodolfo burns his old play (Ex.VI.7b); his account of his work as a writer (Ex.VI.7c); his sense of having been blessed with a rich and fulfilling vocation (Ex.VI.7d). In Scene I these two themes alternate in free variation, creating one of those loose-limbed rondo-like structures which Puccini liked to use to give a schematic backbone to his seemingly naturalistic operatic dialogues.

In the grey skies I watch Paris smoking from a thousand chimneys, and think on that idle...

Ex.VI.7a Puccini, *La bohème* (1896), Act I

Except for 'Nei cieli bigi' itself all these thematic reprises and developments are carried by the orchestra, drenching the commonest things in a transfiguring emotional light, and suggesting a world of feeling beneath the prosaic exterior. And because the orchestra can now do so much, much of the singing is casual, conversational, life-like in a way that Italian opera had never attempted to be before. But Puccini shows that he too understood what Galilei and Metastasio knew so long ago: that, stylishly handled, Italian declamation hovers on the brink of melody. *La bohème* called for a style of song which was 'in some degree realistic' and yet at the same time 'as much *melody*, as possible' (letter to Ricordi, November 1895, in Puccini 1974: 114). Despite all the realistic detail that so pothered Hanslick, popular audiences and the more susceptible critics were thrilled to recognize that here at last was another Italian composer of opera who really understood how to sing. Bellaigue once more:

Here's the first act for you. Over here. Tear it up.

Ex.VI.7b Puccini, *La bohème* (1896), Act I

592

However much you try to protest, perhaps in the depths of yourself, against your too easy and too physical pleasure, your pleasure will be the stronger. Do not be ashamed, because these accents go far, further than the situations, feelings or characters. And they also come from afar: from the old, illustrious land where melody is born, where, fallen and impoverished though it may be, it still survives and does battle. Loved for itself, for itself alone, Italian melody remains the sign or memory, enfeebled but still affecting, of something great, almost sacred. Down there 'they are still singing', and when one of their songs . . . reaches our ears, is it our fault, our great fault, if . . . an ineffable sweetness of life penetrates us and inspires within us a vague desire for tears?

(Groos and Parker 1986: 137)

(Io) re - sto per ter-mi-nar l'ar - ti - co - lo di fon - do del 'Ca -
- storo; Cin-que minuti. Co - nosco il mestier.
Fa pre-sto.

I'm staying to finish the leading article for *The Beaver*. Be quick.
Five minutes. I know my job.

Ex.VI.7c Puccini, *La bohème* (1896), Act I

593

Andante lento ♩=52

RODOLFO

In po-ver-tà mia lie - ta scia-lo da gran si-

P dolce

- gno - re.... rime ed in-ni d'a-mo - re. Per so-gni e per chi-

pp

me - re   e per   ca - stel - li in (aria)

In my happy poverty I throw away like a great lord. . .poems and hymns
of love. With dreams and illusions and castles in the air. . .

Ex.VI.7d Puccini, *La bohème* (1896), Act I

31 · Verdi and Boito

Reconciliation

They were an unlikely pair. Verdi, the senior figure in Italian music, devoted to the Italian traditions of his art, was a man of great simplicity and directness, whose character and ideals had been formed in the heroic decades of the *risorgimento*. Boito, nearly thirty years his junior, was an intellectual and a cosmopolitan – one of the most radical representatives of the *scapigliatura* impatience with old ways and traditional values.

They first met and worked together in Paris in 1862. Verdi was mulling over a commission he had received to contribute an item for the London International Exhibition later in the year; Boito was sojourning there with Faccio on their government bursary. Encouraged by Clarina Maffei to call upon Verdi, the two friends were cordially received and given the kind of encouragement that established masters have traditionally given young aspirants. Moreover, having sampled some of Boito's verses, Verdi charged him with the task of writing a text for him for his London commission: the *Inno delle nazioni*.

A relationship that had begun amiably and promised to become fruitful was soured when Verdi read one of Boito's more foolish poems in a theatre journal. It was the already cited ode, declaimed by the poet at a banquet following the première of *I profughi fiamminghi* in 1863.

> Alla salute dell' Arte italiana!
> Perché la scappi fuora un momentino
> Dalla cerchia del vecchio e del cretino,
> Giovine e sana . . .
> Forse già nacque chi sovra l'altare
> Rizzerà l'arte, verecondo e puro,
> Su quell'altar bruttato come un muro
> Di lupanare . . .[1]

'About the Ode one can only say that, as a high-spirited challenge to the established order, as the extravagant expression of youthful ambitions, it was in place at the banquet in Faccio's honour, among friends. But it should never have been published' (F. Walker 1962: 462). It was published though, and Verdi, as thin-skinned and touchy at fifty as he had always been, found it grossly offensive. It festered in his mind for years; he was forever quoting and misquoting it to his friends. Nor was his opinion of Boito improved by the young man's critical writings on music, which during 1863–64 poured from his pen, and which Verdi found intolerably pretentious and vaporous. 'I have read some articles in the newspapers, where I've found big words about *Art, Aesthetics, Revelations*, the *Past* and the *Future*, etc., etc., and I confess that (great ignoramus that I am) I understand nothing of all that' (to Clarina Maffei, 13 December 1863, *ibidem*: 450).

Boito's attitude to Verdi was in fact far more admiring than the Ode 'All'arte italiana' might lead us to believe, or than Verdi's suspicions about clever young men would allow him to believe for years to come. During the Broglio furore in 1868, he addressed to the Minister a 'Letter in four paragraphs' in which he wrote of 'the Verdian theatre, fascinating, glorious and fecund' (*ibidem*: 461). And by 1871 he was ready to declare himself 'the *happiest*, the most *fortunate* of men, if he could write the libretto of *Nerone* for [Verdi]' (*ibidem* 464–5). This, it must be appreciated, would have represented a tremendous act of self-sacrifice on Boito's part. *Nerone* was to be his own next opera. It was a subject he had lived with and pondered since his student days, and it was to absorb him for the rest of his life. Verdi, however, was slow to forget insults. As late as 1879, when Boito had already begun work on *Otello*, he knew that Verdi still mistrusted him:

Even if Verdi won't have me any more as collaborator, I shall finish the work as best I can, so that he can have proof that I . . . have dedicated to him, with all the affection he inspires in me, four months of my time. By that I would not wish, heaven forbid, to claim any material reward, either from him or from you, if the thing does not turn out well. It would be enough for me to have given Verdi proof that I am very much more truly devoted to him than he believes. (To Giulio Ricordi, *ibidem* 475)

Boito, in all but his enduring Romantic idealism, was himself a much changed man by the 1870s. It is difficult not to believe that he had already come to recognize his own personal tragedy: 'that he and his friends were incapable of the tremendous tasks they set themselves' (*ibidem* 462); that, as he was later to put it in a letter to Verdi, he was being 'slowly asphyxiated by an ideal too exalted for [his] powers' (*ibidem* 489). But Verdi's more recent operas suggested that he did have powers sufficient to realize Boito's dreams; and Boito came gradually to recognize that his primary vocation in life was going to be that of 'making that bronze colossus resound' (to Camille Bellaigue, in Hepokoski 1983: 20). 'You are sounder than I, stronger than I', he wrote in one of his most moving letters to Verdi, 'we tested our strength and my arm bent beneath yours . . . I shall know how to work for you, I who do not know how to work for myself, for you live in the true and real world of art, and I in the world of hallucinations' (in F. Walker 1962: 490). Towards the end of his life he was to tell Bellaigue, 'Nothing moves me so profoundly as to hear myself named when he is spoken of . . . To be the faithful servant of Verdi, and of that other, born on the Avon – I ask no more' (*ibidem* 510).

The extent to which their collaboration was a good thing for Verdi and therefore for the health of Italian opera is more controversial now than once it was. Even outside Italy there is some understanding for those who feel that Verdi's later operas are the fruit of 'a maturity more troublesome than creative . . . [where] learning prevails over invention' (Baldini 1980: 275). And for such as feel like that, Boito has become something of a bogey-man. Here is Bruno Barilli on the subject of *Falstaff*:

A sad, brown shadow stretches out page after page in this score. In the sulphurous glow of the footlights the musical comedy of the old misanthrope often seems cold, prudent, indirect and evasive. He had now . . . met up with a poet who, although imposing, was filled with ideologies and amateurish scribblings. Obliged to underline a tightly packed, complicated dialogue, sprung entirely from fanciful witticisms and literary devices, the old Verdi (who before had built in the simple, scornful manner of the greats) might have sensed the discord, but he lacked the force to dominate, destroy, and reconstruct the material of the libretto along broad, summary, and powerful lines . . .

(Quoted Hepokoski 1983: 142–3)

Few, if any, Verdians north of the Alps would be prepared to go half so far. If there is substance to the complaint of Barilli and Baldini it is that sifted out by Budden, namely

that here [in *Otello*] Verdi does not operate on the same level of musico-dramatic immediacy as in his earlier operas and for the very reason that Baldini gives, namely the recherché artificiality of Boito's language . . . the most memorable tunes of *Otello* often recur to the mind independently [of the text] because such phrases as 'S'inaffia l'ugola' and 'Chi all'esca ha morso' are too self-consciously coined to have any directness; they lack even the emotional charge of Cammarano's agglomerations of adjectives.

(Budden 1973–81, III: 412–13)

Beneficent or not, Verdi's working relationship with Boito was very different from those he had enjoyed earlier with Solera, Cammarano and Piave. Boito was a real poet, a man brimming over with ideas, and a virtuoso with words. He was already a widely experienced librettist before he began to work with Verdi. What is more, as a composer of sorts himself, he understood those qualities of clarification, concentration, metrical variety and so on, which a musician needed of a text. Not least important, he knew that in an opera music's role was bound to be the primary one.

At the same time, for all the reverence he felt for Verdi, he was not overawed by him. The composer's own ideas and wishes were scrutinized carefully and critically, and if they seemed wrong-headed were countered, patiently, cogently and subtly. The nature of the relationship was established very early on when they were seeking a suitable *concertato* finale for Act III of *Otello*. Rather uncharacteristically, one feels, Verdi had suggested a spectacular, non-Shakespearian scene, in which the reception of an embassage from Venice had been interrupted by a renewed Turkish invasion, and Otello, shaken out of his moral torpor, had once more taken up his sword to lead the Cypriot-Venetian forces to victory. He got Boito to write such a finale, and then pressed him to say what he thought of it. Boito replied:

When you ask me, or rather ask yourself: Are these needless scruples or are they serious objections? I reply: They are serious objections . . . That attack by the Turks is like a fist breaking the window of a room where two persons were on the point of dying of asphyxiation. That intimate atmosphere of death, so carefully built up by Shakespeare, is suddenly dispelled. Vital air circulates again in our tragedy and Othello and Desdemona are saved. In order to set them on the way to death we must enclose them again in the lethal chamber, reconstruct the incubus, patiently reconduct Iago to his prey, and there is only one act left for us to begin the tragedy over again. In other words: *We have found the end of an act, but at the cost of the effect of the final catastrophe.*

(Quoted F. Walker 1962: 478–9)

The revision of *Simon Boccanegra*

In this rapprochement of two such dissimilar artists, and in their gradual recognition of the fact that they were going to be able to work magnificently together, the catalytic role was played – as so often in the operatic history of the period – by Giulio Ricordi. For many years it had been his hope that Verdi could be persuaded to undertake a wholesale revision of *Simon Boccanegra*, of all the composer's failed operas far and away the most interesting. When, in 1879, Verdi at last got really interested in the idea, Ricordi suggested that Boito might make the necessary revisions in the text. They worked on it between December 1880 and February 1881. And despite Boito's initial scepticism as to whether anything dramatically worthwhile could be made of Piave's limping plot and lifeless characters, the high standards he set himself, and indeed set Verdi, created the most favourable impression on the composer. The *Boccanegra* revision turned into a kind of trial run for *Otello*, the result of which was to convince Verdi that 'in Boito he had found the poet longed for for so many years' (Gossett 1974: 334), imaginative, eloquent and fearless. Without that experience he would surely have been even more chary about the wisdom of emerging from retirement to undertake so tremendous a task as the composition and production of *Otello*.

When *Simon Boccanegra* was first produced at Venice in 1857 Verdi had felt that it had been 'a fiasco as great as that of *Traviata*. I thought I had written something decent, but it seems I was mistaken' (to Clarina Maffei, 11 April 1857, in Nordio 1951: 55). Coming back to the opera in 1879–80, he realized it was deeply flawed. 'It is too sad', he explained to Ricordi, 'too depressing. There is no need to touch the first act [he meant the Prologue] nor the last, or even the third except for a bar here and there. But I shall need to redo all the second act [i.e. Act I] and give it more contrast and variety, more life' (November 1880, in Budden 1973–81, II: 255).

There follows what Budden calls a 'crotchety diatribe against new-fangled ways'; and Verdi then returns to the matter of Act II (= Act I) and introduces a new *motif*. 'On this point, I recall two superb letters of Petrarch's, one written to the Doge Boccanegra, the other to the Doge of Venice, telling them they were about to engage in fratricidal strife, that both were the sons of the same mother, Italy, etc. How wonderful, this feeling for an Italian fatherland in those days!' (*ibidem* 256). This *motif* is a little surprising, because that aspect of Verdi's work which earned him the soubriquet 'Bard of the *Risorgimento*' had been very little in evidence since *La battaglia di Legnano*, fully thirty years before. Returning at a more exalted level to a theme handled so brashly in the past, Verdi created in the new Act I finale, the Council Chamber scene, his 'political testament, perhaps the highest expression of social idealism in opera ever penned' (*ibidem*: 334). Much of the success of the scene, which ranks among Verdi's supreme achievements, was due to the enthusiasm he felt for Boito's text, 'most beautiful, full of movement, of local colour, very elegant and forceful verses' (28 December 1880, in F. Walker 1962: 481). And from this new centre of gravity the opera acquires an ethical function that was not apparent in the original; it is less a 'conventional tragedy', more a 'dramatic chronicle' (Osthoff 1963: 71).

As he got more deeply involved in revisions that were obviously indispensable, Verdi found it increasingly difficult to leave alone even the passages he had thought could stay as they were. The original *Simon Boccanegra* had belonged to the age of 'cabaletta operas'; by 1880 the more mechanical conventions of that earlier age had come to seem intolerable. To cite one instance, the cadenza of 'Orfanella il tetto umile', the cantabile of the Amelia–Boccanegra duet in Act I, is discarded and a new coda supplied in its place which sustains, indeed raises to a new level of intensity, the poetic tenderness of the movement (Ex.VI.8). moreover, though Verdi might not have cared to hear it put this way, the potential of certain newer musico-dramatic fashions could not be overlooked. So, at the start of Act III he places an orchestral interlude with programmatic intent, such as Catalani or Boito himself might have favoured. Indeed, Boito supplies the best account of its function: 'the idea of an orchestral introduction played with the curtain lowered and accompanied by shouts off-stage I like very much; it is very useful, it binds together wonderfully the end of the [second] act with the beginning of the [third] and it gathers up the events of the last two acts in a temporal unity that is rapid, concentrated, and highly dramatic' (Budden 1973–81, II: 263).

Throughout the opera, in fact, the orchestra is more fully and subtly engaged. Nowhere is this more apparent than in the opening scene of the

Verdi and Boito

Ex. VI.8a Verdi, *Simon Boccanegra* (1857), Act I

How sadly the future was approaching me in my sorrow! . . . If the hope
that now smiles on my soul should be a dream! Might I die when the
illusion vanishes.

Ex.VI.8a *continued*

prologue, which, with its avoidance of formal choral work, and its casual,
naturalistic dialogue, had been highly original even in 1857. But the
material of that dialogue had been conventional enough. Now Verdi gives it
its own unique atmosphere, by enveloping it in a grave, haunting orchestral
theme, 'the smooth flow of which lends the prologue its peculiarly
chronicle-like character' (Osthoff 1963: 72).

The musical language of Verdi's late operas

In Verdi's letters and recorded conversations from the last decades of the
century nothing is more apparent than his sorrowing conviction that Italy's
musical traditions were decaying within and under threat from without.
There can be little doubt that his own last operas were conceived as –
among much else – affirmations of the traditional values of the Italian
musical theatre. Hepokoski puts the point well when he writes that 'in an
increasingly Wagnerian, symphonic, and intellectually sceptical age Verdi
surely believed that he was upholding the primacy of the voice, the
dominance of diatonic melody, the direct outpouring of elemental,
instantly communicable emotions, and the attracting of as large a public as
possible' (1983: 85). And he is right to begin with singing melody, for that
is what Verdi himself saw as the deepest source of the Italianness of Italian
opera.

In 1882, at an early stage in the discussions with Boito about *Otello*, the
question was raised whether it might not be given its première at the Paris
Opéra. Verdi replied: 'Why talk now of a work that does not exist, that will
be Italian in scale and Italian in who knows how many other ways (Open,
oh earth!)? . . . Perhaps a few melodies . . . (if I can find any) . . . And

602

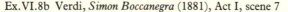

How sadly the future was approaching me in my sorrow! If the hope that
now smiles on my soul should be a dream!. . .might I die when the
illusion vanishes.

Ex.VI.8b Verdi, *Simon Boccanegra* (1881), Act I, scene 7

melody is always Italian, essentially Italian, and can be nothing but Italian,
wherever it comes from' (in Medici and Conati 1978: 65). The first duty of
an Italian composer, he asserted to Gino Monaldi in 1887, was 'to protect
the sovereignty of the human voice and song . . . Young composers must
remember that the human voice, apart from being the finest of all
instruments, is not merely a sound; *poetry* is wedded to this sound, and

poetry requires an ideal form of expression that is both lofty and always intelligible' (Conati 1984: 191). The words 'poetry is wedded to this sound' he understood quite strictly: song was a fusion of the two arts of poetry and music, the one drawing its essential character from the other. One day in 1884 Boito took Giacosa with him to visit Verdi in his villa at Santa'Agata; some years later, in the journal *Vita moderna*, Giacosa recalled the occasion:

Discussions then arose, not, of course, about the music, but the expressive importance of some word and the accentuation it should be given. Verdi would sometimes clutch the libretto and read several pieces aloud. Boito and I looked at each other, our gazes expressing our great admiration: the voice, the accent, the cadences, the force, the anger expressed in that reading betrayed such an ardent kindling of the soul, magnified so immeasurably the sense of the words, that the source of the musical idea was clearly revealed to us. With our own eyes we saw, as it were, the flower of the melody blossom, and the words . . . transmuted into waves of sound.   (Quoted in Conati 1984: 161)

These Italian priorities were preserved in a musical language that in other respects had, during the span of Verdi's life, been transformed out of all recognition. By this time, the subtlety of his harmonic imagination yielded nothing to his north European contemporaries. But it does not lend itself easily to analysis or description, nor are any systematic tendencies to be descried. It certainly does not, as many early critics supposed, reflect an attempt to imitate anyone else. Etienne Destranges's ludicrous notion – proclaimed in a Paris journal in 1890 – that Verdi had reformed himself by 'mugging up with a most youthful enthusiasm the new treatises on harmony' (Conati 1984: 212), may be dismissed, if only because there was nowhere such a harmonic idiom as his to be 'mugged up'.

Above all it is implausible because everything about Verdi's harmony suggests that he would never have thought of it as an autonomous essence with its own rules or principles. In his musical language harmony was a function of dramatic intent or expressive purpose. And therefore, as he might have said, it was neither old nor new, progressive nor archaic, Italian nor German. It ranges in fact from the utmost diatonic transparency to the most formidable chromatic density, from episodes of archaic modality to progressions of extraordinary lability, floating on a stream of second- or third-inversion chords; textures replete with inner-voice chromaticism are neither more nor less typical than organum-like or faburden-like parallelisms.

In two aspects of this extraordinary harmonic art one may see the traces of his early musical training, and of his conservative Italian taste. One is the ineradicable influence of thorough-bass practice, conspicuous signs of which are to be found in the revised *Simon Boccanegra*. Some of the most radical transformations in the new score are in fact accommodated above a bass-line unchanged from the 1857 original (Ex.VI.9). The other is that his boldest harmonic flights are commonly contained within a lucidly articulated phrase structure, in which the cadences provide the clarification, the resolution, the overriding harmony (in the fullest sense of the term) which Italian composers have always regarded as indispensable. His comment on Domenico Scarlatti's so-called 'Cat's Fugue' is instructive: 'with such an odd subject a German would have made something chaotic: an Italian has made it as clear as sunlight' (Budden 1985: 91). He freely admitted that his ear – the comment was prompted by Mascagni's *L'amico Fritz* – 'soon tired of so many dissonances, those false modulations, suspended cadences and tricks . . .' (Conati 1984: 223). Nor should one forget his first impression of *Mefistofele*, when during the Prologue he felt himself to be 'not in Heaven, certainly!' (Budden 1985: 122).

To accumulate further evidence proving that by the last decades of the century Verdi was a master orchestrator, even as a German or French composer would have understood the term, were to heap Pelion on Ossa. Nowhere in opera is the art of atmospheric or dramatic colouring more unerring. With the passage for muted double-basses at the start of the final scene of *Otello* Verdi becomes the first Italian since Spontini to earn a place in Richard Strauss's revision of Berlioz's 'Treatise on orchestration'.

I cannot! Why not? A treacherous fate snatched her away. . . Tell me.

Ex. VI.9a Verdi, *Simon Boccanegra* (1857), Prologue

I cannot! Why not? A treacherous fate snatched her away. . . Tell me.

Ex.VI.9b Verdi, *Simon Boccanegra* (1881), Prologue

And, on the evidence of many an episode in *Falstaff*, one might say that in sheer virtuosity of tone-painting Strauss himself had a formidable rival in the elderly Verdi. His orchestral imagination had become wonderfully liberated from precedent; that is shown by the 'paramusical' clangour – created by drums, gong, cymbals and tone cluster in the depths of the organ – that rumbles in the background of the storm music at the opening of *Otello*.

But to return to the matter of song: the metrical and formal fluidity of Boito's text, the responsiveness of the harmony to mood and verbal nuance, and the 'Chinese refinement' (Tovey) of the orchestral detail of course affect Verdi's melodic writing. Now less than ever, and in *Falstaff* least of all, is song confined to arias, ariosi and ensembles. It blossoms wherever the spirit of poetry gives it life, and the course it follows is dictated by nothing save the thrust and flow of the dramatic action.

Which is not to suggest that these operas are in any way shapeless or unstructured. Boito's own distinction between form and formula (see p. 580) is perhaps helpful. The point is that the dramatic theme is no longer designed, trimmed and bent to fit the preconceived formulas of 'aria, rondo, cabaletta, stretto, ritornello, *pezzo concertato*'; instead the musical form arises from, and in turn gives musical coherence to, the dramatic conception.

So, for example, in Act I of *Otello*, out of the blackness and chaos of the tempest there emerge, quite spontaneously and naturally, two distinct musical shapes: one is a prayer, cried out when the peril is greatest ('Dio, fulgor della buffera'), one an exclamation of joy when danger is past ('Vittoria, vittoria'). Conversely, out of the songs and celebrations that mark Otello's safe arrival more officially, as it were – the bonfire chorus and Iago's *brindisi* – the dramatic action re-emerges with new vigour. Iago's song is the source of the musical figures that propel the brawl, just as the wine of which he sings is the source of the drunkenness that enables him to provoke the brawl.

In *Falstaff*, a very different dramatic theme occasions a very different kind of musical structure. In fact, by far the greater part of the opera moves at such a giddy *scherzoso* pace that we catch only the most fleeting glimpses of musical shapes. The choicest, most heart-easing melodies come and are gone with teasing rapidity, creating an effect as sweet and as poignant as the virtuosic but tender flowering of imagery in Shakespeare's own comedies. But then, in the final scene, the pace broadens: the order of things is re-established and reconciliation is achieved; and this dramatic idea is embodied in a series of what one might describe as musical ceremonies – serenade-sonnet, dance, litany, fugue.

Otello (Milan 1887)

In a famous, or notorious, essay of 1901, George Bernard Shaw remarked how melodramatic Shakespeare's *Othello* was.

The truth is that instead of *Otello* being an Italian opera written in the style of Shakespeare, *Othello* is a play by Shakespeare in the style of Italian opera. It is quite peculiar among his works in this respect. Its characters are monsters: Desdemona is a *prima donna* with handkerchief, confidante and vocal solo all complete . . . Othello's transports are conveyed by a magnificent but senseless music which rages from the Propontick to the Hellespont in an orgy of sound and bounding rhythm; and the plot is a pure farce plot . . .   (Quoted Budden 1973–81, III: 302–3)

More solemnly, some recent Italian critics have said similar things: *Otello* marks Verdi's turning away from tragedy towards a 'positivistic study of behaviour'; it is a story of 'intrigues, of deceit and misunderstanding'; 'the naive spectator respects the passions of Macbeth or of Hamlet, and the madness of Lear, but he would like to jump up on to the stage to prevent Othello's bestiality and to shake Desdemona out of her obtuseness' (Baldacci 1974: 247). Where Baldacci and those who think like him depart from Shaw, and are, I believe, mistaken, is in seeing *Otello* as an

Plate 11 Giovanni Zuccarelli's set for Act I of the 1887 production of *Otello*,
La Scala, Milan

abandoning, under pressure from Boito, of all Verdi's deepest commit-
ments and beliefs.

It is true that the action of the opera no longer hinges round a family
nucleus crossing the generations – father–daughter or father–son. But as an
overpowering, unremitting depiction of the corrosive poison of jealousy
and the destruction of female innocence, as a profoundly pessimistic vision
of love, hope, personality and purpose laid waste, it is a summation of
themes that had haunted Verdi for decades, 'the most Verdian of all Verdi's
operas' (Mendelsohn 1978–79: 139).

In some respects, notably the clarifying of the characterization in terms
that will work operatically, Verdi's *Otello* can be seen as 'the glorious
apotheosis of nineteenth-century ways of reading and mis-reading Shakespeare's play' (Bradshaw 1983: 153). This is most obviously the case in the
'Mediterranean idealization' of Desdemona – who in the opera is unfailingly naive, pure-hearted and trusting – and in the counterpointing against
her of a quasi-diabolical Iago, driven by a fiendish malevolence to destroy
everything good, fair or precious. Given what we have seen of Boito's cast
of mind, it is hardly surprising to find that he has turned Othello's 'ancient'
into something like a double of his own Mefistofele – cynic-intellectual –
complete with Black Credo:

> Credo in un Dio crudel che m'ha creato
> Simile a sé, e che nell'ira io nomo.[2]   (Act II scene 2)

So fascinated were both Verdi and Boito by Iago that for years they were minded to name the opera after him.

It is, of course, only in the Credo, an extended soliloquy, that the diabolic roots of Iago's conduct are revealed. As Boito insisted, it would be 'the crassest of mistakes, the most vulgar error . . . to give him a Mephistophelean sneer and make him shoot Satanic glances everywhere'. Any singer performing the role in that fashion 'would make it all too plain that he had understood neither Shakespeare nor the drama which we are discussing' (Preface to the *Disposizione scenica*, in Budden 1973–81, III: 328). Long before beginning the composition of the opera, Verdi too had his own sharp image of Iago's appearance and manner, 'a manner that is absent-minded, *nonchalant*, indifferent to everything. He should throw off good and evil sentiments lightly, as if he were thinking of something quite different to what he actually says' (letter of 24 September 1881, *ibidem*: 314). And when the role was finished he felt that, 'apart from a few *éclats* [it] could all be sung at half-voice' (to Boito, 9 September 1886, *ibidem*: 321). This was because he had composed for Iago music from which the committed lyrical fervour hitherto so characteristic of Italian opera was entirely absent; the coolness, the lack of symmetrical song, the slitherings and gracings, the fleeting moments of insinuating charm, the spiritual intangibility – all play their part in this astonishing demonstration of what the 'spirit of denial' must mean in musical terms. And it stands in juxtaposition to Desdemona's ardent lyricism, is counterpointed against it, and finally obliterates it with such a terrible finality, that Hepokoski, in his fine essay 'Shakespeare re-interpreted' (in Hepokoski 1987), senses in the clash a reflection of the whole tragic dilemma of Italian opera in a post-humanist age.

In the character sketches of the principals which Boito added to the *Disposizione scenica*, he provided a vivid description of how the integrity of Otello's personality was destroyed:

The whole man changes: he was wise, sensible, and now he raves; he was strong and now he waxes feeble; he was just and upright and now he will commit a crime; he was strong and hale and now he groans and falls about and swoons like one who has taken poison or been smitten by epilepsy.   (Quoted Budden 1973–81, III: 327)

Boito insists on Otello's nobility. But in his libretto he eliminates Shakespeare's Venetian act – save for a handful of crucial passages that can be worked into the first act of the opera – and condenses the final stages of the drama in such a way as to focus very sharply on the pathos of Desdemona's plight. And these structural adjustments, especially when Boito's choice of emphasis and vocabulary is taken into account, result in a portrait of Otello with which some latter-day connoisseurs of Shakespeare would not, perhaps, be entirely happy. We may concede that he is, in

Boito's words, 'simple in his bearing and in his gestures, imperious in his commands', but hardly 'cool in his judgement'. There is a disconcerting emotional vehemence about Otello from the start; even in Act I of the opera he appears as a 'vulnerable, unsettled man, torn apart internally by powerful and turbulent emotions' (Mendelsohn 1978–79: 138). Certain phrases in the love-duet at the close of Act I are exemplary: 'Tuoni la guerra', for instance, or the longer passage beginning 'Pingea dell' armi il fremito.' There is no question here of distant vision, or of emotion recollected in tranquillity; all is experience with an excited immediacy.

One's first suspicion is that, in their operatic portrait of this touchy, excitable, volcanic hero, Verdi and Boito were reverting to the spirit of Giraldi Cinthio (Shakespeare's primary source), as in *Falstaff* they were to revert to the spirit of the Tuscan *novellieri*. In fact, as Hepokoski has shown, they are bringing to its magnificent culmination a distinctive continental interpretation of *Othello* that had its origins in August Wilhelm von Schlegel's epoch-making Vienna lectures, *Vorlesungen über dramatische Kunst und Literatur*. Translated into Italian by Giovanni Gherardini, reprinted to serve as commentary to several nineteenth-century Italian renderings of the play, brought to the Italian stage by the celebrated tragedian Ernesto Rossi, Schlegel's reading of the character of Othello laid heavy emphasis on an 'Ethiopian' core of savage passion and burning barbarism that was but fragilely contained under a veneer of Venetian civility (Hepokoski 1987, 164–7). Of course, this basic premise was developed and qualified and subtilized. But Rossi, whose interpretation struck the American novelist Henry James when he saw it in Rome in 1873 as a surprisingly crude piece of tantrum-throwing, was to be held up by Boito as a model, 'a giant' from whom Verdi's protagonist, the tenor Francesco Tamagno, 'could have learned something' (letter to Verdi, 21 December 1886, quoted *ibidem*: 169). And it is surely not fanciful to detect the influence of this Schlegelian line of interpretation in the paroxismal and explosive spasms by which Otello's music, particularly in Acts II and III of the opera, is so often rent.

If, in relation to the Shakespearian source, characters were in some degree reinterpreted, with certain facets highlighted, others eliminated, there can be no question of the consistency and coherence of Verdi's own vision. He was justifiably proud of it, and boasted of it a little to Boito, incidentally providing us with a clue perhaps to how he had always succeeded in creating characters who were 'all of a piece'. 'I've been over one by one the three leading parts to see if they were clothed in seemly fashion without any patches; and whether they stand up straight and move well . . . and they do!' (letter of 9 September 1886, in Budden 1973–81, III: 321).

The collaboration of Verdi and Boito on *Otello* marked 'the confluence of the mainstreams of Italian literature and music under the aegis of Shake-speare' (*ibidem*: 324). Its première on 5 February 1887 was recognized as a cardinal event in the history of the Italian theatre, and occasioned such tumultuous ovations as had rarely been witnessed in any opera-house. But Verdians of long standing could not fail to recognize in the manifold splendours of *Otello* the fact that a great era of Italian opera had passed for ever. The novellist Antonio Fogazzaro may serve as their spokesman:

Otello marks a new evolution in Verdi's style, a step to what is called music of the future. It could be argued whether or not it was a good thing to have taken this step; but certainly it could not have been more powerfully taken. I believe the operas of Verdi's second manner – *Rigoletto*, *Ballo in maschera*, *Traviata* – to be his best; none the less he has rendered one great service to art; from now on it will not be possible to set to music absurd dramas and lamentable verses. Since this type of music follows the words with strict fidelity, the words will have to be worthy of being followed.

(Quoted Budden 1973–81, III: 325)

Falstaff (Milan 1893)

Verdi had long cherished the desire to compose an operatic comedy – 'for forty years', he told Monaldi in 1890 (Budden 1973–81, III: 417). And perhaps the desire had been sharpened by the publication in 1878 of Giovanni Duprè's memoirs, which revealed to the world Rossini's confidence that Verdi would 'certainly . . . never write . . . an *opera buffa*' (Conati 1984: 20). As a matter of fact, a letter of February 1868 from Giuseppina Strepponi to Verdi's French publisher Escudier suggested that he was carefully considering the possibility of writing a comic opera even then. But, Giuseppina pointed out, it would have to be a subject without buffoonery, and in which there was some sentiment to act as 'a delicate, sympathetic nuance that serves to temper the gaiety and the laughter' (Hepokoski 1983: 20).

It was Boito who eventually resolved any doubts Verdi may have had about attempting the genre, by writing for him 'a lyric comedy quite unlike any other' (letter of 3 December 1890, in Budden 1973–81, III: 417). Boito, the poet who had once been 'half in love with easeful death', the erstwhile dreamer of hashish dreams and worshipper of Gothic idols, had changed profoundly in the time since we first met him as a young *scapigliato*. He had become an ardent apostle of the Latin spirit in art, driven by a sense of mission to 'Mediterraneanize music' – a phrase he knowingly adopted from Nietzsche. *Falstaff* – thanks to the harmonious relationship he now enjoyed with greatest opera composer of the age – was to be the finest achievement in that spirit. And he must have been delighted when his French friend, Camille Bellaigue, enthused over the opera's 'verve and clarity' and acclaimed it 'a masterpiece of *Latin*, classical genius!' (Hepokoski 1983: 34).

611

For all its Latin spirit, *Falstaff* was not an attempt to resurrect the *opera buffa*; Verdi was insistent on that. 'I am not writing an *opera buffa*', he told Italo Pizzi, 'but depicting a character' (Conati 1984: 349). The character in question had long been a favourite of his; Sir John Falstaff he regarded as one of the supreme embodiments of Shakespeare's incomparable gift for 'inventing truth' (letter of 20 October 1876, in Verdi 1913: 624).

Obviously he took that view on the basis of his knowledge of the two *Henry IV* plays. He and Boito recognized from the start that, though the plot of the opera might be that of *The Merry Wives of Windsor*, the characterization must be based on *Henry IV* if Falstaff himself was to be realized in the whole range and depth and amplitude of his glory. So in Boito's brilliant libretto, while the plot of the *Merry Wives* was deftly clarified and condensed, the character of Falstaff was enlarged and enriched, for the most part by the incorporation of elements from *Henry IV*: the 'Honour catechism'; the nostalgic remembrance of his slender youth, 'Quand'ero paggio'; the great comic conception of a Falstaff who is 'not only witty in himself, but the cause that wit is in other men'; and many, many more.[3]

Falstaff is the most brilliant of all operatic adaptations of Shakespeare. But it is an adaptation in which Shakespeare is transfigured by a brighter, Mediterranean light, translated from the soft shadows of the English countryside to, as Boito put it, 'the gardens of the Decameron' (F. Walker 1962: 502). Boito in fact drew freely on Boccaccio to give colour, raciness and an antique tang to his verse, and provoked protest from some early critics in doing so: *La sera* for 10 February 1893 complained of the 'jumbling together of obsolete and old-fashioned words . . . *ciuschero, cerébro, pagliardo, sugliardo, scanfardo, scagnardo, falsardo, castigatoja, crepitacolo, assillo, guindolo,* and a hundred other words that not even Ruscelli dared to put into his famous rhyming dictionary' (in Hepokoski 1983: 30). The refrain which haunts the lovers' music in Acts I and III,

> Bocca baciata non perde ventura.
> Anzi rinnova come fa la luna[4]

is taken direct from the close of Novella 7 of Boccaccio's *Giornata seconda*. In earthier moments, the *commedia*-like tirades poured out by Shakespeare's Falstaff recalled, it has been suggested, 'writers like Aretino, and stimulated Boito to produce a glorious pastiche of scurrilous Renaissance Italian' (Bradshaw 1983: 161).

Falstaff forms the virtuosic climax of Boito's efforts to break down the constricting metrical conventions of the libretto and exploit to the full the rhythmic potentialities of the language. Much of the Alice–Falstaff duet in Act II scene 2, for example, is in the classic alternation of *endecasillabi* and *settenari*:

Ogni più bel gioiel si nuoce e spregio
Il finto idolo d'or.
Mi basta un vel legato in croce, un fregio
Al cinto e in testa un fior.[5]

But, as Boito noted in his manuscript, these lines could equally well, and without damage to the rhyme, be read as *novenari* or *quinari*. Hepokoski believes that this 'playful manipulation of traditional Italian metres' is another of the ways in which the author sought to underline the essentially national character of the opera (1983: 32–3).

The music of *Falstaff* is in every way the culmination of all those Verdian traits that had been developed, transformed, deepened and subtilized through an active career of more than half a century. Nothing shows this more clearly than the density of the lyricism, a quality that might be illustrated from any scene in the opera.

The second scene of Act I provides a particularly glorious illustration of how new melodies spring forth from every action, every mood, virtually every phrase of text. There are themes for the convivial gossips, (Ex.VI.10a), for the mock-passion of Falstaff's love-letter (Ex.VI.10b), for the plan to humiliate the greasy knight (Ex.VI.10c), for the love of Fenton and Nannetta, culminating in the Boccaccio refrain, 'bocca baciata . . .' (Ex.VI.10d). But despite their evanescence, these melodies once heard are unlikely to be forgotten; and more frequently in *Falstaff* than in any other of his operas, Verdi relies on their memorability for the musical design of his opera. Some of the reprises are largely formal: when the wives have laid their plan to rout Falstaff they nourish their determination by recalling the grotesque amorousness of his letters, and they depart at the end of the scene

Ex.VI.10a Verdi, *Falstaff* (1893), Act I scene 2

613

We shall make a pair in smiling love [all with their noses in the letters],
a beautiful woman and a man of substance.

Ex. VI.10b Verdi, *Falstaff* (1893), Act I scene 2

614

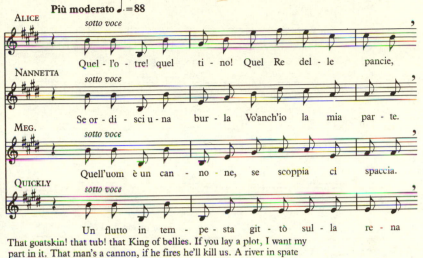

Ex.VI.10c Verdi, *Falstaff* (1893), Act I scene 2

to the same 'gossip' music to which they had entered. But the 'bocca baciata' theme of the young lovers is used to exquisite dramatic effect in the closing scene of the opera. Fenton is alone in Windsor forest waiting for the wives and all the others who are to take part in the masquerade. Naturally Nannetta fills his thoughts, and being alone he can sing of his love at unusual length. The wonderfully beautiful aria rises to an ecstatic climax with the 'bocca baciata' theme, and from farther away in the forest the approaching Nannetta replies (Ex.VI.11).

Verdi knew that he had written an opera which would make unfamiliar demands on the skills of even the best of casts. He warned Ricordi that the new, mellow, benign Verdi that had begun to emerge in the 1880s would not be in evidence at the rehearsals for *Falstaff* – 'No, no; I shall go back to being a bear as I used to be and we shall all gain by it' (letter of 17 June 1892, in Budden 1973–81, III: 432).

The particular problem he foresaw was that the voices would be unable to sink themselves into the melodies, or spread themselves generously over the phrase. 'Generally speaking our singers can only sing with full voice; they haven't vocal elasticity or clear and easy syllabation, and they lack verbal and musical attack (*accento*) and breath control' (*ibidem*). There was no room in *Falstaff* for 'artists who want to sing too much and effect sentiment and action by falling asleep on the notes' (to Ricordi, 2 September 1893, in Hepokoski 1983: 117). For the opera was 'a matter of comedy: music, note and word, stage action, and much energy, not cantabiles' (*ibidem*: 119).

[Singing, he hides himself among the trees, always keeping watch on
Nannetta.] A mouth that is kissed does not lose its freshness. For it
renews itself like the moon.

Ex. VI.10d Verdi, *Falstaff* (1893), Act I scene 2

It is not perhaps surprising if the opera did not at once establish itself as a
favourite. A review of the first Roman performance in April 1893 by T.
Montefiore expressed some of the typical reservations:

There was considerable astonishment – perhaps even disappointment – among many of
the innumerable admirers of Verdi's immortal genius . . . 'Is this our Verdi?', they asked
themselves. But where is the *motive*; where are the broad melodies that decorated his
earlier operas; where are the usual *ensembles*; the *finales*? Alas, all of this is buried in the
past.   (Quoted Hepokoski 1983: 129)

Falstaff became a national classic, rather than a work occasioning
bemused admiration, only when Toscanini insisted on making his super-
latively drilled performances pillars of the repertory in every theatre he
directed.

Verdi and Boito

Ex. VI.11 Verdi, *Falstaff* (1893), Act III scene 2

So I kissed the longed-for mouth! A mouth that is kissed does not lose its freshness. [Off-stage in the distance] For it renews itself [approaching] like the moon.

Ex.VI.11 *continued*

From *Nabucco* to *Rigoletto*, *Trovatore* and *Traviata*, the young Verdi had been one of the national heroes of the age of the *risorgimento*; his operas were performed in every corner of the peninsula, admired and loved as were the operas of no other composer. During the long second period of his career from the mid-1850s to the mid-1890s, as Italian music became more nervous of itself, more prone to imitate or emulate French and German practice, his status in the life of the nation subtly changed. He became the very incarnation of *italianità*, the living embodiment of the finest aspects of a tradition under siege.

It was this fact that gave a peculiar depth and edge to the reverence of such men as Boito and Ricordi. Their feelings went far beyond an admiration for the inexhaustibility of the musician, and the integrity of his character. For them, Verdi had become a bulwark of Mediterranean art and civility, not merely against the menace of Wagnerism, but against the subtler and more all-pervasive danger of self-consciousness and ratiocination that had destroyed Boito's own creative gifts as a musician, and seemed to threaten so many other artists in the last decades of the century

> Or freddo, assiduo, del pensiero il tarlo
> Mi trafora il cervello, ond'io dolente
> Misere cose scrivo e tristi parlo.[6]

exclaimed Carducci. But Verdi was magnificently impervious to such *fin-de-siècle* malaise. And during the last years of his life he was able to become one of the great unifying forces in the life of the new nation. In the words of the journalist Giuseppe Depanis, 'the Italian people . . . recognized in Verdi not only the composer of Manrico, Violetta and Rigoletto, but the patriarch, the guardian deity of the fatherland, and felt attracted to him by a fascination that was at once admiration and gratitude' (Conati 1984: 306–7).

32 · Verismo

Cavalleria rusticana (Rome 1890)

In tracing the influence of *scapigliatura* on Puccini's early operas, and in following through to the end the story of the collaboration of Verdi and Boito, I have passed by one of the cardinal *fin-de-siècle* operatic events in the Italian theatre. In May 1890 a small and sceptical audience gathered at the Teatro Costanzi in Rome to hear a new opera by one Pietro Mascagni, an impoverished young music-teacher who for some years had been eking out a living at Cerignola in Apulia, and who had just won first prize in the second of the Sonzogno competitions. As the opera got into its stride the initial scepticism rapidly melted away. In fact, it was received with the wildest possible enthusiasm, and overnight Mascagni found himself a national celebrity. In little more than a year this first of his completed operas was to be performed all over the world, and more than any other work it was responsible for the vogue for *verismo*, the most clamant of the innovations in taste in the Italian opera-house at the close of the century. Though he showed no comparable enthusiasm for Mascagni's later music, Verdi spoke for all those who were bowled over by *Cavalleria rusticana*: 'he has a very great talent, and has invented a most effective genre: short operas without pointless longueurs' (Conati 1984: 222).

When Sonzogno announced his competition, Mascagni was engrossed in the composition of the opera which he was always to regard as his masterpiece, a version of Heine's Romantic tragedy *William Ratcliffe*. For some time he was inclined to send an act of this to Sonzogno as representative of his best work rather than *Cavalleria rusticana*, which he felt had been over-hastily put together. There were, in other words, 'no aesthetic motivations or innovatory aspirations' behind the decision to set this particular story (Sansone 1987: 35). Mascagni made his debut as a *verista* more by chance than out of any ethical conviction; a fact confirmed by the course he followed in his later operas, where idyll, comedy, historical romance and exoticism are variously mingled with genuine *verismo*. By 1910 he was ready to declare that '*verismo* murders music. It is in poetry, in Romanticism, that inspiration can find its wings' (quoted *ibidem*: 10).

And since Mascagni was no Italian Mussorgsky or Janáček, his opera provides no deeply pondered or comprehensive demonstration of the potential of operatic realism. There is, for instance, nothing remotely realistic in the libretto, written by G. Targioni-Tozzetti and G. Menasci, which veers disconcertingly between the Arcadian, the melodramatic and the folksy. And there is little sense – far less than in Verdi's mature operas – of the characters being the products and victims of their social environment: one needs listen no further than the opening chorus to hear that. With its formality – the men returning from the fields and the women at their spinning are counterpointed almost *alla* Meyerbeer – and its refrain, 'tempo è si mormori da ognuno il tenero canto che i palpiti raddoppia al cor',[1] the movement is incredibly idealized. Theocritus would have found it easier to recognize this Sicily than Verga would; we are nearer to the Golden Age than the 1880s.

Indeed is there not perhaps altogether more of the pastoral in *Cavalleria rusticana* than there is of *verismo*; should one not perhaps emphasize less the extent to which it represents a breakthrough to a new aesthetic, more the extent to which Mascagni was trying to recapture a world of vanished innocence? In 1887, a few years before composing the opera, he had written of Wagner as the 'Pope of all maestri' (Miller 1984: 183), but his perceptions were changing. Rather than following in the paths of Wagnerism he hankered after the values of traditional Italian opera, firmly focused on cantabile melody, and on arias and choruses in the simplest forms. Possibly the chief of the reasons for the extraordinary impact *Cavalleria rusticana* made on early audiences was that they sensed in it an atavistic reassertion of the values of traditional opera against 'the mandarin music-drama, the infiltration of even the Italian operatic world by Wagnerian theories' (Cooper 1974: 154).

Mascagni makes no attempt, as his more sophisticated seniors and contemporaries had done for decades, to mingle and blend the attributes of recitative and song. On the contrary, his opera comprises a series of genre and character numbers linked together by the simplest of recitatives. Sometimes, as when Alfio makes his entrance with an aria in strophic form with choral refrain, we are closer to operetta than to music-drama, let alone music-drama with any aspiration to being realistic. There is scarcely a number in the score that is not startlingly, almost truculently primitive in musico-dramatic terms. Mascagni knows nothing of the *parola scenica*: crucial turning-points in the action, like Santuzza's revealing of Lola's infidelity, are simply tucked into the generous folds of the melody; word-repetition tends to be flabby and pointless; in the same Santuzza–Alfio duet there is not even the kind of effort a composer of Donizetti's generation would probably have made to differentiate between Alfio's shouts for revenge and Santuzza's cries of remorse. And any pretext will do for a song: Lola sings an amorous *stornello* on her way to Mass, Turiddu a *brindisi* on his way out.

The naive fervour with which Mascagni throws himself into his *cantabile* melodies disarms criticism: they are sung in vocal-instrumental doublings against orchestral backgrounds specially designed to set them off – *Trovatore*-like vampings and tremolos; and they tend to recur in 'theme-song'-like manner with no particular purpose save that of insisting on a continuous, vibrant emotional ecstasy. It was the combination of a radical simplicity in the dramatic action with a style of vocal writing in which virtually every phrase is laden with searing lyrical intensity that made *Cavalleria rusticana* irresistible and *verismo* fashionable.

The French sources of *verismo*

The word *verismo* means simply realism. Its most productive period, as far as Italy was concerned, was the last quarter of the nineteenth century, though there were anticipations of it at least thirty years earlier, and echoes of it were still to be heard even after the First World War. Its first literary classics were the Sicilian short stories and novels of Giovanni Verga: *Vita dei campi* 1880 (*Cavalleria rusticana* and other stories), and *I Malavoglia* 1881 (*The house by the medlar tree*); Mascagni's *Cavalleria rusticana*, the first *verismo* opera is, as its name suggests, a setting of one of these tales. *Verismo* was not primarily a native Italian phenomenon – though the *scapigliati* with their contempt for bourgeois ethics and for the exalted and idealistic rhetoric of Romantic art had certainly paved the way for the new ethos; it was, to a large extent, an imitation and modification of a movement that originated in France; and before investigating *verismo* any further it will be useful to describe in the most general terms the characteristics of this French ancestor.

Realism, said the novelist Champfleury, was one of the 'numerous religions ending in *ism*', thrown up by the Revolution of 1848 (Grant 1970: 20). In France it commonly had political overtones. It concerned itself primarily with what was regarded as the 'real' world – the contemporary world as it 'really' was. Among its earliest manifestations in the years around 1850 may be mentioned the first dramas of the younger Dumas, notably *La dame aux camélias*, the source of Verdi's *La traviata*. About the same time were exhibited such early realist paintings as Millet's *The Sower* and Courbet's *Stone-breakers*. In French realism, elegance of manner, polish of form, anything that could be regarded as the mere trappings of the presentation were discarded; they were seen as a kind of pose, a form of artificiality, which stood in the way of directness and honesty of expression. The point is well illustrated by a familiar anecdote told of Courbet. Finding himself one day seated by Corot and painting the same scene, he is said to have remarked: 'I am not so clever as you M. Corot: I can only paint what I see.' Not imagination but reality, not dreams but facts, not elevated rhetoric, but an accurate and frank descriptive style; these were the prerequisites of French realism in its early years. They reflected, or at least they were wholly consonant with, the dominant position in French intellectual life of the ideas of Auguste Comte, the founder of the philosophy of positivism.

According to this philosophy, mankind had outgrown theology and metaphysics; the only reality with which it need concern itself was that of observable 'fact'. There were no mysteries in the world that rigorous scientific investigation would not solve sooner or later. The universe and everything in it, including man, with all his passions, his ideals, his spiritual yearnings, were simply parts of an immense natural machine, explicable in terms of cause and effect. No wonder John Stuart Mill described positivism as 'the completest system of spiritual and temporal despotism which ever yet emanated from a human brain' (Grant 1970: 35).

Nevertheless this philosophy gave some kind of intellectual bolstering to the impulses of the earliest realists. In the last third of the century, still in France, it led to a more extreme and quasi-scientific form of realism, generally distinguished as 'naturalism', and associated especially with the novels of Emile Zola. The object of the naturalist work of art, above all the novel, was to contribute to the understanding of what society was really like – how it functioned, what its effects on the individual personality were. And it did this by a whole-hearted adoption of the scientific methods of observation, documentation and deduction: naturalism was, in Zola's own words, 'the formula of modern science applied to literature' (*ibidem*: 40).

Like realism, naturalism tended to concentrate its attention on areas of society neglected by earlier literary movements: low life, the criminal, the dispossessed, the demoralized. In some measure this was due to the political tendency of the movement, but there were also artistic reasons for the choice. The realists looked to such worlds for simplicity, for 'authenticity', for the absence of pose and artifice; the naturalists preferred them because the relationship between society and its victims was a much more complex and interesting matter to analyse than the relationship between society and the successful men and women of the world.

Much of all this was taken over uncritically and without essential modification into Italy. There no less than in France, intellectual life in the last thirty years of the century was dominated by positivist philosophy. Italian novelists of the period, foremost among them Verga and his friend and fellow-Sicilian Luigi Capuana, aspired to create a realistic art, and they echoed Zola when they described it as entailing 'the application of scientific and positivist methods to the form of the novel, the perfect impersonality of the work of art' (Cattaneo 1968: 331). Like Zola's, their books were concerned very largely with contemporary life in its harsher or more sordid manifestations, with the conditions of working-class life, with the roots of criminality, with the psychological analysis of the morbid and pathological.

All the same, there are significant differences between *verismo* and contemporary French naturalism, as Capuana, the principal theorist of *verismo* recognized: so indeed did Zola. On the occasion of a visit to Italy, the French novelist is said to have remarked of Verga's stories that they were deficient in 'firmly established theories' (*ibidem*: 333). He meant, it is generally supposed, that Verga lacked political commitment. Italian writers and critics could see clearly enough that Zola's novels were an indictment of French society, but the accusatory zeal was an aspect of his work which most of them were not prepared to imitate. Indeed, as Zola's later writings became more overtly political, as he laid claim to be 'the master of good and evil, to regulate Life, to regulate society and ultimately to resolve all the problems of socialism' (Davies 1979: 63), the enthusiasm of his Italian disciplines waned. Verga's pessimistic fatalism knew nothing of programmes of reform; he captured 'the tragic predicament of his people in a mythical stillness hardly stirred by the pounding pulse of history' (Sansone 1987: 7). It was not part of his or Capuana's intention to undermine the social order and bring about in Italy what Capuana, looking back on the events of 1871, described as the 'orgia communarda di Parigi' (Davies 1979: 61).

A second distinction between *verismo* and its French models helps in part to explain that first distinction. Italian writers were less politicized than Zola because of their very different attitude to national institutions. The reason is obvious: while Frenchmen had lived in a powerful unitary state for centuries, Italy was a brand-new creation politically; its unification had been achieved as recently as 1870. And this unification was the realization of a centuries-old dream, achieved against all the odds, against the armed might of the Austrian Empire, and the spiritual authority of the papacy. The problems the new nation-state faced were formidable indeed, and dissatisfaction with the attempts to solve them grew fast, but in the 1870s and 1880s Italians were more disposed to be proud of themselves than otherwise. That wisest of modern Italians, the Neapolitan sage Benedetto Croce, describes the Italy of his youth in these glowing terms: 'All regarded their country as it should be regarded, as a symbol of all that is best in human aspiration, the noblest and also the most familiar social group which could serve as a point of reference for moral ideals' (Croce 1929: 65).

So whereas Zola was digging the grave for an old and hopelessly corrupt society, Capuana and Verga and their compatriots had the task of writing for a society that felt itself to be young, indeed reborn. For the first time for centuries, Milanese and Romans, Genoese and Neapolitans, Florentines and Venetians found themselves part of a single nation-state. And while they knew rather little about one another, scarcely even understood one another's language, they do seem, for the most part, to have been keen to learn. Croce says it was like a great conversation spreading through the length and breadth of the land. And this curiosity about one another is perhaps behind another of the features of Italian *verismo*: in the new-born Italy, objective scientific observation became a way of exploring the unknown land. The methods that the French naturalists had applied to the urban proletariat were more often brought to bear on the peasantry of remote rural areas, of Sicily in Verga, of the Abruzzi in the early d'Annunzio and, a few years later, of Sardinia in Grazia Deledda. Whereas naturalism is urban, *verismo* is more typically rural and provincial.

In one important respect French and Italian writers alike broke away from their theoretical dependence on positivism. Virtually all of them attached a very special importance to the crime of passion, and in some ways this proved to be, for operatic purposes, the most congenial aspect of their work. Verga and his fellows paid lip-service to positivist philosophy and to the scientific pretensions of naturalism, but they sensed that human passion was motivated by something rather more significant than a mechanistic vibration of atoms. Passion was, as the poets had always said, a spark of divinity, the source of life; though certainly circumstances could and did pervert it to tragic or unsavoury ends. Material needs and social conditions could add dimensions of anguish, as they do in *I Malavoglia*, Verga's greatest novel: but what really matters in *verismo* is the passion itself: love, jealousy, pride. The primitive peasant setting enables such passions to flame up in all their savagery, uncomplicated by reason, education or idealism; but in no way does it explain them away. In Romantic Italian art it had been the quality of a man's ideals, his yearnings, his romantic emotions that might set him apart from his fellows, and make him a suitable hero for novel or play or opera; in *verismo* it is savage passion; a passion that drives him beyond reason, beyond morality and beyond the law (at least as the law is understood in progressive, liberal society) to some cathartic deed of perverse heroism. But it is still the individual human being, his raptures and anguishes, in which *verismo* finds its sense of values.

To anatomize the crime of passion became an obsession with writers in the last decades of the nineteenth century; and the fascination forges a link between *verismo* and decadence that is obviously indispensable to any understanding of Puccini. At the same time it explains how the techniques of *verismo* came to be applied to middle-class subjects, as already happened with Capuana's erotic novel *Giacinta* of 1879. Clearly the reason for what Capuana specifically calls the 'pathological case' of his heroine is not to shed light on the workings of society: the pathological case interests him as an artist because she lives life – a life moreover that only a few years earlier would have been regarded as beyond the pale of art – more intensely, at a pitch of frenzy (Davies 1979: 59). By similar tokens *verismo* could look to find promising material in historical themes, provided only that they were set in ages of notorious depravity.

Verismo in opera

In the wake of Mascagni's triumph with *Cavalleria rusticana* there was a surge of interest in *verismo* as a source and model for opera. In the space of a few years there appeared a whole crop of low-life Neapolitan operas: *A Santa Lucia* by Pierantonio Tasca (Berlin 1892) and Nicola Spinelli's *A basso porto* (Cologne 1894, in German); Carlo Sebastiani's *A San Francesco* (Naples 1896) and, most notoriously, Giordano's *Mala vita* (Rome 1892). This featured a labourer and a prostitute as its leading characters, and occasioned something approaching a riot at its first Naples performance when the principal tenor Roberto Stagno appeared in blue overalls. Ruggero Leoncavallo, son of a Naples police-magistrate, was acting in accordance with the best naturalist practice when he modelled *I pagliacci* (Rome 1892) on one of his father's court-cases. Ricordi was sufficiently impressed by *Cavalleria rusticana* to decide that it would be a good investment to commission Verga to write another libretto modelled on one of his *Vita dei campi* stories. Puccini made his own *scenario* for an opera modelled on Zola's 'luridly erotic novel', *La faute de l'Abbé Mouret* (Carner 1974: 99).

The documentary procedures whereby the naturalists had sought to authenticate their materials were transferred to the opera-house. *La lupa* – Ricordi's Verga commission, which had certainly been made with a view to stimulating Puccini's languid genius – was eventually to be set by Tasca, himself a Sicilian, and staged, close to its geographical source, at Noto (Sansone 1987: 82); but back in 1894, Puccini had been sent off on a field trip to Catania, to talk to Verga, to take photographs, to study local costume and local traditional music. The financing of such expeditions was something Ricordi clearly felt was worthwhile: Puccini made several in connection with his various operatic projects. Riccardo Zandonai, regarded by Ricordi as the brightest prospect in the next generation, was treated similarly, sent to Spain to 'collect material' for *Conchita* (Milan 1911) (*The New Grove*, s.v. 'Zandonai').

As for the music of *verismo* opera, one might perhaps begin with that most hackneyed of arias, 'Vesti la giubba' from *I pagliacci*. Canio, the leader of a troupe of itinerant musicians in Calabria, has just discovered that his wife is unfaithful; maddened with rage and jealousy, consumed with lust for revenge, he must nonetheless don his clown's costume and go on with the show. Such excruciating emotional crises are the very essence of *verismo* opera, and they lead to a musical language which, as far as possible, gives the impression of raw, naked passion, and hovers on the borderline between music and histrionics. The vehemence of much *verismo* lyricism is vividly suggested in a remark of Mascagni's about his own *Il piccolo Marat* (Rome 1921): 'It has muscles of steel. Its force lies in the voice, which does not speak or sing: it yells! yells! yells!' (Carner 1974: 259). Some composers seemed to want to turn almost every phrase into a debased *parola scenica*, where music became exclamation, shriek, sob, gesture, flamboyant theatricality. It is typical that in 'Vesti la giubba' one hears more than Leoncavallo's music; there is hysterical laughter too, and sobs of uncontrollable despair; and the composer instructs that, the better to underline Canio's anguish, he should sing holding his head between his hands.

Remembering the 'perfect impersonality of the work of art' extolled by the literary *veristi*, it is more than a little ironic than so self-advertising a form of song should have come to be associated with *verismo* in its operatic form; there is nothing here of the restraint, the quietness of voice, for which Verga's writings are admired. But alongside such a type of *verismo* lyricism, the *aria d'urlo* as it was sometimes called, Puccini was showing how torrid emotionalism could be reconciled with a more genuinely realistic style of song. In many a Puccini aria, the principal melodic idea occurs remarkably late; the opening phrases are inclined to be tentative, casually conversational or ruminative, often barely distinguishable from recitative. We call Cavaradossi's Act III area in *Tosca* by its opening line, 'E lucevan le stelle', but the tune we recall under that title is sung only later, six lines into the lyric, at 'O dolci baci, o languide carezze'; and the orchestral music on which the aria is borne has nothing of the bold urgency of Verdi, of his bright, clear colours. The rhythms are hesitant and unemphatic, the orchestral texture mysteriously sophisticated and shadowy. It may seem paradoxical to associate a style of such manifest artifice with *verismo* at all. But the point is, I think, that in Puccini's hands the aria can often give less the impression of a musical composition being performed, more that of an improvisation, of an experience being lived through.

Which is not to suggest that Puccini altogether eschewed the crasser effects of the *veristi*. With its scenes of torture, attempted rape, murder, execution and suicide, *Tosca* keeps company with the very nastiest operatic dramas. Its arias, and those of Puccini's other *verismo*-inspired operas, are as full of the shrieks and sobs of Mascagni and Leoncavallo as they are of the cooler naturalism evolved from Massenet. The exceptional refinement of Puccini's orchestral writing does not disguise his typically *verismo* fondness for violence of effect: extreme contrasts of dynamics, manic tremolos, grim *ostinati*, rasping explosions of brass and percussion continually assail the spectator's nerves.

Puccini's *ambientismo*

When Verga began, at Ricordi's behest, to turn his short story *La lupa* into an opera libretto, he incorporated Sicilian songs and dances into no fewer than seven of its scenes. Folklore, he felt, might accomplish for musical *verismo* what the proverb – the traditional saying – did for literary *verismo*, by providing an 'uncontaminated, metaphoric expression of the people's ethics and feelings' (Sansone 1987: 100). The first staged opera to make a feature of such musical authenticity was *Mala vita*, into which Giordano incorporated a number of popular Neapolitan dances. It was a practice which Puccini took up enthusiastically. Collections of traditional Japanese music provided him with many a distinctive melodic phrase, sometimes with whole themes for *Madama Butterfly* (Milan 1904) (Carner 1974: 385–6); while for *La fanciulla del West* (New York 1910) popular American music of the 1850s and traditional Red Indian music was laid under contribution (*ibidem*: 405).

The incorporation of popular or traditional melodies to enhance the 'authenticity' of the opera was a facet of that Puccinian preoccupation which we have already met with in *La bohème*, and which Italian critics call *ambientismo*. The ambition was to compose the décor into the music; the evocation of the milieu in which the drama was set became one of the composer's most stimulating tasks. The insistence of *verismo* writers on creating a vivid picture of the scenes of their stories by the precise documentary description of their most ordinary details prompted a sympathetic response in all the *verismo* composers; in none more so than in Puccini. Of course there were precedents for this kind of thing: the Spanish environment depicted by Bizet in *Carmen*, or the sultry tropical atmosphere of Verdi's *Aida* – both works, incidentally, among Puccini's very favourite operas. But these were exceptional, and even in them the milieu evoked remained in the background. With Puccini the setting is an integral part of the drama, built up with the most loving care, and as authentic as a painstaking attention to detail could make it.

Before composing the prelude to the third act of *Tosca*, set on the ramparts of Castel Sant'Angelo at dawn, Puccini travelled to Rome and went up to Castel Sant'Angelo in the early hours of the morning, to hear for himself what the multitude of matin bells ringing over the city sounded like. During the composition of *Suor Angelica* he spent hours in the convent of Vicopelago, where his sister was Mother Superior, in order to absorb the appropriate conventual ethos. Ambience is even more important in *Madama Butterfly*, because here the whole tragedy hinges on the clash of irreconcilable cultures. In preparation for his opera, Puccini studied books on Japanese customs, religion and architecture; he consulted collections of

Japanese music, and listened to gramophone recordings of it; the wife of the Japanese ambassador to Italy was prevailed upon to sing some traditional songs to him (Puccini 1974: 154); and he even arranged an interview with the leading Japanese actress of the day, Sada Jacco, so that he could listen to her recite in Japanese. The object of this exercise was to see whether it might not be possible to suggest the 'peculiar high twitter' of the Japanese female voice in the music he wrote for Butterfly (Carner 1974: 130).

A milieu and the simple objects that evoked that milieu were as stimulating to Puccini's musical imagination as the great characters of literary drama had been to Verdi's. When he paid his first extended visit to London in 1900 for the Covent Garden première of *Tosca*, he spent some time viewing the slums, 'which interested me very much' (Carner 1974: 116). So much, in fact, that he carried the memory of them around with him for the best part of twenty years, until his haunted imagination produced one of the more improbable of his many abortive operatic schemes – a Dickensian opera based on *Oliver Twist*, which advanced as far as a fully worked out *scenario* and a completely versified first act. When he fell under the spell of Didier Gold's *La houppelande*, it was not the characters or the plot that enthralled him but the setting: 'It's a violent thing, brutal, wounding almost, but effective – that life on the river, that colour of the Seine, that background of Notre Dame!' (to Adami, in Carner 1974: 266). The individuality of his operas depends less on the personality of the protagonists or the originality of the happenings in which they are involved than on their distinctiveness of ambience. Industrial riverside Paris, gold-rush California, antique Peking are not just backgrounds to the dramas of Giorgetta, Minnie and Turandot; they themselves 'become "actors" . . . who perceptibly intervene in the action' (Dahlhaus 1982: 119). And, as in the novels of d'Annunzio, the décors acquire a malevolent symbolic force by virtue of 'the ferment of impure, violent deeds which [they] have witnessed' (Praz 1951: 398).

Given these propensities it was inevitable that Puccini should be delighted and thrilled when, on the same London visit in 1900, he made his first acquaintance with the work of David Belasco, and particularly the quasi-cinematographic effects that he was introducing to the American theatre at that time. *Madam Butterfly*, Belasco's adaptation of a novelette by John Luther Long, was the piece Puccini saw, and it inspired what was his own favourite among his dozen operas. In the present context two passages in the play concern us. The first occurred at the start, when the opening scene was preceded by a display of illuminated screens 'depicting in turn a ricefield, a garden of cherry blossom, and a snow-capped volcano in a sunset' (Carner 1974: 128). This effect was surpassed later in the play by the notorious scene of the geisha's vigil, a silent scene lasting some fourteen minutes. While Butterfly remained motionless on the stage, the passing of the night was 'counterfeited . . . by a series of changing effects on the open stage: dusk, the gradual appearance of the stars, the break of dawn accompanied by the chirping of the birds, and sunrise' (*ibidem*). Comparable devices adorned *The girl of the golden West*, which Puccini saw in New York in 1907. When he came to compose the first version of *Madama Butterfly*, he set out to rival Belasco's *tour de force* by writing an extended pantomime for Butterfly's night vigil. This miniature tone-poem, for which attempts were made to invent a new oriental sounding keyboard instrument described by Puccini as a '*cembalo a corde percosse*' (Smith in Maehder 1985: 115), aspired to transpose the *Kitsch* of the original to an altogether more elevated level of art. In the revised *Butterfly*, however (Brescia 1904), the scene had to be abbreviated and dismembered, and the supreme example of Belasco-like *ambientismo* must now be the opening of *Il tabarro*. The curtain rises to reveal Michele's barge, with cabin, flowers, a line of washing, a cage of nightingales, and gangplank; the Seine curls away into the distance, and against a crimson sunset are silhouetted the buildings of old Paris, chief among them Notre Dame, and, nearer at hand, the tenements that flank the quay. Only after the eye has taken in the scene does the music – one of those Puccinian 'celebrations of ambience' (Groos and Parker 1986: 22) – begin. It is a grey Debussian nocturne, evoking the weary, impassive flow of the river, suggesting too from time to time the flaring passions of those who work and live on it, and occasionally punctuated by naturalistic noises – car-hooters, siren whistles. This marvellously suggestive music is as all-pervasive in the first part of *Il tabarro* as is the music of the sea in *Der fliegende Holländer* or *Peter Grimes*.

Eroticism and sadism

Like the librettos of *La bohème* and *Madama Butterfly*, that of *Tosca* was written by Giacosa and Illica working in collaboration. But Illica had himself already written a *Tosca* libretto for Alberto Franchetti as far back as 1894. That year in Paris he visited Victorien Sardou, author of the play which inspired the opera, to read his libretto to him. It happened that Verdi, who was on cordial terms with Sardou, was in Paris at the time and was invited to be present at the reading. He was much impressed by Illica's work, notably by a passage in Act III, a 'Farewell to Life and Art' uttered by Cavaradossi shortly before his execution. When the reading reached this point, Verdi is said to have 'snatched the manuscript from Illica's hand and read the verses aloud in a trembling voice' (Carner 1985: 14). But the episode that moved Verdi so deeply failed to speak to Puccini at all. There is no 'Farewell to Life and Art' in his opera because, at his own insistence, Illica's verses were replaced by those of 'E lucevan le stelle', an aria that indulges itself in sensuous memories of a torrid amorous encounter with Tosca on a summer night; nothing more totally oblivious to all considerations of moral idealism could well be imagined.

It was a telling incident, as commentators have often observed. One of the composer's best-loved arias may serve as a symbol for the fact that, between Verdi and Puccini, the idealism is emptied out of Italian opera. Puccini, and the same must surely be said of his lesser contemporaries, expressed no spiritual aspirations in his operas and had no moral ambitions for them. 'He doesn't set his sights high' is a refrain in Puccini criticism; 'the peasants of Torre del Lago showed the right instinct', remarks Carner, 'when they jokingly referred to [him] as *"il maestro cuccumeggiante"* – "the composer of harlot music"' (Carner 1974: 275).

What Puccini did have, however – like so many *fin-de-siècle* artists – was an acute sensitivity to the pathos of the human condition. The acuteness of this sensitivity was surpassed only by its profound pessimism: he talked of the 'gran sacco di melanconia' he carried about with him (*ibidem*: 169); the refrain of his death-devoted heroes is not – with Verdi's – 'Lassù in ciel', but 'Muoio disperato'. Puccini is at his best and most characteristic in dramas where sweetness and anguish clash and mingle. 'Explain to him my kind of style', Puccini wrote to a friend who was negotiating with d'Annunzio on his behalf; 'tenderness mixed with pain' (*ibidem*: 120). On another occasion he exclaimed to Adami, 'If only I could find *my subject*, a subject full of passion and pain!' (Puccini 1974: 255). No one who has sampled the deplorable tribe of algolagnics, hermaphrodites, necrophiliacs and eteromaniacs anatomized by Mario Praz in *The Romantic agony* will easily be persuaded to regard Puccini as a particularly morbid exemplar of *fin-de-siècle* tendencies, but in admitting to his 'Neronic instincts' he did acknowledge the sadistic basis of his obsession with sex, pain and death. Carner has taught us to recognize that the psychological equation on which all Puccini's operas depend is 'an equation of love with death . . . of Eros with Thanatos' (Carner 1974: 272). Erotic love he perceived as a form of tragic guilt to be atoned for by suffering, death, torture or suicide. A proportion of all his operas is taken up with what one might describe as the celebration of suffering: not only 'muoio disperato' arias like 'E lucevan le stelle', but funeral march episodes that trudge inexorably towards catastrophe; or sequences of balefully tolling chords; or ostinato passages that, so to speak, tie the characters down to torment them.

I suggested earlier that passion uncomplicated by education or idealism, passion that drives characters beyond reason, morality or the law, was one of the hallmarks of *verismo*. In the world of *fin-de-siècle* decadence where Puccini was spiritually more at home, similar passions take a more morbid and wilful form: his characters tend to defy reason, wantonly to flout education and idealism, not because – like the tragic victims of the early

Plate 12 Set design for Act II of *Turandot*, La Scala, Milan, 1926

Mascagni and Leoncavallo – they cannot help it, but because passion and the sensations to which passion gives rise are the only values recognized.

Nowhere is this clearer than in his last opera, *Turandot* (Milan 1926). The eponymous heroine is consumed by such a hatred of men that she insists on the death of everyone who aspires to her hand. Calaf is so obsessed with desire for Turandot that the torture and suicide of his devoted servant Liù leaves him essentially unaffected, and no sooner is the dead body carried away than he tears off Turandot's veil, snatches her in his arms, and kisses her wildly and at considerable length. This physical assault alone melts Turandot's icy heart and miraculously transforms her into the loving woman of the closing scene. In a way the amoral, matter-of-factness of the story is that of fairy-tale or legend, but by treating their passions with all the raw emotional immediacy of *verismo*, Puccini transforms the legendary prince and princess into the sexually disturbed, pathological types so typical of the era. Up to a point, Joseph Kerman's sarcasm is just: 'the inescapable central message of the piece, then, is that the way to proceed with a frigid beauty is to get your hands on her' (Kerman 1956: 256). Except that there is no message. In *Turandot* Puccini was probing those same subconscious sexual impulses of character that were the theme of Pierre Louÿs's notorious erotic novel *La femme et le pantin* – a work the composer long struggled to mould into operatic form – and of many another

631

algolagnic tale of the period. Whether this probing is found to be disturbing and deeply impressive or merely ludicrous and disgusting will depend very much on the eye of the observer. In either case one can only endorse Kerman's view that it is absurd to pretend, as is pretended in the closing scene of the opera, that *Turandot* is about love. Puccini himself sensed the pathological brutishness of the scene surely enough, even if he never succeeded in translating his vision into operatic shape: 'I had thought that her capitulation would be more *prenante*, and I should have liked her to burst into expressions of love *coram populo* – but excessively, violently, shamelessly, like a bomb exploding' (Puccini 1974: 275).[2]

Whatever may have been the case with *Tosca* or *Madama Butterfly*, by the time of *Turandot* neither the *ambientismo*, nor the amorality, nor the cruelty are very deeply rooted in realist principles any longer. With its emphasis on exoticism and legend, on spectacle and ritual, on blood and pain, Puccini's last opera is in fact closer in spirit to Artaud's Theatre of Cruelty than to the *verismo* of the 1890s. 'A primitive ceremonial experience . . . gesture, sounds, unusual scenery, and lighting combine to form a language, superior to words, that can be used to subvert thought and logic'; 'He thought to restore myth and mystery to the theatre, to exploit man's deepest instincts through incantation, movement and the spectacle of cruelty and destruction.' Read any standard reference-book account of Artaud's work – these quotations are from the *Encyclopaedia Britannica*, 15th edition and *The Concise Oxford Dictionary of French Literature* – and they will tend to sound very much like descriptions of *Turandot*. Artaud's concern was not with a philosophically rational, balanced and harmonious work of art; rather his audiences were to be subverted, their subconscious and instinctual selves assailed, their veneer of civilized rationality broken through by an emotional-cum-physical assault to which there could be only a gut-reaction. With Puccini, too, many details cannot be explained by the rational criteria of classical art. Not every part does have an artistic purpose related to and subordinated to a coherent whole; much in his operas is there simply to assault the spectator emotionally. Two examples may be cited.

The first is Liù, the slave-girl in *Turandot*, a character who was invented by Puccini and his librettists on the basis of the merest hints in the literary sources, and who serves no apparently useful function in the drama. That is to say, she serves no rational or logical or plot-forwarding function; her real purpose is, quite simply, to make us weep. Liù is a lovable irrelevance, destined to be loser, to have her heart broken and her body bruised and to die without complaint so that the heartstrings may be tugged. 'I think that Liù must be sacrificed to some sorrow', wrote Puccini (Puccini 1974: 300). His whole philosophy of opera is nicely epitomized in a letter he wrote to his librettists Adami and Simoni in October 1919, immediately after deciding upon the *Turandot* theme:

Put all your strength into it, all the resources of your hearts and heads, and create for me something which will make the world weep. They say that emotionalism is a sign of weakness, but I like to be weak! To the *strong*, so called, I leave the triumphs that fade; for us those that endure! (Puccini 1974: 268)

My other example is the close of *Tosca* where, in Kerman's over-familiar words, 'Tosca leaps, and the orchestra screams the first thing that comes into its head, *E lucevan le stelle*' (Kerman 1956: 19). Again his scorn would be entirely merited if the style of art under discussion were a rational one. But Puccini dealt in theatrical rituals of spectacle and song, whose real purpose was to have a bruising and purging effect on the spectator. If *Tosca* was to end with a melodramatic *coup-de-théâtre*, some matching lyrical cataclysm had to be found, regardless of whether there was or was not a properly logical connection between it and what has gone before. He aimed at a comparable effect in *Turandot*. The opera is of course unfinished, but almost from the start of his work on it he knew that he intended to bring the curtain down with a grandiose reprise of what simply had to be the most emotionally overwhelming music in the opera, Calaf's 'Nessun dorma' from the start of the third act. Here the effect is less crass than in *Tosca*, if only because the reprise is legitimized by the triumph of Eros: 'love must . . . take possession of the whole stage in a great orchestral peroration' (Puccini 1974: 321). All the same, the real issue, one feels, is not the appropriateness of the idea, but its pulverizing emotional impact.

Cavaradossi's cry 'Muoio disperato' served as a kind of motto for Puccini's emotional world: he rewrote the end of *Il tabarro* in 1921 'to end with a *muoio disperato*' (Puccini 1974: 289), and the phrase occurs again to describe 'very nearly' his own condition as he struggled with *Turandot* (*ibidem*: 303). But 'muoio disperato' is not quite the end of the story, for Cavaradossi continues, 'e non ho amato mai tanto la vita'. There may be no great issues in Puccini's art, and no idealism; but what there emphatically is, is a tenderness for the simple everyday things of this world, that we might almost describe as spiritual. In Puccini's hands the most mundane objects – a well-loved overcoat in *La bohème*, the shop-windows of Paris in *Il tabarro* – are magically transfigured by the incantations of song and the colours of the symphony orchestra. It was the same with little people as with little things. Puccini once spoke of his susceptibility to 'grandi dolori in piccole anime';[3] but it was not just a question of sorrows, there were alluring visions too. In his operas seamstresses, and gold-miners, and bargees, and navvies are all poets and dreamers of dreams.

I have already quoted Hanslick's consternation at Puccini's interest in 'the naked, prosaic dissoluteness of our time'. But to speak of 'prosaic dissoluteness' was surely to miss the point, which for Puccini was precisely the poetry of simple things. He had the gift of seeing behind the vulgar, commonplace exterior, and laying hold on what he once described as a 'fluttering of the spirit behind the words; that *non so che* which evokes music, the divine art which begins . . . where the words leave off' (Carner 1974: 192). One can hardly dispute the fact that Puccini's operas are deeply flawed both from a philosophical and moral point of view; but they did have the supreme merit of bringing to 'all sorts and conditions of men' – the audience for which he declared he was writing – a reassurance of what it meant to be alive. And, as Heinrich Mann put it, he set the whole world singing (Mann 1947: 285). That was a gift worthy of a more golden age.

Personalia

Abbatini, Antonio Maria (1609/10–1677/9) Composer and musical scholar
Adami, Giuseppe (1878–1946) Playwright, journalist and librettist
Agazzari, Agostino (1578–1640) Composer and musical theorist
Alberti, Leon Battista (1404–1472) Versatile humanist, esp. influential as architect
Albinoni, Tomaso (1671–1751) Venetian composer, esp. of opera and concertos
Alboni, Marietta (1826–1894) Contralto
Alfieri, Count Vittorio (1749–1803) Poet and dramatist
Algarotti, Francesco (1712–1764) Court counsellor and writer on opera
Ambrogetti, Giuseppe (1780–?) Bass; later a Trappist monk
Andreini, Isabella (1562–1604) Poetess and the first great Italian actress
Anfossi, Pasquale (1727–1797) Composer, active chiefly in Rome, Venice and London
Angiolini, Gasparo (1731–1803) Choreographer, dancer and composer
Apolloni, Giovanni Filippo (c. 1635–1688) Librettist
Archilei, Vittoria (1550–1620s or later) Roman singer
Ariosto, Ludovico (1474–1533) Ferrarese courtier; dramatist and poet
Aristides Quintilianus (fl. AD 200) Neoplatonist philosopher and music theorist
Arrivabene, Count Opprandino (1805–1887) Journalist and editor, a close friend of
    Verdi
Artaud, Antonin (1896–1948) Actor, playwright and dramatic theorist
Arteaga, Stefano (1747–1799) Spanish historian and theorist of opera
Auber, Daniel-François-Esprit (1782–1871) Composer, chiefly of *opéra comique*
Auletta, Pietro (c. 1698–1771) Neapolitan composer of opera
Aureli, Aurelio (fl. 1652–1708) Librettist
Azeglio, Massimo Taparelli, Marchese d' (1798–1866) Painter, novelist and
    statesman, Prime Minister of Piedmont, 1849–52
Bach, Johann Christian (1735–1782) Composer, active in Italy 1754–62
Badovero, Giacomo (1602–1654) Venetian nobleman and librettist
Balzac, Honoré (1799–1850) French novelist
Barbaia, Domenico (?1778–1841) Impresario in Naples, Vienna and Milan
Barberini, family of art patrons, attached to the Papal court
Barbieri-Nini, Marianna (c. 1820–1887) Dramatic soprano
Bardi, Giovanni de' (1534–1612) Florentine nobleman; humanist, musical scholar,
    patron
Baretti, Giuseppe (1719–1789) Man of letters, active at the Italian opera in London
Bargagli, Girolamo (1537–1589) Lawyer and poet
Barilli, Bruno (1880–1952) Journalist and critic
Basevi, Abramo (1818–1885) Florentine doctor and music critic
Bazzini, Antonio (1818–1897) Violinist, composer and teacher
Beaumarchais, Pierre-Augustin Caron de (1732–1799) French playwright
Beccari, Agostino (c. 1510–1590) Scholar and dramatic poet
Belasco, David (1853–1931) American actor, theatrical producer and playwright
Bellaigue, Camille (1858–1930) Parisian music-critic and writer

Bellegarde, Heinrich Graf (1756–1845) Austrian military governor in
     Lombardy-Venetia after the Restoration
Belli, Domenico (?–1627) Court musician and composer
Benedetti, Michele (1778–?) Bass, active chiefly in Naples
Berchet, Giovanni (1783–1851) Writer and poet, an influential advocate of Romantic
     ideas
Beregan, Nicolò (1627–1713) Lawyer and librettist
Berio di Salsa, Francesco (1767–1820) Neapolitan man of letters
Bernacchi, Antonio Maria (1685–1756) *Castrato*, founder of a famous singing-school
Bernini, Gianlorenzo (1598–1680) Sculptor, painter and architect
Bertoni, Ferdinando (1725–1813) Composer and organist, active chiefly in Venice
Biancolelli, Domenico (*c.* 1637–1688) *Commedia dell'arte* actor
Bibiena (Galli-Bibiena), Ferdinando (1656–1743); Francesco (1659–1737) Stage
     designers and architects
Bisaccioni, Count Maiolino (1582–1663) Poet, soldier, political agent and adventurer
Boieldieu, Adrien (1775–1834) Composer, chiefly of *opéra comique*
Boito, Arrigo (1842–1918) Composer, poet, librettist and critic
Bonarelli, Prospero (1580–1659) Poet and dramatist
Bonlini, Giovanni Carlo (1673–1731) Musical amateur and writer
Bontempi, Angelini (*c.* 1624–1705) Composer, singer, historian and architect
Borromini, Francesco (1599–1667) Architect, leading exponent of the Roman baroque
     style
Bottrigari, Ercole (1531–1612) Humanist; musical scholar and poet
Bracciolini, Francesco (1566–1645) Lawyer and poet, long in the service of the
     Barberini family
Breme, Lodovico, Marchese di (1754–1828) Diplomat, courtier and philosopher
Broglio, Emilio (1814–1892) Minister of Public Instruction in the Italian government
Broschi, Carlo, *see* Farinelli
Brown, John (1715–1766) Clergyman, amateur musician and an influential writer on
     musical topics
Bruneau, Alfred (1857–1934) Composer, notably of realist opera, and critic
Bulgarelli-Benti, Marianna (La Romanina) (1684–1734) Soprano
Bülow, Hans von (1830–1894) Pianist and conductor
Buontalenti, Bernardo (1531–1608) Military and hydraulic engineer and architect
Busenello, Giovanni Francesco (1598–1659) Lawyer, poet and librettist
Bussani, Giacomo Francesco (*fl.* 1680) Librettist
Caccini, Giulio (*c.* 1545–1618) Singer and composer in the service of the Medici court
Caffarelli (Gaetano Majorano) (1710–1783) Mezzo-soprano *castrato*
Cagnoni, Antonio (1828–1896) Opera composer and church musician
Caldara, Antonio (*c.* 1670–1736) Composer, active chiefly in Rome and Vienna
Calzabigi, Raniero de (1714–1795) Adventurer, librettist and man of letters
Camerone, Felice (1844–1913) Journalist and polemicist
Cammarano, Salvatore (1801–1852) Neapolitan librettist and playwright
Campan, Mme (1752–1822) Governess, lady-in-waiting to Marie-Antoinette,
     educationist
Cantù, Cesare (1804–1895) Poet and historical novelist
Capuana, Luigi (1839–1915) Sicilian novelist and critic
Carafa, Michele (1787–1872) Prince, soldier and composer, latterly of French opera
Carcano, Giulio (1812–1884) Poet and translator of Shakespeare
Carducci, Giosuè (1835–1907) Scholar, critic, and the most considerable Italian poet
     of the late nineteenth century; Nobel prize-winner in 1906
Carissimi, Giacomo (1605–1674) Roman composer, esp. of cantatas and oratorios

Carpani, Giuseppe (1752–1825) Poet, playwright and critic

Casti, Giambattista (1724–1803) Clergyman, satirist and librettist

Castiglione, Baldassare (1478–1529) Diplomat and author

Catalani, Alfredo (1854–1893) Composer, chiefly of opera

Catalani, Ottavio (?–1644 or later) Composer of church music

Catalano, Antonio (*fl.* 1743–1763) Neapolitan *basso buffo*

Cavalieri, Emilio de' (1550–1602) Composer; from 1588 to 1596 Inspector-General of
    Arts and Artists in Florence

Cavalli, Francesco (1602–1676) Leading composer in Venice after death of
    Monteverdi

Cavour, Count Camillo (1810–1861) Piedmontese statesman, first prime minister of
    Italy

Cerlone, Francesco (1722–after 1778) Playwright and librettist

Cesarotti, Melchiorre (1730–1808) Man of letters, philosopher, translator

Cesti, Antonio (Pietro) (1623–1669) Composer and singer

Champfleury (Jules Husson) (1821–1889) French novelist and critic

Chateaubriand, François-René (1768–1848) Novelist, historian, essayist and journalist

Chiabrera, Gabriello (1552–1638) Poet

Chiari, Pietro (1712–1785) Novelist, poet and librettist

Ciampi, Vincenzo (?1719–1762) Composer, chiefly active in Naples, Venice and
    London

Cicognini, Giacinto Andrea (1606–1651) Lawyer, dramatist and librettist

Cilea, Francesco (1866–1950) Composer and teacher

Cimaglia, Natale Maria (1735–1799) Lawyer, economist and polymath

Cimarosa, Domenico (1749–1801) The most admired Italian opera composer of the
    late eighteenth century

Cini, Giovan Battista (1528–1586) Florentine courtier, diplomat, impresario and
    author

Cirillo, Francesco (1623–after 1667) Composer and singer

Colbran, Isabella (1785–1845) Spanish-born soprano, Rossini's first wife

Coltellini, Marco (1719–1777) Librettist and publisher

Comte, Auguste (1798–1857) Philosopher; founder of positivism

Condillac, Etienne de (1715–1780) Rationalist philosopher

Conti, Carlo (1796–1868) Composer, professor of counterpoint and composition at the
    Naples Conservatory

Conti, Natale (1520–1582) Humanist, poet and historian

Corneille, Pierre (1606–1684) Poet and dramatist, founder of French classical tragedy

Corot, Jean-Baptiste-Camille (1796–1875) Landscape painter

Corradi, Giulio Cesare (?–1701/2) Librettist

Correggio, Niccolò da (1450–1508) Courtier and diplomat; poet and dramatist

Corsi, Jacopo (*c.* 1560–1604) Florentine nobleman; musical amateur and patron

Corsini, Ottaviano (1588–1641) Churchman and politician

Corvo, Nicolò (Agasippo Mercotellis) (?–after 1743) Lawyer and librettist

Cremona, Tranquillo (1837–1878) *Scapigliato* painter

Crescimbeni, Giovan Maria (1663–1728) Literary historian, first *custode generale* of
    Arcadia

Croce, Benedetto (1866–1952) Philosopher, critic and historian

Cuzzoni, Francesca (*c.* 1698–1770) Soprano, one of the most admired *prima donna*s of
    the age

da Ponte, Lorenzo (1749–1838) Adventurer, poet and librettist

Daguerre, Louis-Jacques-Mandé (1787–1851) Painter and physicist

d'Alibert, Giacomo (1626–1713) Courtier, diplomat, theatre manager

d'Ambra, Francesco (1499–after 1552) Florentine dramatist, a leading figure in the
    Platonic Academy
d'Annunzio, Gabriele (1863–1938) Poet, dramatist, novelist; soldier and adventurer
d'Arcais, Francesco (1830–1890) Influential Roman music critic
David, Domenico (?–1698) Librettist, member of Arcadia
David, Giovanni (1790–1864) Lyric tenor
David, Jacques-Louis (1748–1825) French neo-classical painter
de Sanctis, Cesare (?–1881) Neapolitan businessman
de Sanctis, Francesco (1818–1883) Neapolitan literary critic and historian
Delacroix, Eugène (1798–1863) Leader of the French Romantic school of painting
Deledda, Grazia (1871–1936) Sardinian novelist; Nobel prize-winner in 1926
Delibes, Léo (1836–1891) Composer, chiefly of opera and ballet
della Valle, Pietro (1586–1652) Poet, musician and chronicler of the musical scene
Diderot, Denis (1713–1784) Philosopher and man of letters
Dittersdorf, Carl Ditters von (1739–1799) Viennese composer and violinist
Doni, Giovanni Battista (*c.* 1594–1647) Musical scholar
Dossi, Carlo (1849–1898) *Scapigliato* writer
du Locle, Camille (1832–1903) Librettist and theatre manager
du Tillot, Guillaume-Léon (1711–1774) Encyclopaedist, economist and statesman
Dumas, Alexandre (1802–1870) French Romantic novelist and playwright
Duni, Egidio (1708–1775) Composer, most notable for contributions to *opéra comique*
Dupré, Giovanni (1817–1882) Florentine sculptor
Duprez, Gilbert (1806–1896) French *tenore di forza*
Durante, Francesco (1684–1755) Neapolitan composer, esp. of church music, and
    teacher
Durazzo, Count Giacomo (1717–1794) Diplomat and *directeur des spectacles* in Vienna
Faccio, Franco (1840–1891) Composer and conductor
Farinelli (Carlo Broschi) (1705–1782) Soprano *castrato*
Faustina (Bordoni) (1700–1781) Mezzo-soprano, Cuzzoni's great rival, wife of Hasse
Faustini, Giovanni (*c.* 1619–1651) Librettist and theatre manager
Faustini, Marco (?–after 1675) Theatre manager, brother of the preceding
Favart, Charles Simon (1710–1792) Playwright, librettist and impresario
Federici, Vincenzo (1764–1826) Composer, chiefly active in London and Milan
Federico, Gennaro Antonio (?–between 1743 and 1748) Neapolitan librettist
Feo, Francesco (1691–1761) Neapolitan composer and teacher
Ferrari, Benedetto (1603/4–1681) Composer, poet and impresario
Ferretti, Jacopo (1784–1852) Poet and librettist
Festa, Giuseppe (1771–1839) Violinist, orchestral leader and teacher
Ficino, Marsilio (1433–1499) Humanist philosopher; a founder of Renaissance
    neo-Platonism
Filippi, Filippo (1830–1887) Influential music critic, based in Milan
Florimo, Francesco (1800–1888) Teacher and music librarian at the Naples
    Conservatory
Fontana, Ferdinando (1850–1919) Man of letters and journalist
Foscolo, Ugo (1778–1827) Poet and novelist, after 1816 an exile in London
Franchetti, Baron Alberto (1860–1942) Composer, chiefly of opera
Francœur, François (1698–1787) French composer and violinist
Frezzolini, Erminia (1818–1884) Soprano
Frigimelica Roberti, Girolamo (1653–1732) Poet, librettist, architect and librarian
Frugoni, Carlo Innocenzo (1692–1768) Librettist and court poet at Parma
Gabrieli, Andrea (*c.* 1520–1586) Venetian composer, notably of madrigals
Gagliano, Marco da (*c.* 1575–1642) Priest and composer

Personalia

Galiani, Ferdinando (1728–1787) Economist and intellectual

Galilei, Vincenzo (1520–1591) Lutenist, composer, musical theorist

Gallet, Louis (1835–1898) French librettist

Galli, Filippo (1783–1853) Bass, the most admired of his generation

Galuppi, Baldassare (Il Buranello) (1706–1785) Venetian composer, notably of *opera buffa*

Gamerra, Giovanni de (1743–1803) Adventurer and theatre poet

Garibaldi, Giuseppe (1807–1882) Military leader in Wars of Independence

Garrick, David (1717–1779) Actor and theatre director

Gasparini, Francesco (1668–1727) Composer, teacher and theorist

Gastoldi, Giovanni Giacomo (?1550s–1662) Composer, primarily of madrigals and church music

Gavazzeni, Gianandrea (1909–   ) Composer, conductor and writer on music

Gay, John (1685–1732) Poet and dramatist, inventor of the ballad opera

Gazzaniga, Giuseppe (1743–1818) Composer, chiefly of comic opera

Gemistus Pletho (1355–1452) Byzantine intellectual

Gherardi, Evaristo (1663–1700) Actor and playwright

Ghislanzoni, Antonio (1824–1893) Singer, journalist and librettist

Giacosa, Giuseppe (1847–1906) Playwright and librettist

Gigli, Girolamo (1660–1722) Scholar and playwright

Gioberti, Vincenzo (1801–1852) Priest and idealistic patriotic liberal

Giordano, Umberto (1867–1948) Composer, chiefly of opera

Giusti, Giuseppe (1809–1850) Florentine satirical poet

Glareanus (Heinrich Glarean) (1488–1563) Swiss humanist and musical theorist

Goldoni, Carlo (1707–1793) Venetian playwright and librettist

Gomes, Carlos A. (1836–1896) Italianized Brazilian composer, chiefly active in Milan

Gonzaga, family; rulers of Mantua 1328–1627

Gozzi, Carlo (1720–1786) Reactionary controversialist and man of letters

Gravina, Gian Vincenzo (1664–1718) Lawyer and humanist

Grazzini, Anton Francesco (1503–1584) Poet and dramatist

Grétry, André-Ernest-Modeste (1741–1813) French composer, leading master of *opéra comique* in late eighteenth century

Grisi, Giulia (1811–1869) Soprano

Grossi, Tommaso (1790–1853) Milanese novelist and poet

Guadagni, Gaetano (*c.* 1725–1692) *Castrato*, a notable actor as well as singer

Guarini, Battista (*fl.* 1460–1480s) Poet and translator

Guarini, Battista (1538–1612) Diplomat and court poet at Ferrara

Guerrazzi, Francesco Domenico (1804–1873) Writer, chiefly of historical novels

Guglielmi, Pietro Alessandro (1728–1804) Composer, esp. successful with comic opera

Halévy, Fromental (1799–1862) French composer, chiefly of opera, teacher and writer

Hasse, Johann Adolf (1699–1783) Composer, the classic example of an Italianized German

Hayez, Francesco (1791–1882) Historical painter and portraitist

Heinse, (Johann Jacob) Wilhelm (1746–1803) Scholar, translator and novelist

Hoffmann, Ernst Theodor Amadeus (1776–1822) Civil servant, novelist, composer and critic

Hugo, Victor (1802–1885) Poet, dramatist and novelist, the great figure in French Romanticism

Illica, Luigi (1857–1919) Dramatist, journalist and librettist

Imer, Giuseppe (*c.* 1700–1758) Actor and leader of a *commedia dell'arte* troupe

Ivanovich, Cristoforo (1628–1689) Librettist and theatre chronicler

Jacovacci, Vincenzo (1811–1881) Roman impresario

Jommelli, Nicolò (1714–1774) Composer, chiefly of opera and sacred music
Klopstock, Friedrich Gottlob (1724–1803) Lyric, epic and dramatic poet
Krause, Christian G. (1719–1770) German lawyer, composer and theorist
Kretschmann, Karl Friedrich (1738–1809) Lawyer and poet, an imitator of Klopstock
Lamennais, Félicité-Robert de (1782–1854) Catholic democrat and Utopian
Lanari, Alessandro (1790–1862) Impresario, most notably in Florence
Landi, Stefano (c. 1590–c. 1655) Roman singer and composer
Latilla, Gaetano (1711–1788) Opera composer and church musician
Lavigna, Vincenzo (1776–1836) Composer and teacher, notably of Verdi
Legrenzi, Giovanni (1626–1690) Composer and organist
Leo, Leonardo (1694–1744) Neapolitan composer, chiefly of opera and church music
Leoncavallo, Ruggero (1857–1919) Composer and librettist
Leopardi, Giacomo (1798–1837) Poet, philosopher and scholar
Lind, Jenny (1820–1887) Soprano – 'the Swedish nightingale'
Loewe, Sophie (1816–1861) German-born soprano
Logroscino, Nicola (1698–c. 1767) Composer, chiefly of comic opera
Loredan, Giovanni Francesco (1607–1661) Venetian patrician, statesman, man of
    letters
Lorenzi, Giambattista (1721–1807) The outstanding comic opera librettist in Naples
Lotti, Antonio (c. 1667–1740) Composer, organist and *maestro di cappella* at San
    Marco, Venice
Louÿs, Pierre (1870–1925) French novelist and poet
Lucca, Francesco (1802–1872) and Giovannina (1814–1894) Music publishers;
    Ricordi's chief rivals in N. Italy
Maffei, Andrea (1798–1885) Poet and translator, notably of Schiller
Maffei, Clara (Clarina) (1814–1886) Wife of above until 1846; hostess of leading Milan
    salon
Maggi, Carlo (1630–1699) Milanese poet and playwright
Maistre, Joseph de (1753–1821) French moralist and Christian philosopher
Malibran, Maria (1808–1936) Mezzo-soprano, daughter of Manuel Garcia, himself a
    singer and one of the most influential singing-teachers of the nineteenth century
Malvezzi, Cristofano (1547–1597) Composer, *maestro di cappella* to the Grand Duke of
    Tuscany
Malvezzi, Virgilio (1595–1653) Scholar and poet
Mameli, Goffredo (1827–1849) Patriotic republican poet
Mancini, Francesco (1672–1737) Neapolitan composer, organist and teacher
Manelli, Francesco (1594–1667) Composer, poet and impresario
Manfredini, Vincenzo (1737–1799) Composer and theorist
Manuzio, Aldo (1449–1515) Humanist; editor and publisher, esp. of the classics
Manzoni, Alessandro (1785–1873) Milanese poet, playwright and novelist
Marazzoli, Marco (c. 1602–1662) Composer and singer
Marchetti, Filippo (1831–1902) Composer and teacher
Marcolini, Maria (*fl.* 1805–1818) Mezzo-soprano
Marenzio, Luca (c. 1553–1599) Composer, esp. of madrigals
Mariani, Angelo (1821–1873) Composer and violinist; Italy's first specialist conductor
Mariette, Auguste-Edouard (1821–1881) French Egyptologist
Marino, Giambattista (1569–1625) Virtuoso poet of turbulent habits
Marivaux, Pierre de (1688–1763) Dramatist, novelist and essayist
Marpurg, Wilhelm Friedrich (1718–1795) Prussian civil servant, composer, editor and
    theorist
Martini, Padre Giovanni Battista (1706–1784) Musical scholar, teacher and composer
Mascagni, Pietro (1863–1945) Composer and conductor

Massenet, Jules (1842–1912) Leading composer of late-nineteenth-century French opera

Mattei, Saverio (?–?) Poet, scholar and teacher

Mattioli, Andrea (*c.* 1620–1679) Composer and priest

Mayr, Simon (1763–1845) German musician, settled in Italy as composer and teacher

Mayseder, Joseph (1789–1863) Austrian violinist and composer

Mazzini, Giuseppe (1805–1872) Political philosopher, writer and revolutionary

Mazzocchi, Domenico (1592–1665) Roman composer

Mazzocchi, Virgilio (1597–1646) Roman composer, brother of the preceding

Mazzolà, Caterino (?–1806) Saxon, later Viennese, court poet

Mazzucato, Alberto (1813–1877) Composer, teacher and writer

Méhul, Etienne-Nicolas (1763–1817) French symphonist and opera composer

Mei, Girolamo (1519–1594) Humanist; leading authority on Ancient Greek music

Melani, Jacopo (1623–1676) Composer and organist

Mercadante, Saverio (1795–1870) Composer, chiefly of opera, and teacher

Méric-Lalande, Henriette (1798–1867) French singer, the first *soprano drammatica d'agilità*

Metastasio, Pietro (1698–1782) Theatre poet, from 1730 court poet in Vienna

Metternich, Wenzel Fürst von (1773–1859) Austrian statesman

Meyerbeer, Giacomo (1791–1864) German-born composer, notably of French grand opera

Michotte, Edmond (1830–1914) Amateur musician, collector of Rossiniana

Mill, John Stuart (1806–1873) British philosopher and political economist

Minato, Nicolò (*c.* 1630–1698) Lawyer, librettist and impresario

Mocenigo, Count Alvise (?–?) Venetian patrician, president of La Fenice in 1840s

Mondonville, Jean-Joseph (1711–1772) French composer and violinist

Moniglia, Giovanni Andrea (1624–1700) Florentine physician and librettist

Monti, Vincenzo (1754–1828) Poet and dramatist

Moriani, Napoleone (1808–1878) Tenor, celebrated for his death-scenes

Morlacchi, Francesco (1784–1841) Composer, active chiefly in Dresden

Murger, Henri (1822–1861) Chronicler of contemporary Parisian life

Murtola, Gaspare (?–1624) Minor Genoese poet

Muzio, Emanuele (1825–1890) Composer and conductor, Verdi's only pupil

Nelli, Jacopo Angelo (1673–1767) Priest, teacher and comic playwright

Nievo, Ippolito (1831–1861) Novelist

Noris, Matteo (?–1714) Librettist

Noverre, Jean-Georges (1727–1810) Ballet-master and choreographer

Nozzari, Andrea (1775–1832) Dramatic tenor

Obizzi, Pio Enea II, Marchese degli (1592–1672) *Condottiere*, man of letters and musical amateur

Oliva, Domenico (1860–1917) Lawyer, politician, journalist and poet

Orefice, Antonio (*fl.* 1708–1734) Neapolitan composer of opera

Orlandini, Giuseppe (1675–1760) Composer, esp. of *intermezzi*, and church musician

'Ossian' Legendary third-century Celtic bard, fragments of whose works were 'discovered' in the 1760s by James Macpherson

Pacchierotti, Gasparo (1740–1821) Soprano *castrato*, the greatest of his age

Pacini, Giovanni (1796–1867) One of the most prolific and successful of the minor composers of the Romantic period

Paisiello, Giovanni (1740–1816) Composer, chiefly of opera, but prodigiously productive in many genres

Palladio, Andrea (1508–1580) Architect

Pallavicino, Carlo (?–1688) Composer and organist

Personalia

Palomba, Antonio (1705–1769) Neapolitan librettist
Palomba, Giuseppe (*fl.* 1765–1825) Neapolitan librettist, grandson of the preceding
Paolucci, Alfonso (early sixteenth century) Courtier and diplomat in the service of the Este family
Papini, Giovanni (1881–1956) Essayist and controversialist
Pariati, Pietro (1665–1733) Poet and librettist
Pasta, Giuditta (1797–1865) Soprano of exceptional range and dramatic power
Patrizi, Francesco (1529–1597) Philosopher at universities of Ferrara and Rome
Pellico, Silvio (1789–1854) Liberal editor, writer and poet
Pepoli, Carlo (1796–1881) Poet and patriot; spent much of life in exile
Perez, David (1711–1778) Neapolitan composer, latterly chiefly active in Lisbon
Pergolesi, Giovanni Battista (1710–1736) Composer, chiefly of opera and church music
Peri, Jacopo (1561–1633) Organist, singer and composer
Perrucci, Andrea (1651–1704) Dramatic theorist and librettist
Petrella, Errico (1813–1877) Opera composer, chiefly for Naples
Petrucci, Ottavio (1466–1549) Music printer and publisher
Piave, Francesco Maria (1810–1876) Librettist – Verdi's preferred collaborator – and stage-manager in Venice and Milan
Piccinni, Niccolò (1728–1800) Composer, equally influential in Italy and France
Pico della Mirandola, Giovanni (1563–1594) Humanist and philosopher
Pietro da Cortona (1596–1669) Painter and architect
Pindemonte, Giovanni (1751–1812) Poet and dramatist
Pindemonte, Ippolito (1753–1828) Poet, playwright and translator
Piovene, Agostino (*fl.* early eighteenth century) Nobleman and amateur librettist
Pirandello, Luigi (1867–1936) Novelist and playwright
Piroli, Giuseppe (1815–1890) Lawyer and member of parliament
Pizzetti, Ildebrando (1880–1968) Composer, conductor, musical educationalist and writer on music
Pizzi, Italo (1849–1920) Librarian and Orientalist
Planelli, Antonio (1747–1803) Man of letters, author of a substantial treatise on opera (Naples 1772)
Poliziano, [Angelo Ambrogini] (1454–1494) Humanist, scholar and poet
Pollarolo, Carlo Francesco (*c.* 1653–1723) Composer and organist
Ponchielli, Amilcare (1834–1886) Composer, teacher, band-master and church musician
Porpora, Nicola (1686–1768) Neapolitan composer and singing-teacher
Praga, Emilio (1839–1875) *Scapigliatura* poet
Praga, Marco (1862–1929) Son of Emilio; novelist and dramatist inspired by French Naturalism
Provenzale, Francesco (*c.* 1626–1704) First important Neapolitan composer of opera
Quagliati, Paolo (*c.* 1555–1628) Church composer and bureaucrat
Racine, Jean (1639–1699) French classical dramatist
Raimondi, Pietro (1786–1853) Composer (esp. of opera, church music, fugue) and teacher
Rebel, François (1701–1775) Violinist, composer, theatre administrator
Reicha, Antoine (1770–1836) Composer, theorist and teacher
Ricci, Federico (1809–1877) and Luigi (1805–1859) Brothers; among the most successful of the minor opera composers of the time
Ricordi, Giovanni (1785–1853); Tito (1811–1888); Giulio (1840–1912) Milanese family of music publishers
Righetti-Giorgi, Geltrude (1793–1862) Contralto

642

Personalia

Rinuccini, Ottavio (1562–1621) Poet and courtier

Romani, Felice (1788–1865) Poet, journalist, and the most admired Italian librettist of his age

Romanina, La, *see* Bulgarelli-Benti

Ronconi, Giorgio (1810–1890) Baritone; a noted singing actor

Rore, Cipriano de' (*c.* 1516–1565) Netherlandish composer of madrigals and church-music

Rosa, Salvatore (1615–1673) Painter, esp. of landscapes, with a wide enthusiasm for all the arts

Rospigliosi, Giulio (1600–1669) Churchman (Pope Clement IX) and librettist

Rossi, Gaetano (1774–1855) Librettist and stage-manager, active chiefly in Venice and Verona

Rossi, Luigi (*c.* 1597–1653) Composer and virtuoso instrumentalist

Rossi, Michelangelo (1601/2–1656) Composer and organist

Rovani, Giuseppe (1818–1874) Historical novelist

Rubini, Giovanni Battista (1794–1854) Tenor; a supreme vocalist but poor actor

Sacchini, Antonio (1730–1786) Opera composer, his last works in French for Paris

Sacrati, Francesco (1605–1650) Composer

Saddumene, Bernardo (*fl.* 1720–1730) Neapolitan librettist

Salieri, Antonio (1750–1825) Composer and teacher, chiefly in Paris and esp. Vienna

Salvi, Antonio (?–1742) Florentine physician and librettist

Sannazaro, Jacopo (1457–1530) Poet

Sanquirico, Alessandro (1777–1849) Scene painter and stage designer

Sansovino, Jacopo (1486–1570) Architect and sculptor

Santocanale, Filippo (?–?) Palermo lawyer

Sardou, Victorien (1831–1908) French playwright

Sarri, Domenico (1679–1744) The leading musician of his time in Naples civic and court life

Sarti, Giuseppe (1729–1802) Composer, chiefly in Copenhagen, Milan and St Petersburg

Sartorio, Antonio (1630–1680) Composer

Sbarra, Francesco (1611–1668) Aristocrat poet and librettist

Schiller, Friedrich von (1759–1805) Poet, dramatist, philosopher and historian

Schlegel, August Wilhelm von (1767–1845) Poet, translator and scholar

Schopenhauer, Arthur (1788–1860) German transcendental idealist philosopher

Scribe, Eugène (1791–1861) Dramatist and the most productive and admired French librettist of his period

Sebastiani, Carlo (1858–1924) Neapolitan conductor and singing-teacher

Serafino dall'Aquila (1466–1500) Singer, lutenist, poet and composer

Serio, Luigi (?–?) Neapolitan court poet

Serlio, Sebastiano (1475–1554) Architect and architectural theorist

Shterich, Yevgeny (1809–1833) Dilettante composer and pianist

Simoni, Renato (1875–1952) Journalist, playwright and librettist

Sografi, Simeone Antonio (1759–1818) Librettist

Solera, Temistocle (1815–1865) Poet, librettist and adventurer

Soliva, Carlo (1792–1851) Composer and teacher, chiefly in Poland, Russia and Paris

Somma, Antonio (1809–1865) Lawyer and playwright

Sonzogno, Edoardo (1836–1920) Milanese music publisher

Soumet, Alexandre (1788–1845) Poet and dramatist

Spagna, Arcangelo (1631/2–after 1720) Poet and dramatist

Spinelli, Nicola (1865–1909) Composer and pianist

Spontini, Gaspare (1774–1851) Composer, esp. of opera for Paris and Berlin

Stagno, Roberto (1840–1897) Tenor, leading exponent of *verismo* singing
Stampiglia, Silvio (1664–1725) Librettist, founder member of Arcadia
Steffani, Agostino (1654–1728) Churchman, diplomat and composer
Stendhal (Henri Beyle) (1783–1842) French novelist and italophile
Sterbini, Cesare (1784–1831) Roman civil servant and librettist
Stolz, Teresa (1834–1902) Austrian soprano
Strepponi, Giuseppina (1815–1897) Soprano, Verdi's second wife
Striggio, Alessandro [the elder] (*c.* 1535–1592) Composer
Striggio, Alessandro [the younger] (1573–1630) Son of the above; courtier and poet
Strozzi, Giulio (1583–1652) Humanist, poet and librettist
Strozzi, Piero (*c.* 1550–after 1609) Nobleman and amateur composer
Tadolini, Eugenia (1809–?) Lyric soprano
Talma, François-Joseph (1763–1826) Leading tragic actor in early-nineteenth-century France
Tarchetti, Iginio Ugo (1841–1869) *Scapigliato* poet and novelist
Tartini, Giuseppe (1692–1770) Composer, virtuoso violinist and theorist
Tasca, Pierantonio (1864–1934) Sicilian composer, chiefly of opera
Tasso, Torquato (1544–1595) Poet attached to the Ferrara court
Tesauro, Emanuele (1591–1675) Turinese man of letters and historian
Tesi, Vittoria (1700–1775) Contralto *prima donna* of international reputation
Thalberg, Sigismond (1812–1871) Virtuoso pianist, composer and teacher
Tommaseo, Niccolò (1802–1874) Lawyer, politician, scholar and poet
Tommasini, Vincenzo (1878–1950) Composer, writer and Classical scholar
Torelli, Giacomo (1608–1678) Engineer, architect and stage designer
Torelli, Vincenzo (?–?) Neapolitan journalist; later Secretary to the management of the San Carlo theatre
Toscanini, Arturo (1867–1957) Conductor
Tosi, Adelaide (?–1859) Soprano
Tosi, Pier Francesco (*c.* 1653–1732) *Castrato* singer and singing-teacher
Tottola, Leone Andrea (?–1831) Prolific Neapolitan librettist
Traetta, Tommaso (1727–1779) Composer, chiefly active in Parma
Trinchera, Pietro (1702–1755) Neapolitan librettist
Trissino, Giangiorgio (1478–1550) Literary theorist and classicizing poet
Tronsarelli, Ottavio (?–?) Librettist
Tullio, Francesco Antonio (1660–1737) Neapolitan librettist
Vaccai, Nicola (1790–1848) Composer and singing-teacher
Varesi, Felice (1813–1889) Dramatic baritone
Vasari, Giorgio (1511–1574) Artist and historian of art
Velluti, Giovanni Battista (1781–1861) Soprano *castrato*, the last to make a career in opera
Verga, Giovanni (1840–1922) Novelist and short-story writer, the leading Italian representative of Realism
Vinci, Leonardo (*c.* 1690–1730) Leading opera composer in Naples in the 1720s
Vitali, Filippo (*c.* 1590–after 1653) Priest (for a time to the Barberini household) and composer
Vitruvius, Pollio (*fl.* 1st century BC) Roman author of a ten-volume treatise on architecture
Vittori, Loreto (1600–1670) Composer, singer and poet
Vogler, Abbé (1749–1814) Organist, pianist, musical theorist and educationalist
Watteau, Antoine (1684–1721) French painter, admired esp. for his *fêtes galantes*
Werner, Zacharias (1768–1823) Leading Romantic playwright in Germany
Winckelmann, Johann J. (1717–1768) German authority on Classical art

Personalia

Young, Edward (1681–1765) Anglican clergyman, poet and essayist
Zanardini, Angelo (1820–1893) Librettist and composer
Zandonai, Riccardo (1883–1944) Composer and conductor
Zarlino, Gioseffo (1517–1590) Leading music theorist of the humanist age
Zavadini, Guido (1868–1958) Oboist, teacher and musical scholar
Zeno, Apostolo (1668–1750) Literary scholar and theatre poet
Ziani, Pietro Andrea (?1616–1684) Composer and organist
Zingarelli, Niccolò (1752–1837) Neapolitan composer and teacher
Zola, Emile (1840–1902) Chief novelist and theorist of naturalism

Notes

Introduction

1 'It is Music herself.'
2 Cf. Glinka's account of the performance of Bellini's *La sonnambula* in Milan in 1831, p. 398 below.

I The origins of opera

1 The Renaissance intermedi

1 'Songs will declare you to have restored the stage to poetry.'
2 'the beautiful and the good which is shut up in Heaven, to make the Earth like Paradise'
3 For a discussion of the ideals of this group cf. Chapter 2.
4 A discussion of the ideals associated with the *seconda prattica* follows in Chapter 2.

2 The elements of early opera

1 Hathaway 1962 provides a full discussion of the Italian commentators on Aristotle.
2 The earliest, dating from 1506, were Erasmus's Latin versions of Euripides' *Hecuba* and *Iphigenia in Aulis* (Schrade 1960: 26).
3 For a full discussion of Mei's role see Palisca 1954.
4 'The musician was not disjoined from the poet, nor the poet from the musician.'
5 As far as we know, this term was not used by the Camerata themselves; it appears first in Giovanni Battista Doni's *Compendio del trattato de' generi e de' modi della musica*, published in Rome in 1635 (Baron 1968: 426).
6 'If you wish me to weep, you must first experience sorrow yourself.'
7 'The world grows old, and as it grows old it decays.'
8 'Let us love, for the sun dies and then is reborn: but from us he hides his brief light, and sleep leads in eternal night.'
9 'It is not to deaf things that we sing; the woods answer everything.'
10 'But the plains and hills will cry out for me, and this forest which so often I taught to resound with your sweet name. The weeping fountains and the murmuring winds will tell out my plaints.'
11 'Do you then think the sweet spring, which, joyful and smiling, turns the thoughts of the world, of beasts, of men and women to love, is a season for enmity and anger? Do you not perceive how all things love with a love that is filled with joy and well-being?'
12 'sweet carols . . . flowers and streams . . . cupids without bows and without torches'

3 *The beginnings of opera*

1 This was a resetting of a text by Rinuccini, originally composed by Peri.
2 Transcribed and discussed in Porter 1965.
3 'But ah, my dear friends, let us betake ourselves to the grateful shades of that beloved flowery copse. And there, to the sound of the limpid crystal, we shall joyfully sing and dance . . .'
4 'The earth and the ethereal spheres were aflame with the joyful sighs of this pair of loving hearts. And through the serene sky might be heard choirs of winged cupids tuning their sweet songs.'

4 *Monteverdi's* Orfeo

1 'No enterprise is undertaken by man in vain.'
2 'Today pity and love triumph in Hell.'
3 'dear woods . . . beloved hill-sides'
4 Ah, bitter chance! ah, pitiless and cruel fate! ah, injurious stars! ah, avaricious heaven!'
5 'Sigh heavenly breezes, weep oh woods and fountains.'
6 'that sun . . . through whom alone my nights receive their days'
7 'Too much, too much did you rejoice in your good fortune.'
8 I do not understand Pirrotta's objection that to speak of an 'architectonic concept of form' is at this period anachronistic (Pirrotta 1984: 290). If the acts are full of carefully labelled ritornellos, of symmetries and repetitions, and if they are framed with choruses or sinfonias, then one of the 'fruits of intended classicism' to which he alludes must surely have been a musico-dramatic architecture.
9 'who in despair (gives himself) a prey (to grief)'
10 'Sigh heavenly breezes, weep oh woods and fields.'
11 'the unstable plain . . . that he scorned the wrath of Auster and Aquilon . . . that he held the ocean in check with his fragile bark'
12 'cruel trouble . . . who will console us . . . who grant us . . . the two greater lights . . . to be able to weep . . . on this sad day'
13 'beautiful and cold limbs . . . let us go, shepherds'
14 'deepest abysses . . . to see the stars again'
15 'Ah, vision too sweet . . . fields of weeping and of sorrow'
16 'if ever you took amorous delight in these eyes, if the fairness of this face pleased you'
17 'Blessed be the day when first I pleased you, blessed the prey and the sweet deception'

II The Venetian hegemony

5 *Opera in seventeenth-century Rome*

1 It should be noted in passing that there was a break in the tradition between 1644 and 1652, during the early years of the pontificate of Innocent X (Pamphili), when the Barberinis felt obliged to go into exile. During this interlude they were instrumental in bringing opera to Paris. The first opera after their return, the Rospigliosi/Abbatini/Marazzoli *Dal male il bene*, marked a matrimonial reconciliation between the Barberini and Pamphili families.
2 Cf. the incidents recorded in Smither 1977: 160–1.

6 Opera comes to Venice

1 A ducat was worth approximately 6 lire, so this represented a reduction of more than 50 per cent.
2 Cf. the account of Queen Cristina's visit to the Teatro Barberini in Chapter 5 above.

7 The nature of Venetian opera

1 'I do know that you must display your charms somewhere else, captivating souls with the sweetness of your speech, enchanting your listeners. Eloquence has no home in these parts; caprice and bizzarrerie alone dwell here.'
2 'bound together in constancy, these valleys reverberate to the sound of kisses . . .'
3 Mars (Nero)   Now that you invite me to kisses on a bed of roses, come, beautiful one, and lay yourself down naked; my soul calls you to greater delights.
Venus (Gilde)   Gladly I obey you . . .
Mars   But before the soul is bound in sweet chains and the heart is fettered, let us take off our clothes here.
Venus   Readily I obey.   [She undresses.]
Vulcan (Tiridate)   *Is Gilde so bold?*
Bronte   *Do please keep quiet, sir, they're only pretending.*
Mars [Aria]   How I rejoice to see your naked breast; even a cloudless dawn is less delightful to behold. How I rejoice . . .
Venus   That is enough: come to my sweet embrace.
                              [They go to the bed, and each of them reclines upon it.]
4 'The aim of the poet is the marvellous (I speak of the excellent poet, not the clumsy one): he who does not know how to astonish, needs to smarten himself up!'
5 Painting ⎫
  Music   ⎬ à 3   Alas, everything is ruined. This is the fruit of your crazy compasses
  Poetry ⎭

  Architecture   Ah! Ah! You are fools if you believe my contrivances are a catastrophe.

  Painting ⎫
  Music   ⎬ à 3   Uncommon novelties know how to draw ruin in their train . . .
  Poetry ⎭
6 'Come hither, ye zephyrs, and give me back those breaths which you have often collected from my sighs . . .'
7 'But now I see the sheet pregnant with the benign breeze. I entrust myself to the will of destiny!'
8 'Even the inanimate rocks know how to acquire sense and feeling, so that they can enjoy your happiness; even the insensate trees make merry and laugh, rejoicing in your delight.'
9 The extent to which *L'incoronazione di Poppea* should be described as Monteverdi's is controversial: see Alan Curtis's recent edition (1989, Borough Green); the issue does not affect such comments on the opera as are made in this book.

8 The development of the musical language

1 For a fine example from Pallavicino's *Demetrio* (Teatro San Moisè 1666) see Bukofzer 1947: 135.

9 *Cesti's L'Orontea*

1 If Cesti was not the composer of the 1649 *Orontea* (cf. below), this reputation would be owed exclusively to his singing; he wrote no other opera until *Alessandro vincitor di se stesso* (Venice 1651).

2 'Do you but command that my feet be fastened in the chains of servitude; and in those iron rings the astonished world may wonder at your clemency and my pomps.'

3 Or.   How did he insult you?
Cor.   He challenged me to a duel.
Or.   Well?
Cor.   I am a nobleman, he is a plebeian.
Or.   Alidoro is a plebeian?
    And who told you that?
Cor.   He is the son of a pirate and that's enough.
Or.   No more; I shall render Alidoro's name illustrious and famous: I publicly declare him to be a nobleman.

4 'How sweet it is to fondle an amorous beauty, who graciously grants you all the heart could desire. And if that pleasure is sweet, how much sweeter it is to rejoice on her bosom.'

5 See the note on Italian prosody, p. xvii.

6 Cor.   The new dawn broke in the sky, and I return to bow down to you, a more beautiful dawn than the dawn in the sky.
Sil.   The sun rises in lofty majesty, and I come to pay homage to a more beautiful sun, the sun in your handsome face.
Cor.   Silandra, I have no heart: Love robbed me of it and concealed its thefts in your breast.
Sil.   Corindo, I have no life: Love gave me death and wishes my death to live in you.
Cor.   My refreshment.
Sil.   My desire.
Cor.   My treasure.
Sil.   My all.
à 2   How dear is your beauty. Through you this heart departs blessed for the heaven of love.

7 Translated at Ex.II.17.

8 'How angrily he swears! How he threatened me! I'm off to the inn to liquidate my fear.'

9 I say '*might* have anticipated' because although unmistakably lyrical in form, the texts in question are in *settenari* and *endecasillabi*, the metres of recitative.

III *Opera seria*

10 *The* dramma per musica

1 'How very happy you are, innocent shepherdesses.'

11 *'Perfection and public favour'*

1 'Behold, the moment of revolution'
2 'superficially tragic, fundamentally comic'
3 'Gluck before Gluck'
4 Translated at Ex.III.4.

12 *The performance of* opera seria

1 'scandalous philandering'
2 It was Heinse who recorded the ecstatic audience cries of 'O benedetto il coltello, che t'a tagliato li coglioni.'

13 *The collapse of the Metastasian ideal*

1 Metastasio to Farinelli in 1749, cited in Burney 1796, I: 297; in 1751, cited *ibidem*: 402; in 1756, cited *ibidem*: 173.
2 Translated at Ex.III.7.
3 Full details are in Yorke-Long 1954: 14–18.
4 The dedication was in fact written by Calzabigi (Gallarati 1984: 71).
5 'French usage'
6 'In the form of a murderous hand death approaches me; ah, stop! leave off! My mother kills me, an implacable mother indeed if she is not yet sated with blood. Oh God, do you not hear the howls and lamentations? Ah, barbarous woman, hasten the cruel blow; what kind of gift is life if I had it from you?'
7 'a noble simplicity and a calm grandeur'

14 Opera seria *in an age of ferment*

1 'ardent Gluckist'
2 'Greek exploits are but the shadows of more famous adventures among us, and of heroes who with the miraculous and novel achievements of sword and intellect surpassed the proofs of ancient virtue. The tongue speaks of Theseus, but Bonaparte is what the heart means.'

15 *A half-century of* L'Olimpiade

1 'Megacle himself, Megacle abandons me in my greatest need'
2 'Oh! how tiresome you are with this tedious, perpetual scepticism of yours. Close to harbour, would you have me fear shipwreck? Anyone who lends full credence to your doubts never knows whether it is dawn or evening.
    'The steed which is close to the inn quickens its pace all the more: the tightness of the bit does not restrain it, nor does the voice of command.'
3 'Proud of myself, I shall go bearing that dear name before me as I bear it inscribed in my heart. And then Greece will say that we shared our deeds, our thoughts, our feelings, even our names.'
4 'Ah! If Megacle only knew that the contest here today is for me.'
5 'Daughter, everything is ready.'
6 'I should give you cause for pride, were I to tell you all those who have come to compete in the battle for you. There's Olinto from Megara, there's Clearco from Sparta, Ati from Thebes, Erilo from Corinth, and Licida has come even from Crete.'
7 'Do not complain of destiny because it makes you subject to us: you women may be servants, but in your servitude you rule over us. We are strong, you are beautiful, and in every undertaking you are victorious when it come to a contest between beauty and strength.'
8 'Take care to find out where my love is wandering; if he cares for me any more, if he speaks of me any more. Ask if he ever sighs when he hears my name; if he sometimes utters it as he muses to himself.'

9 'Learn, learn [from me], you innocent damsels'

10 'Among a thousand lovers there are no longer to be found even so many as two souls that are constant; and everyone talks about fidelity.'

11 Lic.   Oh! if you win, who will be happier than I? How glad Megacle will be himself! Tell me: won't you be happy in my happiness?

    Meg.   Very.

    Lic.   The moment which binds Aristea to me, tell me, Megacle, will you not think it a happy one?

    Meg.   Very happy. (Ye Gods!)

    Lic.   Will you not be wanting to accompany me to the bridal chamber as my groomsman?

    Meg.   (What anguish!)

    Lic.   Speak.

    Meg.   Yes, just as you wish. (What new type of infernal suffering is this?)

12 'dreadful encounter'

13 'While you sleep, may Love inspire with the thought of my content, the content of your own slumbers.'

14 Meg.   In the days of your happiness, remember me.

    Arist.   Why do you speak like this, my love, tell me why?

    Meg.   Be silent, my beautiful one.

    Arist.   Speak, my sweet love.

    à 2   Ah! how your speech/silence pierces my heart.

    Arist.   (I see him I adore pining, and cannot understand why.)

    Meg.   (I die of jealousy, and cannot speak of it)

    à 2   Who ever felt a direr anguish than this, or a more cruel sorrow?

15 'That is to say, just as the yellow gold is tested in the fire, so is loyalty proved in the time of trial'

16 'Soon I shall return, beloved eyes, to gaze fondly on that face which with its first glance struck fire into my breast. I shall draw strength from those sweet lips, from those fair eyes, so that they will make the time of my heart's content come all the sooner.'

17 Lic.   Dear friend, may that heaven which fate hides from me, look mercifully on your life.

    Meg.   Ah! I wish I might wade across Lethe with you.

    Clis.   What an agonizing moment! Oh God, there can be no greater pain than this.

    Lic.   You must live.

    Meg.   What a command is that.

    Clis.   What a woeful sight!

    Lic./Meg.   One last embrace.

    All   The savage excess of this tyrannical suffering is beyond endurance.

    Meg./Lic.   Prince/friend, oh stars, farewell.

18 'We are ships abandoned on the freezing waves: our passions are impetuous winds: every pleasure is a hidden rock: all life is an ocean.'

IV The tradition of comedy

16 The commedia dell'arte

1 'a tempest in the midst of the calm'

2 'a hundred-year-old child'

17 Contrascene *and* intermezzi

1 It should perhaps be explained that no uniqueness or priority is being claimed for Scarlatti's *contrascene*; they are simply distinguished and comparatively accessible specimens of a genre that had been evolving for three or four decades before his operatic career even began.

2 Serv.   Have you got to take a message to my girl?
  Flac.   You must be crazy; there are no go-betweens anywhere these days, and these love-affairs are things that everyone does for himself.
  Serv.   This modern philosophy brings more freedom into love and deals with the matter of love in a better way. I'm not one to stand upon ceremomy. The social dogma of a past age must yield to that of the present.

3 'Yes, yes, you're a girl, a beast of a girl, a most selfish girl, a most insolent and artful girl.'

4 'For my taste, joy of my heart, you are a veritable Savoy biscuit . . . and you're like a bellyful of sweet pastry pie'

5 'I'm a lovable, alluring little damsel. I'm slender, but there's enough of me; I'm unmarried, I'm competent: that's what makes me appetizing.'

6 Cf. Grout's edition of the opera, p. 3.

7 A detailed list of 'frequently revived *intermezzi*' is given in Troy 1979, Appendix I, pp. 141–52.

8 This, in a rather different form, had been published by the Italian protestant and former Oxford don, Giovanni Florio, as long ago as 1591, in *Second Fruites*, an Italian manual based on a collection of traditional proverbs.

9 'Now every sad memory is silent, and what is past is forgotten: I learned to talk like this from Torquato Tasso. I shall obey you, Bettina, with bowed head.'

10 'from being a servant will finally become mistress'

11 'I know what they talk about and what they get up to: "My dear madam, how are you?" "Well." And then, all of a sudden, "That husband of mine is very odd, very nosy. He expects me to stay indoors all day." And the other woman replies, "What a beast. You should follow my example, neighbour . . ."'

12 'I shall stay here quietly'

13 'most illustrious master'

14 'but why? . . . what majesty'

15 'signorina, you deceive yourself'

16 Full repertory in Reichenburg 1937: 29.

18 The flowering of comic opera in Naples and Venice

1 'Pan loved Echo, nearby; Echo loved a leaping satyr; the satyr loved Lidia; and each of these was loathed by the one he loved.'

2 'Masto Col-Agnolo sharpening his razor in front of his shop; Ciccariello, who is sweeping and singing; Ciomma, in the doorway sewing; Carlo, passing in the distance.'

3 'Listen to me; I'm well off: I've got money: and I'm determined you're going to be mine.'

4 'a vain woman, a wiseacre, a pedant, a braggart, a humbug'

5 It may be noted in passing that one of the great comic roles of the period, in Latilla's *La finta cameriera* (Rome 1738), was that of Don Colascione.

6 Quoted complete in Robinson 1972: 222–4.

7 Goldoni uses a variety of synonyms for *opera buffa*: 'dramma comico',

'divertimento giocoso', 'opera bernesca', 'commedia per musica' and, most
consistently, after 1748, 'dramma giocoso per musica'.

8 'My blessed spade, my dearly loved comforter and sustainer, you are my sceptre,
and these fields my kingdom . . .'

9 'the really thrifty one . . . swashbuckling girl . . . charming woman'

10 On the misattributions of this 'invention' see Heartz 1977–78: 73–5.

11 Fully described in Heartz 1977–78: 70–1.

19 Apogee and decline

1 One should perhaps add that Lorenzi's *Socrate immaginario* was in fact banned in
Naples reputedly by order of the King, but not because of any satirical or critical
intention. The crux of the matter seems to have been indiscretion; an
uncomfortably close resemblance between Don Tammaro and one of the most
respected figures in Neapolitan intellectual life, Saverio Mattei (Scherillo 1916:
401–4).

2 'Oh Excellency, thanks to your generosity, and that of our beloved mistress, we
want for nothing . . . accept everything; Heaven grants the prayers of honest
poverty. Pray for her, that will show your gratitude.'

3 D. Tamm.   Tell me, you ignorant ape, what is it that drives donkeys?
Cal.   The stick.
D. Tamm.   And when the head commands the members, whether by bodily
    force or by the power of thought, what do the members do?
Cal.   They move.
D. Tamm.   Correct! Now tell me, who is the head among scholars?
Cal.   The master.
D. Tamm.   And if the master is the head, what then are the scholars?
Cal.   They are all members.
D. Tamm.   So, since you are a member of Socrates, you must move yourself.
Cal.   I'm persuaded.

4 It may be noted here that because of this association the term 'cavatina' came to be
attached to any entrance aria. By the nineteenth century it indicated not the form
of the aria but its positioning as the 'sortita' of a singer.

5 'Concerning the comic drama I shall say nothing; one might risk causing a fit. The
subject-matter is stupid, the libretto frightful, the whole thing the most horrible
rubbish.'

6 Selim.   You may perhaps have heard tell of a fine old Turkish custom; when a
    wife is a burden to him the husband can sell her off.
Ger.   That may indeed be a fine old custom; but we have an even finer one in
    Italy: the husband breaks the nose of any vile seducer.

7 Poet [enjoying the spectacle]   Carry on . . . keep going . . . excellent! Here . .
there . . . good; that's the way to brawl and wrestle; scratches, bites . . . just
what I wanted . . . what a finale! what a grand finale! Oh! what a sensation it
will be.

8 'Just as the handsome Paris presented the apple to the fairest, so, my enchanting
shepherdess, I present this flower to you.'

20 Il barbiere di Siviglia: *Paisiello's and Rossini's settings*

1 'but good-humouredly, superior to every event'

2 'This is a weight which makes one say, yes. Money always has that effect.'

3 'The leaves return to the trees, the fresh grasses return to the meadow, but peace does not return to my heart.'
4 As for example in the opening lines, where Beaumarchais's 'la caloumnie monsieur! . . . d'abord un bruit léger, rasant le sol . . .' becomes

> La calumnia è un venticello,
> Un'auretta assai gentile
> che insensibile, sottile,
> leggermente, dolcemente,
> incomincia a sussurrar.

[Calumny is a light wind, a very gentle breeze, which begins its murmuring imperceptibly, subtly, lightly, sweetly.]
5 'At the thought of that portentous, omnipotent metal, my mind begins to turn into a volcano.'
6 'what a delicious piece of invention, charming, charming to be sure!'
7 'My head feels as if it were in a fearful forge, where the wearisome crashing noise of the echoing anvils gets ever louder and never rests.'
8 'My tutor will refuse, I shall sharpen my wits. Finally he will be placated and I shall be happy . . . Yes, Lindoro shall be mine; I swear it, I shall get my way.'
9 'But if they touch me on a weak spot I shall be a real viper, and rather than give up I shall think of a hundred traps for them.'
10 Gallarati, to whom this paragraph is indebted, suggests the terms 'parola scenica', 'orchestra guida', 'voce guida' (1977: 239–44).

V Romantic opera

21 Italian Romanticism

1 'The useful for its end, the true for its subject, the interesting for its means'
2 'People of Italy, I urge you (to read) the tales of history'
3 Cf. Romani's valediction to his readers after his dismissal from the *Gazzetta piemontese* on 17 December 1849 (in Rinaldi 1965: 456):

I did all that was possible to ensure that the love of such a mother [Italy] did not die in the hearts of her sons, and at the risk of seeming pedantic, and in the absence of political glory, I rummaged in forgotten bookshelves to rediscover her literary glory, and I cried out aloud: once the patrimony of our forefathers is forgotten, once our language and literature is bastardized, all will be lost and Italy will have nothing left but her geographical position, the one thing Metternich would grant, because it is the one thing he could not take away.

4 'You find me difficult? I know that myself: I make people think. Is obscurity imputed to me? Then liberty will make all clear.'
5 'Those gods are dead which used to lead mortals to the sweet founts of delight, amiably veiling truth in beauteous forms.'
6 Cf. the essay 'Letteratura classicistica' in Croce 1943b.

22 Dramatic themes: the libretto

1 Some of the Cammarano sketches are reproduced in Black 1984: 276–80.
2 'Ossian has supplanted Homer in my heart'
3 The diorama was a partly translucent stage picture, viewed through an aperture and illuminated from above by light of variable intensity. The phantasmagoria was a show of optical illusions, produced by means of a magic lantern.

4 A singer 'di cartello' was one who had 'successfully sung a leading part in a leading theatre' (Rosselli 1984: 178). A 'comprimario' was an intermediate category of singer, able to sustain an independent line in ensembles and to be entrusted with short, single-movement solos, but not with a full-scale double aria.

5 The librettist was also implicated in the rhythmic character of the music; cf. Chapter 24 below.

6 A census taken in 1984 established that, for the first time in history, more Italians were now speaking the national language in the home than were speaking dialect (Weiss 1985: 46).

23 The life of the theatre

1 Cf. the document drawn up by the Marchese di Breme, quoted in Mangini 1974: 184.

2 The Teatro Apollo in Venice, for example, was so converted in 1833 (Mangini 1974: 193).

3 Most of Italian society. Cf. the reservations voiced in Rosselli 1984: 45.

4 Cf. Glinka's account of the performances of Bellini's *La sonnambula* at the Teatro Carcano in Milan in 1830–31, p. 398 above.

24 The musical language of Italian Romantic opera

1 Though it will not come amiss to remind ourselves that Rossini disliked as much as Verdi did what he called 'the vainglorious French expression *créer un rôle*' (letter of 12 February 1851, in Gál 1965: 235).

2 Cf. the account of the first Lady Macbeth, quoted p. 507 below.

25 Rossini in Naples

1 Cf. *Giornale del Regno delle due Sicilie*, 19 July 1819, quoted in Zedda's Preface to the full score of *La gazza ladra* (Zedda 1979, Part I: xxxi).

2 A phrase quoted by Toye 1954: 65.

3 Translated at Ex.V.4.

4 'what do I hear . . . oh! what joy descends into my soul. I owe the peace of my heart to his love. May fortune, honour and glory be always propitious for him.'

5 Conveniently accessible in English in Einstein 1951: 45–6.

26 A franker Romanticism

1 Cf. Romani's remark on *La straniera* quoted in Chapter 24 above, p. 446.

2 The term is discussed on pp. 399 and 445.

3 The Naples censors required the proper title of *Bianca e Fernando* to be changed to *Bianca e Gernando*. For the revised Genoa version, Bellini reverted to the original title.

4 The term is explained on p. 496.

5 Published in the *Atti della Reale Accademia di Archaeologia, Lettere e Belle Arte*, vol. III, Naples, 1867.

27 The young Verdi

1 And probably one does not deceive oneself; cf. Giacosa's account of Verdi reading the *Otello* libretto, p. 604 below.

2 Cf. the comment quoted in Chapter 21 above, p. 396.

3 Literary journal (September 1818–October 1819) edited by Silvio Pellico; suppressed by the Austrians because of its Liberal influence.

4 'staccato e marcato assai: and let it not be forgotten that the speakers are witches'

28 Bellini's Norma

1 'the most beautiful rose in the garland'; *Gazzetta piemontese*, 8 April 1836, in Rinaldi 1965: 277.

2 'The virgin prophetess Veleda, to whom ancient terror offered up incense in the Bructerian forest, where, when invoked, the fierce damsel would, in terrifying words, foretell the fearful secrets of the future.'

3 'Inspire her, dreadful god, with your prophetic spirit; instil in her, oh Irminsul, feelings of hatred and rage against the Romans, feelings that will shatter this peace that is so fatal to us'; cf. Chapter 21 above, p. 394.

4 'War, war! The forests of Gaul produce warriors as numerous as their oak-trees; they will fall upon the Romans like ravenous beasts on the flocks'; cf. Chateaubriand's 'chaque chêne enfanta pour ainsi dire un Gaulois'.

5 'where that fatal Roman offered himself to me for the first time'

6 The phrase is Verdi's; it is quoted in context on p. 472.

VI Cosmopolitanism and decadence

29 Italian grand opera

1 'By that destiny which condemns every tenor to groan, I love the baritone's wife with an immense love.'

2 '*concertato* at the footlights'

3 'delight of my soul . . . execrable'

30 Scapigliati *and bohemians*

1 'I am light and shadow; an angelic butterfly and a foul worm; I am a fallen cherub condemned to roam the world, or a demon climbing up by twisting stairs towards a heavenly dwelling-place.'

2 'Perhaps the man is already born who, modest and chaste, will exalt art upon the altar, upon that altar now defiled like the wall of a brothel.'

3 Cf. his conversation with Felix Philippi, in Conati 1984: 326–30.

4 Budden provides some details of the metrical innovations of *Amleto* (1973–81, II: 21).

5 'a little drama of common-place little bourgeois souls'

31 Verdi and Boito

1 'To the well-being of Italian art! That for a brief moment, young and healthy, it may escape from the confines of the old and the cretinous . . . Perhaps the man is already born who, modest and pure, will raise up art on the altar, on that altar defiled like the wall of a brothel . . .'

2 'I believe in a cruel God who created me in his own likeness, and whom in wrath I worship.'

3 Full details of the borrowings from *Henry IV*, Parts 1 and 2, are given in Hepokoski 1983: 26–9.

4 Translated at Ex.IV.10d.
5 'The most beautiful jewels are all harmful, and I despise the false idol of gold. A veil tied in a seemly fashion, an ornamented girdle and a flower in my hair are enough for me.'
6 'Now coldly, relentlessly, the worm of thought bores into my brain, so that, to my sorrow, I can write only wretched things, speak only sad things'

32 Verismo

1 'Now is the time for everyone to murmur the tender song which redoubles the beat of our heart'
2 A fascinating series of papers on the mythological background and the psychological underground of *Turandot* will be found in Maehder (ed.) 1985; cf. especially the contributions of Lynn Snook, Enzo Restagno and Ottavio Rosati.
3 'great sorrows in little souls'

Bibliography

Abbreviations

AcM	*Acta musicologica*
AMw	*Archiv für Musikwissenschaft*
AMZ	*Allgemeine musikalische Zeitung*
AnMc	*Analecta musicologica*
DBI	*Dizionario bibliografico degli Italiani*. Rome 1960–
ES	*Enciclopedia dello spettacolo* (ed. F. d'Amico). Rome 1954–62, supplement 1966
The New Grove	*The New Grove Dictionary of Music and Musicians* (ed. S. Sadie). London 1980
JAMS	*Journal of the American Musicological Society*
Mf	*Die Musikforschung*
MGG	*Musik in Geschichte und Gegenwart*
ML	*Music and Letters*
MQ	*The Musical Quarterly*
MR	*The Music Review*
MT	*The Musical Times*
NOHM	*The New Oxford History of Music*
NRMI	*Nuova rivista musicale italiana*
PRMA	*Proceedings of the Royal Musical Association*

Abbiati, F. 1959 *Giuseppe Verdi*, 4 vols. Milan
Abert, A. A. 1954 *Claudio Monteverdi und das musikalische Drama*. Lippstadt
    1973 'Opera in Italy and the Holy Roman Empire', in *NOHM*, vol. VII. London
Abert, H. 1907 *Jommelli: 'Fetonte'* (Denkmäler der deutschen Tonkunst, I). Leipzig
    1918–19 'Paisiellos Buffokunst und ihre Beziehung zu Mozart', in *AMw*, 1.
    [Reprinted in F. Blume (ed.), *Gesammelte Schriften und Vorträge*. Halle 1929]
    1978 *W. A. Mozart*, 9th edn. Leipzig
Acton, H. 1961 *The last Bourbons of Naples (1825–1851)*. London and New York
Adamo, M. R. and F. Lippmann 1981 *Vincenzo Bellini*. Turin
Addison, J. 1733 *Remarks on several parts of Italy, &c. in the years 1701, 1702, 1703*, 4th edn. London
Ademollo, A. 1888 *I teatri di Roma nel secolo decimosettimo*. Rome
Algarotti, F. 1969 'Saggio sopra l'opera in musica, 1755', in E. Bonora (ed.), *Illuministi italiani*, vol. II: *Opere di Francesco Algarotti e di Saverio Bettinelli*. Milan and Naples [Originally published 1755; English edn Glasgow 1768; excerpts in Strunk 1950]
Ambrose, M. 1972 '"La donna del lago", the first Italian translation of Scott', in *Modern Language Review*, 67
    1981 'Walter Scott, Italian opera, and Romantic stage setting', in *Italian Studies*, 36
Angermüller, R. 1982 'Grundzüge des nachmetastasianischen Librettos', in *AnMc*, 21

Bibliography

Aristotle 1927 *The Poetics*, transl. W. Hamilton Fyfe (Loeb Classical Library). Cambridge, Mass., and London

Arnold, D. 1963 *Monteverdi*. London

Arnold, D. and N. Fortune (eds.) 1968 *The Monteverdi companion*. London

Arteaga, S. 1785 *Le rivoluzioni del teatro musicale italiano dalla sua origine fino al presente*, 2nd edn, 2 vols. Venice

Ashbrook, W. and J. Budden 1983 'Donizetti', in the *The New Grove masters of Italian opera*. London

Auden, W. H. 1968 *Secondary worlds* (T. S. Eliot Memorial Lectures). London

Austin, W. W. (ed.) 1968 *New looks at Italian opera: essays in honor of Donald J. Grout*. Ithaca and New York.

Baldacci, L. 1974 *Libretti d'opera e altri saggi*. Florence
  1977 'I libretti di Verdi', in *Il melodramma italiano dell'ottocento, studi e ricerche per M. Mila*. Turin

Baldini, G. 1980 *The story of Giuseppe Verdi: 'Oberto' to 'Un ballo in maschera'*, ed. F. d'Amico, transl. and ed. R. Parker. Cambridge

Ballola, G. Carli 1977 'Mercadante e "Il bravo"', in *Il melodramma italiano dell'ottocento, studi e ricerche per M. Mila*. Turin

Balzac, H. 1839 *Massimilla Doni*. Paris

Barbiera, R. 1915 *Il salotto della Contessa Maffei*, 11th edn. Florence

Baretti, J. 1769 *An account of the manners and customs of Italy; with observations on the mistake of some travellers, with regard to that country*, 2nd edn with notes and an appendix added, in answer to Samuel Sharp, Esq., 2 vols. London

Baron, J. M. 1968 'Monody: a study in terminology', in *MR*, 54

Barzini, L. 1964 *The Italians*. London

Basevi, A. 1859 *Studio sulle opere di Giuseppe Verdi*. Florence

Baxter, H. 1962 *The age of criticism: the late Renaissance in Italy*. Ithaca

Beaumarchais, P. A. Caron de 1775/1874 'Lettre modérée sur la chute et la critique du Barbier de Séville', in *Théâtre de Beaumarchais*. Paris

Bell, G. (transl.) 1965 *Giorgio Vasari: Artists of the Renaissance*. London

Bellini, V. 1943 *Epistolario*, ed. L. Cambi. Verona

Belloni, A. 1929 *Il seicento* (Storia letteraria d'Italia). Milan

Benedetti, A. 1974 *Le traduzione italiane da Walter Scott e i loro anglicismi*. Florence

Bent, J. 1968 'Monteverdi and the opera orchestra of his time', in Arnold and Fortune (eds.) 1968

Berlioz, H. 1969 *The memoirs of Hector Berlioz*, transl. and ed. D. Cairns. London

Bettley, J. 1976–77 'North Italian *falsobordone* and its relevance to the early *stile recitativo*', in *PRMA*, 103

Bianconi, L. 1982 Notes accompanying recording of *Orontea* by Harmonia Mundi

Bianconi, L. and T. Walker 1975 'Dalla "Finta pazza" alla "Veremonda", storie di Febiarmonici', in *Rivista italiana di musicologia*, 10
  1984 'Production, consumption and political function of seventeenth-century Italian opera', paper presented at Berkeley Conference of IMS 1977, in *Early Music History*, 4

Binni, W. 1968a 'Goldoni', in *Storia della letteratura italiana*, vol. VI: *Il settecento*. Milan
  1968b 'La letteratura del secondo settecento fra illuminismo, neoclassicismo e preromanticismo', in *Storia della letteratura italiana*, vol. VI: *Il settecento*. Milan
  1968c 'La letteratura nell'epoca arcadico-rationalistica', in *Storia della letteratura italiana*, vol. VI: *Il settecento*. Milan.
  1968d 'Pietro Metastasio', in *Storia della letteratura italiana*, vol. VI: *Il settecento*. Milan

Bjurström, P. 1961 *Giacomo Torelli and baroque stage design*. Stockholm

Black, J. N. 1983 'Salvadore Cammarano's *programma* for "Il trovatore" and the problems of the finale', in *Studi verdiani*, 2

    1984 *The Italian romantic libretto: a study of Salvadore Cammarano* Edinburgh

Blessington, Margaret, Countess of 1839–40 *The idler in Italy*, 3 vols. London

Blom, E. 1927 'The literary ancestry of Figaro', in *MQ*, 13

Bolgar, R. R. 1954 *The Classical heritage and its beneficiaries*. Cambridge

Bonaccorsi, A. (ed.) 1968 *Gioacchino Rossini* (Historiae musicae cultores biblioteca, XXIV). Florence

Boromé, J. A. 1961 'Bellini and "Beatrice di Tenda"', in *ML*, 42

Bradshaw, G. 1983 'A Shakespearian perspective: Verdi and Boito as translators', in Hepokoski 1983

Brizi, B. 1976 'Teoria e prassi melodrammatico di G. F. Busenello e "L'incoronazione di Poppea"', in Muraro (ed.) 1976

Brown, H. M. 1970 'How opera began: an introduction to . . . "Euridice"', in E. Cochrane (ed.), *The late Renaissance: 1525–1630*. London

    1973 *Sixteenth-century instrumentation* (American Institute of Musicology). Rome

    1981 'The geography of Florentine monody: Caccini at home and abroad', in *Early Music*, 9

Budden, J. 1973 'The two *Traviatas*', in *PRMA*, 99

    1973–81 *The operas of Verdi*, 3 vols. London

    1982 'Verdi and Meyerbeer in relation to "Les vêpres siciliennes"', in *Studi verdiani*, 1

    1985 *Verdi*. London

Bukofzer, M. 1947 *Music in the baroque era*. New York

Burney, C. 1771 *The present state of music in France and Italy: or The journal of a tour through those countries . . .* London

    1776–89 *A general history of music*, 4 vols. London

    1796 *Memoirs of the life and writings of the Abate Metastasio*, 3 vols. London

Busch, H. 1978 *Verdi's 'Aida': the history of an opera in letters and documents*. Minneapolis

    1988 *Verdi's 'Otello' and 'Simon Boccanegra' (revised version) in letters and documents*, 2 vols. Oxford

Cametti, A. 1938 *Il teatro di Tordinona*. Tivoli

Carner, M. 1974 *Puccini, a criticial biography*, 2nd edn. London

    1985 *Giacomo Puccini: 'Tosca'* (Cambridge Opera Handbooks). Cambridge

Carpani, G. 1824 *Le Rossiniane ossia lettere musico-teatrali*. Padua

Carse, A. 1940 *The orchestra in the eighteenth century*. Cambridge

Carter, T. 1978–79 'Jacopo Peri (1561–1633): aspects of his life and works', in *PRMA*, 105

    1980 'Jacopo Peri', in *ML*, 61

    1982 'Peri's "Euridice": a contextual study', in *MR*, 43

Casini, C. 1977 'Introduzione a Puccini', in *Il melodramma italiano dell'ottocento*. Turin

Cattaneo, G. 1968 'Prosatori e critici dalla scapigliatura al verismo', in *Storia della letteratura italiana*, vol. VIII: *Dell'ottocento al novecento*. Milan

Celletti, R. 1968 'Origini e sviluppi della coloratura rossiniana', in *NRMI*, 2

    1980 'On Verdi's vocal writing', in Weaver and Chusid (eds.) 1980

Chorley, H. F. 1862 *Thirty years' musical recollections*. London

Chusid, M. 1971 'Schiller revisited; some observations on the revision of "Don Carlos"', in *Atti del IIo congresso internazionale di studi verdiani*. Parma

Bibliography

Cody, R. 1969 *The landscape of the mind: pastoralism and Platonic theory in Tasso's 'Aminta' and Shakespeare's early comedies*. Oxford

Colquhoun, A. 1954 *Manzoni and his times*. London

Conati, M. 1980–81 'Between past and future: the dramatic world of Rossini in "Mosè in Egitto" and "Moise et Pharaon"', in *Nineteenth-century Music*, 4

1982 'Ballabili nei "Vespri . . ." Con alcune osservazioni su Verdi e la musica popolare', in *Studi verdiani*, 1

Conati, M. (ed.) 1984 *Interviews and encounters with Verdi*, transl. R. Stokes. London

Constable, M. V. 1982 'The Venetian "Figlie del coro": their environment and achievement', in *ML*, 63

Cooper, M. 1974 'Stage works: 1890–1918', in *NOHM*, vol. X. London

Cox, C. 1962 *The real Figaro: the extraordinary career of Caron de Beaumarchais*. London

Croce, B. 1914 *La letteratura della nuova Italia*, vol. I. Bari

1926 *I teatri di Napoli dal rinascimento alla fine del secolo decimottavo*, 3rd edn. Bari

1929 *A history of Italy 1871–1915*, transl. C. M. Ady. Oxford

1942 'Problemi di letteratura italiana', in *Conversazioni critiche*, vol. II. Bari

1943a 'L'elemento italiano nella società europea del settecento', in *Uomini e cose della vecchia Italia*, vol. II, 2nd edn. Bari

1943b *La letteratura della nuova Italia*, vol. V. Bari

1943c 'Il romanticismo legittimistico e la caduta del regno di Napoli', in *Uomini e cose della vecchia Italia*, vol. II, 2nd edn. Bari

1946a *Storia dell'età barocca in Italia*, 2nd rev. edn. Bari

1946b 'Interno alla "commedia dell'arte"', in *Poesia popolare e poesia d'arte*, 2nd rev. edn. Bari

1949 *Letteratura italiana del settecento*. Bari

Cusatelli, G. 1971 '"Don Carlos" di Schiller tradotto da Andrea Maffei', in *Atti del IIo congresso internazionale di studi verdiani*. Parma

Cyr, M. 1978 'Rameau e Traetta', in *NRMI*, 12

da Ponte, L. 1823–27 *Memorie*, 4 vols. New York

d'Accone, F. A. 1985 *The history of a baroque opera: Alessandro Scarlatti's 'Gli equivoci nel sembiante'*. New York

Dahlhaus, C. 1974 'Ethos und Pathos in Glucks "Iphigenie auf Tauris"', in *Mf*, 28

1982 *Musikalischer Realismus*. Munich

Dallapiccola, L. 1980 'Words and music in Italian nineteenth-century opera', in Weaver and Chusid (eds.) 1980

d'Amico, F. 1984 'A proposito d'un Tancredi: Dioniso in Apollo', in *AnMc*, 21

Davie, J. M. 1978 *Farce* (The Critical Idiom, XXXIX). London

Davies, J. 1979 *The realism of Luigi Capuana; theory and practice in the development of late-nineteenth-century Italian narrative*. London

d'Azeglio, Massimo, Taparelli, Marchese 1966 *Things I remember*, transl. E. R. Vincent. London [Originally published as *I miei ricordi*, with posthumous completion by G. Torelli, 2 vols., Florence, 1867]

de Napoli, G. 1931 *La triade melodrammatica altamurana: Giacomo Tritto, Vincenzo Lavigna, Saverio Mercadante*. Milan

de Sanctis, F. 1870–71 *Storia della letteratura italiana*, 2 vols. Naples

Dean, W. 1970 *Handel and the opera seria*. London

1973–74 'Donizetti's serious operas', in *PRMA*, 100

1974 'Some echoes of Donizetti in Verdi's operas', in *Atti del IIIo congresso internazionale di studi verdiani*. Parma

1982 'Italian opera', in *NOHM*, vol. VIII. London

Bibliography

Degrada, F. 1969 'Gian Francesco Busenello e il libretto della "Incoronazione di Poppea"', in Monterosso (ed.) 1969

1977 'Prolegomeni a una lettura della "Sonnambula"', in *Il melodramma italiano dell'ottocento*. Turin

Dent, E. J. 1909 'A Jesuit at the opera in 1680', in C. Mennicke (ed.), *Riemann-Festschrift*. Leipzig

1960 *Alessandro Scarlatti*. New impression with preface . . . by F. Walker. London [Originally published 1905]

1968 'Music and drama', in *NOHM*, vol. IV. London

di Stefano, C. 1964 *La censura teatrale in Italia (1600–1962)*. Bologna

Dickens, C. 1846 *Pictures from Italy*. London

Donington, R. 1968 'Monteverdi's first opera', in Arnold and Fortune (eds.) 1968

1981 *The rise of opera*. London

Donizetti, G. 'Scritti e pensieri'. MS, Museo Donizettiano, Bergamo [*See also* Zavadini 1948]

Einstein, A. 1946 *Mozart: his character, his work*, transl. A. Mendel and N. Broder, London

1947 *Music in the Romantic era*. New York

1949 *The Italian madrigal*. Princeton

1951 *Schubert*, transl. D. Ascoli. London

1964 *Gluck*, rev. edn. London

Elwert, W. T. 1968 *Italienische Metrik*. Munich

Fehr, M. 1912 *Apostolo Zeno und seine Reform des Operntextes*. Zurich

Fenlon, I. 1976–77 'Music and spectacle at the Gonzaga court, *c.* 1580–1600', in *PRMA*, 103

1979 'The politics of spectacle', in *The new Golden Age: the Florentine Intermedi of 1589* (BBC). London

Ferrando, E. M. (ed.) 1984 *Tutti i libretti di Puccini*. Milan

Fido, F. 1977 *Guida a Goldoni, teatro e società nel settecento*. Turin

Fiske, R. 1983 *Scotland in music: a European enthusiasm*. Cambridge

Flechsig, E. 1894 *Die Dekoration der modernen Bühne in Italien von den Anfängen bis zum Schluss des XVI. Jahrhunderts*, vol. I. Dresden

Florimo, F. 1880–84 *La scuola musicale di Napoli*, 4 vols. Naples

Folena, G. 1982 'Cesarotti, Monti e il melodramma fra sette e ottocento', in *AnMc*, 21

Fortune, N. 1953a 'Continuo instruments in Italian monodies', in *Galpin Society Journal*, 6

1953b 'Italian secular monody from 1600 to 1635: an introductory survey', in *MQ*, 39

1954 'Italian seventeenth-century singing', in *ML*, 35

1968a 'Monteverdi and the *seconda prattica*', in Arnold and Fortune (eds.) 1968

1968b 'Solo song and cantata', in *NOHM*, vol. IV. London

Freeman, R. 1968 'Apostolo Zeno's reform of the libretto', in *JAMS*, 21

Friedland, B. 1970 'Italy's ottocento; notes from the musical underground', in *MQ*, 56

Gál, H. 1965 *The musician's world: great composers in their letters*. London

Gallarati, P. 1977 'Dramma e ludus dall'*Italiana* al *Barbiere*', in *Il melodramma italiano dell'ottocento*. Turin

1980 'L'estetica musicale di Raniero de' Calzabigi: il caso Metastasio', in *NRMI*, 14

1984 *Musica e maschera: il libretto italiano del settecento*. Turin

Garibaldi, L. A. 1931 *Giuseppe Verdi nelle lettere di Emanuele Muzio ed Antonio Barezzi*. Milan

Bibliography

Gatti, C. 1964 *Il Teatro alla Scala nella storia e nell'arte*, vol. II: *Cronologia completa degli spettacoli . . .*, by G. Tintori. Milan

Gerhartz, L. K. 1968 *Die Auseinandersetzungen des jungen Giuseppe Verdi mit dem literarischen Drama* (Berliner Studien zur Musikwissenschaft, XV). Berlin

    1971 'Il sogno di Fontainebleau. Alcuni riflessioni sulla tecnica dell'introduzione nel dramma schilleriano i nell'opere verdiana', in *Atti del IIo congresso internazionale di studi verdiani*. Parma

Ghislanzoni, A. 1870 'L'arte di far libretti', in *Capricci letterari*. Milan

    1958 'Storia di Milano da 1836 al 1848', in C. Cappuccio (ed.), *Memorialisti dell'ottocento*, vol. II. Milan and Naples [Originally published in *In chiave di baritono*, Milan, 1882]

Gianturco, C. 1975 'Evidence for a late Roman school of opera', in *ML*, 56

Giovanelli, P. D. 1983 'La storia e la favola dell'*Oberto*', in *Studi verdiani*, 2

Girdlestone, C. 1957 *Jean-Philippe Rameau: his life and work*. London

Giudici, E. 1964 *Beaumarchais nel suo e nel nostro tempo: Le barbier de Seville*. Rome

Glinka, M. I. 1963 *Memoirs*, transl. P. B. Mudge. Norman, Okla

Glover, J. 1973 'Cavalli and "Rosinda"', in *MT*, 114

    1975–76 'The peak period of Venetian public opera: the 1650s', in *PRMA*, 102

    1978 *Cavalli*. London

    1982 'Cavalli and "L'Eritrea"', in *MT*, 123

Goldin, D. 1982 'Aspetti della librettistica italiana fra 1770 e 1830', in *AnMc*, 21

Goldoni, C. 1907 *Memorie*, ed. G. Mazzoni, 3 vols. Florence [Originally published 1787 in Paris, in French]

Goldschmidt, H. 1901–04 *Studien zur Geschichte der italienischen Oper im 17. Jahrhundert*, 2 vols. Leipzig

Gossett, P. 1968 'Rossini and authenticity', in *MT*, 109

    1970 'Gioacchino Rossini and the conventions of composition', in *AcM*, 42

    1971 'The "candeur virginale" of Tancredi', in *MT*, 112

    1974 'Verdi, Ghislanzoni and *Aida*: the uses of convention', in *Critical Inquiry*, 1

    1979–80 'The overtures of Rossini', in *Nineteenth-century Music*, 3

    1980 'Fairy-tale and *opera buffa*: the genre of Rossini's *La Cenerentola*', in *La Cenerentola* (ENO Guides, I). London

    1983 'Rossini', in *The New Grove masters of Italian opera*. London

    1985 *'Anna Bolena' and the artistic maturity of Gaetano Donizetti*. Oxford

    n.d. Notes accompanying recording of *La donna del lago* by CBS

Gounod, C. 1896 *Autobiographical reminiscences*, transl. W. Hely Hutchinson. London

Gozzi,C. 1910 Memorie inutile della vita di Carlo Gozzi, ed. G. Prezzolini, 2 vols. Bari [Originally published 1780]

Graf, A.1911 *L'anglomania e l'influsso inglese in Italia nel secolo XVIII*. Turin

Grant, D. 1970 *Realism* (The Critical Idiom, IX). London

Greg, W. W. 1905 *Pastoral poetry and pastoral drama*. London

Groos, A. and R. Parker 1986 *Giacomo Puccini: 'La bohème'* (Cambridge Opera Handbooks). Cambridge

Grosley, P. J. 1769 *New observations on Italy*, 2 vols. London

Grout, D. J. 1947 *A short history of opera*. New York

    1979 *Alessandro Scarlatti: an introduction to his operas*. Berkeley and Los Angeles

Hanning, B. R. 1973 'Apologia pro Ottavio Rinuccini', in *JAMS*, 26

    1980 *Of poetry and music's power: humanism and the creation of opera*. Ann Arbor

Hanslick, E. 1875 *Die moderne Oper*, vol. I: *Kritiken und Studien*. Berlin

Harding, J. 1970 *Massenet*. London

Bibliography

Harnoncourt, N. 1969 'Claudio Monteverdi's *L'Orfeo*, eine Einführung', in booklet accompanying recording by Das alte Werk

Hartmann, A., Jr 1953 'Battista Guarini and "Il pastor fido"', in *MQ*, 39

Harwood, G. W. 1986 'Verdi's reform of the Italian opera orchestra', in *Nineteenth-century Music*, 10

Hathaway, B. 1962 *The age of criticism: the late Renaissance in Italy*. Ithaca and New York

Hazlitt, W. 1826 *Notes of a journey through France and Italy*. London

Hearder, H. 1983 *Italy in the age of the risorgimento 1790–1870*. London

Heartz, D. 1967–68 'From Garrick to Gluck: the reform of theatre and opera in the mid-eighteenth century', in *PRMA*, 94

  1977–78 'The creation of the *buffo finale* in Italian grand opera', in *PRMA*, 104

  1978 'Hasse, Galuppi and Metastasio', in Muraro (ed.) 1978

  1979 'Goldoni, Don Giovanni and the *dramma giocoso*', in *MT*, 120

Heine, H. 1830 *Reisebilder*, vol. III: *Italien 1828*. Hamburg

Heinse, W. 1857 *Sämmtliche Schriften*, vol. V: *Briefe*. Leipzig

Henderson, I. 1957 'Ancient Greek music', in *NOHM*, vol. I. London

Henze, S. 1982 'Zur Instrumentalbegleitung in Jommellis dramatischen Kompositionen', in *AMw*, 40

Hepokoski, J. A. 1983 *Giuseppe Verdi: 'Falstaff'* (Cambridge Opera Handbooks). Cambridge

  1987 *Giuseppe Verdi: 'Otello'* (Cambridge Opera Handbooks). Cambridge

Herrick, M. T. 1962 *Tragicomedy: its origin and development in Italy, France and England*. Urbana

Hibbert, C. 1974 *The rise and fall of the house of Medici*. London

Hitchcock, H. W. 1970 'Vocal ornamentation in Caccini's "Nuove musiche"', in *MQ*, 56

Hitchcock, H. W. (ed.) 1970 *Caccini, Le nuove musiche* (Recent Researches in the Music of the Baroque Era, IX). Madison

Hogarth, G. 1851 *Memoirs of the opera in Italy, France, Germany and England*, 2 vols. London

Holmes, W. C. 1952 'Pamela transformed', in *MQ*, 38

  1968a 'Comedy – opera – comic opera', in *AnMc*, 5

  1968b 'Giacinto Andrea Cicognini's and Antonio Cesti's *Orontea* (1649)', in Austin (ed.) 1968

Huizinga, J. 1949 *'Homo ludens': a study of the play element in culture*. London

Ivanovich, C. 1681 'Memorie teatrali di Venezia', in *Minerva al Tavolino*. Venice

Jacobs, R. 1982 Notes accompanying recording of *Orontea* by Harmonia Mundi

John, N. (ed.) 1980 *Aida* (ENO Guides, II). London

  1982 *Tosca* (ENO Guides, XVI). London

  1983 *The force of destiny* (ENO Guides, XXIII). London

  1985 *Simon Boccanegra* (ENO Guides, XXXII). London

Johnson, M. F. 1971 'Agazzari's "Eumelio", a "dramma pastorale"' in *MQ*, 57

Joly, J. 1978 *Les fêtes théâtrales de Métastase à la cour de Vienne (1731–1767)*. Clermont-Ferrand

Jung, U. 1974 *Die Rezeption der Kunst Richard Wagners in Italien* (Studien zur Musikgeschichte des 19. Jahrhunderts, XXXV). Regensburg

Keller, H. 1963 *Musik und Dichtung im alten Griechenland*. Bern and Munich

Kelly, J. N. D. 1986 *The Oxford dictionary of popes*. London

Kelly, M. 1975 *Reminiscences*, ed. R. Fiske. London

Kerman, J. 1956 *Opera as drama*. New York

Bibliography

1982 'Lyric form and flexibility in "Simon Boccanegra"', in *Studi verdiani*, 1

Keys, A. C. 1960 'Schiller and Italian opera', in *ML*, 41

Keyte, H. 1979 'From De'Rossi to Malvezzi: some performance problems', in *The new Golden Age: the Florentine Intermedi of 1589* (BBC). London

Kimbell, D. R. B. 1981 *Verdi in the age of Italian Romanticism*. Cambridge

1984 'Neo-classical counter-currents in Italian Romantic opera', in *Italian Studies*, 39

Kindermann, H. 1964 'Das romantische Theater in Italien', in *Theatergeschichte Europas*, vol. VI. Salzburg

Kitto, H. D. F. 1939 *Greek tragedy: a literary study*. London

Klein, J. W. 1963 'Pietro Mascagni and Giovanni Verga', in *ML*, 44

1964 'Verdi's "Otello" and Rossini's', in *ML*, 45

1965 'Puccini's enigmatic inactivity', in *ML*, 46

1967 'Toscanini and Catalani – a unique friendship', in *ML*, 48

Kunze, S. 1982 'Ironie des Klassizismus: Aspekte des Umbruchs in der musikalischen Komödie um 1800', in *AnMc*, 21

Lambert, E. Z. 1976 *Placing sorrow: a study of the pastoral elegy convention from Theocritus to Milton*. Chapel Hill

Large, D. C. and W. Weber (eds.) 1984 *Wagnerism in European culture and politics*. Ithaca

Larthomas, P. (ed.) 1977 *Beaumarchais: Parades*, critical edition. Paris

Lawrence, D. H. 1928 'Preface', to G. Verga, *Cavalleria rusticana and other stories*. London

Lawton, D. and D. Rosen 1974 'Verdi's non-definitive revisions: the early operas', in *Atti del IIIo congresso internazionale di studi verdiani*. Parma

Lazarevich, G. 1971 'The Neapolitan intermezzo and its influence on the symphonic idiom', in *MQ*, 57

Lea, K. M. 1934 *Italian popular comedy*, 2 vols. Oxford

Leopardi, G. 1966 *Selected prose and poetry*, ed., transl. and introd. by I. Origo and J. Heath-Stubbs. London

Leopold, S. 1978 'Das geistliche Libretto in 17. Jahrhundert. Zur Gattungsgeschichte der frühen Oper', in *Mf*, 32

Lessona, M. 1869 *Volere è potere*, 2nd edn. Florence

Lichtenthal, P. 1826 *Dizionario e biografia della musica*. Milan

Lindgren, L. 1981 'Ariosto's London years', in *ML*, 62

Lippmann, F. 1966 'Die Melodien Donizettis', in *AnMc*, 3

1969a 'Rossinis Gedanken über die Musik', in *Mf*, 22

1969b *Vincenzo Bellini und die italienische Opera seria seiner Zeit*. Cologne and Vienna

1973–75 'Der italienische Vers und der musikalische Rhythmus. Zum Verhältnis von Vers und Musik in der italienischen Oper des 19. Jahrhunderts, mit einem Rückblick auf die 2. Hälfte des 18. Jahrhunderts', in *AnMc*, 12 [1973], 14 [1974], 15 [1975].

1982 'Über Cimarosas *Opere serie*', in *AnMc*, 21

1983 'Bellini', in *The New Grove masters of Italian opera*. London

Loewenberg, A. 1939 'Paisiello's and Rossini's "Barbiere di Siviglia"', in *ML*, 20

Logan, O. 1972 *Culture and society in Venice 1470–1790*. London

Lumley, B. 1864 *Reminiscences of the Italian opera*. London

Luzio, A. 1947 *Carteggi verdiani*, vol. IV. Rome

McClymonds, M. P. 1980 'The evolution of Jommelli's operatic style', in *JAMS*, 33

Mack-Smith, D. (ed.) 1968 *The making of Italy, 1796–1870*. New York

Bibliography

Maehder, J. (ed.) 1985 *Esoticismo e colore locale nell'opere di Puccini: Atti del I. convegno internazionale sull'opera di Giacomo Puccini . . . 1983*. Pisa

Magnani, L. 1968 'Stendhal e la *musica della felicità*', in Bonaccorsi (ed.) 1968

Mamczarz, I. 1972 *Les intermèdes comiques italiens au XVIIIe siècle en France et en Italie*. Paris

Mangini, N. 1973 'Per una storia dei teatri veneziani: problemi e perspettivi', in *Archivio veneto*, vol. V, no. 135
    1974 *I teatri di Venezia*. Milan

Mann, H. 1947 *Ein Zeitalter wird besichtigt*. Berlin

Manzoni, A. 1970 *Tutte le opere di Alessandro Manzoni*, vol. VII: *Lettere*, ed. C. Arieti. Verona

Marinelli, P. V. 1971 *Pastoral* (The Critical Idiom, XV). London

Martin, G. 1965 *Verdi: his music, life and times*. London

Martinotti, S. 1977 'I travagliati Avant-Propos di Puccini', in *Il melodramma italiano dell'ottocento*. Turin

Mazzini, G. 1910 *Edizione nazionale degli scritti di Giuseppe Mazzini*, vol. VIII. Imola

Mazzuchetti, L. 1913 *Schiller in Italia*. Milan

Medici, M. and M. Conati (eds.) 1978 *Carteggio Verdi–Boito*. Parma

Mendelsohn G. A. 1978–79 'Verdi the man and Verdi the dramatist', in *Nineteenth-century Music*, 2

Mendelssohn-Bartholdy, F. 1899 *Briefe aus den Jahren 1830 bis 1847*. Leipzig

Mercadante, S. 1867 'Breve cenno storico sulla musica teatrale da Pergolesi a Cimarosa', in *Atti della Reale Accademia di Archeologia, Lettere e Belle Arti*, 3

Meyer-Baer, K. 1970 *Music of the spheres and the dance of death: studies in musical iconography*. Princeton

Meyerbeer, G. 1960 *Briefwechsel und Tagebücher*, ed. H. Becker. Berlin

Michotte, E. 1968 *An evening at Rossini's in Beau-Séjour (Passy) 1858*, transl. H. Weinstock. Chicago

Migliorini, B. and I. Baldelli 1964 *Breve storia della lingua italiana*. Florence

Mila, M. 1958 *Giuseppe Verdi*. Bari

Miller, M. S. 1984 'Wagnerisms, Wagnerians, and Italian identity', in Large and Weber (eds.) 1984

Milner, A. 1973 'The sacred capons', in *MT*, 114

Mirollo, J. V. 1963 *The poet of the marvelous, Giambattista Marino*. New York and London

Mitchell, J. 1977 *The Walter Scott operas*. Birmingham, Ala.

Molmenti, P. 1908 *La storia di Venezia nella vita privata*, 4th edn, 3 vols. Bergamo

Monaco, V. 1968 *Giambattista Lorenzi e la commedia per musica*. Naples

Monaldi, G. 1898 *Verdi*. Stuttgart and Leipzig [German edn]

Monelle, R. 1973 'Gluck and the *festa teatrale*', in *ML*, 54
    1976 'The rehabilitation of Metastasio', in *ML*, 57
    1978 'Recitative and dramaturgy in the *dramma per musica*', in *ML*, 59
    1979 '*Opera seria* as drama: the musical dramas of Hasse and Metastasio'. Unpublished dissertation, University of Edinburgh

Monterosso, R. (ed.) 1969 *Congresso internazionale sul tema 'Claudio Monteverdi e il suo tempo': relazioni e comunicazioni*. Verona

Mooney, A. G. 1970 'An assessment of Mercadante's contribution to the development of Italian opera'. M. Mus. dissertation, University of Edinburgh

Morazzoni, G. 1929 *Verdi: lettere inedite*. Milan

Morgan, Lady 1821 *Italy*. London

Mount-Edgcumbe, Richard, Earl of 1824 *Musical reminiscences, containing an account of the Italian opera in England from 1773*. London

Bibliography

Muraro, T. M. (ed.) 1976 *Venezia e il melodramma nel seicento*. Florence
1978 *Venezia e il melodramma nel settecento*. Florence
Murata, M. 1981 *Operas for the papal court 1631–1668*. Ann Arbor
  1984 'Classical tragedy in the history of early opera in Rome', in *Early Music History*, 4
Muratori, L. A. n.d. *Della perfetta poesia*, ed. G. Falco and F. Forti. Milan and Naples [Originally published 1706]
Nagler, A. M. 1964 *Theatre festivals of the Medici*. New Haven
Nardi, P. 1944 *Vita di Arrigo Boito*. Verona
  1949 *Vita e tempo di Giuseppe Giacosa*. Milan
Nichols, P. 1973 *Italia, Italia*. London
Nicolaisen, J. R. 1977–78 'The first "Mefistofele"', in *Nineteenth-century Music*, 1
  1980 *Italian opera in transition, 1871–1893*. Ann Arbor
Nicoll, A. 1963 *The world of Harlequin: a critical study of the* commedia dell'arte. Cambridge
Niklaus, R. 1968 *Beaumarchais, le barbier de Seville*. London
Nordio, M. 1951 *Verdi e la Fenice*. Venice
Noske, F. 1973 'Ritual scenes in Verdi's operas', in *ML*, 54
Nulli, S. A. 1918 *Shakespeare in Italia*. Milan
Ogden, D. H. 1978 *The Italian baroque stage. Documents by Giulio Troilo. Andrea Pozzo, Ferdinando Galli-Bibiena, Baldassare Orsini*, transl. with commentary. Berkeley, Los Angeles, London
Oreglia, G. 1968 *The commedia dell'arte*, transl. L. F. Edwards. London
Orrey, L. 1969 *Bellini*. London
  1974 'The literary sources of Bellini's first opera', in *ML*, 53
Ortolani, G. 1962 'I melodrammi giocosi del Goldoni', in *La riforma del teatro nel settecento ed altri scritti*. Venice and Rome
Osborn, P. 1982 '"Fuor di quel costume antico": innovation versus tradition in the prologues of Giraldi Cinthio's tragedies', in *Italian Studies*, 37
Osborne, R. 1985 'The new Rossini edition', in *MT*, 126
  1986 *Rossini*. London
Osthoff, W. 1954 'Die venezianische und neapolitanische Fassung von Monteverdis "L'incoronazione di Poppea"', in *AcM*, 26
  1960 *Monteverdi-Studien*, vol. I: *Das dramatische Spätwerk Claudio Monteverdis*. Tutzing
  1963 'Die beiden "Boccanegra"-Fassungen und der Beginn von Verdis Spätwerk', in *AnMc*, 1
Pacini, G. 1865 *Le mie memorie artistiche*. Florence
Palisca, C. V. 1954 'Girolamo Mei: mentor to the Florentine Camerata', in *MQ*, 40
  1956 'Vincenzo Galilei's counterpoint treatise: a code for the "seconda prattica"', in *JAMS*, 9
  1960a 'Girolamo Mei, letters on ancient and modern music . . . a study with annotated texts', in *Musicological studies and documents*, vol. III. Rome
  1960b 'Vincenzo Galilei, and some links between "pseudo-monody" and monody', in *MQ*, 46
  1963 'Musical asides in the diplomatic correspondence of Emilio de'Cavalieri', in *MQ*, 49
  1968 'The Alterati of Florence, pioneers in the theory of dramatic music', in Austin (ed.) 1968
  1972 'The "Camerata Fiorentina": a reappraisal', in *Studi musicali*, 1
  1978 'G. B. Doni, musicological activist, and "Lyra Barberina"', in E. Olleson (ed.), *Modern musical scholarship*. Stocksfield

Parker, R. L. 1981 'Studies in early Verdi (1832–1844). New information and perspectives on the Milanese musical milieu and the operas from *Oberto* to *Ernani*'. Unpublished dissertation. London
    1983 '"Un giorno di regno": from Romani's libretto to Verdi's opera', in *Studi verdiani*, 2
Peattie, A. (ed.) 1985 *Norma* (programme book). Cardiff
Perusse, L. F. 1981 'Tosca and Piranesi', in *MT*, 121
Pestelli, G. 1977 'Il cento anni di Rovani e l'opera italiana', in *Il melodramma italiano dell'ottocento*. Turin
Pirandello, L. 1974 *On humor*, transl. A. Illiano and D. P. Testa. Chapel Hill
Pirrotta, N. 1954 'Temperaments and tendencies in the Florentine Camerata', in *MQ*, 40
    1955 '*Commedia dell'arte* and opera', in *MQ*, 41
    1968 'Early opera and aria', in Austin (ed.) 1968
    1969a *Li due Orfei: da Poliziano a Monteverdi*. Turin
    1969b 'Teatro, scene e musica nelle opere di Monteverdi', in Monterosso (ed.) 1969
    1980–81 'The tradition of Don Juan plays and comic opera', in *PRMA*, 107
    1982 *Music and theatre from Poliziano to Monteverdi*, transl. K. Eales. Cambridge
    1984 *Music and culture in Italy from the Middle Ages to the Baroque: a collection of essays*. Cambridge, Mass.
Pizzetti, I. 1921 'L'immortalità del Barbiere di Siviglia', in *Intermezzi critici*. Florence [Also published in Bonaccorsi (ed.) 1968]
Plumb, J. H. 1961 *The Horizon book of the Renaissance*. London
Poggioli, R. 1975 *The oaten flute: a study of pastoral poetry and the bucolic ideal*. Cambridge, Mass.
Porter, A. 1967 'A lost opera by Rossini', in *ML*, 48
    1972 'Donizetti's "Belisario"', in *MT*, 113
    1978 '"Les vêpres siciliennes": new letters from Verdi to Scribe', in *Nineteenth-century Music*, 2
    1983 'Verdi', in *The New Grove masters of Italian opera*. London
Porter, W. V. 1965 'Peri and Corsi's "Dafne": some new discoveries and observations', in *JAMS*, 18
Portinari, F. 1977 '"Pari siamo". Sulla struttura del libretto romantico', in *Il melodramma italiano dell'ottocento*. Turin
Pougin, A. 1881 *Giuseppe Verdi, vita anneddotica*, with notes and additions by 'Folchetto' (Jacopo Capponi). Milan
Povoledo, E. 1982 'Origins and aspects of Italian scenography', in Pirrotta 1982
Praz, M. 1951 *The Romantic agony*, transl. A Davidson, 2nd edn. Oxford
    1956 'Shakespeare translations in Italy', in *Shakespeare-Jahrbuch*, 92
Procacci, G. 1970 *History of the Italian people*, trans. A. Paul. London
Prout, E. 1900 'Auber's "Le philtre" and Donizetti's "L'elisir d'amore": a comparison', in *Monthly Musical Record*
Puccini, G. 1974 *Letters of Giacomo Puccini*, ed. G. Adami, transl. E. Makin; new edn rev. M. Carner. London
Pulver, J. 1916–17 'The *intermezzi* of the opera', in *PRMA*, 43
Quadrio, F. S. 1743 *Della storia, e della ragione d'ogni poesia*, vol. III. Milan
Qvamme, B. 1974 'Verdi e il realismo', in *Atti del IIIo congresso internazionale di studi verdiani*. Parma
Radiciotti, G. 1905 'Teatro e musica in Roma nel secondo quarto del secolo XIX (1825–50)', in *Atti del IIIo congresso internazionale di scienze storiche (Roma, Aprile 1903)*, vol. VIII. Rome

1921 'Un opéra fantastique de Rossini', in *La Revue musicale*, 2
1935 *Pergolesi*. Milan
Raimondi, E. (ed.) 1960 *Trattatisti e narratori del seicento*. Milan and Naples
Reichenburg, L. 1937 *Contribution à l'histoire de la 'Querelle des Bouffons'*. Philadelphia
Reiner, S. 1961 'Collaboration in "Chi soffre, speri"', in *MR*, 22
Ricci, C. 1930 *La scenografia italiana*. Milan
Ricci, L. 1954 *Puccini interprete di se stesso*. Milan
Rinaldi, M. 1965 *Felice Romani: dal melodramma classico al melodramma romantico*. Rome
Rinuccini, G. B. 1843 *Sulla musica e sulla poesia melodrammatica italiana*. Lucca
Ritorni, C. 1841 *Ammaestramenti alla composizione di ogni poema e d'ogni opera appartenente alla musica*. Milan
Robb, N. A. 1935 *Neoplatonism of the Italian Renaissance*. London
Robertson, J. G. 1910 'Shakespeare in Italy', in *Cambridge history of English literature*, vol. V. Cambridge
Robinson, M. F. 1966 *Opera before Mozart*. London
1972 *Naples and Neapolitan opera*. Oxford
Rolandi, U. 1951 *Il libretto per musica attraverso i tempi*. Rome
Rosand, E. 1975 '"Orminda travestita" in *Erismena*', in *JAMS*, 28
1976a 'Aria as drama in the early operas of Francesco Cavalli', in Muraro (ed.) 1976
1976b 'Comic contrast and dramatic continuity: observations on the form and content of aria in the operas of Francesco Cavalli', in *MR*, 37
Rosen, C. 1971 *The Classical style: Haydn, Mozart, Beethoven*. London
1980 *Sonata forms*. New York and London
Rosen, D. and A. Porter (eds.) 1984 *Verdi's 'Macbeth': a sourcebook*. Cambridge
Ross, P. 1983 'Amalias Auftrittsarie in "Maskenball". Verdis Vertonung in dramaturgisch-textlichem Zusammenhang', in *AMw*, 40
Rosselli, J. 1983 'Verdi e la storia della retribuzione del compositore italiano', in *Studi verdiani*, 2
1984 *The opera industry in Italy from Cimarosa to Verdi*. Cambridge
Rossi, G. 1637 'Descrizioni dell'opera *Andromeda* rappresentata al Teatro di S. Cassian nell'anno 1637', in 'Storia delle leggi e de' costumi veneziani', vol. XI, fos. 80–7. MS, Biblioteca Marziana, Venice
Rousseau, J.-J. 1953 *The confessions of Jean-Jacques Rousseau*, transl. M. Cohen. Harmondsworth [Originally published 1743–44]
Rubsamen, W. H. 1961 'Music and politics in the "Risorgimento"', in *Italian Quarterly*, 5
Russell, B. 1961 *History of Western philosophy, and its connections with political and social circumstances from the earliest times to the present day*, 2nd edn. London
Rutherford, A. 1970 *Byron, the critical heritage*. London
Sachs, H. 1978 *Toscanini*. London
Sadie, S. (ed.) 1989 *History of opera* (The New Grove Handbooks in Music). Basingstoke
Salvetti, G. 1977 'La scapigliatura milanese e il teatro d'opera', in *Il melodramma italiano dell'ottocento*. Turin
Sansone, M. 1987 '*Verismo* from literature to opera'. Dissertation, University of Edinburgh
Santi, P. 1971 'Etica verdiana ed etica schilleriana', in *Atti del IIo congresso internazionale di studi verdiani*. Parma
Santini, P. 1939 'Opera – papal and regal', in *ML*, 20
Savage, R. 1989 'Operatic production in the eighteenth century', in Sadie (ed.) 1989

Bibliography

Schaeffner, A. 1968 'L'Italiana in Algeri', in Bonaccorsi (ed.) 1968

Scherer, J. 1954 *La dramaturgie de Beaumarchais*. Paris

Scherillo, M. 1916 *L'opera buffa napoletana durante il settecento, storia letteraria*. Milan [Anastatic reprint, Bologna 1975]

Scherliess, V. 1982 '"Il barbiere di Siviglia": Paisiello e Rossini', in *AnMc*, 21

Schlitzer, F. 1954 *Mondo teatrale dell'ottocento*. Naples

Schmidgall, G. 1977 'Donizetti: *Maria Stuarda* and *Lucia di Lammermoor*', in *Literature as opera*. New York

Schmidt, C. B. 1975 'Antonio Cesti's "La Dori": a study of sources, performance traditions and musical style', in *Rivista italiana di musicologia*, 10

  1978 'An episode in the history of Venetian opera: the "Tito" commission', in *JAMS*, 31

Schrade, L. 1951 *Monteverdi, creator of modern music*. London

  1960 *La représentation d'Edipo Tiranno au Teatro Olimpico*. Paris

Schumann, R. 1914 *Gesammelte Schriften über Musik und Musiker*. Leipzig

Simhart, M. 1909 *Lord Byrons Einfluss auf die italienische Literatur*. Leipzig

Smith, J. 1969–70 'Carlo Pallavicino', in *PRMA*, 94

Smither, H. E. 1977 *A history of the oratorio*, vol. I. Chapel Hill

  1979–80 'Oratorio and sacred opera, 1700–1825: terminology and genre distinction', in *PRMA*, 106

Snell, B. 1953 *The discovery of the mind: the Greek origins of European thought*, transl. T. Rosenmeyer. Oxford

Solerti, A. (ed.) 1903 *Le origini del melodramma*. Turin

Somville, M. F. 1984 'Vocal gesture in "Macbeth"', in Rosen and Porter (eds.) 1984

Sonneck, O. G. T. 1912–13 'Il giocatore', in *Musical Antiquary*, 4

Spohr, L. 1860–61 *Selbstbiographie*, 2 vols. Kassel and Göttingen

Stendhal (M. H. Beyle) 1817 *Rome, Naples et Florence en 1817*. Paris

  1956 *Life of Rossini*, transl. R. N. Coe. London

Sterling-Mackinlay, M. 1908 *Garcia the centenarian and his times*. Edinburgh and London

Sternfeld, F. J. 1975 'La technique du finale: des intermèdes à l'opéra', in *Les fêtes de la renaissance*, vol. III. Paris

  1978 'The first printed opera libretto', in *ML*, 59

  1979 '*Intermedi* and the birth of opera', in *The new Golden Age: the Florentine Intermedi of 1589* (BBC). London

  1980 'Repetition and echo in Renaissance poetry and music', in *English Renaissance Studies presented to Dame Helen Gardner in honour of her 70th birthday*. Oxford

Stevens, D. (ed. and transl.) 1980 *The letters of Claudio Monteverdi*. London

Strainchamps, E. 1976 'New light on the Accademia degli Elevati of Florence', in *MQ*, 62

Stringham, S. 1971 'Schiller and Verdi: some notes on Verdi's dramaturgy', in *Atti del IIo congresso internazionale di studi verdiani*. Parma

Strohm, R. 1977 'Handel, Metastasio, Racine', in *MT*, 118

  1978 'Zu Vivaldis Opernschaffen', in Muraro (ed.) 1978

  1979 *Die italienische Oper im 18. Jahrhundert*. Wilhelmshaven

  1985 *Essays on Handel and Italian opera*. Cambridge

Strong, R. 1973 *Splendour at court: Renaissance spectacle and illusion*. London

Strunk, O. 1950 *Source readings in music history*. New York

Surian, E. 1978 'Metastasio, i nuovi cantanti, il nuovo stile, verso il classicismo, osservazioni sull *Artaserse* (Venezia 1730) di Hasse', in Muraro (ed.) 1978

Tammaro, F. 1977 'Ambivalenza dell'*Otello* rossiniano', in *Il melodramma italiano dell'ottocento*. Turin

670

Bibliography

Tartak, M. 1969 'The two Barbieri', in *ML*, 50

Termini, O. 1978 'The transformation of madrigalisms in Venetian opera of the late seventeenth century', in *MR*, 39

    1981 'Singers at S. Marco in Venice – the competition between church and theatre (*c*. 1675–*c*. 1725)', in *RMA Research Chronicle*, 17

Tesauro, E. 1960 'Il cannocchiale aristotelico, Venice 1655', in Raimondi (ed.) 1960

Tiby, O. 1957 *Il Real Teatro Carolina e l'ottocento musicale palermitano*. Florence

Tilmouth, M. 1972 'Music on the travels of an English merchant: Robert Bargrave (1628–61)', in *ML*, 53

Tintori, G. 1964 *Cronologia completa degli spettacoli* . . . [Vol. II of Gatti 1964]

Tomlinson, G. A.1975 'Ancora su Ottavio Rinuccini', in *JAMS*, 28

Tosi, P. 1723 *Opinioni dei cantori antichi e moderni, o sieno Osservazioni sopra il canto figurato*. Bologna [English translation by J. E.Galliard, *Observations on the florid song*. London, 1742]

Towneley, S. 1968 'Early Italian opera', in *NOHM*, vol. IV. London

Towneley Worsthorne, S. 1948 'Venetian theatres, 1637–1700', in *ML*, 29

    1954 *Venetian opera in the seventeenth century*. Oxford

Toye, F. 1954 *Rossini: a study in tragicomedy*, 2nd edn. London

Troy, C. E. 1979 *The comic intermezzo: a study in the history of eighteenth-century Italian opera*. Ann Arbor

Vaccai, N. 1978 *Metodo pratico di canto italiano per camera*, transl. J. Bernhoff. London, Frankfurt and New York [Originally published 1832]

Varese, C. 1967 'Teatro prosa poesia', in *Storia della letteratura italiana*, vol. V: *Il seicento*. Milan

Verdi, G. 1913 *Copialettere di Giuseppe Verdi*, ed. G. Cesari and A. Luzio. Milan

Walker, D. P. 1941–42 'Musical humanism in the 16th and early 17th centuries', in *MR*, 2–3

    1953 'Orpheus the theologian and Renaissance Platonists', in *Journal of the Warburg-Courtauld Institutes*, 16

    1973–74 'Some aspects of the musical theory of Vencenzo Galilei', in *PRMA*, 100

Walker, D. P. (ed.) 1963 *Les fêtes du mariage de Ferdinand de Medicis et de Christine de Lorraine, Florence 1589*, vol. I: *Musique des intermèdes de 'La Pellegrina'*. Paris

Walker, F. 1949 'Two centuries of Pergolesi forgeries and misattributions', in *ML*, 30

    1952–53 'Mercadante and Verdi', in *ML*, 33–34

    1962 *The man Verdi*. London and New York

    1968 *Hugo Wolf: a biography*, 2nd edn. London

Warburg, A. 1932 'I costumi teatrali per gli Intermezzi del 1589', in *Gesammelte Schriften*, vol. I. Leipzig

Weaver, R. L. 1961 'Sixteenth-century instrumentation', in *MQ*, 47

    1964 'The orchestra in early Italian opera', in *JAMS*, 17

Weaver, R. L. and N. W. Weaver 1978 *A chronology of music in the Florentine Theater 1590–1750: operas, prologues, finales, intermezzos and plays with incidental music* (Detroit Studies in Music Bibliography, XXXVIII). Detroit

Weaver, W. and M. Chusid (eds.) 1980 *The Verdi companion*. London

Weinstock, H. 1964 *Donizetti and the world of opera in Italy, Paris and Vienna in the first half of the nineteenth century*. London

    1968 *Rossini: a biography*. London

    1972 *Vincenzo Bellini: his life and his operas*. New York

Weiss, P. 1982 'Verdi and the fusion of genres', in *JAMS*, 35

    1984 'Venetian *commedia dell'arte* "operas" in the age of Vivaldi', in *MQ*, 70

    1985 '"Sacred bronzes": Paralipomena to an essay by Dallapiccola', in *Nineteenth-century Music*, 9

Bibliography

1986 'Ancora sulle origini dell'opera comica: il linguaggio', in F. Degrada (ed.), *Studi Pergolesiani – Pergolesi studies*, vol. I. Scandicci, Florence

Westrup, J. A. 1940 'Monteverdi and the orchestra', in *ML*, 21

1958 'Two first performances: *Orfeo* . . . and *La clemenza di Tito*', in *ML*, 39

Whenham, J. (ed.) 1986 *Claudio Monteverdi: 'Orfeo'* (Cambridge Opera Handbooks), Cambridge

White, D. M. 1979 'Italy: comedy', in D. M. Grimsley (ed.), *The age of enlightenment 1715–89* (Pelican Guides to European Literature). Harmondsworth

Whitfield, J. H. 1960 *A short history of Italian literature*. Harmondsworth

1976 'Introduction', to *Battista Guarini: 'Il pastor fido'* (Edinburgh Bilingual Library). Edinburgh

Wiesend, R. 1983 'Metastasio's Revisionen eigener Draman und die Situation der Opernmusik in den 1750er Jahren', in *AMw*, 40

Winternitz, C. 1979 *Musical instruments and their symbolism in Western art*, 2nd edn. New Haven and London

Witzenmann, W. 1971 'Domenico Mazzocchi 1592–1665, Dokumente und Interpretationen', in *AnMc*, 8

1978 'Die römische Barockoper "La vita humana ovvero Il trionfo della pietà"', in *AnMc*, 15

1982 'Grundzüge der Instrumentation in italienischen Opern von 1770 bis 1830', in *AnMc*, 21

Wolff, H. C. 1975 'Italian opera from the later Monteverdi to Scarlatti', in *NOHM*, vol. V. London

Woodward, W. H. 1906 *Studies in education during the age of the Renaissance*. Cambridge

Wolff, S. 1969 *The Italian risorgimento*. London

1979 *A history of Italy 1700–1870*. London

Wright, E. 1730 *Some observations made in travelling through France, Italy* . . . London

Yorke-Long, A. 1954 *Opera at court: four eighteenth-century studies*. London

Zamboni, G. 1953 *Die italienische Romantik*. Krefeld

Zavadini, G. 1948 *Donizetti: vita – musiche – epistolario*. Bergamo

Zedda, A. 1969 'Introduzione', in *Il barbiere di Siviglia*. Milan [Reduction for voice and piano of the critical edn of the score]

1979 'Prefazione', in *La gazza ladra* (Edizioni critiche delle opere di G. Rossini, XXI), 2 parts. Pesaro

Index

Index

Index

Mattei, Saverio 192
Mattei, Stanislao 126, 189, 354, 440
Mattheson, Johann 318
Mattioli, Andrea: *Perseo* 132
Mayr, Simon 238, 247–8, 355, 442–3, 468;
 Che originali 340, 342, 345; *Lodoiska* 247,
 443; *Medea in Corinto* 247, 434, 443;
 Saffo 238; *Zibaldone* 247
Mayseder, Joseph 442
Mazzini, Giuseppe 312, 393, 396–7, 399,
 401, 411–13, 492, 501, 506–7, 535, 536
Mazzocchi, Domenico: *La catena d'Adone*
 102, 106, 289
Mazzocchi, Virgilio 100; *Chi soffre, speri*
 289
Mazzolà, Caterino: *La clemenza di Tito* 276
Mazzucato, Alberto 571–2
Medici family 19, 20, 53
Méhul, Etienne-Nicolas: *Joseph* 490
Mei, Girolamo 25, 42, 44, 46
Melani, Jacopo 315
Menasci, Guido: *Cavalleria rusticana* 620
Mendelssohn-Bartholdy, Felix 417, 422,
 490
Mercadante, Saverio 239, 399, 402, 409–11,
 422, 435, 445, 467–8, 475–82, 493, 504,
 513, 538; *Adriano in Siria* 410, 480; *Il
 bravo* 435, 477, 478; *I briganti* 479; *Le
 due illustri rivali* 477; *Elena da Feltre* 399,
 435, 438, 477, 478, 480; *Elisa e Claudio*
 468; *Ezio* 410, 480; *Il giuramento* 438,
 439–40, 477, 478, 479; *Il lamento del
 bardo* 399; *I Normanni a Parigi* 468, 477,
 479; *La Vestale* 435, 438, 477, 478, 480
Mercotellis *see* Corvo, Nicolò
Méric-Lalande, Henriette 435, 485
Metastasio, Pietro 9, 182, 185–90, 192–205,
 210, 212–13, 216–18, 220, 227–9, 231,
 235–7, 238–44, 278, 305, 316, 330, 334,
 342, 430, 480, 591; *Adriano in Siria*
 204–5, 410, 480; *Artaserse* 186, 192, 194;
 Attilio Regolo 193, 202; *Catone in Utica*
 186, 194; *La clemenza di Tito* 194;
 Demofoonte 194, 195, 211; *Didone
 abbandonata* 193, 199; *Ezio* 185, 194,
 410, 480; *L'impresario delle canarie* 304,
 305, 306; *L'Olimpiade* 193–4, 250–78
metrics 73–4, 92, 167–70, 260–1, 414,
 517–18, 547, 613
Metternich, Wenzel Fürst von 393
Meyerbeer, Giacomo 427, 443, 480, 541–2,
 572, 579, 620; *Les Huguenots* 478, 541;
 Robert le diable 541
Michelangelo Buonarroti 410
Michiel family 113
Milan 13, 209, 214, 268, 312, 393, 490,
 492, 573–4; Teatro dal Verme 536;

Teatro La Scala 13, 394, 403, 410, 420,
 424, 426–9
Mill, John Stuart 622
Millet, Jean-François 621
Minato, Nicolò 135–6; *Antioco* 132;
 Artemisia 135; *Scipione Affricano* 132–3
Molière, Jean Baptiste 52, 227, 243, 291,
 305, 363; *Tartuffe* 291
Molina, Tirso de 165
Moncalvo, Meneghino 393
Mondonville, Jean-Joseph: *Titon et l'Aurore*
 228
Moniglia, Giovanni Andrea 315
monody 25–6, 45–6, 55, 60, 86–9
Montani, Giuseppe 392
Monteverdi, Claudio 48, 138, 142, 150,
 154, 157, 172; *Arianna* 53, 55, 61, 68,
 106, 127, 152; *Bello delle ingrate* 53, 97;
 Il combattimento di Tancredi e Clorinda 97,
 157; *La finta pazza Licori* 140;
 L'incoronazione di Poppea 124, 135, 137,
 140–1, 145, 160, 164, 167, 296, 648;
 Lamento della ninfa 152; *Le nozze di
 Tetide* 140; *Orfeo* 3, 5–6, 26, 29, 40,
 60–2, 63–93, 106, 137, 140–1, 150, 157;
 Il ritorno d'Ulisse in patria 137, 140, 141,
 145, 150; *Vespro della Beata Vergine* 78
Monti, Vincenzo 246, 494, 514; *I Pitagorici*
 246; *Sulla Mitologia* 392, 396; *La supplice
 di Melpomene* 354; *Teseo* 246
Morgan, Lady 422, 424, 426
Moriani, Napoleone 409
Morlacchi, Francesco 448
Mount Edgcumbe, Lord Richard 450
Mozart, Wolfgang Amadeus 196, 238, 246,
 248, 275–6, 329, 331, 338–9, 355, 358,
 367, 369–70, 373, 382, 422, 440, 454,
 465, 472; *La clemenza di Tito* 239, 275–6;
 Don Giovanni 429; *La finta semplice* 329;
 Idomeneo 238, 347; *Le nozze di Figaro* 347
Muratori, Ludovico Antonio 135, 207, 290
Murger, Henri 588; *Scènes de la vie de
 bohème* 570, 589
Murtola, Gaspare 125
music of the spheres (*musica humana,
 instrumentalis, mundana*) 21–4, 51, 64, 67,
 69, 93, 546
music publishers 539–40
Mussolini, Benito 535, 536
Mussorgsky, Modest Petrovich: *Boris
 Godunov* 545
Muzio, Emanuele 446, 509

Naples 13, 112–13, 164–5, 181–2, 192,
 197–207, 215, 238, 311–12, 314–19, 331,
 334–6, 368, 403, 417, 429, 448–66, 477,
 538–9; **theatres**: dei Fiorentini 315, 409;

Index

Index

Index